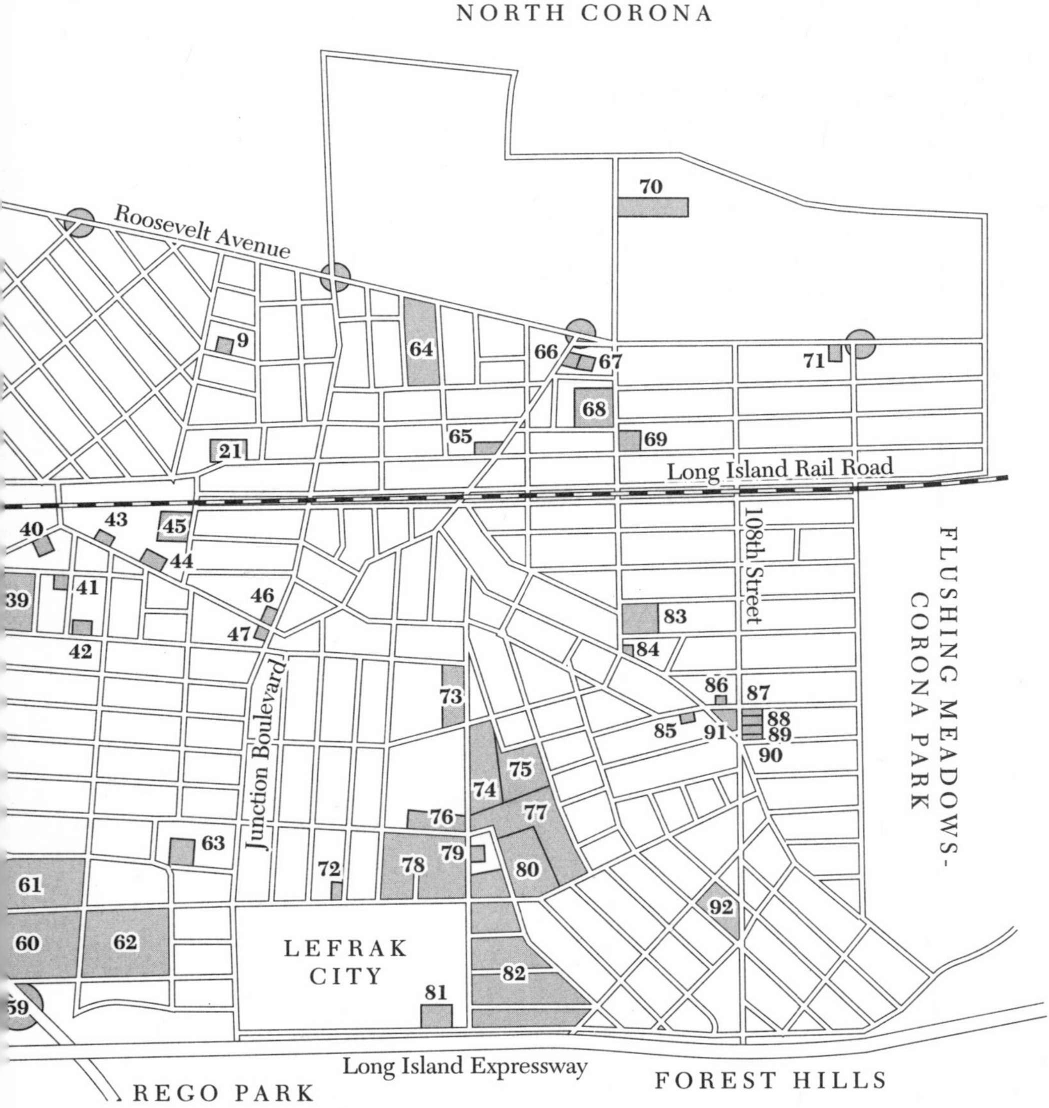
NORTH CORONA
Roosevelt Avenue
Long Island Rail Road
108th Street
Junction Boulevard
FLUSHING MEADOWS-CORONA PARK
LEFRAK CITY
Long Island Expressway
REGO PARK
FOREST HILLS
9
21
39
40
41
42
43
44
45
46
47
59
60
61
62
63
64
65
66
67
68
69
70
71
72
73
74
75
76
77
78
79
80
81
82
83
84
85
86
87
88
89
90
91
92

72 C-Town (former Waldbaum's)
73 IS 61
74 Corona high school site (proposed public housing; later PSS & TWU senior citizen housing)
75 Louis Simeone Park
76 St. Paul's, R.C.
77 Corona high school site (sixty-nine homes)
78 Sherwood Village rentals
79 Eternal Light Baptist Church
80 Rego-Forest Pool Club (later Queenswood)
81 Lefrak City Branch Library
82 Sherwood Village co-ops
83 St. Leo's, R.C.
84 Joyce's candy store
85 Lucchese bookie parlor, raided 1990
86 Park Side restaurant
87 Army's Restaurant
88 Lucchese gambling casino, raided 1987
89 Veterans of Foreign Wars Hall
90 Northside Democratic Club
91 William Moore Park
92 PS 14

The Future of Us All

The Future of Us All

Race and Neighborhood Politics in New York City

Roger Sanjek

Cornell University Press

Ithaca and London

A volume in the series

Anthropology of Contemporary Issues

Edited by Roger Sanjek

First published 1998 by Cornell University Press

Printed in the United States of America

LIBRARY OF CONGRESS CATALOGING-IN-PUBLICATION DATA

Sanjek, Roger, 1944–
The future of us all : race and neighborhood politics in New York City / Roger Sanjek.
p. cm.—(Anthropology of contemporary issues)
Includes bibliographical references and index.
ISBN 0-8014-3451-3 (cloth : alk. paper)
1. Elmhurst (New York, N.Y.)—Race relations. 2. Elmhurst (New York, N.Y.)—Ethnic relations. 3. Corona (New York, N.Y.)—Race relations. 4. Corona (New York, N.Y.)—Ethnic relations. 5. Minorities—New York (State)—New York—Political activity—Case studies. 6. Immigrants—New York (State)—New York—Political activity—Case studies. 7. New York (N.Y.)—Race relations. 8. New York (N.Y.)—Ethnic relations. I. Title. II. Series.
F128.68.E53S26 1998
305.8'009747'1—dc21 98-21179

Cornell University Press strives to use environmentally responsible suppliers and materials to the fullest extent possible in the publishing of its books. Such materials include vegetable-based, low-VOC inks and acid-free papers that are recycled, totally chlorine-free, or partly composed of nonwood fibers.

Cloth printing 10 9 8 7 6 5 4 3 2 1

Illustrations

Figures

Plates

Illustrations

Figures

Plates

Acknowledgments

Many people helped move the "New Immigrants and Old Americans" research project and this book along their courses. Our sources of funding were the Ford Foundation (1984–1985, 1987–1989), National Science Foundation (1985–1988), PSC-CUNY Anthropology panel (1984, 1985), Queens College, and (for a survey of local businesses) the Elmhurst Economic Development Corporation and Con Edison. I am grateful to Diana Morris and William Diaz at Ford, Daniel Gross and Stuart Plattner at NSF, and Nick Jordan, Renée Zarin, and Frank Spencer at Queens College for facilitating this support. In addition, Hsiang-shui Chen received funding from the Wenner-Gren Foundation, and Steven Gregory from the National Research Council and NSF. At the Queens College Asian/American Center where I served as acting director and Chen, Ruby Danta, Kyeyoung Park, and Madhulika Khandelwal were housed, we benefited from the collegiality of Wu Hong, Lori Kitazono, and Lamgen Leon.

Early on, Josh DeWind suggested important bibliographic leads, and Roger Waldinger shared his street survey of sewing shops in Community District 4. The staff of the Long Island History Collection of the Queens Borough Public Library assisted in locating and photocopying newspaper clippings and other documents. Richard Bearak of the Queens Department of City Planning gave me his unpublished paper on zoning struggles and a set of historical maps of Elmhurst-Corona that he had prepared for his architectural thesis; his colleague Deborah Carney made 1970s and early 1980s district cabinet and community board minutes available. Master Queens County historian Vincent Seyfried sent me a prepublication copy of his book on Elmhurst.

Several anthropologist friends joined me on walking tours of Elmhurst-Corona and shared their reactions: Ulf Hannerz, Helena Wulff, Laurel Kendall, Moshe Shokeid, Carol Kramer, Mona Rosendahl, Alan Harwood, Parminder

Bhachu, Catherine Besteman, Kevin Birth, and Nilanjana Chatterjee. In 1988 I visited research teams in Miami, Chicago, Philadelphia, Houston, and Garden City, Kansas, all part of a Ford Foundation "Changing Relations" project modeled on our Elmhurst-Corona study. I thank Marvin Dunn, Alex Stepick, Max Castro, Paul Friesema, Dwight Conquergood, Judith Goode, Nestor Rodriguez, Jacqueline Hagan, Don Stull, Ken Erickson, Janet Benson, Mark Grey, Roy Bryce-Laporte, Sally Merry, Greta Gibson, Niara Sudarkasa, Karen Ito, Louise Lamphere, and other project participants for the stimulation these visits and other exchanges provided.[1]

I am grateful to Åke Daun and Ulf Hannerz for inviting me to a 1990 conference in Botkyrka, Sweden; this visit to a very different established resident–newcomer setting was illuminating.[2] I also thank Monona Yin and the staff of the Committee Against Anti-Asian Violence, and the 1995–1996 Columbia University Charles H. Revson Fellows, for engaged discussions of major themes of this book.

Several participants in this Elmhurst-Corona story read portions of this book. In 1989 the Asian/American Center and the Queens Federation of Churches cosponsored a conference at which papers by our team were discussed with clergy and lay leaders, and I thank Reverend Lyn Mehl and Reverend Charles Sorg for their comments, incorporated here in Chapter 15.[3] In addition, John Rowan read Chapters 3, 4, 5, and 12; Rose Rothschild, Chapters 9 and 14; Carmela George, Lucy Schilero, Haydee Zambrana, Sung Jin Chun, and Seung Ha Hong, Chapter 13; Edna Baskin, Judy D'Andrea, and Richard Bearak, Chapter 14; and Al Blake and Sung Soo Kim, Chapter 15. (I regret deeply that Bob Tilitz died before he could read Chapter 12.) This is a better book for their reactions and suggestions, but I am aware that my interpretations may portray Elmhurst-Corona local politics as more instrumental than every participant will see it. As political scientist David Lloyd-Jones notes, political effectiveness "is probably [more] the result of empathy . . . than a rationally calculated matching of means to ends."[4]

For also reading various sections and chapters, I thank Yasmine Castillo, Hsiang-shui Chen, Ruby Danta, Margaret Fung, Steven Gregory, Monica Jimenez, Madhulika Khandelwal, Stan Mark, Maria Matteo, Silvie Murray, Kyeyoung Park, Milagros Ricourt, Nan Rothschild, Marty Sonnenfeld, Judy Wessler, and Shane White. For reading and commenting on most or all of the manuscript I am indebted to Peter Agree, Karen Brodkin, Ying Chan, Ulf Hannerz, Justine Previdi, and Susie Tanenbaum. For a final editorial polishing, I am grateful to Patricia Sterling.

Lani Sanjek waded through many drafts, and I have depended on her advice, criticism, and support through the years. Whatever I could have accomplished alone is better immeasurably for all the big and little things we have shared.

R. S.

Abbreviations

AD	New York State Assembly District
AFDC	Aid to Families with Dependent Children
BAN	Bond Anticipation Note
BOE	Board of Education
BSA	Board of Standards and Appeals
CB	Community Board
CBD	central business district
CCA	Concerned Community Adults
CCDC	Corona Community Development Corporation
CCN	Community Conciliation Network
CCQ	Ciudadanos Conscientes de Queens/Concerned Citizens of Queens
CD	Community District
CDA	Community Development Agency
CDBG	Community Development Block Grant
COMET	Communities of Maspeth and Elmhurst Together
C-POP	Community Patrol Officer Program
CTF	Community Task Force
CUNY	City University of New York
DLMA	Downtown–Lower Manhattan Association
EAU	Emergency Assistance Unit
EEDC	Elmhurst Economic Development Corporation
EFCB	Emergency Financial Control Board
FAR	floor-area ratio
FCLG	Financial Community Liaison Group
HHC	Health and Hospitals Corporation
HPD	Department of Housing Preservation and Development
HRA	Human Resources Administration
ICIB	Industrial and Commercial Incentive Board
ICIP	Industrial and Commercial Incentive Program
IDA	Industrial Development Agency

IND	Independent subway line
INS	Immigration and Naturalization Service
IRCA	Immigration Reform and Control Act of 1986
IRT	Interborough Rapid Transit subway line
IS	Intermediate School
JIB	Job Incentive Board
KAAMQ	Korean American Association of Mid-Queens
KPA	Korean Produce Association
LCTA	Lefrak City Tenants Association
LIRR	Long Island Rail Road
M&A	mergers and acquisitions
MAC	Municipal Assistance Corporation
NCA	Newtown Civic Association
NECL	New Elmhurst Civic League
NPP	Neighborhood Preservation Program
NSA	Neighborhood Strategy Area
NSP	Neighborhood Stabilization Program
NYPD	New York Police Department
OMB	Office of Management and Budget
OME	Office of Midtown Enforcement
PDC	Public Development Corporation
PRLDEF	Puerto Rican Legal Defense and Education Fund
PS	Public School
PSS	Presbyterian Senior Services
PVB	Parking Violations Bureau
QBPL	Queens Borough Public Library
QCBCA	Queens County Builders and Contractors Association
RAN	Revenue Anticipation Note
SB	School Board
SD	School District
SSI	Supplemental Security Income
SSRC	Social Science Research Council
TAN	Tax Anticipation Note
TNT	Tactical Narcotics Team
TWU	Transit Workers Union
UCA	United Corona Association
UDC	Urban Development Corporation
ULAQ	United Latin Americans of Queens
ULURP	Uniform Land Use Review Procedure
USTA	United States Tennis Association
VVA	Vietnam Veterans of America
WTC	World Trade Center
YBA	Your Block Association

The Future of Us All

Figure 1. Location of Elmhurst-Corona within New York City.

Introduction:
A Window on America's Great Transition

The United States is in the midst of a great transition. In less than one hundred years Americans of African, Asian, and Latin American ancestry will outnumber those of European origin. According to one demographic projection, by 2080 the proportion of whites will fall from its present 74 percent to 50 percent, and the rest of the U.S. population will be 23 percent Latin American, 15 percent black, and 12 percent Asian. The great transition among America's children will arrive even sooner. By the year 2035 only 49 percent of children under age eighteen will be white.[1]

The pace of multiracial change is faster on the nation's coasts and in its cities than in its heartland and suburbs. New York City crossed the "majority-minority" threshold in the early 1980s, and by 1990 the city's white population stood at 43 percent, down from 52 percent in 1980.[2] It is in New York's diverse, changing neighborhoods such as Elmhurst-Corona, the subject of this book, that clues about the future of us all may first be glimpsed.

Elmhurst-Corona underwent its majority-minority transition in the 1970s. The neighborhood's white population fell from 98 percent in 1960 to 67 percent in 1970, 34 percent in 1980, and 18 percent in 1990. Over these same decades immigrant and African American newcomers arrived in substantial numbers, and by 1990 Elmhurst-Corona was 45 percent Latin American, 26 percent Asian, and 10 percent black. Established residents of German, Irish, Polish, Italian, Jewish, and other European ancestries now lived among African, African American, Chinese, Colombian, Cuban, Dominican, Ecuadorian, Filipino, Haitian, Indian, Korean, Mexican, Puerto Rican, and other new neighbors. In 1992 New York's Department of City Planning called Elmhurst-Corona "perhaps the most ethnically mixed community in the world."[3]

In the years since liberalization of U.S. immigration law in 1965, the numerical impact of immigration on Elmhurst-Corona has been three times as great as on the city overall.[4] Other New York neighborhoods have also experienced heavy immigrant settlement, but only in northwest Queens, with Elmhurst-Corona at its epicenter, has such a diverse stream of newcomers moved in.[5] Other historically "white ethnic" New York neighborhoods have also experienced the arrival of African Americans, sometimes responding with militant opposition and incidents of violence.[6] Few neighborhoods, however, have experienced heavy immigration and white-black encounter simultaneously. Elmhurst-Corona has, and with relatively little overt conflict. Following initial white resistance to newcomers in the 1970s, its arenas of civic politics, decentralized local government, churches, and public rituals have become more open and inclusive. The experiences of Latin American and Asian immigrants, who are dispersed throughout the neighborhood, and those of blacks, who are concentrated in just three of thirty-five census tracts, have not been identical, however. Still, channels of communication among all of Elmhurst-Corona's diverse residents have broadened, and this is the story of *The Future of Us All.*

As the anthropologist Nancy Foner noted in her comparative study *New Immigrants in New York,* "Little has been written on . . . relations among new immigrants, old minorities, and native whites in concrete social settings." This book traces these relations in Elmhurst-Corona from the 1960s to the mid-1990s. The overarching goal is to assess how far Elmhurst-Corona's diverse population has come in forming what the legal scholar Lani Guinier terms "an integrated body politic in which all perspectives are represented, and in which all people work together to find common ground."[7]

The unit of study, Elmhurst-Corona, presents a large canvas. As its population grew more diverse, it also increased in size, from 88,000 in 1960 to 137,000 in 1990 (undoubtedly an undercount). An anthropologist whose fieldwork involves observing ongoing behavior and listening to spontaneous speech-in-action cannot cover fully such sizable terrain. One possibility was to carve out a small corner of the neighborhood in which to study ethnic and racial relations face-to-face, but this was not the course I selected.[8] Instead I focused on the district-level political field as conceptualized by Jane Jacobs in her classic *Death and Life of Great American Cities.*[9] Jacobs distinguished three levels of urban existence: "the city as a whole," in which people find jobs, visit museums, support baseball teams, and vote for mayor; "the street neighborhood" of immediate daily interaction; and "the district," which "mediate[s] between the . . . inherently politically powerless street neighborhoods, and the inherently powerful city as a whole." In New York City, she noted, districts ranged from 80,000 to 200,000 residents in size.

Jacobs envisaged district-level political power emerging from "churches, PTA's, businessmen's associations, political clubs, local civic leagues, [and] block improvement associations." For a district "to be big and powerful enough to fight City Hall" or to obtain "public improvements and services," political "interweav-

Figure 2. Elmhurst-Corona sections and White, Black, Latin American, and Asian population in 1970, 1980, 1990.

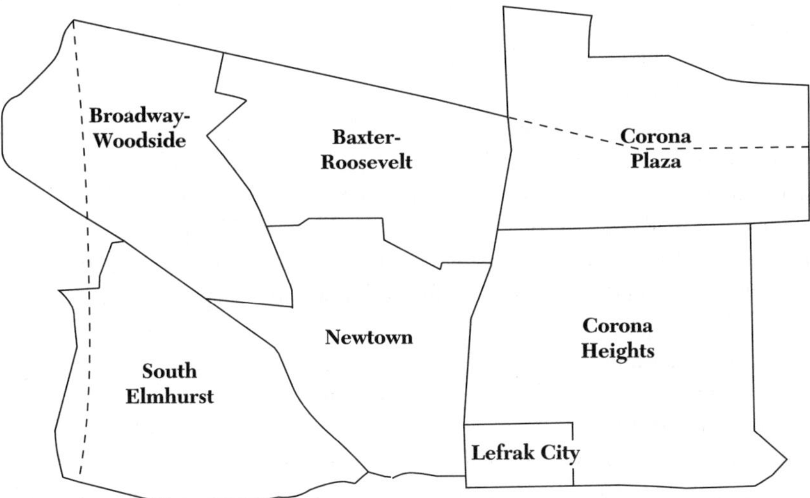

Note: The thirty-five Elmhurst-Corona census tracts extend into Community District 3 in Corona Plaza, and overlap with Community Districts 2 and 5 in Broadway-Woodside and South Elmhurst; dotted lines show the boundary of Community District 4 in these sections. Section census tract numbers are given in parentheses: Broadway-Woodside (265, 267, 481, 483, 485); Baxter-Roosevelt (269, 271, 463, 465, 467, 469); South Elmhurst (475, 479, 499); Newtown (457, 459, 461, 471, 473, 683); Corona Plaza (375, 399, 401, 403, 405, 407, 409); Corona Heights (411, 413, 415, 427, 437, 439, 443); Lefrak City (455). John Rowan analyzed Corona Plaza block groups for 1970 and 1980 and found that nearly all black residents lived in the CD3 portion of this section. "Broadway-Woodside" and "Baxter-Roosevelt" are my designations for these areas; the other section names are used by residents.

	1970	1980	1990
Whites	82,245	46,778	28,483
Broadway-Woodside	12,059	7,169	4,569
Baxter-Roosevelt	16,898	9,031	4,757
South Elmhurst	9,112	7,172	5,020
Newtown	11,052	6,696	4,323
Corona Plaza	7,863	4,128	2,114
Corona Heights	17,238	10,751	7,065
Lefrak City	8,023	1,831	635

	1970	1980	1990
Latin Americans	31,178	52,598	69,837
Broadway-Woodside	3,779	5,465	6,830
Baxter-Roosevelt	8,402	14,870	17,125
South Elmhurst	1,034	1,516	2,476
Newtown	3,765	5,159	6,766
Corona Plaza	8,392	15,465	19,549
Corona Heights	4,202	8,666	14,832
Lefrak City	1,604	1,457	2,259

	1970	1980	1990
Blacks	5,531	13,809	15,249
Broadway-Woodside	190	317	442
Baxter-Roosevelt	442	1,051	1,029
South Elmhurst	17	28	103
Newtown	71	400	420
Corona Plaza	3,384	2,752	2,143
Corona Heights	438	2,150	2,406
Lefrak City	989	7,111	8,706

	1970	1980	1990
Asians	4,696	19,937	40,569
Broadway-Woodside	1,006	4,393	9,636
Baxter-Roosevelt	1,190	6,261	11,710
South Elmhurst	104	1,392	3,844
Newtown	697	4,461	7,839
Corona Plaza	318	663	2,606
Corona Heights	496	2,460	4,741
Lefrak City	885	307	220

ing" of its groups and associations was required. In a "successful" district, "working relationships [exist] among people, usually leaders, who enlarge their local public life beyond the neighborhoods of streets and specific organizations or institutions, and [who] form relationships with people whose roots and backgrounds are in entirely different constituencies. . . . It takes surprisingly few people to weld a district into a real Thing. A hundred or so . . . do it in a population a thousand times their size."[10]

The composition and scale of Elmhurst-Corona's district-level political field matched Jacobs's description. Within it I could readily observe ongoing events and listen to speech-in-action. Its participants included black and immigrant newcomers, but the majority continued to be long-established white residents. Some local whites were antagonistic or indifferent to their new neighbors. Others sought accommodation and even formed new friendships. All were intensely aware of change going on around them.

This book examines the full range of interracial relations as they emerged within Elmhurst-Corona's district-level political field. In this regard, it differs from the sociologist Jonathan Rieder's *Canarsie: The Jews and Italians of Brooklyn against Liberalism,* which deliberately focuses on white resistance to black arrival during the 1970s and neglects countervailing activity arising within Canarsie's white and black population. Born in Manhattan's Washington Heights of Croatian and Irish immigrant grandparentage, and having lived a portion of my childhood in Queens, I am skeptical of unidimensional portraits like Rieder's of "outer-borough white ethnics," or the political scientist Andrew Hacker's sweeping depiction of "neighborhood New Yorkers": "To be a 'neighborhood New Yorker' . . . is to be less a denizen of the entire city than of one of its circumscribed segments. . . . [Here] several generations of a single family live side by side and . . . schools, churches, and synagogues enlist the emotions and energies of local residents. . . . Not . . . terribly sophisticated by cosmopolitan standards . . . neighborhood people seem all alike."[11] Senator Barbara Mikulski, product of a white ethnic neighborhood in Baltimore, also rejects such broad-brush generalizations. "Women of working class ethnic roots have usually been portrayed in patronizing, perjorative or pathological manner," she writes. "They have voiced to me their deep pain at perceiving . . . their life style [depicted] as unhip and their values as unsophisticated."[12]

In contrast to the conclusions of Rieder and Hacker, my fieldwork in Elmhurst-Corona uncovered complexity, variety, and differences in action and opinion among local white residents. I did not find that their attention to overcrowded schools or to their now racially diverse churches overwhelmed their awareness of living in "the city as a whole." To the contrary, I found that people operated quite easily at all three of the levels of urban life identified by Jane Jacobs.

Fieldwork in Elmhurst-Corona, Queens

My research began in 1983 when Hsiang-shui Chen and I analyzed 1980 U.S. census data for northern Queens. Our objective was to locate an area containing substantial numbers of whites, blacks, Asians, and Latin Americans, and we quickly settled on Elmhurst-Corona. This neighborhood, officially Queens Community District 4 (CD4), falls at the socioeconomic midpoint of New York City's fifty-nine community districts. In 1990 its median household income was $30,100, nearly the same as the $29,800 figure for the city overall. In addition, average household incomes by race in CD4 were closer than anywhere else in Queens. In 1990 they stood at $36,000 for Asians, slightly over $35,000 for blacks, $35,000 for whites, and $33,000 for Latin Americans.[13]

In fall 1983 Chen and I were joined by Ruby Danta and Jagna Wojcicka Sharff in familiarizing ourselves with Elmhurst-Corona on foot. Already by 1960 the most densely settled portion of Queens, CD4's quiet blocks of homes and apartments were alive with people traveling to and from schools, workplaces, libraries, houses of worship, parks, coin laundries, restaurants, local shopping strips, and the neighborhood's nine subway stations. The area was well endowed with the features that Jane Jacobs identified as providing neighborhoods with vitality: a mix of residential, commercial, and recreational uses; short blocks with unexpected junctions and turnings; distinctive architectural sites, including diverse houses of worship, scattered throughout; and a variety of old and new buildings.[14]

In 1984 we launched our "New Immigrants and Old Americans Project," a team study of Elmhurst-Corona's residents by researchers of the same linguistic and cultural backgrounds. Chen began fieldwork in the Taiwan Chinese immigrant population; Danta (born in Cuba) initiated study of the diverse Latin Americans; Sharff (who left the project in 1987) and I did the same among white Americans. Our team was augmented later in 1984 by Kyeyoung Park, working in the Korean community; in 1986 by Milagros Ricourt (from the Dominican Republic), joining Danta to study Latin American immigrants; and in 1987 by Steven Gregory, focusing on African Americans, and Madhulika Khandelwal on South Asian Indians. Several team members also branched into surrounding Queens neighborhoods: Chen and Park in Flushing, Gregory in North Corona–East Elmhurst, and Khandelwal in Flushing and Jackson Heights.[15]

Although each researcher conducted participant observation and interviews within a specific population, our common concern was interaction among the different groups. In addition to staff meetings where information was exchanged, during 1985–1989 our team jointly studied the annual Queens Festival attended by hundreds of thousands in Flushing Meadows–Corona Park, and in 1986–1987 we surveyed 1,428 businesses along CD4's commercial strips. Mar-

Figure 3. Queens Community Districts (numbered) and Neighborhoods.

itza Sarmiento-Radbill and Queens College students Martin Michel and Xiaoxia Yuan joined us in the business survey. Five more Queens students, all Elmhurst-Corona residents, also conducted research with the project: Elena Acosta, May Guerrier, Maria Matteo, Priti Prakash, and Tom Rodriguez.[16]

My own fieldwork began in December 1983 when I attended my first meeting of Community Board 4 (CB4) and interviewed John Rowan, the board's district manager. At the board meeting Bill Donnelly, an Elmhurst Lion, gave me his card and asked, "Are you our Margaret Mead?" At the next CB4 meeting Rowan introduced me as a Queens College professor of anthropology and explained the nature of our project. Board member Rose Rothschild laughed and exclaimed, "We're going to be studied!" I later gave CB4 members a statement of the goals, methods, and auspices of the New Immigrants and Old Americans Project; this document was also printed in Spanish, Chinese, and Korean and distributed widely during our work (see page 15).

Between 1983 and 1996 I attended sixty-two CB4 monthly meetings and twenty-seven CB4 public hearings and committee meetings, each of these evening events lasting from two to four hours. The board was composed of forty to fifty civic activists; a majority remained white, but I was present as African American, Latin American, and Asian numbers grew. Beginning in 1987 I also attended thirty-four monthly CB4 district cabinet meetings. These daytime meetings of city agency personnel were chaired by the district manager Rose Rothschild, who had succeeded Rowan in 1986 and who gave me permission to attend. On three occasions I addressed CB4 and the district cabinet about our research.

From CB4 I moved into various community settings. Local political meetings introduced me to mainly white civic associations but also to racially diverse groups and to organizations of Korean, Latin American, and African American CD4 residents. I attended the Queens hearings of Mayor Edward Koch's commissions on Hispanic and Asian American affairs in 1986, a local town hall meeting with Mayor Koch in 1989, and public hearings on city council and school redistricting in 1991 and 1994. During 1991–1992 I participated in seventeen meetings of a predominantly African American Community Task Force formed after an incident of black-Korean conflict at a local supermarket. In all, my fieldnotes cover fifty such political meetings.[17]

The most unanticipated aspect of my fieldwork involved the eighty-three public ritual events I attended between 1984 and 1996: Christmas tree lightings, ethnic festivals, protest rallies, block cleanups, award ceremonies, anti-drug marches, and pan-ethnic harmony programs. Anthropologists have long paid attention to rituals in small-scale, culturally homogeneous communities, and since Max Gluckman's 1940 "Analysis of a Social Situation in Modern Zululand," they have also been attuned to secular rituals in complex societies.[18]

I recalled Gluckman's account of black and white South Africans participating in a bridge-opening ceremony when in 1985 I attended the dedication of a renovated playground in Corona. The white American local "chiefs" (the CB4 chair and two Democratic Party district leaders) were in attendance, as were higher-level officials (the borough president and the city parks commissioner). Following an opening prayer by an Italian American Roman Catholic priest, a chorus of Latin American, Asian, black, and white schoolchildren sang the national anthem and "We Are the World." The African American park leader then gathered her pre-school children at the new play equipment, forming a backdrop for ribbon cutting, speeches, and photographs. These children's Latin American, South Asian, and white mothers, elderly Italians from the neighborhood, and uniformed park workers all looked on.

Rituals in CD4 shared common features with those elsewhere. They marked special occasions or purposes, occurred in central or symbolically transformed locations, and broke the flow of ordinary events with formal behavior including invocations, speeches, music, processions, dance, and the sharing of food. They were planned and enacted rather than spontaneous, and they sorted and positioned those present into organizers, participants, and audience.[19]

Like other anthropologists, I viewed the rituals I observed as interlinked events that were part of local politics.[20] Elmhurst-Corona's district-level leaders appeared at these rituals and interacted with one another. Public rituals also provided these leaders points of articulation with elected officials and city agency personnel, and with local residents who participated or watched. And through their use of the dramatic qualities of rituals—temporary but memorable focused assemblages, the display of symbols (such as flags and anthems), and orations and exhortations—Elmhurst-Corona's district-level leaders communicated messages.[21]

Some rituals in this multiracial, multiethnic, multilingual neighborhood reinforced existing social and political arrangements; others presented critical or competing visions. Memorial Day observances and Christmas tree lightings staged by white civic groups stressed their role in neighborhood continuity. Korean and Latin American protests and festivals asserted and celebrated new cultural presences. Ethnic and racial harmony programs in schools and at Elmhurst Hospital emphasized the inclusion of newcomers. Park openings and block cleanups crossed lines of ethnicity and race to underscore "quality-of-life" values sharable by all. In each ritual, however, overt messages and implicit meanings might differ for organizers, participants, audience members, and those who read or heard about it. Memorial Day meant one thing to an elderly white Elmhurst resident whose brother died in World War II; it meant something else to the Latin American or Asian parent of a junior high school bugler playing "Taps."[22]

Another strand of my fieldwork was the study of three Presbyterian, Baptist, and Lutheran churches among which I shuttled on Sunday mornings during 1987–1989. Each had a white American core membership, but worshipers also included Chinese, Cuban, Filipino, Guyanese Indian, Haitian, Indonesian, Mexican, Nigerian, and other immigrants. In addition to attending seventy-five services and social events in these houses of worship, I visited three of CD4's five Roman Catholic churches; African American, Latin American, and Haitian Protestant congregations; and a Hindu temple.

I also took numerous walks through Elmhurst-Corona: on planned surveys; before and after meetings, rituals, and church services; alone, with team members, and with visiting anthropologist friends. I spent many hours at parks, playgrounds, an indoor shopping mall, and commercial strips. I ate in local restaurants and visited schools, libraries, senior centers, the police station, and Elmhurst Hospital. I rode buses, subways, and the Long Island Rail Road through CD4, both during fieldwork and to my classes at Queens College. I observed persons and events on Elmhurst-Corona's streets, visited locations mentioned in meetings, collected flyers and posters, recorded the contents of commemorative plaques and hand-lettered signs, and watched changes in the neighborhood over a dozen years.

I used formal interviewing sparingly and strategically. On twenty-eight occasions I sat down with persons at arranged times and asked questions. Eighteen interviews covered the biography, work history, and neighborhood attachments of white Americans (and one Japanese American, a longtime friend who moved to Elmhurst) whom I met at meetings (three were CB4 members), local events, churches, and Queens College. Other interviews with school principals, clergy, Korean and Latin American civic leaders, and district manager John Rowan concerned public matters.

This book depends far more on natural speech-in-action than on interviews, however. As I mastered local codes, I listened and took notes.[23] I bore in mind the advice given to the ethnographer William Whyte by "Doc," a resident of Boston's North End: "Go easy on that 'who,' 'what,' 'why,' 'when,' 'where' stuff, Bill. You ask those questions, and people will clam up on you. If people accept you, you can just hang around, and you'll learn the answers in the long run without even having to ask the questions."[24] As my face became familiar to them, people told me about events, other persons and groups, and themselves. In my 1,230 pages of fieldnotes the ratio of participant observation to interviews is 10 to 1.

In addition to my own notes I have used a variety of documentary sources. I draw heavily on the *Newtown Crier,* since 1971 the bimonthly newspaper of Elmhurst's Newtown Civic Association. Most *Crier* reportage between the late 1970s and 1991 was by Bob Tilitz, a retired social worker who lived in Elmhurst from 1917 until his death in 1996. I use the *Crier,* like my fieldnotes, without specific citation. I make similar use of eight Corona Community Development Corporation newsletters produced during 1986–1990 by director Tom Rodriguez, and a few documents from other civic organizations. Although my account of CB4 and district cabinet activities before 1983 utilizes minutes of these bodies, many of the participants then were individuals I came to know later, and my reconstruction of these events incorporates this "upstream" familiarity.[25] Other than for precise details, I depend very little on minutes of the CB4 and district cabinet meetings I attended, relying instead on my own fieldnotes.[26]

I also make extensive use (and cite in notes) newspaper reports of local, city, and national events and factual information. With census and other government documents and academic and policy studies, these materials provide context for my ethnographic fieldwork. In addition, I regard the many reporters whose Elmhurst-Corona stories I cite as an extension of my fieldwork team: working on their own at events we could not attend and with many people we never met, these journalists produced a record that added to ours.

Time, Space, Power

My fieldwork and writing between 1983 and 1996 were sandwiched among other activities. I had only one year of full-time research support, and that coincided with the death of my father and attendant responsibilities in 1986. Although the project and this book were always on my mind, my days included teaching, writing research proposals and reports, advising team members, and, during 1987–1990, full-time administration of the Queens College Asian/American Center—all of which turned out to be a blessing in disguise, for long-term, part-time fieldwork provided a time perspective that one or two years of full-time intensive study could not have done, and in writing this book I blend ethnography and history. Elmhurst-Corona was no self-contained urban village, and I bore in mind Frederica de Laguna's caution that anthropologists "perceive only one aspect of a greater reality that has spatial and temporal extensions beyond our immediate range of vision."[27]

To understand these broader dimensions of time and space and how they shaped the events I observed, I utilize ideas of the social theorists Fernand Braudel and Anthony Leeds. Like ethnographers, Braudel and Leeds begin with concrete, observable events. (Each well understands, as do I, that what is "seen" in events is determined as much by the observer's substantive and theoretical interests as by the events themselves.) And Braudel and Leeds both ground their schemes in geography and ecology. Their more abstract analytic concepts are compatible if not identical, and the two scholars attune us to time and space in complementary ways.

Leeds proceeds from events to the dialectic of structure and process, seeing the impress of past events affecting the present, and that of the present structuring but not determining the future. All this occurs within the interlinked local, regional, national, and global social orders and their class and power relations.[28] Braudel moves from events to "conjunctures," shorter-term temporal trends that help order key events ("those which will bear fruit") in terms of their political-economic implications. A longer-lasting, more fundamental social arrangement he terms *longue durée;* such structures are similar to Leeds's social orders persisting through time. These too may change, but when they do, they remain subject to underlying features of geography and ecology.[29]

Neither Braudel nor Leeds is a rigid thinker. They offer their concepts to help interpret specific settings, not to squeeze past and present events into inflexible formulas. Their ideas are useful for this book in four ways: to isolate the "conjunctures" that shaped events in CD4 during 1960–1996; to delineate the social order of New York City and place Elmhurst-Corona within it; to identify the city's long-enduring social arrangements; and to understand how these are now changing.

Arising consecutively in the 1960s and 1970s, four major "conjunctures" transformed the white ethnic neighborhood of Elmhurst-Corona. Two were national in scope—increasing white-black engagement, and renewed immigration—and two were particular to New York City: political decentralization, and the 1975 fiscal crisis. The combined impact of these changes continued to "orchestrate" (as Braudel puts it) the flow of events I observed in CD4 in the 1980s and 1990s.

First, the mass migration of African Americans to northern cities in the 1950s and 1960s intensified white-black contacts. White-to-black population ratios in New York City moved from 6 to 1 in 1960 to 2 to 1 in 1980, and are projected to reach 1 to 1 by 2010. White Elmhurst-Corona residents increasingly interacted with black persons in public settings, workplaces, and Democratic Party councils. Housing throughout the city remained strongly segregated by race, but in the 1970s a substantial black population moved into Lefrak City in Corona. By the 1980s civic politics in CD4 brought white and black leaders into regular face-to-face interaction.[30]

Second, in 1965 the United States government loosened restrictions on immigration from regions beyond Europe, and since then Latin America, Asia, and the Caribbean have supplied the majority of new immigrants. Elmhurst-Corona quickly became a focus for new arrivals who by the mid-1970s outnumbered the waning white population. Established whites were now likely to have immigrant neighbors and to encounter immigrant shopkeepers on local commercial strips and immigrant worshipers in their churches. Immigration transformed the face of the entire city. By 2010 Latin American New Yorkers will outnumber both whites and blacks by 1.3 to 1, and by 2030 the Asian-to-white ratio will be 1 to 1.

Third, during the 1966–1973 mayoralty of John Lindsay, "the nation's most ambitious attempt at urban decentralization" resulted in a new layer of city government: district-level community boards with land-use and city budget purview; district cabinets of municipal agency personnel (linked, after 1975, to the community boards); and district school boards. These new "city trenches" redefined local politics: they channeled civic group activity toward the new political bodies and connected neighborhood activists more directly to municipal-agency representatives and elected officials.[31]

Fourth, in 1975 Manhattan's major banks cut off credit to the city and precipitated a fiscal crisis. Ultimate budgetary and policy control passed from public to private hands, and massive cuts in municipal services followed. The aftereffects of the 1975 fiscal crisis—reduced building inspections, declining public safety, crowded schools, inadequate youth recreation facilities, and other consequences of fiscal austerity—have defined the content of neighborhood politics for more than two decades. These assaults on what Elmhurst-Corona residents call "quality of life" have troubled whites, blacks, and immigrants alike.

In Elmhurst-Corona the shift from a white to a multiracial population and the appearance of new decentralized political arenas and new post–fiscal crisis issues produced a pattern of change resembling sociologist Norbert Elias's general depiction of established resident–outsider relations. "The established group of old residents . . . had lived in [their] neighborhood for two or three generations [and had developed] a stock of common memories, attachments and dislikes. . . . [T]he newcomers . . . were strangers in relation not only to the old residents but also to each other." Established leaders initially mobilized sentiments against the newcomers through "gossip, stigmatizing beliefs about the whole group modeled on observations of its worst sections, degrading code words and, as far as possible, exclusion from all chances of power." As the political demography changed, however, and as assaults on neighborhood quality of life deepened, the newcomers themselves organized. Some leaders among the established then began to see that "outsider groups are in some way needed." At this point, "outsider . . . representatives [began to] move into positions previously denied them." Elias holds that "what is central [in] the complex polyphony of the movement of rising and declining groups" *is not* "perceiving people with another skin color as belonging to a different group." He points out that established-outsider situations also arise where no such differences exist. What *is* central is "the balance of power."[32]

Power for theorist Anthony Leeds is a concept linked to social order and class. Many scholars have formulated all-purpose definitions of "power," his being "the exercise of some control, as individual or group, over one's own situation and [that] of others."[33] Of greater interest to Leeds than definitions, however, are the three components of power in complex social orders: material resources, organization, and numbers. Leeds identifies the power of resources as the ownership of wealth, property, banks, and corporations and the control over others that this ownership allows. Organizational or "lubricatory" power resides in the possession and manipulation of information, communications, bureaucratic rules, and legal procedure. The power of numbers emerges when people mobilize in common effort—voting, petitioning, marching, demonstrating, striking, boycotting. Upper, upper middle, and working and lower middle classes may be associated respectively with these three forms of power, but in actual situations their interaction is more complicated than this.

Upper-class owners of resources occupy leading positions in public and private organizations that include middle-class and working-class employees and members. Day to day, the social order operates to maintain and advance upper-class position; rarely is the power of resources questioned in political debate or electoral campaigns. Only when the disposition of resources is threatened openly by the power of numbers does upper-class power become evident. Then legal and ultimately police power is enlisted to preserve the existing social order.

Lubricatory power greases and oils the smooth flowing of the social order. In the contemporary United States, upper-middle-class professionals have secured their own share of power through mastery and elaboration of technical, managerial, and bureaucratic functions. Advanced training and professional certification are largely controlled by this class itself. It also uses its power of numbers in lobbying and voting. Most often lubricatory power maintains the overall balance of power, but at times renegade lubricatory specialists ally with working- and lower-middle-class groups to change that balance.[34]

Whereas upper-class power is "supra-local" in its citywide or national span, and upper-middle-class lubricatory power is lodged in professional occupations and bodies, working-and lower-middle-class power is dispersed in many specific neighborhoods and workplaces. Leeds identifies "mobilizable" numbers of people in neighborhood settings as the basis for "locality" power (or what Jane Jacobs would call district-level power). Although this power of numbers is disorganized and weak most of the time, conflict in complex social orders arises repeatedly when cross-locality (and cross-workplace) linkages emerge to oppose a distribution of power and resources favoring the upper classes.

Leeds's conceptualization of social orders begins not with classes but with events. Local, citywide, regional, national, and global social orders and power arrangements are constructed from observable links and alliances among persons, households, friendship sets, neighborhood groups, religious congregations, political associations, workplace and professional organizations, and private and public agencies. These alignments and arrangements are in constant flux as a result of ecological constraints, political struggles, and individual leadership. Anthropologists do not apprehend a social order directly, Leeds advises. Rather they construct descriptions of it from observations and records of the flow of everyday events.

Plan of the Book

In Part I, "A Neighborhood in New York City," Chapter 1 sketches the history of Elmhurst-Corona from its settlement in 1652 to 1960. Chapter 2 introduces the opposition between neighborhood New York and the city's "permanent government," and discusses the impact of city land-use policies on local politics.

Part II, "City and Neighborhood Remade: 1960–1980," focuses on Elmhurst-Corona during the 1960s and 1970s. These chapters trace the arrival of African Americans and immigrants, the creation of "decentralized" city government, and the origin and impact of the 1975 fiscal crisis.

Part III, "City and Neighborhood at Odds: 1980–1996," adopts a top-down perspective on economic trends and city policies that have affected life in Elmhurst-Corona. It contrasts the ideologies of the city's past three mayors with the underlying continuity of their regimes in satisfying permanent-government demands and reducing services in neighborhood New York. It then outlines how Elmhurst-Corona's civic activists themselves define "quality of life."

Part IV, "The Transformation of Neighborhood Politics," portrays CD4's ethnic and racial diversity during the 1980s and 1990s, and examines political change in the "urban trenches" of civic politics and Community Board 4. It also focuses on bonds of interracial cooperation in neighborhood life, and on episodes of conflict and division which have tested those bonds.

The conclusion, "The Future of Us All," assesses the strengths and limits of the cross-racial politics that have arisen in Elmhurst-Corona. With new technologies steadily dispersing economic activities long housed in Manhattan, New York's *longue durée* is coming to a close, and opportunity now arises to redirect public resources toward growing the city's real economy and reversing the quality-of-life assaults experienced in Elmhurst-Corona since 1975.

New Immigrants and Old Americans Project

The New Immigrants and Old Americans Project of Queens College seeks to document the changing political, social, and cultural nature of life in Queens. As the borough—home to the vast majority of Queens College students—has grown more religiously, ethnically, and racially diverse, so also has the College. The Project arises from a desire to understand better the varied backgrounds of the Queens College student body.

During 1987–88 the Project will be based in Elmhurst-Corona, one of the most diverse urban neighborhoods in Queens, and in all of urban America. The Project staff will visit public institutions and commercial establishments, observe daily events and special occasions, and speak informally and in arranged interviews with residents, business people, clergy, and private and public organizational personnel.

The Project seeks to understand life in Queens from all points of view: old, middle-aged and young; women and men; long-time residents and newcomers; "old" Americans of diverse ethnic and racial backgrounds; and new immigrants to America from Asia, Latin America, Europe, and elsewhere. No one will be interviewed who does not wish to be. The Project depends upon the continuing good will and cooperation that Elmhurst-Corona residents have already shown us. Arranged formal interviews with residents will be confidential; to protect people's privacy, the Project will make up names for those we interview, and details that might reveal a person's identity will be altered. Interviews with representatives of organizations and community groups will seek information of a public nature; the same protection of privacy will apply to any personal information that is mentioned during the interview.

The Project seeks to obtain a many-sided view of life in Queens, not that of any single person, group, or organization. Project reports will reflect the diverse viewpoints of those we learn from. We hope the results of our work will be helpful to Queens College, and may be shared with residents and organizations in Elmhurst-Corona, as well as with the scholarly and general public. We will seek ways in which the work of the Project and its staff can be harmonized with the goals of residents and community organizations. Please feel free to ask questions, or to bring to our attention concerns we may be able to address.

The Project Director is Dr. Roger Sanjek, Associate Professor of Anthropology at Queens College. The staff includes Ms. Elena Acosta, Mr. Chen Hsiang-shui, Mrs. Rosalia Danta, Dr. Steven Gregory, Ms. Kyeyoung Park, Mrs. Priti Prakash, and Ms. Milagros Ricourt. The Project is funded by Queens College, the City University of New York, the Ford Foundation, the National Science Foundation, the Wenner-Gren Foundation, and Con Edison. The Project may be contacted through Dr. Roger Sanjek, Asian/American Center, Queens College, Flushing NY 11367; (718) 670 4226.
[1987 version]

Figure 4. New Immigrants and Old Americans Project flyer.

PART I

A Neighborhood in New York City

[1]

Elmhurst-Corona, 1652–1960

Free and enslaved labor created the agrarian landscape that sustained Elmhurst-Corona for its first two hundred years and is still discernible on its map today. A product of glacial deposit, the area in the early 1600s contained wooded upland, swamp, freshwater streams, salt meadow, wild strawberries, and game, fish, and shellfish. In 1652 English farmers from New England crossed Long Island Sound, ascended the Flushing River, and traveled up Horse Creek. At the center of present-day Elmhurst they established "the New Town." (An earlier settlement to the south in Maspeth had been evacuated during Dutch-Indian conflict in the 1640s.) Farms and pasture surrounding Newtown village were cleared, a watering pond and gristmill created, and wheat and food crops planted. Soon barreled flour and meat were marketed in the port of New York and exported to Europe and to the southern and Caribbean plantation colonies.[1]

The 250 English settlers were Puritan Congregationalists who governed their affairs by town meeting. After the British crown replaced Dutch rule in 1664, a larger township was created by uniting Newtown village with "the out-plantations." These farms along the Queens shore facing Manhattan had been settled as early as 1638, and extended through present-day Long Island City and Astoria to La Guardia airport. Mainly Dutch, but including Swedish, German, French, and English settlers, the out-plantation farmers now traveled to Newtown village to register land transactions, attend the yearly town meeting, and participate in annual "Training Day" militia ceremonies. By 1700 the Newtown village population had also gained one Italian and a few French, Welsh, and Danish farmers, and a tailor, carpenter, cooper, and blacksmith who were granted house plots.

Native American Munsee had previously used the Newtown vicinity for hunting, but their claims were bought out in 1666. Some reappeared late in the century as wolf bounty hunters on lands to be cleared for farming. A few other Indians from southern colonies were among the slaves of Newtown farmers. In 1708 an enslaved Indian man and black woman murdered their out-plantation owners when they were denied the customary Sunday freedom other Newtown slaves enjoyed; the pair was publicly executed in Jamaica, the county seat. The last mention of an Indian slave in the area was in the 1720s.

Africans arrived as enslaved laborers with the European farmers, and property transactions involving them were long noted in Newtown records. By 1700 the township population included one thousand whites and one hundred blacks. Like the Europeans, the Africans were of diverse cultural and linguistic roots. By the 1750s nearly one-quarter of Newtown township's 1,400 residents were black, and in 1790 blacks accounted for 28 percent of the 2,100 residents.

White and black men did farm labor, cleared swamps, and transported flour and market produce by wagon. Roads connected Newtown village southwest to Brooklyn and the ferry to Manhattan, and northwest to the out-plantations and a second Manhattan ferry in today's Astoria. Other roads ran southeast to Jamaica, north to a wool fulling mill on Long Island Sound, and east to Flushing. White and black women did housework, spun wool from local sheep and cotton imported from the Caribbean, wove cloth, and performed garden and occasional farm work.

By the 1720s families had multiplied, land prices had risen, and cultivation had expanded throughout the township (which comprised today's Maspeth, Middle Village, Ridgewood, Glendale, Rego Park, Forest Hills, Corona, East Elmhurst, Jackson Heights, and Woodside). Farms now passed to a single heir; other sons pioneered new agrarian settlements elsewhere or moved to Manhattan for careers in commerce or the professions. Marriage ties knit together the two dozen Newtown families who remained landowners between 1698 and 1790. By the late 1700s these included English-Dutch marriages in increasing number.

The prosperity of the 1720s and onward was evident in the oak frame, shingled homes that replaced earlier stone and thatch cottages, in imported and locally manufactured furnishings and clothing purchased in Manhattan, and in the array of crops and livestock: corn, barley, rye, peas, potatoes, peaches, pears, "Newtown Pippin" apples, tobacco, cows, sheep, pigs, and chickens. A brickworks, tannery, starch factory, and brewery were established in Newtown village, and wheelwrights, saddlers, and weavers worked for hire. The school begun in 1684 had grown to five schools by the 1730s. In that decade new Dutch Reformed and Anglican houses of worship joined the former Congregational, now Presbyterian, church in Newtown village, and families from all over the township traveled there on Sundays.

British troops occupied Newtown between 1776 and 1783, and the population was forced to house and provision them. Several black residents escaped slavery during the Revolution, but manumissions in the decades before then were few

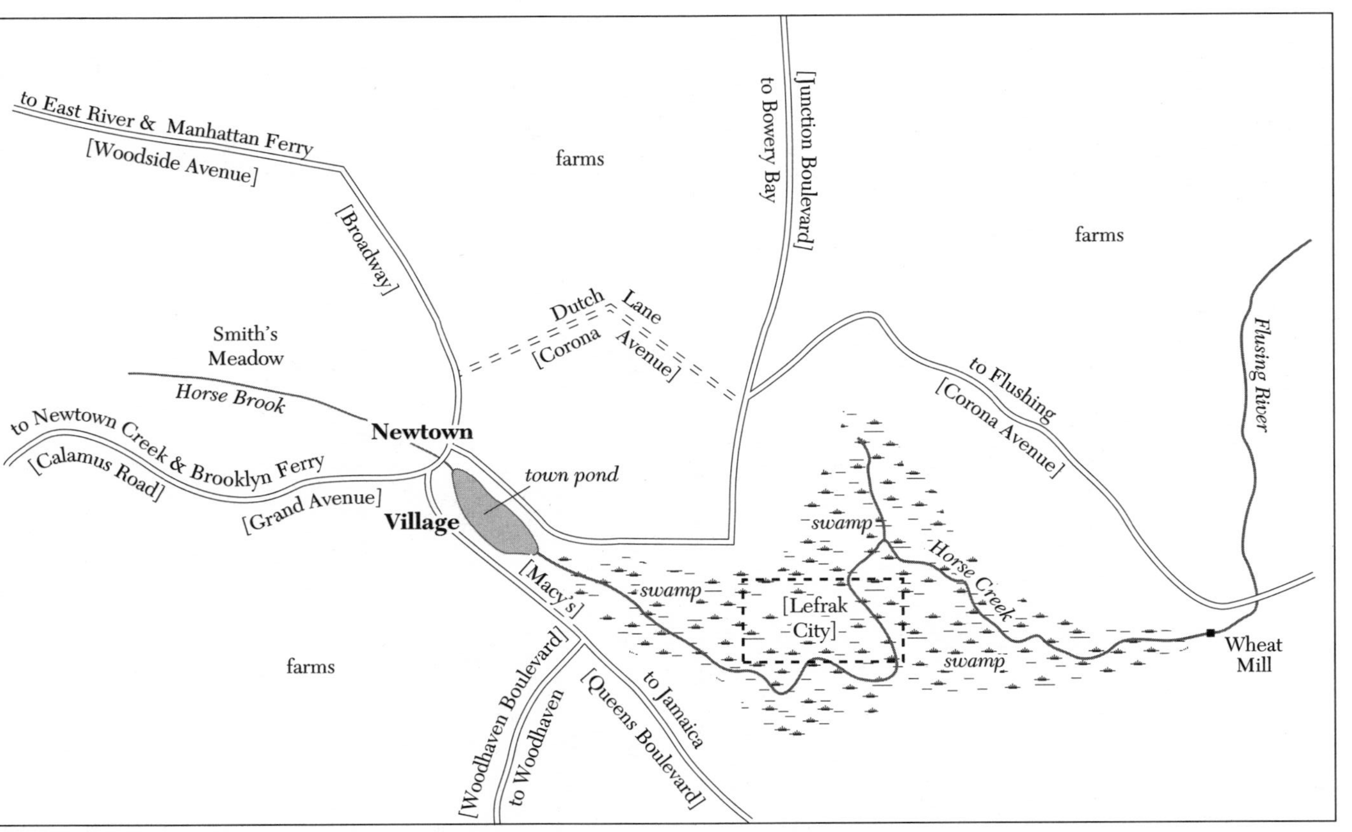

Figure 5. Colonial Newtown.

(one "free Negro" is mentioned in an account of a 1754 incident). A "gradual" phasing-out of slavery began in New York State in 1799. Persons born after that year were free but were required to serve "apprenticeships" with their owners until they reached age twenty-eight; in 1817 those born before 1799 were declared free as of July 4, 1827. Many black persons left surrounding rural areas for Manhattan during these years. Still, as late as the 1820s land-owner Richard Leverich, descendant of a 160-year-old Newtown family, rode to church with two black male slaves driving his carriage and two black female slaves seated behind.

By 1830 Newtown was changing. The township population had grown only slightly, to 2,600, but the opening of the Erie Canal in 1825 reordered the local agricultural regime. With flour from upstate and the Midwest now arriving in New York City, Newtown farmers concentrated on truck gardening for the burgeoning Manhattan population. Over the next century they cash-cropped potatoes, corn, oats (for horse fodder), asparagus, peas, cabbage, turnips, carrots, tomatoes, watercress, fruits, and flowers. Some 75,000 yards of woolen cloth were still hand-produced in 1845, but sheep raising was in decline. Dairy production, however, was increasing and lasted into the 1940s.

Newtown's farm labor force shifted from blacks, who by 1845 numbered only 375, to European immigrants, then already 1,950 in a population of 5,500. Germans were most numerous. A forerunner of larger numbers arriving from the 1840s onward, German immigrant Ascan Backus settled in Newtown in 1829. He leased and bought farms, and at his death in 1880 owned four hundred acres and employed more than a thousand farm workers. Backus attended Newtown's Dutch Reformed church, and his children mixed with offspring of the Rapelye, Lawrence, Moore, and other old families at the Newtown Academy. Many Germans, however, were Roman Catholics, and in 1854 St. Mary's parish, one mile from Newtown village, was organized, with German priests serving through the 1880s. In 1874 a short-lived German-language newspaper was begun by the American publisher of the township's *Newtown Register.*

The Germans settled into local life and operated a growing number of village stores. So did Irish immigrants, including William O'Gorman, Newtown's town clerk in the 1880s. In 1869 a mainly Irish Our Lady of Sorrows parish was organized in Corona, and in 1891 a Polish St. Adalbert's parish in Elmhurst. Beyond farm work, immigrant laborers found employment in the massive cemeteries created in the township after Manhattan banned burials in 1850, and in the new factories and oil refineries along the Long Island Rail Road (LIRR) lines, on Newtown Creek separating Queens and Brooklyn, and in Long Island City, which seceded from Newtown township in 1870.

Newtown village's male gentry, both the well-educated scions of old families and Manhattan business commuters with homes "in the country," disdained the "foreigners . . . coming over by the thousands." In the 1880s they formed a Newtown Law and Order Society to press for enforcement of laws banning recreation and drinking on Sundays. In fact, German and Irish baseball enthusiasm, beer-garden and saloon patronage, and public urination resembled the horse racing, drunkenness at funerals, and boisterous Training Day revelry that had marked old Newtown into the 1850s.

That way of life, however, had begun to fade with a "plank road" turnpike to Brooklyn in 1852 and the arrival of the LIRR in 1854. By then, elite offspring of Newtown landowners had moved to New York City, and numbered a Manhattan district attorney, an Anglican bishop of New York State, presidents of the New York Medical Society and Columbia College, and a U.S. senator. As carriage-to-ferry travel time dropped, life in "country seats," with farmland increasingly worked by immigrant managers, became more attractive.

Charles Leverich moved from Newtown to Manhattan to begin his commercial career in 1827, but after becoming a bank director in 1840 he built a large home near the family estate. He commuted during the following decades while he invested in southern cotton plantations, helped broker $150 million in loans to the Lincoln government to finance the Civil War, and became president of the Bank of New York in 1863. Country life also attracted Manhattan businessman Samuel Lord (of Lord & Taylor) to Newtown village in 1840. In the 1850s he built and sold six mansions on his holdings next to the new railroad station.

Near a second LIRR stop, entrepreneurs sold "Corona" house lots, and by the 1870s another colony of commuters had sprung up there. This area had already drawn Manhattan and Brooklyn amusement seekers to its picnic groves and a large race track that flourished in the 1850s and 1860s. In 1869 banker Leverich endowed a picturesque nondenominational chapel (still standing in 1998) in Corona village, and a memorial service was held there when he died in 1876.

A bucolic life of country homes, elm- and cherry-lined lanes, sleigh rides, and first-name friendliness flourished among Newtown's well-to-do in the 1860s and 1870s. The arrival of fixed-rail horsecar lines to the Brooklyn and Manhattan ferries in 1876, however, and then trolleys in the 1890s, increased the appeal of the area to upper-middle-class commuters. Beginning in 1896 the Cord Meyer family, children of a German immigrant industrialist, transformed farmland north of Newtown village into the more densely populated "Elmhurst," a 1,700-lot tract of elegant six- to ten-room detached homes and rowhouses. Professionals, middle managers in the growing number of Manhattan corporations, and a colony of "theater folk" moved in. "Restrictions" applied: no Jews and no blacks.

African Americans continued to dwindle in number, and many of those remaining in Newtown village worked for wealthy white families, but their sense of local rootedness was strong. In 1862, in response to President Lincoln's request for the views of "colored" Americans about possible "resettlement" overseas, black Newtown residents affirmed, "We love this land, and contributed our share to its prosperity and wealth . . . by cutting down forests, subduing the soil, cultivating fields, [and] constructing roads."

Rigid segregation nonetheless marked local social life. The first black juror was called only in 1883, and a segregated school for the handful of Newtown village black children existed until 1884. African American community life revolved around a church on the village outskirts. It housed black Presbyterians, then Methodists, and finally a small African Methodist Episcopal congregation organized in the early 1900s. With few members still residing in Elmhurst, it relocated in 1929 to the expanding North Corona black community that had emerged in the early 1900s.

Between 1880 and 1900 the population of Elmhurst and Corona grew from 1,250 to 4,400. The heart of old Newtown village remained a service center for the rural economy with stores selling seeds, hardware, provisions, and hay and oats for livestock. A score of other villages and railroad hamlets now filled the rest of the township, and during these two decades the total population quadrupled from 10,000 to 40,000. In 1886 the North Beach amusement park, a rival to Coney Island, opened on the site of today's La Guardia airport; a trolley line through Newtown village to North Beach operated until the park closed in 1919.

Around the elite and upper-middle-class Elmhurst and Corona commuter enclaves, the working- and lower-middle-class community that would flourish between 1900 and 1960 was already emerging. Immigrant and second-generation Germans, Irish, and Poles continued to settle as farms were subdivided for housing. A Chinese laundry opened in Elmhurst in 1883. Beginning in the late 1880s, Italians moved in increasing numbers from Brooklyn and Manhattan to Corona Heights, south of the Corona LIRR station and village, where they bought land and built homes. An Italian Roman Catholic parish, St. Leo's, was established in 1903, although it was served by Irish priests until the 1940s. A number of Jewish immigrants also settled in Corona Heights along with the Italians.

Vestiges of rural Newtown still existed early in this century. Boys swam in Horse Creek and hunted muskrats in the surrounding swamp into the 1920s. Barges of horse manure for farmers arrived from Manhattan on the Corona bank of the Flushing River. A fox was killed in fields just north of Elmhurst as land was being "improved" for housing. The death knell for old Newtown, however, had rung in 1900 when the New York City Council approved construction of the Queensborough Bridge.

That structure opened in 1909, and trolley lines over it connected Elmhurst-Corona to Manhattan for a single fare. Queens factory production boomed, as did housing demand and land prices. Developers and businessmen formed a Queens Chamber of Commerce in 1910 to press for transit extensions to their urbanizing borough. In 1912 the LIRR was connected by tunnel to the new Pennsylvania Station in Manhattan. The elevated Interborough Rapid Transit (IRT) arrived in Elmhurst and Corona in 1917, and the underground Independent (IND) subway in Elmhurst during 1933–1936. The IRT in Elmhurst was built on empty land along newly created Roosevelt Avenue, but in Corona forty homes had to be condemned. Excavation for the IND necessitated destruction of most of the old buildings in Newtown village.

These transportation developments led to intensification of residential land use. Single- and multiple-family homes, rowhousing, and by the 1920s five- and six-story apartments replaced existing structures, including most of the Cord Meyer homes in Elmhurst. Laborers, operatives, skilled artisans, clerical workers, city employees, small business proprietors, and the clergy, doctors, lawyers, and real estate agents serving them increasingly dominated the scene. During the booming 1920s Elmhurst jumped from 15,000 to 28,000 residents, and Corona (including the portion now in Community District 3) from 27,000 to 61,000.

Many of Elmhurst-Corona's conspicuous architectural features date to the two pre-1929 decades: the 230-foot-tall Elmhurst gas tanks (built in 1910 and 1921—and torn down in 1996), 200-foot-wide Queens Boulevard (1914), the block-long Newtown High School addition (1922), the Elmhurst Masonic Temple (1923), the Elks' Club Lodge (1924), the American Legion Hall (1926), William Moore Park commemorating Corona's first World War I casualty (1929), and several churches and public and parochial schools. Movies also arrived, the first theater opening in Corona in 1910 and in Elmhurst in 1916. During these years, 6:00 A.M. whistles from several large factories started the day for male and female workers. And the aroma from Durkee's spice and condiments plant in Elmhurst, which opened in 1917 and employed three hundred women, pervaded the area.

Neighborhood memories of older persons still living in the 1980s dated to these years. The Zaccarias arrived in Corona from Italy in 1912. Husband and wife both worked as their seven children grew up: he in Corona and Flushing factories, later as a window washer, and finally in his own laundry delivery service; she at home making paper flowers, on a truck farm, and in one of the many Jewish-owned garment shops located in Corona from the 1890s on. The German-Austrian Tilitz family moved from Manhattan to Astoria and then to Elmhurst, neighborhoods where the father worked as a baker. His son Bob recalled a farm down the block when they arrived in Elmhurst in 1917, and horses stabled across the street. When he began college in 1927, Bob Tilitz took the Queens Boulevard trolley from Elmhurst across the Queensborough Bridge and then transferred to a Bronx-bound subway. (The trolley ended service in 1937, put out of business by the IND.)

In the 1930s one of the few remaining members of the old elite registered her snobbish opinion: "The neighborhood isn't what it used to be, anyway. It has gone through a transition that's not for the better." New housing continued to rise during the Depression decade though at a slower pace; Elmhurst-Corona increased by only one-third the number of new residents it had added during the 1920s. In the late 1920s and early 1930s, however, all the residential streets were paved, and new factories and businesses appeared, including what was reputed to be the nation's largest drive-in restaurant: Howard Johnson's on Queens Boulevard with its famous "28 Flavors" of ice cream.

At the end of the 1930s CD4 lost the forty-foot-high "Corona dumps," the mounds of Brooklyn ashes and garbage carted after 1910 to the salt meadow bordering the Flushing River. The location of Wilson's garage in F. Scott Fitzgerald's 1925 novel *The Great Gatsby,* this odiferous landfill had been a haven to mosquitoes and rats. In 1939 the futuristic New York World's Fair opened on this site, giving Elmhurst-Corona residents a glimpse of technological marvels that World War II delayed until the 1950s and 1960s. When the fair closed, Flushing Meadows–Corona Park replaced it and provided much appreciated recreational space.

World War II restrictions on residential construction ended in 1947, and housing activity resumed. Many remaining open sites in CD4 had been filled in by the 1950s. New apartments appeared, as did more Jewish residents and a synagogue: Temple Emanu-el opened in Elmhurst in 1949. More Italians also moved to Elmhurst, from both Corona and elsewhere. During the 1940s and 1950s the family of Antonin Scalia—President Ronald Reagan's 1986 Supreme Court appointee—lived in Elmhurst, where "Nino," still remembered by some, went to school and joined a local Boy Scout troop. The center of the Horse Creek swamp was occupied by temporary veterans' housing from 1947 to 1954. Apartment construction began there later, and the large Lefrak City rental complex opened in 1962.

Civic involvement has a long history in Elmhurst-Corona. Colonial Newtown was governed by town meeting, though as elsewhere only white, male property owners voted. Ordinances affecting quality-of-life issues were enacted and enforced by citizen officials. In 1662 the town voted "that whosoever has cats or dogs or hogs lying dead in any place to offend their neighbors they must either bury them or throw them into the creek." Annual town meetings continued until 1898, when Queens joined "Greater New York City."

As their numbers and their stake in local affairs increased, the out-plantation Dutch established their own church in English-dominated Newtown village in 1730. In 1828 black freedmen formed a United African Association to administer their church and cemetery. Later, German, Irish, Polish, and Italian immigrants organized not only religious congregations but ethnic associations. These ranged from a German men's chorus in Corona Heights (until World War I) to Italian Charities of America, a service organization formed by Queens residents of Italian ancestry in 1936 and since 1950 headquartered in Elmhurst.

Facing a growing immigrant population in nineteenth-century Newtown, the old English-Dutch elite created their own associations. The Wandowenock Volunteer Fire Company began in 1843, composed of men from landowning families; only in the 1880s did German and Irish names appear on its roster. Members of established families also founded the Newtown Library Association in 1845 and a Masonic Lodge in 1873. These same Newtown "farmers and citizens" appealed unsuccessfully to the state legislature in 1855 to close the Corona racetrack; they sought to prevent the "gambling, drunkenness, profanity and . . .

rowdyism" they predicted would accompany its Brooklyn and Manhattan patrons and investors.

In 1892 a short-lived United Improvement Association of Corona was formed by 125 male residents to bring sidewalks and streetlights to their village; the membership list comprised English, Dutch, German, Irish, and a few Italian and Jewish names. After the end of home rule in 1898, civic associations arose to lobby New York City officials on issues affecting their areas. In 1916 Elmhurst and Corona civic groups formed a Roosevelt Avenue Rapid Transit Committee to monitor IRT construction, and a Newtown Taxpayers Association flourished in the 1920s. The South Elmhurst United Civic Association pressed for better municipal services during the 1930s, and in the 1940s it joined the Corona Civic Association to demand that the name of the new park on the World's Fair site be amended to Flushing Meadows–*Corona* Park. Civic leaders were usually also members of the political party clubs, business associations, and fraternal, religious, and service organizations that flourished in Elmhurst-Corona between 1900 and 1960.

Public rituals also marked the area's long history. After the Training Day festivities of the colonial and national periods ended, a more solemn Memorial Day featured processions of Civil War veterans and children carrying flowers to the gravesites of Newtown men killed in that struggle. Rituals to mark the departure of local men, and then to commemorate those who died, accompanied and followed both world wars. Fourth of July crowds gathered by the thousands for band concerts and fireworks in Corona's Linden Park beginning in 1910. Ceremonies marked the opening of the Corona IRT station and the many public buildings erected in the 1920s. And in Elmhurst a large Christmas tree appeared in front of the Durkee's factory.

European immigration largely halted after 1924, and the working- and lower-middle-class Elmhurst-Corona of the 1950s was the culmination of its immigrant history begun a century earlier. More family members now went to college, but with rising incomes, veterans' housing benefits, and massive federal highway construction, many also were attracted to the suburbs, especially those farther out on Long Island. Family roots remained in CD4, but branches were increasingly far-flung. While still amounting to 98 percent of the 1960 census count, the neighborhood's white population numbers were beginning to contract.

[2]

The Social Order of New York City

Elmhurst-Corona is located near the geographic center of New York City. In common parlance, however, it is part of "the outer boroughs"; the city's center or core is downtown and midtown Manhattan. Every day legions of outer-borough residents pour into this Manhattan core to work. New York's upper and upper middle classes live mainly in central Manhattan and in a few high-income outlying sections (Riverdale, Douglaston, Brooklyn Heights). The overwhelming majority of working- and lower-middle-class New Yorkers reside in the neighborhoods, such as Elmhurst-Corona, which make up the rest of the city.[1]

The imagery of core versus outer boroughs easily lends itself to simplified notions of New York as a "dual city," a view harking back to the "marble palaces and dark dens" metaphors of nineteenth-century observers.[2] From this perspective the "cosmopolitan" and "urbane" values of the higher classes are extolled by scholars and policymakers, and the "local" and "parochial" life-styles of the lesser classes are disdained.[3] The sociologist Gerald Suttles castigates this "continuing tendency . . . to describe urban society as a stratum of [upper-] middle- and upper-class conventionality suspended over a layer of self-defeating and self-imposed irrationality." He urges that we break with this top-down viewpoint and calls on urban ethnographers "to reduce the distance between strata and make intelligible the conduct" of the working- and lower-middle-class urban majority.[4]

In doing so we need to bring both outer-borough and Manhattan-centered viewpoints into sharper focus. We embark on this analysis of New York City's social order somewhat unconventionally, however, beginning from the outside in.

Neighborhood New York

Neighborhood New York is where the city's working and lower-middle classes reside, and where its new immigrants settle. It contains many languages and many local and occupational codes. It is a city of small businesses, diverse houses of worship, well-used parks, schools that children walk to, civic and ethnic associations, little-noted public rituals, neighborhood hangouts, local memories and traditions, old-country and down-home survivals, foods of delicious variety, and ways of getting around formal rules, oversized bureaucracies, and labor market rigidities. There are differences to be sure among the Italians of Belmont, the African Americans of Bedford-Stuyvesant, the Puerto Ricans of El Barrio, and the Chinese of Flushing.[5] Still, the routines and aspirations of neighborhood New Yorkers have more in common with one another than with the financial, business, and political elites of the city, or with its upper-middle-class professionals.

"Neighborhood" is an ambiguous word. It may refer to both the "street neighborhood" and the "district" levels of urban life. The first level connotes neighborly interaction and pleasantries, children's play groups, corner stores, people-watching, familiar strangers, and personal feelings about "my neighborhood" and its safety. The most immediate forms of neighborhood political organization—block, tenant, and merchant associations—arise at this street-neighborhood level.[6]

At the district level, New York neighborhoods are amalgams of named subareas (often the domains of organized civic groups), commercial strips, and public school, park, and hospital catchment areas. Many residents identify only vaguely with their district, and few know its political activists by name. District boundaries—usually expressways, railroad tracks, parks, or major streets—often have more physical than historic reality.[7] When Community District 4's boundaries were established in 1961, Corona was divided at Roosevelt Avenue between CD4 and CD3, and the southern portion of Elmhurst, cut off since the late 1950s by the Long Island Expressway, was assigned to CD5. Since then, however, it is these new boundaries that have set the parameters of district-level politics.

Inhabiting neighborhood New York's streets and districts are its pink- and white- and blue-collar income earners and their families. They include manual laborers, machine operators, clerical and sales personnel, government workers, schoolteachers, and supervisory and technical employees. Present also are lower-middle-class retail shopkeepers, owners of small manufacturing and repair firms, rank-and-file professionals, and local clergy.[8] And there are poor neighborhood New Yorkers as well, those who depend upon kin, friends, charity, or government for survival. They include persons who lose or cannot find jobs; others who lose household income through death, divorce, or desertion; still others who succumb to physical or mental illness or to addiction; elderly persons whose incomes drop after retirement; and dependent family members of all these persons.

Rather than separating the poor as an autonomous "underclass," it makes ethnographic sense to locate them within neighborhood New York. Even in neighborhoods such as Elmhurst-Corona, which their residents see as "middle class," poor persons are part of the local mix.[9] In 1984 I spoke about housing issues before an audience of three hundred white, mainly Italian members of St. Leo's Golden Age Club in Corona Heights. At the conclusion of my talk a handful of men and women approached me individually. All had incomes low enough to qualify for state and city property-tax or rent-increase exemption programs for senior citizens, and they wanted more information about them. Several described living situations that included adult children troubled by unemployment or divorce, and a few hinted at worse problems. Two elderly women lived in female-headed, three-generation households and played central roles in raising their grandchildren.[10]

The proportion of poor, working-class, and lower-middle-class residents varies from one New York neighborhood to another, and it shifts as the city's economy rises or falls. It also varies as neighborhoods change with the arrival of newcomers and with the upward and outward mobility of established residents and their children.

Both historically and in the present, when poorer newcomers—often immigrants—first move in, many willingly or unwillingly accept more crowded living conditions than established neighborhood residents are accustomed to. Landlords profit from this situation by providing quickly renovated or even new lower-quality accommodations. In addition, the younger demographic profile of newcomer populations leads to more intensive use of housing and also of public spaces, transportation, and city services. What frequently follows is diminished accessibility or even reduced provision of municipal amenities for children, the elderly, and the more economically secure established residents. Sometimes an increase in crime by a small proportion of newcomers and the use of criminally controlled services by others also occur. Predictably, some of those at the upper end of the established population begin to move to other neighborhoods or suburbs. In time, they are followed by successful newcomers and by members of the new, locally raised second generation.

Although neighborhood New York today is home to an increasingly diverse white, black, Latin American, and Asian population, it remains marked by substantial racial segregation. In 1990 twenty of the city's fifty-nine community districts were 63 percent or more white, eight were 60 percent or more black, and four were 65 percent or more Latin American; many other districts contained sub-areas where one racial category was numerically dominant.[11] In only nine community districts, including CD4, were the white, black, Latin American, and Asian categories each less than 50 percent of the total population. Only in

Elmhurst-Corona's neighbor, Community District 3, however, did the relative numerical balance among the four racial categories approach the situation in CD4. Although neither of these two districts mirrored perfectly the racial demography of New York City, they came closer to the citywide picture than did any of the fifty-seven others.[12]

The Permanent Government

When turning to the opposite end of the social order, it does little good to speak generically of "the upper class" or "the rich." There certainly are upper-class and rich persons in New York City, but linkages among them are loose. Some are members of the white Protestant upper class whose Social Register connections and integrating institutions are well studied. This group includes both old New York families and arrivals from elsewhere in the United States who come to join prestigious firms or manage and direct corporations based in the city. A Jewish upper class with its own traditions and institutions is also well established.[13] Among the city's wealthy residents there are in addition foreigners whose investments and business interests bring them from Europe, Canada, Japan, and other countries. And there are the newly rich, persons with little social entrée to established upper-class gatherings, particularly when their wealth arises outside corporate business channels. Individuals from all these groups may live in the same areas of Manhattan and frequent the same expensive restaurants, stores, and galleries, but they organize their lives in separate networks.

Within these higher circles, however, and maintaining connections as needed to all of them, is a much smaller group which in 1977 journalists Jack Newfield and Paul DuBrul christened "the permanent government." In a general sense its members' activities ensure perpetuity of upper-class wealth and power and a city that radiates a wholesome corporate "business climate." But in a particular sense they serve a narrower interest: the molding of public policy for the private gain of permanent-government figures themselves.

> Ultimate power over public policy in New York is invisible and unelected. It is exercised by a loose confederation of bankers, bond underwriters, members of public authorities, the big insurance companies, political fund-raisers, publishers, law firms, builders, judges, backroom politicians, and some union leaders. The power of this interlocking network of elites is based on the control of institutions, money, property, and the law-making process. It endures no matter who the voters elect as mayor, governor, or president. Its collective power, when organized, is greater than the elected, representative government. . . . [T]here are about 1500 to 2000 people in New York City who have pieces of a power that is decisive, concealed, and therefore unaccountable. . . . These 1500 to

> 2000 people all know each other and deal with each other as members of the same club.[14]

The permanent government's base is "the Golden Triangle of politics–real estate–banking" and not, as in other cities, the control of natural resources or major manufacturing firms.[15] Much New York City political history can be read as the jockeying for ascendancy of politicians, landowners and developers, and financiers and as competition and alliances among them. What ties them together is a common interest in Manhattan real estate and in profits generated by maintaining and increasing its value.

Economist Robert Fitch argues that land in the downtown-midtown Manhattan core, not merely the buildings on it, acquires value as the entire regional economy grows. As the paper value of this centrally located property increases, it in turn absorbs more and more capital through higher and higher rents. This benefits those who own this prime real estate, but it deflects capital investment from other, productive uses. As core Manhattan land costs rise, the process inexorably shifts investment to land uses that provide the highest return: commercial office buildings, upscale retail business, and "luxury" housing for the upper and upper middle classes.

Throughout the city's history the expansion of these highest-return uses in Manhattan's core has squeezed outward such other uses as manufacturing, shipping, warehousing, mass-market shopping, and housing for neighborhood New Yorkers. Openly or behind the scenes, members of the permanent government direct public policy to support and speed up this process. As a result, public expenditures are championed that make Manhattan office buildings and luxury housing more feasible and more profitable—mass transportation connections, tax exemptions, park and landfill creation, subsidies for "high culture" institutions, and removal (rather than in-place upgrading) of "slum" housing and "unsightly" manufacturing. This process sends ripples and waves across neighborhood New York, spinning working- and lower-middle-class jobs farther outward, relocating masses of ordinary people, transforming the nature of existing neighborhoods (if not eliminating them), and providing only minimal transportation and quality-of-life services to the outer boroughs.[16]

The returns to the permanent government come in the form of rents, bank investments and loans, and myriad other upper- and upper-middle-class rewards generated by new office towers and luxury housing in Manhattan. Moreover, as Newfield and DuBrul point out,

> an amazing number of individuals can become involved in any building project in New York City: the seller of the site, the builder of the project, architects, dozens of separate construction trades, title-search insurance brokers, contractors, property insurance brokers, truckers, building inspectors, bankers (to fi-

> nance the sale of the land, the cost of construction and ultimately a long-term mortgage)—and almost all of them will be accompanied by legions of lawyers, accountants, and tax experts. . . . In turn each of these groups has its own lobbyists, string-pullers, and political godfathers operating at City Hall and the State Capitol, and each is a source of campaign contributions, favors and political foot-soldiers for "sympathetic" politicians.[17]

The public expenditure and borrowing that support all this compete with municipal services and "welfare" payments benefiting neighborhood New York.[18] In boom periods the fulfillment of these latter needs may be uncontroversial, but when economic downturns occur, the permanent government demands cuts and retrenchment so that public subsidy for its favored projects can go forward.

During both boom and bust some permanent government interests hammer unceasingly at "high taxes" in order to retain even greater amounts of private capital. In this they are joined by those segments of the city's upper class whose interests do not lie directly in Manhattan land and its profits but who have little desire to devote any of their wealth to taxes. Others within the permanent government are less upset about prevailing tax rates. They are more concerned to ensure that city government expenditures are channeled to desired uses: interest to bondholders, capital budget infrastructure investment, office building and luxury housing subsidies and tax exemptions, and business services and promotion campaigns. Still others support planned social spending, cautioning that excessive zeal either to limit tax revenues or to spend them too conservatively could result in political unrest in neighborhood New York. These efforts are assisted by upper-middle-class "good government" spokespersons and charity-minded "experts" on the poor.

Elected officials and political party leaders receive campaign contributions, investment tips, financial kickbacks, patronage positions, and postretirement jobs from private-sector permanent-government associates. Periodically, however, they seek to enlarge their own cut of the tax-generated pie, thus limiting the flow of public expenditures for the enhancement of land values. The cry of "scandal!" is then raised by "reform" leaders and the press, most recently during the "City for Sale" decade of the 1980s.[19]

Robert Fitch views this disruption *within* the permanent government as a contest between political party "kleptocrats" and real estate developer and financial investor "plutocrats": "The goal of the kleptocrats is to sell (discreetly, of course) franchises, contracts and gentrification rights to the plutocrats for as high a price as possible until retirement or incarceration, whichever comes first. To stay in the contest, however, the kleptocrats must maintain their power base in the outer boroughs and be at least somewhat responsive to neighborhood concerns on some occasions." Fitch points out that the "plutocrats" prefer a weak city council with budgetary decision-making centralized in a small group of leaders or, ideally, a like-minded or malleable mayor. Periodic municipal charter reform accomplishes precisely this outcome and serves to curb the "kleptocratic" cut into the molding of public policy for private gain.[20]

Roots of Political Change in Neighborhood New York

As the Manhattan core of offices and luxury housing expands not only vertically but laterally, the land-value politics governing this process result in continuous pressure on neighborhood New York. Existing structures and neighborhoods are either "upgraded" as investment capital for new construction and renovation flows in, or "downgraded" by "disinvestment" in repairs and maintenance and an intensification of housing stock usage (that is, more crowding).[21] In consequence, neighborhoods "change": either upper and upper middle classes begin to appear or immigrants, lower-paid workers, and poor persons start moving in. When New Yorkers speak of "healthy" and "deteriorating" neighborhoods, these are the changes they are talking about, whether or not they understand the impetus provided by permanent-government policies.

There is nothing "natural" or "ecological" about these processes, despite generations of urbanologists who have used such metaphors to describe them. Neighborhood change is the result of deliberate action by persons and networks within the urban social order that seek to maintain or increase the value of their investments in land. To understand politics in neighborhood New York, one must ask, how do its residents organize to maintain their own interests?

The early signs of upgrading or downgrading are quickly recognized by established residents. More often than attributing such changes to government policies, bank lending decisions, or real estate profit-seeking, however, neighborhood New Yorkers allocate responsibility to the various newcomers themselves. For downgrading, they blame poorer new arrivals whose accommodation in more crowded, or less well maintained, rental housing they sense correctly will "change" their neighborhood. They also blame the newcomers for the lower prices that real estate speculators now offer for privately owned homes, and they nervously try to decide whether and when to sell, hoping to leave before a stampede begins. When upgrading occurs, some residents at first welcome the early wave of developers, selling their own homes at a profit or hoping that the new arrivals will "clean up" the neighborhood—which often does occur as increased municipal services follow. Renters, however, soon discover that the pace of upgrading is pricing them out, and homeowners who resist offers to buy are burdened by higher property taxes as the neighborhood around them "improves."

Both sorts of pressure have affected Elmhurst-Corona since the 1960s—contradictorially, perhaps, but in tune with ups and downs in the regional economy and permanent-government policies. Though not always clearly or correctly, change has been seen by established residents as coming from both below and above, and thus threatening continuity. The local political responses to these changes, their wider context, and their implications for ethnic and racial relations are the central themes of this book.

The Social Order of New York City

A summary view of the city's social order appears in Figure 5. The upper and upper middle classes reside in the Manhattan core and a few outer-borough enclaves. (Some also own additional homes outside New York City.) The majority of these two classes are U.S.-born white Americans, but a segment of global elites from other countries now also live in Manhattan. The upper middle class includes some U.S.-born and immigrant Asian, Latin American, and black members. These groups, however, confront "glass ceilings" that limit promotion and influence in the professional and managerial careers they enter. Opportunities for upper-middle-class advancement, particularly in the corporate sector, are still open overwhelmingly to whites, including many who come to New York City as adults from elsewhere in the United States.[22]

The lower middle and working classes and the poor reside in neighborhood New York. The particular mix of these categories varies from inner-city areas, where rising land values may eventually displace them, to "stable" areas in the outer boroughs. Immigrants and U.S.-born persons of all races and ethnic backgrounds live in these neighborhoods, but to a substantial degree they are divided residentially by race.

At the upper edge of the lower middle class, movement out of neighborhood New York to the suburbs is a highly desired and continual process. Mobility of neighborhood New Yorkers into the city's upper middle class through education and professional training often involves suburban exit and later reentry.[23] (Many upwardly mobile suburbanites also move to other parts of the United States.) Private schools to reproduce upper- and upper-middle-class status for their own offspring are supported by Manhattan-core dwellers. A few children from neighborhood New York do achieve mobility to the upper middle class locally, through scholarships or exceptional effort.

Six distinctive forms of politics occur at particular points in the social order of New York City:

1. The politics of the upper class involves strategies to maximize wealth accumulation, either through limiting taxes or through molding public policy for private gain. Particular upper-class segments are also dedicated either to retrenchment in public social spending or to maintaining political stability through targeted spending on social needs.

2. Most upper-middle-class professionals maintain their lubricatory power base by supporting upper-class policies, but one section of this class consists of "reformers" or "liberals" who advance the cause of "good government" against kleptocratic politicians; they also provide "expertise" for public and private

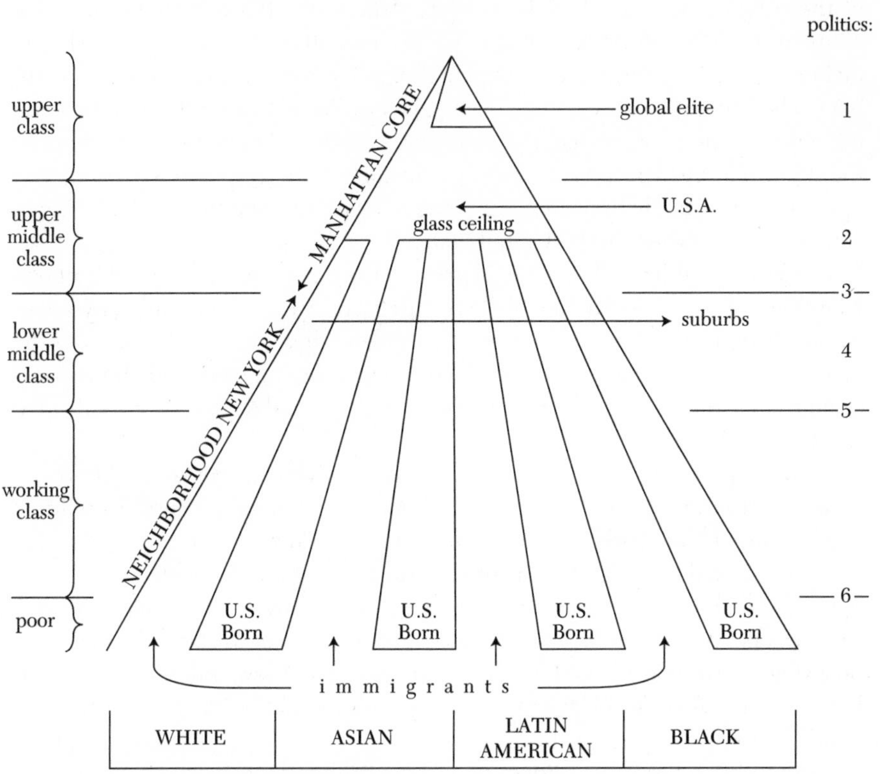

Figure 6. The social order of New York City.

spending on social needs. A few upper-middle-class professionals, however, become "advocates": class renegades who utilize lubricatory power to expand the flow of resources to neighborhood New York.[24]

3. Elected and party officials are themselves part of the upper middle or upper class via the emoluments of office if not by education and social origin. Their prime objective is political predictability and reelection. Although they reward faithful voters, according to John Mollenkopf, "neither the regular nor the reform faction of the Democratic party" in New York City is "interested in mobilizing potentially challenging groups" and thus expanding the electorate and its demands.[25] A few maverick politicians without organized party support, however, occasionally create independent electoral followings in neighborhood New York and manage to survive.

4. The strategies of upwardly mobile, lower-middle-class New Yorkers are highly personal, oriented to college education for their children and, for many, a move to suburban housing when they can afford it. Because they are, in Oliver Cox's definition, "members of a class [who] are constantly striving away from their fellows, a situation which leads to their individuation," their interest in local politics is curtailed by their desired exit from the city.[26]

5. Politics in lower-middle- and working-class neighborhoods is oriented to quality-of-life issues arising from permanent-government polices and neighborhood upgrading or downgrading. Civic associations and local leaders use the power of numbers to press for improvements when municipal services are overused or declining; they also work to supplement services through their own efforts. Elected officials are one potential resource in these struggles but not the only one. Neighborhood surveillance and volunteerism by local leaders seeks to accomplish what politicians and "liberals" cannot be counted on to achieve.

6. The politics of New York neighborhoods that house mainly poor and lower-paid working-class residents is characterized by demands for social and health services, which have never been adequate. In African American neighborhoods these demands may be expressed through a rhetoric of "empowerment," which calls attention to race and historic political neglect; this contrasts with quality-of-life politics, which underplays race and ethnicity.[27]

PART II

City and Neighborhood Remade: 1960–1980

[3]

Racial Change and Decentralization

The 1960s and 1970s were decades of enormous change in Community District 4. The white population fell from 84,000 to 47,000, and African Americans and Latin American and Asian immigrants became the new Elmhurst-Corona majority. The immigrants moved in continually over these two decades, into homes and apartments already vacated by whites in every census tract. African Americans arrived in substantial numbers, however, only after a 1970 federal housing discrimination suit at the Lefrak City apartment complex. Here blacks replaced whites, most of whom rapidly moved out. Thus, while immigrants and whites were interspersed on the same streets and in the same buildings throughout most of CD4, blacks in Lefrak City and whites in the rest of Elmhurst-Corona faced each other across a new racial border.

Black-White Engagement in Neighborhood New York

Between 1960 and 1970 the city's white population fell by 700,000, and its black population grew by half a million. The demand for housing by black New Yorkers rose not only from their growing numbers but also from loss of residential units due to demolition, arson, and landlord abandonment. By the early 1970s, reports John Mudd, "New York was losing more housing units each year . . . than it was gaining through new construction," and this affected African American neighborhoods disproportionately.[1] New York's racially segregated housing market persisted, and with black concentrations expanding at their margins, blockbusting realtors aroused white fears that home prices would drop, and then reaped profits by reselling white homes to new black owners. Speculators in the rental market further induced white flight by cutting back on maintenance, subdividing units, and renting to low-income tenants.[2] The growing African American lower middle class had little choice but to move into virtually all-black areas of private homes and apartments, including parts of Queens.[3] The housing they left was occupied by the city's black working class and poor. In 1960 some 55 percent of all black Americans lived in poverty. National initiatives during the 1960s reduced this figure substantially, but one-quarter of black New Yorkers were still living below the poverty line in 1970.[4]

Black-white racial politics gripped America during the 1960s, and New York was one of many stages in this drama. The 1960 sit-ins in the South targeted public accommodations, settings already desegregated in New York, but the city's numerous black-majority schools *were* racially segregated—not by law but by residential patterns and school-district gerrymandering. Following the 1954 Supreme Court decision outlawing "separate but equal" schools, black protest stirred in Brooklyn and Harlem.[5] The realization that a movement for racial equity was under way registered upon all New Yorkers, reinforced by the federal civil rights legislation passed between 1964 and 1968.[6]

The drama of racial change soon arrived in the North Corona–East Elmhurst area directly north of CD4. In 1950 the African American population of this neighborhood numbered 7,200 and included a small but growing poor and working-class segment in North Corona as well as East Elmhurst's lower-middle-class homeowner population. During the 1950s white flight occurred throughout North Corona, and 70 percent of its largely Italian population moved out. By 1970 few whites remained, and the North Corona–East Elmhurst black community numbered 25,000.[7]

Although North Corona–East Elmhurst was one of the smaller black concentrations in the city, its elementary school was among the 22 percent of all New York City schools declared racially segregated in a 1964 State Education Commission report. Public School 92 in North Corona, built in 1910 and holding a low priority on the Board of Education's repair list, was 97 percent black. Just six blocks away in Jackson Heights, PS149—built in 1935 and renovated in 1962—was 87 percent white. In 1963 the board announced that the two schools would be "paired": all students from both schools would attend first and second grade at PS92, and higher grades at PS149.

Though initiated by a group of white Jackson Heights parents, the school pairing plan ignited a storm of protest from other local whites, as did pairing proposals for other city neighborhoods. After an anti-pairing demonstration brought 15,000 angry white residents to City Hall, the Board of Education reduced its desegregation plan from twenty to just five pairs of schools. Among these were the North Corona and Jackson Heights schools, where pairing began in fall 1964.[8]

Many of the Jackson Heights whites opposed to pairing had moved there from city neighborhoods where black populations were increasing.[9] The neighborhoods they had left were symbolized to them by "the strip," a cluster of blocks in North Corona where one- and two-family homes had been divided into rooming houses. Landlords "milked" these properties for whatever rents their low-income tenants could pay, and bank loans for housing repairs were unavailable. Unemployment was high; several hundred households received public assistance; youth facilities were scarce; and drug and alcohol use were visible on the streets. Here also the black civic leadership of East Elmhurst worked with city agencies throughout the 1960s to ameliorate neighborhood decline.[10]

Both conditions on "the strip" and the 1964 anti-pairing movement were on the minds of many white Corona Heights residents when in 1965 the city announced plans for 214 units of public housing near Flushing Meadows–Corona Park, then the site of the 1964–1965 World's Fair. At a meeting of the Corona Homeowners Civic Association four hundred residents agreed to protest construction of the two proposed ten-story buildings. Using Democratic Party channels they convinced the Queens borough president, Mario Cariello, to object, and within two weeks the plan was killed by the City Planning Commission.[11]

The housing project had been announced in the final year of Democratic Mayor Robert Wagner's administration. In 1966 his Republican-Fusion successor John Lindsay took office, elected with a 45 percent plurality composed of white Republicans, African Americans and Puerto Ricans, and upper-middle-class white Democrats, many of them Manhattan "cosmopolitans." Soon after his election Lindsay proposed a civilian review board for the Police Department, a step advocated by African American and Puerto Rican leaders and supported by liberal whites. The Patrolmen's Benevolent Association immediately began a petition drive to place the issue on the 1966 ballot, where it was defeated by a 63 percent vote. Republicans and white outer-borough Democrats opposed the review board and voted against Lindsay's 1969 reëlection, which he won with only 42 percent of the vote.[12]

Although Lindsay had entered office with few connections to neighborhood New York, his governing ideology, drawn from President Lyndon Johnson's 1964 Economic Opportunity Act, called for "maximum feasible participation" by local residents. During Lindsay's 1966–1973 mayoralty a new layer of local school, land-use, hospital, antipoverty, and service-coordinating bodies was created, structures that transformed the shape of city government.[13] During these years activism in both black and white New York neighborhoods gave life to Lindsay's notion of participation. Yet throughout this decentralization revolution, the most persistent thorn in the mayor's side was grassroots protest in Corona.

City versus Neighborhood

The Corona housing proposal defeated in 1965 had been part of New York City's response to President Johnson's mandate to increase racial integration via federally funded public housing. When Lindsay took office in 1966, he promptly announced twelve locations (none in Manhattan) where 3,500 units of "scattered-site" public housing would be built in white neighborhoods. The African American beneficiaries of this housing would have low incomes, and their new white neighbors would be "middle class." White opponents claimed that they objected to the crime rates associated with low-income projects, not the race of the tenants, and they pointed to "middle-class" blacks who agreed with them.[14] Public officials mounted no efforts to take them at their word, however, and racial steering and blockbusting persisted in New York's private housing market.[15]

One of Lindsay's public housing proposals was for 509 units on a 4.5-acre parcel of city-owned land next to heavily Italian and working-class Corona Heights.[16] On the opposite side of the site stood the Lefrak City and Sherwood Village complexes of apartment buildings, whose largely Jewish and lower-middle-class residents preferred to say they lived not in Corona but in Rego Park or Forest Hills, neighborhoods across the Long Island Expressway to the south.

The Corona Homeowners Civic Association and local Democratic Party leaders again mobilized borough president Cariello in opposition. As a counterproposal to Lindsay's housing project they suggested that a new high school be built on the site, pointing out that the two closest schools, Forest Hills and Newtown in Elmhurst, were overcrowded. The Board of Education welcomed this idea. The high school plan also suited the interests of developer Samuel Lefrak. He was still trying to fill Lefrak City's 4,650 units, a task that public housing next door would not make easier.

Busloads of white Corona and Lefrak City residents, backed by Lefrak's personal lobbying, were successful; the public housing project was relocated from the Corona site to a vacant plot in Forest Hills. Following similar objections in other white neighborhoods, Lindsay retreated from his scattered-site initiative and announced that new public housing thenceforth would be built in low-income, inner-city areas. Lefrak was pleased, but the "victory" for Corona was short-lived. Board of Education plans for the high school required eight additional acres, and to meet this requirement five local businesses and sixty-nine homes would be condemned.

The affected homeowners banded together to fight and early in 1967 hired a thirty-four-year-old lawyer, Mario Cuomo. This time they received no support from Lefrak City; in fact, Samuel Lefrak began to list the planned high school as an amenity in his rental ads. Only the owner of the Rego-Forest Pool Club aided the embattled Corona property owners. This newly opened recreation complex facing Lefrak City was located on leased city land now included in the high school plan.

The four hundred people living in the designated sixty-nine houses included some of the most deeply rooted families in Italian Corona. Their streets had been settled after 1909 by immigrants who bought the land and built their own homes, many of which were later expanded to meet family needs. Several mortgages had been paid off by the veterans' benefits of men killed in World War II. Scores of successful offspring had moved up and out, and the population remaining in 1967 included many elderly, retired, and disabled residents. Some persons lived in homes they had been born in and later inherited. Others cared for relatives or neighbors who could not manage on their own. Many households were linked by ties of kinship, marriage, and friendship.

Under the Corona Taxpayers Civic Association banner, the residents raised $27,000 over the next four years with bingo games, raffles, picnics, and individual contributions. This supported bus trips, publicity, and court appearances by Cuomo, who argued that alternative sites were available—if not for the high school, then at least for the athletic field, which alone would displace sixty-five of the homes. The residents broadcast their positions with homemade signs: "Lindsay Uproots Italian Community," "Lindsay Ignores Middle Class Pleas and Answers Lefrak Pressure," "Is This Russia?" "John Lindsay—New York City's Greatest Mistake."

Meanwhile, Forest Hills residents pressured the mayor to begin construction in Corona to alleviate high school overcrowding in their neighborhood. In 1969, just weeks before the mayoral election, Lindsay did condemn the sixty-nine Corona homes. When his reelection effort had started earlier that year, the Corona protestors had begun a telephone campaign urging his defeat. After the condemnation they staged street demonstrations against city relocation officers and burned an effigy of the mayor in front of an assembled press corps.

In 1970 a splinter group of Corona residents was joined at a noisy City Hall demonstration against condemnation by Lindsay-nemesis Vito Battista, a state assembly member from Brooklyn. The city's low cash offers for their homes had provoked this breakaway faction, but the rest of the Corona homeowners stuck with Cuomo while he negotiated a compromise with the Lindsay administration. Lindsay's intransigence toward Corona had isolated him, and several Democratic and Republican elected officials served their own interests by criticizing him. Following newspaper columnists Jimmy Breslin and Jack Newfield's espousal of the Corona homeowners' cause, Lindsay was even criticized by his liberal Manhattan supporters.

The 1970 Cuomo-Lindsay compromise reduced the size of the athletic field, returned thirty-one condemned homes to their owners, and promised to move twenty-eight homes to an unused part of the site if their owners did not elect to sell. It called for demolishing only ten, already vacated houses. A few of the Corona sixty-nine held out, still insisting the school could be built elsewhere. They were encouraged by the Rego-Forest Pool Club owner, who hoped to retain his investment at the site, and by Battista, who maneuvered to block state legislation permitting return of the condemned homes to the original owners.

Corona residents traveled to Albany to lobby for the compromise. Lindsay further sweetened the deal by shifting the school building one hundred feet, thereby preserving fifteen more homes—and saving the city the expense of moving them. Finally, Corona state assembly member Joseph Lisa Jr.'s bill to permit return of the condemned homes passed in 1972.

No homes were ever moved, however, and no high school was built. The city had learned that higher buyout offers were cheaper than moving costs, and by 1974 only one house slated for relocation was not already in city hands. In addition, falling pupil numbers in Forest Hills schools and a new annex for Newtown High School's ninth grade elsewhere in Corona resulted in revised plans for a smaller high school building. Then, in January 1975, Mayor Abraham Beame rescinded funds for the Corona high school in response to the city's mounting fiscal crisis.

All this was hardly a victory for Corona. A dozen of the sixty-nine homeowners had moved away, and the struggle had divided the remaining residents and embittered some in both the pro-compromise and holdout camps toward each other. "Battista Destroyed Corona" signs had joined the anti-Lindsay ones. The city-owned site now contained vacant homes, a deserted bocce court, and an empty lot where five houses had been razed. It had become an illegal dumping area, an eyesore of old mattresses, abandoned cars, and rats where teenagers hung-out in the empty buildings. Throughout the turmoil, however, the Rego-Forest Pool Club—serving Lefrak City, Rego Park, and Forest Hills patrons—had survived.

Decentralization in Neighborhood New York

In July 1964 Harlem blew up. Thousands poured into the streets after an African American teenager was shot by a white off-duty policeman, and violent disruption continued for three nights.[17] President John F. Kennedy had been assassinated eight months earlier, and the white anti-school-pairing rally had occurred in March. In Washington and throughout the nation, racial debate and protest were roiling and would result in the Civil Rights Act of 1964—which John Lindsay, then a member of Congress, helped floor-manage—and the Voting Rights Act of 1965.[18] Still, over the next several years a potential "long hot summer" loomed annually. Taking office in 1966, Mayor Lindsay was as much concerned with cooling out further racial protest as with his participatory ideals when he initiated plans to bring government closer to New York City's neighborhoods.

As a first step, he kept several campaign offices open after the election as "neighborhood City Hall" complaint centers. Next, following a summer 1966 racial incident in Brooklyn, in 1967 he formed a preventive Summer Task Force composed of twenty neighborhood teams. These each brought together local clergy, businessmen, civic group leaders, and youth under an appointed liaison with direct ties to City Hall. Lindsay and his agency heads soon discovered that the task force's detailed intelligence about local problems and service glitches was different from what came up through the city bureaucracies. In 1968 it was renamed the Urban Action Task Force, and its now year-round local units were charged to bring recreation programs and technical assistance to block and tenant associations in an expanded number of neighborhoods. No task force team would arrive in Elmhurst-Corona, however, until 1973.[19]

A second Lindsay-era experiment, again limited to neighborhoods of potential disturbance, was the creation of three locally controlled demonstration school districts in 1967. The plan was backed by African American and Puerto Rican parents and civic activists, upper-middle-class "Lindsay longhairs," and Ford Foundation advisors. Hardly enthusiastic about the new decentralized bodies, the school bureaucracy rebelled when local decisions over personnel threatened its power. A thirty-six-day teachers' strike in 1968 heightened racial tensions. What resulted was a weakened decentralization plan extended to the entire city in 1969. Its unfamiliar cumulative-voting electoral procedure for local school boards, and low turnouts, allowed organized interests such as the teachers' union and the Catholic Church to attain power in several of the thirty-two new school districts.[20]

It was while these task force and demonstration school-district efforts were unfolding elsewhere that opponents of scattered-site housing and the high school were in revolt in Corona, where neither ongoing City Hall liaison nor devolution of decision-making was yet in play. Lindsay's third decentralization step, however, the empowerment of community boards to make land-use and capital budget recommendations, hold public hearings, and monitor services, came to all city neighborhoods in 1969. The boards were expanded from a handful of members appointed by the five borough presidents to as many as fifty local residents and business proprietors.[21] As the 1970s began, Corona and Elmhurst were incorporated into the decentralized structures of the Lindsay revolution as the northern tier of School District 24 and with Community Board 4 in place.

Queens Democratic Party politics was in flux during the Lindsay years. The man who would dominate the county from 1974 until his suicide in 1986, Donald Manes, did not yet have his sources of power lined up.[22] A Flushing city council member since 1965, Manes supported Democrat Sidney Leviss for Queens borough president in 1969 but bolted his party that year to back Lindsay, then running on the Liberal Party line. When several established Queens Democratic leaders retired to judgeships in 1970, Manes allied with the new county leader, Matthew Troy. They displaced Leviss (to another judgeship) in 1971 and awarded the borough presidency to Manes by appointment. He was elected in his own right in 1973, and again in 1977, 1981, and 1985.

In 1974 Manes ran for governor, gaining name recognition and sizable campaign contributions (and a taste for more) but few voters outside Queens. Next, with support from the new Democratic mayor, Abraham Beame, whom Manes but not Troy had supported in 1973, Manes ousted Troy as Democratic county leader in 1974 and would hold this post in addition to the borough presidency for the next dozen years.

From his new base Manes conducted a hidden life of corruption which did not become known publicly until indictments and trials of several of his associates in 1986. Manes had grown up in graft-ridden Brooklyn Democratic politics, and when first elected to the New York City Council he used a phony Queens address while actually residing in Nassau County. After his 1973 borough presidency race his deputy Robert Groh, a former Elmhurst resident, was indicted for shaking down a hotel corporation for a $7,000 Manes campaign contribution in exchange for a favorable zoning variance vote. Several grand jurors protested that Manes should have been the one indicted; Groh, later also promoted to a judgeship, was acquitted.[23]

In 1977 Manes secured a top position in the city's Parking Violations Bureau (PVB) for Geoffrey Lindenauer, his partner in real estate deals. Established in the Lindsay era to collect unpaid parking tickets, the PVB had become a cash cow; it was netting the city $128 million a year by 1985. Michael Lazar, a Queens Democratic colleague of Manes, had been overseeing the PVB while serving as city traffic commissioner. In 1976 he left for a consultancy with Datacom, a collection agency to which he had awarded a five-year, no-bid PVB contract in 1975.[24] With Manes's associates in charge of the PVB after Edward Koch became mayor in 1978, Lazar approached Manes in 1979 to expand Datacom's PVB business in exchange for a $500 monthly bribe. Lindenauer received the cash from Lazar and transferred it to Manes at Queens diners, including the Sage on Queens Boulevard in Elmhurst. Between 1979 and 1986 Manes and Lindenauer expanded their contracts-for-kickbacks operation to other firms and pocketed $2 million in bribes.

What all this meant with respect to the new Elmhurst-Corona community board was that borough president Manes paid it little attention. Since its recommendations on zoning and budget matters could be overturned when they countered his opportunities to solicit bribes and campaign contributions, or to use his Board of Estimate vote for political advantage, he let the dozen sitting CB4 members continue when he became borough president in 1971. In 1972 he placed oversight of appointments in the hands of his new director of community boards, Claire Shulman.

A nurse and former PTA president and civic association officer, Shulman had been chair of CB11 in Bayside, Queens. She became Manes's eyes and ears in Queens neighborhoods and shepherded the boards during the 1970s as they grew in size and power. Knowledgeable about local events and personalities throughout Queens, Shulman became deputy borough president in 1980 and was appointed to the borough presidency following Manes's suicide. She was elected to this office later in 1986 and reelected three times.

Other elected officials paid CB4 even less attention than Manes. Board members complained repeatedly through the 1970s that the two city council members representing Elmhurst and Corona rarely attended meetings, as mandated by law. Council districts were not coterminous with community district lines, and both these council members resided, depended for votes, and belonged to Democratic clubs outside CD4.

Corona was home to the numerically shrinking Northside Democratic Club, and its leader, Joseph Lisa Jr., lost his state assembly seat to an opponent from Jackson Heights in 1976. (Lisa later served in the city council during 1982–1991.) Elmhurst had no Democratic club, but it did have a powerful Democratic Party leader in Queens Supreme Court Judge William Brennan. A state assembly member and state senator during the 1950s and 1960s, he was rewarded with a judgeship in 1968. During the 1970s, however, he was no political advocate for his neighborhood. Until his own indictment in 1985 he busied himself soliciting at least $73,000 in bribes from organized-crime figures appearing in his court. Brennan and his clients transacted their deals at a restaurant in the Pan American Motor Inn on Queens Boulevard in Elmhurst.

Around the corner from the Pan Am lived Elmhurst native Michael Dowd, a criminal lawyer who chaired CB4 from 1969 to 1974 and was a member, though rarely in attendance, through 1981. Dowd was a law partner of Thomas Manton, a city council member who represented Elmhurst but lived in Woodside, where his Democratic club was located. (Manton went to Congress in 1984, filling vice-presidential candidate Geraldine Ferraro's seat; in 1986 he became Democratic county leader in Queens, replacing Manes.)

Dowd ran unsuccessfully for the state assembly in 1972. In 1977 he managed the losing mayoral primary campaign of Mario Cuomo, whose Corona high school site negotiations he had supported at CB4. That year Dowd also formed a firm to bid for PVB traffic-ticket collection contracts and in 1982 was directed by Manes to begin paying bribes through Lindenauer. Dowd's confession of remitting $36,000 in kickbacks—against $1.9 million in PVB contracts—proved critical to Manes's downfall. Dowd was suspended from legal practice but later given a New York state job by Governor Mario Cuomo.

Much like borough president Manes and local city council members and Democratic Party leaders, the city's mayors showed little interest in CB4 during most of the 1970s. Lindsay heralded enhanced citizen participation via the boards but quickly recognized that this channel led not to him but to the borough presidents who appointed the board members. To counter that tendency, in 1972 Lindsay's Office of Neighborhood Government began phasing in still another layer of decentralization: the district cabinets. These bodies brought together field-level municipal personnel from police, fire, parks, city planning, sanitation, traffic, and other agencies, chaired by a Lindsay administration official and staffed by a mayor-appointed, full-time district manager.[25]

The district cabinet that covered CD4 and CD3 first met in October 1973, just three months before Lindsay's successor Abraham Beame became mayor. In addition to agency representatives, several neighborhood civic leaders and CB4 and CB3 members attended its monthly meetings. This brought together white Elmhurst-Corona residents and their black North Corona–East Elmhurst counterparts, facilitating acquaintance across racial lines as well as recognition of common local concerns.

As his attention focused increasingly on the fiscal crisis that consumed his mayoralty, Beame showed little interest in the community boards but assumed a command-and-control stance toward the district cabinets.[26] In 1974 the Beame-appointed district manager formed an "Elmhurst-Corona Federation" of civic and block associations, crossing black, white, and Latin American lines. It met a few times, but without continuing top-down backing its leaders found more self-directed forums in CB4 and CB3, which Claire Shulman was increasingly configuring as bodies of civic group representation. In 1975 Beame's chair for the CD3-CD4 district cabinet—Sanitation Commissioner Robert Groh, the Manes associate—tried to create a "victory garden" to cover up part of the unsightly Corona high school acreage, but this plan was rejected by the Corona Taxpayers Association.

Considerable duplication between district cabinet and community board agendas was evident. Following approval of a new city charter in 1975, in January 1977 the CD3-CD4 district cabinet was split in two and transferred to the respective community boards, each of which now had the power to hire its own district manager. The charter also mandated that all municipal agencies except the schools (overseen by their own decentralized boards) and the Fire Department must reorganize their service districts to be "coterminous" with the boundaries of the city's community districts.[27] In 1977 CB4 hired Elmhurst native John Rowan as district manager, a position he held until 1986. A six-year veteran of CB4 and former assistant to Benjamin Rosenthal, Elmhurst's U.S. Congress member, Rowan quickly organized his office to track complaints about city services from Elmhurst-Corona residents. As these data accumulated, Rowan (and other district managers) could gauge more and more precisely the quality and quantity of work that city employees and contractors were performing. The charter now permitted community boards to make recommendations for the city's expense budget as well as its capital budget, and for both these tasks the new service performance data were critical.

With ongoing contact between community boards and city agencies at the monthly district cabinet meetings and via frequent district manager–agency phone conversations and field visits, a new bottom-up check on agency operations was available to counterpose bureaucratic reporting at the top. During the 1978–1989 Koch years the community boards, using uniform complaint forms ("pinks"), would become much more important to mayoral budget preparation and management oversight. To this end, Koch was represented at both district cabinet and board meetings by liaisons from his new Community Assistance Unit.[28]

Community Board 4 in the 1970s

The membership of CB4 was predominantly white and male at the beginning of the 1970s, and remained 90 percent white and three-quarters male at the decade's end. Many of the same members would serve during the 1980s, and although some moved away or died, several continued into the 1990s. Aside from Michael Dowd, however, none used CB4 as a stepladder to elective office or big-league political corruption. With relatively little oversight, the board developed its own political culture, reflecting the neighborhood interests of its members. CB4 mirrored its district's aging, ethnically diverse Italian, Irish, German, and Jewish majority in 1970, but by 1980 this population constituted only one-third of Elmhurst-Corona's residents.

Of the 1970s CB4 members, many "represented," as they and Claire Shulman saw it, Democratic clubs, civic and tenant associations, local school and social service organizations, and the business sector.[29] Corona Northside Democratic Club members included Tony Caminiti and Norma Cirino, both district leaders. Though Elmhurst had no club of its own, Dowd was a member of the Maspeth Democrats, and Miriam Levenson of Manton's Woodside-Elmhurst Democrats. Like other board members, they also had multiple ties to other civic arenas.

Rose Mazzarella, like Dowd, was a member of South Elmhurst's New Elmhurst Civic League, founded in the 1940s. The Newtown Civic Association, begun in 1971 in central Elmhurst, included several board members, among them John Costello, Tom McKenzie, and Charles Stidolph. Ron Laney of Elmhurst founded the civic group Your Block Association in 1977. Tony Quondamatteo and Anthony Piazza were officers of the Corona Taxpayers Association, which had expanded its Corona Heights base beyond the high school site's homeowner group. Late in the decade Carmela George, Judy D'Andrea, and Al Fernicola, leaders of Corona block associations, joined CB4, as did Rose Rothschild, an Elmhurst PTA president.

Retired contractor Steve Trimboli, chair of CB4 from 1974 to 1979, was director of the Italian Charities Senior Center, founded in Elmhurst in 1973. Lillian Manasseri, one of the Corona high school protest leaders, was director of the Corona Preservation Senior Center, begun the same year. Corona insurance man Lou Simeone, the 1979–1981 CB4 chair, was president of School Board 24. CB4 member Sister Thomas Francis was executive director of St. John's Hospital in Elmhurst. Architect James Giacopelli represented local business members of the Elmhurst Lions and the Elmhurst Chamber of Commerce; Dino Guiducci, a builder, was a Corona Lion. Restaurateur Ira Meyer owned a McDonald's on

Queens Boulevard in Elmhurst. Steven Spinola of the Off-Track Betting Corporation, which operated three branches in CD4, served on CB4 before becoming president of the city's Public Development Corporation as a result of Manes's recommendation to Koch; he later became a spokesperson for citywide developer interests as head of the Real Estate Board.

Some appointees quickly came and went. Of the seven Latin Americans who were CB4 members during the 1970s, only two served more than one year. Peter Nefsky, an Argentinian whose Spanish Community Council sponsored youth programs, was a member from 1972 to 1975, and Lucille Martinez, a Corona resident, from 1977 to 1981. The first African American member, Rose Miller, a Lefrak City Tenant Association (LCTA) president, joined the board in 1976; so did Ken Daniels, a white Lefrak City tenant leader. Until then, no one from this large apartment complex had been represented on the board. A second black member, Richard Isles, the new LCTA president, joined the board in 1979 after Miller had left.

CB4 took its planning mandate seriously, even if during the 1970s its recommendations went largely ignored. From 1971 onward the board unsuccessfully called for the creation of a "multipurpose center" to meet senior citizens', teenagers', and day-care needs in the Corona Heights–Lefrak City vicinity. It even identified a potential site, as it did locations for vest-pocket parks, but none of these was accepted by the Department of City Planning. Also without success, CB4 pressed this department to extend its study of Queens Boulevard from Forest Hills and Rego Park to Elmhurst, hoping to spark city interest in commercial and office development along this seedy strip. The board formulated locally oriented proposals for changes in subway and Long Island Rail Road service, but schedules designed to move Nassau County and eastern Queens commuters through CD4 remained unchanged.

On several occasions CB4 antagonized the political hierarchy. It angered borough president Leviss, a Forest Hills resident, by opposing the Corona high school plan, which he supported. Defending "our parks, our blood, and our tears," CB4 filed an injunction against Lindsay's Parks Department for permitting a profitmaking roller-skating rink to open in Flushing Meadows–Corona Park without board consultation. It sued Beame's Traffic Department for changing bus routes on Queens Boulevard without notifying CB4, as required by law. In 1977 it even passed a resolution urging Manes to drop the two ex-officio city council members from CB4 for failure to attend meetings.

On other occasions the board was more compliant. In 1977 its chair, Steve Trimboli, defended the city's lease of seventeen acres in Flushing Meadows–Corona Park to the private United States Tennis Association (USTA). He insisted that as a Parks Department franchise the lease did not have to go through the Uniform Land Use Review Procedure (ULURP) and CB4 vote which other members insisted were required by the new city charter. The USTA had threatened to leave New York City unless a larger site than its Forest Hills location was found. Beame wanted it to stay in the city, and Manes wanted to keep it in Queens.

As director of the Italian Charities Senior Center, Trimboli had been unsuccessful in placing his members in the Forest Hills public housing, which had been displaced from Corona. After the city dropped the Corona high school from its capital budget in 1975, Trimboli persuaded CB4 to "approve the concept" of senior citizen housing on the site, and then filed a proposal for construction funds with the federal Department of Housing and Urban Development.

If the city wished to sell or make any other use of the high school site, the matter would first have to come to CB4.[30] In 1977 the city announced its intention to sell a portion of the site, and CB4 voted to oppose the sale. In the city's 1978 capital budget the Corona high school reappeared. A few months later CB4 learned that the city again planned to sell a portion of the site, and Trimboli and district manager John Rowan now proposed that the board create a Corona Task Force to develop a plan for the entire site, and oppose any sale before the plan was ready. Trimboli appointed Tony Caminiti as chair, and in 1979 the Corona Task Force recommended selling one parcel on the site; permitting the Rego-Forest Pool Club to continue its city lease; renting a third parcel at a dollar a year to the Corona Taxpayers Association for a garden for local residents; and retaining a fourth parcel for senior citizen housing. No task force member supported a high school on the site.

From White to Black in Lefrak City

In 1970 some 2,150 black people resided in Elmhurst-Corona.[31] Lefrak City's 1,000 black residents constituted 9 percent of that apartment complex's population; the rest of Corona and all of Elmhurst were less than 4 percent black. In eighteen of CD4's thirty-five census tracts black residents were less than 1 percent, and in seven of these tracts no blacks were counted at all.

By 1980 Elmhurst-Corona's black population had grown five times to 11,000. In Lefrak City, 7,100 black tenants made up 65 percent of the complex's population, and another 2,200 black residents lived in adjoining apartments and co-ops. As CD4's black numbers grew, black racial concentration intensified. In 1970, 46 percent of Elmhurst-Corona's black population resided in Lefrak City; a decade later, 64 percent of the much larger black population lived there. Little change had occurred throughout the rest of CD4, where by 1980 nineteen census tracts were still less than 2 percent black.

Lefrak City opened its first units to tenants in 1962. The forty-acre complex comprised five "sections," each consisting of four connected eighteen-story apartment towers, with swimming pools, doorman service, and surrounding shopping strips. Residential construction ended in 1964, but an adjoining office building was added in 1968. This "Magic World of Total Living" was named for builder Samuel Lefrak, who ran his real estate empire from this flagship development. Most of the early renters were white young professionals and older couples; many were Jewish. They had little in common with Italian Corona Heights nearby. Even Lefrak City's transportation links to Queens Boulevard, the Long Island Expressway, and the IND subway turned its residents in the opposite direction from the Heights. Lefrak City's platoons of well-dressed Manhattan commuters—first white, later black—traveled to and from work unseen by Italian Corona.

Samuel Lefrak did not easily fill his 4,650 units. In 1963 he offered a six-year rent freeze to attract tenants. He faced competition from the neighboring Sherwood Village co-ops, which opened in 1961 and would continually cream off more economically advantaged Lefrak tenants, and also from newer apartments that continued to rise nearby. In 1966 Lindsay's plan for low-income housing next door made the rental task more difficult. Lefrak favored the high school proposal, which would make his apartment complex more attractive to families, and continued to support it into the early 1970s, even as Corona and CB4 opposition hardened.

During the late 1960s Lefrak opened his mainly white development to a more racially diverse tenantry, something he did not do in his other properties. By 1970 Lefrak City was only 70 percent white; Latin Americans, largely Puerto Rican, were 14 percent; Asians, 8 percent; and blacks (including many Africans), 9 percent. For the first time since the colonial era, black people in Elmhurst-Corona were increasing in numbers.

Many African American New Yorkers were convinced that Lefrak practiced racial discrimination widely in the more than one hundred buildings he owned throughout the city. In 1961 the Brooklyn chapter of the Congress of Racial Equality (CORE) staged a sit-in at his Forest Hills realty office to protest denial of apartments to blacks. The Lefrak Corporation admitted that this had occurred in the six instances CORE cited but claimed that each one "was simply a case of one employee doing something absolutely out of line with our policies."[32]

Following passage of the 1968 federal Fair Housing Act banning residential racial discrimination, the New York Urban League began using white and black "testers" to determine whether Lefrak rental agents gave different information according to the race of an apartment-seeker, or steered them to mainly white or mainly black buildings. Evidence that this was indeed the case in Lefrak's solidly white Brooklyn apartments was turned over to the federal Justice Department. A 1970 federal suit against Lefrak recounted this incident at Lefrak City in 1968: "A salesman allegedly told three [black] women that Lefrak did not rent to single women. A second salesman, however, filled out their applications and stamped them 'approved.' Afterwards, the second salesman allegedly told the women they would be rejected because Lefrak City had a quota on Negroes. After the case then went to the State Division of Human Rights, the women were offered an apartment."[33]

The 1970 suit was the Justice Department's first New York City housing discrimination case under the 1968 law. It no doubt had political overtones: to assuage the fears of Nixon's southern white supporters that their region would be the only target of civil rights enforcement, and to embarrass Mayor Lindsay, whom Nixon detested.[34] The suit charged that renters in Lefrak's Brooklyn and Queens apartments were "channeled" and "steered" on the basis of race, thereby keeping forty buildings virtually all white. It also claimed a practice of reduced maintenance in predominantly black Lefrak-owned buildings.

Without admitting past discrimination, Lefrak signed a consent decree in 1971 and agreed to reserve the next fifty vacancies within his "white" Brooklyn apartments for eligible black tenants. The decree, which covered Lefrak City, also called for new rental procedures that suggested how black tenants were being discriminated against in the wider housing market: weekly public posting of vacancies; time-stamping of tenant applications to assure non-race-based, "first come, first served" rentals; standardized credit checks (apparently a wife's income had been counted for white couples, but not for black ones); and stipulation that a weekly paycheck equal to 90 percent of monthly rent was sufficient for tenant qualification. Lefrak also agreed to equalize maintenance expenditures in mainly white and mainly black buildings.

In 1971 Lefrak City's still majority-white population was stable. The three thousand Social Security Administration workers in its office building provided daytime patronage for its commercial strips, and the three swimming pools, which charged admission, were well used. But the lobby furniture had been replaced by floor-bolted metal fixtures. The doormen were gone. The growing numbers of youth had inadequate recreational facilities. There was no senior center, and no multipurpose center nearby for the elderly, teens, and day care as CB4 recommended. Drive-by drug sales on 57th Avenue in front of Lefrak City, mainly of marijuana but also heroin, had become a problem and would remain so into the 1990s. The white president of the newly formed Lefrak City Tenants Association, a drug counselor, observed in 1971, "I know half the junkies in Queens. I know that junkies come here to make their deals. It's the biggest narcotics traffic center in Queens. And nothing is done about it."[35]

Over the next few years, white flight occurred from Lefrak City. The black population rose from 9 percent in 1970 to 70 percent in 1976.[36] During the same period the security staff fell from seventy in 1971 to thirty in 1975.[37] Annual tenant turnover soared to 20 or 25 percent. Maintenance went down. Vacancies went up. And with Mayor Beame's decision in January 1975 to kill the Corona high school, half-billionaire Samuel Lefrak, New York City's biggest landlord, had a crisis on his hands in the "city" that bore his name.

Crisis and Resolution

In January 1975, CB4 member William Weisberg, a lawyer who lived in an Elmhurst apartment two blocks from Lefrak City, informed the board that the Lefrak complex was "being loaded with welfare cases." Other members expressed fear for the surrounding community if the "balance between welfare cases [and] residents" should "tip." In fact, Lefrak management had avoided accepting tenants who were on public assistance, believing this would drive up vacancies, then nearing 700 apartment units.[38] White CD4 residents had indeed begun to see more black faces at Lefrak City, but they were the faces of black teachers, professionals, municipal employees, and office and sales workers—persons who qualified financially and were moving to Lefrak because the 1971 consent decree offered them a fair chance at obtaining an apartment.

In 1972, CB4 chair Michael Dowd had objected to a planned Elmhurst Hospital alcoholic-treatment center on the grounds that it would bring "blacks in [the] community." Dowd lived in a white Elmhurst census tract where in 1970 there was no black resident. Then in 1974 a Newtown Civic Association report that "welfare tenants" were replacing "residents" in northern Elmhurst was brought to a CB4 meeting. This led to discussion of Lefrak City, where, some board members noted, "people have moved out because of the bad conditions there, attributed to welfare tenants." Chair Steve Trimboli added, "As soon as landlords rent to them, the buildings deteriorate and we will have another South Bronx. The people contribute nothing to society." Like Weisberg, many CD4 whites reflexively equated the arrival of African Americans in their neighborhood with "the problem" of keeping out or limiting the number of "welfare cases."

In 1947, when New York City was 90 percent white and a million manufacturing jobs supported its working-class households, 223,000 persons had been welfare recipients. By 1972 blue-collar jobs had declined drastically, and most of the 1.1 million New Yorkers living below the poverty line depended on public assistance. The largest segment, 71 percent, received Aid to Families with Dependent Children (AFDC), and the rest either Supplemental Security Income (SSI) for the disabled and elderly poor or Home Relief for other single adults. More than half of New York's poor in 1970 were black or Puerto Rican, but 43 percent were white, including many "hidden poor" in white neighborhoods. A third of the white poor were elderly, as opposed to only 5 percent of the black and Puerto Rican poor. More blacks than whites were AFDC mothers and children, the stereotypical image of "welfare cases" for most white Americans.[39]

In 1970 Mayor Lindsay was excoriated by the press for placing a thousand AFDC families in private hotels that were expensive, dangerous, and a temporary measure at best. In poor neighborhoods, residential units were diminishing in number. Public housing offered little escape because welfare tenant numbers were restricted, amounting to just 23 percent in 1970, and many of those being elderly SSI recipients. Private-sector construction of low-rent housing had halted, and public-sector expansion was stymied by protests such as those in Corona. Pent-up housing demand affected all economic levels of the city's residentially circumscribed African American population.[40]

The Lindsay administration pressed Lefrak to accept welfare tenants in the early 1970s. Lefrak management was even sued by the city for racial discrimination because it adhered to the "weekly income must equal 90 percent of monthly rent" formula of the 1971 consent decree. The city argued that this effectively kept out welfare recipients, most of whom were not white. But Lefrak was sustained in a court decision announced just five days before Weisberg's false alarm at CB4 about "welfare cases" amassing in Lefrak City. The vacancy problem, however, and the steps that Lefrak management was taking to solve it, would lead to a real crisis—one made more difficult by white CB4 members' mistaken equation of black faces and "welfare."

Representatives from the still mainly white Lefrak City Tenants Association and from Lefrak management came to the March 1975 CB4 meeting. The LCTA spokesperson acknowledged racial change and the presence of more lower-income tenants than in the past. His members were not aware of any "welfare cases" at Lefrak, but they had entered discussion with management about reduced security, now at fifty men, and maintenance problems: unsanitary interior conditions, broken elevators and lighting, and facilities that had been vandalized and not repaired, including the holding units for compacted garbage.

The Lefrak management official explained that the complex did not accept welfare recipients because of its income eligibility standard, recently sustained by the court ruling. He said that some tenants might have gone on public assistance later but were not expelled as long as they paid their rent. He emphasized vandalism as the major problem at the site, and pot smoking and loitering by youth, some of whom were not Lefrak residents. He suggested revived LCTA patrols as a solution. A city Human Resources Administration representative added that there were in fact 129 Lefrak City families receiving public assistance in fall 1974 and stressed that this was less than 3 percent of the complex's population, a figure below the overall percentage for Queens.

Meanwhile, Lefrak management was taking steps to deal with the financial loss caused by vacant units. This included further cuts in security (to thirty men by October 1975); "rent sales," which in effect lowered the income eligibility threshold and angered tenants who held existing leases at higher rents; and contracts with social service agencies to lease apartments for group homes.[41]

At the June 1975 CB4 meeting, with no Lefrak tenant on the board to help filter continuing "welfare" rumors from fact, reports of a worsening situation were aired. The board moved to ask the city's human rights commissioner, Eleanor Holmes Norton, to investigate whether the rent reductions amounted to "blockbusting," as some CB4 members labeled the racial shift now visibly in progress.

In October 1975 the crisis emerged full blown in a *Long Island Press* series highlighting tenant complaints. In September a petition protesting lowered maintenance, security, and tenant-screening standards had been signed by five hundred residents. The white LCTA president, Ken Daniels, had reinstituted tenant patrols, and he told reporters that lack of maintenance by management, rather than vandalism or unruly tenants, was the real problem. A dissident black tenant group, however, blamed Daniels for a "lack of leadership."

Commissioner Norton now announced a study; CB4 scheduled a public hearing; and the Beame-appointed district cabinet chair for CD4-CD3, Martin Gallent, also entered the fray. Vice-chair of the City Planning Commission, Gallent was a Jackson Heights resident and a sage interpreter of Queens civic politics. Over the next two years he would pilot concerned parties through the Lefrak crisis.

Gallent understood that both Lefrak City and the surrounding community would deteriorate if black middle-class Lefrak tenants began to leave. He pressed Lefrak management to upgrade maintenance and security, which climbed back to fifty men in 1976. Lefrak tightened its screening procedure, adding home visits to prospective tenants, and instituted eviction proceedings against several disruptive "problem tenants." Gallent informed CB4 that only eight of the 130 problem tenants were on public assistance, thus deflecting suggestions that "welfare" was the root of the problem. In March 1976 Ken Daniels joined CB4, as did Rose Miller, a black tenant dissident who would replace Daniels as LCTA president that year. Their presence finally gave CB4 direct lines into Lefrak City.

The solution to Lefrak's vacancy problem was Section 8, a Nixon administration rent-subsidy program intended to redirect federal funds away from public housing and into the private market.[42] By 1977 Lefrak City was "full," and Section 8 tenants occupied 12 percent of the units. The program guaranteed landlords a federally determined "fair market rent." Low-income persons awarded a Section 8 certificate applied 25 percent of their monthly income to this rent, and the feds paid the rest. The first Section 8 tenants Lefrak management accepted were white and elderly. When Gallent reported this to CB4 in 1976, seeking their support for the Section 8 solution, they gladly approved, construing "white elderly" as the tenantry that would fill Lefrak's vacancies.

But AFDC families were also eligible for rent subsidies, and legally Lefrak management could not discriminate among Section 8 tenants by age or race. Section 8 families were especially welcomed to fill three-bedroom apartments. CB4 leaders, including LCTA's President Miller, had assumed they could "screen" the applications and were upset to find in June 1976 that four of the next six Section 8 tenants were black. By 1978 half the several hundred Section 8 tenants were elderly and mainly white; the other half, families and mainly black.

Feelings about the Section 8 solution soured among CD4 community leaders. Lefrak City's image had improved since the 1975 low point, and Martin Gallent now hoped that the complex could "lean away" from reliance on the rent-subsidy program. The two Lefrak City CB4 members were more blunt: "Mrs. Miller [said] that the people living there now do not like the connotation . . . because most people associate Lefrak City with a large population of Section 8, and Section 8 is subsidy. Agreeing with Mrs. Miller, Mr. Daniels said if the buildings were turned into Section 8, it would bring back the welfare rumors."

The effects of the Lefrak City crisis on the surrounding area were also of concern. Trimboli told the press in 1975, "If you bleed in Lefrak City, you bleed in Corona and Elmhurst." And as quickly as Lefrak management evicted "problem tenants" in 1976, some found apartments in the Sherwood Village rentals across the street. The owner of three of these six-story buildings, distinct from the well-maintained Sherwood co-ops, was milking them in slumlord fashion: maintenance had halted, any tenant was accepted, and diminishing rent collections were pocketed. In 1977 the landlord defaulted on his government-backed construction loans, and the federal Department of Housing and Urban Development became the landlord.

City Human Rights Commissioner Eleanor Holmes Norton recognized the wider local context of a successful Lefrak solution. Her first report called for improved maintenance, expanded youth facilities, and a strengthened tenant association at Lefrak, and her 1976 report outlined a Neighborhood Stabilization Program (NSP) that would encompass Lefrak City, nearby apartments including the Sherwood rentals, and surrounding Corona private homes. Both CB4 and the LCTA voted their support.

In November 1976 Yvette Schiffman, who had written Norton's first report, became director of the NSP (under a Ford Foundation grant secured by Martin Gallent) and opened an office in the Sherwood rentals. In February 1977 CB4 agreed to apply for $68,000 in federal Community Development Block Grant (CDBG) funds for the NSP, thus becoming its fiscal sponsor. With these funds Schiffman hired a staff of three in July 1977. She did not keep CB4 informed of NSP activities on a regular basis, however, and questions arose when she requested that the board reapply for a second year of federal funding. Meanwhile, bickering at CB4 among Daniels, Miller, and Weisberg about the Lefrak situation deflected attention from the NSP.

The new CB4 district manager hired in 1977, John Rowan, soon joined the round of meetings encompassing the NSP, the LCTA, Lefrak management, government agencies, and others. In addition to involvement in the Section 8 solution and the Sherwood foreclosure crisis, the NSP promoted government loan and tax abatement programs for apartment and homeowners, intending to counter any bank redlining that would hasten local neighborhood deterioration.

It also worked to develop a Lefrak area merchants' association and sponsored a block fair on 57th Avenue in 1978.

By the time the NSP ended in September 1979, tenant associations had been organized in the Sherwood buildings, and the LCTA structure of section, building, and floor captains was rebuilding under Richard Isles, the black LCTA president elected in 1978. Other signs of resident organization in Lefrak City also appeared. In 1978 a group of ninety mainly black senior citizens formed, secured rent-free space from Lefrak management, and applied to the city Department for the Aging to expand its lunch program. And in 1979 the Youth in Progress Association, a group of black adults living in Lefrak City, obtained grants to begin a youth training, tutoring, recreation, and counseling storefront program, which CB4 supported with a city budget request.

In 1979 the LCTA focused its negotiations with Lefrak management on maintenance—utilizing tenant report forms it developed—and on the security force, which had dwindled to twenty-five persons who were showing increasing insensitivity to residents. Lefrak management reverted to a "tenant vandalism is the problem" hard line, and negotiations deteriorated. An LCTA rent strike in November 1979 led to a twenty-nine-point agreement with management, one the tenant organization would need to monitor. The United Corona Association, an alliance that included white Corona Heights civic organizations, had written a letter backing the LCTA (also a member) just before the rent strike. In addition to black-white interaction in this association, and at CB4 since 1976, one more channel between Lefrak City and white Corona Heights had also emerged.

As white Democratic voter numbers in Corona fell during the 1970s, the white-over-black balance shifted in the 34th Assembly District (AD), which included both Corona Heights and North Corona–East Elmhurst. In 1974 Helen Marshall, an African American schoolteacher and East Elmhurst civic activist, was elected the first black district leader in the 34th AD, serving alongside those from the white Northside Democratic Club in Corona Heights.[43] Marshall and white CD4 leaders also became acquainted during 1973–1976 at CD3-CD4 district cabinet meetings. In 1979 she made her first appearance at Community Board 4 and would return regularly following her 1982 election to the state assembly.

Substantial numbers of African Americans had moved upward in income and job ranks during the 1960s and 1970s. By 1970 black New Yorkers could count a higher number and percentage of college graduates (104,000, or 11 percent) than could the city's Italians (80,000, or 9 percent). By 1980 a quarter of black Queens residents held professional and technical jobs, as compared with 18 percent of Queens Italians.[44] These black advances were well represented in Lefrak City's African American population. In 1979 mean black family income in Lefrak was $18,699, and mean white family income in Corona Heights was $17,894. CD4's whites and blacks had more in common than many yet realized by the time the Lefrak City crisis abated in the late 1970s.

[4]

The Impact of the New Immigration

Elmhurst-Corona's population swelled by more than half between 1960 and 1980. Against a loss of 37,000 whites, black numbers increased by 11,000, Asians by nearly 20,000, and Latin Americans by more than 50,000. Most of the growth, a total of 36,000 additional residents, occurred in the 1960s and was heavily Latin American. The smaller 1970s net increase of 13,500 included substantial numbers in all newcomer groups, with the pace of Latin American arrivals diminishing and that of black and Asian arrivals accelerating.

White numbers fell by 1,500 in the 1960s and then by more than 35,000 in the 1970s. In fact, a "white flight" of 8,000 from Corona Plaza and the departure of 10,000 more whites from other Elmhurst-Corona sections during the 1960s was counterbalanced by 16,500 new white residents in Lefrak City and other new apartment buildings. White flight again took place at Lefrak in the early 1970s, but most white loss in that decade occurred throughout Community District 4 as households aged and contracted in size, moved to suburbs or other states, or sold out when home prices rose. Some white residents departed because they "couldn't take the changes," district manager John Rowan recalled; the parents of one friend were "getting older and just didn't like not knowing what half the stuff in the corner grocery was. With a Spanish clientele there, they no longer felt comfortable."

Although most whites and blacks in CD4 were American-born and most Latin Americans and Asians were immigrants, all groups contained both persons born in the United States and those born overseas. New immigrants from Europe continued to arrive, and Italian, Greek, and Russian could be heard on the streets. And a substantial segment of the black population consisted of West Indians and Africans. There were also U.S. mainland–born Latin Americans, many of them Puerto Ricans. And there were Asian Americans whose parents or grandparents had arrived in the United States at the same time as those of most Elmhurst-Corona whites—among them, families that had moved out of Manhattan's Chinatown during the 1950s.

In the early 1960s scores of Taiwan Chinese immigrant households also appeared in Elmhurst. The New York Chinese used the IND subway for direct travel to Chinatown for shopping or work. The immigrant Chinese, however, were mainly Mandarin and Taiwanese speakers who did not understand the Toysan and Cantonese spoken by most of Chinatown's established or newly arriving residents.[1] Cuban refugees in the late 1950s added to a Latin American mix of long-settled Colombians and growing numbers of Puerto Ricans. By the early 1960s they were joined by even larger cohorts of Dominicans, who used political connections to obtain visas or left their island following Trujillo's assassination in 1961. The Dominicans settled mainly in Corona Plaza, where they rented and bought homes from both whites and African Americans. By 1964 Latin Americans in Corona Plaza were numerous enough that a Spanish-language congregation of Puerto Ricans, Dominicans, and Cubans reopened the First United Methodist Church, which had been closed since its Italian congregation disbanded in 1957.[2]

Immigration Reform

In 1965 Congress passed the Hart-Celler Act, which would widen the flow of Latin American and Asian immigration, although that was hardly the original intent of this legislation.[3] During the 1950s pressure to eliminate the 1924 National Origins Act quotas favoring northern Europe came from Senator John F. Kennedy and other Democratic legislators who had South and East European constituents. By the early 1960s, Poland, Italy, and Greece had large backlogs of immigrants waiting for visas, and Americans of these ancestral nationalities were lobbying for immigration reform.

After Kennedy's assassination, President Lyndon Johnson endorsed the immigration bill and signed it in 1965. The law set an annual maximum quota of 20,000 per country within an overall Eastern Hemisphere immigration ceiling of 170,000. Spouses, unmarried minor children, and parents of U.S. citizens were admissible above this ceiling, as were designated groups of refugees. The expectation was that backlogged European nations would fill their expanded quotas, and relatively few other Old World immigrants would apply for visas.

The anticipated European immigration occurred and then diminished in the 1970s. By the early 1980s Europeans amounted to only 11 percent of U.S. immigrants as economic prosperity at home and intra-European migration led to a reduction in visa applications. According to the Italian American proprietor of a Corona Heights homemade wine business, few Italian immigrants were arriving by the mid-1980s, whereas in the late 1950s and early 1960s Italians had been coming "every week, [and] then people had to wait for visas."

During the 1970s an increased volume of Asian immigrants filled the annual Eastern Hemisphere ceiling by applying for occupational or "family reunification" visas. Under the Hart-Celler Act, 10 percent of annual visas were allocated to immigrant professionals and scientists, and another 10 percent to workers in occupations for which the U.S. Department of Labor certified that American job-seekers were in short supply. Designed for European immigrants, the family reunification provisions covered 74 percent of annual visas: 30 percent were for adult children of U.S. citizens, 24 percent for their brothers and sisters (the spouse and minor children of a qualified adult immigrant could be admitted under that person's visa category), and 20 percent for spouses and unmarried adult children of "permanent residents," those legally admitted immigrants who were not citizens. The 6 percent of visas allocated to refugees from Communist countries were added in 1980 to those for dependents of permanent residents.

Latin American and Caribbean immigrants were treated less favorably in the 1965 immigration act. Within an annual ceiling of 120,000, Western Hemisphere immigrants could apply only for occupational visas. The per-country limit of 20,000 did not apply, however—mainly to placate Mexico, supplier of the majority of New World immigrants before 1965. As with Eastern Hemisphere immigrants, the spouses, minor children, and parents of U.S. citizens were admitted above the annual ceiling. And in addition to the annual Western Hemisphere quota, 370,000 Cuban refugees entered the United States between 1965 and 1979.

Latin American and Caribbean health professionals were especially well represented, as they were among Asian immigrants with no U.S. kin. In 1965 President Johnson signed the Medicare and Medicaid legislation, which expanded health coverage for elderly, disabled, and poor Americans, and this vastly increased health-care funding and jobs. Even before 1965, however, several hundred Latin American professionals, half of them doctors, were immigrating each year; in 1962 a third of the civil engineers graduating in the Dominican Republic migrated to the United States, and by the mid-1970s they all did.[4] Between 1961 and 1975 some 60,000 Latin American professionals arrived, and professionals from India, South Korea, Taiwan, and the Philippines also joined this "brain drain" exodus. In many countries medical education had become oriented to producing U.S.-bound graduates trained in high-tech hospital care.

Elmhurst Hospital recruited staff at all levels throughout the 1960s and employed many Latin American and Asian immigrants, who found housing nearby. Indeed, one Korean nurse who settled in Elmhurst during the 1960s later became a real estate agent and built her business by locating homes and apartments for Korean nurses and other medical professionals.[5] During the 1970s large numbers of Asian immigrants also became citizens and used the family reunification preferences to obtain visas for relatives. This created constantly expanding networks of kin, and a widening spectrum of age and class backgrounds as older and less well-educated relatives arrived.

Family reunification became even more important after 1976 when the occupational preference for medical doctors ended, and all new occupational visas required a specific job offer. In 1977 the annual per-county limit of 20,000 visas was applied to Western Hemisphere nations, and the separate Western and Eastern Hemisphere ceilings were merged into one of 290,000 per year. The full visa preference system was also extended to the Western Hemisphere, allowing Latin Americans to build kin-based migration chains through family reunification.

The 1965 immigration law also permitted Asians and, after 1977, Latin Americans to "regularize" temporary student or business visas within an immigrant visa category while in the United States. This benefited mainly foreign students, of whom there were 300,000 by 1981. Persons who overstayed student or tourist visas, or who worked while holding them, entered the category often termed "illegal aliens." Relatively few undocumented immigrants in New York City arrived clandestinely; most were "visa overstayers." There were, however, some individuals who purchased phony documents, bribed American officials, arranged marriages of convenience to U.S. citizens, or traveled on tourist visas to Puerto Rico and then flew to New York, representing themselves as Puerto Ricans.[6]

The Local Impact of Immigration

The immigrants of the 1960s and 1970s internationalized Elmhurst-Corona. " 'Plaza de las Americas': That's What They Ought to Call Corona Plaza," proclaimed a 1968 *Long Island Press* report of Colombian and Argentinian newspapers for sale, Mexican features at the local movie house, and a "Shango" *botanica* where spiritualists purchased religious articles. Headlined "Queens Swaying to a Latin Beat," a 1970 *Daily News* story explored the nightclub scene on Roosevelt Avenue, including appearances by *salsa* musicians Tito Puente and the Orquesta Broadway. In 1975 the *New York Post* noted that Corona Plaza was known to Dominicans as "Sabana Iglesias," named for a town in their country's Cibao region, and Elmhurst and Jackson Heights were "Chapinerito" to Colombians, referring to the Bogotá suburb Chapinero. In 1979 the *New York Times* reported that a quarter of Elmhurst's 11373 zip code was composed of "registered aliens"; Colombians were most numerous, followed by Chinese, Filipinos, Ecuadorians, Indians, Koreans, Dominicans, Argentinians, and others.[7]

Shopping Strips

Many immigrants soon established businesses. To white residents their stores dramatized ongoing change, opening next to or replacing familiar ones. More than 140 immigrant firms still in operation in 1986 had opened during the 1960s and 1970s. Ninety were owned by Latin Americans, including Colombians (twenty businesses), Cubans (thirteen), Argentinians (twelve), Dominicans (nine), Ecuadorians (nine), Puerto Ricans (six), a Chilean, a Honduran, a Peruvian, and a Salvadoran (one each), and others whose nationality our team did not learn. Another fifty-three businesses were owned by Asians: Chinese (twenty-one), Koreans (sixteen), Indians (eleven), Pakistanis (two), Thais (two), and one Filipino.

Immigrants arriving in Queens during the 1960s and 1970s found a borough losing its retail base as white American proprietors moved away or retired, and at the same time increasing its population of potential customers. While retail businesses fell by 1,200 during the 1960s—an average loss of ninety stores per community district—Queens gained 177,000 residents, and annual retail sales grew from $1.7 billion to $2.4 billion.[8] The majority of immigrant-owned businesses in Elmhurst-Corona were of the very types being abandoned by white Americans—gift and electronics shops, laundries and dry cleaners, newsstands and liquor stores, meat and fish stores, convenience groceries and fruit and vegetable stands, drugstores and florists, barbers and beauty salons, furniture and pet stores, clothing and shoe stores—and they competed for customers of all backgrounds.

A few other stores offered services familiar to Americans but using the immigrants' own languages: auto repair shops, driving schools, real estate offices, travel agencies.[9] Only a small proportion of the new firms were oriented to customers of the owners' ethnic or regional background. These included two Argentine butcher shops and a pizzeria; a Colombian bakery, record store, and two restaurants; a Cuban restaurant; an Ecuadorian record store and two restaurants; a Puerto Rican *botanica;* two Chinese groceries; a Filipino grocery; two Indian groceries and a *sari* (women's clothing) store; a Pakistani grocery and *halal* (Islamic) butcher; and a Thai grocery.[10]

Overall, Queens was a profitable frontier for immigrant entrepreneurs, but few of them had had small-business experience in their homelands. Most were downwardly mobile professionals facing an English-language barrier, or upwardly mobile workers. Funds from home countries were not their major source of capitalization. Neither were the rotating credit arrangements (called *hui* by Chinese, *san* or *sociedad* by Dominicans, and *kye* by Koreans) in which a group of acquaintances pooled equal cash contributions, each member periodically taking the total amount. Instead, immigrant proprietors drew primarily on personal savings to open their enterprises, and on family-member labor to operate them.[11]

Housing

As immigrant newcomers settled on residential blocks and in apartment buildings in CD4, Latin Americans generally preceded Asians. Many Latin Americans who came before 1960 were "white" in appearance—Colombians, Cubans, and other "Spanish" families, as their white American neighbors called them. A son of Swedish immigrants who grew up in South Elmhurst in the 1930s and 1940s recalled "some discrimination" on the part of a white neighbor when "Argentines" replaced an Irish family on their block in 1954. More Latin Americans followed, and in 1974 the Swedish man moved back to the block with his Mexican wife. Then, "in the late 1970s Asians, from China, India, moved in, one at a time. . . . Now [in 1987] there is a Dominican Republic–Costa Rican couple—black Hispanics. I joke [to my neighbor] that he didn't sell when *I* took over the house."

For those who bore the brunt of discrimination, the experience remained indelible. A Puerto Rican medical technician who sees himself as "dark" encountered racial prejudice while living in California in the 1960s. When his light-complexioned children began to speak about "those blacks," he decided to move back to New York. In 1967 he bought a house in Corona, and "when I moved in, the people on the block all put up 'For Sale' signs." Not until years later did he realize that this was meant to show him he wasn't wanted. In the 1970s he became active in his block association and at St. Leo's Church. "*Now* [in 1989] this is a very mixed block—Italian, Oriental, Dominican, Puerto Rican, Polish."[12]

It was primarily space made available by whites who had already left that brought Latin American and Asian residents to CD4. From the perspective of Herman Gaillard, a white Elmhurst real estate broker since the late 1940s, "a major residential attraction of the area was the availability of reasonably priced apartments just outside the [Manhattan] core. With a surplus of units [by 1964], apartment owners were not 'too choosy' about whom they accepted as tenants."[13] As John Rowan remembered, "My generation were leaving in the 1960s. Their parents were left behind—some moved out, some died. This created a vacuum, and at that time the new immigrants arrived and moved in [and] everyone mixed around rather than establish ethnic enclaves. Take my [apartment building] floor—Chinese, Spanish, Greek, an old Irish lady, and me."

By the early 1970s several white American realtors had added Colombian associates to service this new group's desire to buy homes. In addition, new real estate businesses were formed by immigrants themselves; a Dominican agency was operating in Corona Plaza by the late 1960s.[14] Of the twenty-four real estate offices from the 1960s and 1970s that were still active in Elmhurst-Corona in 1986, only six were owned by white Americans. Nine were owned by Latin Americans (Colombian, Cuban, Ecuadorian, Peruvian), and two by Spaniards; three were Korean, one Chinese, and one Indian.

The entrance of Latin American and Asian immigrants into the CD4 housing market had little impact on its long-standing closure to African Americans. Aside from Lefrak City, growth in black numbers was mainly in census tracts adjacent to the Lefrak complex. In part a predictable expansion of African American residents on the perimeter of a new black enclave, this was facilitated by "fair housing" regulations in buildings constructed with government financing, such as the

Sherwood Village rentals. Overall, then, immigrant newcomers moved into a "white" housing market and made it their own. White residents increasingly found they had immigrant neighbors, and in most of Elmhurst-Corona any black neighbor was more likely to be an immigrant than an African American. In the 1980 census, 3 percent of Elmhurst-Corona's Latin American residents identified themselves as "black," 60 percent as "white," and 36 percent as "other."[15]

One small point of "non-Hispanic black" population growth beyond Lefrak City was the Baxter-Roosevelt section of Elmhurst, where 440 black residents were recorded in 1970 and 1,050 in 1980. The 250 Haitian households established there by 1970 no doubt accounted for most of this census count. Many Haitians who immigrated in the 1950s were light-skinned and may have designated themselves "white" or "other" on U.S. census forms. But as Haitian immigration grew during the 1960s and 1970s, more of that nation's black majority arrived, among them most of the Elmhurst Haitians I encountered in the 1980s.[16]

Some Haitians probably entered the CD4 housing market via accommodating real estate agents, as did Latin American immigrants of color. In addition, however, numbers of immigrant Haitian women took jobs in Elmhurst during the 1970s as household workers or caretakers for elderly whites; some then bought homes from their employers or their employers' neighbors when these white residents moved.[17]

Houses of Worship

Changes in Elmhurst-Corona's houses of worship brought many established whites into contact with immigrant newcomers. During the 1960s Latin Americans revived the declining Our Lady of Sorrows Roman Catholic parish in Corona Plaza, and by the early 1970s Dominicans and South Americans made up half of the congregation. Conflict over liturgical music and over an Irish pastor's reluctance to offer more than one Spanish mass or permit Spanish-language church organizations was exacerbated by the lack of a Latin American priest. Nonetheless, Dominicans traveled weekly from Manhattan and Brooklyn to join family members at Our Lady. At St. Bartholomew's in Elmhurst there was not only a Spanish mass but a French one for Haitian communicants. At Ascension in South Elmhurst a charismatic group led by a Colombian priest attracted hundreds of Latin American worshipers in the 1970s. The first Spanish mass at St. Leo's in Corona Heights was held in 1977.[18]

White Protestants also encountered immigrants at churches where white membership was diminishing, and congregations that could not replenish their numbers were in trouble. Indeed, the white American Elmhurst Methodist and Christian Science churches disbanded in the early 1980s, and both buildings were sold to Korean congregations. Other churches welcomed newcomers and survived. In 1980 the Reformed Church of Newtown included congregants from thirteen Asian, Caribbean, and Latin American countries, and it began a Chinese-language ministry that would eventually involve a majority of its members.[19] Still other Protestant churches survived by dividing Sunday worship time with independent congregations that rented space in their buildings. The Reformed Church rented to a Korean Methodist congregation for seven years during the 1970s and more briefly to Filipino and Latin American groups. Initiating non-English ministries or renting space, however, brought risks. The fledgling congregations dreamed of acquiring their own buildings, and several eventually did.

Meanwhile, other immigrants organized their own houses of worship. By 1978 there were three Spanish-language Baptist and Evangelical congregations in renovated commercial buildings, and a Korean Unitarian-Universalist group was meeting in an Elmhurst home.[20] There was also a Southern Baptist church in Lefrak City, the only black church in this now sizable African American community, though several well-established denominational and smaller storefront black churches existed not far away in North Corona–East Elmhurst.[21]

Less familiar to Elmhurst-Corona whites, blacks, and most immigrants were the Hindu and Muslim forms of worship that were becoming part of the neighborhood. The Geeta Hindu Temple began in a storefront near Newtown High School in 1972. When its doors were open, passersby could see the several large statues of deities which faced its North Indian Hindi and Gujarati worshipers. By the mid-1970s four hundred were attending its Sunday afternoon services.[22] Muslim worship was inaugurated in 1961 by a group of Kuwaiti, Libyan, Pakistani, and Sudanese medical residents at Elmhurst Hospital. In the 1970s the Sunni Muslim Masjid al-Falah was established in Corona Plaza by a group of Pakistani Punjabis. It was defaced with anti-Iran graffiti during the period when American hostages were imprisoned in that country, and in 1979 men in ski masks threw firebombs, causing $2,500 in damage. White and Latin American residents, however, told a reporter they knew of no community antagonism toward the mosque, and it remained in Corona through the 1990s.[23]

Schools

Between 1970 and 1975 pupil numbers fell by 4 percent in New York City's public schools, but during these same years immigration produced the opposite effect in CD4.[24] Most immigrants were young adults, and as their families matured and their kin networks expanded via family reunification, the numbers of both American-born and newly arrived immigrant children grew, overcrowding the district's schools.

In Elmhurst-Corona's five primary schools, whites dropped from 89 to 28 percent of the student body between 1960 and 1976; by that time, Latin American children made up 50 percent, Asians 12 percent, and blacks 10 percent. In Newtown High School (which drew students from beyond CD4) whites fell from 93 to 38 percent between 1960 and 1976, while Latin American students rose to 37 percent, Asians 9 percent, and blacks 16 percent. In addition, all these schools were packed. In 1960 the five primary schools were at 70 percent of capacity, but by 1976 they were at 114 percent. Newtown High School was already at 113 percent of capacity in 1960, years before the Corona high school was even proposed. In 1976, even with a four-year-old annex, it stood at 143 percent.

The crisis in the primary schools would have been even worse if makeshift plans had not been approved by the local School Board 24.[25] As crowding overwhelmed PS89 in the heavily immigrant Baxter-Roosevelt section of Elmhurst, a "mini-school" was approved for its kindergarten classes in 1971—a prefabricated, one-story structure to be erected on a school playground, thus diminishing recreation space. When it was proposed to place it instead on the spacious grounds of PS102 in South Elmhurst, that school's parent association objected. Seeking support against the mini-school, a group of PS102 parents brought the matter to a 1971 CB4 meeting chaired by South Elmhurst resident Michael Dowd. The ensuing discussion of "illegal aliens" (the first mention of this phrase in CB4's minutes) indicated that the parents' objection was to an influx of Latin American children in their mainly white school. They won. A six-room mini-school opened in 1973 at PS89, covering most of its small playground. Enrollment continued to increase at PS89, however, and in 1976 its kindergarten classes began to be bused to a school three miles away in the southern tier of School District 24. This "temporary" solution continued into the 1990s.

Community Board 4 had no formal purview over public education, but it became an arena for politicking over school crowding. As immigration into Elmhurst-Corona climbed during the 1970s, requests for help in obtaining mini-schools were brought to CB4 by parents from PS13 in Newtown and PS19 in Corona Plaza, where they also staged a boycott over school conditions in 1976. Eventually mini-schools were built on playgrounds at both schools, and also at PS102, where by 1976 Latin American and Asian enrollment from its own catchment area amounted to 45 percent.

From the start of school decentralization in 1969, School Board 24 was controlled by a "Parochial Slate" majority that represented the interests of local Roman Catholic schools. SB24's major concern, preserved even at the expense of public-school daytime programs during the city's fiscal crisis, was to fund afterschool programs to benefit parochial school students. The majority of the nine SB24 members, all white, were from the southern portion of the district—Maspeth, Middle Village, Ridgewood, and Glendale. Elmhurst was represented by the Reverend John Garkowski, a priest at St. Bart's who was elected to the board in 1977 and each election thereafter as part of the well-executed, get-out-the-vote campaign in SD24's network of twenty-two Catholic parishes.[26] Corona's representative, Lou Simeone, a CB4 member, fought for more classrooms and new schools in Elmhurst-Corona but was frustrated by the city's fiscal crisis and by what he called "a bunch of Archie Bunkers from Ridgewood" who dominated SB24.

Just as PS102 had lobbied to keep PS89's immigrant students out of its mainly white school, so SB24 maneuvered with busing, mini-schools, and carefully drawn school catchment lines to keep the Latin American, Asian, and black children of its northern tier in place. SD24's southern tier schools were not overcrowded during the 1970s. SD30 to the north of Elmhurst-Corona (see Figure 7) also had underutilized schools, but as Simeone reported to CB4 in 1976, its school board wanted an "ethnic breakdown" of Corona students before making seats available to relieve overcrowding. By the mid-1970s the black and immigrant children of CD4 had thus become a political football in school district politics in western Queens.

The Great "Illegal Aliens" Panic of 1974

Much as white CB4 leaders misdefined Lefrak City's growing black population as "welfare cases," they also misdefined Elmhurst-Corona's immigrant population as "illegal aliens." But unlike "welfare cases," whose numbers might be contained but not ejected, the phrase "illegal aliens" suggested a law-and-order problem solvable by arrest and deportation. Both misdefinitions masked real issues: Lefrak's overbuilding and maintenance reductions, and African American social and political equality in the first instance; population implosion and overcrowded schools and housing in the second. In both cases, progress in facing these issues was made only after definitions were revised, hysteria over newcomers subsided, and leaders began to reconsider the problems as matters affecting the "quality of life" of all CD4 residents—white and black, American and immigrant alike.

At the 1971 meeting where South Elmhurst parents objected to a proposed mini-school, CB4 member Steve Trimboli announced his intention to protest in writing to the Immigration and Naturalization Service (INS) about the numbers of foreign students remaining in the United States after their visas expired. Then in March 1972 the issue of illegal room rentals in private homes—the emergence of "rooming houses," as John Rowan put it—was first discussed. Again debate was phrased in terms of "illegal aliens" and expired visas, and a motion calling for INS investigation of undocumented immigrants was passed.

At the May 1972 CB4 meeting Rowan reported that federal relocation funds were available to help alleviate rooming-house overcrowding. Peter Nefsky, an Argentinian and the sole Latin American member of the board, offered to work on this with Rowan. But John Costello, a retired post office official and World War II air force major, interjected that the Newtown Civic Association (NCA) to which he belonged was planning to meet with the INS. As far as he was concerned, if illegal aliens were dealt with properly by the INS "the housing and

Figure 7. Queens School Districts

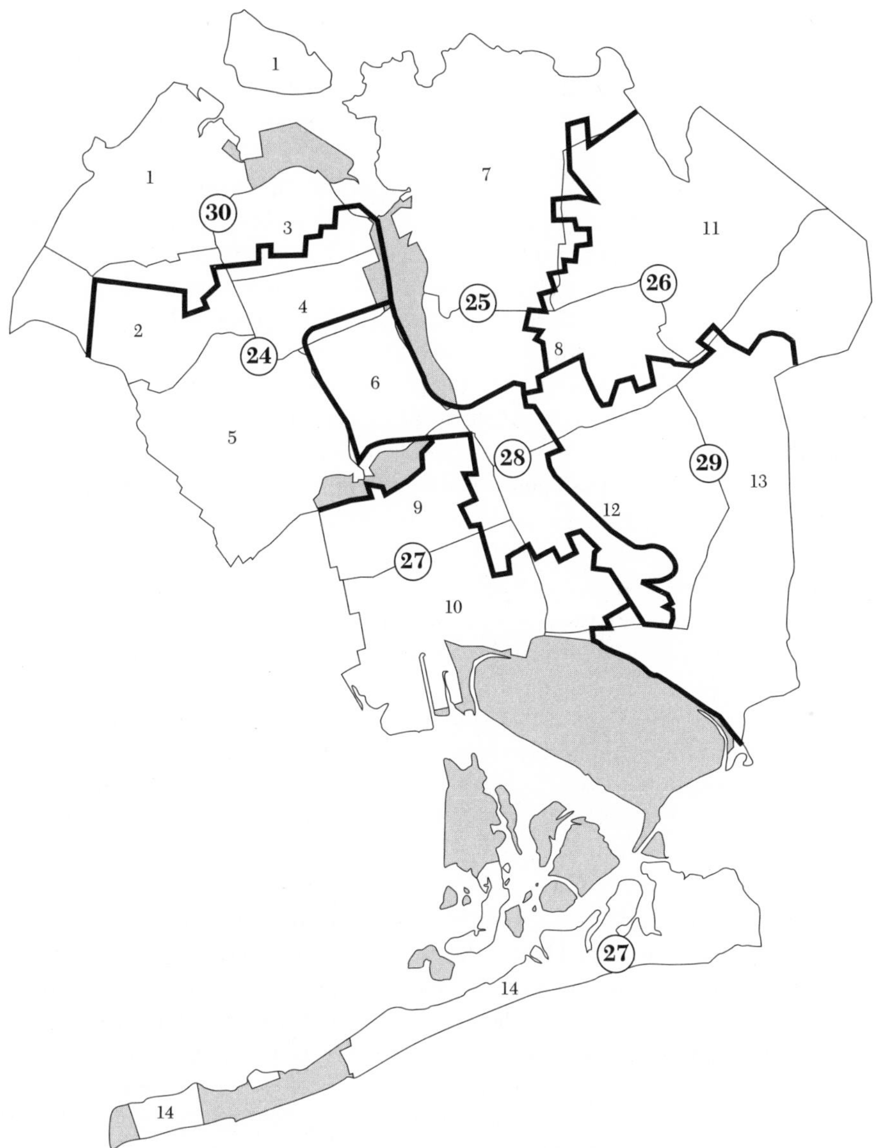

Heavy lines demarcating seven Queens School Districts are overlaid on light lines dividing fourteen Queens Community Districts

neighborhood deterioration problem would solve itself." The meeting closed with a garbled report that the PTA at PS19 in Corona Plaza was about to sponsor a "vote on turning PS19 into a Spanish-speaking school with English as a second language."

Panic was setting in and would soon erupt. In June 1974 a CB4 meeting was called to air the "illegal aliens" issue. Costello's NCA had sent notices with the addresses of overcrowded Elmhurst buildings to all elected officials in the area. One of the usually absent city council members reported that he had spoken with the INS and learned that they rarely operated in CD4, and then only on raids; he suggested that residents ask their congressional representatives to pressure INS for more enforcement. Costello declared that the INS had "all the information they need" to apprehend undocumented immigrants in Elmhurst. "Illegal aliens are causing overcrowding [in] our schools," he added, and "if teachers must take time to explain to non-English-speaking children, they are taking time away from English-speaking children."

Two days before the August 1974 CB4 meeting the *Daily News* ran a story headlined "Illegal Aliens, a Flood Tide in Elmhurst." It quoted CB4 chair Steve Trimboli's reference to the Baxter-Roosevelt section as a site of "people pollution. . . . Thousands of illegal aliens live here," most of them from "Colombia, Ecuador, and Venezuela," he asserted. He added that they worked "off the books" and that neither employers nor immigrant workers paid withholding tax. In a formula he would repeat many times, Trimboli stated, "My parents were immigrants, and this country was built by immigrants. But this is getting ridiculous. Our community is being overrun. Our schools, housing, and many jobs are being taken by people who have no legal right to be here." The *Daily News* story also reported that Henry Wagner, the Manhattan INS chief of investigations, had been receiving reports about undocumented immigrants in CD4 "for years. But the problem in Elmhurst-Corona is just the tip of the iceberg." Wagner estimated there were "more than a million" illegal aliens in metropolitan New York, and with only 196 agents it was impossible to respond effectively.[27]

Following the *News* story, a conservative radio talk-show host, Bob Grant, announced that "illegal aliens" were on the agenda at the next CB4 meeting. Although no public hearing had been scheduled, an angry crowd of 150 showed up and demanded one "here and now." Ethnic slurs were hurled, and speakers who tried to mollify the crowd were shouted down. Martin Knorr of Ridgewood, a state senator, arrived to pump his bill (just vetoed by Governor Malcolm Wilson) making employment of undocumented workers a felony and their employers subject to fines. CB4 passed a resolution demanding that the INS enforce "the laws on the books" in Elmhurst-Corona.

At the September CB4 meeting Steve Trimboli admitted that he had been shocked by some of what was said in August, and after conferring with borough president Manes he had asked persons pursuing the issue "to cool it." CB4 then approved Trimboli's request to convene a meeting on immigration with federal and city agencies, to be followed by a public hearing "not for an emotional confrontation along ethnic lines, but in order to meet this problem for the betterment of the entire community."

The interagency meeting was held in October 1974 at U.S. Representative Benjamin Rosenthal's Elmhurst office. INS officials emphasized their insufficient manpower to mount the illegal alien dragnet that some NCA members proposed. They explained that with 3 million aliens entering Kennedy Airport each year, just the task of checking their visas was enormous. Moreover, when undocumented immigrants were apprehended, they were freed on $500 pretrial bonds, which many simply forfeited. Rosenthal appointed a task force to pursue the issue.

That same month some three thousand Queens residents, including six busloads of Elmhurst NCA members, attended a Sunnyside "Town Meeting" on illegal aliens addressed by thirteen elected officials—including Knorr, Rosenthal, and Bronx Congress member Mario Biaggi—and CB4 chair Trimboli and talk-show host Bob Grant. The chair of CB3 opened the meeting with a call for five thousand federal marshals to sweep through New York City and enforce the immigration laws. Biaggi spoke about his employer sanctions bill, a federal equivalent of Knorr's state legislation, and Rosenthal outlined his bill addressing the lack of coordination between visa issuance by the State Department and visa enforcement by the Justice Department.

A tense CB4 public hearing that filled the 1,100-seat Newtown High School auditorium followed in November 1974, with Bob Grant again attending in person and announcing it on radio. A State Department representative promised efforts to tighten issuance of student and tourist visas. Biaggi's bill was discussed again and endorsed by CB4 later that month.

In early 1975 CB4's attention turned to Lefrak City, but the NCA continued to focus on "illegal aliens" in Elmhurst. Its January *Newtown Crier* headline, "Our 'Silent Invasion,' " was followed by John Costello–style rhetoric about "the possible social and economic death of our community" because "illegal aliens [were] usurping jobs that could be filled by American citizens, . . . spong[ing] on public services while paying little, if any, taxes, [and constituting] a cancer on the city's health." Mass roundups and detention sites were called for. The *Crier* also spotlighted the all-too-real "squatters quarters [in Elmhurst] made available by absentee landlords. These business men cash in on the fact that the existing building codes and housing laws are not being enforced."

Increasingly, the "illegal alien" problem in CD4 was being redefined as a housing issue, and this was the thrust of Representative Rosenthal's task force recommendations later in 1975. The same redefinition was evident in the *Crier*'s report of a 1976 tour arranged by the NCA for U.S. Senator James Buckley.

> The first stop . . . was at a three-family [infill] house built within the last year and selling in the price range of $120,000. . . . On this house were three mail-

> boxes—one for each apartment. The first box had three Hispanic names on the outside and on the inside of the lid there were four more Hispanic names taped on! The next house attached to the above had a sign on the balcony—"ROOMS TO LET." . . . Another house, at least fifty years old and possibly at one time a two-family house, had eight door bells around the door-jam. . . . We stopped at a grouping of apartment houses. One was known as having mostly tenants from Columbia [*sic*], the other from Ecuador. . . . The Senator spoke with people outside who stated the conditions within were awful. These people were Hispanic-speaking [*sic*] Americans who stated these problems were caused by South American immigrants who, they believed, were illegal aliens.

By now it was clear even to the NCA that not all Latin Americans in CD4 were illegal immigrants. The majority, undoubtedly, were not. Elmhurst's combined Latin American and Asian 1980 census count (excluding Puerto Ricans) was 39,000. This figure included a substantial (if unascertainable) number of naturalized citizens and American-born children; 18,000 more were valid visa holders and permanent residents who had voluntarily registered with the INS in 1979. And this number was itself an undercount of legal immigrants, as compliance with the poorly publicized INS annual registration regulation was so spotty that it was discontinued in 1981.[28]

Some undocumented immigrants in Elmhurst-Corona did escape the 1980 census, but in fact 2.1 million undocumented aliens nationwide *were* counted, including 188,000 in New York City. Careful demographic analyses indicated that the total number of undocumented immigrants in 1980 was no greater than 3.5 million. It is reasonable to infer that two-thirds of CD4's undocumented immigrants, like those elsewhere, *were* included in its census enumeration.[29]

The panic stirred by Costello and Trimboli was abetted by inflated estimates of illegal aliens from government officials. If an upper estimate of 375,000 undocumented immigrants could be projected for New York City in 1980, then the New York INS estimate of "more than a million" in 1974 was misleading. The Koch administration's 1979 "conservative estimate" of 750,000 to a million, reprinted by the *Newtown Crier,* was baseless, a ploy to bolster the city's later call for upward adjustment of the census count. Even more bogus were INS Commissioner Leonard Chapman's 1975 pronouncement that there were 4 to 12 million illegals in the United States, and President Gerald Ford's 1976 statement, "The main problem is how to get rid of those six to eight million of aliens." Still more irresponsibly, Representative Biaggi told CB4 in January 1975 that "Mr. Chapman, of Immigration privately estimates it as high as forty (40) million."[30]

Even while the clamor over illegal aliens was peaking in Elmhurst-Corona, some voices acknowledged that immigrant residents and their needs should be part of the neighborhood's agenda. In November 1974 Argentinian CB4 member Peter Nefsky told the *Daily News,* "Sometimes I think that all this talk is a conspiracy to get rid of Hispanic immigrants. We hear the most bitter charges imaginable being made about Hispanic immigrants. The vast majority of the so-called illegal aliens in Elmhurst and Corona are here legally. The flap is caused by those who simply don't like it."[31]

The message began to sink in. In December 1974 John Rowan informed CB4 that the Rosenthal task force would deal with "aliens, both legal and illegal." Helen Marshall, the African American Democratic district leader in East Elmhurst, told the CD3-CD4 district cabinet in May 1975 that discussion of "illegal aliens" should "avoid implicating the legal residents of Hispanic origin who are good hard-working people." And that same month Reverend Kelly Grimsley of Elmhurst Baptist Church wrote in the *Newtown Crier*, "We have allowed fears and prejudices to erect barriers between different national and ethnic groups. . . . Elmhurst will not improve by increasing hostilities among sub-groups."

School crowding was no simple matter to be solved by rooting out "illegal aliens" but a result of immigrant family formation and the policies of SB24. Even local parochial schools were filled with immigrant children as the white student pool diminished. By 1983 St. Bart's students were 40 percent Latin American, 25 percent Asian, and 5 percent black. Immigrant public school enrollment in fact made possible the only "impact aid" for localities such as CD4 which were disproportionately affected by the post-1965 immigration. Federal bilingual education funds began to flow to PS89 in 1973 for Spanish, French, and later Mandarin, Cantonese, and Korean instruction, and to other Elmhurst-Corona schools thereafter.[32]

Immigrants and Jobs

Charges that immigrants were working "off the books," failing to pay their "fair share" of taxes, and taking jobs away from Americans reverberated nationally.[33] Opponents of immigration failed to appreciate that tax evasion and off-the-books economic activity were expanding ubiquitously and involving citizens as well as immigrants at every economic level.[34] Advocates oversimplified issues by insisting that immigrants took only the jobs Americans did not want. Neither side acknowledged the longtime role of low-wage immigrant labor in the New York and national economies. And neither side examined the impact of growing numbers of immigrant professionals on the job market and its educational infrastructure.

The size and composition of post-1965 immigration emerged with little legislative consideration of their impact on the U.S. labor force. The annual ceiling of 290,000 was not derived from projected manpower needs, despite demographic forecasts of a future worker shortage due to the declining U.S. birthrate. With immediate relatives of U.S. citizens permitted to enter above the numerical ceiling, by 1978 the total amounted to 600,000 legal immigrants a year. Those admitted under occupational preferences had no obligation to remain in the jobs for which their visas were issued; those admitted under family reunification were free to take any job at all.[35] It was the actual impact of immigrant workers on the labor force that triggered popular reaction, not the specifics of immigration law. This impact varied at different points in New York City's work force.

Jobs Americans Don't Want

Legal and illegal immigrants, largely from Mexico, constituted the bulk of American farm labor by the 1970s, with little U.S.-born competition.[36] Low-paid immigrant workers also permitted America's upper and upper middle classes to employ Caribbean, Latin American, and Asian child-care and household workers; African-American women having largely deserted this occupation in the 1960s, U.S. workers willing to take such jobs were in short supply.[37] Only a few household workers were employed in Elmhurst-Corona, but poorly paid sewing-machine operator jobs were available in increasing number by the 1970s. While employment in the New York City garment industry dropped from 267,000 to 148,000 between 1960 and 1975, sewing shops in CD4 proliferated.

Much apparel production was shifting overseas, and imports accounted for half of all garments sold in the United States by the 1980s. Standardization, particularly of casual styles popular since the 1960s, made it profitable to ship production to U.S. regional or overseas contractors who paid cheap wages. Design, cutting, and marketing, however, remained in New York. The sewing jobs that also stayed in the city were more and more limited to skilled custom work and to rapid "spot market" production of styles that were in demand and sizes or colors that ran short.

As the total number of apparel jobs was falling, older white, black, and Puerto Rican garment workers were retiring faster still, and Latin American and Asian immigrants were replacing them. Jewish and Italian shop owners were increasingly joined by Chinese, Dominican, and other immigrant entrepreneurs. The industry also decentralized from its Manhattan "Seventh Avenue" core. Garment shops in Chinatown grew from 16 in 1960 to 430 by 1980—and Chinatown accounted for only 10 percent of the apparel work force; hundreds more Latin American and Asian sewing shops appeared throughout upper Manhattan, the Bronx, Brooklyn, and Queens. In 1981 the sociologist Roger Waldinger counted 57 shops in CD4; five years later our team counted 60 on Elmhurst-Corona's commercial blocks and residential streets.[38]

Working conditions in the "new sweatshops" were appalling. Poor heating, little ventilation, and fire hazards were common. Wages were often paid in cash, taxes and benefit deductions fudged and evaded. Children were employed illegally. Books were doctored so that piece work earnings over sixty-hour (or longer) weeks were recorded as the product of forty hours—a fiction that made substandard wages appear to meet the 1970s minimum of $2.90 per hour. Immigrant women knew their pay was low, but they understood that earnings could rise to twice the minimum wage with increased skill. Moreover, they appreciated the lack of a language barrier, the ease of finding a job and receiving training, the proximity of work to home and children, and the opportunity to be paid in cash and work extra hours if they wished.[39]

In 1977 CB4 members gained a glimpse into the shady maneuvers by which the sweatshop industry was expanding in their neighborhood. At the December meeting real estate agent George Perrotta spoke on behalf of the owner of a building in Corona Plaza, where a "prospective tenant" wished to operate "a dress-type factory." The change in site use required permission from the city's Board of Standards and Appeals, with a vote by CB4 the first step in the process.

Several CB4 members who had visited the site noted that "Hispanic and Oriental" sewing-machine operators were already at work there and were "probably . . . illegal aliens." Perrotta responded that the building owner needed the rental income and that illegal immigration was a federal responsibility. Since "the neighborhood is of Hispanic, Central American origin," he added, it was better for residents to work than to receive welfare. One board member retorted that "the neighborhood is Italian," a perception no longer reflecting demographic reality.

Lucille Martinez, CB4's only Latin American member and a Corona Plaza resident, said that when she had spoken in Spanish with women at the site, they were evasive, asking if she was "from the Police." Martinez nevertheless favored approval of the new sewing shop because it "would create jobs for our community." But board members were angry that site owner Pasquale Postiglione had already illegally rented the space, and they voted to table their decision until he appeared in person.

At the January 1978 meeting Postiglione explained that for several years he had been unable to sell the building. When approached by a sewing shop owner, Hone Lee, he offered him a temporary lease and hired Perrotta to pursue a change-of-use application. Postiglione assured the board that the twenty employees were legal residents, and his request was approved. CB4 members, however, now understood that local whites were complicit in the evasion and illegality that accompanied the growth of sweatshops in their neighborhood.

Working-Class Employment

Although Elmhurst-Corona's apparel shops provided some 1,500 local jobs, most working-class immigrants entered the citywide labor market, where the issue of competition with American-born workers was murkier. By the mid-1970s many white and black Americans in blue-collar and clerical positions found immigrants working in similar jobs or alongside them. But it was for reasons other than immigrant competition that they worried about the security and earning power of their own jobs.

In the seven years following the 1969 recession New York City lost 600,000 jobs, and employment fell to its lowest point since 1950. In 1974 the cost of living jumped 14 percent, and President Gerald Ford only reminded Americans of this by wearing a "Whip Inflation Now" button on his lapel. Increasingly, job openings in New York City called for college education and advanced training. "Good" working-class jobs—with high wages, fringe benefits, steady employment, safe working conditions, security, and advancement opportunities—were disappearing. Those readily available were "bad" jobs, with low wages, no benefits, intermittent employment, poor working conditions, no security, and no room for advancement.[40]

Many of the 180,000 manufacturing jobs that disappeared during the 1960s were "good" blue-collar jobs. This hemorrhage worsened in the 1970s as the city lost 270,000 more factory jobs. By 1980 only 496,000 manufacturing jobs remained, a fifth of them in the garment industry. Many others were what Spanish-speaking immigrants called *trabajos chiquitos* (little jobs): low-wage, "bad" work in the jewelry, machine parts, office supply, toy, and other light industries of Long Island City, the south Bronx, and Brooklyn. In these factories legal and illegal immigrants worked together, as they did in apparel shops. Similar "bad" conditions characterized jobs in restaurants, whether owned by Americans or fellow immigrants. Elmhurst-Corona immigrants on their way to jobs like these constituted a sizable component of the 35,000 subway riders who by 1970 left the neighborhood each morning. Others traveled to work in vans and carpools.[41]

The immigrant working class included many who were downwardly mobile in relation to their home-country education and occupation. They took low-wage jobs because of their unfamiliarity with English or, for some, their undocumented status. They were often willing to pare living costs by sharing accommodations, and they restricted expenditures in order to save money or send funds to family members back home. Employers welcomed such workers. They worked steadily and accepted overtime even when not paid overtime rates. Many put up with what they well understood were "bad" jobs because earnings were greater than in their home societies. Some hoped eventually to invest in property or commercial ventures in their own countries, or in businesses in New York.[42]

Trabajo chiquito employment was at minimum wage or slightly higher. The journalist John Crewsdon discovered that employers who sought to hire Americans at these wage levels found few who would accept the working conditions or remain in the job beyond a few weeks. By accepting these low pay levels, immigrants may have kept afloat some enterprises that would have closed if employers had had to pay higher wages and upgrade workplaces to attract U.S.-born employees. Such has long been the "function" of immigrant labor, according to several economists and sociologists—a function employers who resisted immigration restriction or workplace regulation well understood. Indirectly, then, the supply of willing low-wage immigrant workers affected the availability, working conditions, and wage levels of jobs for some low-skilled Americans, and also for earlier immigrants.[43]

No one conducted a careful evaluation of this labor-market "impact," but during the 1970s some U.S.-born working-class New Yorkers clearly were falling behind, relative to immigrants. African Americans and Puerto Ricans had gained a sizable share of New York's "bad" working-class jobs as their populations increased in the 1950s and 1960s. During the 1970s the black population grew by only 150,000, while Latin Americans (overwhelmingly *not* Puerto Ricans) increased by 205,000 and Asians by 130,000. Researchers studying Dominicans and Colombians during the 1970s and later repeatedly found evidence that Latin American immigrants were displacing Puerto Rican workers. And surveys recorded employer's stated preferences for immigrant over black employees.[44]

Between 1970 and 1980 the proportion of employed, working-age U.S.-born black males dropped sharply in New York City, from 81 to 67 percent; for Puerto Ricans it dropped from 80 to 71 percent. During this "stagflation" decade the U.S.-born white proportion also fell, from 88 to 83 percent, yet it remained higher at the end of the decade than the figure for blacks and Puerto Ricans at the beginning. Immigrant Latin American men fared like whites, their employment falling from 90 to 82 percent. The proportion of employed, working-age Asian immigrant males actually *rose,* from 84 to 87 percent. Black employment relative to white had begun to decrease during the 1950s, before the impact of immigration. Its acceleration during the 1970s, however, occurred in a job market where immigrant employment was rising.[45]

Manufacturing jobs fell by 8,000 among African American New Yorkers during the 1970s, while Latin American immigrants gained 26,500 manufacturing jobs, and Asian immigrants gained 19,000. During this same decade immigrants also moved into low-wage jobs generated by New York City's expanding financial and business services sectors; these included office cleaners, security guards, messengers and deliverers, and maintenance staff for residential buildings. For these sectors, however, careful study of competition between immigrants and black and Puerto Rican New Yorkers was lacking.[46]

Some immigrants were also finding employment in the job sectors that whites worried most about holding or losing. White New Yorkers dominated "contract construction," the office-building and residential projects that employed well-paid unionized workers. Office construction peaked during 1970–1972 and remained anemic during the rest of the decade. As construction workers looked elsewhere, they found the "additions and alterations" market dominated by nonunion immigrants who worked at lower wages.[47] Here, as in garment, restaurant, and factory work, some employment was off the books, but much was not; immigrant workers were generating tax revenues and payroll deductions.[48]

The immigrant impact was also felt in pink- and white-collar "good jobs." As immigrants improved their American English, acquired citizenship, and "learned the ropes," upward job mobility followed. Clerical positions in New York City dropped by 118,000 during the 1970s, but the falloff among the declining white population was even larger at 163,000. African Americans filled 12,000 clerical job openings; Latin American and Asian immigrants together, 20,000. Immigrants registered stronger gains than blacks in financial and business services: foreign-born Latin Americans and Asians gained 37,000 jobs; African Americans, 15,000. In contrast, African Americans took a larger share of government job openings during the 1970s, 21,000, while Latin Americans and Asians together gained 15,500.[49]

Small-Business Employment

When some of Elmhurst-Corona's Latin American and Asian immigrants moved into small-business proprietorship, both locally and elsewhere in the city, few established whites made accusations of "taking jobs away from Americans." Quite the reverse: "Thank God for the Chinese," said an Irish-American resident, explaining that immigrant businesses had revitalized Elmhurst's Broadway shopping strip as white storekeepers retired or moved away. The long business hours, convenient access, and low prices immigrant businesses offered, moreover, were widely appreciated.

Nonetheless, there was ambivalence about unfamiliar names, writing, items, and odors, especially in shops serving mainly immigrant clienteles. After telling me about the good prices at a "Hindu" electronics store on Broadway, a white Elmhurst-raised man added, "The shopping might have gotten better, but it's gotten too specialized toward the new wave of people coming in. You have to go closer to Rego Park if you want more Americanized shops. If you walk in the Korean stores, you really have to have a gas mask because of some of the stuff there. . . . I guess if you're used to it, it doesn't bother you. But not for people like us."

Retail employment in New York City contracted during the 1970s, falling from 444,000 to 377,000 jobs, yet the numbers of Latin American immigrant in retail jobs grew from 19,500 to 30,000, and Asians from 10,000 to 27,000. With family labor deployed in most immigrant businesses, it was nonrelated sales personnel and local teenagers seeking part-time jobs whose work opportunities diminished. In the 1970s this affected African American New Yorkers in particular, and their retail employment numbers fell from 52,000 to 42,000.[50]

White-Collar Salaried Employment

The jobs that expanded most dramatically during the 1970s and thereafter were those that "demand[ed] technical proficiency and emphasize[d] interpersonal communication," as sociologist Roger Waldinger characterized them. It was these professional, technical, and managerial positions, amounting to a quarter of all U.S. jobs by 1975, that the college-educated children of all Elmhurst-Corona residents hoped to attain. In 1980 white New Yorkers held the majority of such "best" jobs, and despite population decline, whites added 5,000 to their share during the 1970s. African Americans, one-quarter of the 1980 population, held 10 percent, having increased their share since 1970 by 25,000. Immigrant

Asians and Latin Americans, most of whom arrived during the 1970s, together outstripped this African American advance: Asians increased their professional, technical, and managerial jobs by 27,000, and Latin Americans by 12,000.[51]

What accounted for these substantial immigrant numbers was the "brain drain" visa preference of the 1965 immigration act. By 1980, 26 percent of the immigrants who arrived during the 1970s were in professional and technical occupations, as compared with 16 percent of U.S.-born Americans. That year immigrants accounted for 25 percent of New York State's health technicians, 20 percent of nurses, 20 percent of scientists, 16 percent of architects and engineers, and 14 percent of dentists.[52]

As immigrant professionals filled employment needs in industry, hospitals, and colleges—if frequently in the less prestigious locations, shifts, and fields—the question arose of what indirect effect this absorption of highly educated manpower was having on the U.S. social order. From one perspective, importing skilled professionals saved the United States the costs of training them. From another, educational investments that would produce similar numbers at home were not being made.

Between 1965 and 1975 some 75,000 foreign-trained doctors entered the U.S. By 1973 there were 7,000 immigrant Filipino doctors, compared with 6,000 African American physicians. As immigration lawyer Franklin Abrams observed in 1976, this shift to professional recruitment from abroad "to some extent injures many Americans by lessening the incentive to develop the skills of our own manpower." Political scientist Christina Brinkley-Carter was more blunt, pointing to the lack of "human capital investment . . . for native-born citizens who attend U.S. schools but are not educated," affecting in particular "minority populations" who in 1970 amounted to 17 percent of the total U.S. population but only 8 percent of professionals. "The number of immigrants and their rate of entry into professional occupations generally exceeds the corresponding numbers and rates for native minority entrants. . . . A sufficient number of openings may exist to accommodate both groups. But both groups are not being accommodated. . . . Given the patterns of institutionalized racism in our social and economic structure, a supply of immigrant labor represents an alternative to hiring native minorities."[53]

Immigrants were not responsible for U.S. immigration policy, employer hiring preferences, or national disinvestment in education, but the United States was indeed turning more and more to foreign skilled professionals. In 1980 U.S. citizens earned 25,900 doctoral degrees in American universities, and by 1992 the number had dropped slightly to 25,400 (those awarded to African Americans declined from 1,030 to 950). Over these same years, however, foreign recipients of American doctoral degrees jumped from 5,080 to 11,840. The 20 percent expansion in doctoral training over this period thus accrued entirely to the benefit of foreign students, many of whom stayed in the United States. The demand for science and engineering Ph.D.'s was expected to double by the year 2000, yet with 40 percent of these degrees going to foreign students, U.S. universities were making less effort to recruit and train U.S.-born students.[54]

The ripple effect of these employment and educational trends was a lessened labor-market demand for potential professionals educated in New York City. Coupled with crowding in Elmhurst-Corona schools and cuts in education funds after the 1975 fiscal crisis, the prospects for their children's upward mobility into professional, technical, and managerial jobs worried American and immigrant parents alike. Several anthropologists who studied New York City schools in the 1960s and 1970s uncovered low academic expectations for "minority" students among their teachers and an emphasis on pupil discipline. As class sizes increased, and peer pressures and oppositional youth cultures strengthened, the fulfillment of parental desires for educational excellence during the 1980s and 1990s would require even greater civic involvement.[55]

[5]

Fiscal Crisis and Land-Use Struggles

New York City is the engine that drives the largest, densest regional economy in the United States. In 1960 the tristate, thirty-one-county New York region contained 40 percent of all national-market wholesaling jobs, a third of the nation's financial sector, a quarter of business services employment, and 12 percent of manufacturing jobs—and all this with only 9 percent of the U.S. population. Occupying just 2 percent of this 12,000-square-mile domain, New York City housed 37 percent of the region's population, with the rest residing in a ring of 550 suburbs. An even smaller slice, the nine square miles of downtown and midtown Manhattan, provided a quarter of the region's 8 million jobs. Despite ups and downs, this giant economy continued to grow, but jobs and income have shifted more and more to the suburbs. Herein lies the key to understanding New York City's fiscal crisis and its continuing aftermath.[1]

Roots of the Crisis

The region's expanding economy was the rising tide that permitted 1.5 million white New Yorkers to move to suburban homes during the 1950s and 1960s. It was also the beacon that attracted African American and Puerto Rican job-seekers—but they arrived at a time when working-class employment in the city was shrinking. Some of this job loss was due to relocation outside the region, but while the city lost 174,000 manufacturing jobs during 1952–1969, its suburbs added 129,000. Total suburban job growth was enormous. Whereas New York City employment expanded by 2 percent during the 1950s and 7 percent in the 1960s, suburban jobs grew by 38 and 33 percent, outpacing even the national rate.[2]

Although these trends encouraged white city residents to move to the suburbs, few black or Puerto Rican New Yorkers could follow because of racial housing segregation.[3] In addition, zoning restrictions closed off 90 percent of the region to all but the upper and upper middle classes. Even working-class whites were channeled into densely packed suburbs that frequently were far from their places of work.

Each suburb set its own land-use policy. Those with spacious minimum plot sizes and restrictions on apartment buildings kept out working- and lower-middle-class residents. Some exclusive areas also zoned out manufacturing, although other communities offered tax concessions to attract businesses, often directly from New York City. In short, a "free market" for homes and jobs did not exist in the suburbs, and developers were unable to construct sufficient affordable residential units to relieve New York City's crowding and housing loss. And despite the increase in suburban jobs, few poor and working-class city residents could afford to travel to them on the expensive commuter railroads designed to transport suburban residents into the city.

As suburban population numbers increased, so did suburban political power. A decisive defeat for New York City came in 1971 when a bill was considered to set statewide standards for suburban plot sizes, and to require inclusive zoning for worker housing in suburbs that permitted manufacturing. Suburban sovereignty prevailed in Albany, and the bill failed.[4]

A bleak employment picture thus faced the city's newest residents, especially the many African Americans arriving from southern states who had been denied first-rate schooling. As Lindsay bureaucrat Charles Morris put it, "The civil rights movement was confirming the black claim to full legal equality with whites, but equality in fact would require massive investment . . . by the government."[5] Progress toward this goal, benefiting neighborhood New Yorkers of all colors, was certainly made between the 1950s and early 1970s. Mayor Robert Wagner built 130,000 units of public-sector housing, three hundred schools, and five public hospitals, plus libraries and thousands of acres of parks. He added to the police force, and crime rates dropped. Wagner and then Mayor John Lindsay oversaw expansion of the tuition-free city university from 93,000 to 271,000 students; CUNY campuses doubled from nine to nineteen and, after 1970, provided a place for all city high school graduates. In addition, the city's public assistance and Medicaid safety net expanded, totaling nearly $1 billion by 1975.[6]

All this put mounting pressure on the city's tax base. What kept government investment going was the double-edged sword of deficit spending, which began in Wagner's last year and enjoyed a decade-long run. In 1965 Wagner borrowed $256 million to fill the gap in his budget; his source of repayment was to be an increase in property taxes that he hoped voters would later approve. He then announced he would not seek a fourth term. Arriving in 1966, Lindsay scuffled to fill Wagner's rolled-over deficit and his own new one. By the 1970s he had expanded deficit spending and fallen more deeply in debt as he borrowed to pay interest on earlier borrowing. (New York State under Governor Nelson Rockefeller and other municipalities around the country were all doing the same thing.)

This occurred with the active participation of New York's major banks. They bought and marketed the city's tax-free bonds and notes, reaping underwriter profits on the difference between what they paid the city and the price to investors. Short-term revenue, tax, and bond anticipation notes (RANs, TANs, BANs) proliferated, even as receipts fell short of the "anticipated" figures supplied by the city comptroller, Abraham Beame. By 1972 New York City accounted for one-fourth of *all* state and local government short-term debt in the United States. Nonetheless, in 1973 the city retained an A credit rating. By 1975 the city's budget deficit was $2 billion, its accumulated debt was $13 billion, and its overall borrowing to meet short-term note obligations the year before totaled $8 billion.[7]

Four components of the budget gap merit attention: rising municipal employee costs; declining tax receipts due to job loss and recession; the near-defeat of a commuter tax; and permanent-government policies that diminished the city's tax base. Other factors were less important. New York City welfare and Medicaid costs did increase during 1965–1975, in line with the national trend, but so did federal and state aid. Measures to reduce excessive Medicaid payments to hospitals, pharmacists, and proprietary nursing homes required state and federal, not city, action. Construction of public-sector housing ended with Lindsay's scattered-site fiasco in 1966 and did not resume until 1973 under the much smaller Section 8 program.[8]

Municipal Employees

In his 1961 mayoral campaign, having lost regular Democratic Party support, Wagner allied with the city employee unions. Salaries and pension benefits then increased, if productivity did not, and in 1962 at the unions' behest Wagner repealed the rule dating from 1937 which required municipal employees to live in the city. During Lindsay's first year city workers went on strike, but the mayor and a new union coalition then reached accord, and raises averaged 12 percent over the next three years. By 1969 Lindsay viewed the unions and their campaign contributions as an important base for his reelection. During his second term 30,000 workers were added to the municipal payroll.

In the 1930s city jobs had become more desirable and accessible to working-class families than previously, but pay remained low. In the 1960s the unions brought wages up to private-sector levels, as did the burgeoning public-sector labor movement nationwide. The consensus of economic analysts was that New York's pay levels were now in line with compensation elsewhere, but pension benefits were on the high side. Ironically, city employees' wage increases also made suburbanization more feasible, particularly for the better-paid police, firefighters, and teachers. By 1977 half the members of the police force were commuters. Lower-paid clerical and service workers, mostly members of American Federation of State, County, and Municipal Employees (AFSCME) District Council 37 led by Victor Gotbaum, were more likely to live in the city, but they now enjoyed better incomes.[9]

Job Loss

Between the 1969–1970 national recession and 1976, New York City lost 600,000 jobs. Its 1968 unemployment rate of 3 percent climbed to 11 percent by 1974. The recession hit more deeply than in the rest of the country, and the city's population fell by 440,000. Those who remained included a greater proportion of elderly residents—heavy users of health and social services—and youth aged sixteen to twenty-four, now facing fewer job choices.

Much was made of the loss of corporate headquarters, but this in fact indexed continuing vigor in New York's regional economy: twenty-five of the thirty-eight Fortune 500 headquarters that left the city between 1965 and 1975 relocated to its suburbs. These moves were not made to flee higher business taxes, which remained at 1950s rates, or to reduce rents, which were higher in Connecticut—where many corporations relocated—than in Manhattan. Rather, as urbanologist William H. Whyte discovered, corporate offices moved to be more convenient to the residences of their top executives. Suburban corporations continued to draw on Manhattan-based business services. In all, only 27,000 city jobs were lost because of corporate exits.[10]

The 1969–1976 job decline was more significantly an acceleration of longer-term changes already in gear. The construction of 340,000 miles of federal highways and 44,000 miles of oil pipelines between 1950 and 1975 resulted in massive geographic dispersion of economic activity. Suburban relocation within the New York region, part of this larger process, affected manufacturing jobs and wholesale, retail, and service employment as well as corporate headquarters. Within New York City only government employment, health care, and banking continued to grow. And ominously, the city budget now depended more heavily upon financial and business services sectors staffed disproportionately by commuters.[11]

The Commuter Tax

An additional impetus toward suburbanization of New York's economic base was the city income tax begun in 1966—although clearly this was not its intended purpose. The proposal Lindsay sent to Albany would have taxed all income earned in New York City at the same rate. Both commuters and city residents already paid property taxes to support services in their own localities (renters did so indirectly). Commuters, however, received tax-free the benefits of New York City fire and police protection, sanitation services, and transportation infrastructure. Many Long Island commuters drove to Elmhurst and other Queens neighborhoods, parked in city streets or municipal lots, and rode to work by subway. In view of the deficit, Lindsay called for *all* users of city services to make an additional contribution to balancing the budget.

Suburban legislators did not see it this way. They approved the new income tax but set the commuter rate at one-eighth that of city residents. The unstated message to city residents was that their city income tax could be reduced by 87.5 percent if they moved to a suburb. Many did. According to the Twentieth Century Fund analyst Masha Sinnreich, "From 1960 to 1970 the proportion of those working in New York but living outside the city rose from 14 percent to 18 percent, an increase of 150,000 commuters. If [they] had chosen to live in New York, they would have provided 500,000 additional jobs in the city for sales clerks, building superintendents, teachers, bakers, and shoemakers." Undertaxing commuter income continued to hamstring the city; by 1988 Manhattan earnings totaled $105 billion, with $33 billion accruing to commuters still paying the one-eighth rate.[12]

Permanent-Government Policies

The dispersion of working-class jobs within the New York region was accelerated by actions of New York's permanent government, particularly the expansion of high-rent-yielding Manhattan office buildings between 1960 and 1975. As this commercial space turned to glut by 1974, the banks that mortgaged or owned these buildings sought to redirect city resources to policies that would fill the underutilized space. Doing so required massive cuts in services benefiting neighborhood New York and produced a quality-of-life crisis that has persisted ever since.

Publicly funded "urban renewal" projects of the 1950s—the United Nations, the West Side bus terminal, Lincoln Center—enriched the owners of the commercial and residential real estate surrounding them; against this, the city lost working-class jobs and property-tax revenues.[13] The growth of tax-exempt real estate was substantial, rising from 28 percent of all New York City land in the mid-1950s to 40 percent by 1976—mostly because of private uses encouraged or subsidized by renewal projects: tax-exempt foreign embassies, cultural and educational institutions, hospitals, and foundations. In addition, projects of such public agencies as the Port Authority and the Metropolitan Transportation Authority expanded. By 1976 tax-exempt private real estate was worth $4.1 billion, and tax-exempt public authority real estate was worth almost as much.[14]

Manhattan's World Trade Center (WTC) exemplified the permanent government's contribution to the city's fiscal crisis. Concerned that most recent projects were in midtown, in 1958 David Rockefeller, head of the Chase Manhattan Bank, had formed the Downtown–Lower Manhattan Association (DLMA), a group of Wall Street banking, real estate, and corporate interests, to lobby for public spending to enhance real estate values below Canal Street—including Chase's holdings. DLMA priorities were a crosstown expressway to facilitate commuter travel, a trade center, and luxury housing built on landfill. Mayor Wagner was indifferent to these plans, but Lindsay was a supporter and bore the brunt of neighborhood opposition to the expressway plan, which he abandoned in 1967. David's brother Nelson Rockefeller, governor of New York State from 1959 to 1973, was enthusiastic; he brokered approval for construction of the trade center by the Port Authority, from which Chase in turn earned fees for marketing the construction bonds.[15]

New Jersey's price for permitting the Port Authority to issue the WTC bonds was an agreement in 1962 for the Port Authority to assume operation of the Hudson River commuter subway, and to stipulate that its bridge and tunnel income would not be invested in mass transit. New York City got twin 110-story towers (dubbed "David" and "Nelson" by lower Manhattan residents) but was denied Port Authority funds for its own subway. To fill the towers, the governor announced a relocation of New York State office workers from elsewhere in the city to the WTC once it was completed, and in 1969 he authorized a forty-year state lease for one-quarter of the WTC's 11 million square feet.

Completed in 1972, the WTC did little to benefit New York City when the 1975 crisis arrived. The city had already lost 400 businesses and the tax revenues and jobs they generated when local commercial printing and electrical districts and a wholesale produce market were razed to make room for the twin towers. The tax-exempt WTC gave the city a small "in lieu of taxes" yearly fee, far less than the $65 million in property taxes it would have paid if privately owned. The still-unfilled WTC's operating deficit, moreover, was subsidized by city residents through their state income taxes. In addition, the city granted "hardship" property-tax reductions to owners of office space vacated by tenants who moved to the WTC.[16]

Overall, the permanent government's promise of "job growth" from office-building construction was illusory. Working-class jobs were lost as sites were cleared, and rising rent levels forced small businesses to move or close down. Total employment in the downtown-midtown core declined from 2.5 million to 2 million between 1956 and 1980. In the early 1960s there was already a 9 percent office vacancy rate, yet 44 million square feet were added during the 1960s and another 49 million between 1970 and 1975—*after* the 1969 recession had begun. In 1974, office rents fell and property-tax collections stagnated. By 1975, 32 million square feet of Manhattan office space stood empty.[17]

The "headquarters city" ideology that had promoted the 1960–1975 office construction boom held that economic well-being depended on creating space for personal interaction among the male white-collar elite, and not on working-class jobs. Its spokesperson William H. Whyte wrote in 1976, "There is likely to be an increase in the kind of face-to-face and brain-intensive work for which a central location is important. . . . What we ought to be talking about is New York as a *work* place, and how subtly, intricately, and superbly it functions. . . . It's mostly people—meeting, talking, listening, not listening, arguing, gossiping, swiping ideas, agreeing."

Oddly enough, Whyte drew this conclusion after documenting the increasing number of corporate headquarters dispersing from Manhattan. He noted that "computer operations" might also leave but considered it merely a loss of "routine clerical work" (this was the era of keypunch machines and batches of IBM cards). Whyte evoked a nostalgic vision of the epoch when white men in Manhattan office buildings *had* directed the American economy and its global operations. By the mid-1970s that world was decentralizing; foreign competitors were already renting offices in New York; and the city's permanent government was in trouble. Like Samuel Lefrak in Community District 4, it had overbuilt.[18]

Viewpoints different from Whyte's saw New York in the mid-1970s at a historic turningpoint, not simply at the "recession" setting of a repetitive business cycle with "recovery" on its way. Economist Matthew Edel noted that the corporate headquarters and financial-sector jobs that had expanded since the 1950s, and the office buildings that housed them, "were all financed out of profits made elsewhere." These streams of capital owed no allegiance to New York City as economic activity dispersed and new investment opportunities arose elsewhere. Economist Robert Fitch suggested that the early 1970s overinvestment in office buildings resulted from a lack of other profitable investments as one economic era neared its end and new opportunities were as yet unclear. Lindsay bureaucrat Charles Morris recognized that the headquarters city boom "was built on a peculiarly fragile base" and that during the 1969 recession corporate and financial-sector employment had declined, offices closed, and tax collections fallen off.[19]

A restoration of the permanent government's headquarters city honey-pot would take more than market forces. It would require tax forgiveness and new subsidies from the city budget, which would mean austerity for neighborhood New York—something elected officials were unlikely to undertake on their own.

The Sequence of Events

The year 1973 brought several unconnected events that would soon intertwine to help precipitate the crisis. First, the Organization of Petroleum Exporting Countries (OPEC) quadrupled the price of oil; this worsened the U.S. economic slowdown and led to rising inflation and interest rates. In November Abraham Beame was elected mayor, and in December Manhattan's West Side Highway collapsed, highlighting the city's ongoing public investment needs. Also in December Governor Nelson Rockefeller resigned (in less than a year he became President Ford's vice-president).[20]

These events rattled the men who directed New York City's major banks. Between 1960 and 1974 tax-exempt municipal bonds had grown from a quarter to half of their investment portfolios. With interest rates rising, locked-in bond returns were less attractive than new investments at higher rates. In addition, mounting job loss and office vacancies threatened the profitability of their Manhattan real estate loans and holdings.

Beame they knew well. As city comptroller in the early 1960s he had moved employee pension-fund investments out of New York City bonds into corporate securities, and the banks then gladly bought up the tax-exempt bonds. They also knew the gimmicks—overestimating revenues, moving operating expenses to the capital budget—that Beame used to pronounce the city budget "balanced." Since 1965 they had heard warnings from the Citizens Budget Commission about the budget deficit, but they continued to buy city bonds and notes, both to lessen their own tax obligations and to earn underwriter fees.

The highway collapse signaled that the city's deficit was likely to increase. And with Nelson Rockfeller gone from Albany, the bankers feared that his replacement, Malcolm Wilson, might not be able to force the legislature to pay bondholders if recession diminished state revenues. Under Rockefeller, New York State debt had expanded from $2 billion to $13 billion, much of it in the high-yield "moral obligation" bonds he promoted. If the overextended state defaulted, might the overextended city be next?[21]

The banks had other reasons to reconsider their holdings of New York City paper. With losses in real estate investment trusts, corporate bankruptcies, and loans to Third World governments, they had less income to shelter with tax-free municipals. They also enjoyed new lending opportunities and foreign investment tax credits via federal banking and tax law changes. Then the investment community was shaken when in June 1974 Governor Wilson repealed the Port Authority agreement prohibiting use of its revenues for New York City mass transit. (The repeal was overturned in 1977.)

In July 1974 the banks ratcheted up the loan rate they charged the city to 7.9 percent. A week later it was 8.5 percent; and by December, 9.5 percent. More important, several banks began to sell their holdings of city bonds and decided not to buy new city issues for their trust clients. Still, as underwriters they marketed $4 billion in city paper between October 1974 and March 1975, and they supported the city's issuance of $10,000 notes to attract individual investors (until then, $25,000 was the smallest note issued). Meanwhile, Democrat Hugh Carey was elected governor in November 1974.[22]

As 1975 began, Mayor Beame was borrowing unprecedented amounts, and his operating deficit was exploding; he admitted to $450 million, but comptroller Harrison Goldin set it at $670 million. Goldin's office leaked a sobering memo estimating that $2.7 billion in property-tax arrears and other receivables would not materialize. At the banks' urging the city instituted layoffs of municipal workers in November 1974, and Beame claimed in January 1975 that the work force was down by 12,700—though it was soon clear that actual dismissals were only 1,900. To the banks, this was more gimmickry and indicated collusion with Victor Gotbaum's union coalition.

At this point the Financial Community Liaison Group (FCLG) was formed; chaired by a Morgan Guaranty Trust official, it included David Rockefeller of Chase and top officers of Citibank, Bankers Trust, Chemical Bank, Manufacturers Hanover, Merrill Lynch, and Salomon Brothers. Meetings between the FCLG and the city over budget cuts and new borrowing began immediately. FCLG underwriters and creditors were finding city paper increasingly difficult to market, and although they had reduced their own holdings to a quarter or less of their investment portfolios, they still had much at stake in a potential default. And they could be held criminally liable if they sold city issues that they knew might not be paid on time or in full.[23]

In February 1975 the Urban Development Corporation (UDC), which Nelson Rockefeller had created, defaulted; Governor Carey refused to meet the "moral obligation" to pay its bondholders with New York State tax revenues. Public default had become a reality. (One month later Carey and the legislature learned their lesson and paid off UDC creditors.) To meet the city's February debt service and payroll, Goldin and Beame maneuvered a purchase of city BANs with municipal pension funds. By July, however, they would need to borrow another $2 billion. More disturbingly, the city had less than half that amount left in legal borrowing authority.

At the end of February, Bankers Trust said it wished to inspect the city's books before buying more notes. A March 13 offering of three-month RANs was bought by underwriters only after the city agreed to dedicate New York State aid funds to repay them. Even so, the underwriters were able to sell only half the RANs and had to keep the rest themselves. That was it: on March 17 the FCLG leadership met with Beame to tell him they would no longer lend the city money unless it cut jobs and services. The next day they gave the city's congressional delegation the same message and told them federal assistance would soon be needed.[24]

With the banks on strike, the city ran out of money in April 1975. The state advanced $800 million for April and May expenses, but when Beame asked for more, Carey appointed an advisory committee headed by Felix Rohatyn to find a solution. "Felix the fixer" was a partner and corporate merger specialist at Lazard Freres, a Wall Street investment bank. In May, Rohatyn's committee devised the Municipal Assistance Corporation (MAC) plan, which Carey shepherded through Albany in June. MAC's board consisted of eight bankers and corporate executives plus one academic. No city council members, municipal workers, or residents of neighborhood New York were represented at its meetings. MAC was empowered to sell $3 billion in long-term bonds backed by New York City sales and stock-transfer taxes. The banks could redeem their outstanding city paper at maturity with MAC receipts or exchange it for longer-term MAC bonds, which paid a higher return.

When only half the first MAC issue of $1 billion was sold on the investment market in July and underwriters had to keep the rest, the MAC solution was imperiled. The bankers demanded more city cuts, and cuts were made, but MAC bonds still would not sell. In September 1975 Carey created the Emergency Financial Control Board (EFCB), which effectively became New York City's government. It had power to approve budgets and expenditures, and authority to abrogate labor contracts, all to assure that deficit spending would end by 1978. This briefly reassured investors, but by October MAC bonds were sinking in value.[25]

The unions protested but finally accepted job cuts. With a large suburban membership among the uniformed and teacher groups, service cuts affecting neighborhood quality of life were not a first-order concern. As leader of the union coalition Victor Gotbaum had led 10,000 city workers in a June 1975 demonstration on Wall Street to protest the banks' call for retrenchment, and he withdrew $15 million in union funds from First National City Bank. But over the summer Gotbaum grew increasingly chummy with Rohatyn and became more concerned about loss of collective bargaining rights and pension payments if default occurred. By early fall, abandoning the union insistence on job cuts through attrition only, he had agreed to layoffs. After a September 1975 school strike, so did the teachers union leader Albert Shanker. Nonetheless, forty-five demonstrations over job and service cuts tied up lower Manhattan from September through November.[26]

The federal aid that the FCLG said would be needed arrived in November 1975. At first President Ford balked, and on October 30 the *Daily News* ran its famous "Ford to City: Drop Dead" headline. Governor Carey then made *his* message plain to Ford—"Federal money or Federal troops"—and in November Washington approved $2.3 billion in annual loan guarantees. Beame's closest aides were dismissed, and EFCB reins were tightened. The banks still found MAC bonds unpalatable, and Gotbaum endorsed an EFCB plan for the unions to buy them with their pension funds. Over the next three years the unions invested $3.8 billion in MAC—three times what the banks put in—and thus became financially dependent upon the success of EFCB austerity.[27]

The unions in fact drew closer to the banks in 1977 through creation of the Municipal Union-Financial Leaders group, consisting of six union leaders and six commercial bank CEOs plus Rohatyn. It endorsed the budget cuts that Mayor Edward Koch would begin to implement in 1978. One consequence of this link was that the unions did in fact achieve most of the required job cuts through attrition, and seniority rules and collective bargaining rights were preserved.

Despite the cuts, the city budget was still in deficit in 1978, with 24 percent of revenue going to debt service. Rohatyn and Carey then engineered a second solution. The "emergency" was dropped from the name of the Financial Control Board (now FCB), and its power over city finances was extended for thirty years. New annual loan guarantees of $1.6 billion over three years were approved by

President Jimmy Carter. The banks and union pension funds agreed to additional MAC bond purchases. To congratulate themselves, Rohatyn and Gotbaum celebrated a joint birthday party in Southampton, Long Island. (In 1981 Gotbaum's son joined Rohatyn's firm and later became a partner.)

By 1979 the municipal work force was less than 80 percent of its 1975 size, and the city was able to sell and repay its notes in the credit market. By 1981 the city budget showed a surplus. In 1986, the city having balanced its budget unassisted for three consecutive years, FCB oversight was lessened but not lifted.[28]

Effects on the Quality of Life

To Southampton partygoers or suburban commuters, service cuts following the 1975 fiscal crisis made little difference. But to residents of neighborhood New York they were devastating. At a July 1975 meeting of MAC, permanent-government leaders David Rockefeller, Felix Rohatyn, Walter Wriston of Citibank, and Frank Smeal of Morgan Guaranty demanded a wage freeze, job reductions, a transit fare increase, and tuition at the City University of New York. Mayor Beame waited outside the meeting room until the list was handed to him. By the end of his mayoralty two years later the demands had all been met.[29]

Overall, the city budget shrank 22 percent between 1975 and 1983, and service cuts affected every aspect of neighborhood New York life. The transit fare was raised from thirty-five to fifty cents, yet because of "deferred maintenance," subway breakdowns tripled between 1977 and 1981 and out-of-service buses made up a fourth of the fleet by 1980. After six members of the Board of Higher Education resigned, 129 years of free college education ended with the imposition of tuition in 1976; by 1980 the number of CUNY students dropped 30 percent. Public school layoffs resulted in 15,000 fewer teachers and paraprofessionals, and a 25 percent increase in class size. Library hours were curtailed. Summer youth jobs, senior citizen programs, and recreational and cultural services were scaled back. Five city hospitals were closed by 1980, services at others reduced, and twenty-eight drug rehabilitation clinics shut down.

Fire Department response time increased. The number of building inspectors fell from 625 in 1975 to 382 by 1980. Sanitation department staff had declined 48 percent by 1984. Park and playground workers were cut 25 percent during 1975, 29 percent more by 1984, and shifted from fixed assignments to mobile teams servicing several locations. City-financed construction projects were frozen until 1983, even though the City Planning Commission reported in 1978 that there were bridges, sewers, water tunnels, and parks "fac[ing] collapse." For ordinary citizens New York became a more expensive, slower-moving, shabbier, less well-maintained city.[30]

Police Department cuts made life more dangerous. NYPD strength fell 14 percent in 1975 and by 1984 stood at three-quarters of its 1974 level. Narcotics, organized crime, and youth crime units were curtailed severely; police were told to make arrests only for "serious" crimes. The reductions were particularly evident during the 1977 power blackout when NYPD numbers were insufficient to prevent theft and damage totaling $135 million throughout the five boroughs. Unlike the peaceful 1965 blackout, the 1977 event resulted in open looting with little risk of arrest. Some 1,600 stores were hit; food, clothing, and household goods were the main items stolen.[31]

In Elmhurst-Corona the district cabinet was informed in June 1975 that the 110th Precinct would take its share of NYPD job losses, that half the nineteen district park laborers were to be laid off, and highway and pothole repair crews reduced. In September it learned that nineteen school-crossing guards had been terminated. At the January 1976 CB4 meeting a demonstration to protest more cuts at Elmhurst Hospital was announced, 250 employees already having been fired. In March 1976 the *Newtown Crier* reported, "Home burglaries and muggings have been on the rise. . . . Our police are trying to do their job, but do not have enough manpower. . . . The sanitation pick-ups have dwindled to one a week in some sections and overall our streets are filthy. We are informed some of the classes in our schools are so large that teachers are having problems maintaining control." By June 1976 the Elmhurst Branch Library was reduced to a three-day schedule, and PS89 announced that staff would be laid off, the dental clinic eliminated, and class size increased in the fall.

At a 1979 CB4 meeting comptroller Harrison Goldin summarized the impact of the city's four-year capital budget freeze: "The collapse of the city physically is overwhelming and is the result of failure to invest limited amounts of money on highways, sewers, parks, subways, all of which now require huge sums of money to bring them back to acceptable standards. . . . Much of the city's essential equipment such as garbage trucks, police cars and fire vehicles are in an advanced state of deterioration. . . . In Queens, beautiful hospitals and libraries have been built and now the City cannot generate funds to staff them."

The Beginning of Koch Policies

National and local economic woe began to reverse in 1977, and by 1980 the city's economy was improving. Jobs in the financial sector and business services were expanding. Vacant office space filled, and ten new office buildings arose between 1976 and 1980. New residential construction and upgrading of housing by upper-middle-class gentrifiers were on the upswing. The recovery was largely Manhattan-centered, however, and affected mainly the higher reaches of the job market. Compared with 1970 recession levels, jobs were up 8 percent in business services and holding their own in the financial sector, whereas jobs were down 14 percent in wholesale employment, 15 percent in retail trade, 19 percent in manufacturing, and 30 percent in construction.[32]

In 1978 former Greenwich Village city council and congressional representative Edward Koch became mayor. The cuts in city jobs and services remained in effect, and FCB, MAC, and federal-loan supervisors continued to scutinize and approve city budgets. Koch embraced the tax policies that were priming the Manhattan-based recovery and filling up office space. Businesses taxes had been cut after 1975, and by 1980 reductions in the general corporation and commercial rent taxes and the phasing out of the stock transfer tax amounted to $480 million in lost city revenues. Koch also expedited publicly funded construction projects that benefited permanent-government bond purchasers, underwriters, and owners of surrounding real estate; these included midtown's Javits Convention Center and Times Square redevelopment, and downtown's Battery Park City built on World Trade Center landfill.

Tax cuts for office-building construction were administered through an Industrial and Commercial Incentive Board (ICIB) created in 1977. In 1979 Comptroller Goldin criticized some $62 million in ICIB tax abatements as unnecessary, awarded to projects that would have been built without them. By 1982 ICIB was costing the city $47 million a year, with 90 percent of its subsidies going to Manhattan office buildings. The similar New York State Job Incentive Board (JIB), created in 1968 to foster manufacturing employment with ten-year tax cuts, was reprogramed after the fiscal crisis to assist Manhattan's real estate market. One Wall Street firm was given $1.3 million in JIB tax credits when it moved to midtown. Even larger JIB awards were made to financial and corporate offices that remained in Manhattan after threatening to leave or had already planned to move there.[33]

Tax policies to subsidize housing for Manhattan's business elite also expanded under Koch. The 421a property-tax exemption for new residential construction cost the city $150 million in 1979, most of it going to luxury units. J-51 tax abatements, awarded for up to twenty years, were originally designed to upgrade rental tenements. In 1975 J-51 was extended to co-op and condominium units, and to residential conversion of industrial and commercial buildings, including single-room occupancy (SRO) low-rent hotels. J-51 had cost the city $100 million by 1983 and subsidized the loss of 31,000 SRO units, thus contributing to the homelessness crisis which city and state officials estimated was affecting 36,000 persons by 1979. Koch continued underassessing one-family homes in higher-income neighborhoods such as Riverdale, Bayside, Douglaston, and Little Neck while overassessing in lower-income areas. This meant that poorer New York homeowners paid property taxes at higher rates than wealthy ones.[34]

In 1980, five years into New York's fiscal crisis, sociologist Eric Lichten concluded:

> New York's working class and poor were forced to sacrifice disproportionately; its capitalist class actually benefited from austerity. There was a redirection of tax benefits and city and state funds to improve business conditions and lower the costs of doing business in New York. . . . Austerity was further justified by an ideology of scarcity . . . yet this scarcity was the direct result of deliberate decisions by investors and financiers, and especially New York's major banks, to withhold funds until their needs were met by a redirection of government priorities. There was no absolute scarcity of investment money; rather, it was redirected to more profitable ventures.[35]

Land-Use Struggles

During the 1960s a wall of apartment buildings arose in the swampy southern stretches of Newtown and Corona Heights. This zone, including Lefrak City and scores of six-story buildings, housed 24,000 residents by 1970, 80 percent of them white. Their arrival during the 1960s, however, was not greeted by their white neighbors on the opposite side of the Corona high school site. As the City Planning Commission put it in 1969, "There is little communication between the new residents of Lefrak City and the old, tightly-knit Italian-American community. Their different backgrounds, needs, and aspirations cause friction: the new apartment dwellers have higher incomes and more urbane tastes. The older residents are fighting to maintain the village character of their neighborhood. They feel threatened on two fronts: by a spreading pocket of decay to the north [the North Corona "strip"] and by middle-income development on the south."[36]

The patronage of this new "middle-income" white population and the confluence of Long Island Expressway and IND subway links made the Newtown portion of Queens Boulevard a choice site for large-scale retail development. In 1964 Macy's opened a 340,000-square-foot store with a distinctive round architectural design and parking for 1,500 cars. In 1971 CB4 approved a zoning variance for the new Queens Center indoor shopping mall one block away and twice the size of Macy's. The mall's seventy-five shops, anchored by department stores Abraham & Strauss and Orbach's, opened in 1973.

Apprehensive about the increased traffic the mall would bring, in 1971 an Ad Hoc Committee for Justice in Elmhurst proposed street reroutings and an underground entrance to the IND subway station, noting that Gimbel's department store had built such an entrance in Manhattan. Instead, the city widened an avenue next to the mall, destroying twenty street trees in the process. Elmhurst civic activists carefully monitored their promised replacement, and in 1975 Tom McKenzie told CB4 that ten of the new trees were dead. (In 1993 I counted eighteen trees; nine were large and flourishing, and nine were small and recently planted.)

By the early 1970s the larger tracts of remaining residential space in CD4 were filled in. New apartment buildings were now economically viable only if zoning variances permitted extra floor space, and requests for such variances brought developers to Community Board 4. In 1972 CB4 voted down a variance for construction of two fourteen-story office-and-apartment towers in Elmhurst's Broadway-Woodside section; board members objected that the 800 luxury units would overburden schools, street parking, and subways. At a 1973 CB4 meeting the Newtown Civic Association urged opposition to a variance for a 120-unit apartment in their section for similar reasons.

The arguments that civic leaders raised against these and other developers' proposals all referred to CD4's ongoing population implosion. As the *Newtown Crier* put it in 1973, "We are choking in density of population, unmanageable traffic and too much housing. . . . We do not have enough schools, hospitals and transportation for the people we have now. Real estate interests and speculators eye our locale with greed in mind."

This was *before* the city's fiscal crisis. After 1975 the likelihood of new schools or subway improvements ended, but population increase did not. Political realism led Your Block Association (YBA), a civic group in the Broadway-Woodside section, to locate a developer for an empty factory whose owner had moved to the suburbs. CB4's 1974 recommendation for a vest-pocket park on this location had been turned down; next, its designation as a school site was killed by the 1975 capital budget freeze, and YBA leader Ron Laney feared that the building might be razed for high-rise apartment construction. A developer was found; with the support of CB4 chair Steve Trimboli a variance for residential conversion of the existing structure was secured; and in 1979 a ninety-seven-unit condominium opened.

Two-thirds of CD4's population increase during the 1960s occurred in the apartment-building zone, but 85 percent of new Latin American and Asian residents moved instead into the older areas of Elmhurst-Corona, replacing whites who had left. In 1960, 63 percent of Elmhurst's housing units and 89 percent of Corona's had been built before 1940. Half the dwelling units were in one- and two-family homes, a fifth in three- to nine-unit walkups, and almost a third in apartment buildings, most of them in Elmhurst.[37] Overwhelmingly in sound condition, this older housing stock in the Baxter-Roosevelt, Broadway-Woodside, and Newtown sections was where CD4's population implosion first appeared. And here in 1971 the newly formed Newtown Civic Association began to point to problems of crowding, "infill" housing, and illegal occupancy. Crowding in schools, subways, and streets was particularly evident to longtime residents. Some of this was the result of young immigrant families replacing older departing whites—larger households replacing a single person or a couple. One-family homes were also being converted into two-family units. In Elmhurst the number of one-families on the property-tax rolls dropped from 3,200 to 2,100 between 1960 and 1978, while units in two-family homes grew from 3,900 to 6,500.

Infills

As the development frontier shifted to the older Elmhurst-Corona sections, where by 1975 some 4,800 units had been added, a new pattern began to alarm established residents: the demolition of existing housing and its replacement by brick-box "infill" units. Between 1970 and 1975, 350 units of standing housing were torn down, three-quarters of them in the Baxter-Roosevelt, Broadway-Woodside, and Newtown sections of Elmhurst.

What made this possible was the city's 1961 Zoning Resolution, designed to benefit developers and facilitate Manhattan "recentralization."[38] Like many outer-borough districts, CD4 had been overzoned. Most of it was designated R-6, a "medium density" zoning that fit the existing housing and population profile of Greenwich Village but not most standing Elmhurst-Corona housing, which conformed to R-5 zoning (half the density of R-6) or to R-4 (less dense still).

R-6 zoning permited developers a floor-area ratio (FAR) of 2, meaning that newly built floor space could be twice the square footage of the lot (thus a 1,000-square-foot lot could yield 2,000 square feet of floor space). R-6 also required that 30 percent of the lot remain unbuilt open space, including a back yard of at least 30 feet and, for detached one- or two-family homes built in R-6 zones, two side yards at least five feet wide. No side yard, however, was required for R-6 dwellings of three or more units. On-site parking was also mandated for each dwelling unit in detached homes but for only 70 percent of units in multiple dwellings. Finally, a bonus FAR of 2.43 was permitted for buildings that provided open space on at least 33.5 percent of the lot.

When developers turned to CD4's small remaining unbuilt lots in the early 1970s, the impact of R-6 zoning began to register. Since a multiple-unit building on vacant land could be built to the lot lines of neighboring homes, residents of older Elmhurst-Corona houses that did not conform to R-6 conventions might find their windows abutting a new infill-building wall. And with parking places required for only 70 percent of R-6 multiple-dwelling units, available street parking began to shrink. Even worse, a developer could buy an existing frame house, demolish it, and erect a three- or four-story brick box with a 2.43 FAR. Most existing homes were in the R-4 and R-5 range of .75 to 1.25 FAR. Thus a developer could build two or three times the floor area of the demolished home and produce an infill rental building with three to six (or more) legal units in place of a one-family home. The development potential of the land was now worth more than the structure standing on it. And housing demand by the 1970s ensured that home prices and real estate agents' activity would escalate.

Many residents of the new infills were immigrants. A white Elmhurst man born in 1960 recalled, "When we were kids we called [the infills] 'Chinese houses' [and] we called all the Orientals 'Chinese.' My [Chinese] friend Art lived in one. He said the Oriental families like to buy these houses and use them as stepping stones." But other infill tenants were white, as were many developers and agents in the infill housing market. The *Newtown Crier's* frequent columns about "predatory real estate interests" and "exploitation by unscrupulous landlords" never mentioned whether they were American or immigrant. Plainly, both were involved.

In 1971 both CB4 and the Newtown Civic Association called for downzoning to R-5 or R-4 to limit the size of the "garden apartments" beginning to appear on vacant plots. Few civic activists, however, yet understood the full implications of R-6 zoning. Without realizing its actual message, the *Newtown Crier* in 1972 carrried a strangely worded ad from a builder: "WANTED . . . *Vacant* lots any size *with or without house*" (emphasis added). In its next issue the *Crier* lamented "the present tearing down, by small builders, of older frame homes . . . and replacement of such with three-story brick houses . . . built on the neighbor's line. . . . This type of construction is now prevalent in Elmhurst." At a 1975 brunch with elected officials, NCA leaders communicated their dissatisfaction over the infills' lack of side yards. That year a city official explained to CB4 that housing demolition and infill replacement were perfectly legal, and that the board needed to petition the City Planning Commission if it wanted a zoning change.

A 1977 open letter from the NCA to CB4 mentioned "past zoning errors" and noted that Elmhurst-Corona contained "approximately 200 real estate offices (with individual operators . . . many times that number). This many persons engaged in the real estate business is far in excess of what is found ordinarily in a community such as ours." A formal request for change from R-6 to R-5 zoning was approved by CB4 in 1978, studied for two years by the Queens Department of City Planning, and with its approval submitted to the City Planning Commission. In 1980 this developer-oriented body of Koch appointees turned it down.

Illegal Occupancy

The "rooming house" problem, first identified by CB4 member John Rowan in 1972, concerned illegal units in one- and two-family homes and older apartments, and also in infills. In 1977 the *Newtown Crier* reported on a building in Broadway-Woodside where Rowan had discovered "six-room apartments with each room rented to a different family." The *Crier* wrote sympathetically of "intimidated tenants who are victimized by the over-crowding [but] do not complain." According to Rowan the situation was worsening: "The most severe examples of illegal occupancy involve two or three-family homes which are turned into rooming houses by landlords and rental agents. In some cases ten or more people . . . may be using one bathroom. The danger of fire is increased by the overcrowding and firemen are often surprised by the number of persons they have to evacuate from what appears to be a two-family house."

Some established whites, like one NCA member who spoke at a 1977 CB4 public hearing, thought that the rooming-house situation was not equivalent to the two-family homeowner (perhaps like him) who rented an illegal third unit—

say, a converted garage or basement. More people than one might realize had become involved in providing illegal housing, and reductions in building inspectors during the fiscal crisis made the situation worse.

In 1977, as district manager, Rowan submitted an unsuccessful joint CB4-CB3 budget request for increased code enforcement by the city's Department of Housing Preservation and Development (HPD). (CD3, also receiving many new immigrants, was experiencing similar housing problems.) Later that year Rowan told CB4 that the Community Development Agency (CDA), the city's conduit for federal Community Development Block Grant (CDBG) antipoverty money, might be a funding source for the code enforcement project, but in 1978 CDA also turned it down. The two community boards again included code enforcement in their 1978 budget requests, and the city once more rejected their proposal.

This all changed when portions of Corona in CD4 and CD3 were designated a Neighborhood Strategy Area for 1979 CDBG funding. After negotiating to expand the designated area, Rowan met opposition from NCA and Elmhurst CB4 members. His proposal combined the stick of enhanced HPD code enforcement in all of CB4 with the carrot of rehabilitation loans and technical assistance to landlords and homeowners via the city's Neighborhood Preservation Program. The recalcitrant CB4 members wanted only the stick. The package was accepted by an acrimonious 14-to-13 vote with support from chair Lou Simeone and Judy D'Andrea, a new Corona CB4 member who worked on the proposal with Rowan. Located in CD3, the Neighborhood Preservation Program began operation in 1980.[39]

A Neighborhood Remade

On the eve of the 1980s Elmhurst-Corona was a neighborhood vastly different from what it had been in 1960. Then it was overwhelmingly white; now its 47,000 whites were a third of the population, and 1 in 6 of them were residents of a new apartment district that had sprung up during the 1960s. Many of the newer whites were Jewish, whereas most established Elmhurst-Corona whites were Roman Catholics and Protestants of Italian, Irish, German, and other European ancestry. These differences, however, were considerably muted by 1980, since leaders from both old and new white populations had served together on Community Board 4 during the 1970s.

Their neighbors now included 11,000 black residents centered in Lefrak City. African American political ties with whites on CB4 had begun to form only during the late 1970s. Black residents, moreover, had established ties with the North Corona–East Elmhurst African American community in CD3. Their immediate concerns in CD4 focused on Lefrak and Sherwood managements. They did not experience the crowding, the illegal occupancy, and the march of infills that confronted established Elmhurst-Corona whites and their new immigrant neighbors.

Latin Americans, largely immigrants, numbered 50,000 by 1980, and Asians, also mainly immigrants, numbered 20,000. No immigrant group had yet made a significant entry into local civic politics. Asians were not represented on CB4, and Latin Americans only minimally. But the growing immigrant presence on Elmhurst-Corona's shopping strips was evident to all. And differences were becoming clear between immigrant households that owned homes, or rented units in new or older apartment buildings, and less advantaged immigrants who resided in crowded, sometimes illegal units.

A two-decade political history had also remade Elmhurst-Corona. The Corona high school struggle had left the scar of a still-empty site. Ten-year-old School Board 24 and Community Board 4 were the legacy of the Lindsay revolution. Crises over "welfare cases" and "illegal aliens," though misunderstood, had been weathered. The city's 1975 fiscal crisis had reduced neighborhood services and set an agenda for local politics. A zoning resolution drafted for Manhattan's permanent-government and outer-borough developers had created havoc on quiet streets, and more would follow.

Population, if fully counted, had almost doubled in twenty years.[40] Schools were overcrowded. Cultural symbols from all over the world were visible daily. Some houses of worship brought together established residents and newcomers; others underscored differences of language and religion. As the 1980s began, Elmhurst-Corona was a neighborhood struggling to evolve patterns of coexistence, accommodation, and interaction. It was also part of a metropolitan region whose elites held their own vision of a Manhattan-centered city, one that paid little heed to the lives, employment opportunities, or opinions of neighborhood New Yorkers.

Plates

Plate 1. One-family homes in Corona. Photo author.

Plate 2. Apartment buildings in Elmhurst. Photo author.

Plate 3. Lefrak City and 57th Avenue. Photo author.

Plate 4. Infill building in Elmhurst. Photo author.

Plate 5. Sewing factory in Corona. The sign, translated, reads "Singer and Merrow machine operators needed. Year-round work." Photo author.

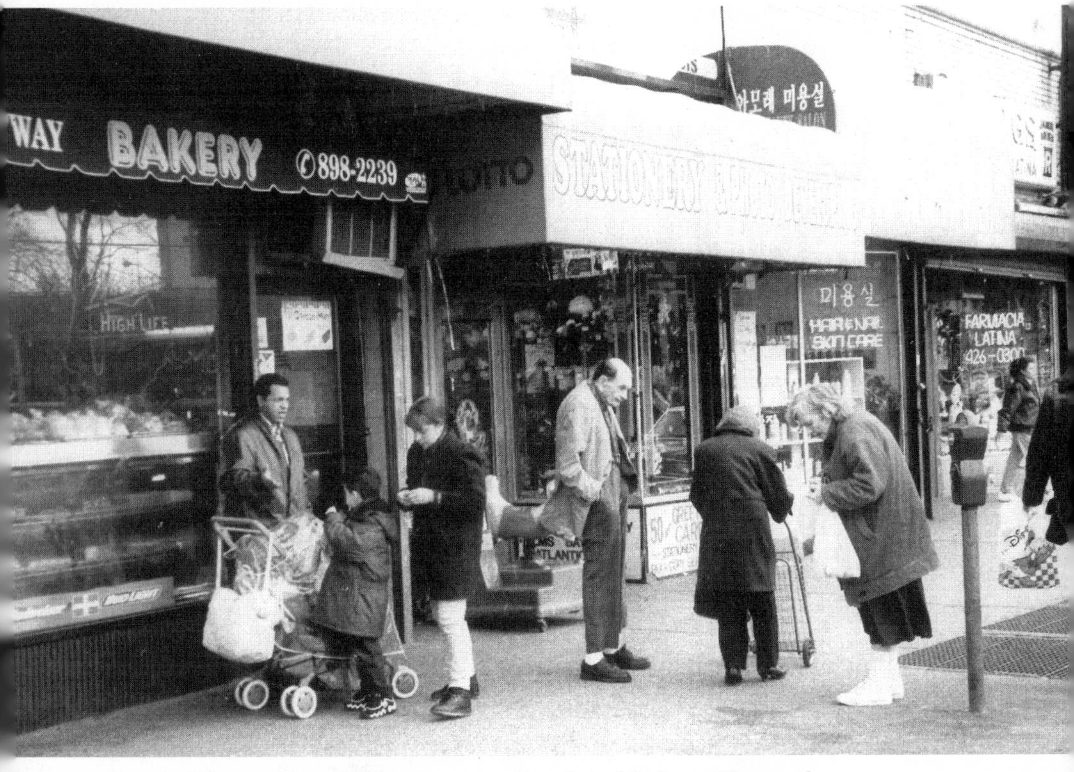

Plate 6. Baby carriage and shopping cart on Broadway, Elmhurst. Photo author.

Plate 7. St. Leo's Roman Catholic Church, Corona. Photo author.

Plate 8. Masjid al-Falah Mosque, Corona. Photo author.

Plate 9. Elmhurst Baptist Church. Photo author.

Plate 10. Geeta Hindu Temple, Elmhurst. Photo author.

Plate 11. Picknickers at 1993 Korean Harvest and Folklore Festival in Flushing Meadows–Corona Park. Photo Elena Roldán.

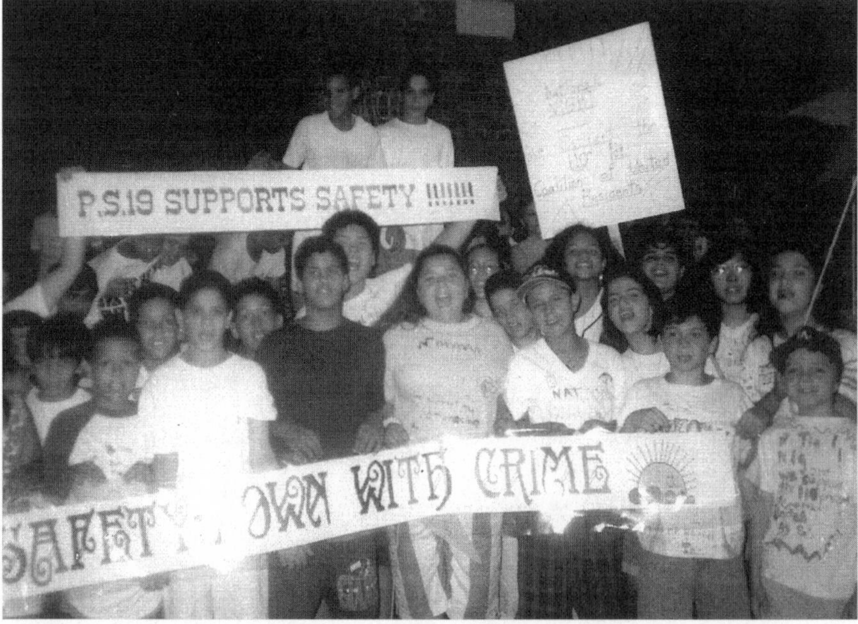

Plate 12. Elmhurst–Corona children at 1992 National Night Out March. Photo Lucy Schilero.

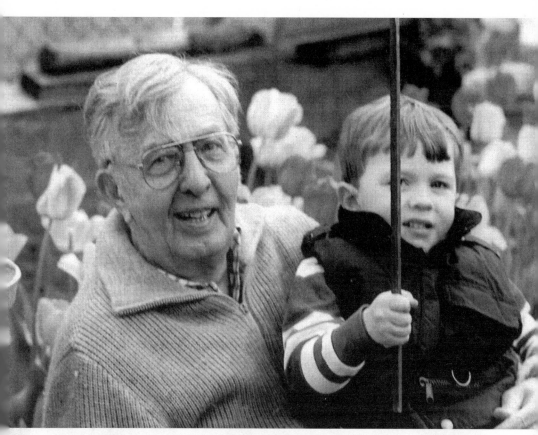

Plate 13. Bib Tilitz with grandson Alex Tilitz. Photo Thomas Tilitz.

Plate 14. Seung Ha Hong and Sung Jin Chun. Photo Sung Jin Chun.

Plate 15. Carmela George.
Photo author.

Plate 16. District manager Rose Rothschild (right), with son Robert, receiving photo montage of civic activities from Edna Baskin at tenth anniversary celebration. Photo Lucy Schilero.

Plate 17. City council member Helen Marshall, Lucy Schilero, and Ana Lopez, head of the Father Billini Association. Photo Lucy Schilero.

Plate 18. Haydee Zambrana. Photo author.

Plate 19. State assembly member Jeff Aubry, mural opposite Lefrak City. Photo author.

Plate 20. C-Town supermarket, Lefrak City. Photo author.

Plate 21. Park Side restaurant, Corona. Photo author.

PART III

City and Neighborhood at Odds: 1980–1996

[6]

New York's Three Economies

Contemporary New York City has three economies, each increasingly diverging from the others, each operating according to its own dynamics. The "speculative-electronic economy," what used to be called "Wall Street," is based on global trading in currency and security values. It is subsidized by city and national coffers and periodically requires bailouts. Since 1980 the speculative-electronic economy has employed fewer and fewer city residents and has been dispersing nationally and worldwide. For those at its command posts, enormous compensation, bonuses, and investment income permit opulent life-styles and political influence, via campaign contributions, unrivaled in U.S. history.

The city's "real economy" of goods and services provides the basics of daily life: food, clothing, machinery, housing, transportation, health care, repairs. Its decline as a source of employment for neighborhood New Yorkers between 1980 and 1996 was due in part to job dispersal to the suburbs and other regions of the United States, and in part to new productive technologies and downsizing policies that required fewer workers. Damage to the real economy occurred as the speculative-electronic economy siphoned off productive capital to pursue paper gain. This resulted in job loss, wage stagnation and decline, erosion of health insurance, and pension insecurity.

As opportunities and rewards in the real economy diminished, New York's "underground economy" grew massively. Sophisticated tax avoidance was its largest component, but other off-the-books pursuits flourished at all economic levels. These included not only flea markets, street peddling, and scavenging but less visible activities producing quality-of-life problems in Elmhurst-Corona: illegal rooming houses, sweatshops, gambling, car theft, drug dealing, and prostitution. The growth of the underground economy resulted partly from cuts in the number of city inspectors and police officers after 1975, and partly from the declining real economy.

The Speculative-Electronic Economy

When New York's fiscal crisis began in 1974, the yearly volume of domestic stock, bond, and currency transactions was roughly the same dollar amount as the U.S. gross national product. By the 1990s, however, these transactions were forty times the size of GNP and still expanding. Most of this more complex and computerized trade in securities, money (dollars, marks, yen, and so on), commodity futures, and "derivatives" (intricate speculative hedges against rises or falls) redistributed paper increases in value. Only $25 billion of the $800 billion in currency churned daily was capital raised for the production of real goods and services. A gigantic balloon inflated with more and more money was floating over the workplaces and stores where most Americans made and spent their earnings.[1]

Federal policies during the Carter and Reagan presidencies freed or attracted vast amounts of capital to fill this balloon. First, Federal Reserve monetarist policies of high interest rates were established in 1979 to cool the economy. As real investment opportunities thus diminished, capital shifted into speculative investment. High interest rates also attracted foreign investment, and during the 1980s federal borrowing to meet enormous budget deficits kept rates high. European and Japanese banks increased their activities in the United States, enjoying Federal Deposit Insurance Corporation (FDIC) protection after 1978. Domestic and foreign investors alike capitalized on high-return opportunities proliferating in the speculative-electronic economy.[2]

Next, after millions in deposits left savings and loan banks for money-market funds during the high-inflation 1970s, the S&Ls were deregulated in 1982 and permitted to pay higher interest rates and invest more freely beyond the home mortgages to which they had been limited. This moved enormous sums from housing loans into the speculative market, particularly to fund upscale malls and office buildings. Commercial banks were also permitted to increase real estate investment, and an ever larger portion of construction activity shifted to speculative investments.[3]

Tax cuts for wealthy individuals also swelled the volume of money feeding the speculative-electronic boom. The capital gains tax fell from 49 to 28 percent in 1978 and to 20 percent in 1981. Inheritance taxes were eliminated on estates of up to $600,000. The top personal income tax rate was cut from 70 to 50 percent in 1981 and to 28 percent in 1986 (though it was raised to 31 percent in 1992). Corporate tax rates also fell, and new tax credits were created; the share of federal revenue collected from corporations dropped from 12 percent in 1980 to 6 percent by 1983. The federal deficit caused by these tax cuts was covered in large part by borrowing from individuals who had additional money to lend *as a result* of the same tax cuts, and the interest paid them was tax free. By the beginning of the 1990s interest payments, going mainly to the wealthy, exceeded federal income support for the elderly and poor.[4]

The monetarist-induced recession of the early 1980s, moreover, spurred a wave of investor and corporate borrowing to acquire (or retain control of) existing companies. In 1981, $82 billion was borrowed for this purpose; by 1990 the decade's accumulated corporate debt totaled $1,300 billion. This M&A (merger and acquisition) borrowing drove up interest costs for all other investors, including the federal government, but produced little growth in the real economy. To the contrary, its increasing pace reduced employment and worker security as "assets" (stores, factories, pension funds) were liquidated to raise stock prices and dividends and pay off M&A debt. As Sony's Akio Morita saw it, Americans were making money "by playing 'money games,' namely mergers and acquisitions, by simply moving money back and forth . . . instead of creating and producing goods with some actual value."

All this speculative activity was in fact subsidized by the federal government because interest on funds borrowed for M&As was deductible from corporate and personal income taxes. North Dakota Representative (later Senator) Byron Dorgan introduced a bill in 1981 to eliminate this subsidy, but like later attempts to limit high-interest "junk bond" M&A financing, it was thwarted by lobbyists representing speculative-electronic firms. The volume of merger deals continued to accelerate, reaching an annual total of $659 billion in 1996.[5]

As the speculative-electronic economy began its takeoff, it was centered in New York City's commercial banks and brokerage houses, stock and commodities exchanges, and legal and accounting firms. Between 1978 and 1983 the city gained 200,000 financial-sector jobs. "New York is now unquestionably the financial center of the world," David Rockefeller proclaimed in 1983. That year the city processed $200 billion in global transactions each day. Signs of the rising financial-sector tide were noted in the co-op market, upscale restaurants and shops, limousine rentals, and arts and entertainment patronage.[6]

Neighborhood New York, however, was not benefiting. As business school graduates (MBAs) and other professionals arrived to work in the financial sector, many chose to live in the suburbs. Between 1978 and 1981 city residents netted fewer than 30,000 new jobs, while more than 140,000 went to commuters. This Manhattan-anchored suburban prosperity continued through the 1980s with commuters accounting for one-fifth of the city's work force and two-fifths of its income. By 1991 a fifth of all earnings in New York's suburbs came from New York City employment; in nearby Nassau and Westchester Counties city jobs provided 40 percent of total earnings.[7]

The 1980s speculative-electronic boom was not based on old headquarters-city routines. Gone was face-to-face interaction between senior dealmakers and favored customers over two-hour, three-martini lunches. Gone also were the legions of outer-borough women who answered telephones, typed, and filed. Now microcomputers (introduced by IBM in 1981), prepackaged and customized software, copiers, fax machines, modems, cellular telephones, satellites, computer networking, voice mail, e-mail, teleconferencing, and desktop financial-information services all compressed the time and space in which business was done. By 1982 one computer "work station professional" at Citibank performed the operations formerly done by fourteen paper-office workers. Over the next decade $800 billion in information technology was added by companies in the service sector, including speculative-electronic firms. The derivatives market, worth $16 trillion by 1994, was built on electronic risk computation and instantaneous global communication. As the new technology improved, trading volume rose, but in the early 1990s "job compression" became the watchword: increased output no longer meant more employees.[8]

On October 19, 1987, David Rockefeller's "financial center of the world" began to come apart. The stepped-up pace of borrowing and leveraging had so inflated paper investment that the bubble burst, and the stock market fell by 508 points, a 22 percent loss in value. By 1991 "other key Wall Street business activities [had] also turned sour [and] many of the heroes of the 1980s [were] now either in financial difficulty, in jail, or indicted."[9] Overextended S&Ls were going under nationwide, prompting a $10 billion federal bailout in 1987. As the 1990s began, it was clear that at least $500 billion would be needed to compensate S&L depositors, and additional funds required to bolster commercial banks against sinking investments.

In 1989 massive job loss began in New York City. Manhattan's financial sector had axed 56,000 jobs by 1991, and stalwart firms E. F. Hutton and Drexel Burnham Lambert disappeared. The 1977–1987 boom had produced 400,000 jobs, but during 1989–1993 the city lost 330,000. For decision-makers in speculative-electronic firms, however, jobs were not an issue. They opposed President Bill Clinton's 1993 job stimulus program—which would have pumped $1 billion into New York City—and applauded Federal Reserve interest rate hikes, which dampened growth in the real economy and prompted 1995 headlines such as "Bonds Surge on New Sign of Slowdown." Despite a nationwide gain of 10 million jobs after 1993, only 57,000 New York City jobs had been added by 1997. Had the city's "recovery" matched that of the rest of the country, jobs would have increased by 310,000.[10]

New York's weak gain in jobs (a third of them going to commuters) was again largely tied to the speculative-electronic economy. After federal bailouts and much personnel downsizing, the stock market rose 1,000 points in 1992. The Federal Reserve then raised interest rates in 1993–1994, and long-term bond returns became less attractive than the panoply of short-term options. In 1994 Paine Webber's CEO David Marron announced, "We have had a crash in the bond market at least as great as the stock market crash of 1987"; low year-end bonuses were followed by firings and internal turmoil at a dozen major brokerage houses and commercial banks. What reprieved Wall Street during 1995–1996 was a national boom in M&A activity and in stock investments, especially via mutual funds, and the Dow-Jones average rose from 4,000 to 6,500, more than twice its 1987 high point. Now, however, investors could be serviced as well by brokers across the nation and around the globe as by those in New York.[11]

The technologies that stoked Manhattan's 1977–1987 financial boom also dispersed and deconcentrated the speculative-electronic economy. Between 1976 and 1986, 63,000 financial and business-services jobs left Manhattan—30,000 to New York's suburbs and 33,000 to Delaware, South Dakota, and other states. In 1987 the Manhattan securities analyst Reid Nagle opened a consulting firm in Hoboken, New Jersey, and in 1990 moved it to Virginia. "Technology in the last five years," he said, "has made it possible for us to locate in a lower-cost area that has a more attractive lifestyle" and still serve customers in New York or elsewhere. By 1993 suburban New Jersey's 16-million-square-foot Bridgewater Mall housed AT&T's world headquarters and offices of Chase Manhattan, Dun & Bradstreet, the NYNEX phone company, and four insurance companies; their executives used the Morristown airfield just fifteen minutes away, a private international jet facility with its own U.S. customs clearance. By the mid-1990s, Charlotte, North Carolina, was the nation's third-largest commercial banking center.

In 1995 New York had 13,000 fewer jobs in the securities industry than in 1987, whereas the rest of the country had gained 85,000. A 1996 *Wall Street Journal* survey of leading brokerage houses found that companies located in Chicago, St. Louis, and St. Petersburg, Florida, outperformed the top New York firms in predicting stock-price gains. More ominously, the securities accounts already serviced by internet brokers in 1996 were predicted to grow from 100,000 to 9 million by 2001. "The Internet is more than a new market," a Morgan Stanley executive stated. "It allows end users to bypass the middleman. It allows them to bypass us."

In 1980 New York's commodity exchanges faced no foreign competition; in the 1990s seven of the top ten exchanges were located overseas. The Tokyo Stock Exchange carried more tradable equity than the New York Stock Exchange in 1988, and the NYSE itself anticipated moving to a twenty-four-hour trading day by the year 2000 to participate in what was becoming one continuous worldwide market. By 1995 three-quarters of the 49,000 Bloomberg financial-information terminals were located outside New York, both across the United States and in seventy-eight other countries. The speculative-electronic money balloon had expanded beyond New York City to float over far more of the United States and the world than it did in 1974.[12]

As deregulation, tax cuts, and bank bailouts enhanced capital flow into the speculative-electronic economy during the 1980s and 1990s, its leading firms increased their power in Washington through lobbyists (both Republican and Democratic), think-tank sponsorship (largely tax deductible), and government appointments (Clinton's treasury secretary, Robert Rubin, was a Goldman Sachs cochairman). Campaign contributions from financial-sector political action committees tripled during the 1980s, and their "soft money" gifts to both parties in 1992 amounted to one-fifth of all such presidential-election-year contributions.[13]

The Real Economy

If one measures economic growth not by stock and bond prices or derivatives earnings but by rising living standards, declining unemployment, and decreasing poverty, then the 1980s and 1990s were an era of stagnation in New York City. A warning was sounded by the Municipal Assistance Corporation chair and investment banker Felix Rohatyn: "[People] who have a place in the mainstream are being pushed along by the tremendous wave of technology and the rapid accumulation of wealth. But those who are out of the mainstream . . . are falling further behind. . . . The challenge to New York is not just to create jobs for jazzy takeover attorneys and snazzy municipal-bond traders. The challenge is to hang on to what is left of the garment industry and light manufacturing." The increasing divergence between beneficiaries of the speculative-electronic economy and the mass of neighborhood New Yorkers was epitomized in the response of one corporate CEO to a 1991 *New York Times* query, "How can we save New York City?" He said, "The city has to send a signal to . . . people in commercial offices—that . . . the central business district [will] be kept clean and safe. . . . It would take political will, because the outer boroughs want a share of the budget, but the fact is, most businessmen and tourists don't visit the outer boroughs."[14]

In 1981 Ronald Reagan promised that his tax cuts would create 13 million jobs, and 12 million were added by 1987. But the tax-cut-induced savings and investment that were supposed to produce this job growth did not materialize. Instead, savings and investment rates both fell, and most corporate "investment" was in mergers and acquisitions, not in job creation. It was massive defense spending that primed the real economy, and a sharp drop in the dollar's value during 1985–1987 which reignited overseas demand for now-cheaper U.S. exports. The falling dollar was a result of the high interest rates the Reagan administration was paying to cover its deficits. With dollars piling up and the U.S. economy in recession during the early 1980s, the paper dollar was worth more than the "real" goods and services for which it could be exchanged. In 1985 all this unraveled, and the dollar collapsed.[15]

The new jobs that appeared during the Reagan years came mainly in two varieties: high-skill, high-pay and low-skill, low-pay. A vast recomposition of the U.S. labor market was under way. Financial and business services accounted for 3.3 million new jobs, a quarter of the increase. Most of these jobs paid well, but that total also included low-paid data-entry, messenger, and office-cleaner positions. At the same time, low-paying retail and food service jobs grew by 4.5 million;

clerical employment stagnated; and manufacturing jobs, paying twice the wages of service jobs, decreased.

As these shifts gathered steam, the economists Barry Bluestone, Bennett Harrison, and Lucy Gorham warned in 1984, "We are entering an era in which, for those who were employed in the older industrial sectors and regions of the country, downward skidding rather than traditional upward mobility may become the norm. And for new entrants to the labor force, those who do not have advanced skills may be relegated permanently to the lower rungs of the employment distribution." By 1991 manufacturing jobs were down 1.8 million from 1981, and 3.4 million more low-wage food service, hotel, and department store jobs were projected by 2000.[16]

New York City underwent a more extreme job-market bifurcation than the United States overall. Manufacturing employment dropped by 30 percent during 1977–1987, and the Manhattan speculative-electronic job boom largely bypassed unemployed blue-collar workers or unskilled labor-market entrants. In 1982 a Bureau of Labor Statistics official predicted that 70 percent of the decade's new jobs would be white-collar slots requiring "computer and communications skills." By 1987 employers expected at least one year of college for positions where a high school diploma had previously sufficed. In 1990, just after the job hemorrhage began, city employment was up by 406,000 white-collar service jobs since 1980 but only 20,000 in retail and wholesale positions, and down 202,000 in manufacturing.[17]

As economist Robert Fitch pointed out, New York's situation was exceptional. In 1993 the city had a far lower share of workers in manufacturing (9 percent) than Los Angeles (18 percent), Chicago (16.5 percent), or Philadelphia (15 percent), the next three largest cities. At the same time it had roughly double the percentage of financial-sector employment (14.5 percent) as Los Angeles (6.5 percent), Chicago (8.5 percent), and Philadelphia (7.5 percent). Nonetheless, New York had only the same number of financial jobs in 1994 that it had in 1969. The speculative-electronic economy had provided no lasting job growth over twenty-five years; in fact, the city's total employment had fallen from 3.8 million to 3.2 million, and 600,000 manufacturing jobs were gone.[18]

The loss of U.S. manufacturing jobs, and the more severe manufacturing drop in New York, can be attributed only in part to "factory flight" of jobs moving abroad. By the beginning of the 1980s, Europe, Japan, and the United States each produced virtually the same array of goods and competed in one another's markets according to price and quality; the advantage U.S. manufacturing had enjoyed when these other economies were rebuilding in the decades after World War II was gone. Still, things were not static. The overvalued dollar made foreign imports cheap during the early 1980s, but U.S. exports rebounded after the dollar fell in the mid-1980s, and U.S. manufacturing was in fact growing in the 1990s. Third World imports from the much publicized "new international division of labor," moreover, amounted to less than 3 percent of the U.S. real economy in 1990. By 1993 only 11 percent of real economic activity in the United States was attributable to imports, and most of this was balanced by exports.[19]

More important to New York's job losses than foreign competition was the relentness dispersion, deconcentration, uprooting, and churning of manufacturing and other jobs *inside* U.S. borders—from cities to suburbs and across regions. Between 1979 and 1995 thousands of workplaces moved, contracted, or closed; new jobs appeared, but re-employment entailed a downward shift in wages for two-thirds of the 43 million workers who lost their jobs. Many firms moved to suburban "edge city" locations which by the 1990s housed two-thirds of all offices in the United States. Although New York City gained 400,000 jobs during 1977–1987, its suburbs gained 470,000. The number of Fortune 500 headquarters in New York City fell from 117 to 43 during the 1970s and 1980s, and those that left New York deconcentrated; in 1970 half these companies were in ten large cities, but by 1990 less than a third were. Nationally, employment shifted to sunbelt states. While the Northeast and Midwest added 8.5 million jobs during the 1980s, the West and South gained 16 million.[20]

The reasons firms moved at all, and why they left New York, involved more than the conservative lament over "high taxes." As researchers who studied business location decisions pointed out, many New York City firms that moved after taxes fell in 1975 had not left earlier when taxes were higher. The Clinton-era ten-million-job expansion, moreover, occurred after taxes were increased in 1993 to 36 percent on incomes over $115,000, and to 39.6 percent above $250,000.

Tax levels were gauged as "high" or "fair" in relation to services—public safety, transportation, an employable work force, livable neighborhoods. As the supply of educated and available labor in the suburbs and sunbelt increased through the 1980s, including the growing number of women seeking full-and part-time jobs, a wide spectrum of firms moved to these locations. The lower pay accepted by suburban and sunbelt job-seekers, particularly by second or third wage earners in households struggling to maintain living standards, was one attraction. And prime considerations continued to be top executives' travel time and life-style choices, especially proximity to outdoor recreation. Employers also welcomed tax cuts or other financial inducements awarded to "attract" or "retain" jobs, and learned to play competing offers against each other.[21]

In New York City the declining quality of life after 1975 diminished the value in services for taxes paid. The failure of crowded, underfunded public schools to produce employable job entrants discouraged business leaders; New York Telephone, Time Inc., and several commercial banks withdrew from high school partnership programs that failed to deliver job-ready candidates in sufficient number. City attention to the infrastructure for manufacturing, moreover, was miniscule. Rents rose as publicly subsidized office buildings and luxury housing competed for space with factories and warehouses. New York land zoned for manufacturing was threatened by city plans for residential and office "waterfront development" in the 1980s, and for retail megastores in the 1990s. The lack of a trans–Hudson River rail-freight connection disadvantaged New York manufacturers wishing to reach national and export markets. With no city strategy to water the roots of the real economy, manufacturing jobs were thus lost at four times the national rate during the 1980s. Retail, wholesale, and service firms dependent on local markets all faced a shrinking real economy, and many cut jobs or closed.[22]

"Job compression" through computerization and new communications technology also moved into New York's real economy during the 1980s and accelerated in the 1990s. Managerial, clerical, wholesale, retail, and manufacturing employment were all affected. Fewer employees meant fewer supervisors, and some of them were replaceable by electronic monitoring of worker output. Automated teller machines displaced bank staff. Computerized bar-coding and electronic scanners reduced labor needs in sales and inventory. Technological advances made "just in time" delivery possible, cutting back warehouse and wholesale jobs. Smaller numbers of higher-skilled manufacturing workers replaced larger numbers of lower-skilled workers, and their output grew.

Computerized design and tooling enhanced productivity. By 1994 it was possible to customize women's blue jeans by entering individual measurements on a touch-screen computer in New York (or anywhere), relaying the information by modem to computerized cutting machinery and production lines in Tennessee, and mailing the bar-coded product to the buyer's home. Telemarketing reduced the number of retail sales workers, and catalogue and television shopping-channel buyers made credit-card purchases by phone; by 1994 commercial 800-number calls accounted for 40 percent of AT&T's telephone business.[23]

Wealth Polarization

In 1994 Secretary of Labor Robert Reich warned, "America has the most unequal distribution of income of any industrialized nation in the world." The inequality grew as tax policies, employment trends, and divergence between the speculative-electronic and real economies polarized income and wealth. In 1980 the top fifth of households received 42 percent of national income, and the bottom fifth received 5 percent. By 1993 the top fifth was receiving 48 percent, the bottom fifth, 3.6 percent. A stream of government reports, economic studies, and best-selling books pointed to mounting income inequality during the 1980s and 1990s. Even Alan Greenspan, chairman of the Federal Reserve and an architect of Reagan-era policies, observed (in economist talk), "A potentially significant factor in the current state of long-run concerns is that the distribution of family income has become more dispersed."[24]

In blunter terms, the rich were much richer, and the poor were poorer and more numerous. The boom at the top was astonishing. By 1989 four-fifths of income gains since 1977 had gone to the top one-fifth of households, with the top 1 percent taking 44 percent of all income growth. The total wealth of this richest 1 percent amounted to $5.7 trillion, a sum greater than the $4.8 trillion held by 90 percent of Americans. This top 1 percent, 800,000 households, owned 45 percent of all commercial real estate, 49 percent of stocks, 62 percent of business assets, and 78 percent of bonds. Ultrarich "supernovas" earning more than $500,000 a year mushroomed from 17,000 in 1979 to 205,000 in 1993.[25]

At the opposite pole, the reductions in poverty achieved during the 1960s and 1970s had been nearly wiped out by the 1990s. In 1960, 40 million persons (22 percent of the population) lived below the poverty line. As a result of safety-net programs and rising wages, the poor decreased to 25 million in 1970 and remained at that number until the 1980s. Then, with Carter-era policies to restrain the economy and Reagan-era budget reductions, the number of poor persons rose to 35 million in 1983 and 39 million (15 percent of Americans) in 1993. This new poverty was more concentrated among children than in previous decades, and by 1994 more than a fifth of the nation's children lived below the poverty line.[26]

For the majority of Americans between rich and poor, income trends sloped downward. As world competition increased, U.S. corporate profits dropped from 10 percent in the 1960s to 6 percent in the 1970s. A "wage squeeze," as economist David Gordon termed it, then began: worker pay flattened and declined; the value of the minimum wage fell; and by 1993 spendable take-home pay for four-fifths of the American labor force was 3 percent lower than in 1979. As income tax cuts in the 1980s were counterbalanced by Social Security tax increases, many Americans wound up paying more in total federal taxes. As a result, consumer borrowing—to keep in place—expanded voluminously during the 1980s and 1990s, especially with credit cards.

U.S. corporate profits recovered after 1983 as the result of lower taxes and wage costs, federal defense contracts, and rising exports; by 1996 they stood at 11.5 percent. Corporate CEO pay increased by 5 percent a year, and in 1995 CEO-to-worker pay ratios were as high as 212 to 1. The ranks of managers and supervisors doubled over 1960s levels, and between 1973 and 1993 their compensation grew by 50 percent. In contrast, half of IRS returns in 1989 were for incomes of $20,000 or less, and in 1990 some 18 percent of full-time workers earned below-poverty-level wages. Economist William Frey spoke of a "hollowing out of the middle" during the 1980s, "with growing numbers of men both above $50,000 and below $20,000 and fewer men in between." Those who fell most behind were workers with less than high school education and African Americans. Black workers had moved steadily toward wage parity with whites in the 1970s, but during the 1980s they lost ground.[27]

This wage squeeze was achieved in three ways. First, antiunion policies were embraced by employers, a development encouraged by the Reagan administration, which crushed its own union of air traffic controllers and slowed or reversed pro-worker regulatory activities. Labor contracts after 1981 increasingly included benefit givebacks, wage concessions, and "two-tier" arrangements under which new workers were simply paid less.

Second, with a less secure wage base, American households swelled the labor supply as they took on second or third jobs and sent more members to work; women's labor force participation rose from 42 to 60 percent between 1973 and 1994. In 1983 economist Alvin Schorr noted that the single-worker "family wage" was dead; only 40 percent of jobs paid enough for one worker to support a family of four.

Third, employers converted or "outsourced" full-time work with benefits into part-time or temporary jobs without them. New job entrants often found these the only jobs they could get; so did millions of workers who had lost full-time employment. In 1994 the business magazine *Fortune* celebrated "how the 'job' itself may disappear and be remembered only as an artifact of the industrial age, to be replaced by meaningful, market-driven work assignments in post-job organizations."[28]

Wealth polarization was accompanied by spatial polarization. The upper "fortunate fifth" of Americans pulled apart to suburbs and "gated communities" removed from urban neighborhoods, immigrants, and racial diversity. During the 1980s a large-scale, primarily white internal migration occurred to booming metropolitan areas in Florida, Georgia, North Carolina, Virginia, Arizona, Colorado, Oregon, and Washington. And everywhere, Robert Reich warned, this upscale elite was

> quietly seceding from the rest of the nation. . . . In many cities and towns, the wealthy have in effect withdrawn their dollars from the support of public spaces and institutions shared by all and dedicated the savings to their own private services. As public parks and playgrounds deteriorate, there is a proliferation of private health clubs [and] golf clubs. . . . The number of private security guards in the United States now exceeds the number of public police officers. . . . The new elite is linked by jet, modem, fax, satellite and fibre-optic cable to the great commercial and recreational centers of the country, but it is not particularly connected to the rest of the nation.[29]

This new geography of privileged enclaves tied to the speculative-electronic economy increasingly overlay the old geography of localities and political units rooted in the real economy. The "fortunate fifth" voted in higher percentages than the bottom four-fifths, supporting school choice, lower taxes, and their benefactor Ronald Reagan. In the rest of America, journalists Donald Barlett and James Steele asked "what went wrong" and discovered that "life for the working class is deteriorating, and those at the bottom are trapped. For the first time in this century, members of a generation entering adulthood will find it impossible to achieve a better lifestyle than their parents."[30]

Income polarization in New York City went further than anywhere else. Here real per capita income rose 33 percent during the 1980s, even while the numbers in poverty swelled. By 1990 the average household income of Manhattan's "fortunate fifth" was $174,000 (for the *nation's* upper fifth it was $94,000). Income growth was led by the financial sector, where average pay (from secretary on up) jumped from $65,000 in 1987 to $134,000 in 1993. At the height of the 1980s boom the financial community's "top 100" earners all made $4 million or more. In 1992 Robert Rubin of Goldman Sachs earned $28 million, but this was a pittance next to currency speculator George Soros, who made $800 million. The gap between rich and poor continued to grow, and 58 percent of New Yorkers believed it was still widening in 1995.

Many of New York's wealthy lived in the suburbs. When the coffee-sugar-cocoa and cotton exchanges threatened to move to New Jersey in 1995, they announced that less than 30 percent of their 5,000 employees resided in New York City. In Manhattan the rich were concentrated on the Upper East Side, where in 1990 a quarter of all households had incomes above $100,000 (only 6 percent of all city residents had incomes that high). In 1995 Upper East Side landlords attempted to secede from the rest of New York City by proposing a "security district" tax of $100 to $200 per apartment to pay for 500 private guards to patrol the neighborhood. Although Mayor Rudolph Giuliani backed the plan, residents and local elected officials objected, and the proposal died.[31]

In 1980 a fifth of New Yorkers lived below the poverty line. As national numbers of poor persons grew, New York's grew faster—to 24 percent in 1982, and 27 percent in 1993. Poverty among New York City children increased from 32 percent in 1979 to 44 percent in 1993. That year 24,000 homeless persons slept in city shelters each night—up from 18,000 in 1984—and ten times that many, or 239,000, had spent some time in a public shelter during the previous five years. Access to shelter tightened and numbers remained stable under Giuliani, but between 1994 and 1996 meals served at soup kitchens and emergency pantries rose from 67,000 to 115,000 per week.

The public assistance rolls climbed from 1.4 million in 1982 to nearly 1.8 million in 1993. Despite the conservative dogma that New York's shelters and income support were a "magnet" for poor people, few welfare recipients were new arrivals; in 1990 only 3 percent of welfare clients had not lived in the city five years earlier. The faltering real economy was the main culprit. During the 1980s and 1990s unemployment in New York City outpaced national levels, standing at 9 percent in the city versus 6 percent nationwide in 1984, and 8.5 versus 5 percent in 1996. The number of single adults qualifying for Home Relief surged after job loss began in 1989, rising from 204,000 to 298,000 between 1990 and 1994. "We're seeing people who were living on the margin, off the books, holding minimum-wage jobs, . . . single adults who can no longer find work or support themselves," a city Human Resources Administration official stated in 1991. By 1995 half of all welfare recipients had worked full time the year before they applied for public assistance.[32]

In 1990 Elmhurst-Corona's reported income distribution was more clumped in the middle than that of the city overall: only 23 percent of households fell below $15,000, versus 28 percent in all New York City; 55 percent were between $15,000 and $50,000, compared with 45 percent citywide; and 22 percent were over $50,000, versus 27 percent. Between 1980 and 1990 blue-collar production, operator, and transport jobs held steady at 28 percent in CD4 but declined from 23 to 19 percent citywide. Clerical employment in Elmhurst-Corona dropped from 25 to 18 percent, compared with the less severe 25 to 21 percent citywide decrease; and sales jobs for CD4 residents rose from 9 to 11 percent, paralleling a 10 to 11 percent citywide increase. Service employment, mainly in education and health, grew from 16 to 21 percent in CD4, while rising only from 15 to 16 percent citywide. Administrative, professional, and technical workers remained at 22 percent of the CD4 labor force, but citywide they increased from 28 to 34 percent.

Life for Elmhurst-Corona residents became harder in the 1990s. Between 1990 and 1994 the number qualifying for public assistance (under Aid to Families with Dependent Children, Home Relief, Supplemental Security Income, and Medicaid) jumped from 16,000 to 28,500.[33]

The Underground Economy

Combined with job dispersal and downsizing, New York City's policy of starving the real economy produced unique results. Here more than anywhere else people vanished from the economic radar screen. At the height of the job boom in 1986 only 56 percent of the city's adult population had jobs (the percentage had not changed since 1980) versus 65 percent nationwide. By 1996 the gap widened to 55 percent in New York against 67 percent nationwide. Had the city's labor force participation rate matched the nation's, there would have been 650,000 more New Yorkers holding jobs in 1996. Yet somehow this vast army managed to survive. Some people received public assistance, others begged on the streets, still others labored in the unreported, unrecorded, underground cash economy. Underground transactions also provided cheaper goods and services, and supplementary earnings, to many who labored in the real economy.[34]

Economists variously estimated the total U.S. underground economy at 4 to 33 percent of GNP. As Internal Revenue Service audits fell from 5 percent of tax returns in the 1960s to 2.5 percent in 1980 and less than 1 percent in 1994, the estimates rose. In a 1981 survey 80 percent of U.S. households admitted to underground cash transactions: for auto and home repairs by moonlighters, roadside produce purchases, child-care and housework services for which Social Security and IRS taxes were avoided, and street peddler and flea market goods. Such cash transactions, however, paled in dollar amount to business and landlord tax fraud, paper shifts of corporate profits to overseas subsidiaries, embezzlement, and organized-crime proceeds. All these activities together accounted for a 1993 income-tax shortfall estimated by the IRS at $150 billion.[35]

In 1986 the IRS estimated that 20 percent of New York City's economy was unreported and totaled $40 billion a year, including $15 billion in criminal activities. Despite a computerized record-matching program begun that year, by the 1990s the city's estimated underground economy increased to $50 billion. Off the books, on the side, skimmming, scamming, hustling, and scavenging, New York's underground economic activities were all illegal in big or little ways.[36]

Making Crime Pay

Participants in the underground economy spanned the city's racial and ethnic mix. Elmhurst-Corona's car thieves, chop-shop owners, illegal dumpers, gambling operators, drug importers and sellers, bordello proprietors, prostitutes, and gang-member extortionists included whites, Latin Americans, Asians, and blacks—with African Americans the least involved (see Chapter 9). These activities publicly disturbed neighborhood quality of life, but more hidden underground criminality also occurred, unknown to most residents: criminal profits were laundered through legal businesses; stolen, smuggled, and counterfeit merchandise appeared in Elmhurst-Corona stores, as it did citywide.

A Gambino "family" associate arrested in 1994 for airport cargo theft was a white South Elmhurst resident; his "crew" had stolen and fenced tens of millions of dollars' worth of champagne, sneakers, video games, and camera film. That same year an Ecuadorian cargo theft ring was busted at Kennedy Airport; it specialized in electronics and airplane parts. In 1995 two white truck drivers were arrested for bribing Board of Education warehouse employees to "overload" school supplies when packaging deliveries; the drivers then sold the extra items to Queens retail outlets. In 1992 Sergeant Pete Petrone of the 110th Precinct arrested a Latin American Elmhurst bodega owner for buying "hot" cigarettes, and the following year the city's Department of Finance agents arrested a Chinese Elmhurst resident who smuggled cigarettes from Virginia, evading New York excise taxes, and sold them to local stores. By the mid-1990s ten million cartons of untaxed cigarettes were being sold in New York City each year.[37]

The marketing of brand-name "knockoffs" involved ethnically diverse chains of producers, distributors, sellers, and customers, including the Chinese–Pakistani–Latin American linkages that sold bogus 1994 World Cup soccer merchandise in CD4. That year 300,000 phony "designer" T-shirts were seized at an illegal Manhattan factory run by three Koreans, one of them an Elmhurst resident. In 1995 three West Africans were arrested for illegally copying videocassettes in a Corona basement, and knockoffs of 3,500 movie titles, including *The Lion King* and *Cinderella,* were impounded. Most audacious of all were the Colombian father and son whose Elmhurst jewelry shop sold counterfeit subway and bridge tokens, silver dollars, credit cards, and police shields before it was closed in 1993. The availability of knockoff merchandise was a major New York tourist attraction, and by 1996 the city estimated counterfeit clothing, perfume, software, and other items at $2 billion a year in lost revenue and enforcement costs.[38]

The history of telephone scams during the 1980s and 1990s was an underground counterpoint to technological innovation in the speculative-electronic and real economies. "Stuffers" in the early 1980s jammed telephone coin boxes so that although calls went through, New York Telephone—which then owned all pay phones in the city—lost the revenue. In the mid-1980s, when credit cards and multiple long-distance companies transformed the business, hustlers appeared at public phone banks offering cheap long-distance calls; they purchased numerical credit-card codes from hackers who programmed computers to dial consecutive numbers until a call went through, identifying an active code. Immigrants as well as Americans were willing customers, allowing the hustler to dial for them and then enjoying unlimited phone time. When credit-card owners discovered such calls on their bills, they notified the carrier and those charges were cancelled, but the losses were absorbed through higher phone rates for legitimate callers.

Cellular phones in the 1990s decentralized long-distance hustling. Phone criminals now obtained numerical cellular codes out of the air by electronic scanner, cloned microchips containing valid codes, and placed the chips in store-bought phones. Four Latin American Elmhurst men arrested in 1991 were operating from parked jeeps in which customers placed calls on cellular phones; waiting lines next to these vehicles became a neighborhood distraction. As Sergeant Petrone told the district cabinet, "They sell a half-hour to call anywhere in the world for a flat fee." By 1995 cloned cell phones themselves were available on the street for $100, and a Latin American Corona Heights resident was arrested at an apartment "factory" that sold ready-to-use phones for $50 to middlemen. In addition, 18,000 illegal pay phones were in operation on city streets by 1994. Unlike NYNEX, which operated 8,700 legal street phones, owners of these phones paid no franchise tax, an annual loss to the city of $6 million.[39]

Avoiding Taxes

Tax evasion occurred widely in occupations and legitimate businesses dealing in cash. The IRS estimated that self-employed professionals and small-business proprietors were reporting only 60 percent of their income; hairdressers, barbers, waitresses, and waiters similarly underreported cash earnings and tips. During the 1980s city inspectors uncovered sales tax evasion in several retail shopping areas, among them the South Asian shopping district on 74th Street in Jackson Heights. Here an Indian undercover agent of the Finance Department found merchants who told him no sales tax would be charged if he paid in cash. Hsiang-shui Chen learned that many Chinese Elmhurst residents sought out such stores: "To pay the extra fee of a sales tax beyond the label price is very hard for Chinese people to understand because there was no such charge in Taiwan."

Tax avoidance was also pervasive in the housing market. One Wall Street executive who invested in a five-unit building on Manhattan's Upper West Side instructed his tenants to make out rent checks to "cash," and reported only two-thirds of his landlord income to the IRS. Tax evasion in Elmhurst-Corona was widespread in illegal units. Landlords underreported income from rooming houses and subdivided apartments; homeowners avoided property-tax increases by failing to register illegal rental units.[40]

Paying Subminimum Wages

Employers in restaurants, groceries, sewing shops, construction, and household work frequently paid less than the minimum wage to undocumented workers. The situation worsened after the 1986 Immigration Reform and Control Act, which required employers to ascertain the citizenship or visa status of all employees and made hiring undocumented immigrants a finable offense. As labor organizers from the Chinese Staff and Workers Association discovered, employers used their knowledge that a job-seeker was illegal to push wages below the legal minimum.

> Employers have in fact replaced legal residents or U.S. citizens with undocumented workers. The employer could take the chance because of INS's ineffective enforcement . . . and the ease with which legal obligations under the law can be circumvented. . . . Wages for undocumented workers, who are paid mostly off-the-books, are as a rule 20 to 30 per cent below [those] of legal residents and citizens. . . . By hiring undocumented workers, the employer saves on payroll taxes including Social Security taxes and statutory insurance payments. Finally, undocumented workers living in fear supply a more docile workforce.[41]

The 1986 law created a bull market in subminimum wage jobs, and immigrants had little trouble finding such employment. By 1990 Chinatown garment shop wages of $20 for ten-hour days were not uncommon, and restaurant employees worked twelve-hour, six-day weeks for $1,100 a month. Caribbean and Latin American women found similar wages in sewing factories, office cleaning, child care, and household work; so did Mexican and Central American men in restaurants and Korean greengroceries, and West African men as security guards. Malaysian Chinese men were hired for construction and other day labor at streetside sites in Flushing and Chinatown; Latin American, Polish, and Korean men assembled for day work in Astoria, Woodside, Elmhurst, and Flushing.

New streams of undocumented Mexican and Chinese immigrants fed this post-1986 underground labor market. Among the "snakeheads" apprehended for smuggling economically indentured men and women from Fujian Province in southern China was Elmhurst resident George Huang, a 1970s immigrant who had worked as a waiter, run a garment shop, and owned a restaurant on Manhattan's Upper East Side. Some 150 passengers had each pledged $20,000 to Huang for a four-month journey on a ship with one bathroom and wooden shelves for beds.[42]

Not Reporting Income

Stagnant or falling earnings and periods of unemployment led many New Yorkers to initiate or intensify cash-producing businesses and sidelines, and most of this income went unreported. In Elmhurst-Corona I encountered white Americans with home-based, cash-earning activities: beauticians who gave off-the-books facials; persons who tutored and gave music or art lessons; men who earned income in bowling leagues and tournaments; and collector-traders of old fountain pens and postcards. Milagros Ricourt discovered similar activities among Latin American residents: babysitters and tutors; women who sold cooked food from their homes or in Corona sewing shops; and men who did automobile repairs on the street.

Cash sidelines brought people more visibly into the underground economy when they paid fees for spots at annual street fairs and weekend flea markets. I interviewed one diverse group of sellers in 1984 at Elmhurst Day, an annual festival held in the playground opposite Elmhurst Hospital. A white Elmhurst woman with her young daughter sold old household articles, and by helping to organize the event, she had saved the $25 fee other vendors were charged. An African American woman selling clothing told me she saw a newspaper ad for the fair and wrote for a spot. A Latin American man who worked many street fairs with a machine that printed designs on T-shirts had been at Elmhurst Day the year before: "They have lists," he told me, "they contact you." An Indian couple with two children sold new clothes from racks. Two Thai women displayed the imported Chinese blouses and toys that they also sold elsewhere on weekends. An Uruguayan mother and adult daughter displayed secondhand knickknacks; a pair of Ecuadorian women sold shoes, wool shawls, and caps. A white woman from Long Island sat by a tableful of handmade wooden shelves and picture frames, which she sold each weekend at Long Island and Queens fairs and flea markets.

Organized flea markets mushroomed nationwide in the 1970s; from fifty large outdoor markets in 1975, some two hundred were in operation by 1980. The largest one opened in 1976 at Roosevelt Raceway; it was attended each Sunday by 35,000 Long Island and Queens customers to whom 1,600 vendors—including schoolteachers and civil servants—sold clothing, brand-name sneakers, housewares, and food. By 1990 dozens of weekly parking-lot and schoolyard markets, including several purveying farm produce, existed in Manhattan. Annual city street fairs sponsored by neighborhood organizations grew to 3,500 in 1984 and 5,000 by the early 1990s.

At many of these events, among them ethnic festivals in Flushing Meadows–Corona Park (see Chapter 10), restaurants and other legal businesses moved into the underground economy. Prices at these markets were lower than in stores, and sales tax was irregularly collected, although by the 1990s state tax inspectors were appearing more frequently. New York City charged vendors $10 for merchandise permits and $20 to $30 for food permits; with these fees plus its 20 percent share of street rentals from sponsoring organizations, the city was earning $1.3 million annually from street fairs and flea markets by 1992.[43]

Earning Cash on the Streets

Street peddlers have existed throughout the city's history, and they increased after the 1975 fiscal crisis. Reduced police numbers meant less attention to misdemeanors, including unlicensed street vending and selling in restricted locations. With high unemployment among neighborhood New Yorkers, city estimates of peddler totals rose from less than 1,000 before 1980 to 10,000 in 1994. Numbers increased in the early 1980s as the speculative-electronic boom produced more customers. A second boost in peddler numbers occurred after the job bust that began in 1989.[44]

The peddling explosion began in midtown Manhattan, where laws barred sellers from locating within a hundred feet of a store offering the same merchandise; after 1983 large sections were banned to street selling of any goods other than printed materials. Nonetheless, both licensed peddlers (whose numbers were capped by law at 850 in 1979) and unlicensed vendors worked the midtown area. What they sold often replicated what was in stores—they followed sales ads and offered the same goods—but most brand-name items were knockoffs. Licensed food vendors expanded to 7,000 during the 1980s but fell to the capped total of 3,000 after the 1989 job slump reduced patronage. Many food carts were portable kitchens costing up to $5,000, and they offered a wide array of ethnic cuisine as well as traditional hot dogs.

The peddling tide washed beyond midtown to the rest of the city during the 1980s and 1990s. Tailgate vendors sold hats, auto parts, and fruit on highways, and rugs and clothing near factories. Peddlers appeared with audio cassettes, umbrellas, toys, and sunglasses near subway stops, and with a panoply of goods on major shopping strips in all boroughs. Chinatown food and produce sellers clogged sidewalks; Chinese women sold underwear and costume jewelry purchased from Orthodox Jewish wholesalers. In lower Manhattan, West African traders sold "African" goods that they bought from Korean wholesalers and paid a Chinese restaurant to store overnight. Roosevelt Avenue in Elmhurst offered streetside coconut milk, roasted corn, Mexican tacos, Ecuadorian *humitas* (sweet-corn tamales), and Colombian *obleas* (wafers spread with sweet condensed milk). In the late 1980s Mexican flower vendors selling from supermarket shopping carts blanketed the city.[45]

Peddling attracted free spirits such as one white woman from Connecticut: "For the last two years I've been making my own jewelry to sell [in Times Square] for a dollar, and I make $40 to $50 a day. . . . Who needs a license?" It also appealed to immigrants with trading backgrounds, such as the Ecuadorian Otavalo Indians whose distinctive textile, handbag, and clothing designs and men's long hairbraids appeared throughout the city during the 1980s (many Otavaleños lived in Corona). It was the stalled and failing real economy, however, that pushed most into street selling.

Tilman Tomlin, an African American, lost his telephone company job in 1982 and eventually found a $150-a-week factory job; in 1986 he began selling roses and stuffed animals after work at a subway stop in Queens where most weeks he matched his factory salary. White American Albert Linder sold knockoff Gucci and Chanel sweatshirts on Fifth Avenue; a former Sanitation Department worker, he claimed in 1993 to have made more on the street than the $35,000 he earned as a city employee. Dominican immigrants Luis Mendoza, an unemployed construction worker, and his wife Charo Blanco, a former supermarket cashier, sold fresh-pressed sugarcane juice and mangos from street-corner vans; rising at 4:00 A.M. to buy supplies, the couple netted up to $800 during summer weeks in 1994.[46]

Store owners complained that peddlers evaded taxes, paid no rent, and undercut them in price. Pressure from the Fifth Avenue Merchant Association led in 1983 to the formation of a Peddler Task Force of twenty-five police officers to issue summonses in Manhattan south of 59th Street. Midtown sweeps followed, and summonses rose from 29,000 in 1981 to 50,000 in 1985, but many were ignored or the small fine was paid. After Mayor David Dinkins took office in 1990, anti-vendor pressure on City Hall shifted to outer-borough small-business owners who faced both the jobs recession and increased peddler competition. Sung Soo Kim of the Small Business Congress protested, "The police see the street peddlers as just people out there trying to make a living. They don't realize that they're choking the small business owner."[47]

Dinkins increased the Peddler Task Force to eighty police officers and deployed it beyond Manhattan. Mayors Koch and Dinkins, however, both professed sympathies with street vendors, Koch noting that his father and grandfather had been peddlers in Poland, and Dinkins recalling his youthful hawking of shopping bags in Harlem. Mayor Rudolph Giuliani had no such sympathies. In 1994 he placed unlicensed peddling on his *Police Strategy No. 5* agenda, vetoed a city council bill permitting increased numbers of food vendors in midtown, and cleared 125th Street in Harlem of hundreds of African, African American, and Caribbean peddlers.[48]

At a 1985 meeting of Community Board 4 the Greek owner of a Corona gas station was asked about peddlers who appeared on his property each weekend;

he claimed that he did not rent out the space: "I call the police [but] they do nothing." Renting space to vendors did occur elsewhere in CD4, even though a law against doing so was passed in 1984. By 1986 merchandise peddlers were encamped daily on sidewalks next to the Queens Center mall and near three heavily trafficked subway stations.

With mounting complaints of parked vendor vans coming to CB4 from local business owners, district manager Rose Rothschild focused on the issue at a 1990 district cabinet meeting. Reflecting the Dinkins administration's attention to outer-borough peddlers, the 110th Precinct's commanding officer announced that he was sending ten officers for "peddler enforcement training. . . . We will make seizures—the Board of Health is cooperating—with a truck and lift-gate. Summonses are ineffective; we must take the property and the vehicle." A Department of Health official explained food-vending regulations but added with a sigh, "I have only two inspectors for all of New York City." Shocked by this, Rothschild responded, "I feel like I'm in the Twilight Zone." "So do I," answered the official.

Another component of New York's underground street economy was the proliferation of artists. During the 1980s scores of Chinese art students arrived in the city, many settling in Queens, and supported themselves by drawing portraits for $10 to $30 in Manhattan public spaces. Unable to obtain peddler's licenses because of the numerical cap, however, they faced "constant moving" by police. The ancient street-music tradition also reblossomed. Many musicians literally went underground—into subways where, if they passed an audition, they could occasionally get a choice performance spot at a major station. Subway music encompassed many genres: white folk; African American blues, jazz, soul, and hip-hop; Caribbean steel pan; Andean string, panpipe, and percussion; and European and Chinese classical. At one Elmhurst station I even heard an African American man play a remarkable gamelan-like ensemble of discarded metal objects.[49]

Verbal artists too appeared on city streets. Three-card-monte hustlers ("Red you win, black you lose, it all depends on the card you choose") invited their marks to guess which of three rapidly shuffled, face-down cards was the red one. The "art" reposed in both the skill of the dealer (the mark won only if the hustler wished) and his verbal patter. In 1976 twenty three-card-monte teams of dealer, shills, and lookouts operated throughout midtown Manhattan; by 1993 there were 1,500 three-card-monte arrests a year. Other verbal hustlers plied bus, rail, and airplane travelers with offers to take them and their luggage, for a fee, to "arranged" transportation; this turned out to be just a taxi in Manhattan but was often an overpriced limousine at airports. The "hand collector" who appeared periodically at one Elmhurst subway stop was uncreative by comparison; he told riders the token box was inoperative, opened the slam-gate, and pocketed fares himself.[50]

Providing Unregulated Transportation

Unlicensed passenger vans appeared in the Bronx in the early 1970s and quickly spread to Queens and Brooklyn; by 1995 there were 5,000 such vans citywide. They ran parallel to bus routes, carrying riders to and from subway stops or directly to Manhattan. Traveling faster than buses, making stops wherever requested, and holding local fares to $1.00 as bus fares rose to $1.50, the vans were popular with outer-borough riders. Some van drivers held other jobs and worked only morning and evening rush hours; others, including Caribbean and Chinese immigrants, drove full time. Haitian immigrant Dorelus Bernardo, after losing factory and valet parking jobs, bought and operated a van during the early 1990s. Unable to eliminate the vans, the city designated side roads and parking areas for their use in the early 1990s, and in 1995 licensed two van companies.[51]

Drivers of legal for-hire vehicles adopted underground practices as well. In 1987 taxi mechanics estimated that one-quarter of yellow cabs were using various methods to speed-up meters and overcharge riders; arrests of those caught doing so continued through the 1990s. In areas of Queens not served by vans, yellow taxis and licensed radio-call cars traveled along bus routes, illegally soliciting shared-group business. During the 1977-1987 boom luxury sedans servicing corporate accounts numbered more than 10,000. After the stock market crash many began illegally negotiating fares when hailed on the street, becoming higher-priced versions of the city's thousands of unlicensed "gypsy" cabs. By 1995 illegal yellow cabs operating without licenses had become a new target for police seizure.[52]

Scavenging at the Margins

The most labor-intensive work in the underground economy was turning abandoned items into cash; one Latin American immigrant collected mattresses at illegal dump sites and sold them for $5 each to a refurbishing firm. When the price of recycled newsprint rose in 1994, vans appeared on pick-up days to steal bundled newspapers before the sanitation trucks arrived, costing the city $2 million. Some people in the South Bronx collected unused bus transfers from passengers as they exited and resold them for half price.

Among poor and homeless New Yorkers, "canning"—hunting for soda and beer cans and bottles to redeem for deposits—became a ubiquitous occupation. White, black, Asian, and Latin American men and women could be seen canning everywhere, including in Elmhurst-Corona parks and wire trashbaskets. In lower Manhattan 200 elderly Toysan Chinese women rummaged for cans, sometimes waiting next to persons still drinking from them. Uptown canners included African American men such as Robert Williams, who separated recyclables for apartment building supers in exchange for cans and bottles and averaged $50 a day. Others were "two-for-one men" who paid half the deposit price to canners unwilling to wait at stores and redemption centers. Some canners also scavenged for discarded books, magazines, records, clothes, appliances, and housewares, which found their way to streetside secondhand sellers in many parts of the city.[53]

More circumspect were scavenger-thieves of commodities like copper and building appointments. From the late 1970s on they stripped abandoned buildings of pipes, wire, plumbing fixtures, and architectural ornaments, selling them to junkyards and construction suppliers. By the early 1990s the 2,600 miles of copper subway cable had become a target of scavengers, who sold it for a dollar a pound; the Transit Authority paid seven times that much to replace it.

Tragedy at the very bottom of the underground economy occurred in 1993 when Wilfredo Nuñez died in a sewer tunnel. With friends, he often opened manhole covers and descended with wading boots, flashlight, and shovel in search of coins, jewelry, and even gold teeth. On this trip an unexpected rush of water knocked him over, and he fractured his skull.[54]

[7]

Mayoral Ideologies

New York's contracting real economy, widening wealth polarization, and growing underground economy were hardly signs of successful mayoral stewardship. None of the city's three mayors during the 1980s and 1990s claimed credit for these trends, but neither did their policies do anything to counter them. Rather, each promulgated a governing ideology that served his political interests and diverted attention from the worsening quality of life in neighborhood New York. Edward Koch embraced the "world city" imagery that celebrated the 1980s speculative-electronic boom. David Dinkins proclaimed New York "a gorgeous mosaic," thus seeking to allay apprehension over incidents of racial violence but beclouding persistent inequalities intensified by economic trends. Rudolph Giuliani campaigned to improve New York's quality of life and defined what he meant in *Police Strategy No. 5.*

The World City

As Koch prepared for his 1981 reelection campaign (challenged from the left by state assembly member Frank Barbaro of Brooklyn, who received 36 percent of the Democratic primary vote), he needed a theme to deflect attention from the subsidies given to New York's permanent government. "Planned shrinkage" presented one possibility. Proposed in a 1976 *New York Times Magazine* piece by Beame housing official Roger Starr, planned shrinkage meant the deliberate withdrawal of public resources from the city's poorest districts, even beyond the post–fiscal crisis service reductions already affecting neighborhood New York. The aim, in Starr's words, was "making New York smaller" by so reducing the quality of life that poor people would move away.

In 1978 President Jimmy Carter's Department of Housing and Urban Development adopted planned shrinkage in its directives for distributing antipoverty funds to selected "Neighborhood Strategy Areas." The Koch administration selected its first ten NSAs, including Corona, in 1979, and they excluded the city's poorest neighborhoods. Planned shrinkage was thus tacitly accepted by the Koch regime; because the phrase itself had the drawback of reminding all city voters that neighborhood quality of life had shrunk since 1975, however, the mayor avoided using it.[1]

In 1980 a Twentieth Century Fund Task Force on the Future of New York endorsed planned shrinkage in its *New York—World City* report[2], but more important, it offered a positive, even classy alternative by anointing New York "the true world capital." The task force pointed to the foreign banks, corporate offices, and real estate investment then increasing in the city and predicted that "the revival of economic activity . . . visible in Manhattan" would soon make New York "the global marketplace for business, finance, communications, the professions, and the arts." The report located the engine of world city emergence in the "legal, financial, consulting and communication [firms] servicing national and international corporations." Only one task force member, a former AFL-CIO official, dissented: "The Report fails to emphasize the need for blue-collar and rank-and-file white-collar jobs," he stated. "It concerns itself primarily with the problems of bankers and financiers."[3]

Like "headquarters city" in its heyday, Koch's "world city" depended on government subsidy, but the Twentieth Century Fund report opposed this: "Special incentives are not now needed to attract or maintain business. . . . Public . . . financing of new luxury housing represents a diversion of public funds." Mascha Sinnreich, a Fund staff member branded such public subsidies "elitist," providing "services to the wealthy at the expense of the poor . . . [and] jobs mainly for commuters and new arrivals." The report instead called for public investment in education, mass transit, and infrastructure maintenance.[4]

During what Annmarie Hauck Walsh termed "the [1980s] decade of the developers," the permanent-government alliance with Koch heeded no such criticism of its alphabet soup of tax breaks, insisting that "the benefits of increases in real estate values [and] job expansion . . . are essential to the city's well being and will filter down to the city's low-income population." It welcomed world city enthusiasts such as the Rutgers University urbanologist George Sternlieb, who asserted, "We can't go back. The city's future is as a world financial capital," and Boris Pushkarev of the Regional Plan Association, who announced, "The primacy of Manhattan as a world city will not be challenged in the forseeable future." Deputy Mayor Kenneth Lipper, a former investment banker, agreed: "It's the place to be, it's the Rome of the modern era."[5]

In 1985 Koch appointed Deputy Mayor Robert Wagner Jr. to head a Commission on the Year 2000. Its report, *New York Ascendant,* arrived just months before the October 1987 stock market crash. "We see a city ascendant—with a basically healthy economy," it began. "By the turn of the century, it should be the unrivaled world city." The report predicted that New York would add 300,000 jobs by 2000 and called for public initiatives to build office buildings to house them. (Over the next six years the city would lose 330,000 jobs.) Like the Twentieth Century Fund report, it downplayed manufacturing and recommended rezoning manufacturing land for residential and commercial uses. Job growth for neighborhood New Yorkers, it advised, would occur in low-wage clerical, office-cleaning, security-guard, and food-service jobs spun off by an expanding speculative-electronic economy.[6]

Beginning in 1988 a series of think tank and academic volumes joined the world city chorus. In *New York Unbound,* subsidized by the conservative Manhattan Institute, Louis Winnick of the Ford Foundation described New York as a "world city whose central business district is the core of the economic planet." Echoing past enconiums to the headquarters city, Winnick emphasized the "extraordinary premium on face-to-face communication rendering much of New York's economy resistant to the powerful dispersive pulls of modern communications technology." In the same volume Koch official Mark Willis affirmed that "the mass exodus" of firms from New York "was now over," citing the withdrawn "threat by AT&T to move its headquarters to New Jersey." (AT&T would make that move in 1991.)[7]

Also in 1988 the first anthology of the Social Science Research Council's Committee on New York City was published by the Russell Sage Foundation. Here political scientist John Mollenkopf declared New York "the premier location of the largest, most specialized, and most international corporate service firms. . . . Its primacy has not been threatened." In a 1991 SSRC volume as well, Mollenkopf and Manuel Castells stuck to the world city script: "Although the 1987 stock market crash has slowed their growth, over the long term [advanced corporate service firms] will continue to drive the city's economic transformation." Contributor Matthew Drennan retold the tale of the 1977–1987 Manhattan boom and assured readers that the 19,000 jobs lost by 1990 were "not the beginning of another long economic decline." (Unfortunately, they were.)[8]

The high point of world city studies was the sociologist Saskia Sassen's book *The Global City,* published in 1991. Paying little attention to the real economy, it stressed the "strategic role" of New York and Tokyo and London "as highly concentrated command points in the organization of the world economy"; New York's "agglomeration" of interlinked "producer services"; and the importance of "face-to-face" communication in "the advanced corporate service sector." None of this was new. The "command point," "agglomeration," and "face-to-face" ideas had appeared two decades earlier in influential essays (one cited by Sassen) of the economist Stephen Hymer, who wrote in 1971 that "New York has become a major capital of the world" along with "Tokyo, London, Paris, and Frankfort."

Hymer's thinking in turn drew on a 1926 essay by Regional Plan Association economist Robert Haig.[9] By 1991, moreover, these ideas were obsolete. Sassen acknowleged that "producer services" had grown at a higher rate nationwide during 1977–1987 than they did in New York. During that decade New York's national employment share *declined* from 8.4 to 6.2 percent in business services, 10.1 to 7.5 percent in real estate, 6.5 to 4.8 percent in insurance, and 9.4 to 8.2 percent in legal services. Agglomeration occurred only in banking and finance, where the city's national share rose from 11.7 to 11.8 percent. Even in the highly agglomerated securities sector the city's national employment share dropped from 39 to 35 percent.

Sassen discounted the threat to New York's global ascendance from technological change. "Established telecommunications centers have what amounts to an almost absolute advantage. . . . Development . . . requires massive investments and continuous incorporation of new technologies, discoveries, and innovations [and such] facilities have not been widely dispersed." (In fact they had, as Elmhurst-Corona phone hustlers, among others, understood.) More tellingly, Sassen cited a 1988 study concluding that "advances in computerization and communications technology are 'making it increasingly feasible to design [producer services] in the form of software.' " In fact, the "advanced sectors" were shifting from the old face-to-face agglomeration era to a new dispersed economy operating screen-to-screen.[10]

In a 1993 SSRC volume, the bloom was off the world city rose. Contributor David Vogel warned that "mobilization of capital through computers and satellites" was undermining the financial dominance of New York, Tokyo, and London, since "a particular financial transaction can take place anywhere." Countering world city agglomeration were the loss of New York Stock Exchange business to regional and overseas competitors; the growth of currency and other speculative trading in Chicago, Singapore, and Japan; and the rise of financial activity in Los Angeles rivaling that of New York.[11]

That same year the economist Robert Fitch branded world city praise-singing as "globaloney." "What the higher real-estate consciousness fervently hopes is that . . . low-rent blue-collar workers, factories, [and] poor people will go away [and] high-rent elite workers, office buildings, [and] luxury residential buildings will be attracted to their property. . . . The basic ideas . . . bubble up to the elevated university precincts [where] social scientists simply formalize, provid[ing] evidence and academic ballast for received business opinion [from] bankers and real estate men." As 49 million square feet of Manhattan office space arose during the Koch years, private investment capital and $1 billion a year in public subsidy were diverted from other uses, Fitch explained. The space was filled by persons "trading stocks, selling bonds, suing people, . . . activities which transfer [claims on wealth] rather than [produce] wealth." By the 1990s New York's speculative-electronic boom was over, and "lights were going out all over the global city." International investment in New York peaked at $12 billion in 1987 and had fallen below $4 billion by 1991, but the "boosterism of [financial-sector] and planning elites seeking to market New York as the global capital" continued.[12]

Koch left office just as the job hemorrhage was beginning. In 1991 his successor, David Dinkins, received a report from his Economic Policy and Marketing Group titled *New York City 1991: The World's Capital in Transition.* It included a measure of world city optimism: "This City is poised for another period of growth stemming from its success in the past decade in building the world's single most important producer services sector." Its sections examining components of this sector, however, were decidedly gloomy:

> Wall Street, in its heyday, was ruled by a tight fraternity of the biggest securities firms [which] controlled the market's machinery, held a lock on proprietary information and benefitted from entrenched relationships with Wall Street's best clients. Today . . . many of Wall Street's best customers, particularly corporate financial and pension executives, have become disenchanted with Wall Street and the services it provides. . . . They are directing more of their business to alternative markets or conducting it themselves. Complaints include outrageous fees, poor quality deals promoted by investment bankers, and . . . trading by firms for their own accounts, often in conflict with their customers. . . . Technology is also . . . making once-exclusive market information instantaneously accessible to anyone with a computer terminal.

Local prospects for banking, insurance, advertising, law, and accounting were likewise negatively assessed.[13]

World city puffery returned in 1992 with Dinkins's appointment of Deputy Mayor Barry Sullivan, who deemed New York the "hub of the global economy." Dinkins joined Sullivan's travels to Tokyo and London, hoping to recruit firms from one world city to another. Dinkins's successor Rudolph Giuliani continued to proclaim New York a world city. In 1994 he asserted, "New York City is the place to be if you're a player in global industry," and then awarded to the Mercantile Exchange tax incentives worth $22,700 per employee to stay in it. At that point New York ranked thirty-third in Class A office rents among the world's cities; commercial tenants were willing to pay rents four times higher for prime London, Beijing, and Shanghai office space, and six times higher in Tokyo and Hong Kong. More realistically than his boss, Deputy Mayor John Dyson admitted that "with modern telecommunications and other innovations, virtually no company *has* to be in New York to operate." Giuliani, however, persisted in world city cheerleading. In 1996 he announced, "New York is, I think, increasingly being seen . . . again, almost without reservation, as the Capital of the World. The Pope said it when he was here, which solidifies it."[14]

A Gorgeous Mosaic

Racial and ethnic diversity in their own globalized neighborhood mattered more to Elmhurst-Corona residents during the 1980s and 1990s than world city rhetoric. And their local and workplace cross-racial interactions were influenced more by media coverage of a series of high-profile racial incidents, each followed by commentary from mayors and public figures, talk-show hosts and callers, and friends and acquaintances.

White-black tension had risen during the 1968 teacher strike, and African American frustration over ineffective schools continued. Jewish fears of anti-Semitism were stoked by Jesse Jackson's "Hymietown" reference to New York City during his 1984 presidential campaign. Then in 1991 a car in the motorcade of the leader of the Lubavitcher Hasidim, a Jewish sect in predominantly black Crown Heights, Brooklyn, ran a red light and killed Gavin Cato, a seven-year-old black Guyanese boy. Three nights of black-Hasidic clashes followed. Anti-Semitic slogans were shouted, and Lubavitcher Yankel Rosenbaum was stabbed; he died in Kings County Hospital.[15]

Tensions also intensified between the largely white police force and New Yorkers of color. The deaths at police hands of black New Yorkers Michael Stewart in 1983 and Eleanor Bumpers in 1984 were deemed "police brutality" by African American spokespersons. Their suspicions were vindicated when the chief medical examiner, Elliot Gross, resigned in 1985 following accusations by colleagues that his autopsies were biased to exonerate police misconduct. Instances of police violence against black citizens continued to occur.

So did those involving Puerto Ricans, and they culminated in the 1994 death of Anthony Baez following an illegal chokehold applied by a white police officer on whose record were eleven previous complaints of excessive force. Baez, a Pentecostal Christian visiting from Florida where he had applied to be a police officer, was playing touch football with his brothers when their ball hit the car of the officer who then killed him. In 1994 the Mollen Commission, studying police corruption, confirmed that NYPD officers in predominantly black and Latin American neighborhoods routinely used excessive force. A year later Police Commissioner William Bratton admitted that he had never met a New Yorker of color who could not relate a story of bad experiences with police.[16]

As the cocaine trade grew in the mid-1980s, crime rates spiked up. Reported robberies, mainly "muggings" in which criminals confronted their victims, grew to 86,000 in 1988, and 100,000 in 1990. The experience of crime was cumulative, with the proportion of New Yorkers who had been mugged rising each year. Most muggers were young men from the city's now majority-minority population; victims were of all races, but statistically, white victims were more likely to be mugged by a perpetrator of color than by a white assailant. In a 1987 poll, 47 percent of white New Yorkers admitted assuming that any "mugger" mentioned in crime reports was black; so did 44 percent of black New Yorkers. These interpretations had been reinforced by the 1984 subway shooting of four black male teenagers by white Bernhard Goetz, who maintained that their demeanor indicated their intention to rob him. Whites often interpreted muggings as "racial" whether or not evidence of racial hostility was present. Black and Latin American mugging victims more often perceived these crimes as acts without racial motivation.[17]

Incidents in which whites were the perpetrators and persons of color the victims included a series of high-profile killings that were unambiguously "racial." In 1982 William Turks, a black transit worker, was beaten to death by a white mob in Gravesend, Brooklyn. In 1986 Michael Griffith, a black Trinidadian immigrant, was herded into highway traffic, where he died, by white youths who resented his presence in "white" Howard Beach, Queens. In 1989 Yusuf Hawkins, a sixteen-year-old African American, was shot to death by one of the forty young white men objecting to his presence in "white" Bensonhurst, Brooklyn. In 1994 Manuel Aucaquizphi, an Ecuadorian immigrant, was killed by white youths angered that "Mexicans" had "invaded" a park in Bay Ridge, Brooklyn.[18]

Tensions between Koreans and blacks mounted after black picketing of Korean stores in Harlem in 1984. A 1988 boycott in Bedford-Stuyvesant, Brooklyn, produced a flyer reading, "Korean Merchants are vampires! *Our* money in *their* blood. Let's cut off their supply! Don't patronize those who disrespect and abuse you! BUY BLACK!" An extended black boycott of a Korean store in Flatbush, Brooklyn, followed in 1990. According to protesters, the incidents igniting the boycotts were the shortchanging of customers, accusations of shoplifting, and discourteous treatment. Koreans denied such charges. Flyers urging boycotts of Korean and Chinese businesses also appeared—in English and Italian—in "white" Gravesend and Bensonhurst in 1987.

In 1990 a firebomb ruined the home of a black Grenadian couple who had moved to a "white" block in once solidly white Canarsie, Brooklyn. The following year a Pakistani-owned grocery was torched by a white youth; a realty under court order to end racist practices was firebombed twice; and an African American father was knifed by white youths while playing with his daughter in a public park. In 1992 the porch light of the Forest Hills home into which an African American police sergeant and his two children had just moved was smashed by a white neighbor shouting, "Niggers, get out of here!"[19]

Koch and Black New Yorkers

Edward Koch had marched for civil rights in Mississippi in 1964 and espoused liberal positions in Congress. In 1972, however, he traveled to Forest Hills to support anti-public-housing pickets and soon began to argue that black New Yorkers preferred to live in black neighborhoods. Koch named African American

Basil Paterson a deputy mayor in 1977, but after he resigned two years later Koch's black support began to crumble. Things worsened with the mayor's 1980 closure of Sydenham Hospital in Harlem and his resistance to a 1984 congressional investigation of police brutality. Koch continued to practice affirmative action in his top appointments, naming the city's first African American police commissioner, Benjamin Ward, but dragged his feet on developing legally mandated affirmative action plans for the municipal work force.

Buoyed by the strong vote for Jesse Jackson in the 1984 presidential primary, a coalition of black politicians and leaders tried but failed to designate a viable "minority" challenger to Koch in 1985. Throughout Koch's third term the city's leading black newspaper, the *Amsterdam News,* ran weekly "Koch Must Resign" front-page editorials. African American antagonism to Koch increased with his blandishment that Jewish voters "would have to be crazy" to vote for Jackson in his 1988 presidential run. Dinkins, beating Koch in the 1989 Democratic primary, carried 93 percent of the black vote.[20]

Ethnic Ed

As Koch's black support weakened, he cultivated other sources of votes. By 1984 his Ethnic Advisory Council included representatives of twenty-five Old World immigrant groups and was convened monthly by Koch aide Herbert Rickman, who also coordinated mayoral appearances at ethnic parades and festivals, selected persons for annual "Ethnic New Yorker" awards, and organized ethnic rallies during Koch reelection campaigns. Some ethnic council members became political operatives; during the 1985 campaign, for example, the Korean representative defended the mayor's opposition to commercial rent regulation, even though most Korean business leaders favored it.[21]

Koch also courted the city's Latin American population, both Puerto Ricans (still the majority of Latin American voters) and immigrants. In 1982 he praised Queens Latin Americans for "rejuvenating once half-empty churches and opening up many new restaurants and small businesses." A 1985 poll indicated that 66 percent of Latin American Democrats planned to vote for Koch in the primary (compared with 22 percent of black Democrats), and 62 percent did. He then announced that the plight of Puerto Ricans and other Latin Americans would become a priority of his third term and appointed a Commission on Hispanic Concerns consisting of sixteen Latin American business, education, judicial, and social service leaders. "Having a decent place to live and raise a family, going to school and getting a job are simple things," the mayor stated, "but things many Hispanics don't have. The commission will look at these issues and develop workable, pragmatic initiatives the city can implement."[22]

The mayor got what he asked for. The commission took testimony in English and Spanish from 120 organizations and individuals at hearings in all five boroughs. Its inch-thick 1986 report contained 178 policy recommendations, among them the elimination of overcrowding in heavily Latin American school districts (including Elmhurst-Corona's SD24), the training of unemployed city residents by businesses receiving tax breaks, increased assistance to Latin American–owned small business, and more English-Spanish bilingual staff in city hospitals.

Even before the report was delivered, however, Koch rejected its anticipated recommendations to appoint a Latin American to the Board of Education and to increase the number of Latin Americans in city agencies. "That is the equivalent of a quota," he said, citing a poll showing that for "75 percent of the Hispanic people and 63 percent of the blacks questioned . . . ability, and not preferential treatment, should be the main consideration in hiring and promotion." The commission agreed, but by comparing city hiring numbers with the Latin American employment pool, it countered that "ability" was not the criterion being applied. *Daily News* columnist Miguel Perez called the report "an indictment on the Koch administration for neglecting Latinos," and Angelo Falcón of the Institute for Puerto Rican Policy termed it "more hardhitting than many of us expected." At his public meeting with the commission, Koch unveiled a sixty-nine-page rebuttal. Chair Edgardo Vasquez of Banco Popular responded, "The mayor, with no apparent reason or explanation, . . . rejected some of the Commission's most important recommendations," dealt with others "in vague terms," and ignored the rest. Koch replied that thereafter his own administration would evaluate progress on "Hispanic concerns."

Meanwhile, Koch had appointed a similar panel of African Americans, and in 1988 rejected this commission's recommendations. Among other findings, its *Report of the Mayor's Commission on Black New Yorkers* called for Koch's ineffective Equal Employment Opportunity Committee to be replaced by deputy mayor–level oversight of affirmative action. Koch also appointed a panel on Asian issues, but to avoid a third "runaway commission," it consisted solely of city officials—who never issued a report.[23]

Race and the Housing Market

New Yorkers perceived that they lived in a highly segregated city. In a 1985 poll, 70 percent of whites stated that their homes were in predominantly white neighborhoods, 60 percent of blacks that they resided in mainly black districts, and 44 percent of Latin Americans that they lived in mostly Latin American areas. A 1987 poll revealed that most black New Yorkers did *not* want to live in all-black communities, contra Mayor Koch and a third of city whites, who believed they did. Three-quarters of black New Yorkers preferred a half-white, half-black or otherwise racially mixed neighborhood; only 10 percent wanted to live in an all or mainly black area. In contrast, 45 percent of white New Yorkers preferred all or mainly white surroundings, and only 36 percent favored racially mixed neighborhoods. Black preferences were pragmatic; as the *New York Times* columnist

Sam Roberts pointed out, "One reason that many people of color prefer to live in mixed neighborhoods is their fear that city services will suffer if whites leave."[24]

More than a fifth of black New Yorkers reported that they had encountered racial discrimination when looking for housing. Evidence to support these poll results was not difficult to find. Claims of discrimination in the private housing market were investigated by the city's Commission on Human Rights. Despite staff cuts after the 1975 fiscal crisis, it used teams of white and black or Latin American "testers" to visit real estate and rental offices; team members were matched in income, occupation, and other criteria except race. When white and nonwhite testers were consistently given different information about apartment or home availability and price, or were "steered" to white, black, or Latin American neighborhoods, this constituted evidence of discrimination. (A 1984 Supreme Court decision validated the use of testers in housing discrimination cases.) In 1991 a federal study found that in New York black testers faced discrimination 44 percent of the time when buying homes and 40 percent when renting; for Latin American testers, the likelihood of discrimination was 61 percent when buying and 53 percent when renting. "For blacks, the New York area is about as bad as any place in the country," the study concluded. "For Hispanics, it is easily the worst."[25]

In Queens, housing discrimination was widespread. Black and white incomes converged more than in other boroughs, but by 1990 some 60 percent of black residents still lived in only two of fourteen community districts. When confronted with tester evidence of racial discrimination, in 1984 a dozen brokers and apartment owners in Forest Hills, Rego Park, Kew Gardens, and the 3,200-unit Fresh Meadows apartment complex signed consent decrees to end such practices. Instances of landlords who told black or Latin American apartment-seekers that advertised units were no longer available, and then offered them to whites, were uncovered in Ridgewood, Flushing, and Fresh Meadows in 1986, Glendale in 1987, and Middle Village in 1988. In 1989 the Commission on Human Rights challenged a Jackson Heights co-op that withheld sale of an apartment to an economically qualified white mother of two half-black children. In 1990 even the New York Public Housing Authority admitted that it had been assigning tenants to projects on the basis of race since at least the 1960s, despite a federal warning in 1983.

Cases of overt racism also surfaced. In Forest Hills another white mother and her half-black daughter were harrassed and denied use of the back yard by one landlord and refused a lease by a second after he saw the child. In 1986 a Ku Klux Klansman image was spray-painted outside Puerto Rican Francisco Caballero's Astoria apartment. In 1991 Lucy Jimenez's Ozone Park home was firebombed and a note was left: "Hear [*sic*] we have a nice class of Italian and Irish. When spics move in you people ruin it." And in 1995 Middle Village tenant Maria Sanchez found a disemboweled rabbit in front of her door with a note reading, "Move Out, Spics, Or You'll Burn."[26]

Race and Jobs

The 1980s Manhattan boom largely bypassed New Yorkers of color. As private-sector jobs grew between 1975 and 1982, black and Latin American unemployment increased, and by 1983 unemployment among black college graduates was higher than for white high school graduates. Black New Yorkers remained concentrated in the employment sectors they had entered before 1980: retail banking, department stores, hospitals, social service agencies, telephone communications (the result of a 1973 discrimination suit at AT&T), and government. Latin American employment was concentrated in light manufacturing, hospitals, hotels, and building service jobs. Employment gains in the city's financial, advertising, communications, cultural affairs, and construction sectors went primarily to whites. In 1992 New York legal firms employed 60,000 lawyers, but the number of black, Latin American, and Asian partners was less than 100.[27]

In 1980 black and Latin American New Yorkers constituted 40 percent of the city's overall work force but held only 28 percent of private-sector jobs. Government employment was more open to New Yorkers of color, and blacks rose from 29 to 41 percent of the municipal work force during the 1980s. Latin Americans remained underrepresented, however, accounting for only 11 percent of municipal workers in 1989. Within the city work force, blacks were concentrated in the Department of Health, the Human Resources Administration, the Juvenile Justice agency, and the Youth Bureau (in all of which they constituted half to three-quarters of employees) and in the Board of Corrections (where half of uniformed officers were black). In the Police, Sanitation, and Fire Departments whites made up 71, 73, and 90 percent of employees in 1986. By 1994, whites had increased to 73 percent of the police force, which since 1983 had registered the smallest percentage gain in black officers of the fifty largest U.S. cities. Whites were also 70 percent of public school teachers in 1992, and city economic development and policymaking employees were also predominantly white.[28]

Interpersonal Racial Friction

In 1987 polls 46 percent of black New Yorkers reported having been a target of racial slurs and slights, 35 percent of them within the preceding year. A college professor was regarded with panic by white residents of his apartment building and shadowed by security guards while shopping; a schoolteacher and part-time investor was denied a co-op apartment when the board refused to believe that her $250,000 in assets had been accumulated lawfully; a six-foot, four-inch publishing executive who was clean shaven was frisked by police in their search for "a five-foot, ten-inch black male with a moustache." Other New Yorkers of color shared similar experiences. A Dominican student at a high school sports rally was told by a white classmate, "I don't want a nigger sitting in front of me." A Chinese American magazine editor crossing the street was shouted at by a passing driver, "You fucking Asian bitch, why don't you go back where you came from!"

After a 1983 police beating of an African American seminary student, many black New Yorkers were incensed at Mayor Koch's response that it was "possible, but nevertheless strange, that in the heart of Harlem two white cops would intentionally, in violation of the law, harass a minister." Koch typified widespread white opaqueness to what the black journalist Derrick Jackson called "the slow, monotonous currents of day-to-day racism. . . . When I tell [white] colleagues about racist encounters . . . most stare at me in utter disbelief and say, 'Really?' " As the white political scientist Ira Katznelson observed, "Most whites have concluded that enough has been done for blacks, that the doors of opportunity are open, [and] it's up to blacks to go through. Blacks are likely to see white incomprehension of racial barriers and feel . . . more despairing."[29]

At the same time, the increasing pace of cross-racial encounters was bringing New Yorkers of different races into positive relationships. A 1985 poll revealed that half of white New Yorkers had "at least two work friends of another race," as did three-quarters of blacks and Latin Americans; and half of whites and two-thirds of blacks and Latin Americans had "spent a social evening with [a] friend of another race in recent months." Several poll respondents added that their interracial socializing did not take place in their own neighborhoods, but a 1987 poll found that a third of white and a quarter of black New Yorkers had entertained persons of the other race in their homes.

Newspaper coverage of high-profile racial incidents also exposed cross-racial channels of contact in historically white neighborhoods. Following anti-Asian harassment in Bensonhurst in 1987, "a coalition of about fifty community and church leaders" denounced the racist flyers being distributed and met with Mayor Koch, who advised them to "make a special effort" to recruit an Asian member to their community board. Despite a rash of racial violence in Canarsie in 1991 the 150 parishioners at Holy Family Church were just "two-thirds white," and sixty-year-old white usher Sal Fiore "embraced everybody who walked by, whether they were black, white, Hispanic, or Asian." And in Forest Hills, after a black police sergeant faced vandalism and racist catcalls in 1992, a white neighbor stopped by to tell him, "Welcome to the neighborhood. You've got as much right to be here as anybody. This garbage has got to stop."[30]

Dinkins the Healer

Koch's third term was marked by the Manes suicide in 1986, the stock market crash and the Howard Beach trial in 1987, and boycotts of Korean stores in 1988. In a January 1989 poll 88 percent of blacks, 79 percent of Latin Americans, and 65 percent of whites agreed that "it was time for someone else to take the mayor's job." Race relations in the city then took a coarse and violent turn. The white *Newsday* columnist Jimmy Breslin openly addressed a Korean colleague as "slant-eyed" and "a yellow cur." A gang of black and Latin American youth engaged in what they called "wilding," beat and raped a white female jogger; police found no evidence of racial bias, but many white New Yorkers saw it as "racial" nonetheless. The August shooting of teenager Yusuf Hawkins in Bensonhurst seemed like a last straw as the September 1989 primary neared.

Koch's racial divisiveness had alienated many. Following his anti–Jesse Jackson remark in 1988, Rabbi Alexander Schindler reminded him he was "Mayor of the City, not just of New York Jewry." A rebuke from Manhattan borough president David Dinkins had a measured tone: Koch was "not helpful to our efforts to create an atmosphere whereby tensions can be eased." Courtly and nonconfrontational, the African American Dinkins pledged to advance the "healing" he thought the city needed. He defeated Koch and other candidates in the primary, and beat Republican Rudolph Giuliani by 50 to 48 percent in the November election. Dinkins voters were 44 percent white, 43 percent black, and 13 percent Latin American; Giuliani voters were 87 percent white, 7 percent Latin American, and 6 percent black.[31]

Proclaiming New York "a gorgeous mosaic," Dinkins formed an administration that "looked like New York City." His deputy mayors included two Jews, an Irish American, two African Americans, and two Puerto Ricans, and he appointed the first Asian department commissioner. Dinkins reorganized Koch's ethnic council and black and Latin American offices into four coordinate Offices of African American/Caribbean, Asian American, European American, and Hispanic Affairs. He advertised city jobs in ethnic newspapers and named a black-owned investment firm as an underwriter for the sale of city securities. Businesses owned by "minorities" and women were permitted to qualify for some city contracts with bids 10 percent above the lowest entry. And as directed by the 1989 city charter, an affirmative action plan was drafted with "flexible goals and timetables" to fill positions marked by "manifest underutilization [of available] minorities."[32]

Dinkins's mosaic, a metaphor suggesting group boundedness rather than connection, lost its gloss with the midtown killing of a white tourist by a multiracial youth gang, the racial incidents in Canarsie, and a Bronx attack on two black children, who were robbed, insulted, and squirted with white liquid shoe polish by four white youths. Koreans were displeased that the black boycott in Flatbush dragged on until September 1990 before the new mayor visited the store; in May 1990 Korean leader Sung Soo Kim had implored, "David Dinkins, supreme leader of New York, must open his mouth and make judgment. What about this 'gorgeous mosaic'?" Some black New Yorkers were glad when the Flatbush affair finally ended, but boycott leaders felt that underlying issues remained unresolved, and they criticized mayoral negotiations that forestalled still another Korean store boycott.

Lubavitcher leaders and some white politicians castigated Dinkins for "holding back" police during the early stages of the 1991 Crown Heights conflict;

other New Yorkers believed he had averted further bloodshed. Many Jews were displeased that there was no conviction for the stabbing of Yankel Rosenbaum; many blacks were equally displeased that the Lubavitcher leader did not acknowledge the death of Gavin Cato. Then, following a July 1992 police shooting of a Washington Heights Dominican man, a crowd of Dominican residents clashed with police. Dinkins paid the funeral expenses of the dead man, and this incensed NYPD officers, who said that the victim was a drug dealer and the shooting was justified. In September 1992, 10,000 off-duty police held an unruly anti-Dinkins rally in front of City Hall. Racist signs and shouting were evident, and Una Clarke, a black city council member was addressed as "nigger" as she passed the crowd.[33]

In short, Dinkins's "healing" efforts of mediation and visiting victims of racial violence satisfied too few. A 1993 poll of voters indicated that 55 percent of whites, 52 percent of Latin Americans, and 34 percent of blacks saw race relations as having worsened during his tenure.

Giuliani's "One Standard"

The 1989 and 1993 mayoral elections were like two flips of a coin, with 1.8 million votes cast each time. Dinkins won in 1989 by 47,000 votes; four years later Giuliani won by 52,000. Half of Giuliani's winning share came from Staten Islanders who had not voted in 1989 but turned out in response to a 1993 secession referendum. Overall, Dinkins's black support grew by four points and Giuliani's white backing increased by six points, but fewer whites voted and Dinkins's white following was smaller in 1993. Giuliani's Latin American vote increased marginally, and he carried two-thirds of the tiny Asian vote, including three-quarters of Koreans.[34]

"Gorgeous mosaic" symbolism disappeared as Giuliani pledged to run the city by "one standard." He ended the inclusiveness measures instituted by Dinkins: the African American/Caribbean, Asian American, European American, and Hispanic offices were abolished; advertising of city jobs in ethnic newspapers ended; and the 10 percent bid advantage for firms owned by "minorities" and women was eliminated. The new mayor also tried to dismiss the black firm that Dinkins had hired to underwrite city securities, but Comptroller Alan Hevesi objected, and Deputy Mayor John Dyson's inopportune racial characterization of the company as "a watermelon" temporarily foiled the attempt.

Black New Yorkers, a quarter of the population, noted that there was no African American among the mayor's close advisors and, for the first time in sixteen years, no black deputy mayor. In mid-1996 a black deputy mayor was appointed, but part of his portfolio was taken over by a white deputy mayor. After two years under Mayor Giuliani there were 4,600 fewer blacks working for the city, 640 fewer white women, and 385 more white males; among senior positions, black numbers were down 300, and white numbers up 600. Overall, the proportion of "minority" city employees fell from 52 to 50 percent, a fact the mayor first denied but later admitted. Giuliani insisted, "My government's representative, made up of people of merit and quality. I look for the best person to do the job." His appointments included six of his and his wife's relatives; his childhood friend Lou Carbonetti, later dismissed as head of the Community Assistance Unit for failing to report personal financial and driving-license irregularities; two of Carbonetti's sons; Communications Director Christyne Lategano's best friend; and Corrections Commissioner Anthony Schembri, who resided illegally in Westchester County and doctored time sheets to cover up days spent out of the city.

The Giuliani administration's first high-profile police action was a forced entry of the black Nation of Islam mosque in Harlem; this severed a long-standing protocol for communication between police and mosque leadership when problems arose, a procedure used with other religious institutions as well. Later in 1994 the mayor chided Bronx borough president Fernando Ferrer, a Puerto Rican, after he called for the resignation of a Yankee Stadium official who had referred to Bronx children as "monkeys" and "little colored boys." "Calm down," the mayor told Ferrer, "leadership is trying to get *control,* understanding we've got a forty or fifty year future to think about—and not just trying to get our feelings out." Then in 1995, just after Alfonse D'Amato apologized on the U.S. Senate floor for using a mock-Japanese accent to demean Judge Lance Ito, Giuliani began a reception for Mayors Beame, Koch, Dinkins, and himself by saying, "I think I'll start with four or five ethnic imitations. You should hear my Mafia accent."

New Yorkers of all colors wondered what the mayor meant when he said, "I think I've moved the city to a deeper understanding of how people unite with each other, not based on excessive concern over differences." Giuliani courted Latin Americans, who had provided his 1993 margin of victory, by appointing a handful of Puerto Ricans to top-level positions (though three of them were gone by 1996). After poll results showed his Latin American support falling to 42 percent in 1994 and 20 percent in 1995, he donned a tropical *guayabera* shirt and sash reading "*Alcalde* [Mayor] of New York" and marched in the 1995 Puerto Rican Day parade. He was jeered but criticized the press for not reporting that he received more cheers than boos. By 1997 only 35 percent of New Yorkers described the city's race relations as "good."[35]

Police Strategy No. 5

In 1972 the Knapp Commission on police corruption had exposed pervasive payoffs from heroin sellers, gambling operators, and other criminals. One consequence was the replacement of most of the NYPD leadership. Another was a shift from foot patrols, considered ripe for renewed corruption, to radio cars responding to 911 calls. Two decades later the Mollen Commission again uncovered police corruption, this time violence, theft, and cocaine selling by "crews" of "rogue cops."[36]

Problems at the 110th Precinct

Elmhurst-Corona's 110th was not among the half-dozen corrupt precincts named by the Mollen panel, but between the two commissions the 110th had had a series of internal scandals. In 1982 seven officers were indicted for accepting bribes to overlook drug sales and liquor-law violations in local nightclubs, upsetting many CD4 residents. Another 110th officer scheduled to testify died of head injuries received at a fund-raising party before the trial; his wounds, inconsistent with chief medical examiner Gross's conclusion that his death was due to a fall, indicated homicide. In 1990 a $25,000 overtime scam was uncovered, and the 110th's commanding officer was transferred. In 1992 a female 110th officer testified to sexual harassment by male colleagues, and in 1993 a black officer found racist messages on his precinct locker.[37]

More than scandals, however, it was day-to-day operations that concerned Elmhurst-Corona civic activists and CB4 members. Following the 1975 fiscal crisis NYPD strength fell, and nonviolent quality-of-life complaints received low priority. By 1984 dissatisfaction with the police was being aired at nearly every CB4 meeting.[38] Rose Mazzarella protested the lack of response to calls about late-night noise near L'Amour East, a rock-music club two blocks from her South Elmhurst home; almost proving her point, a 110th officer countered that after the windows of Mazzarella's car were shot out, "the 110th, they came." Other complaints were voiced by CB4 members who witnessed drug sales or lived on streets where vehicles parked illegally: "The 110th doesn't know what is going on." "No tickets!" "The police at the 110th stink." In 1984 Terri Gerrish of the Newtown Civic Association told CB4 about three recent muggings and two afternoon rapes of children in the Baxter-Roosevelt section of Elmhurst. "We need the police to be more visible on the street," she said. "The only time I see police is when I drive by the precinct house."

The attitudes of 110th officers also troubled Elmhurst-Corona residents. NCA members complained in 1983 that telephone calls were answered in an "argumentative, rude, or sarcastic" manner; they later voted "no confidence" in the precinct and its commanding officer, Thomas Connelly. CB4's public safety chair, Al Fernicola, a volunteer auxiliary policeman who knew the precinct well, summed up complaints in a 1984 letter to NYPD Commissioner Benjamin Ward. Officers were observed "parked in cars, drinking coffee, and loafing," Fernicola wrote. "A majority just do not care." A month later Fernicola reported a police car parked for more than an hour with "young girls" in it, and no record of them in the officers' logbook.

By fall 1985 dissatisfaction with the police was ready to boil over. Several CB4 members, including Rose Rothschild, Judy D'Andrea, Angela Sonera, and

Helma Goldmark, had been victims of burglaries or muggings. "The next thing we will do is go picket them," Rothschild said at the September meeting. In October vandals broke into St. Leo's Church, and Monsignor Anthony Barretta called the 110th. He waited half an hour before a police car arrived; to his comment about how long it took, an officer replied, "*I* have to wait three hours at the doctor's office." In December, when CB4 learned that the precinct was looking for temporary quarters while its building was renovated, Miriam Levenson remarked, "Just eliminate them. Who'll know the difference?" CB4 member Haydee Zambrana, a 110th civilian employee, reported in March 1986 that evening drug sales on Roosevelt Avenue were "an epidemic." Don Mallozzi responded, "Connelly's a lot of hot air," and his motion to demonstrate at the precinct passed overwhelmingly.

The April 1986 Saturday demonstration began at twelve noon. When I got there, Rose Rothschild and Miriam Levenson were grousing about the absence of several outspoken CB4 members. Member Angela Sonera, a Puerto Rican, and her husband were likewise disappointed at the sparse turnout; she recalled that when she was a schoolgirl in Corona during the 1950s, police walked the beat and everybody knew them. Sung Jin Chun and Seung Ha Hong of the Korean American Association of Mid-Queens arrived next, followed by Al Fernicola carrying a sign:

Are You Satisfied With Response From the Police of the 110 Pct.??
Are You Happy With:
1. Drug Dealing
2. High Robbery + Burglary Rate
3. Houses of Prostitution
4. Illegally Parked Vehicles

Our band was completed by CB4 member Carmela George, her neighbor, and Elmhurst civic activist Ron Laney (all white Americans), Chinese School Board 24 candidate Evelyn Yang, and Chinese and white newspaper reporters. We were invited inside and served coffee by Captain Connelly, who said the 110th was making progress on drug arrests and closures of prostitution houses, but there was little he could do about illegal parking without a towing program for Queens. Rothschild brought up police attitudes, mentioning one officer who told a burglary victim, "You should move out of this area." Angela Sonera complained about officers sitting in parked cars for long periods and a rash of burglaries near her home. Fernicola recounted the treatment received by Monsignor Barretta.

As a result of the demonstration, NYPD Commissioner Ward set up a meeting for Al Fernicola and Rose Rothschild with a deputy police commissioner. There they emphasized the lack of courtesy from 110th officers. Later in 1986, when Rothschild and CB4 member Howard Riback addressed the 110th at its monthly "community meeting," Riback reported to CB4, "They reversed the situation and attacked the community. They said they can't afford to live in the city." Rothschild added, "They were sarcastic, and put their feet up while we spoke."

Cops on the Beat

Important changes at the 110th had begun a year before the 1986 demonstration when ten foot-patrol officers were assigned to twenty-square-block beats under the Community Patrol Officer Program, known as C-POP. Their duties included meeting with merchants and tenant and civic groups, giving crime prevention advice, and maintaining radio liaison with patrol cars. Commissioner Ward had instituted C-POP in Brooklyn during 1984 to "put cops back on the street"; by 1987 residents of precincts where it did not yet exist were clamoring for it, and Ward promised to make C-POP citywide by 1989.[39]

CB4 members were skeptical at first, and the year-old program was not even mentioned at the 1986 protest. By 1987, however, Elmhurst-Corona civic leaders were requesting additional C-POP coverage, and in 1988 CB4 member Norma Cirino credited C-POP's presence for quieting youthful boisterousness in the vicinity of Intermediate School 61. By 1989 Rose Rothschild was referring to the officers by first name. "They've gotten really good ones in the C-POP program," she noted at a district cabinet meeting. "You see their presence. They're on the street—not all at first, but now it's settled in." An eleventh C-POP beat was added in 1990, but radio-car police still outnumbered foot-patrol officers by 9 to 1.

One exception to dissatisfaction with police responsiveness and attitudes came from COMET (Communities of Maspeth and Elmhurst Together), a civic organization in South Elmhurst and nearby Maspeth in CD5. "They like the police over there," Miriam Levenson told me at a COMET meeting in 1986. Indeed, during the same week as the 1986 demonstration, COMET's "Cops for Community" program at St. Adalbert's Church honored two 110th C-POP officers who patrolled their area.[40] Two years later COMET sponsored a "National Night Out" rally, an event begun in 1983 and held each year at several sites throughout the city. One 110th officer told me that the precinct itself had organized a National Night Out a few years earlier, "but nobody came."

COMET's 1988 "Night Out against Crime" took place on a warm August evening in a bank parking lot just over the Elmhurst-Maspeth border in CD5. A trio of electric guitar, bass, and drums began the program with an Irish song and then played rhythm-and-blues, Duke Ellington, show tunes, and an Elvis Presley medley. Some six hundred people—half elderly and a quarter children—enjoyed free pizza and McDonald's orangeade, visited NYPD and other city agency exhibits, mounted police horses, and clambered around radio cars, a bomb squad's van, EMS and Fire Department vehicles, and a see-through glass garbage truck.

The crowd was overwhelmingly white (South Elmhurst shifted from 70 to 43 percent white between 1980 and 1990; CD5 remained 80 percent white in 1990), but I noted two Boy Scouts who were East Asian, a dozen Latin American and East Asian children from a 110th Precinct youth program at St. James Episcopal Church in Elmhurst, and a few black and Latin American police.

Candidates in the upcoming fall election handed out literature, and elected officials addressed the crowd. COMET's president, Rosemarie Daraio, led a mass balloon launch "to let other neighborhoods know we're here, and that we're looking out for our neighborhood and each other." She introduced "our terrific Police Commissioner, Ben Ward," who spoke about rising drug and crime rates and told the crowd, "National Night Out is the good people of America." Queens borough president Claire Shulman exclaimed, "COMET has done it again!" and told the audience that she had "put in [from city budget funds allocatable by her] money over what the Mayor did for 900 more police, and for civilians to free up police officers." By then the crowd had thinned to two hundred and, though scheduled to attend, Mayor Koch never arrived.

Koch on Crime

New York's crime rates escalated during Koch's third term. Elmhurst-Corona senior citizens were accosted on their way home from banks. An elevator robber preyed on women in Lefrak City and Sherwood Village. Muggers frequented the 74th Street subway arcade and followed victims from Elmhurst subway exits. Burglaries increased in Corona Heights. A bingo game was held up at St. Paul's Church. Murders in CD4 rose from 12 in 1984 to 30 in 1988. During 1989 the city experienced 5 murders, 200 robberies, and 365 car thefts a day.[41]

Even though Koch could take credit for the popular C-POP program, he did not give it prominence in his list of accomplishments. Neither did he show much understanding of what neighborhood New Yorkers meant by "quality of life." He hectored an Elmhurst COMET meeting about the need for more jails, which had already doubled in capacity during his mayoralty, but he was unresponsive to issues raised by his audience: school and subway crowding, housing overoccupancy, infills, too few police. As CB4 member Pat Carpentiere summed up a 1988 mayoral visit, "Koch came, and didn't see anything. . . . It was a joke. His body was in Corona but his mind was on Manhattan."

Koch used 1980s budget surpluses to return overall city employee numbers to pre-1975 levels, including a big increase in jail guards. He did not, however, direct resources or hiring toward restoring pre-1975 neighborhood quality of life, and only in his last budget did he expand school construction. The number of police in 1989, 26,300, remained below the 1975 level and was actually 1,200 lower than in 1987—the result of retirements without replacements. Nonetheless, with Dinkins an unknown quantity to many white Queens residents, in the

1989 primary Koch carried the 30th Assembly District, which included Woodside, Elmhurst, and Rego Park. Dinkins, however, won the adjoining 35th AD with its strong black voting ranks in North Corona–East Elmhurst and Lefrak City.[42]

Safe Streets, Safe City Hall

Six months after Dinkins assumed office, CB4 held a public hearing on police issues. Frustrated that little more could be done, given the 110th's current staffing level, a delegation of Elmhurst-Corona civic leaders scheduled a September meeting with the NYPD Queens borough commander. There they learned that C-POP numbers were about to be increased.

During the summer of 1990 city tabloids highlighed a string of murders, and one headline pleaded, "Do Something, Dave." In fact, New York stood thirteenth in the FBI's ranking of reported crime in large cities, but this gave little comfort to crime victims, who amounted to 10 percent of the city's population that year. Responding to press and city council pressure, Dinkins drafted an anticrime "Safe Streets, Safe City" tax-increase package which was approved in August. It provided funds for a return to the 1975 level of 31,600 police and for crime prevention and youth programs. In addition, Police Commissioner Lee Brown planned to quadruple C-POP, now called "community policing," to an average of forty officers per precinct.[43]

On the basis of its population and crime statistics, the 110th was slated to grow from 187 to 265 officers, a 42 percent increase. Numbers climbed to 205 in 1992, with more scheduled to arrive in 1993 and 1994, and C-POP officers increased to 34. The precinct's greater attention to the quality-of-life problems troubling CD4 residents—prostitution, illegal vendors, "noise pollution"—was facilitated by the larger number of officers. It was also a priority of Queens District Attorney Richard Brown, appointed in 1991.

Auto thefts soon declined in CD4, as they did citywide. Murders in Elmhurst-Corona peaked at 36 in 1990 and fell to 20 in 1993 (in part because of the victory of one cocaine-importing "cartel" over another; see Chapter 9). Reported robberies—mainly muggings—in the 110th, however, crept up from 1,600 in 1989 to nearly 2,000 in 1992. And street-level drug arrests actually fell during the Dinkins years as Commissioner Brown redirected police efforts to higher-level importers and distributers.

The Newtown Civic Association charged in 1992 that the 110th was shortchanged in additional police because of a 1990 census undercount and the reluctance of undocumented immigrants to report crimes. But two-thirds of the new officers were slated to arrive only after July 1993—after which reported crime in the 110th decreased in all categories except burglaries, with robberies falling to 1,100 that year. As a consequence of this "backloaded" phase-in of new police, however, Dinkins's reelection campaign could not take advantage of the full impact of his Safe Streets, Safe City program. This was left to his opponent, Rudolph Giuliani, who became mayor in 1994.[44]

Bratton's NYPD Makeover

Giuliani's Police Commissioner William Bratton, who had been Dinkins's Transit Police chief, took office just as the NYPD reached its 31,600-officer level. Under his tenure, crime citywide fell by 12 percent in 1994 and 17 percent in 1995. By 1996 New York City's crime rate ranked it 136th among U.S. cities of 100,000 or more.

In a report detailing problems with C-POP, Bratton denounced "lazy cops" during his first month and proclaimed, "I'm shaking this department up more so than it's ever been shaken up." In 1994 he replaced top NYPD officials and appointed new commanding officers in thirty-one of the seventy-five city precincts, including the 110th. Central directives empowered precincts to seize unlicensed guns, arrest drug dealers, round up school truants, and investigate domestic violence—activities previously assigned to special units. Bratton also instituted weekly "comstat" (computer statistics) sessions at which printouts of the types, locations, and timing of crimes were used to prod borough and precinct commanders and to deploy patrol strength.[45]

The approach was not new. During the 1980s hundreds of police in TNT (Tactical Narcotics Team) units had flooded drug-selling locations, and in 1990 a 110th Precinct "Operation Takeback" had concentrated seventeen foot-patrol officers in the high-robbery area around Elmhurst Hospital. What was new was that Bratton and Deputy Commissioner Jack Maple began to run the entire department this way, with computer-assisted strategies targeting specific spots or problems. In 1995, for example, Chief Gertrude LaForgia of Queens North unveiled a Roosevelt Avenue Task Force of twenty-five uniformed and undercover 110th and 115th (CD3) Precinct officers to focus on prostitution, drug selling, and parking violations. The unit operated from a trailer placed at varying locations along a thirty-block strip; arrest bookings and computer analysis took place directly inside.

Bratton and Maple attributed the continuing drop in crime to their "comstat" approach. Criminal justice experts too credited comstat but also pointed to the incarceration of potential offenders (New York State's prison population doubled during 1983–1993), the ravages of AIDS among drug users, a lessening of internecine violence among drug sellers, an increase in heroin use and decline in crack (crack users commit more frequent and violent crimes than heroin addicts), and new auto-theft prevention methods. In addition, they underscored the Safe Streets, Safe City increase of 5,000 NYPD officers in itself.[46]

The most controversial initiative was *Police Strategy No. 5: Reclaiming the Public Spaces of New York,* announced by Giuliani and Bratton in July 1994. Improving the quality of life had been a theme in Giuliani's mayoral campaign, and the meaning he attached to this phrase was delineated in *Police Strategy No. 5.* Eight "signs of a city out of control" were listed as indicators that "the quality of life in [New York] has been in decline": peddlers and panhandlers; street prostitution; boombox, motorcycle, and nightclub noise; mentally ill street people; graffiti; illegal dumping; alcohol sales to minors; and hazardous traffic violations. The strategy outlined precinct-level procedures to control these "conditions" and instituted a requirement (which also applied to public drinking or urination) that alleged offenders present "government-issued photo identification" before being issued a summons or a desk appearance ticket releasing them until their arraignment date. Persons without such ID and anyone with "a history of misdemeanor arrests, warrants, and low-level imprisonment" would now be detained in jail.

The new initiative had two rationales. Giuliani stated that incarceration itself would reduce crime: violators would need to be jailed for only a few days "to make your point." Bratton and Maple stressed interrogation. They believed that the relatively small number of persons who committed most of the crimes were in contact with one another (socializing, buying drugs or guns, selling stolen goods); questioning quality-of-life offenders could identify other such persons, and "relentless follow-up investigation" would penetrate criminal networks.

In the seven months before *Police Strategy No. 5* went into effect, a quarter of uniformed NYPD officers had made no arrests and another quarter only one or two. But now city jails became clogged with petty offenders, including unlicensed Chinese portrait artists and Caribbean immigrants rehearsing for the West Indian-American Labor Day carnival. Overtime for police and corrections officers went up, and in September 1994 Giuliani announced he would build three new jails. Arrests in 1994 were 19 percent higher than in 1993, but 1995 criminal indictments were down 2 percent. A Legal Aid attorney stated, "We are shocked at the quality of arrests on quality of life. We can't understand why they are putting them through the system." Increased police aggressiveness produced a 56 percent jump between 1993 and 1996 in accusations of officer misconduct filed with the Civilian Complaint Review Board.[47]

Giuliani also centralized numerous city operations within the Police Department. In 1994 he merged the Housing and Transit Authority police forces with the NYPD, expanding its venue and increasing total strength to 38,500. Police took over traffic direction in downtown Manhattan from lower-paid Department of Transportation employees, enforcement duties from Parks Department staff, and vehicle inspections from the Taxi and Limousine Commission. NYPD officers posted in city hospital emergency rooms superseded unarmed hospital guards, and a thirty-five-member police squad replaced city outreach workers to move homeless persons from public places to city shelters.

When the city council established an agency to monitor police corruption following the Mollen Commission report, Giuliani vetoed the bill; he was overridden but took the council to court and won. Meanwhile, he created a police corruption monitoring unit accountable directly to him. He also campaigned to place school security guards under police control and to absorb the Port Authority police into the NYPD.[48]

Community Policing Shrinks

As overall crime rates dropped, the number of precinct officers assigned to C-POP beats and patrol cars fell, and larger numbers were deployed in task forces, special units, and administrative activities. "They're in Manhattan," said CB4 chair Richard Italiano, "on corners, in twos and threes." Many neighborhood New Yorkers felt less protected, and in September 1995 district manager Rose Rothschild confronted the new 110th Precinct commander: "This administration is not committed to community policing. It looks like it's dying out." He responded, "The department philosophy is that everybody is doing community policing. In the 110th, the Community Policing Unit is intact, downsized a bit." "I want more cops walking the beat," Rothschild replied. "When we had that, it was the best of times. When [criminals] see the patrol officers they know you're there, and they go someplace else." Nevertheless, by 1996 there were only eight 110th C-POP officers left.

Precinct staffing in Queens was 10 percent below 1994 levels that year, and the 110th's officer complement stood at 233, not the 265 promised by the Safe Streets, Safe City Program. Police response time to 911 calls in Queens had risen to ten minutes—two minutes more than in 1995 and three minutes more than in Manhattan. In 1993 Giuliani had campaigned "to support our neighborhoods—the seedbeds of civic life. That's why community policing is important, . . . officers walking the beat to keep our neighborhoods safe." And once elected, he argued that merging the city's three police forces would allow him to put more officers on the streets. By 1996, however, he insisted that "patrol strength means nothing" if crime statistics were down.

COMET president Rosemarie Daraio, a single mother whose next-door neighbor was murdered while waiting for police to respond to his 911 call, was upset: "I know the Police Department worries about the crime statistics and they're always patting themselves on the back that crime is down, but what doesn't reflect in statistics is the quality of life." Walter McCaffrey, Elmhurst's city council representative, believed that with patrol strength diminished more residents were staying home: "People feel less safe in their neighborhoods. In this case perception is reality. When people feel safer, they're more likely to go out. That ends up adding to the level of real safety."

By fall 1996 less than half the C-POP beats citywide were staffed, and only 15 percent of Queens residents felt that they were safer than during the last year of the Dinkins mayoralty. "Our police officers are being taken away," NCA vice-president Angie LaChapelle lamented. "Elmhurst's loss of its quality of life by lack of police presence can only be brought back by community residents banding together and demanding our elected officials get our police officers back to our precinct all the time." Convinced that police statistics did not reflect the true level of crime, she urged, "Every crime must be reported to the 110th Precinct so it goes on the record." By 1997 patrol strength was no longer included in the mayor's management report, and police at the 110th numbered 188—just one more than the pre–Safe Streets, Safe City level.[49]

[8]

Mayoral Practice

The "world city," the "gorgeous mosaic," and *Police Strategy No. 5* were each an ideological formulation of how a mayor promised to better the lives of New York's citizenry. Koch's world city presumed that a city-subsidized economic boom would grow jobs and enhance neighborhood quality of life, presumptions that were dead by 1989. Dinkins's gorgeous mosaic addressed high-profile racial conflicts but was silent about everyday interactions and housing market inequities. Giuliani's police strategy focused on a limited agenda of quality-of-life concerns, and his cuts in patrol strength imperiled even this.

Although these three New York mayors differed in their symbolic visions, their economic policies were remarkably similar. As poverty and unemployment rose, as city-resident job growth stagnated, and as an underground economy of lapsed city regulation and last resort expanded, Koch, Dinkins, and Giuliani offered New York's permanent government an open hand and a filled cup. And each added to the list of budget cuts and service reductions that further diminished the quality of life in neighborhood New York.

Koch and the Permanent Government

As the 1980s speculative-electronic economic bubble expanded, empty Manhattan office space filled up. Construction of new office buildings slowed during the 1975 fiscal crisis, and only 2 million square feet were built during Koch's first mayoral term. In 1981, however, construction picked up: 23 million square feet were added in the second Koch term and 24 million more in his third, including Canadian firm Olympia & York's 7.5-million-square-foot World Financial Center in Battery Park City. Rents for new leases rose, and by 1983 office vacancy rates fell below 5 percent downtown and 6 percent in midtown. Property taxes on this real estate and income taxes from financial-sector employees now constituted an increasing contribution to the municipal coffer.[1] Even so, the plethora of tax breaks and favors subsidizing the real estate boom did not diminish; in fact, tax exemptions, cuts, and individual reductions all expanded. The city's corporation tax rate fell 12 percent during the Koch years, and as earnings ballooned for those at the top, income tax revenues declined from 12 percent of total personal earnings to 10 percent. In 1982 Mayor Koch joined building owners in lobbying (unsuccessfully) to repeal a state capital-gains surcharge on property sales of $1 million or more. The idea behind this levy was to let the state share in windfall profits spurred by the gathering real estate boom.

Heating Up the Alphabet Soup

By 1983 the Industrial and Commercial Incentive Board was under so much criticism that Koch created a panel to "review" it. The ICIB awarded property-tax reductions to new or rehabilitated buildings in return for "job creation"; the overwhelming share of benefits went to Manhattan projects, including large tax breaks for AT&T (which later left for New Jersey) and Olympia & York. Critics complained that the ICIB did not follow up on promises of job creation, and as Charles Brecher and Raymond Horton of the Citizens Budget Commission concluded, its tax breaks "have not induced new investments so much as they have increased the profitability of those that would have been made anyway." As if to prove this point, the brokerage firm Smith Barney applied for an $11 million ICIB tax abatement to renovate new offices, was turned down, and made the renovations anyway. In 1984 the ICIB was renamed the Industrial and Commercial Incentive Program (ICIP), and tax breaks were then awarded automatically to projects beyond an excluded downtown and east midtown zone. City tax losses via ICIP increased, amounting to $325 million between 1984 and 1989.[2]

Despite a healthy market, tax breaks for residential housing also expanded under Koch, accruing largely to luxury projects in Manhattan. After much criticism the J-51 tax abatement for upgrading existing housing was amended in 1983 to limit benefits on high-priced units and deny them to SRO hotel conversions, but Koch successfully pressed the city council to waive these restrictions in large areas of the city. The 421a tax exemption for new construction, also tilted heavily toward Manhattan luxury apartments (such as the Park Avenue Trump Tower, which received a $70 million benefit), was eliminated in the Manhattan core after 1985; during a one-year grace period, however, more than one hundred downtown and midtown construction projects broke ground and qualified for 421a exemptions if completed by 1989. Between 1984 and 1989, J-51 and 421a tax losses together cost the city $1.4 billion.

The Koch-appointed City Planning Commission accommodated Manhattan developers by upzoning west midtown in 1982 and negotiating with builders to permit extra stories or floor area in return for "amenities," usually open plazas or seating areas. In addition, real estate owners could appeal to the City Tax Commission for "hardship" reductions in property assessments. So could individual homeowners, but the largest awards went to Manhattan office-building owners who employed specialized property-tax lawyers. Whereas commercial property was assessed at 60 percent of market value, the Pan Am building was assessed at 25 percent, the Manufacturers Hanover Bank headquarters at 20 percent, and Rockefeller Center at 22 percent—all "hardship" cases. As with other tax favors, such reductions subsidized real estate owners whose buildings were easily filled by the booming speculative-electronic economy, and they indicated their gratitude with campaign contributions to the mayor.[3]

Policies to strengthen the real economy and "create jobs" were channeled through the city's Industrial Development Agency, founded in 1974, and its Public Development Corporation, dating to 1966. Empowered to issue tax-free bonds, the IDA provided individual firms with below-market-rate loans from its bond proceeds. By 1985, 38 percent of the companies receiving IDA loans had failed to create any new jobs, and another 45 percent produced fewer jobs than promised. Similar unkept promises marked the PDC, which, as the public administration scholar Annmarie Hauck Walsh noted, "had a rocky history of unsuccessful industrial developments and negative management audits" during the Koch years. Expanded from a staff of ten to more than two hundred, the PDC under Steven Spinola, a Donald Manes ally, sold city-owned land without competitive bidding to firms that pledged to create jobs. (One sale went to Kleinsleep, a mattress retailer whose chair was a PDC board member.) In 1987 the PDC listed 1,150 new jobs at a Queens Pepsi-Cola site where by 1995 ground had still not been broken. "Job statistics were put together simply for public relations purposes," concluded investigative reporter Doug Turetsky. In downtown Brooklyn the PDC assisted in closing more than one hundred small businesses to clear the manufacturing-zoned MetroTech site for speculative-electronic office development. Between 1984 and 1989 the IDA cost New York City $43 million in tax losses, and the PDC at least $12 million.[4]

Spurning Conditionality

Koch's economic development policies imposed no closely audited conditions on beneficiaries. Tax incentives to business entail calculable investments and returns that can be measured with the same criteria as direct budgetary expenditures. As the economist Michael Kieschnick noted in 1981:

> Public investment decisions should count only the costs and benefits . . . which would not have occurred without the tax subsidy. . . . The benefits . . . include net increases in [city] income due to induced investment or hiring, reduced welfare or transfer payment costs, and any increased tax revenues from the ex-

> panded economic activity. If the tax incentive does not induce greater investment or hiring, there are no net benefits to the [city] although there will be to the private firm. The costs . . . include the revenue initially forgone through the subsidy . . . and any increased public service costs or new infrastructure required by induced investments and hirings.

In 1988 four city council members sponsored a "conditionality" bill requiring that firms receiving city loans and tax breaks reserve a set number of jobs for low-income city residents; it also established fines for noncompliers. Both these practices were used by other U.S. cities. But Koch official Sally Hernandez-Piñero, overseer of IDA, and Steven Spinola, then head of the Real Estate Board, representing large developers, testified against it. The bill died.[5]

No one disputed that tax policy *could* nourish the real economy. Martin Paint Stores received $3.5 million in IDA funding and created 81 jobs, 32 more than promised; Loehmann's, a women's clothing retailer, received $2.9 million and produced 206 jobs, 132 more than projected. The biggest tax breaks, however, went to landlords and firms tied to the speculative-electronic boom. City tax incentives did not create this boom, but they did subsidize office rents at below "free market" levels. And the city bypassed opportunities to direct economic development subsidies to more firms like Martin Paints and Loehmann's, to the creation of resident rather than commuter jobs, and to the real economy rather than the speculative-electronic economy. Lessening the tax burden on some businesses and property owners, moreover, shifted it to others: small businesses shared little in the breaks and favors and paid their taxes in full. By 1985 they were mobilizing against Koch for regulation of the rising commercial rents that Manhattan's subsidized development was spiraling out into neighborhood New York.[6]

Neighborhood New York Critics

Relatively little tax-incentive largesse arrived in such neighborhoods as Elmhurst-Corona.[7] CD4 leaders nonetheless understood its indirect effects, and they criticized and resisted Koch policies that appeared inequitable. Elmhurst civic activist and CB4 member Ron Laney ran as a Republican in the early 1980s against Democratic city council member Thomas Manton; he attacked Manton's support of the ICIB and campaigned to use tax abatements to lure small businesses that were leaving Manhattan to empty sites on Elmhurst commercial strips. Citing a report by a state senator, Franz Leichter, Laney noted at a 1988 CB4 meeting that $200 million in ICIP tax abatements had gone to doctors' offices, eating establishments, and retail stores in Queens—uses that the market could support without subsidies. "The city wants to raise property taxes [for] homeowners," Laney said, "and they are giving tax abatements like this! This results from developer contributions to the mayor's campaigns." Don Mallozzi seconded Laney: "I'm damned if I'm going to pay more taxes and give the mayor's curly-haired boys tax abatements. Let them pay taxes like everyone else."

Koch's residential tax breaks were also unpopular. At a 1985 CB4 meeting the City Planning Commission's vice-chair, Martin Gallent, outlined plans to upzone Queens Boulevard for housing development. Elmhurst COMET member llsa Vasko asked Gallent, "Will there be tax abatements?" "Yes," he replied. "Our monies are being wasted in order to destroy us," she retorted. In 1987 CB4 zoning chair Raoul LaFaye announced his committee's recommendation against a 421a tax exemption for a forty-eight-unit condominium in Elmhurst: "They are making enough money on this, and should pay taxes."

Koch Cuts

In 1982, when the *New York Times* published an eight-part series on the impact of immigration in Elmhurst, the editors of the *Newtown Crier* objected that "the whole Elmhurst story" was not told: "At the same time that Elmhurst was being called upon to absorb the new wave of immigrants it was required also to cope with appalling cutbacks in all municipal services. . . . Sanitation, police, educational and health services are under great strain." In 1984 the Newtown Civic Association began annual breakfast meetings with elected officials and city agency respresentatives; agenda items included deteriorating subway service, insufficient garbage collections, housing code violations, school overcrowding, and drug sales. Following the 1988 breakfast the *Crier* reported, "A thread which ran through reports and comment by spokespeople for all agencies: Fire, Police, Buildings, HPD, Traffic, Taxi and Limousine, was that they do not have sufficient staff to get their jobs done."

At CB4 the frustration was much the same. In 1984 the City Planning Commission's vice-chair, Martin Gallent, was barraged by complaints about illegal housing units, gambling, and prostitution. He responded candidly, "Other community boards in Queens have these problems too. . . . Since the fiscal crisis of 1974 the city has not concentrated on these quality-of-life issues." In 1986 two Transit Workers Union officials, one a former subway car inspector, told CB4 that before 1975 trains had averaged 20,000 miles before breakdown, and buses 10,000 miles; with no preventive maintenance since then, "trains are down to 9,000 miles before failure, and buses to 1,100 miles." That same year the city's Office of Management and Budget (OMB) scored only 73 percent of Elmhurst-Corona streets "clean," and the Parks Department rated conditions in a fifth of CD4 parks as less than "acceptable."[8]

New budget cuts were announced after the 1987 stock market crash. Parks Department hiring was frozen at the beginning of 1988, and tree pruning and maintenance were curtailed; with decreased recreation personnel, participation in city-run children's programs had declined 35 percent by 1989. The Playground for All Children, a Flushing Meadows–Corona Park facility accessible to children with disabilities, reduced its daily programs from ten to two. Cuts in sanitation personnel were announced, and refuse tonnage collected had dropped 22 percent citywide by 1989. The number of "clean team" street-sweepers, which Koch had doubled, fell from 1,300 to less than 600.

At the beginning of the 1989 election year, 72 percent of New Yorkers agreed that "city life [had] worsened" under Koch. As Korean Elmhurst resident Carol Kim put it, "In this neighborhood, we need much help. The drug men come up to you. The garbage piles up to the sky."[9]

Dinkins and the Permanent Government

Dinkins's 1989 support included many voters energized by the 1984 and 1988 Jesse Jackson campaigns. As a candidate, moreover, Dinkins criticized the ICIP and pledged to phase out other tax incentive programs. Yet as his administration took shape, Koch officials occupied all the top economic policy positions. At a forum just weeks before the new mayor assumed office, the journalist Juan Gonzalez remarked, "My sense is that you get a people's movement that develops, it elects a people's candidate, and then there is a coup, right? . . . When the establishment in this city realized that a people's movement was about to come to power, they grabbed Dinkins so fast that he still hasn't stopped turning around." In January 1990 Dinkins's electoral troops gathered for his inaugural address in the cold outside City Hall. A reception for his financial backers followed—indoors at Olympia & York's World Financial Center.[10]

During Dinkins's first year 45,000 private-sector jobs disappeared, and after two years employment was down 270,000. By mid-1991 there were 43 million square feet of empty office space (remember, 49 million had been added in the Koch years), and 65 million by 1993. Vacancy rates in Manhattan office buildings hovered between 16 and 20 percent throughout the Dinkins years. Given all this empty space, rents on new Class A offices collapsed from a high of $52 per square foot in 1990 to $32 in midtown and $30 downtown by the end of the Dinkins mayoralty.[11]

New York City's permanent government was in trouble. Its prime commodity, office space, was in glut and losing value. The city was also in trouble. Tax collections depended heavily on the speculative-electronic economy, and three-quarters of additional private-sector earnings during the 1980s had come from financial-and business-services employees. Income tax revenues dropped with job loss in these sectors, and the property tax rose from 40 percent of city revenues in 1985 to 45 percent by 1992. Residential property-tax arrears and mortgage foreclosures, however, increased to 1 in 6 properties between 1988 and 1992, most of them occurring in low-income neighborhoods. As the situation worsened, rather than maintain its upscale real estate revenue base and target neighborhood New York for relief, the Dinkins administration moved to bail out the permanent government by expanding the full panoply of Koch-era tax policies.[12]

Reheating the Alphabet Soup

ICIP property-tax reductions doubled under Dinkins, averaging $144 million in forgone city revenue each year during 1990–1993. Downtown and east midtown remained excluded, but ICIP continued to subsidize west midtown commercial projects, despite the abundance of existing space. In Times Square, four buildings constructed by developer William Zeckendorf, a Dinkins campaign contributor, had property taxes reduced from $23 million to $7 million. Then, with encouragement from permanent-government leaders, Dinkins extended ICIP benefits to the excluded Manhattan areas in 1992 and added a clause allowing projects already under way to qualify retroactively.

J-51 tax losses totaled $842 million between 1990 and 1993, and in 1992 benefits were extended to a wider range of high-end co-op and condominium conversions. The 421a tax exemption for new apartments amounted to $718 million over the Dinkins years, and during his last weeks in office the mayor signed a bill restoring 421a to downtown and midtown Manhattan. Critics saw this as a favor to developer Zeckendorf, who planned a large midtown apartment complex, and an unnecessary boost to Manhattan luxury housing against stagnant outer-borough residential construction. Even Republican city council member Charles Millard objected to expanding 421a: "Developers, just like everyone else, need to be subject to the market."[13]

Commercial real estate clearly *was* losing value "subject to the market." In 1991 city assessors lowered the taxable value of Manhattan office buildings from $26 billion to $23 billion, a 12 percent decline. They decreased assessments on other commercial property from $25 billion to $20 billion, a 20 percent drop and an indication of greater economic distress in the rest of the city. The City Tax Commission nonetheless continued to award property-assessment reductions disproportionately to Manhattan office buildings. In 1992 Goldman Sachs received a 28 percent reduction, the same year its vice-chair, Robert Rubin, earned $28 million. For buildings worth more than $1 million, the commission did no independent audits but accepted the owners' income and expense figures.

IDA and PDC subsidies also expanded under Dinkins, totaling $123 million and $36 million respectively. The wisdom of such tax-incentive policies became questionable in 1991 when Citibank eliminated 500 jobs at the Long Island City office tower for which it had received $90 million in tax breaks in 1989; and again in 1992 when Taystee Bread, a beneficiary of $780,000 in IDA-subsidized loans since 1985, moved 400 jobs from its Flushing factory to Pennsylvania; and yet again in 1993 after CBS was granted $50 million in tax breaks to "retain"

4,600 jobs, although chairman Laurence Tisch admitted, "We never threatened to leave. . . . I just wanted to be treated like everyone else."[14]

New Directions in Tax Breaks

In 1991 Dinkins announced a public-private partnership between the City Planning Commission and a group of downtown realtors owning 25 million square feet of empty office space. Named "the Lower Manhattan Project," it was chaired by John Zuccotti, head of the Downtown–Lower Manhattan Association and New York president of Olympia & York, which alone held 16 million square feet of downtown real estate. Owners of lower Manhattan Class B space—older buildings unsuitable for computer-run business—were lobbying City Hall for tax abatements to convert their buildings to apartments. The Lower Manhattan Project studied 650 such buildings, but no recommendations emerged before Olympia & York and several other downtown landlords went bankrupt in 1992. In 1993 the project reported that 45 buildings, about 4 million square feet, were potential residential conversion sites, but no legislative initiative addressing the depressed downtown situation appeared before Dinkins left office.[15]

At the time the Lower Manhattan Project was begun, a viewpoint at odds with its save-the-permanent-government mission was emerging from within the Dinkins adminstration. In 1991 the Economic Policy and Marketing Group under Deputy Mayor Sally Hernandez-Piñero released a report questioning across-the-board tax favors. It stated that although 163,000 jobs left the city during 1976–1986, and 37,000 were added by firms moving in, some 464,000 jobs were created by new companies formed within the city. The report called for a city economic policy to support start-up firms. "Tax exemptions are a very inexact way to address economic development needs," Hernandez-Piñero told the *New York Times*. "It shouldn't be the cornerstone of our philosophy, which it is." Dinkins found it hard to embrace the report's message of shifting city largesse from permanent-government real estate owners to up-and-coming firms. So did the permanent government. In 1992 a *New York Times* op-ed piece by Ronald Shelp, head of the David Rockefeller-backed New York Partnership, called for "an experienced and distinguished business executive" to replace Hernandez-Piñero, and praised city efforts "to prevent the relocation of . . . major corporations." Hernandez-Piñero soon left the Dinkins administration (though she returned later in 1992 to head the New York Public Housing Authority).[16]

With modern technology, as Shelp put it, permitting "many jobs to be done as effectively in Kansas, Florida, or even Ireland" as in New York City, the permanent government's resource base was shrinking. Its leaders understood that only continuing tax subsidies would keep in New York those firms liberated by the new technology. This would require either (1) retaining the existing regime of across-the-board tax breaks to property owners who thereby enjoyed lower costs, or who leased space to others at subsidized rents, or (2) providing a new system of tax breaks for specific companies who agreed to stay in New York, whether in their own space or as renters—or both. Hence, the existing system, written into the as-of-right tax programs, continued, but a new regime of "designer packages" of city subsidies awarded to individual firms began as well.

Longtime permanent-government leaders such as David Rockefeller took advantage of both the old and new systems. The deputy mayor who replaced Sally Hernandez-Piñero in 1992 was Barry Sullivan, who had spent twenty-four years of his thirty-two-year career at David Rockefeller's Chase Manhattan bank and was appointed by Dinkins at Rockefeller's suggestion. Sullivan got Dinkins to declare a four-year property-tax freeze and, with Shelp's partnership and Rockefeller's support, traveled overseas to drum up tenants for New York City office-building owners. In 1991, moreover, Chase had shifted 4,600 workers to the city-subsidized MetroTech site in Brooklyn and received $234 million in job-retention tax breaks, and by spring 1992 its downtown headquarters was 24 percent vacant. In summer 1992 Sullivan negotiated a $106 million "designer package" of subsidies in return for which Prudential Securities "saved" 5,000 jobs and signed a twenty-year lease for a million square feet of empty Chase Manhattan space. (In 1995 Chase merged with Chemical Bank and downsized 4,000 jobs.)[17]

Including Prudential, Sullivan crafted twelve designer packages worth $471 million in tax forgiveness and energy credits during 1992–1993; eight of these were for speculative-electronic financial firms and three for information/media corporations, including the $50 million CBS deal. Three of the deals would unravel. Mastercard, which in 1993 pledged to remain in the city, moved to Westchester in 1994. Kidder Peabody agreed in 1993 to retain 3,500 jobs; two years later it eliminated 2,500 New York City positions. The commodity and mercantile exchange, which received $178 million in tax breaks to retain 11,700 jobs in 1992, was offered another $209 million from the city and state in 1994 to keep until 2009 what had become 8,100 jobs.[18]

Dinkins Cuts Deeper

Budget cutting intensified during Dinkins's mayoral term, and its effects were duly announced at the Elmhurst-Corona district cabinet. The five Queens Human Rights Commission offices dealing with housing discrimination were reduced to two. City inspectors for home-based day care were eliminated, making it impossible for parents using such facilities to deduct the cost on their income taxes. Sewer repair personnel were reduced from sixty to thirty for the entire city. The Sanitation Department "clean team" was eliminated, and mechanical street-sweeping and wire trashbasket collections were cut back. The ranks of sanitation enforcement officers fell by two-thirds, leaving only two to patrol CD4. In all, the number of sanitation workers fell from 26,000 to 18,000, and department representatives joked about "safe streets, dirty city" when they addressed CB4 in 1993.

The Parks Department lost 28 percent of its workers under Dinkins, including 40 percent of those posted in Queens. Forestry workers decreased by 90 percent, recreation staff by 50 percent. The schedules for swimming pools and mobile recreation units were drastically reduced, and the three pre-school programs in Elmhurst-Corona parks were eliminated. Maintenance staff for CD4's twenty–three public parks, sitting areas, and triangles fell to just five.[19]

Privatization Begins: The USTA

The largest Dinkins-era reduction in park facilities was the leasing of 10 percent of Flushing Meadows–Corona Park to the United States Tennis Association. Created by Robert Moses for the 1939 World's Fair, the 1,255-acre grounds were one and a half times the size of Central Park, but two large lakes, wetlands, Shea Stadium, and Transit Authority train yards left only 450 acres of usable space. The park housed a zoo, carousel, botanical gardens, art and science museums, and a half-scale eighteen-hole golf course, but its primary attraction for 8 million visitors each year was open space for recreation and picnicking. On spring, summer, and fall weekends it was filled by soccer teams and spectators, baseball players, family groups, couples, and youth. During the annual Colombian, Ecuadorian, and Korean festivals and other special events, gigantic crowds arrived.

In existence since 1871 to promote tennis, the USTA sponsored the U.S. Open each September, one of four "grand slam" tournaments that determined world champion status. After television coverage began in 1968 both the audience for tennis and the USTA's profits—from broadcast rights, tickets, and stadium concessions—grew enormously. In 1978 the USTA had moved from Forest Hills to a seventeen-acre site in Flushing Meadows–Corona Park, a deal brokered by borough president Donald Manes. Upon Dinkins's election it began negotiations for a lease to succeed the one expiring in 1994. Dinkins was a daily tennis player and ardent fan. In 1991 he announced a plan to award the USTA an additional thirty-one park acres—including the golf course—on which it would invest in new facilities. "The world's greatest tennis tournament remains in the world's greatest city," he said, and boasted of retaining an undocumentable "$150 million" in annual hotel, restaurant, and tourist business which his Economic Development Corporation assured him the U.S. Open stimulated. Borough president Claire Shulman, though having negotiated with the USTA throughout 1990 to prevent the taking of even more parkland, supported the plan.

Opposition quickly mounted in Queens. Legislators asked where the $11 million in promised road improvements would come from when the city budget was being cut. Civic activists who had resisted a plan by Manes to use the park for speedcar racing regrouped in a Committee for the Preservation of Flushing Meadows–Corona Park, an alliance that included dozens of civic groups plus the American Institute of Architects, Queens chapter, and the New York Hispanic Soccer Leagues Association, whose members played in the park. The committee declared that equivalent space in Manhattan's Central Park would never be transferred to a private organization.

Critics also faulted the USTA for being a poor neighbor. Its courts were open to the public during the off-season only at $12 per hour or higher rates; their use was not covered by the $50 annual Parks Department tennis court fee. U.S. Open ticket policies discouraged ordinary fans; the bulk of tickets were available only in blocks purchased by corporations or as $2,000 passes for the two-week-long season. Sentiment against USTA expansion was epitomized in a September 4, 1991, letter to the *New York Times:* "The Mayor's love of tennis and the well-heeled crowd that supports and attends the Open is obviously greater than his love of the thousands of non-elite people of all races and economic classes who enjoy the park. . . . Now New York City plans to take a piece of that away." Opposition hardened in 1992 when the USTA announced that it was moving its Manhattan offices to Westchester.

At CB4 opinion was divided. Corona residents had long complained about traffic during the Open, particularly on days when Mets baseball games were also being played at Shea Stadium. And they were assaulted by USTA noise. "There are two humming blimps over our heads for the last two weeks," said Judy D'Andrea. "The noise is terrible." Under the new plan the noise would only worsen: La Guardia Airport flights paths were to be diverted from over Flushing Meadows–Corona Park to surrounding Queens neighborhoods. Richard Isles declared he was "incensed at Mayor Dinkins when he asked to reroute the flight patterns [over Lefrak City] for the USTA." Ron Laney thought the deal one-sided: "The USTA made $134 million last year [actually half that amount], and paid New York City $251,000, or two-tenths of one percent of their profit. So they rent seventeen acres for 3.5 cents per-square-foot. And now they want [more] of the park . . . so they can enjoy their BMWs and Perrier . . . and live in Connecticut." Some CB4 members, however, saw an opportunity to secure additional funds for the rundown park. As Tony Caminiti, chair of the CB4 parks committee put it, "We feel the USTA should do more security and maintenance, and pay to replace everything they take. . . . We're in favor, but we want something from them."

Pro-USTA lobbying was extensive. Parks Commissioner Betsy Gotbaum (wife of former labor leader Victor Gotbaum) vigorously supported it, as did Dinkins, although the mayor never appeared before Queens audiences to answer opponents. USTA efforts were directed by Sid Davidoff, a former Lindsay official and a tennis partner of Dinkins and First Deputy Mayor Norman Steisel. Davidoff arranged visits by tennis celebrities to the five community boards that bordered the park and would vote on the plan. He also invited eight hundred Queens community board and civic group members to the USTA stadium for a lavish reception and demonstration match between tennis stars Gabriela Sabatini and Jennifer Capriati.

Misinformation accompanied the lobbying. During a 1991 USTA debate at CB4, Lucy Schilero declared, "We're losing space for our kids. If they want to encourage kids on tennis, they should do more—[like] programs for kids." City council member Helen Marshall replied, "They do have extensive training programs—free—as they agreed when they moved from Forest Hills." "It's not free," Judy D'Andrea shot back, "I paid." "That's not what Betsy Gotbaum told me," Marshall responded. Despite reservations, CB4 voted in 1993 to approve the plan, as did three other community boards.

The city's negotiator with the USTA was Steisel's chief of staff, Ellen Baer. (Baer and lobbyist Davidoff "acknowledge a social relationship" the *Daily News* reported.) The ninety-nine-year lease Baer produced included an estimated $800,000 payment from the USTA to the city each year, and an $8 million endowment for Flushing Meadows–Corona Park. Financing for the $172 million project was provided by city-subsidized IDA bonds. Two city council members representing CD4, John Sabini and Walter McCaffrey, opposed what one called a "sweetheart deal," but the agreement passed the council by a 33-to-15 vote. As a concession, the USTA exchanged the thirty-one-acre portion of the park it wanted for a different twenty-six-acre parcel, thus saving the golf course. In his last week in office Dinkins signed the agreement, thus privatizing forty-three acres of city parkland until 2093.[20]

Giuliani and the Permanent Government

As a candidate, Republican Rudolph Giuliani assigned blame for post-1989 job losses to his Democratic predecessors: "There's no question that the [existing] policies and programs have aggressively driven jobs out of New York City by failing to get control of government spending, and then having to subsidize government by confiscating increasing amounts of money from the private sector." The spending that Giuliani referred to was for neighborhood quality of life and education, areas cut by Koch and Dinkins, and for rising welfare costs, more a consequence of the failing city economy than its cause. And like Koch and Dinkins, Giuiliani would increase spending on jails and police. The new mayor, however, had no intention to "get control" by reversing Koch-Dinkins tax polices, which in fact decreased revenues "confiscated from the private sector." ICIP, J-51, 421a, IDA, and PDC cost the city $594 million in Dinkins's last year, and $600 million in Giuliani's first. Also like his Democratic predecessors, Giuliani dismissed calls for closely audited conditionality on permanent-government and corporate tax breaks, standards now common in other cities.[21]

Giuliani's campaign reference to "*the* private sector," moreover, was ambiguous. As Brecher and Horton explain, "The city's businesses are numerous and differ in several ways: size (big versus small); control (managers versus entrepreneur-owners); products (services versus goods); markets (local versus national and international)." And within the private sector, interests diverge: "The 'advanced business service sector' [includes] headquarters of manufacturing enterprises, financial institutions, law firms, advertising and public relations firms, management consultants. . . . Closely allied are the realtors, who develop and/or own the buildings that house the advanced business sector firms. . . . [T]he realtors' interests are not identical to those who buy or rent commercial real estate."[22]

The Dinkins regime had seen this divergence grow. It had not moved to satisfy the collective interests of distressed lower-Manhattan realtors, but it had chosen to advance the specific interests of particular speculative-electronic and information/media corporations. Giuliani's pro-business message promised help to everyone.

By 1994 jobs in lower Manhattan had fallen by 100,000 from their 1988 peak of 475,000. Downtown's Class A vacancy rate climbed from 15 to 18 percent that year; overall vacancies hit 28 percent; and several buildings were "mothballed," or fully closed down. In June, Giuliani established his own lower Manhattan project; in December he revealed its members' recommendations to an appreciative audience of real estate owners. He proposed new tax breaks for leases, renovations, and residential conversions in pre-1975 buildings, a package estimated to cost the city $234 million over the first three years (Steven Spinola figured it would subsidize new rents by 10 to 20 percent). In addition, zoning restrictions would be eased on new construction, and rail linkages to Long Island and Westchester commuter terminals would be constructed, including a three-mile tunnel from Grand Central Station to Wall Street. By early 1995 new downtown leases had plummeted to $20 per square foot, and that fall New York State approval for the mayor's tax package was granted.[23]

Opinion on both left and right cautioned that the bailout plan was bad economics and unlikely to work. Progressive economist Robert Fitch observed, "Downtown [is] not needed anymore. It can't compete. . . . The only way it has been made viable is through immense subsidy." New York University economist Emanuel Tobier stated, "I'd let nature take its course." Historian Fred Siegel, a Giuliani campaign advisor, warned against "prop[ping] up lower Manhattan. . . . Does the city need a second major business district? It's not clear that it does. . . . Meanwhile, the crying need is for small-business growth in the outer boroughs." Peter Salins of the conservative Manhattan Institute declared, "I'm a great believer in letting markets find their own level. . . . Cities . . . think they can invent the business base they want . . . but to a large extent they can't because those things are subject to worldwide factors."[24]

"The plan is to make lower Manhattan precisely what it it used to be," Giuliani told downtown supporters, "a generator of jobs." But with flat job growth and continuing speculative-electronic dispersal, a plan to subsidize downtown rents would more likely be a *shifter* of jobs, inducing moves to downtown from higher-rent locations elsewhere. Brooklyn borough president Howard Golden worried that speculative-electronic firms attracted by MetroTech might now be pulled to lower Manhattan by cheaper rents.

Midtown real estate owners, with 14 percent vacancy rates, were concerned that subsidized rents in lower Manhattan might reverse an ongoing migration of downtown firms to their newer, technology-friendly buildings. New midtown leases rose from $25 to $28 per square foot between 1994 and 1995, and state senator Franz Leichter observed that midtown "might be primed for a turnaround without any City intervention." Giuliani, however, proposed yet another tax break: an expansion of ICIP benefits for midtown office renovations. Midtown developer Seymour Durst complained that new city intrusion disadvantaged owners of existing Class A real estate and contributed to the tax-break drain on municipal services. Nonetheless, the city council approved Giuliani's midtown plan in June 1995.[25]

In early 1996 owners of 1,300 city office buildings provoked the first maintenance staff strike in forty-eight years when, hoping to trim operating costs, they proposed a 40 percent wage cut for new workers (the eventual settlement cut wages 20 percent). Midtown rentals improved during 1996, reaching $40 per square foot for Class A space, and vacancies fell to 9 percent. The picture downtown remained dire, despite Giuliani's tax breaks and the substantial space rentals by city and state agencies. The World Trade and World Financial Centers were 17 percent empty, and downtown rents of $20 per square foot set a historic low relative to midtown. By 1997 this disparity was beginning to attract midtown firms, and a shift to the heavily subsidized downtown was under way. Nonetheless, some 34 million square feet of core Manhattan office space still remained vacant.[26]

Giuliani also continued the Dinkins-Sullivan "designer packages," concluding twenty-two deals worth more than $653 million in forgone city revenues. In charge of these corporate retention packages during 1994–1995 was Clay Lifflander, a thirty-one-year-old merger-and-acquisitions executive from the Smith Barney investment firm. Lifflander admitted that 40 percent of the jobs he "saved" were held by commuters, and like Sullivan, he focused on speculative-electronic firms and media companies (including ABC, which—as CBS had done—admitted it had no intention of moving). Also like Sullivan, Lifflander negotiated a deal benefiting his former employer—in his case a 1994 agreement with Smith Barney worth $22 million. Two of the packages, moreover, subsidized foreign-owned firms: $50 million to CS First Boston, a Swiss investment bank; $2 million to Tullent & Tokyo Forex, a British-Japanese currency broker.

Three of the Giuliani deals were soon in trouble. In 1994 Republic National Bank and Donaldson Lufkin & Jenrette pledged to retain jobs; in 1995 both announced that they were cutting positions. Then CS First Boston unveiled plans to lay off 900 employees, just one month after agreeing to increase its New York City work force. Neither the Dinkins-Sullivan nor the Giuliani-Lifflander packages did much to grow the real economy. Only one blue-collar employer, Blue Ridge Farms of Brooklyn, received a tax break—$4 million to retain 600 food-industry jobs under Dinkins.[27]

Giuliani Cuts Deeper Still

David Dinkins's reduction of the city work force by 15,000 positions fell short of the New York Partnership's call to "get rid of 50,000 [municipal] jobs." Rudolph Giuliani pledged to cut the rest, and through severance payments and attrition municipal employment had fallen another 21,000 by 1997. At the Department of Transportation only one pothole-repair crew remained for all of Queens. The Sanitation Department lost 20 percent of its employees, leaving only one enforcement officer for CD4, and its annual hazardous-waste collections were canceled. In 1994 the CD4 sanitation supervisor told the district cabinet, "The city expects us to meet the same standards with seven less [garbage] trucks per week. For the first time in twenty-five years—and I never thought I'd see it—we don't have the men to man the trucks we have." District manager Rothschild responded, "They're firing who does the work—the people we work with—and the supervisors stay. The mobile litter crew and clean team are fired. There is no one to send out to do the work."

Subway car and station cleaning jobs were cut. The Parks Department fell to 1,200 workers, and skilled employees were not replaced. There were "wild, dying, and not-pruned trees" in Elmhurst-Corona's parks "and [on] every side street," CB4 parks committee chair Tony Caminiti announced in 1996. "William Moore Park looks like a forest; it's being choked." The number of Home Relief recipients who were paid subminimum wages for park litter removal, however, grew from 250 in 1994 to 7,000 by 1996, and another 27,000 "workfare" laborers and cleaners worked in other city agencies. Community board budgets, which included rent, were cut from $152,000 to $110,000, forcing the CB4 part-time staff to drop from four to one.

Cuts canceled all CD4 Department of Youth Services programs in 1994, and after disarray and reorganization in this agency, only half its funds for community programs were restored in 1995; more cuts came in 1996. Library book budgets fell by a third. Tuition at CUNY was raised one-third, to $3,200, by the city and state. In supporting this increase, the mayor stated, "They might have to work harder and take out a loan. Learn a little civic responsibility." Most CUNY students already held tuition loans and worked, a third of them in full-time jobs.[28]

Despite annual increases of 20,000 new students, the Board of Education budget was cut $1.1 billion during the Dinkins years, and another $1.3 billion by Giuliani. In effect, the student body increased by 12 percent during 1990–1996, while per-pupil spending fell by 12 percent. City council member Helen Marshall told CB4 in 1995, "One thing our mayor seems to go after is education. He goes after it with a vengeance." Class size went up; retiring teachers were not replaced; afterschool programs decreased; supplies and equipment were in shortage; textbooks were out-of-date; music, art, physical education, and school health programs were curtailed.

In addition, many schools were in poor physical condition. PS102 in Elmhurst was surrounded by scaffolding to prevent falling bricks; students wiped plaster dust off their desks each day; and water leakage made third-floor classrooms unusable when it rained. With a shortage of 150,000 seats estimated by the year 2000, in 1994 School Chancellor Ramon Cortines requested $7.5 billion in capital budget funding to build thirty-three new schools and repair others. Giuliani agreed to $3.4 billion, and Cortines canceled plans for new construction, deploying the funds for renovations and additions. Then in 1995 the mayor reduced capital funding to $2.7 billion, and Cortines resigned. (The city council restored $1.4 billion in 1996.)

In 1995 the report of a blue-ribbon panel of eleven business leaders was released. Headed by Harold Levy, vice-president of Salomon Brothers investment bank, the panel concluded that $4.6 billion in "wholesale modernization" was needed at 424 of the city's 1,069 existing schools, including 340 still heated by coal, and 125 with "dangerous window conditions." "No one would tolerate this in the private sector," the Levy report stated. "Unless immediate and far-reaching steps are taken to fix the buildings, we believe that it is probable that school children, teachers, and staff will be hurt or even killed in the near future." The panel's recommendation of a property-tax increase to fund renovations was summarily rejected by Giuliani.

During 1995, while reiterating his calls for more "administrative" cuts and for NYPD control of school security guards, the mayor insisted that he offered a "complete vision for the schools." Staten Island Board of Education member Lou DeSario disagreed: "I don't understand his rhetoric or why he's taking that approach. . . . I've never had one conversation with the mayor and had no opportunities to air concerns or educational goals." Diane Ravitch, a Reagan administration education official, was also critical: "All he's talked about is cutting. I would like to hear him talk at least once about what kind of school system we should have five years from now, ten years from now." In 1996 the mayor amplified his vision: "Learning isn't about the number of children in school. It isn't about what the facilities are like. It isn't about space. It's about reading. It's about accessing knowledge yourself."[29]

Privatizing Public Hospitals

As a candidate Giuliani had pledged to "privatize" New York's public hospitals, and in February 1995 he announced plans to sell three, including Elmhurst Hospital Center. Opened in 1957, Elmhurst Hospital by the 1980s had expanded dietary offerings to accommodate its immigrant patients and developed a volunteer translation corps speaking a score of languages. Beginning in 1989 it underwent a $200 million renovation and expansion, and in 1991 it initiated English classes and retraining for foreign nurses residing in New York City. "Why go to another country to look for nurses," said the executive director, Pete Velez, "when almost every country in the world is represented in our neighborhood?" During 1994 Elmhurst's staff of 4,000 treated more than half a million patients in its emergency room, outpatient departments and clinics, regional trauma center, and 646 beds.

Defending privatization, Giuliani mistakenly told a television interviewer that private hospitals had to admit patients for nonemergency care, regardless of ability to pay. In fact, private hospitals were required only to evaluate patients and provide emergency treatment, which resulted in the practice of "dumping," or transferring poor and uninsured persons to public hospitals for further care. Consequently, the city's Health and Hospital Corporation facilities served a poorer and sicker population. In 1994, 63 percent of inpatients at HHC hospitals were covered by Medicaid; the 13 percent uninsured were primarily low-income persons. At private hospitals the profile was 29 percent Medicaid and 7 percent uninsured, many of the latter higher-income, self-paying patients. While accounting for only one-fifth of New York City's hospital beds, HHC units treated 30 percent of all hospitalized infants and mothers, 35 percent of AIDS patients, 40 percent of tuberculosis and drug abuse cases, and 50 percent of psychiatric hospitalizations.

Giuliani asserted that privatization would result in savings, but a 1995 Twentieth Century Fund report by Charles Brecher and Sheila Spiezio disputed this. They pointed out that Mount Sinai Medical Center, a potential purchaser of Elmhurst Hospital, charged $978 a day for a hospital room versus $620 at Elmhurst; in addition, administrative personnel at Mount Sinai were twice as numerous as at Elmhurst, and their salaries were higher. Elmhurst, moreover, was generating a surplus at the time its intended sale was announced in 1995. "The case for selling Elmhurst seems particularly weak," Brecher and Spiezio maintained. "It is a new facility serving numerous uninsured patients," and a public hospital system to serve the city's 1.3 million uninsured residents would be needed "for the forseeable future," they concluded.

Giuliani's pronouncement that privatization would reduce costs for the city was also challenged. The city contributed $300 million to HHC's annual budget—the other 95 percent came from Medicaid, Medicare, and other sources—yet it received more than twice this amount in the services that it mandated HHC to provide: medical treatment of police and firefighters, health services to prisoners, operation of the EMS ambulance system (which Giuliani transferred to the Fire Department in 1996), and care for Medicaid patients beyond government reimbursement, in addition to treating the uninsured. The city would still have to pay private hospitals the cost of these services if HHC units were sold or closed.[30]

Community Board 4 first discussed privatization of Elmhurst Hospital in 1994. Steve Trimboli favored it, and Richard Italiano suggested that the mayor's refusal to answer questions meant "It's a done deal." Carmela George, who—like Rose Rothschild, Miriam Levenson, and Clara Salas—had served on the hospital's Community Advisory Board, spoke about its standard of care: "I've been using Elmhurst Hospital for ten years. I advise people to go there. They're courteous. It *is* working—it's gotten better. They call you if you miss an appointment. That's something even a private doctor won't do." Rothschild added, "If you go to St. John's emergency room [a private hospital in Elmhurst], if you don't have some classy health insurance, they tell you to go to Elmhurst. A lot of people have had to drop their insurance—it's $600 to $700 a month for a family, and it's getting more expensive. If we didn't have a hospital like Elmhurst, we'd have a lot of epidemics and sick people walking around."

At a 1995 district cabinet meeting just days after Mayor Giuliani's announcement of his intention to sell Elmhurst Hospital, Rothschild related a personal experience. "It's not only the working poor who will be affected. My [twenty-five year-old] son was treated [at Elmhurst Hospital], and I paid. He was covered when he was a student, but now he has no health insurance. The care was top-notch. . . . We don't need another private hospital in Queens, we have enough; they tell them on their death bed, 'Go to Elmhurst.' We need a city hospital. Since 1978 its gotten bigger and better. We're proud of it. . . . I think the mayor should, like, tour around and see the real world, and maybe he'll see what's going on."

At the April 1995 CB4 meeting an HHC vice-president scheduled to answer questions about the Elmhurst sale failed to appear. Priscilla Carrow moved to support a request from CB2 in Manhattan for a letter opposing the sale. City council member John Sabini said that over eighteen months he had received no response from the mayor's office to his calls about the hospital. Council member Helen Marshall said that she had met with Giuliani health advisor Maria Mitchell but received no answers either, and she was worried about care for "indigent people" should the hospital be sold. Clara Salas spoke against privatization, as did Domingo Genao, who emphasized that poor people were not welcomed at private hospitals. "They push you out after emergency care. . . . It's not good to privatize Elmhurst Hospital. If people say there are problems, we should try to improve it." The board voted 28 to 3 to oppose privatization, and a letter affirming this outcome was sent to Mayor Giuliani.

In 1996 the city council sued the mayor over denying it a vote on the sale of city hospitals, and CB4 went on record once more against privatization. Press accounts stressing that 23 percent of Queens residents had no health insurance reinforced opposition to the mayor's plan, now expressed by 58 percent of Queens residents. In 1997 a State Supreme Court judge ruled Giuliani's hospital sales illegal, but the mayor vowed to appeal and continue privatization.[31]

The Return of Planned Shrinkage

The Giuliani administration's reluctance to build schools and its enthusiasm to sell hospitals were complemented by its housing, homelessness, and welfare initiatives. The Koch-Dinkins policy of seizing tax-delinquent residential properties—mainly undermaintained, low-income housing—ended. With no threat of seizure, and with building inspection cutbacks, pressure on landlords to correct housing code violations was lifted. An example of what could result occurred in 1995 when a Harlem building with $96,000 in tax arrears and 337 outstanding violations collapsed, killing three tenants. Under the previous two mayors the city had upgraded 50,000 units in buildings it had seized, but this program was severely reduced, and a new policy of selling blocks of such housing to private landlords was announced in 1995.[32]

For persons becoming homeless because of housing deterioration, overcrowding, or domestic disputes, the path to city shelter narrowed. At a 1994 district cabinet meeting a Human Resources Administration (HRA) spokesperson announced that city staff assisting homeless persons was being cut from ninety-four to fifteen, and borough-level Emergency Assistance Units (EAUs) where homeless families could apply for shelter were reduced to one Bronx site that would accept clients only by telephone appointment. A person seeking shelter now called an 800 number, and "the operator tries to divert them from coming to the facility," telling them to go to an HRA office the next day. There "diversion teams" would "try to get you to stay in housing." Only if there was no alternative would clients be accepted at the Bronx EAU, and they had to arrive there on their own: "There will not be vans." Ivonne Garcia, Claire Shulman's liaison, said, "I saw that, at eleven [o'clock] at night. Chinese. She didn't know your 800 number. I sent her to the 114th precinct."

"Boy, we have to get out of this city if we get in trouble," Rose Rothschild declared. "We should all realize 'there but for the grace of God.' . . . This is disgraceful. Ivonne, I hope the borough president knows this. . . . What about battered wives, thrown out with no money. It's being made more and more difficult. We used to have [an HRA] family center on 99th Street in Corona. Now they might as well go to Idaho. . . . There were only three people [at the Queens EAU], and they were great. They helped a lot of people, even senior citizens, who came in. They couldn't have saved a lot of money by closing it."

The HRA spokesperson explained that 3,000 HRA staff had been "downsized," and that eligibility determination for income assistance was being "contracted out. . . . Community groups will do the paperwork before clients come to HRA, to be more user-friendly." Rothschild responded, "So, a Korean group can help a Hispanic person? How is this more sensitive?" The HRA representative then added that the community groups, not HRA, would publicize the locations where welfare eligibility determinations were to be initiated. "If they don't know where to go, they go to the police. . . . The system is actually changing. Eventually it's hoped that it will be improved services." "Children don't vote," Rothschild replied, "and some of their parents don't vote. That's what scares me. So that's who's gonna get hurt—the kids. I gave all these years to my community and they're our future. And now I think there's going to be no one left to help them."

In 1995 Mayor Giuliani hired five hundred "fraud detection" investigators to screen applicants for Home Relief and Aid to Families with Dependent Children; their efforts were projected to reduce by half the number of single adults on Home Relief (now limited to ninety days), according to mayoral advisor Richard Schwartz, architect of Giuliani's education, hospital, and welfare policies. The investigators' background checks and home visits uncovered few cases of fraud, but they did use evidence of underground income-producing activities as a basis to deny Home Relief and AFDC. By 1997 these efforts had pared the two programs' rolls by 235,000, a 20 percent drop from 1995.[33]

What linked Giuliani's school, hospital, and social services policies was the "planned shrinkage" idea of the late 1970s. In 1995 senior Giuliani officials explained "what this mayor believes" in press interviews. One told the *New York Post,* "Making the city inhospitable to the poor is the best way to 'clean it up.' " Another told the *Village Voice* that if Giuliani's policy "leads to people making the decision that they'd be better off getting welfare in other places where the cost of living is lower, fine." Mayoral advisor Peter Salins, director of research at the Manhattan Institute, reinforced the message in *Newsday:* "In the Third World, you really see patterns of migration towards centers of opportunity. [In New York] the poor are anchored by welfare that puts a premium on staying put. . . . Some of that population should leave. The modern welfare city has undermined mobility."[34]

At a 1995 budget briefing Giuliani was asked, "Is it your unspoken strategy that poor people should move to another city or state?" He responded, "That's not an unspoken strategy. That's the strategy. We just cannot afford it. Those left out will have the option of moving elsewhere. That will help make New York City more like the rest of the country." The next day he added, "Mobility would be a good thing."

Giuliani officials insisted that the city's future continued to lie with the speculative-electronic economy and pointed to his 1995 budget message affirming that New York's "special economic genius is to be the nation's business and financial headquarters, with a vast number of white-collar jobs for which skill and talent requirements have been increasing." Tax breaks would subsidize this world city, and planned shrinkage was the mayor's vision for neighborhood New York.[35]

[9]

Assaults on the Quality of Life

At the heart of neighborhood politics in Elmhurst-Corona was "quality of life," a phrase I heard repeatedly. It was used as an adjective ("a quality-of-life problem"), a noun, and even an exclamation in the midst of debate ("Quality of life!"). The most succinct definition I heard was offered during a 1993 Community Board 4 meeting by Angie LaChapelle: "Quality of life—the problems that are important to us."

As I listened during CB4, district cabinet, and civic association meetings, and at marches and rallies, the quality-of-life issues mentioned most frequently were school crowding, housing code violations, drug sales, lack of youth recreation facilities, and dissatisfaction with police response.[1] These and other "quality-of-life" problems that were "important to us," problems resulting from the 1975 fiscal crisis, were intensified by continuing mayoral budget cuts.

Subway Crowding

Despite fare increases and service reductions, Elmhurst-Corona residents' daily subway ridership rose 13 percent and reached 35,500 during the 1980s, and continued to grow in the 1990s. Riders from neighboring community districts also used CD4's stations, as did the eastern Queens and Nassau County commuters who left their cars in the 1,100-space municipal parking lot near the Woodhaven Boulevard IND station. By 1992, 108,000 daily riders were entering the nine Elmhurst-Corona subway stations, five of which ranked among the ten busiest of the seventy-nine stations in Queens.[2]

Riders were affected by two major bottlenecks. The first was at Woodhaven Boulevard, where 15,000 fare-payers entered each weekday. This long, underground station provided just one entrance for Lefrak City and other apartment zone residents, plus the municipal parking lot commuters. During rush hours its two-abreast entry staircase and narrow platform were tightly packed. In 1991 the Transit Authority closed an exit at the opposite end of the station, and the situation worsened. Edna Baskin, head of Concerned Community Adults in Lefrak City, began a series of protest demonstrations with support from district manager Rose Rothschild. After several meetings, the Transit Authority agreed in 1993 to a $6 million renovation to reduce crowding and refurbish this dingy station.

The second bottleneck was at the 74th Street station, were staircases and (frequently inoperative) escalators connected the underground IND and the elevated IRT. The IND's E and F express lines passing through this station afforded faster service to Manhattan than local IND trains, and a greater range of destinations than the IRT. Thus, thousands of riders transferring to IND expresses joined 28,000 passengers who entered at this station, giving 74th Street the most severely crowded morning rush hour platforms in the entire system. In 1988 nine "passenger controllers" began "assisting" riders onto E and F trains. (Only one other station, also in Queens, had morning passenger controllers; two Manhattan stations had them at evening rush hour.) By the time E and F trains left Queens, they were a third more crowded than those of any other line entering the Manhattan core.[3]

In 1983 the Transit Authority presented Queens community boards with five options for expanding subway service. Only one would benefit Elmhurst-Corona riders: a plan to connect the IND to a new East River tunnel and thus schedule fifteen more trains per hour. (The existing E and F tunnel was already carrying its maximum of thirty trains per hour.) For a decade nothing happened, though the Newtown Civic Association pressured elected officials, met with subway executives, protested service cuts, and clocked performance time; in 1989 it surveyed one hundred daily riders who described subway conditions as "dehumanizing" and "outrageous." But not until 1994 did construction of the $645 million tunnel connection begin, with completion scheduled for 2001.[4]

Parking

By 1990 Elmhurst-Corona residents owned 5,000 more cars than in 1980.The increased number of infill houses with on-site parking for only two-thirds of their dwelling units not only added to street parking but also reduced existing street space as their driveways cut through curbs. Parking congestion on Sundays was exacerbated by the proliferation of new houses of worship.

Trucks and vans compounded the problem. Parking a commercial vehicle on a residential street for more than three hours violated the traffic code but was commonplace by the 1980s. In 1984 CB4 member Tom McKenzie cited five delivery trucks parked each night on one Elmhurst street. "No tickets. They sweep their garbage out onto the street." In 1989 McKenzie reported "two eighteen-wheeler trailer trucks from Brattleboro, Vermont, parked overnight in a Queens Boulevard bus stop, with their refrigeration compressor grinding all night." Police from the 110th Precinct insisted that thousands of summonses were issued each year, but the problem continued. (Before writing a summons an officer had to observe the illegally parked vehicle twice within a three-hour interval.) Some offenders, like one van owner with twenty-four citations in a single year, merely paid the fines; out-of-state vehicles ignored them.

Radio cars also competed for street space as they parked or waited near their bases on residential streets. Dozens of livery companies were operating in CD4 by the mid-1980s, serving the 23,000 Elmhurst-Corona households owning no automobile. Legally they could respond only to telephone calls, but in practice they cruised for street hails and massed in triple-parked ranks at subway exits and in front of Macy's and the Queens Center mall. In 1987, when the city's car services were required to register with the Taxi and Limousine Commission, there were 40,000 livery cars (compared with 11,000 yellow cabs). Some radio cars also ferried prostitutes, drugs, and drug money. District manager Rose Rothschild and 110th Precinct officers testified against two companies whose drivers had been arrested on these counts, and local suspicions about car services were reinforced in 1994 when police found $150,000 in cash in a livery car in Jackson Heights. By the 1990s there were forty-two licensed bases in CD4, each with a minimum of ten cars, and still others operating illegally from unlicensed bases.

As the parking crunch worsened in CD4, alternate-side-of-the-street parking compliance diminished, and garbage collection and street cleaning became more time consuming and less effective. Some frustrated livery drivers and parkers removed "No Standing" and "No Parking" signs; still other signs were faded, a problem all over New York City, and parkers ignored them, knowing that a photograph of an unreadable sign would void a summons. By 1987 sign replacement was two years behind schedule, and with Department of Transportation cuts under Mayor Dinkins, signage staff in Queens fell from twelve to six. By 1992 it was official policy to replace only missing "Stop" and "One Way" signs. "They have a warehouse full of signs—we were on a tour," Rose Rothschild informed a 1992 district cabinet meeting, "but they don't have the people."[5]

Auto Repairs and Chop Shops

With more cars, auto service and repair businesses increased in CD4, numbering 118 by 1986. Illegal repair activities also grew, including work done openly on the street (a finable offense) and in shops in residential locations (a zoning violation). As police and inspector numbers fell, the situation intensified. CB4 members complained about street congestion and grease and oil on sidewalks and in catch basins. On one corner, Don Mallozzi reported, "they are tearing cars apart, leaving parts on the street. Nothing is being done. People in our community are sick and tired."

Abandoned cars on Elmhurst-Corona streets added to these problems. In 1985 the Newtown Civic Association called for speedier Sanitation Department tagging and removal, but four years later it found that the interval between reporting and removal had lengthened from two or three days to four or five. Locations for repeated abandonments included a supermarket parking lot and a dead-end street in Elmhurst, and the grounds of IS61 in Corona. By the summer of 1994 removals of abandoned cars in CD4 averaged fifty-five per month—most of them stolen vehicles divested of salable parts.

Between 1975 and 1990 New York City's car-theft rate doubled, rising to 146,000 vehicles in 1990, or one for every fifty residents. By 1984 "grand larceny auto" was the most common 911 complaint at the 110th Precinct. In 1988 CB4 member Judy D'Andrea's car was stolen in broad daylight, and member Delores Rizzutto's while she attended the CB4 Christmas party. Rose Rothschild told the district cabinet in 1989 that the Baxter-Roosevelt section was "worse than ever. A woman left a car for ten minutes and it was dismantled." A prime location for auto thieves was the municipal parking lot near the Queens Center mall. "The pros—they steal cars!—are in and out in fifteen seconds," 110th Precinct's Sergeant Pete Petrone explained at a 1992 district cabinet meeting. "They know the cars to go to."

New York's auto-theft profile also changed during the 1980s. Bill Richards of the NYPD auto crime division told CB4 in 1994 that "joy rides" now accounted for only 5 percent of stolen cars. Thefts for parts accounted for 55 percent, and owner-arranged insurance fraud for another 25 percent. "Tag jobs" constituted the remaining 15 percent: in these thefts, top-line models were stolen, their VIN (Vehicle Identification Number) plates replaced with those from junked cars, and the vehicles sold or exported. Tag-job thieves were an elite corps tied to organized crime. Parts thieves, the grunts of the auto-theft army, stole "front ends, windows, trunk lids, computers, etc.," Officer Richards explained, "and sell for $20 or $40 to a chop shop. There are about ten to fifteen thieves per chop shop." These shops, some of which also bought junked cars legally to sell for replacement parts, maintained a telephone network over which information about parts needed or for sale was exchanged.

In 1985 a twenty-seven-person auto-theft ring operating three legal body shops and six illegal chop shops was busted by the auto crime division; responsible for 2,000 thefts and worth $20 million per year, it was headquartered at a Corona auto salvage business which was raided again in 1995. Due to VIN plating of all new cars after 1987 and to increased police numbers after 1990, auto thefts began to decline and had fallen to 68,000 by 1995. In Elmhurst-Corona, auto thefts dropped from 3,000 in 1991 to 1,500 in 1995.[6]

Housing Code Violations

In 1983, at the request of Newtown Civic Association president Miriam Levenson, district manager John Rowan convened a meeting on illegal housing units, attended by city agency representatives and elected officials. The immediate concern was "slapdash" conversions in one- and two-family homes. Plywood room partitions, basement and garage units, and self-installed water, sewage, and electrical connections created dangerous, overcrowded conditions. "Greedy or unscrupulous landlords find renters with the complicity of the real estate community," Rowan explained. A recent fire in one such Elmhurst house uncovered "eight tenants, including two . . . in a six-by-six-foot attic room."

The illegal conversion problem was distinct from the practice of both tenants and homeowners who rented rooms to lodgers (*bordantes* in Spanish). Hsiang-shui Chen discovered Chinese tenants who sublet bedrooms or living rooms, sometimes telling landlords the new residents were relatives. Milagros Ricourt learned that Latin Americans frequently saved rooms for arriving kin or friends, or asked neighborhood, church, and workplace acquaintances if they knew of available rooms. Ricourt herself rented a room in a house owned by a Dominican woman, and Kyeyoung Park rented an apartment room from a Korean tenant family.[7] Many immigrants did not realize that this was against the law, and to Elmhurst-Corona civic activists it was not as serious a problem as illegal building alterations.

Housing code violations flourished in CD4 during the 1980s and 1990s. At a 1984 CB4 public hearing an Elmhurst resident related that the owner of a three-unit building on his block had secretly installed two cellar units and thus was renting to five families. In 1987 CB4 member Don Mallozzi cited a Corona street where "they are building two three-family houses and putting in plywood dividers for separate rooms that you can see from the window." Even more openly, a mimeographed flyer discovered by Tom McKenzie described "a $256,000 home for sale in Elmhurst. It advertised more than $4,000 monthly rental income from units in the basement, the first floor, four rooms on the second floor, and the attic, or seven rental units . . . in a legal two-family detached home." "In our area," New Elmhurst Civic League (NECL) leader Linda Walsh told CB4 in 1991, "every one-family [home] sold is converted to two or three families. The garage goes, street parking gets worse, a wall is put in, and they rent it out."

The dangers of faulty electric wiring and a lack of fire exits in illegally converted homes became all too evident in 1989 when Kamaljit and Harjinder Kaur, the eleven- and four-year-old daughters of a Corona Indian immigrant, were killed in a fire. Their "legal three" building was occupied by twenty-two people, and the fire had started in an illegal basement factory. In 1987 the owner had received citations for its illegal conversion and lack of smoke detectors, but these violations had not been corrected.

The homelessness crisis of the 1980s produced a citywide slowdown of code enforcement. In 1984 the director of Elmhurst-Corona's Neighborhood Preservation Program (NPP) told CB4 that even in buildings with violations, evictions were "something we cannot do with the Mayor's concentration on housing the homeless." In 1987 Don Mallozzi said bluntly, "The man higher up ["The Mayor!" Norma Cirino interjected] does not want to stop [illegal conversions] because if people didn't live there, they'd be on the street." When the topic arose again in 1991, Lucy Schilero declared, "The city doesn't want to move. They won't do anything. But at least make it safe."

Issues of divided agency jurisdiction and denial of access to private homes compounded the problem. The NPP offered owners rehabilitation loans to correct code violations in both private homes and multiple dwellings, but its inspectors could freely enter only buildings of five or more units. A citywide Department of Housing Preservation and Development (HPD) "cellar-to-roof" inspection program came to CD4 in 1986; five hundred multiple-dwelling buildings (including Lefrak City) were inspected, and owners of more than half of them signed agreements to correct violations.

In buildings of fewer than five units, which included most illegally converted rooming houses, inspectors could enter only with the owner's permission or a court warrant issued in response to a tenant complaint. HPD inspections concerned safety and habitability; Buildings Department inspections covered zoning code compliance. Both the NPP and CB4 referred suspected structural violations in these smaller buildings to the Buildings Department. Few actual inspections resulted, however, and where violations were found, reinspections did not occur promptly—as the death of the Kaur sisters indicated.

Only seven Buildings Department inspectors served all of Queens in 1994, down from forty-two in 1975; they also certified zoning code compliance at construction and building alteration sites, and for owners making sales or applying for loans. As state assembly member Helen Marshall put it, "Code enforcement is only a skeleton of what it should be." Even worse, twenty-six Buildings Department inspectors and supervisors, nearly half the citywide enforcement staff, were convicted in 1992 of extorting payments from owners of buildings with violations, including some in Elmhurst-Corona.[8]

During the late 1980s the Fire Department's 46th Battalion became the de facto agency combatting illegal conversions in CD4. As the number of fires in Elmhurst-Corona increased over that decade, so did firefighter discoveries of illegal units in one- and two-family homes, and these were reported to the Buildings Department with little effect. In 1986 Rose Rothschild began reporting illegal conversion locations directly to the 46th Battalion. Fire marshals could inspect any building considered a potential fire hazard, and although they could not enforce the zoning or habitability laws, they could issue a "vacate" order for overcrowding and were required to reinspect before lifting the order. A 46th Battalion chief told the district cabinet in 1989, "If a one-family is broken into two units, that's not bad. But if units are also in the cellar, and rooms are divided into cubicles, that's dangerous. Cellar occupancy is the worst." Rothschild added, "A man who got a vacate [order] made four cubicles in a room, with two [persons] in each cubicle. They pay $200 per week for cubicles. They're not cheap."

With Koch's budget cuts, however, Fire Department building inspections fell 19 percent between 1987 and 1989, and under Dinkins the Queens fire marshal office was closed in 1992. That year a 46th Battalion chief told the district cabinet, "We're down to 200 fire marshals for all of New York City. We had a cellar fire [in Elmhurst] yesterday, and it took the marshal one and a half hours to arrive from the Bronx." In 1991 routine HPD and Buildings Department inspections in larger buildings were eliminated, and by 1996 the number of inspectors had dropped citywide from 460 to 162 at HPD (there had been 800 before 1975), and from 95 to 47 in the Buildings Department.

In her 1993 "District Needs" report Rose Rothschild called for coordination between the Fire Department and "other city agencies to combat the rise of illegal conversions, illegal occupancies in multiple and private dwellings . . . and sweat shops. Fire Department personnel seem to be the only ones able to gain access and vacate the dangerous situations." In 1995, with CB4 prodding, an informal "buildings task force" of Fire, Police, Sanitation, and Buildings Department personnel was working one day each month to coordinate inspections, summonses, and fines at suspicious Elmhurst-Corona locations.[9]

Sewing Shop Abuses

At the February 1985 CB4 meeting, Norma Cirino called attention to a *U.S. News and World Report* story about the return of sweatshops. "The worst sweatshops are in Corona. One had a dirt floor and was located in a basement." At the May meeting Rose Rothschild held up the story and stated, "Now we become . . . the sweatshop capital of the world. Some sweatshops use secret openings through barber shops and karate shops. We should be applying ourselves. It gives our area a bad name."

"Some [shops] are legal," Judy D'Andrea continued, "but not those in an apartment house." Al Fernicola added, "People are using industrial sewing machines doing homework in apartments. The Labor Department must get on it. There are dozens in apartments." John Rowan concluded the discussion: "If anyone has a location, bring it in. Places [like storefronts and garages] are sealed up, or look like something else. We'll have them investigated. Apartments are very difficult—the Department of Labor doesn't have the authority to open up doors. In apartments, tenants have to complain."

Rosalia Almonte, a thirty-five-year-old Dominican immigrant, arrived in Corona in 1986. Knowing no English and afraid to travel beyond walking distance, she found a job at a sewing shop two blocks from her home. It was owned by a Cuban and Ecuadorian couple and located in the living room of a private home. Mrs. Almonte sewed sleeves, seams, and buttons, earning at most $130 for a forty-five-hour week—less than minimum wage. Within a few months she was laid off but discovered several more apparel firms in Corona employing Latin American and Asian women. She chose a small shop where she did piecework for $70 to $90 per week and could work less than a full day. By the end of eleven months in New York she was ready to travel by subway to better-paying factory work in Manhattan.[10]

Some Corona sewing shops had the firm's name on windows and door. Others had nameless, graffiti-covered windowgates and doors left open only on hot summer days, then providing glimpses of rows of women working at sewing machines under fluorescent lights. Still others were revealed only when garage doors were opened, drapes drawn back or blinds raised in private homes, or when garment racks were moved in and out of residential buildings.

During the 1980s and early 1990s New York City garment industry employment fell officially from 139,000 to 94,000, but sewing shops increased from 4,000 to 6,000—2,000 of them unlicensed—mostly in Brooklyn and Queens. Workplaces became more dispersed, a result of the outward push from Manhattan's garment center where tax incentives and zoning favors flowed to office towers, land prices soared, landlords shortened leases and increased rents, and shops closed or moved to Chinatown and the outer boroughs.[11]

A federal General Accounting Office study in 1989 concluded that two-thirds of the city's apparel firms were "sweatshops" that violated safety or minimum-wage laws; in addition, hundreds of children worked in New York garment shops, and at least 20,000 women did homework on sewing and knitting machines—a practice illegal since 1935. Underpinning these abuses was a freer "free market." Cuts in the city's Buildings and Fire Department inspection force meant reduced pressure to comply with zoning and safety regulations. Reagan-era cuts also decreased the number of federal wage-and-hour and safety inspectors; by 1996 there were only 800 nationwide. And New York State's Labor Standards Enforcement Unit, the most active government agency, dropped from sixty-nine staff members in the 1970s to twenty-four in the 1980s, and stood at twenty-eight in 1996.[12]

Illegal Dumping

For residents of CD4's cramped illegal units, storage of garbage over even a few days was unpleasant; landlords, moreover, did not want to advertise overoccupancy with masses of garbage. As a consequence, bags of household garbage were deposited in overflowing park trashbaskets or on streets or in front of stores. "We're living in a mountain of garbage," an exasperated Rose Rothschild stated in 1987.

Since New York City requires businesses to pay for private waste disposal (city trucks remove only residential garbage), some of this "mountain" was also commercial garbage (packing boxes, unsold stock, paperwork); when the business of origin could be determined, Parks Department workers "returned" it. The problem worsened when the city doubled its "tipping fee" at the Fresh Kills landfill in 1988, and private carters in turn raised their prices. By 1989 some stores had dropped private carting service to economize, and illegal dumping in CD4 was on the increase. Then in 1991 the Department of Health pest control unit was cut to nineteen people serving the entire city. Rat infestation at dump sites grew, and complaints inundated CB4. By 1994 there were rats in Corona's William Moore Park.

Several locations became targets for large-scale dumping of commercial and industrial refuse, auto parts, and discarded household items. "We picked up 100 tires on 45th Avenue," Sanitation Department supervisor Phil Pirozzi reported at a 1988 district cabinet meeting, "and there was another bunch of tires dumped while we were away to get another truck." Other "drops" included the vacant Corona high school site and areas next to Conrail and Long Island Rail Road tracks. Residents complained, and Rose Rothschild pressed the LIRR to clean its corridors and prune vegetation, noting that LIRR sidings in Nassau County were well maintained.

City sanitation workers removed tons of garbage from these locations, but removals diminished when the number of workers assigned to clean illegal dump sites fell from seventy-nine in 1991 to nineteen in 1994; the situation became so overwhelming that the Giuliani administration later restored twelve workers. In 1995 I inspected the Conrail siding at the northwest corner of Elmhurst. A fence on the adjacent street was broken, and the thirty-foot slope down to the track was covered with doors, rugs, construction materials, tires, produce boxes, and other waste. CD4's Sanitation Department supervisor was convinced that some dumping on railroad sidings was done by private carters. Because much of this business was controlled by organized crime groups, however, residents who observed surreptitious dumping were afraid to sign the affidavits needed for legal action.[13]

Gambling

One did not have to look far to see the attractions of gambling in Elmhurst-Corona. St. Adalbert's Church in South Elmhurst had a large sign announcing "BINGO Every Wed. 7:30 p.m. Air-conditioned." The Off-Track Betting parlor at the 74th Street subway arcade drew a diverse white, black, Latin American, and South and East Asian male crowd. At four social clubs in Corona Heights elderly Italian American men played cards, as did Italian immigrants and other men on concrete chess tables in William Moore Park. Bus tickets to Atlantic City were sold at newsstands and travel agencies throughout CD4. Advertisements in Chinese newpapers listed Hong Kong and Taiwan entertainers at Atlantic City casinos, where Chinese blackjack and poker players accounted for 10 percent of the clientele.[14]

More hidden gambling also occurred. Corona residents told me that the storefront with reflecting-glass windows opposite William Moore Park was a card parlor. White and black CB4 members mentioned a coin laundry and two fast-food shops opposite Lefrak City where numbers bets were taken. I observed sports betting at a pizzeria. All these forms of gambling were ubiquitous throughout neighborhood New York.[15]

In 1987 an illegal casino over a tailor shop facing William Moore Park was closed by the Queens district attorney. Run by members of the Lucchese crime family, its blackjack and craps tables had been open four nights a week as part of a $1-million-a-year operation. Thirty customers holding $30,000 in cash were let go, and sixteen employees arrested. In 1990 police raided a $4-million-a-year bookie parlor on the opposite side of William Moore Park. Located in a building rented by a Lucchese member, it "mostly catered to neighborhood people. Everybody knew everybody," a police captain said. Two roof-top satellite dishes tuned to racetrack broadcasts were confiscated and four employees arrested, including one Corona Heights man.[16]

Neither of those organized-crime operations had disrupted neighborhood life to the point of quality-of-life complaint. This was not the case with a Genovese crime family's blackjack and slot-machine casino in Elmhurst, worth $3.6 million a year, which was raided in 1989. Five employees were arrested, and slot machines were smashed; customers, including one East Asian man, were released. This basement operation beneath a row of stores faced Elmhurst Memorial Park; nearby residents, who had received leaflets and business cards advertising its location, were disturbed by nighttime traffic. "We don't need that type of thing here," said Jorge Ocasio. Betty Ross, another resident, explained, "We have children here. You know there's going to be problems when you have gambling like that. How far behind will the shooting be when someone gets cheated?"[17]

Gambling was a major profit center for New York's five "Mafia" crime groups: the Bonanno, Colombo, Gambino, Genovese, and Lucchese families—or, as some white Corona residents referred to them, "you know, the *men.*" Their other cash-generating activities during the 1980s and 1990s included automobile and cargo theft, private waste carting, loading activities in the garment industry and at the city's produce and fish markets, labor union and construction industry rackets, loan sharking at interest rates of 150 percent or more, and heroin importation and distribution. They also operated legitimate businesses through which illegally acquired cash was laundered.[18]

Physical force and interpersonal intimidation came from "made men": the soldiers (*soldato*) and captains (*capo*) who formed "crews" (*regime*) to carry out various operations and shared profits with the bosses heading each family. These men were of Italian ancestry, but non-Italian "associates" participated in their enterprises, and lower-level employees included non-Italians as well. Arrested at gambling locations in CD4 were persons with Italian, Irish, Polish, and Spanish surnames, and three East Asians were visible in television coverage of the Corona casino bust.[19]

Estimates of the number of made men varied from 870 in 1983 (including 110 in the Lucchese and 200 in the Genovese group) to 700 in 1996; associates were estimated at four to ten times as many. Arrests and convictions of upper-level leaders during the 1980s and 1990s depleted the five groups, and prosecutors hailed the "decline" and "toppling" of the Mafia. But as investigative reporter William Bastone put it, "While bosses may be at the top of those nifty FBI flowcharts, the Mafia's real power comes from the ground up." New leaders arose, and day-to-day illegal activities persisted.[20]

The pervasiveness of "Joker Poker" and other illegal video gambling machines in neighborhood New York made this clear. In 1984 Norma Cirino told CB4, "Two weeks ago I saw a slot machine in a grocery store. This wasn't a video *game*, but a real slot machine. I called the police." At the next meeting she added, "[When you win,] you get the money from the [store] owner, not from the machine." Reports followed of video gambling machines at a Corona Heights bodega, which also sold beer to minors.

Hsiang-shui Chen learned about video gambling from the Chinese owner of a candy store in Elmhurst.

> In August 1984, a "Joker Poker" machine was installed. Mr. Lou said that the owner of the machine had come to talk about installing it six months earlier, but they were afraid because it was illegal and they might be fined if they agreed to install it. But the video-game store next door had installed one, and nothing had happened over six months. . . . "Joker Poker" profit was shared fifty-fifty: Mr. Lou and the owner each took half after players' winnings were deducted. . . . This business grew as more and more people learned that there was a poker machine in the store. According to his calculation, Mr. Lou received a monthly average of $1,750 over ten months from the poker machine.[21]

I played Joker Poker at this store in 1985. For twenty-five cents I drew a "hand" of five cards; I could exchange this for a new hand, or draw from one to three "face down" cards. The machine listed the number of points (actually quarters) for winning hands, ranging from three of a kind to a royal flush. (I didn't win anything.) Mr. Lou told Chen that one man had played between 800 and 1,000 quarters the day before.

Joker Poker machines became illegal that year but did not disappear. I spotted one near the entrance to a Dominican restaurant in Corona in 1986, and saw one that had been confiscated by police sitting next to the 110th Precinct booking desk in 1988. Lucchese, Gambino, and Bonanno "sit-downs" were held to divide gambling machine territories, and hundreds of Joker Poker and other machines continued to be seized in neighborhood New York bars, pizzerias, beauty parlors, video rental shops, and bodegas over the next decade.[22]

In 1992 an attempted robbery of gambling machine proceeds at an illegal after-hours club in Corona Plaza resulted in open fire between police and three men using Uzi submachine guns. The regular club clientele who came to drink and gamble were Latin Americans, as were the three robbers, one of whom was killed. A Pakistani carpenter, a member of the Masjid al-Falah Islamic community, was taken hostage and killed in the gun battle. Some local residents had patronized the three-year-old club, but others such as José Grullon felt that "every time they open up one of these places, it's trouble for the neighborhood." Two more Corona Plaza residents, both Dominican, were killed in 1994 in an attempted robbery of a baseball-betting operation at a long-distance telephone and money-transfer business. And at another illegal Corona Plaza gambling club, one hundred persons betting on cockfights were arrested in 1995.[23]

Drugs

Street sales of marijuana, cocaine, and other drugs plagued Elmhurst-Corona throughout the 1980s and 1990s. Focused on 57th Avenue in front of Lefrak City and along Roosevelt Avenue, drug trafficking intensified after 1984 when crack, a cheap, smokable form of cocaine, first appeared. Though less visible, cocaine and heroin importation and distribution rings also operated in CD4, and press coverage of large drug seizures was unsettling to residents. So were the drug-related killings which by the late 1980s were threatening uninvolved bystanders.

Marijuana on 57th Avenue

The layout of the six-block 57th Avenue strip facing Lefrak City facilitated the drive-by drug trade that existed there from at least 1971. Three-way traffic connections at each end afforded convenient coming and going. Dealers congregated at the center of the strip in a supermarket parking lot—shunned by customers—from which they approached passing cars; on rainy days, they did business under a beach umbrella. Another sales location a block away, a secluded street ending in a circular roundabout, allowed drivers to exit off 57th Avenue, make drug purchases, turn around, and drive away. When police were sighted, dealers escaped into Lefrak City's underground parking garage, or through street-level and basement doors in the Sherwood Village rental buildings. Three walk-in telephone booths were monopolized by dealers until residents and CB4 pressured the telephone company to replace them with wall phones. Drugs were stashed in cars or inside buildings, including a Sherwood Village laundry room that residents avoided after 4:00 p.m.; they were carried in amounts smaller than felony quantity, or in larger amounts by youths under age sixteen.

Marijuana was the main attraction on 57th Avenue. Sellers were black, both Jamaican (some with dreadlocks and outsized hats) and African American. "All the buyers are white," Sergeant Pete Petrone told the 110th Precinct Community Council in 1985. "Buyers come from all over, including Washington, D.C., Westchester [County], Connecticut." White local residents, among them CB4 members Pat Carpentiere and Rose Rothschild, were approached by drug sellers when they drove by, but so was state assembly member Helen Marshall and her husband, both African American. She told CB4 in 1987 that buyers were from "Lefrak City, New Jersey, other areas too. It's very middle-class people, non-blacks in cars, [and] every hue under the sun." On an evening in 1987 Steven Gregory and I witnessed sales to two scruffy young white men, a casually dressed Korean man, and a young, well-dressed black male professional.

Several block-watcher residents, including one man whose son had been a crack addict, regularly surveyed the 57th Avenue drug scene. They knew dealers by sight, recorded buyers' license numbers, and called the employers of purchasers who were driving company vehicles. They were particularly angered by pot sales through bus windows to school children. Ken Daniels, a Lefrak City resident and CB4 member who provided police with block-watcher intelligence, was also known to dealers, and in 1984 his car was set on fire in retaliation.

In 1985 two drive-by shootings between drug-selling groups occurred on 57th Avenue, and four addicts died from heroin overdoses in Lefrak City stairwells. By 1987, as a Sherwood Village resident put it, "The tenants want it cleaned up. We can't have company over, it's so bad." In 1989 three bystanders were hit when two drug sellers, both living in Lefrak City, were gunned down in front of a phone booth by Uzi-wielding competitors; many residents also understood that some youths' colored bandanas signaled which drug they were selling. By the early 1990s four "crews" shared the trade, selling drugs both on 57th Avenue and in Lefrak City apartments. Anti-drug marches and meetings were organized repeatedly by Lefrak area residents, politicians, CB4, and the police.

Uniformed police could not make arrests, a 110th Precinct officer explained to CB4 in 1984, because judges did not believe that dealers would conduct business in their presence. Only arrests by undercover narcotics division cops would stick, and few were assigned to the Lefrak area. In 1985 the precinct's plainclothes officers were authorized to make drug arrests, and numbers climbed to more than two hundred in 1987. The 110th also began "Operation Neighborhood," an increased uniformed presence on 57th Avenue, including scooter- and horse-mounted officers. When this program slackened in 1987, dealers returned, and residents concluded that only a visible police presence would diminish street selling. Some Lefrak residents, however, were glad to see Operation Neighborhood go; as member Richard Isles told CB4, "We got cops harassing local residents. It backfired."

By then, crack was on the rise, and much drug selling moved indoors. Sergeant Petrone told a Lefrak City community meeting in 1987 that soon after police discovered a drug stash in a twelfth-floor apartment, a hand-lettered sign appeared reading "Crack house bust. To 7th floor." A major undercover investigation led to a sweep by three hundred police officers in 1996; twenty-four dealers were arrested, ending their estimated $4.4 million annual marijuana and cocaine business.[24]

Cocaine on Roosevelt Avenue

Elsewhere in CD4, drug use by white Corona Heights youth in William Moore Park during the 1970s ended after a 1979 park renovation. But drug traffic was reported from the 1970s through the 1990s in Linden Park in Corona, and in Clement Clarke Moore Park and near the 90th Street IRT station in Elmhurst. In 1984 Don Mallozzi told CB4 that "at 2:00 to 4:00 p.m." he saw "a car with two women and two men with needles" near his Elmhurst home. The following year Lou Simeone described drug activity in Corona Plaza: "At night cars are coming in. I observed this last night around 10:00 p.m. There were New Jersey plates. They are shooting up right in the hallways of buildings. There was a white college kid shooting up. I chased him off."

These were probably observations of heroin use, but after 1984 it was the crack epidemic that increased local drug selling. Produced from the coca plant grown in Peru and Bolivia and imported via Colombia, cocaine was an expensive "champagne drug" during the 1970s. When the highly addictive derivative called crack appeared, prices came down, and the market expanded.[25] In Elmhurst-Corona, Roosevelt Avenue became a retail market for crack, cocaine powder, and bazooka, another smokable form of cocaine. Sales spread along streets near each IRT stop, and by 1990, 80 percent of 110th Precinct drug arrests were for cocaine.

Drug arrests citywide grew from 56,000 in 1984 to 94,000 in 1989. Jails filled, and courts were gridlocked. After a police officer was killed by southeast Queens crack dealers in 1988, a Tactical Narcotics Team descended on the area and made mass arrests. In response to community pressure, TNT came to CD4 in 1989 and returned in 1992; it focused on Roosevelt Avenue and largely ignored the 57th Avenue marijuana scene. In 1990 Police Commissioner Lee Brown decreased the narcotics division and TNT ranks and turned from street arrests to undercover investigation of higher drug-trade levels; arrests fell to 69,000 in 1991. After 1994, however, street-seller incarcerations were again emphasized under Commissioner William Bratton.[26]

At a 1988 meeting of the Coalition of United Residents for a Safer Community, residents of Elmhurst's Baxter-Roosevelt section offered a bird's-eye view of local drug selling.

Older white man: In private homes near Roosevelt Avenue, sellers plant things on the property, in the bushes and under cars. They don't hold the drugs themselves. You can't risk confronting people on your property.

Latin American woman #1: One man runs a drop at 90th Street. He's been described. He never carries drugs. He gives drugs to men in a huddle. We've made many calls. He's there. Stores are involved; they go in there. A fat guy.

Latin American woman #2: Last year, with calls, [my] street was cleaned up for a while. Now it's starting again. Boom!

White woman: A drug pusher urinates against cars. Can he be arrested?

On an Elmhurst street off Roosevelt Avenue in the Broadway-Woodside section, residents took matters into their own hands in 1988 and invited the Guardian Angels youth patrol to board up an empty house where bazooka was sold. Addicts smoked it near the Conrail tracks and then burglarized cars and homes, or engaged in prostitution. "They've broken into my cars three times," said business proprietor Mohammad Shah. "At night there are messengers on every block, complete with beepers," a female resident added. "The gypsy cabs drive up, the rider places their order, and the crack is delivered to the car. I've seen them with guns. I've seen pregnant fourteen- and fifteen-year-olds selling their bodies for crack." Ellie Noviello, whose family had lived in Elmhurst for four generations, complained. "I've had people in my driveway smoking crack and called the police and they never came."[27]

From her Elmhurst home and her Corona office, district manager Rose Rothschild monitored the drug scourge. One dealer was arrested in her building; another operated at a store on her block. In 1987 she learned that "St. John's and Elmhurst [hospitals] are getting cocaine overdoses by the dozens." She was shocked to find drugs sold over the counter at a Roosevelt Avenue delicatessen, "with the milk!" The transformation of her neighborhood disturbed her. "Now Roosevelt Avenue is a sewer. We can't even shop. . . . I saw a young woman yesterday, she couldn't even stand up. . . . Kids see the drug dealers, and the money, and that they get out easily."

Wholesale Cocaine

In 1975 a *Daily News* article identified Elmhurst and Jackson Heights as "probably the major cocaine distribution point for the entire city." Press coverage of drug seizures, murders, and money-laundering over the next two decades reinforced this "drug capital" reputation. All-too-real linkages to Colombian cocaine "cartels" in Medellín and Cali tarnished the image of the mass of law-abiding Colombian immigrants who, with CD4's other Latin American residents, patronized Roosevelt Avenue businesses that were also frequented by drug dealers (*los mágicos*). Colombians, moreover, understood the havoc cocaine brought to their homeland, where politicians, judges, journalists, and ordinary citizens were killed at the order of drug barons.[28]

Colombian cocaine importers and wholesalers first arrived in Elmhurst in the 1970s and blended in among Colombian immigrants. In 1982 Newtown High School teacher Thomas Tilitz noted, "This underworld activity is largely invisible and has had no effect on the average person residing in the neighborhood." But between the late 1970s and early 1980s annual cocaine imports to the United States were estimated to have grown from twenty to eighty tons; by 1986 the figure was 150 tons, and in 1994 just one Cali "cell" operating in Queens distributed one to five tons of cocaine *per month.* Profits were enormous. In 1983 a kilogram (2.2 pounds) of coca paste cost Colombian traders $350; a kilogram of refined cocaine brought into the United States was worth $30,000 to importers and six times that much in retail street sales. Wholesale prices fluctuated with supply in the late 1980s and 1990s and fell to a low of $13,000 a kilo in 1996.[29]

Medellín and Cali refiner-exporter groups were in daily telephone contact with U.S. operatives who received the cocaine and sold it to distributors. Medellín dealers had controlled most of the Elmhurst–Jackson Heights trade through the 1970s but increasingly focused on their operations in Miami and Los Angeles; by the time their Queens lieutenant was arrested in 1983, the Medellín role in New York had diminished. Cali honcho José Santacruz first visited New York in 1977, frequenting Roosevelt Avenue nightclubs, and by the early 1980s Cali-based importers dominated the Queens drug business.

More than 130 drug-related murders occurred in Queens between 1984 and 1996. The growth of crack profits intensified conflict between Medellín and Cali groups in Colombia, and this spread to Queens as Medellín exporters attempted to regain their share in the New York market, worth an estimated $10 billion by 1986. In addition, cartel leaders (*los grandes mafiosos*) sent gunmen to New York, youths who used intimidation and force to make creditors pay and were assigned to kill those who did not. With key Medellín leaders arrested in the United States in 1987 and killed in Colombia in 1993, by the 1990s Cali operatives in Queens controlled 80 percent of the New York cocaine business. In 1992 Cuban investigative journalist Manuel de Dios was murdered in an Elmhurst Argentinian restaurant on orders from José Santacruz in Cali; his offense was a series of articles about the Queens-Cali drug connection. The arrest in 1995 of top Cali leaders in Colombia led to rising cocaine prices that year and yet another round of violence in Queens. Santacruz himself was killed by police in Colombia in 1996.[30]

During the 1970s cocaine first arrived in Queens inside Colombian human "mules" who ingested sealed condoms containing the drug. As the U.S. market grew, staging sites in Central America and the Caribbean were established for airflights across the U.S. border, and for seacraft which landed illegally or were met by boat offshore. Cocaine was also smuggled in air and sea cargo, on cruise ships, by airline personnel, and in trucks across the Mexican border. Once it arrived in East Coast, Florida, or California locations, it was transported to Queens. Importers stashed cocaine in Queens and Long Island safehouses (*caletas*) obtained through Roosevelt Avenue real estate agents. Tons of cocaine were seized by law enforcement teams in most Queens neighborhoods, including Elmhurst (80 pounds in 1991) and Corona (500 pounds in 1986; 230 pounds in 1992; 1.6 tons in 1997).[31]

Cocaine dealers also utilized Roosevelt Avenue long-distance telephone parlors, car services, and travel agencies to transfer money internationally. Federal law prohibited moving amounts of more than $10,000 out of the country without registration, and banks had to report all cash transactions of $10,000 or more and, after 1990, keep records of cash purchases of money orders or cashier's checks exceeding $3,000. In New York State, licensed international currency-transfer businesses had to report transactions of $3,000 or more. Drug dealers responded by colluding with compliant businesses and money-wiring firms in Queens to "smurf," or illegally bundle, cash transactions into amounts of less than either $10,000 or $3,000. One Roosevelt Avenue business, Ecuadorian-owned Delgado Travel, was charged with smurfing $260 million for Colombian drug dealers between 1985 and 1990; in 1991 it forfeited $1 million to U.S. agents and was fined $50,000 by New York State.[32]

While the top level of the cocaine trade was Colombian, importing and distribution cells included white Americans, Chinese, and other Latin Americans. At each of the two or more distribution levels leading to street sales, ethnic diversity increased, involving Dominicans, Jamaicans, white Lucchese, Genovese, and Gambino operatives, and others. In 1990 Colombians accounted for only twenty-one of three hundred Elmhurst-Jackson Heights drug arrests. Violence over unpaid accounts and drug-selling turf occurred among lower-level distributors as well and spilled into CD4 streets. In 1988 a sixty-one-year-old white American woman was killed in Corona Heights during a shootout involving Chinese and Latin American drug dealers.[33]

The Return of Heroin

Heroin importation from southeast Asia to New York was dominated by white American and Sicilian criminal groups until the 1980s. In 1985 the arrest of a Corona Indian restaurateur with thirteen pounds of heroin, and the seizure of twenty-two pounds at Little India of Queens—an Elmhurst spice and grocery shop—signaled a shift to Asian importers. By 1987 heroin seizures from New York Chinese importers—one of whom was an Elmhurst resident—had netted 1,000 pounds, worth $1 billion in street sales. Pound for pound, heroin was worth ten times as much as cocaine.

The Chinese sold heroin into the same multiethnic distribution networks that cocaine entered. In 1987, for example, federal agents raided the stash of lower-level Dominican dealers in Corona and discovered heroin packets wrapped in

Chinese newspapers. In 1989 police arrested heroin importer Peter Woo at his Corona home and seized 820 pounds, the largest single heroin bust since the 200-pound "French Connection" in 1971. Two Thai sisters who received heroin shipments from their homeland were also arrested in 1989; they operated an Elmhurst warehouse from which the drug was distributed to Chinatown dealers.

By the early 1990s the Lucchese crime group had established its own import links for Asian heroin. More ominously, South American poppy production was rising, and on arrest rosters at Queens airports Colombians carrying packets of heroin were increasingly joining the Nigerians who transported Asian heroin. In 1996 the twelve members of a Colombian heroin distribution gang based in Corona were arrested. Two-thirds of heroin seized was by now of Colombian origin, and heroin was rivaling crack in popularity on U.S. streets.[34]

Prostitution

Both streetwalkers and bordellos appeared in CD4 during the 1970s. In 1976 two dozen male transvestite street prostitutes were arrested on Roosevelt Avenue near the 74th Street subway arcade, a location where this activity continued into the 1990s. That same year a "massage parlor" opened on Roosevelt Avenue, but female prostitution arrests quickly resulted in its closure. In 1978 Mayor Koch created an Office of Midtown Enforcement (OME) to close down indoor prostitution in Manhattan; in 1984, when City Planning Commissioner Martin Gallent told CB4 that the problem was still centered in that borough, he was jeered. "It's more open in Manhattan." "One is next door to me." Since 1982 CB4 had been protesting against the Venus, a Queens Boulevard bordello. The Venus was closed in 1985, but a new phase in the local sex industry was about to begin.

While walking on Broadway in Elmhurst, CB4 member Tony Caminiti was handed a "palm card" advertising "twelve Oriental women" at an Elmhurst address. Later in 1985 the Newtown Civic Association became alarmed over the Honeybee, a Korean massage parlor above an Elmhurst grocery. CB4 learned that the Honeybee, like other sex businesses, advertised in *Screw* magazine; two Columbia journalism students, moreover, tape-recorded offers of sexual services costing from $50 to $100 at the Honeybee. Pressure on elected officials from civic groups and CB4 finally brought the OME to Queens, and it closed the Honeybee in 1986, just before a planned NCA demonstration. The publicity so embarrassed the massage parlor's Korean landlord, an officer in the Korean American Association of Mid-Queens, that he moved out of Elmhurst.

The Elmhurst bordellos discovered in 1985 were among two dozen that opened in western Queens during 1984–1986. The OME had by then reduced the number of midtown Manhattan sex businesses from 120 to 50, but as a Queens police captain put it, "The rents are lower here, there's good access to highways, and there's lots of adequate parking." The Queens bordello prostitutes were mainly Korean, many of them ex-wives of U.S. servicemen and recruited near military bases. Others were Chinese women from Taiwan for whom visas were obtained by massage parlor operators. Although most of these female-run, East Asian bordellos were closed in 1986, new ones continued to open through the 1990s. In 1992 a call-service prostitution ring was busted, and four Chinese and Korean women aged sixteen to eighteen were arrested with their twenty-one-year-old Chinese male pimp; their pickup point was the Elmhurst Burger King restaurant featured in Eddie Murphy's 1988 film *Coming to America.*[35]

These sex businesses served both East Asian and other male customers. Prices at massage parlors were $40 for admission, with sexual services negotiable up to $100; the Burger King call girls charged from $100 to $200. Less expensive Latin American bordellos, with immigrant women providing services mainly for immigrant men, also began to appear in Elmhurst in 1985. By 1992 they included seventy locations over stores and in apartments on and near Roosevelt Avenue in Elmhurst, Corona, and Jackson Heights. Palm cards were distributed by male *chica-chica* touts. In the dingiest places the price was $20 for twenty minutes (kitchen timers were used) with half going to the house and half to the prostitute.

Elmhurst civic activist Lucy Schilero was shocked when three bordellos opened on Junction Boulevard near her home in 1990. "They're beautiful girls, just fourteen or fifteen, from Peru and Bolivia. They say as bad as things are here, they are worse where they come from." In 1991 pressure from CB4 and civic associations resulted in a Queens Anti-Prostitution Task Force organized by the district attorney, Richard Brown. By 1994 seventy-five bordellos were closed, but forty remained, many having reopened in new locations. Civil proceedings against landlords were the preferred enforcement tools, complemented in 1996 by a 110th Precinct "Operation Inside" using undercover female officers to arrest male patrons.[36]

Crack-addicted street prostitutes of various ethnic backgrounds, both female and male, were appearing along Roosevelt Avenue and in Linden Park in Corona by 1987; some charged as little as $5.00. Streetwalkers also worked on Queens Boulevard at the Elmhurst-Woodside border near several "hot sheet" motels ("$25 for four hours, and $5 off if you bring the ad coupon"). Civic groups aroused by massage parlors here in 1986 returned in 1990 with street rallies, traffic stoppages, posters warning of AIDS transmission, and threats to expose "johns" whose license plates they photographed.[37]

Homeless Hotels

Homeless adults in New York's public spaces became commonplace during the 1980s. Though media attention focused on midtown Manhattan, the problem became visible in neighborhood New York as well. One cold November night in 1986 I saw a man sleeping on a bench in an Elmhurst subway station. In 1987 homeless people were living in Linden Park, and by the summer of 1990 as many as eighty were sleeping there on cardboard and grass. In 1994 an "encampment" of the homeless near the Conrail tracks in Elmhurst was dispersed by city outreach workers and the 110th Precinct. Other encampments still existed in parks and in a Long Island Expressway underpass in 1995.

Some of CD4's homeless population were in regular contact with city agency personnel. By 1985 Elmhurst Hospital had homeless persons sleeping in its emergency room, and the hospital's patient advocate told CB4's health committee, "Some people probably live in the lobby. The staff know them." At a 1988 district cabinet meeting a Transit Authority policeman asked, "If we move them, where do we move them to? They're not giving us problems with crime—it's the odor. If you move them to the community, they create more problems." In 1992 another Transit Authority officer told of repeated dealings with two homeless persons in Elmhurst subway stations. "We take them to Elmhurst Hospital, they clean them up, and after two days, they're back." Sergeant Pete Petrone recounted his story of one homeless man: "I've been present when 'Red' has been taken off Broadway twenty-one times to the hospital, and then released. He runs screaming into banks. I once got a standing ovation when I chased him on Broadway."

Homelessness worsened with the loss of 100,000 SRO hotel units during the Koch and Dinkins years, and with rising unemployment and poverty. In addition to single adults there were families who could not afford rent increases or who left the 15,000 housing units that became uninhabitable each year. They arrived at Emergency Assistance Unit (EAU) offices which, if no cash-benefit solution to a rent problem could be found, sent them to city shelters. As these filled up, families were placed in hotels paid for by the city. By 1988 some 15,000 homeless persons were residing in hotels.[38]

One evening after 11:00 P.M. I met an overweight white woman in her late-twenties exiting with two children from the subway in Elmhurst. She asked directions to the Mets Motel, and I pointed west, saying it was a long walk (actually three-quarters of a mile). She said she had no money anyway, picked up her bags, and set off.

Just across the Elmhurst-Woodside border, the Mets ("Special Day Rates—Exotic Adult Movies") housed homeless families between 1983 and 1990. In 1987 it charged the city $910 for a two-week stay and was so profitable that its owner built an eighty-five-room addition. Heating and cleaning were atrocious; one women said she preferred municipal shelters. As chair of CB4's health committee, Rose Rothschild visited the Mets and was appalled at the conditions and costs. "I have nothing against the homeless," she told CB4 in 1986, "but they should go into regular apartments."[39]

To deflect criticism for placing families in hotels like the Mets, in 1987 Mayor Koch proposed building four shelters in Queens, each to house one hundred families waiting to move into renovated city-owned apartments. Borough president Claire Shulman counterproposed one twenty-five-family shelter in each of the fourteen Queens community districts. CB4 rejected the Corona shelter location that Shulman suggested, a site the Corona Taxpayers Association wanted for a library. CB4's debate over shelters, however, revealed more complicated perceptions of homelessness than simple "not in my back yard" resistance.

> *Haydee Zambrana:* We have needs in addition to the homeless—such as schools in our area—for vacant sites here. There are other sites in the city, multifamily buildings. . . .
>
> *Ken Daniels:* It may seem we're selfish saying put it somewhere else, but we oppose everything, even middle-income and luxury housing, because of congestion in CB4.
>
> *Howard Riback:* The homeless have no place to go. The middle class also has no place to go with rents in Manhattan and now in Queens. If we rehab existing units, the middle class will have places, and the homeless will have them too. Now it's only patchwork. . . .
>
> *Judy D'Andrea:* [Koch] wants to sell off the south Bronx and parts of Brooklyn to developers. He must build and rehabilitate housing for the people *there.* The homeless today are not just poor people.
>
> *Don Mallozzi:* They come from welfare.
>
> *Miriam Levenson:* Not all of them. They come looking for jobs in New York City, and some can't find them and become homeless.

The city had secretly opened a temporary shelter for thirteen women in Elmhurst in 1985 and informed CB4 by letter afterward. No objection was raised, and it remained forgotten in a quiet infill building until a new director contacted the district manager in 1989. Rose Rothschild visited the shelter and commended it at the district cabinet meeting. She was also supportive of the Human Resources Administration office in Corona, which in 1987 began a homelessness prevention program, offering pre-eviction cash and legal assistance. It was later closed by Dinkins-era budget cuts.

In 1991 CB4 united with civic groups to protest a proposed homeless shelter in Elmhurst and the conversion of a Corona hotel into a private seventy-four-unit women's shelter with rents even higher than those at the Mets. A sign carried by one Corona demonstrator read, "School Is Overcrowded As It Is!" Both proposals were Dinkins administration efforts to comply with a court order to end the placement of homeless families in hotels. The new shelters were not built; instead, a program to rent private apartments for homeless families was begun by Dinkins—but ended by Giuliani in 1994. Even with new diversion teams restricting access to the city's only remaining Emergency Assistance Unit, by 1995 nearly two hundred families were sleeping there, and placement of homeless persons in hotels began once more. By 1996 their number had climbed to 940.[40]

School Crowding

In 1986 Pat Carpentiere told CB4 that his children at PS14 in Corona Heights were in classes of forty-five, or ten more than the teachers' contract permitted. In 1988 I saw PS14's doubled-up kindergartens where fifty children occupied a single classroom; one art station was located in a former bathroom; the library, gymnasium, and part of the lunchroom were filled by classes separated by room dividers. PS14's new wing, approved by School Board 24 in 1985, did not open until 1995. In Corona Plaza, PS19's 2,200 students made it by 1994 the largest primary school in the city. At 140 percent of capacity it was so crowded that storage closets were commandeered for classes, and one teacher used the men's room as his office, exiting when other teachers used it as a bathroom. In 1996, PS19's first grade classes each contained forty to forty-two students, and its fourth grades, forty-six.

At South Elmhurst's PS102, a building designed for 440, the student body rose from 650 in 1987 to 1,000 in 1994. Classrooms contained up to thirty-nine desks, and teachers' lounges, the assistant principals' offices, and the gymnasium were all used for instruction. By 1987, PS89 in the Baxter-Roosevelt section of Elmhurst had sixteen "double classes": two classes with two teachers sharing one room. The next year the PS89 kindergarten—which since 1975 had been bused thirty minutes to a school in Glendale—returned, and the school's fifth grade was then bused to Maspeth. PS89 was so crowded by 1994 that English as a Second Language classes were conducted on staircases and in halls. In 1995 some 600 more pupils registered than in 1994.

School crowding was a frequent topic at CB4 meetings. "I'd like to run a tour of PS89 for the City Planning Commission," said Lou Simeone in 1984. "Nobody cares about the kids." Said Rose Rothschild, "I've been involved with schools for twenty years. I know what it is to have a child in an overcrowded school—a Tower of Babel. Kids come home with headaches. Teacher absenteeism is high. . . . Our kids go to overcrowded primary school, overcrowded intermediate school, and overcrowded high school. It's a wonder they do as well as they do."

While serving as president of SB24 in 1984, Simeone secured a Board of Education budget commitment for an 1,800-seat primary school in Elmhurst-Corona. He then pushed CB4 to declare a moratorium on zoning variances for new housing until a school site was selected. The BOE rejected several proposed locations, and Simeone died at the end of 1984. Under the new president, Mary Cummins of Middle Village, SB24 returned to its policy of "temporary" mini-schools for Elmhurst-Corona, and three were approved in 1985.

Both as CB4 chair and as district manager, Rose Rothschild continued to press for new schools. She worked closely with Richard Bearak, a Department of City Planning staffer assigned to CD4, who supplied technical land-use expertise. They suggested two city-owned sites for schools in 1986, but objections arose from the BOE, SB24, neighboring residents, and the city agencies that controlled the sites. They next proposed to use the private property housing L'Amour East, a rock music nightclub. The site was accepted; the club was condemned and demolished. But engineers then discovered that ancient Horse Brook beneath it was contaminated, and the plan for a school there was abandoned. (A Korean supermarket opened on this site in 1990.)

Primary schools were eventually approved for both the sites Bearak and Rothschild had recommended in 1986, and ground was broken in 1992. But even with two new buildings and additions to PS14 and PS89, CD4's primary schools remained over capacity. One new school, PS7, opened in 1995, but by 1996 its kindergarten was being bused elsewhere because of overcrowding.[41]

Lack of Youth Recreation Facilities

In 1981 NCA president Bob Tilitz lamented that "recreational and other services for the youth of Elmhurst have been inadequate. Indeed . . . these services have actually dwindled at the same time that the Elmhurst youth population has increased." School gyms were used as classrooms. Hours at the Elmhurst and Lefrak City Branch Libraries were cut. The large, grassy Newtown High School athletic field was closed to public use during the 1975 fiscal crisis; it was not reopened until 1985, and then only part time. CD4's playgrounds were heavily used; even on a cool March evening in 1995 the basketball courts of Elmhurst's Clement Clarke Moore Park were packed with mixed teams of Latin American, Asian, white, and black youth. But in Lefrak City, where 10 percent of CD4's youth lived, only one of three swimming pools was open—for paid admission—and the single basketball court had no lights for evening use.

Some efforts were made. CB4 awarded its annual youth services allocation of approximately $2 per child to civic associations for afterschool and summer programs. Other civic groups and churches ran youth activities with volunteer adult labor, private donations, and contributions from local merchants.

During the 1980s and 1990s there were 24,000 children between the ages of five and nineteen living in Elmhurst-Corona, or 10,000 per square mile. With crowded schools, a shortage of recreational space and programs, and parents who often worked long hours, CD4's youth interacted intensively with one another. Dress styles, jewelry, and "big hair" for girls and sculptured haircuts for boys reflected the appeal to some of oppositional youth cultures and mass media imagery. When young people gathered, they were often noisy and boisterous. "What causes the problems," said Edna Baskin of Lefrak City, "is that there are all these kids hanging around with nothing to do."

Youth gangs were not the problem in Elmhurst-Corona during the 1970s that they were elsewhere in neighborhood New York, but in 1978 a 110th Precinct "youth conditions car" was assigned to monitor "disorderly kids." In 1981 Bob Tilitz noted "complaints of after-dark unruly or disorderly behavior, of drug use and dealing in local parks and playgrounds, of destructive acts against property." In the mid-1980s, CB4 members reported evening teenage drinking in two small Corona Heights playgrounds, and Don Mallozzi noted "forty to fifty kids" hanging out late at night in Corona Plaza. Teenagers "congregating" in Lefrak City lobbies were an annoyance to some adult residents. And South Elmhurst residents complained of youth smoking marijuana near the LIRR tracks and drag racing at night.

Residents of blocks near L'Amour East, which opened in 1983, suffered late-night and early-morning noise, and intimidation from some heavy-metal music fans leaving the club or refused admission by its bouncers. Some of the white "burnout" crowd that arrived to hear such stars as Greg Allman or former Kiss guitarist Vinnie Vincent also parked, urinated, and threw beer bottles on streets and driveways. By 1987 wooden police barriers provided some relief to residents, but three deaths and a dozen assaults, rapes, and weapons violations at the club frightened them. In 1988 residents cheered at CB4's public hearing on a proposed school at this location; they favored it as a way to close down L'Amour East.[42]

Still, the 110th's commanding officer insisted in 1986, "We do not have a youth problem"; in his view most Elmhurst-Corona youth were orderly and law-abiding. Police opinion shifted in 1989 when the new commanding officer, Gerald McNamara, announced, "Gangs are springing up." He explained that these "loose-knit" groups were organized on a "turf" basis, not by ethnic origin. "Some are of one group by the geographical area—82nd Street [in Baxter-Roosevelt] is predominantly Hispanic, but there are whites, blacks, and Orientals in the gang. There is not a bias or ethnic problem between the groups, but they use language to each other I wouldn't [use] before the Human Rights Commission. They're not violent—no guns. They use fists, but may have knives or baseball bats. They are not drug users [but] one or two may smoke marijuana."

NcNamara's immediate objective was to establish neutral "safe corridors" at a Jackson Heights movie theater and the Queens Center mall, both frequented by numbers of teens. He had participated in "youth dialogue" meetings with gang leaders at Newtown High School, but so far the only fight there was "over a girl" and did not involve whole gangs. Problems at that school were intensified by youth milling outside. They included both some of Newtown's 4,300 students, who arrived early or waited for classmates, and students from other high schools coming to meet friends. At a 1992 district cabinet meeting Rose Rothschild reported that youth outside the high school were accosting residents—a problem that still continued in 1995, according to staff of the nearby Bethany Lutheran Church day-care center.

The new locally based "gangs" arose from the common experiences of the enormous cohort of youth who had grown up in Elmhurst-Corona and reached their midteens by the late 1980s; a man who had moved to Lefrak City as a teenager in 1984 told me in 1992, "I still feel like an outsider to Lefrak boys who grew up here; they're very tight." In 1987 I wondered if named youth gangs were emerging when I heard two male African American teens talk about the "the 111s"—named, I supposed, for 111th Street in Corona. By 1989 the "gang" in Elmhurst's Broadway-Woodside section was called "the 78th Street Boys." And that year youth in each of Lefrak City's five sections wore bandanas of a different color, in part spurred by *Colors,* a 1988 film about Los Angeles gangs. As one young man told me, "You shouldn't go into another section. It would be bad to wear your bandana there."

In South Elmhurst up to forty teens convened at night in Crowley or Hoffman Park, and noise, marijuana, piles of beer bottles, and graffiti became problems. As a Parks Department worker put it in 1990, "We paint over every week, and there is graffiti again—on signs, the building, the fence. They are also ripping up the fencing. They write 'UPS' for United Pot Smokers, and 'Wasted.' These are the two graffiti groups."

In Corona Heights by 1990 some two dozen teens had moved from playgrounds to a corner opposite William Moore Park, at the far end from the Park Side restaurant and a cafe where "the *men*" gathered. Their beer drinking and nightly firecrackers were upsetting local residents, said Northside Democratic Club leader Tony Caminiti. "We expect this on the Fourth of July, fine! But we've been putting up with it for weeks." The problem persisted, and in 1992 Rose Rothschild observed the scene one night: "I didn't realize we had so many white kids in the area. The leader is the son of the flower shop owner."

Contemporaneously with the appearance of these "gangs" in CD4, youth violence was occurring elsewhere in Queens. Early in 1989 three members of DTC (Down to Crash), a fifty-member "crew" with some Elmhurst members, killed another youth in CD3. In 1990 five Chinese and Korean "good-grade guys," including one from Elmhurst, were assaulted in a Bayside shopping mall by thirty members of TMR (The Master Race), a mainly white but racially mixed gang. Later that year one of eight FTS (Fuck That Shit, or Flushing Top Society) youths killed a twenty-two-year-old Utah tourist during a midtown Manhattan robbery. FTS members, who were also graffiti "writers," were of diverse racial identities (the murderer, "Rocstar," was Guatemalan) and lived in Flushing, Corona, and Woodside.[43]

The most dangerous youth gang in CD4 between 1986 and 1990 was the Green Dragons. Like other Chinese gangs headed by an adult *dai lo* (elder brother) involved in gambling and drug distribution, the Green Dragons were immigrant teens. They were recruited by heroin importer Paul Wong to ferry drugs and cash, and received spending money. And like other Queens Chinese gangs, the Dragons—who included Taiwan, Hong Kong, Cambodian Chinese,

Vietnamese, and Korean members—frequented the Golden Q pool hall on Queens Boulevard in Elmhurst. They also patronized Linda's Beauty Salon in the Broadway-Woodside section to have their hair permed and streaked to complement their tattoos and all-black dress. After their *dai lo* moved to China in 1989, the Dragons increased extortion activities in Elmhurst Chinese restaurants, killing two owners who refused to pay. Before the last members were arrested in 1990 at their Elmhurst safehouse, the two dozen Green Dragons had killed eight people in Elmhurst, including an Irish immigrant bystander and three members of rival Chinese and Korean gangs.[44]

The violent gangs attracted non-collegebound, working-class youth. Other teens banded together in protection and affected a tough demeanor. "We have to gang up to go over the [Long Island Expressway overpass] bridge to the school playground because that is the territory of other groups of kids," some Lefrak City youth told Edna Baskin. "Gangsta" rap music and movies, as well as word-of-mouth knowledge of violent gangs, influenced the dress and language of some teens. A group of Filipino, South Asian, and Latin American girls age twelve to fifteen met during the summer of 1993 at the Queens Center mall and called themselves BGC (Bitches Going Crazy); they occasionally drank malt liquor in parks, but mainly they delighted in tough talk, low-slung jeans, striped boxer shorts, and big earrings.[45]

Notwithstanding the notoriety of Elmhurst-Corona teenage "gangs," their numbers were small. Problems were worse in other neighborhoods. In 1993 the Citizens' Committee for Children ranked Elmhurst-Corona seventeenth or eighteenth among the city's fifty-nine community districts in terms of community safety, crime risk, and child health factors. It fared worse in educational risk as part of SD24, which was ranked twenty-third of the city's thirty-two school districts. Still, despite ranking thirty-fifth among the community districts in income, CD4 scored sixth in child safety as measured by reported abuse and neglect.[46] Elmhurst-Corona parents evidently cared about their children, and youth issues were central to local definitions of the quality of life.

Voices at a Mayoral Town Meeting

In May 1994 Mayor Giuliani held a town meeting in East Elmhurst, and residents from both CD3 and CD4 attended.[47] Lucy Schilero, president of the Coalition of United Residents for a Safer Community and a CB4 member, told the mayor that her organization congratulated the police for attention to drug dealing and prostitution on Roosevelt Avenue. Other issues came up—auto theft, the Mayi murder (see Chapter 15), and the idea of police substations (which began on Roosevelt Avenue in 1995)—but the largest number of questions were about schools and youth programs.

"There's really only one answer on schools," the mayor told his audience. "We are spending the money unwisely, I think immorally. . . . The majority of money is not going to schoolrooms and children. . . . We have got to crush the administration in the school system. Not reduce it [but] crush it, remove it. . . . I am engaged in a mission to accomplish that." A black woman from the United Parents Association objected that the mayor was cutting the school budget. He told her, "I'm not reducing the money for the school system. I'm increasing it." (This was simply not true; moreover, the annual salaries of all central and district bureaucrats amounted to $164 million, or just one-eighth the amount of Giuliani's 1994–1995 education cuts.)[48]

A Latin American woman asked why there would be no summer classes or adult education, and Giuliani replied, "The chancellor decides, not me." Paul Lewis, chair of CB3, and Joan Shuck of School District 30, both white, emphasized that schools in their district were at 150 percent of capacity, and that the growing number of elementary and intermediate school pupils signaled the need for a new high school in northwest Queens. "We agree with you about putting money into the classroom," Shuck told the mayor, "but there is no space in our classrooms. We need lease space, modules, whatever kind of help you can give us."

Ortner Murray, a black sporting-goods store owner and former policeman, was applauded for objecting to reduced youth services. "When we cut back," Murray said, "we have a bunch of kids on the street with nothing to do. I have seen it, and I'm not speaking only for the [North] Corona–East Elmhurst community. This is a problem in the entire area, the whole of Queens. Can you please tell the youth from our community what you will do for them?" Giuliani insisted that nothing had been cut yet. (His budget that year in fact proposed such cuts, and in 1995 youth services funding was reduced by half.)

The most eloquent speaker was a young Latin American woman from a youth program at Our Lady of Sorrows Church in Corona Plaza.

> I work for the Father Billini Association, and we have an afterschool center and outreach programs that not only employ the youth of our community, but give the youth . . . a safe haven to go to afterschool. And many parents who unfortunately can't afford childcare look to us as a form of being able to work those extra two and three hours so that we don't have to become dependent so much on the welfare system. So I believe that outreach programs and [Safe Streets,] Safe City programs lighten the burden of the city, not necessarily make it heavier. . . . The kids, who are of different ethnicities, different religions, different racial backgrounds, can all play together, and we all learn together. . . . I believe that there might be another channel of income the city may use instead of cutting the outreach programs, the Safe Streets, Safe City programs, the crime prevention programs that our children need so desparately.

When a 1995 poll showed a falling percentage of New Yorkers who expected quality of life to improve, the mayor responded, "I think that life is actually going to get better over the next year to two years." But only 25 percent of New Yorkers agreed with him; 40 percent expected it to worsen, and 31 percent felt there would be no change. These results paralleled a 1995 survey of the city's community board district managers and chairpersons. Although nearly all districts credited Mayor Giuliani and Police Commissioner William Bratton for improved public safety, in only sixteen of fifty-nine districts did they say that quality of life had improved; in twelve they felt it was worse, and in thirty-one—including CD4 and CD3—they saw no change, or a mixture of decline in some areas and improvement in others. In 1996, 58 percent of all New Yorkers rated Giuliani negatively on handling quality-of-life issues.

The 1995 poll also found that 81 percent of New Yorkers wanted more public funding for education, and 59 percent wanted more spent on youth services. Another 1995 poll revealed that 53 percent of New Yorkers were willing to pay more taxes if school funding was increased. Giuliani's disapproval ratings on education stood at 61 percent in 1995, 69 percent in 1996, and 60 percent in 1997, and only 18 percent of New Yorkers felt the schools had improved during his tenure. To neighborhood New Yorkers, schools and youth programs were clearly at the heart of their definition of quality of life.[49]

PART IV

The Transformation of Neighborhood Politics

[10]

The New Multicultural Geography of Elmhurst-Corona

A Belizean raised in Elmhurst once told me, "I'm from two places that no one would believe!" The population of Belize includes Creoles of African descent, Mestizos of Spanish and Native American ancestry, Mayan Indians, Garifuna (black speakers of a Native American language), German Mennonites, Asian Indians, and Chinese. Like Belize, Elmhurst-Corona is, in Louis Winnick's phrase, "an ethnic cross section of the planet."[1] In 1990 its 28,000 whites were a mix of European ancestries (see Chapter 11). Its Asian residents included 16,300 Chinese, 8,900 Koreans, 7,600 Indians, 4,000 Filipinos, and smaller numbers of Thais, Vietnamese, Pakistanis, and Guyanese of Indian ancestry. The Latin American population comprised 13,600 Colombians, 12,000 Dominicans, 6,800 Ecuadorians, 6,500 Puerto Ricans, 2,900 Cubans, 2,700 Mexicans, 2,700 Peruvians, and other South and Central Americans. Black immigrants included 3,900 West Indians (among them at least 1,200 Haitians) and 1,850 Africans.[2]

Rituals of Ethnic Celebration

A variety of new public rituals arose in Elmhurst-Corona during the 1980s. Some of these rituals celebrated particular ethnic identities: Colombian, Ecuadorian, Korean, African American, and Italian. With one exception, they took place not in the midst of CD4's ethnically diverse neighborhood terrain but rather in nonresidential locations. And whatever their celebratory purposes, they attracted multiethnic audiences and dignitaries; indeed, such participation was a testament to their success.[3]

Colombian Independence Festival

In 1984 the Centro Civico Colombiano sponsored its first Colombian Independence Day celebration in Flushing Meadows–Corona Park. By the 1990s this was the park's largest event, attracting crowds in the hundreds of thousands. Located in Elmhurst, the Centro had been formed in 1978; a president was elected annually from among its business and professional membership. In addition to the festival, the Centro offered classes in English, U.S. citizenship, Spanish (for U.S.-born youth), and Colombian history. It also collected relief funds from Colombian New Yorkers after a 1985 volcano eruption and landslides in their homeland, and it organized a blood drive following the 1990 crash on Long Island of a Colombian airplane in which seventy-three persons died.

After riding an IRT subway packed with festivalgoers, I arrived in Flushing Meadows–Corona Park on a sweltering July Sunday in 1987. An enormous crowd, with many dancing in place, flowed outward from a large stage where a succession of *cumbia* bands and folkloric troupes performed, amplified by a pulsating sound system. Yellow, blue, and red balloons, the colors of Colombia's flag, were everywhere. Beneath a large "Festival Independencia de Colombia" banner were logos of commercial sponsors: Banco de Bogotá, Goya food products, Juvenia watches, and Aguadiente Taba Rojo, a liquor company. On stage, representatives of Governor Mario Cuomo and Mayor Edward Koch read proclamations honoring the event.

In rows of wooden kiosks with striped roofs, Queens restaurants sold *empanadas, arepas* (Colombia's corncake staple), roast pig, *chorizo* (sausage), fruit juices and ices, and *obleas* (round wafers with sweet condensed milk spread between); the lines were long. Ecuadorian food carts present each weekend near the park's soccer fields were also doing business, and unlicensed vendors sold beer from plastic bags and baby carriages. A few picnickers on the outskirts had brought grills and home-prepared dishes. In the shade of some trees two men played a flute and a drum in Colombian folk style; couples danced, and a small audience encouraged them with laughter and comments.

Elena Acosta, a Colombian raised in Queens, said the crowd looked "very Colombian" to her, and one saw white, black, and Indian faces and every combination of mixed background. In addition to "Cali," "Cartagena," and "Medellín" T-shirts, however, others read "Puerto Rico" and "José Marti" (a Cuban national hero). Spanish-language television Channel 41, broadcasting live, interviewed persons from Costa Rica, El Salvador, and Ecuador. There was also a fundraising table for a Nicaraguan group.

The 1992 festival crowd was even larger, extending beyond visual or aural range of the stage. The colorful El Ballet de Sonia Osorio performed, bands played, and the Colombian consul read a message from his country's president. Colombia's official colors appeared on paper flags, streamers, and hats, and when a group on stage shouted "Que viva Colombia!" and "Viva Latinoamerica!" flags waved throughout the crowd. Corporate sponsors that year included American Airlines, Pepsi-Cola, *El Diario* (a New York Spanish-language daily newspaper), and Ria Envia (a money-transfer firm with offices in Queens).

More picnickers than in 1987 arrived with loaded shopping carts, beach chairs, umbrellas, and even hammocks. More kiosks offered food, and more vendors worked the crowd with beer, *obleas,* fruit ices, green mangoes, and plates of *chorizo.* Peddlers sold toys, hats, baby clothes, and jewelry; dozens of Ecuadorian Otavaleños offered distinctive woven bags, garments, and wristlets; and four West Africans sold gold-plated knickknacks. Musical performers beyond the range of the sound system—an Andean panpipe, drum, and guitar ensemble; a keyboardist and singer; an alto saxophonist—passed the hat and sold cassette tapes.

The political significance of this festival grew yearly. In 1993 Mayor David Dinkins, running for reelection, greeted the crowd; so did U.S. Congress member Nydia Velazquez, who represented Elmhurst-Corona, and Roberto Ramirez of the Bronx, a state assembly member and candidate for city comptroller—both Puerto Rican. In 1994 Queens borough president Claire Shulman declared July "Colombian Heritage Month"; in 1995 Mayor Rudolph Giuliani attended the Centro Civico Colombiano Independence Day dinner.

Each August an Ecuadorian Independence Day Festival was also held in Flushing Meadows–Corona Park, organized by the Comite Civico de la Colonia Ecuatoriana. Crowds were smaller than at the Colombian event, but other aspects were similar.

Korean Harvest and Folklore Festival

In 1982 the Korean Produce Association held its first celebration of the centuries-old *ch'usok* festival in Flushing Meadows–Corona Park. Organized in 1974 to represent the interests of Korean greengrocers, the KPA maintained an office in the Hunts Point produce market, regulated competition and mediated disputes among its members, and negotiated with the city over sanitation inspections and fines. By the early 1980s the KPA was the dominant organization in the city's Korean community.[4]

In Korea, *ch'usok* is a family-oriented harvest celebration during which ancestors are honored. In New York it has become an occasion for the city's Koreans to gather on a September Sunday and be entertained. Tradition was not slighted; an ancestor-worship ceremony, a *song-pyon* pine-cake-making contest, and a closing *kang-gang-su-wol-lae* circle dance all recalled *ch'usok* in Korea. Folk dance groups performed, and Korean games were played; a fashion contest was held for women in traditional *chogori* blouses and long, high-waisted *chima* skirts. Particular crowd-pleasers were a folksong contest for senior citizens, and male *ssirum* wrestling matches. By late afternoon and evening the major draw was movie stars and entertainers flown in from Korea, among them three hip-hop dancers in 1993. Raffle prizes included airline tickets, televisions, and automobiles.[5]

Attendance in 1986 and 1987 was estimated at 20,000 to 30,000, but the 1991 crowd was several times that size. That year the KPA joined other organizations to celebrate the admission of both South and North Korea to the United Nations. The audience filled thousands of chairs in front of the stage, including a reserved section for senior citizens. Larger numbers milled through tents selling Korean food; around promotional displays of Korean packaged foods, cosmetics, and children's books; and in and out of the corporate booths of Citibank, AT&T, American Express, Pepsi-Cola, the *Daily News,* and Metropolitan Life Insurance, where a costumed Snoopy was available for pictures with children. Still more people sat on mats around grills in three-generation family groups. Korean was spoken by announcers, handbill canvassers, and nearly everyone except groups of teenagers. (I also heard English spoken by youth at the Colombian festival.) By 7:30 P.M. some in the dwindling crowd were drunk, and they sang and danced along with the stage performers until 9:30, when the festival broke up.

At this largest gathering of Koreans outside Korea, the *ch'usok* audience was itself a resource for Korean organizations. Groups that rented booths to distribute literature and raise funds included Elmhurst's Association for Korean American Education and Culture and several churches. In 1984 Korean American Women for Action registered voters; in 1991 Rutgers students petitioned and raised funds for Korean language classes at their university; in 1993 flyers circulated from a group seeking an apology and redress from Japan for its use of Korean "comfort women" during World War II.

A handful of whites, blacks, and Latin Americans was visible each year, some attending with Korean wives or friends. Several white American parents brought their adopted Korean children for exposure to Korean culture; in 1993 the KPA reserved seating for adoptees and parents, and also for American Korean War veterans and for African American students returned from visits to Korea. By 1991 many Central American employees were visible working in Korean restaurant tents. A platoon of white, black, Asian, and Latin American canners scoured the festival grounds for refundable containers, and a few Indian balloon sellers and Latin American beverage and cigarette vendors circulated through the crowd.

The number of American politicians making appearances or sending representatives and telegrams escalated over the years. Manhattan borough president Ruth Messinger, who championed a commercial rent regulation bill supported by Korean merchants during the 1980s, appeared several times. In 1991 the director of the Justice Department's Community Relations Office addressed the audience, and the program included a message from President George Bush on White House stationery. In 1993 mayoral candidates Dinkins and Giuliani both spoke to the crowd.

Black Heritage Book Fair

In 1988 flyers appeared in the Lefrak City area announcing a "Multicultural Book Fair Specializing in Black Heritage Children's Books," to be held in front of the Queens Center mall. It was sponsored by Concerned Community Adults (CCA), an organization founded by Edna Baskin, an African American Lefrak City resident. After Baskin had mentioned to CB4 district manager Rose Rothschild that she was seeking support from local merchants for her summer youth activities, Rothschild spoke to Queens Center mall director Lorraine O'Neill, who offered to help, and Baskin requested space for a book sale. "This is the first event from Lefrak City outside the Lefrak area in the nine years I have been living here," Baskin said.

When I arrived at the Saturday event, three folding tables on the sidewalk in front of the mall were covered with books. They included *Black Indians, Poems* by Nikki Giovanni, biographies of Marcus Garvey, Richard Pryor, Jesse Jackson, Oprah Winfrey, and Paul Robeson, *Black English* by J. L. Dillard, *The Africa News Cookbook, Traditional African Musical Instruments, What Color Was Jesus?* and many children's books on black heritage themes. The stock came from black-owned Nkiru Books in Brooklyn, which split the profits with the CCA. Baskin wanted to raise enough to spend $50 per month on additions to the Lefrak City Branch Library's holdings. "I know what a Black Heritage collection should be, and I was disappointed to see what's there. They also need books on Chinese and Indian cultures." By the end of the day she had taken in more than $500.

Edna Baskin had planned to hold the sale at the library, but the location in front of the mall "gives us a bigger population. People can see who we are, and learn about our position." Black, white, Latin American, and Indian passersby stopped to browse or to talk with Baskin and her helpers. One Indian man said nothing but studied the tables and then bought $23 worth of books. Several Lefrak City parents Baskin knew arrived during the day. One African American woman bought a Martin Luther King board game as a graduation present. It turned out she lived in Baskin's building, and Baskin proceeded to recruit her as a chaperon for a CCA bus trip.

Other CCA members who helped with the book sale included two African American couples and a single woman; Toyin Chukwuogu, a Nigerian woman who had arrived in the United States just three months earlier and worked with Edna Baskin throughout the summer; an Indian Lefrak City Branch librarian; the white CD4 youth coordinator; and Elena Acosta, a Colombian Queens College student.

During 1988–1990 Baskin held ten more Black Heritage book fairs to raise funds and recruit support for CCA. These occurred at Lefrak City, however, in the lobby of her own building or in front of the branch library, and publicity for them was directed to Lefrak residents through flyers and CCA's newsletter.

Corona Heights Fourth of July

Posters for a "100th Birthday of Corona" on July 4, 1985, listed the Corona Community Development Corporation and the Corona Heights Businessmen's Association as sponsors. At 6:00 P.M. the street on the north side of triangular William Moore Park was closed off by police barriers and flooded with people, many of them lined up between wooden sawhorses to receive free hot dogs and beer or soda. These were available at tables in front of the Park Side restaurant's parking lot, where men and teenage boys were cooking on portable grills. Behind them in the lot were a dozen tables topped with umbrellas and bearing reservation cards; at one of them I recognized city council member Joseph Lisa Jr., who represented Corona Heights.

Fifteen more tables in the closed-off street were occupied by elderly white neighborhood residents, for whom a man was barbecuing chicken on the park's brick grill. American and Italian flags were strung across the barricaded street, and smaller paper flags hung throughout the park. Near the Park Side a band made up of trumpet, electric keyboard, bass, and drums accompanied a man singing in Italian. The bandstand was surrounded by people enjoying the music, and a handful of older Italians danced in the street as the crowd swept back to make room.

At 7:00 P.M. council member Lisa came to the bandstand and directed everyone not registered to vote to two tables set up for that purpose in the park, and invited people to sign his reelection petition if they wished. Tony Giordano, owner of a meat store opposite the park, greeted the crowd for the Corona Heights Businessmen's Association. Twenty minutes later a trim man in his fifties, wearing gold medallions and an open shirt, came to the microphone and sang two Italian songs, the first dedicated to "Mr. Tony of Park Side." "We're all Italian here," he asserted welcomingly—though this was hardly the case. As the crowd grew into the thousands, half the many teenagers and most of the children were Latin American. There were also two or three groups of East Asians, an Indian family, and a dozen blacks, some perhaps Latin American. Many of these non-Italians moved along the hot dog line, as I did, twice.

At 7:30 P.M. a score of young men policing the food line departed for Baldi's, an Italian bakery a block away, and returned carrying a ten-foot birthday cake decorated with an American flag. Most of the young men wore the red "100th Birthday Corona" T-shirts that were being sold near the Corona Pizzeria, another business facing the park. They cut the cake in front of the bandstand and served it to the crowd on paper plates. With the band playing, people sang "Happy Birthday" to Corona. There was also a large "Happy Birthday Corona" streamer from the park to the Northside Democratic Club, where district leaders Norma Cirino and Tony Caminiti and his wife, Josephine Andreucci—all members of Community Board 4—sat with others on beach chairs. I left at 8:30, but Ruby Danta stayed until 10:00 P.M., listening to speeches from Caminiti and a representative of Governor Cuomo, and watching the fireworks that ended the evening.

The principal sponsor of this event was Anthony Federici, owner of the Park Side restaurant, opened when William Moore Park was renovated in 1979.[6] The Park Side's white-tablecloth service and Italian cuisine brought patrons from all over Queens and Long Island. I discovered its notoriety at a Corona playground opening when borough president Donald Manes spoke about his midnight dinner at the Park Side with U.S. Senator Alphonse D'Amato: after the meal they strolled into William Moore Park, and "Senator D'Amato challenged me to a game of bocce," Manes recounted. "Maybe because I'm not Italian, he thought he could beat me. I beat him 5 to 1."

William Moore Park was clean, safe, and used round the clock. "You never see even a candy wrapper on the ground here," council member Lisa told me. The park and its impressive flowers and shrubbery were maintained by an employee of Anthony Federici, and both these men were often thanked during public events there. Federici also used the brick grill and kept cooking gear in the park, and in 1989 *Newsday* restaurant reviewer Cara De Silva, invited to eat there, reported: "He led us, astonished, to an open-air kitchen, complete with refrigerator, a sink for dishwashing, a large grill, and a picnic table. There, Ralphie, Frankie, and Figgy—among a number of others who do their wining and dining here—were helping put together a late-afternoon barbecue."[7] "Much of it is illegal," a Parks Department employee told me. "Electricity lines are run in, and other things. But they keep it very well, so we don't bother them."

Anthony Federici continued to sponsor Fourth of July celebrations in William Moore Park during the 1980s and early 1990s. In 1988 at 6:30 P.M. firecrackers were being set off by young Latin American boys on the edges of the park, as they were throughout Corona Heights, and Italian and American flags again appeared. But fewer elderly Italians sat at tables than in 1985, and there was no food line. Free steak sandwiches and beer were available near the brick grill only to those who asked.

By 9:00 P.M., though, the crowd was in the thousands. It was more than half Latin American, with smaller numbers of whites, blacks, and Asians, and included many visitors whose parked cars filled the surrounding streets. Suddenly about thirty men in their late teens, twenties, and thirties walked onto the stretch of Corona Avenue next to the park and moved police barriers to block traffic at both ends. Most were Italian, and those in charge included "Figgy," who supervised valet parking at the Park Side; I also noted some youth from St. Leo's teen club (see Chapter 12), who were skipping a party there, and a young Latin American who worked at Army's, a second Italian restaurant facing William Moore Park. Although surrounded by throngs of sidewalk spectators standing behind wooden sawhorses, the men on the street joked with each other as if no one else were there. Most wore running shoes, white socks, sweat pants, and colored T-shirts. They strutted with feet splayed outward and elbows bent back, and several puffed on cigars. At this point half a dozen cannonlike metal pipes, ten inches across and two feet high, were placed on the center line along Corona Avenue. Then Anthony Federici arrived from the Park Side. Boxes of fireworks came next; they were put in the pipe cannons and lit with cigars. From 9:30 P.M. onward one after another of the cannons exploded. The noise was very loud; sparks caused the crowd to push back; and only a third of the fireworks rose into the air. People grew restless and by 10:30 P.M. were beginning to drift away. On a bus the next day, however, I heard an African American teenager from Lefrak City say he remained at "the party at Corona Heights" until midnight.[8]

No Corona civic leaders addressed the crowd at this Fourth of July celebration; indeed, nobody spoke.[9] As I was leaving, I saw many Italian Corona Heights families out in front of their homes watching smaller fireworks displays on nearly every corner, or observing the spectacular show visible in the sky over Flushing Meadows–Corona Park.

Ethnic Particularity at the Community's Margins

In September 1984 ten members of the Gleane Street Block Association arrived at CB4 to protest events at a Colombian festival held near their Elmhurst homes the previous July. These white, Latin American, Indian, and Filipino neighbors were upset that drugs and alcohol were consumed on their street, men urinated openly, and residents were harassed. Ed DeCordova, an Argentinian CB4 member and Gleane Street resident, said that no police were present; "It is okay for each group to have their affairs, but it must be orderly." Another Latin American man who complained at the 110th Precinct stated, "We take care of our homes and street. It was just a bunch of hooligans, and people trying to sell stuff." District manager John Rowan explained that the festival's sponsors had a permit for one commercial block but that turnout exceeded expectations; the crowd spilled over onto residential Gleane Street, and police protection was insufficient. The event had not created problems in the past, but no permit would be issued for it again.

In that same year Centro Civico Colombiano began its Colombian Independence Day festival in Flushing Meadows–Corona Park and, like the Ecuadorian and Korean festivals, attracted a metropolitan-area-wide audience, one that would have overwhelmed a residential neighborhood. These rituals, like Puerto Rican, Cuban, Indian, and Pakistani parades in Manhattan, were spatially removed from the residential terrain of CD4. Posters and flyers advertised them, but multiethnic neighborhood public space was not utilized for these particularistic events. Similarly, the first Black Heritage book fair was held at a central location in front of the Queens Center mall. Its purpose, however, was not to celebrate African American culture before a black audience from the whole metropolitan area but to raise funds for youth programs within CCA's immediate local arena; it relocated to Lefrak City in order to solidify support.

The Fourth of July celebration of Italianness, held in a neighborhood that had become half Latin American and half white, was exceptional in its assertion of ethnicity in the midst of a mixed residential setting, albeit one that still had a strong Italian presence. The Italian men who occupied Corona Avenue did so only one night a year, sufficient to mark their presence symbolically, but the event remained marginal to most Corona Heights Italians; their attendance waned after the 1985 celebration, and Italian neighborhood leaders thereafter made neither speeches nor appearances.

The Colombian, Ecuadorian, Korean, African American, and Italian rituals of ethnic celebration were the only ones held in CD4 during my fieldwork. Though memorable for those who attended, they were tangential to Elmhurst-Corona neighborhood politics, which focused on issues other than particularistic ethnic assertion.

Local Color

As in Belize, cultural juxtaposition characterized Elmhurst-Corona, and peoples and languages ran into each other in a mix never seen before. Their businesses, whether ethnically distinctive or not, were interspersed, and many depended on a mixed clientele. On a heavily Latin American block of Roosevelt Avenue in Elmhurst, an Indian, a Chinese, and a Korean store coexisted with seven Colombian, Dominican, and Argentinian firms; and facing William Moore Park in Corona, one Jewish, one Korean, two Greek, and two Dominican stores were scattered among fourteen Italian businesses.

Neither in Belize (which I visited in 1991) nor in Elmhurst-Corona were people perpetually in awe of the multicultural complexity around them. As anthropologist Ulf Hannerz points out, places like these are not just "mosaics" composed of "pieces of more or less the same kind and size, each of a single color, and . . . distinctly bounded toward one another." Rather, their diverse residents fashion connections within "a single field of persistent interaction and exchange [where] each [person] comes into some, if only fleeting, contact with a larger part of it." Like it or not, people were caught up in countless scenes and encounters where cultures flowed into one another.[10]

Neighborhood Vignettes

In 1989 the Transit Authority flooded Elmhurst-Corona IRT stations with a flyer printed in English, Spanish, Chinese, and Korean hailing the return of express service. Nearly everywhere in CD4 during the 1980s one could see a poster of a middle-aged Indian woman with the heading, "Sahaja Yoga, Shri Mataji Nirmala Devi—La Yoga de la Grande Madre." It listed the rented PS69 location where instruction was offered on Wednesday evenings and explained: "You cannot know the meaning of your life until you are connected to the power that created you. . . . Tu no puedes conocer il significado de su vida hasta que te conectes al poder que te creo."

On a Sunday afternoon in the playground opposite Elmhurst Hospital, a group of six Chinese men did flowing *tai ch'i* exercises. Two Thai sisters in their twenties practiced tennis against the wall of a handball court. Latin American and Indian mothers with young children filled benches near the swings and slides. A group of four junior high school girls stood watching the scene; they were "Irish and Scottish," Dominican, Dutch-Filipino, and "from Iowa." Two elderly men with shopping carts, one white and one East Asian, methodically worked through the park collecting soda cans and bottles.

On a July evening a dozen men, several speaking Italian, played cards at the cement chess tables in William Moore Park. About sixty people, mainly middle-aged and elderly white men, many in undershirts, were gathered at the bocce court. A handful of Park Side's and Army's customers in summer dresses and white pants and white shoes strolled through the park to the Lemon Ice King of Corona with its twenty-eight flavors. A group of white male teenagers, a few older Italian women (one in house slippers), and white and Latin American girls minding toddlers chatted by the park entrances or sat awhile. On one park bench two Punjabi men contentedly drank a sixpack of Heineken's.

In 1993 an unemployed garment worker, Wu Da Pei, killed his wife and two children at their South Elmhurst apartment after hearing voices ordering him to do so. The murder was discovered when neighbors noticed that the children's shoes were not outside the door, something they were used to seeing among Chinese families. That same year a male family friend obsessed with twenty-year-old Hema Sakhrani murdered her fiancé at his Long Island home. Hema then killed herself by jumping sixteen stories from her Queens apartment. A joint funeral service with a Brahman priest officiating was attended by hundreds at Elmhurst's Gerard J. Neufeld funeral home, established in 1936 and now a regular location for Hindu funeral rites in Queens.[11]

During the 1980s attendance at the Elmhurst Senior Center grew, and by the 1990s its 2,000 registered members were 20 percent white, 35 percent Asian, and 35 percent Latin American. Irish, Germans, Italians, and Poles—many of them long-settled immigrants—joined Argentinians, Colombians, Cubans, Ecuadorians, Puerto Ricans, Spaniards, Chinese, Filipinos, Indians, and Koreans at breakfast and lunch, each group speaking a different language. The center was run by the Spanish-, English-, Chinese-, and Korean-speaking staff of the Institute for Puerto Rican/Hispanic Elderly. For years the landlord, the Chinese Christian Testimony Church, objected to Friday dancing, card and domino playing, and most of all to Chinese mahjong, and finally refused to renew the lease. In 1997 the center moved to new quarters.[12]

Inside Restaurants

In 1984 I had dinner at Shamiana, an Indian restaurant in Elmhurst. The manager, a Sikh from New Delhi with a magnificent beard, told me 75 percent of his customers were Indian, but Chinese and Koreans also ate there. From a stack of credit card receipts he pulled out one for Yee Fuk Shin, who had eaten there four times; the manager was not sure whether he was Chinese or Korean. Shamiana occupied a building that had previously housed an Irish bar and before that a German restaurant; it was itself later replaced by a Chinese restaurant, and then a mini-mall of Asian and Latin American stores and offices.

In 1986 I saw a group of nine Korean men sharing a mixed grill of meat and sausage at El Chivito D'Oro, an Uruguayan restaurant in Jackson Heights. A year later I noted a group of construction workers, half Korean and half Latin American, sharing Korean barbecue at Chung Kiwa, an Elmhurst restaurant. Both Koreans and Uruguayans are hearty meat-eaters, and their restaurants featured their specialties of *kalbi* and *bulgogi* (grilled beef), and *parillada* (steak, short ribs, sweetbread, pork sausage, and blood sausage).

At La Gran Victoria, a Dominican Chinese restaurant in Corona Plaza, a Chinese waiter speaking fluent Spanish served four young Latin Americans who ordered Chinese dishes, and nothing from the *comidas criollos* side of the menu. In Elmhurst at the Taiwanese Broadway Noodle Shop I heard a Chinese female cashier take orders in Spanish from a table of Latin Americans. Around me sat a mix of white, black, and Asian customers.

Soccer Madness

Soccer is the sport of passion for CD4's South Americans. In Flushing Meadows–Corona Park half a dozen simultaneous matches are played on weekends among Argentinian, Bolivian, Chilean, Colombian, Ecuadorian, Paraguayan, and Peruvian teams. During the 1980s the Elmwood movie theater in South Elmhurst showed closed-circuit broadcasts of soccer matches in South America, and tickets were sold at Delgado Travel on Roosevelt Avenue. By the 1990s satellite dish and cable transmissions were available on large-screen televisions in many of Elmhurst-Corona's Latin American restaurants and bars.

Hemispheric title games and the quadrennial World Cup matches bring special police details to CD4 to contain soccer exuberance. Following Argentina's World Cup victory in 1986, a thousand fans took to the streets around the cluster of Argentinian restaurants on the Elmhurst-Corona border known as "Esquina Diego Maradona" in honor of Argentina's star player. In 1989, 5,000 rowdy supporters waved Colombian flags and honked car horns along Roosevelt Avenue in Elmhurst to celebrate a Medellín club's defeat of a Paraguayan team for the South American championship. In 1990 after Argentina's defeat of Italy in the

World Cup semifinals, Argentinians poured into Esquina Maradona with pots and pans, firecrackers, and air horns, and chased one Italian flag waver; no celebration followed the West German victory over Argentina in the finals, and the 150 police officers on hand left Esquina Maradona quietly. In 1993 an America Cup defeat of Colombia by Argentina produced a victory foray from Esquina Maradona to Roosevelt Avenue by carloads of flag-waving Argentines; bottles, eggs, and insults were hurled, but no arrests were made.

Two months later Colombians savored their 5-to-0 defeat of Argentina, thus qualifying, as Argentina already had, for the 1994 World Cup. Neither Colombia, Argentina, Bolivia, nor Mexico—the Latin American teams among the twenty-four contenders—survived to the finals, but World Cup fever raged in CD4. The area was deluged with flags and World Cup paraphernalia, including bogus items purchased in Chinatown or distributed in Queens by a Pakistani canvasser; inspectors from Time Warner Sports, the official World Cup marketer, arrived to impound knockoff items. Some two hundred hardcore Argentine fans departed to Boston for the first-round match, in which their team defeated Greece, and others celebrated at Esquina Maradona. After the United States beat Colombia, a lone Puerto Rican honked and waved an American flag on Roosevelt Avenue until police detained him for his own safety. Bolivians consoled themselves over their team's defeat on their soccer-fan turf in Jackson Heights. And following a tie match with Italy, Mexicans demonstrated noisily along the Corona portion of Roosevelt Avenue where their restaurants were located; police arrested thirty-seven.[13]

Scenes from a Mall

In 1993 the Queens Center mall celebrated its twentieth anniversary with four weekends of free entertainment. Customers were no longer solely the "middle income" whites for whom the mall was designed, and anniversary performers reflected its multiethnic clientele: They included Chinese lion dancers, Korean fan dancers, the Indian Carnatic Music Association of North America, Andean music by Tahuantinsuyo (two Peruvians and two Ecuadorians), the Latin Jazz Coalition, a flamenco dancer, "Afro-American jazz," Greek music, Irish dance, Andy Statman's Klezmer Ensemble, the country-and-western Stonewall Band, St. Benedict's Ancient Fife & Drum Corps, and a Queens Symphony Orchestra string trio.

I arrived one Saturday afternoon to hear vibraphonist Bill Jacobs's septet, including alto saxophone, trombone, electric keyboard, bass, drums, and percussion. As they performed Dizzy Gillespie's "Night in Tunisia," Horace Silver's "Nica's Dream," Duke Ellington's "Satin Doll," and Thelonious Monk's "Rhythm-A-Ning," I saw a large Indian family group, a Chinese couple with a young child, and some Russian adults all stop to listen. A Latin American mother and her two preteen daughters stayed longer. An African American woman I knew from Lefrak City was watching with her granddaughter. Four elderly African American men and women were the most intent listeners, beaming through the set. At the height of the performance there were a hundred persons in front of the bandstand or looking down from atrium balconies. Most shoppers went on shopping: teens, elderly people, family groups, mothers and children; U.S.-born and immigrant; black, white, Latin American, Asian.

Race and Place

Elmhurst-Corona streets, once solidly white, were filled with Latin American and Asian residents by 1990. In most of CD4, however, the black population was 4 percent or less, and in a quarter of the census tracts blacks amounted to just 1 percent. Only in two tracts next to Lefrak City, where blacks were the majority, did black numbers rise to between 12 and 15 percent.

By 1980 Latin Americans already owned 22 percent of the 9,000 owner-occupied housing units in Elmhurst-Corona, and Asians owned 15 percent. Blacks (including black immigrants), then 17 percent of homeowners citywide, owned less than 3 percent in CD4.[14] African Americans had established themselves in the Lefrak vicinity but barely appeared elsewhere in Elmhurst-Corona's rental and homeowner markets. It was immigrants, not African Americans, who continued to purchase Elmhurst-Corona homes during the 1980s and 1990s, even as blacks increased to constitute one-quarter of New York City's population.

Home sales and apartment rentals were facilitated by white and immigrant-owned realties, many of which diversified their staffs but not to the point of hiring African Americans. In our 1986 survey of Elmhurst-Corona businesses, we asked about the ethnicity of owners and employees. In real estate firms that served customers who spoke only one immigrant language, their staff reflected this fact, but most of the sixty-eight employed a mix of whites, Latin Americans, and Asians. The Chinese-owned Century 21 Sunshine Realty had staff members who spoke Mandarin, Taiwanese, Cantonese, Hakka, Spanish, Italian, German, Polish, Korean, and "Indian" [*sic*]; the Colombian-owned Woodside Realty Corporation employed speakers of Spanish, Hebrew, Korean, and Mandarin. The same pattern was evident in a brochure distributed at the 1994 Queens Festival in Flushing Meadows–Corona Park by the Re/Max realty, with offices throughout Queens. Of twenty-four Re/Max agents, each with a photograph in the brochure, ten were Latin American, five white, four South Asian or Indo-Guyanese, three Chinese, one Korean, and one Filipino. None was black.

Elmhurst-raised Newtown High School teacher Thomas Tilitz observed in the early 1980s that "the one group not to come into the community in any significant numbers is North American blacks. It is a notable fact that housing discrimination has broken down in this area for every group except this one. Blacks of Hispanic, West Indian, and Haitian descent live in Elmhurst, but . . . racism in this country is apparently reserved for its natives of dark complexion." In 1982 a *New York Times* reporter profiled an Elmhurst apartment building inhabited by white Americans; Latin Americans from Chile, Colombia, Peru, and Uruguay; Asians from Bangladesh, India, Korea, and Vietnam; and black immigrants from Haiti and Nigeria.

By 1990 some 800 African Americans lived in Elmhurst as compared with 1,200 black immigrants; African Americans in CD4 overall, however, outnumbered black immigrants by 3 to 2. In the 1990s Elmhurst-Corona's housing market remained largely closed to African Americans. This situation was perpetuated by individual white landlords such as the building owner I overheard discussing prospective tenants with a real estate agent: "Afghanistan is okay. Anything, but not black."[15]

[11]

Solidarity and Conflict among White Americans

By 1990 Community District 4's white residents were a residual population, only a third of their 1960 total. Numbers tell us little about who these people were, however, or how they saw themselves and their neighbors. For many deeply rooted Elmhurst-Corona whites, a sense of continuity balanced their awareness of change. As Elmhurst-born Thomas Tilitz put it, "In the midst of this [arrival of newcomers], the proportion of more indigenous white Americans has clearly been reduced. However, in the approximately twenty years of ethnic transition . . . it is not only the elderly who have remained. Large numbers of non-immigrant [white] families including all age groups continue to make Elmhurst their home."[1]

The stayers recognized differences between themselves and other groups of whites: the Manhattan elites who formulated economic and governmental policies affecting the neigborhood; local business proprietors, police, and school board members who lived outside CD4 but influenced its quality of life; recent European immigrants, particularly Italians, Greeks, and (by the 1990s) Russians; upper-middle-class "liberals," mainly residents of Manhattan; and "yuppies," the beneficiaries of the 1980s boom.[2]

Most white Elmhurst-Corona residents in their fifties and older were children of Germans, Irish, Italians, Poles, and other Europeans who had come to New York during the 1880–1924 immigration wave. This second-generation cohort had lived through the 1930s depression, World War II, and the relatively prosperous 1950s, and many had married other sons and daughters of immigrants, frequently across European nationality lines. Their own children, grandchildren of the immigrant generation, constituted most of Elmhurst-Corona's younger white population in their twenties, thirties, and forties. This third generation, growing up in the 1950s and more turbulent 1960s and 1970s, married across white ethnic lines to an even greater extent.

By the 1980s the neighborhood's 3,600 white children under age eighteen were a numerical minority, amounting to just 12 percent of Elmhurst-Corona's youth. For elderly whites the opposite was true: in 1980 the 10,700 whites age sixty-five and over made up three-quarters of CD4's senior citizens.[3] Both generational continuity and racial discontinuity were evident in the neighborhood, and along Broadway in Elmhurst I repeatedly encountered elderly white men and women pulling shopping carts amid young Latin American and Asian mothers pushing baby carriages. These older whites, a quarter of Elmhurst-Corona's white population, were "aging in place." Their homes were paid for, and their apartments were rent-controlled or rent-stabilized. Their neighborhood contained senior centers, medical offices, pharmacies, and two hospitals; churches, familiar stores, friends, and kin were close at hand.[4]

Portraits

Norma Fee and Patsy Baird

Norma and Patsy are sisters whose four grandparents migrated from Germany in the late nineteeth century; their mother and father were born in Manhattan.[5] In 1917 their paternal grandfather, a barber, bought land in a former Newtown fruit orchard. He moved a renovated farmhouse to the site, each of its three floors with its own kitchen and bathroom. In 1919 infant Norma, her parents, and her grandparents moved in to occupy the second floor, where Patsy was born in 1922; the families of an aunt and an uncle and one boarder lived on the other floors—fourteen persons in all. Both sisters grew up understanding German.

As children they watched residential streets replace farms, and they remember the trolleys that connected Elmhurst to Manhattan and to Jamaica, Flushing, and Ridgewood. They went to PS89 and Newtown High School, and in 1935 Norma began work as a secretary in Manhattan. In 1938 Patsy married a printer of Scotch-Irish and German ancestry and moved to Ridgewood. In 1941 Norma married; her Scottish-English husband worked at an automobile factory and later for a utility company, and they lived in Astoria. In 1943 the sisters' grandmother died, and their grandfather asked Patsy and her husband to move back to the family home; Norma and her husband also moved there in 1945. In 1948 Patsy's husband left her and their four children. She began working as a secretary, first in Queens while her children were growing up, and then by the mid-1960s in Manhattan. Norma, who had no children, became "a second mother" to Patsy's. These children now live in Illinois, Pennsylvania, North Carolina, and Flushing.

Over the years the sisters' grandfather, father, and mother all died, and by the 1980s only Norma and her husband (both retired) and Patsy (still working) were living in the family house. The three ate together on weekends, sometimes at a German restaurant in Middle Village, the Park Side in Corona, or "occasionally Roy Rogers." The sisters shopped at the Elmhurst grocery, butcher, bakery, and pharmacy as they had for years, but other stores they had known "now are all gone." They used a Korean dry cleaner and greengrocer, and bought clothes at Macy's and Loehmann's in Lefrak City. Patsy took the subway to work, and both sisters used it to go shopping. "Elmhurst is convenient to Manhattan—the activity, it's alive, [and] the museums. If [only] people were cleaner and more polite," Norma said, "it would be better."

The sisters were raised as Lutherans, but Norma has been a member and chorister at Elmhurst Baptist Church since 1945 and participates in a women's society—"a merry group!"—that meets for devotion, lunch, and fellowship once a month; Norma's husband and Patsy also attend Sunday services there. Norma belongs to an AARP (American Association of Retired Persons) chapter that meets at the church twice a month and sponsors trips. Norma also takes her husband, "an avid golfer" before his stroke in 1986, to a weekly exercise class "done by a former Rockette" at the Elmhurst Senior Center.

When the sisters were growing up, the family next door was Italian, and other neighbors were Italian, Irish, and Czech. "We were the only Germans," Patsy recalled, "but it never occurred to us. We didn't make a distinction. People were all family-oriented and took pride in the neighborhood. Now they don't seem to care. People are pulling it down." Today the ten households on their block are "Armenian, Chinese, Italian, Indian, Greek, Italian-Irish, Korean, Filipino, Hispanic, and us."

The sisters are disturbed when their newer neighbors' garbage is inappropriately packaged or sits on the curb longer than from the evening before a scheduled pickup. Norma "spoke to Sanchez, our neighbor, to keep the area nice," and Patsy admonished another neighbor: "The garbage of the Chinese family—out in the streets! I told the son to get a pail, and next week, there was a pail." Dog litter is another problem. "A Chinese lady—her dog runs all over," Norma said. "I spoke to her and she slammed the door in my face. The dog still runs. Sanchez is okay, the only one."

When the sisters began attending Elmhurst Baptist in the 1940s, "members were English, Irish, German, typical of the area." Since 1970 several Filipino, Latin American, and Jamaican families have joined. "Without the Filipinos," Patsy said, "the church would have gone down." Like other longtime white members, Norma and Patsy serve on committees with the newer members and kiss and embrace them when greeting. "We in church never think of color or background," Norma said. "[One member] is Puerto Rican. Once someone remarked, 'These Puerto Ricans . . . ' at a business meeting. Never anything else. We are one big family."

Norma told me that one of the checkers at their supermarket is "a black girl, very attractive. Her mother was a home attendant to our mother, from Barbados." One day Norma mentioned this connection to the daughter, but "she said they all look alike to me. I told her we used to say that about black people."

Norma's husband died in 1989, and the following year the two sisters sold their house and moved to Long Island.

Mary Walensa

Mary was born in Pennsylvania in 1928. Her Russian immigrant father, a construction worker, converted from Russian Orthodox to Roman Catholic when he married Mary's Czech immigrant mother. Both parents died when Mary was fourteen, and her eldest sister "raised us six kids, and four of her own." Mary first visited New York in 1940 to spend the summer with a sister in Washington Heights. At seventeen she moved with her eldest sister to an apartment in Woodside and enrolled in a three-year nursing program at St. John's Hospital in Elmhurst. As an R.N. (registered nurse) she then worked at a Manhattan hospital for ten years, but in 1958, when another sister died of cancer, she decided to go into cancer research. She applied for a job at a Manhattan research institute, which hired her only after she agreed to attend college. By 1965 she had completed B.S. and M.A. degrees; during the late 1960s and early 1970s she was an administrator at the research institute and taught at New York University.

In 1956 Mary married her second-generation Polish husband, an electrical engineer, and in 1960 they moved from her sister's house in Elmhurst to an apartment building nearby. They had one son who now lives in Florida. In 1973 Mary and her husband were in an automobile accident, after which she worked only part time. Soon thereafter he developed leukemia and died in 1980. "I was bankrupt. Friends and relatives helped me. I lived on presents until my husband's pensions and annuities rolled through. Now, I'm fine financially."

Mary often has brunch after Sunday mass with her eldest sister, who now lives in a Jackson Heights co-op. Her other sisters and brothers live in Queens, upstate New York, New Jersey, and California, and their children are scattered in Chicago, South Dakota, Colorado, Singapore, and Flushing. Each summer her two brothers organize a one- or two-week "yearly reunion," and "we all rent beach houses together on the south Jersey shore." Mary also keeps in touch with a friend "I've know since age four," now living in Baltimore, and two nurses whom she met through work.

"I'm also friendly with neighbors," she said. "Rosie, across the hall, owns a bakery in Corona. Her husband's from Argentina; she's from San Juan [in Puerto Rico]. And Mr. and Mrs. Kim are Korean. Mrs. Kim runs a beauty parlor near Bloomingdale's [in Manhattan]; Mr. Kim works for Korean Airlines. Rosie's two boys are Raul and Pedro, and the Kims' children are Robert and Susan. The parents don't understand American homework. I help them. I check their report cards. So I have four kids." On Friday nights she plays poker with them, or takes them bowling or to a movie, "and then for hamburgers. The other nights they do homework. . . . The mothers often bring me dinner, especially Rosie—chicken with rice. I've also had Korean food a few times. Mrs. Kim takes care of my nails because I help her kids. The kids go to public schools. I push them to get books at the libraries to read more about something they are interested in. I got Rosie and Mrs. Kim to English school. You need it to understand running a bakery or beauty salon."

Mary shops at Macy's and the Queens Center mall, and buys groceries on Broadway in Elmhurst. She has her hair done at a Korean beauty parlor. Her doctor is in Jackson Heights. "I don't know if he is Indian—Dr. Arshad? He took over when my doctor retired." In 1985 she joined the local civic group, Your Block Association. "I hate the broken trash cans, the benches in the park, the uncleanliness of the streets, those things bother me. And the drugs." She is also troubled by Elmhurst's multilingual complexity. "I don't hear English at the post office, the dry cleaner, or my own beauty parlor. I feel like I'm a minority living in a foreign country."

The lobby of her building, she says, "was gorgeous when we moved in. Now things are broken or stolen." Today Mary sees "a lower class of people" in her building, "but not specific to any culture. The Orientals are of a higher class, the Spanish are lower, but not all, not Rosie. It's more the Indian and Spanish, but not all Indians and Spanish. You can't generalize. I don't have any bias; I judge people individually. I have some good black friends at NYU, some smarter than I am. I judge people as I find them. The ones that stay in Elmhurst don't have the prejudice. When we moved here in 1955, my sister's best friends, an Italian couple, tried to get into one of the Jackson Heights buildings. They were not approved because they were Italian."

She labels herself "a staunch conservative" and points to her family members "who lost our parents, and could pull ourselves up. I don't mind helping the sick, crippled, or disabled, but I hate liberals. Or those who get a welfare check and then walk to a tavern, keep having babies every year, or hide their husband in the next room. I would throw all liberals in the Potomac River. I write to [U.S. Senators] D'Amato and Moynihan when I disagree with them. If I have a problem I don't bother with underlings."

Phil Pirelli

Phil's parents emigrated from Apulia in southern Italy in 1924 and lived in East Harlem, where he was born in 1930. They moved to Corona Heights in 1934, and Phil attended PS14. "My first language was Italian, and I learned English in school." By age seven he was working in the family food business and had progressed from sweeping the store to bagging and packaging by age nine. In 1941 the business moved to a larger building, a former speakeasy, and the Pirelli family lived upstairs. During World War II Phil worked afterschool as an apprentice mechanic at a Corona Plaza knitting mill owned by his godfather. He attended Newtown High School but then began working full time in the family business, completing his education at night.

Phil met his second-generation Hungarian wife in 1951. They married in 1955 and lived in her Queens neighborhood for two years but in 1957 moved to the single-family home in Elmhurst where they still live. "My hobby is to invent food-processing machinery. I've developed a lot of the factory machinery—that's the secret of our success—in the plant machine shop. If I retire, I'll be a consultant." The business grew and in 1969 moved to a larger site in eastern Queens. Since then its work force has expanded from thirty to three hundred employees.

Phil's three siblings work in the family firm and now live on Long Island (their widowed mother lives with one of them) and elsewhere in Queens. Phil's two adult children, who also work in the firm, live on Long Island and in Queens, and he sees them twice a week. Phil is active in many Queens business and service organizations. "I have no close friends, but I know many people. I know the whole block. I have plenty of friends at work, and through my wife and children. My hobby is traveling. We've been all over the world, on tours."

At home, Phil enjoys cultivating the flowers and hedges in his well-kept front yard, and he and his wife go to the movies twice a month. They do much of their shopping locally at Waldbaum's (later C-Town) near Lefrak City, Macy's, the Queens Center mall, and Leo's Latticini, an Italian food store in Corona Heights. Phil is a parishioner at St. Leo's Church, but "I only attend." Both he and his wife are members of their block association.

Having lived more than sixty years in Corona and Elmhurst, Phil has seen much change, yet he also notes continuities. At PS14—"a great school, only Corona knew"—his fellow students were Italian, Jewish, and Irish. "Who paid attention? It didn't make any difference to kids." His family firm's customers then were mainly Italian, but some were Jewish. At the knitting mill where he worked as a teenager, "the women were all mixed. I never paid attention to what nationality. People got along better; it didn't mean anything. Jews and Italians got along, insulted each other, but I've never seen nationalities fight." After World War II, however, he remembers "racial fights" at a junior high school in Corona Plaza, conflict that spilled into Linden Park. "Black and white. Black kids were from Northern Boulevard [in North Corona]. You didn't see fights at Newtown High School."

At his family company the workplace language shifted from Italian to English in the early 1950s, and Puerto Ricans began to replace the Italian labor force. In the early 1960s commercial activity nearby "was dying. The Spanish revived it in the 1970s, a fabulous job. Then the Chinese came in." After the 1970s, "South Americans" became the dominant group at the Pirelli company, but the delivery drivers were "mixed. I even had a Vietnamese mechanic up to 1982."

His block was "Irish and German" when his family moved there in 1941; today it is more diverse. Still, "it's easy to unify the people. If there is a problem, they come out. Sometimes there are a hundred people at block association meetings.

People all show up; Oriental, Spanish, Irish, German, all show up. The only difference is that the houses and streets got cleaner. We miss the big trees, replaced by small streets. Everybody minds their own business, like they always did, the same way." And things are now better as far as sanitation is concerned. "I remember rats in Corona, from the dumps, and mosquitoes. And horses—all over—for ice, coal, fruit and vegetable wagons, and milk and junk men, into the 1930s. Corona was ugly. People say 'good old days.' They weren't so good."

Ed Gullin

The parents of Edward Gullin were Swedish immigrants who met and married in New York. His father learned tailoring in Sweden, worked in London, and then came to the United States. Ed's mother was a household worker on Long Island and "learned English with an Irish brogue from the other girls." An only child, Ed was born in 1930. Two years later the family moved to the South Elmhurst house where Ed lives now, next door to his Swedish godparents. He was baptized at First Presbyterian, the closest Protestant church. The family moved to Sweden for two years when he was five, and when he returned in 1937 he spoke only Swedish. He learned English "right on the block, but I had a Swedish accent for four years."

He graduated from PS102 in 1944. "I still know many I went to school with, and those who lived here. Of my class, some are in Long Island, California, three in Elmhurst, one in New Jersey. One moved and another sold his house, both recently." He attended Newtown High School, finishing in 1948. He worked for two years in architectural and engineering firms, then served in the army during the Korean War from 1950 to 1954. Upon returning he enrolled at Queens College, majored in anthropology, and graduated in 1958. After that, he studied architecture at Columbia University from 1958 to 1963. Throughout his schooling he worked part time as a draftsman.

In 1963 Ed met Laura, a daughter of Mexican immigrants, "at church—the first Spanish family." Her parents were from Yucatan, a place Ed was familiar with from reading the work of anthropologist Robert Redfield in college. Laura grew up in Manhattan—"neither of us could speak English in first grade"—then went to Mexico for stenographic training and returned to New York to work as a bilingual secretary. The Gullins married in 1964 and lived for ten years in Laura's parents' three-family house in Woodside. During this period Ed was licensed and began working as an architect. In 1974 he was hired by a New York City municipal agency.

Ed's parents died in 1970 and 1973, and in 1974 he and Laura moved into his South Elmhurst family home. Many local families, he explained, have transferred homes from one generation to the next through inheritance, or self-arranged sale. As an example, Ed pointed to his godparents' house next door; they sold it to their niece, and she later sold it to a member of another neighborhood kin group. Ed's home is half of a two-family house, "like most around here. But most of them [also] have one or two extra units, legal or illegal." Laura's parents later moved to a South Elmhurst house a block away from the Gullins, and Laura sees them every day.

Ed and Laura have one son serving in the army, and they go to Long Island and Connecticut to visit the wife and daughters of Laura's deceased brother. Both are active members of First Presbyterian, as is their son's Colombian godfather, who lives across the street. Ed is a block captain in the COMET civic association (see Chapter 12), and reads about local events in the NCA's *Newtown Crier.* He shops (Laura does not drive) for both his own household and Laura's parents, mostly at supermarkets in Maspeth and Middle Village. Both households patronize Macy's, the Queens Center mall, and Queens appliance stores. Ed and Laura go to a private doctor in Forest Hills and use St. John's Hospital for emergencies; Laura's mother is a clinic patient at Elmhurst Hospital.

South Elmhurst "was heavily Irish, with some Italians and more Germans" when Ed was growing up. "There was one Negro family that also went to PS102. When I came back from the Korean War, it was still mainly Irish. A few Swedes and Norwegians." Ed's high school class "was mainly white, about 2 percent black and 1 percent other. The blacks were from East Elmhurst, by La Guardia airport. It was a working-class to upper-class black neighborhood."

An Argentinian family moved into South Elmhurst in 1954. By 1974 "there were other Spanish people. In the late 1970s, Asians, from China, India, moved in, one at a time. The Irish are still here. They are dominant, but the white total is down. They have big mouths and are the community leaders. Ascension [Roman Catholic Church] is mainly Irish." Ed's own church was heavily Scottish when he was younger, but "in the 1960s First Presbyterian changed. Filipinos came in the 1970s. Koreans came and left in the early 1980s, and established their own church. In the last twenty years it's become very international."

At work Ed's staff consists of "three [white] Americans, and one French Jew, Indian, Russian immigrant, Ecuadorian, Jamaican, Chinese, Korean, and black American men and women." The client population his agency serves is mainly black. "We don't have any prejudice [within our staff], and 60 percent of blacks don't [either]."

Kenneth and Linda Witter

Kenneth was born in 1960 and still lives in the Newtown section of Elmhurst. His Manhattan-born father was the son of German and English immigrants. His mother's Polish and Russian immigrant parents lived in Mount Vernon, New York, but in the late 1930s moved to Manhattan, where Kenneth's parents married. After World War II they moved to the Elmhurst house of Kenneth's paternal uncle, an engineer at a local factory. Kenneth's father, a machinist, died in 1963, and Kenneth was raised in his uncle's house. In 1974 the uncle relocated with his factory to New Hampshire. Kenneth and his mother stayed in Elmhurst, moving to a nearby apartment.

Kenneth attended PS13, Newtown High School, and Queens College, where he majored in geology and graduated in 1982. That year his mother moved to her aging father's house in Mount Vernon, but Kenneth remained in Elmhurst. "I didn't want to move, or work for an oil company, so I worked at Macy's where I had worked part time while in college." In 1986 he became an urban park ranger at Flushing Meadows–Corona Park; he teaches about animals, plants, weather, astronomy, and local history in schools and at the park. The rangers also conduct summer children's programs and weekend park tours, and do "crowd control" during special events.

Kenneth met his wife, Linda, while working at Macy's. She is Jewish, of mixed German, Russian, and Austrian background, and grew up in Forest Hills and Jackson Heights. She now works for a media firm in Manhattan. They married in 1987, and she moved into his Elmhurst apartment. Kenneth parks their car on the street, but with difficulty: "Renting [out residential units in] garages is big business around here, so [many] people park on the street." Since their building does not have a laundry room, Kenneth and Linda drive to Mount Vernon, where "my mother does it."

Kenneth and Linda enjoy old movies and camping, and are Grateful Dead fans, owning dozens of concert tapes. They patronize Karl's, a German delicatessen where Kenneth has shopped since childhood, and a nearby bodega for soda and cigarettes, but buy most of their food at a Pathmark in Long Island City: "The selection and prices are better; the stores here are smaller." They eat out occasionally in Elmhurst at a diner and an Italian restaurant, and order takeout from a Chinese restaurant. They shop at Macy's, the Queens Center mall, and a mall on Long Island.

Kenneth's uncle and mother were members of the Newtown Civic Association, and he recalls its Christmas events at the Elmhurst Branch Library and Clement Clarke Moore Park in the 1970s. He is not an active NCA member but does read the *Newtown Crier.* As a child he attended St. James Episcopal Church, but "I stopped, and consider myself an atheist today." He bowled in a Methodist church league from his teens until he was married, and played softball in a Middle Village league and football in Queens parks.

"Growing up, I could play on the streets," Kenneth said. "The neighborhood has changed tremendously since my youth. Almost all the storekeepers I grew up with have moved away. All the delis were German, and only Karl is left." In high school, "I had a lot of friends who were Jewish and Oriental. I was in the honors school at Newtown; there were only one or two blacks and Hispanics in it." In the 1980s the street where Kenneth has lived his whole life became "all Hispanic. Karl's deli carries *El Diario;* he needs to sell newspapers to survive." Kenneth added, "We've never tried the Latin restaurants near here. We wouldn't feel comfortable."

The users of Flushing Meadows–Corona Park where Kenneth works "are heavily Hispanic, and in some areas Indian. The Hispanics use the soccer fields. We banned national flags in the park; it invites arguments at games. I don't see many Chinese or Koreans." The other rangers are "Korean, two Cuban, one Basque, black, two white (I don't know their background; they have Irish names but don't look Irish), Italian, WASP [White Anglo-Saxon Protestant], and black women bosses." These work colleagues are also friends; "We're a small group. I invited them to parties here," and one of the Cubans "once took me to a good [Latin American] meal in Jackson Heights." Kenneth's friends in Elmhurst include childhood friend Art Wong and his non-Chinese wife, a white "married to a Puerto Rican," and a white couple who recently moved back to the wife's family house.

Linda's friends are mainly "Jewish or half-Jewish, from my neighborhood as a kid." One "is Ecuadorian, but not his wife. She's Spanish, I'm not sure of the nationality. I had black friends in junior high and high school. I sang in the choir [with them]; they didn't live in my neighborhood." Linda's boss is "WASP"; her colleagues include "two Nigerians, two Italians, one WASP, and the rest are Jewish, about eight of them."

Kenneth and Linda's apartment building used to be owned by the Cord Meyer company. "I've heard from the older ladies there were 'No dogs, No Jews' signs in the Cord Meyer days. When they sold it, the owners didn't keep it up. The janitor when it was Cord Meyer used to mop the floors every night. Now it's once a month. Two old ladies on this floor died this year, and Latin American families moved in." The landlord profited from this turnover: "The two old ladies were paying less than $100 [a month]. New apartments are renting at $650 to $700."

Outside, "the nature of the block has changed. People come to the alley to smoke marijuana and coke. The stores put up corrugated sheet metal gates. The Ecuadorian and Colombian nightclubs draw cars on the weekends. People used to sit out with chairs at night." In 1988 Kenneth was assaulted by four men in his building's courtyard. "There was a man urinating in the halls. I asked him to go elsewhere. He called three friends. They used the courtyard as a john for beer drinkers at the bodega. Today I wouldn't let my wife walk home from the train station alone at night. My assault was the first time in this area. It's definitely going downhill. We're looking to get out now. They're drinking beer on the street at 8:00 A.M."

The Declining Significance of Ethnicity

The ancestral nationalities of Elmhurst-Corona's white population have been strikingly diverse. In 1980 the largest group was 11,100 persons of Italian ancestry (60 percent of them in Corona); another 2,200 were of part-Italian ancestry, and together they made up 28 percent of CD4's white population. The next groups in size were 4,100 Irish and 5,900 part-Irish, 2,600 Germans and 3,200 part-Germans, and 1,750 Poles and 1,200 part-Poles. The rest included 2,800 Greeks, about 2,000 English, about 1,400 French, 1,300 Russians, 800 Austrians, 700 Czechs, 700 Hungarians, 540 Yugoslavs, 525 Ukrainians, 460 Romanians, 300 Portuguese, 180 Lithuanians, 110 Scots, 100 Dutch, 100 Swedes, 70 Slovaks, and 40 Norwegians. (Partial ancestry figures for Greeks and other nationalities are not readily available.)[6]

The substantial numbers of mixed European ancestry were one indication of the cross-ethnic marital ties that existed among Elmhurst-Corona whites.[7] But beyond persons such as Russian-Czech Mary Walensa and German-English-Polish-Russian Kenneth Witter, others of unmixed ancestry were married to spouses of European ethnic backgrounds different from their own. One could not assume from a surname that the person's parents or spouse were of the ethnic identity that surname indicated. Married women were frequently of different ethnic ancestry from their husbands: Mrs. Fee and Mrs. Baird were German, Mrs. Pirelli was Hungarian, Rose Rothschild was Italian. Kinship networks involved ethnically diverse relatives and surnames; it was not unusual, for instance, to hear a third-generation Italian say, "I have Jewish cousins."

As a location of continuing Italian residential and commercial concentration, Corona Heights was the only identifiable white "ethnic neighborhood" in CD4. In 1980 Italians accounted for 50 to 75 percent of the white residents in the seven census tracts surrounding Willam Moore Park, but this was no isolated Italian urban village existing beyond the larger white melting pot. Maria Matteo, herself from a local Italian family, collected information on second- and third-generation marriages in five long-established Corona Heights Italian families and found that in twenty-two marriages only seven spouses were Italian. The others were German (six spouses), Irish (three), German-Polish (two), Italian-Irish, Polish, Swedish, and Ukrainian.[8]

What then did ethnicity mean to Elmhurst-Corona whites who intermarried so frequently and were often of mixed European ancestry themselves? David Halle, a sociologist who studied a similar population in New Jersey, found ethnicity "a phenomenon of secondary and fading importance. . . . [People] rarely use ethnic categories to understand and explain their own position in contemporary America. . . . Very little happens because they are Italians or Poles or Irish or Germans. . . . As a third-generation [man] of Irish origin explained: 'You know, years ago in the 1930s if you wanted to marry an Italian or Pole your family would give you all kinds of trouble. . . . Now things have changed. It doesn't matter anymore.' Beliefs that those of similar ethnic origin should spend their social life together are even weaker. No one [I met] ever expressed such a view."[9]

Italian and its regional dialects were spoken in Corona Heights by elderly first-generation immigrants and recently arrived Italians, and other European tongues could be heard elsewhere. Some second- and third-generation whites (such as Norma Fee and Patsy Baird, Phil Pirelli, and Ed Gullin) spoke or understood an ancestral European language because their parents or grandparents had spoken it at home, but many others spoke only English. At one Corona Heights Christmas tree lighting in William Moore Park the master of ceremonies was Anthony Quondamatteo (known as Tony Q). He called attention to his own unease with Italian when he told the audience he had rehearsed four times the pronunciation of "Tu Scendi dalle Stelle," an Italian carol to be sung by the PS14 glee club.

White people were aware of one another's European surnames, better-known ethnic foods, and holiday customs, but in block and civic associations or Community Board 4, white ethnicity was irrelevant. In relation to their newer neighbors, people referred to themselves as "American," not as European ethnics. At a meeting between Queens community leaders and the Korean American Association of Mid-Queens, Rose Rothschild called attention to the latter's banner; she thought they should call themselves "Americans of Korean ancestry," noting that she was "an American of Italian ancestry."[10]

The only official recognition of white ethnicity on any CB4 meeting agenda during my fieldwork was a request to string an *eruv* wire along streetlights in Elmhurst to permit "observant Jews" to carry items within the enclosed area during the weekly sabbath. Board members were uncharacteristically silent and appeared uncomfortable with this ethnically exclusive matter. The two men making the request, both wearing beards and yarmulkes, explained that they were from the Young Israel congregation in Jackson Heights, and that an *eruv* had been approved in the Forest Hills–Rego Park area. The motion for approval elicted no discussion and was quickly passed.

On two occasions I heard Italian ethnicity interjected into CB4 meetings in remarks interpreted as ethnic slights. In 1984 Tom McKenzie reported that he had written on CB4 stationery about litter at the Elmhurst Burger King, and he wondered why the reply from its owner, a Mr. della Monica, came to his home address. A Jewish male member said jokingly, "What's the name? You've got the answer"—a remark intended to link the owner's Italian surname with personal intimidation. "I object," shouted Norma Cirino, conveying her anger over this ethnic slur. "It's like being in Germany." At another meeting Cirino herself asked, "Who's supposed to remove the snow at Spaghetti Park?" the name commonly used in Corona for William Moore Park. "I resent that as an ethnic remark," Rose Rothschild responded. "I also resent that," said Miriam Levenson, who was Jewish. By characterizing the query in ethnic terms, the two women deflected Cirino's questioning of their performance as district manager and CB4 chair.

Rothschild and others occasionally used self-directed ethnic humor, however. At a playground dedication she joked about telling someone making demands of her, "Listen, I'm from East Harlem, so you better worry about your knees." And at one district cabinet meeting she commented, "That Transportation Commissioner—Riccio—I hate that he's Italian. Oops!"

Although white ethnicity had little scope or force in Elmhurst-Corona civic politics, privately some people did maintain a "concern with identity, with the feeling of being Jewish or Italian, etc.," and in some cases, an assertive "ethnic pride."[11] For a few, ethnicity became a mission. My one exposure to this attitude occurred at the 1987 Queens Festival in Flushing Meadows–Corona Park when I placed our English-Spanish-Chinese-Korean project statement in the Queens College tent. A white Corona Heights resident in her late fifties demanded to see me. "You have Asian, Hebrew, Spanish, and English. No Italian!" (she mistook Korean for Hebrew). I expained that we were not studying Italian-speaking immigrants, but she continued to berate me.

This in-your-face ethnic assertion contrasted with sociologist Donald Tricarico's assessment that "Italian American ethnicity has been taken for granted, reserved, ambivalent."[12] Such a taken-for-granted ethnic identification was probably more salient for persons of Italian ancestry living in Corona Heights than for others of any European ethnic identity, including Italians, elsewhere in CD4. As Maria Matteo viewed it,

> To me, Corona has always been "Italian" in the sense that neighboring families were from an Italian background as were most of my [St. Leo's parochical school] classmates. . . . I think that a large part of the personality of Corona is defined by the merchants and types of businesses along Corona Avenue. These include the Lemon Ice King, Corona Pizzeria, the Salumeria (or Nucci's), the Corona Heights Pork Store, Baldi's Italian Pastry Shop, . . . the Park Side Restaurant and Army's Restaurant. In some way, these businesses manage to cater to the demands of the older, established Italians and first generation Italian-Americans while giving the younger residents, those who are second and third generation, a sense of identity.[13]

This handful of stores received frequent press coverage and, in addition to local customers, attracted an outside clientele in search of Italian food and atmosphere.[14] As in other Italian neighborhoods in New York City,[15] eating and food-shopping in Corona provided visitors who wished to "feel" or "assert" Italianness with a dose of what sociologist Herbert Gans calls "symbolic ethnicity," an individualized form of white ethnicity "characterized by a nostalgic allegiance to the culture of the immigrant generation, or that of the old country; a love for and pride in a tradition that can be felt without having to be incorporated in everyday behavior."[16]

Symbolic ethnicity is self-initiated and self-cultivated; in some cases it becomes, in effect, a hobby. I did not discover much of this among Elmhurst-Corona whites. Phil Pirelli, who spoke Italian and whose family firm produced Italian food items, downplayed ethnic identification. He mentioned his trip to

Italy only when listing tours he had taken around the world. Joe Frascatti, a Corona Heights resident who had visited Italy twice and traveled there with his mother's sister, a nun who lived in Genoa, spoke warmly of these visits in the language of family and kinship, not of "roots" and symbolic ethnicity.

A more assertive attachment to Italianness was expressed by Ed Gullin, the Swedish architect. He told me, "Our relatives are basically Italian American," referring to the Italian American widow of his Mexican brother-in-law and their two daughters, both of whom had married Italian Americans. Ed was himself a professed "Italophile" and injected several Italian phrases while telling me about his visits to Italy.

An even stronger case of symbolic ethnicity was the pursuit of Irishness by German-English-Polish-Russian Kenneth Witter.

> I wanted an ethnic identity in high school. I felt it was lacking. I couldn't speak Polish, and didn't have a Polish name. I didn't feel it [when I first went to] college. My best friend [then] was Irish, and we went to different bars. I tried Guinness; I loved it. We went to Liffey's [bar] on Broadway [in Elmhurst]. There was a guy with a guitar and fiddle. I loved it. . . . I had another Irish friend, who plays guitar. We go to bars and sing. . . . In the [mid-]1980s, the Irish [began to] disappear, and more Indians and Pakistanis came to play pool [at Liffey's], but I was there in the golden days—with two guitars, fiddles, and tin whistle. . . . Now there is a new surge of Irish in Jackson Heights and Woodside, and the young Irish are going to Liffey's again. I've been to Ireland, with Art [Wong]. I took Irish history at Queens College. I learned about Irish politics at bars. I was jealous of real Irish and their names when I first started. I assumed an Irish accent and manner of speech. So who is Irish? I know more Irish history, music, than they do. I belong to the Irish society at work, for political reasons. I feel so at home now with Irish people, or in going to Ireland. I've learned it all in the past ten years. I became an Irish person in college. Sometimes I meet people who find out I'm not Irish, and won't speak to me.[17]

Bonds of Local Solidarity

What white Elmhurst-Corona residents shared most was local knowledge, common experience, and lifelong memories. They viewed their streets and neighborhood through layers of reminiscence, which surfaced in everyday conversation. New sights, structures, events, and neighbors were registered on long-held, shared mental templates of what "Elmhurst" and "Corona" are and were, and how to navigate and live within these neighborhoods. These understandings and routines constituted what anthropologists call "culture"—a way of life that was reproduced daily along predictable pathways and in ordinary interactions, grew more meaningful over years and decades, and at the same time was continually adjusted to new circumstances.

This local culture was constructed and replenished through what A. H. J. Prins calls "a patterned set of recurrent events."[18] While I was interviewing Norma Fee and Patsy Baird, a friend who had lived on their block since 1922 dropped by, and the three women reminisced—about farms and orchards, stores on Broadway in the 1930s, the movie theater that later became Temple Emanu-el synagogue, and Bamman's ice cream parlor, a Newtown High School student hangout from the 1930s to the 1960s. I heard similar remembrances of things past from many white residents, recited sometimes with a sense of loss and other times as a layered history of what had preceded a store or building's current use. Recent change was so pervasive that even twenty-four-year-old Elmhurst college student Steve Aron had a stock of reminiscences: the amusement park "that used to be where the [Queens Center] mall is now," the Elmhurst lane where he bowled before it was "bought by Koreans," the first Geeta Hindu Temple on a site now occupied by "a Spanish church."[19]

This sharing of remembrances, with continual fine-tuning for ongoing change, occurred as white Elmhurst-Corona residents conversed with household members, kin, and friends. Forty-four-year-old Joe Frascatti spent Saturday afternoons with old "Corona boys" over lunch and drinks at Army's restaurant. Most of these men were Italian, but links of neighborhood experience and friendship easily crossed white ethnic lines. At the 1992 retirement party for Pastor Charles Sorg at First Presbyterian Church, I sat across from Bunny Schwartz, who was Jewish and a close friend of Lois Sorg. They had met soon after the Sorgs arrived in Elmhurst. In 1966 Schwartz approached Pastor Sorg to ask if her VFW chapter could celebrate Memorial Day at the church's monument commemorating men killed in World War II. He agreed, and Mrs. Sorg invited Schwartz "in for tea." The two women "found our sons were both entering kindergarten at PS102, and we've been friends ever since."

White Elmhurst-Corona men were often linked through bowling leagues. One night I accompanied Steve Aron to Maspeth Bowl, just over the Elmhurst-Maspeth border, where he bowled and worked part time. The bowlers, predominantly white, had Italian, German, Polish, and other European surnames and ranged from late teenagers to men in their fifties. Constant banter marked the scene, a locker-room democracy in which trim twenty-year-olds in tight jeans and razor haircuts mixed with less clothes-conscious men in their thirties and forties, some with advanced potbellies under T-shirts identifying their employers.

In Steve's 6:30 P.M. league eighty men bowled in four-man teams; his 9:00 P.M. league consisted of one hundred men in five-man teams. After a man bowled, he reached to touch the hand of each of his teammates, and sometimes of opposing team members, in a sweeping movement around the lane's seats and scoring table. A strike elicited hand-slapping; a man who performed poorly would skip the touching, disappointed at himself, but one or two teammates often touched him in reassurance. Friends who dropped by to watch joined in, and this physical camraderie embraced each bowler, no matter how he or his team scored.

Civic associations (see Chapter 12), senior centers, and churches also knit established white residents together. Elmhurst-Corona's senior citizen programs all began during the 1970s, when increasing numbers of second-generation whites were reaching retirement. They included AARP chapters at the Reformed Church of Newtown, First Presbyterian, and Elmhurst Baptist; Golden Age Clubs, featuring bingo, at Ascension, St. Leo's, and St. Paul's Roman Catholic churches; and city-funded programs with activities and meals at the Elmhurst Senior Center, Italian Charities in South Elmhurst, and the Corona Preservation Senior Center and the Spanish-language First United Methodist Church, both in Corona Plaza. At St. Paul's the group was Italian and African American, and the mainly Latin American program at First United Methodist also included a group of local whites.[20]

A remarkable chapter had opened at Elmhurst's white houses of worship in 1972 when a monthly lunch meeting of Protestant ministers began, and the clergy and laity from three Protestant and two Roman Catholic churches held their first joint "Week of Prayer for Christian Unity" service. During 1973 three Protestant congregations conducted common summer services, rotating weekly from one church to another. The dormant Elmhurst Federation of Churches revived in 1974 and sponsored a joint Thanksgiving service that year at First Presbyterian, with Temple Emanu-el's new rabbi as the main speaker; its 1975 Thanksgiving service was held at the rabbi's synagogue. The following year, eleven clergy participated in the Week of Prayer service along with choirs from St. Bart's and the Reformed Church.

By 1983 federation lunches were drawing fourteen Protestant and Catholic clergy from Elmhurst and Jackson Heights, all of them white except Chinese Pastor Bill Lee from the Reformed Church and the Korean minister of Ban Suk Methodist. During the 1980s, however, the historically white churches focused on attracting new immigrant worshipers, and the annual Thanksgiving and rotating summer services ended. Temple Emanu-el, whose shrinking congregation had no Jewish immigrant population to draw on, sold its building and moved to Forest Hills. The spring Week of Prayer service continued but by 1988 involved only four churches. The audience of fifty that year consisted mainly of older white women, among them Norma Fee and Lois Sorg.

White Outsiders in Elmhurst-Corona

White diners and shoppers from outside the neighborhood came to the Park Side restaurant and the Queens Center mall and Macy's. White Long Island and eastern Queens commuters traveled through CD4 on crowded subways, provoking some resentment. More resentment, however, simmered and occasionally boiled over between Elmhurst-Corona whites and white local business owners who resided outside CD4, white police who lived outside New York City, and the white School Board 24 members from other neighborhoods who controlled Elmhurst-Corona's schools.

Antagonism toward particular landlords and business proprietors arose repeatedly. White civic activists knew the identity of some bordello owners who lived outside their neighborhood, such as the "landlord from East Setauket, Long Island, who had three [Roosevelt Avenue] houses of prostitution," cited by Rose Rothschild at a 1995 district cabinet meeting. Legitimate businesses, however unwelcome, were often more difficult to fight. Their owners hired attorneys adept in the intricacies of zoning regulations, and they used the power of resources to cultivate community support.

In 1972 the Mancusos came to CB4 to protest the ice machine on a residential property next to their Corona home. They had complained for three years to the absentee owner, a Mr. Steiner, about the machine's noise, ice trucks parked on their sidewalk, and nighttime customers who banged on the machine and rang the Mancusos' doorbell when it was out of order. They had confirmed that the machine's operation was illegal, but the owner was now requesting a zoning variance to permit its continuance. CB4 chair Michael Dowd objected to legalizing an illegal use, and Rose Mazzarella said it "would mean going backwards in terms of zoning." The board voted against the variance and advised the Mancusos to attend the Board of Standards and Appeals (BSA) hearing, the next step in the variance-request process.

In 1986 attorney Sid Davidoff, later the lobbyist for the USTA expansion in Flushing Meadows–Corona Park, came to CB4 representing the Queens Center mall.[21] He spoke against a proposed new shopping mall at a nearby site in Rego Park, arguing that it would harm local quality of life with increased traffic and air pollution and would represent "a $40-to-50 million loss to surrounding mom-and-pop stores." Davidoff's presentation opened old wounds, and CB4 member Howard Riback exploded. "We fought Queens Center in 1973 and raised the same problems, such as traffic. You're not fighting for our community. You're fighting for business. I was a businessman. I'm one of those mom-and-pop businesses *you* put out of business." Founded in 1922 by his father-in-law, an Austrian immigrant, Riback's variety store in Elmhurst had closed soon after its fiftieth anniversary. Other board members likewise expressed little sympathy for Davidoff and his client.

Fighting McDonald's

Commercial zoning along most Elmhurst-Corona shopping strips was designed "to accommodate stores and services for the neighborhood's residents."[22] At several locations, however, nearby residents and commercial real estate owners skirmished over business expansion intended to serve wider markets. The longest-running battle pitted Elmhurst homeowners against a McDonald's restaurant.

The McDonald's opened in 1972, occupying both a corner commercial lot on Queens Boulevard and a residential (R6) parcel behind it on Cornish Avenue, which ran directly into Queens Boulevard. While it was still under construction, Joseph Morsellino, a lawyer representing the restaurant, came to CB4 to request a zoning variance that would permit parking on the R6 plot. Morsellino stated that without this parking the business would not be profitable. He also said that no drive-through exit would be built to Cornish Avenue, and shrubbery would be planted along the entire Cornish side of the property. If this parking was necessary to make the McDonald's profitable, asked CB4 member Steve Trimboli, then why had they waited to seek the variance until after the building was already going up? Despite the concern of some members that Morsellino had "not sufficiently answered" this question, however, CB4 approved the variance.

In 1982 Ira Meyer, the McDonald's owner since 1975, applied for another variance to construct a drive-through exit to Cornish Avenue, arguing that he needed it to compete with other fast-food drive-ins. CB4 member Tom McKenzie was furious. He lived on Cornish Avenue, and like its other residents he objected to the increased traffic and inconvenience a drive-through exit would bring to this street. He argued that owner Meyer was aware of the existing traffic pattern when he purchased the business, that the restaurant was already profitable, and that an exit onto Queens Boulevard—avoiding Cornish Avenue—could be added with only slight modification of the existing building. CB4 nonetheless approved the variance, and so did the BSA.

Early in 1983 residents noticed that the McDonald's addition and drive-through did not conform to the plan approved by CB4. McKenzie notified Elmhurst's city council member Thomas Manton, and the building permit was suspended. At CB4 McKenzie detailed owner Meyer's noncompliance, adding that the shrubbery planted earlier to block off the parking lot from Cornish Avenue was too low. Charles Stidolph, a building engineer and chair of CB4's zoning committee, responded that the BSA had not yet ruled on Meyer's claim that the addition was in "substantial compliance." Meyer himself was now also a member of CB4, and Rose Rothschild commented, "There's plenty of conflicts of interest here."

The next act in McKenzie versus McDonald's occurred in 1985 when Ira Meyer applied for still another zoning variance to permit commercial use of a Cornish Avenue house he had bought next to the R6 parking lot. This time Meyer hired both lawyer Morsellino and CB4 zoning chair Stidolph, who recused himself from voting. The public hearing on the variance was attended by a dozen local residents and a half-dozen CB4 members. Meyer admitted that he had bought the house in 1981 to use illegally as an office but had occupied only the basement until 1984, when his expansion to the first floor was noticed by Cornish Avenue residents. Morsellino added that they were requesting a second variance to permit commercial activity in a wooden building, also an illegal usage.

An elderly man asked, "Isn't it now operating against the law?" to which Morsellino replied evasively, "The application is pending." Tom McKenzie, a court officer, stated that the variance requests, which he had read, claimed an "economic hardship" because Meyer would have difficulty selling the house to a residential buyer, given its proximity to a commercial property—namely, his own McDonald's restaurant. "Isn't this a self-created hardship?" McKenzie retorted.

A woman asked, "Why did he buy it if he knew the office was wrong?" Meyer replied, "It was my assumption that since it was next to a warehouse [on the opposite side], no one would care. I'm asking for permission now." Ilsa Vasko, a South Elmhurst homeowner said, "There is a danger that a precedent may be set. I do not live in this area, but on [my] street, it happened. A house was used for selling automobiles. It was closed down [only] after it was brought to CB4." "This case is unique," Morsellino responded. Vasko, however, urged "the illustrious members of CB4" not to allow commercial uses in residential areas. "The problem is commercial block-busting," McKenzie added.

At this point an older man said, "I've been here for forty-five years. We want to keep the block residential. Other houses *would* make more money renting the first floor as offices. It is illegal, and should be padlocked." Another woman added, "He [Ira Meyer] has power. He wanted a driveway and he got it. We don't have power. This is a little at a time." Ilsa Vasko, speaking with a European accent, agreed: "Certain things are just being pushed down our throat." Lawyer Morsellino then said, "Here in America people have a right to ask for a variance." Shaken by this innuendo, Vasko declared, "I'm an American too, here thirty-seven years."

At the next CB4 meeting the McDonald's variances passed by 22 to 2, with Stidolph and Meyer abstaining, a result facilitated by the "explanatory approach" of attorney Morsellino. In this mode of argument, according to political scientist Jeffrey Davidson, a knowledgeable, confident spokesperson seeks "to provide [board] members with sufficient information and with an interpretation of that information which enables the [board] member to see the . . . reason behind the lobbyist's position and to vote accordingly. . . . Individuals . . . using the explanatory approach act as if they were the [board] member's equals." Morsellino had done zoning work since 1963, knew the law and facts of his cases, and was familiar with the CB4 and city agency cast of characters.

The dissenting Elmhurst residents, in contrast, exemplified the "exclamatory approach," presenting their view of "what is 'right,' 'fair,' or 'moral' [more] than what is 'reasonable,' [an approach] often used by neighborhood groups opposing some 'intrusion.' . . . Those who use the exclamatory approach seem unsure of themselves, as if a great social distance existed between themselves and the [board] member. . . . They are not optimistic about their chances of obtaining a fair hearing or of winning."[23]

Although Tom McKenzie combined both explanatory and exclamatory appeals to his CB4 colleagues, he lost. In addition to enlisting Morsellino's lubricatory power and hiring the CB4 zoning chair, McDonald's owner Ira Meyer relied on the good will he had cultivated through cash and kind gifts to Elmhurst-Corona community groups. CB4 member Pat Carpentiere testified to Meyer's support of the Corona Ambulance Corps, to which Carpentiere belonged, and member Richard Isles called Meyer "a good neighbor in the commmunity. When people ask for things, he gives to them, for street fairs, etc. There are no problems with McDonald's."

When Ira Meyer later resigned from CB4, having moved out of New York City, the board voted him a citation for his service. He continued to operate his Elmhurst McDonald's, and Tom McKenzie continued the struggle. In 1987 McKenzie complained about compressor noise during food deliveries "at 4:30 [to] 6:30 A.M. They come at daylight hours in Manhattan." An agreement eventually banned the compressors before 7:00 A.M. on weekdays and 11:00 A.M. on weekends. In 1989 Meyer applied for a zoning change to combine the three restaurant, parking, and office properties into one commercially zoned lot. Understanding that future changes would then require no public hearing, McKenzie and his neighbors again mobilized against "commercial blockbusting." Both the Newtown Civic Association and CB4 questioned why the rezoning was needed if, as Meyer pledged, he planned no changes to his building. But CB4 voted in Meyer's favor, and commercial zoning for the entire parcel was granted in 1990. Additions to the existing building followed in 1991.

"What's good for business may not be good for Elmhurst," McKenzie concluded after this last defeat. He noted, moreover, that Corona and Lefrak City supporters of the Elmhurst McDonald's variances over the years were now opposing a twenty-four-hour, two-story McDonald's drive-through restaurant in *their* neighborhood. Meetings, petitions, and a public hearing followed, and in 1995 CB4 learned that the City Planning Commission had denied this proposed McDonald's its required variance.

110th Precinct Police Officers

White Elmhurst-Corona residents were well aware that many 110th Precinct police lived outside the city. During a CB4 discussion of the unavailability of police officers of captain's rank on weekends, Miriam Levenson said sarcastically that the 110th Precinct commanding officer "can't come in because he lives on [Long] Island." In 1988 the Queens borough commander told the Newtown Civic Association that "ninety-nine of the 105 officers at the 110th Precinct reside outside New York City," as compared with 40 percent for the department overall. Some NCA members suggested that "if the 60 percent city-dwelling [figure was] reflected in the 110th . . . these police officers might have a different attitude on enforcing Elmhurst's quality-of-life problems."

Many white residents remembered police officers who had lived in the neighborhood. Tom McKenzie recalled growing up in the 1950s when "McLennihan, the deskman at the 110th, lived on this block. You were afraid he would tell your parents if you were in trouble." Some Elmhurst residents also remembered their neighbor Michael Codd, who took the subway to work every day even while serving as New York City's police commissioner in the 1970s. Two popular 110th officers, Sergeant Pete Petrone and the 1989–1990 commanding officer, Gerald McNamara, emphasized their local ties: Petrone had grown up in Elmhurst, where his parents still lived; McNamara resided in Woodside, just three blocks outside CD4.

A president of the city Police Sergeants Benevolent Association told author Charles Morris, "We lost something when so many men started to live in the suburbs. Some men even avoid making an arrest if it means missing their car pool." And a veteran city labor negotiator explained, "Hell, it's simple. These guys don't live in the city any more and don't care what happens to it."[24] CB4 member Pat Carpentiere, a Queens court officer, affirmed that "[police] officers who live on the Island don't care about the problem. New officers should live in New York City." A city residency requirement, however, was fiercely resisted by the Patrolmen's Benovolent Association.

By 1994 almost half of the entire NYPD lived outside New York City, and 55 percent of new white recruits were suburban commuters.[25] The attitudes of some of these young white police toward CD4 were problematic. At the 1987 Queens Festival a young white 110th Precinct officer stood next to me facing a map of the borough. "Half of Queens is shot," he told me. "Douglaston and Little Neck are still nice. Glen Oaks is integrated. Queens Village is okay. [All of southeast Queens] is gone. Richmond Hill is okay I hear. Glendale is nice. Woodside, no. Jackson Heights, Corona is all gone. . . . I grew up in Astoria. It's going." His comments reflected the racial geography of Queens. White areas were "nice," mixed areas with white populations were "going," and areas of black and immigrant settlement such as Elmhurst-Corona were "gone."

At a Lefrak City community meeting, McNamara was candid about Police Academy trainees assigned to the 110th. He acknowledged that they were "holding hands" at one end of 57th Avenue, "afraid of the middle of the block" where drug selling took place: "These kids are about twenty. They have no life experience, and most do not come from the city. They have no street smarts, and would not know a drug sale if they were standing next to it. But after their training they have learned. This is the first job they have ever had except for working at Burger King, or as a stockroom clerk, or a lifeguard."

School Board 24

In 1988 Norma Cirino told CB4, "I and Father [John] Garkowski are the only two representing Elmhurst and Corona on . . . School Board 24. The other seven represent Middle Village, Maspeth, Ridgewood, and Glendale. They pull for their area" (see Figure 7). Rose Rothschild responded, "He [Father Garkowski] doesn't hold a meeting to tell us what's happening." Garkowski had lived in Glendale for ten years before coming to St. Bart's in Elmhurst in 1975, and he was also a lawyer for the Brooklyn-Queens Roman Catholic Diocese. The only priest on any city school board, he was elected to SB24 in 1977 and took particular interest in the afterschool programs that the district sponsored at parochial as well as public schools.

CB4 members knew that schools in the southern tier of SD24 were not overcrowded during the 1980s. "Is this only because we have minority children?" asked Norma Cirino, who knew first hand the attitudes of her all-white SB24 colleagues. Clara Salas said bluntly, "School District 24 has been a very racist board. It favors Middle Village, Maspeth, and Ridgewood." Proposals during the 1980s to redraw school district lines in order to shift Elmhurst-Corona children into less crowded neighboring districts went nowhere. "I don't think they like the makeup of our children," commented Tom McKenzie about SD30 to the north. "The Forest Hills area [SD28 to the southeast] doesn't want our kids," said Rose Rothschild. Like many other white CB4 members, McKenzie and Rothschild ordinarily spoke of "our" children when discussing school district policies.

In 1987 the Newtown Civic Association invited SB24 president Mary Cummins, a Middle Village resident, to "discuss overcrowding in Elmhurst public schools [and] measures being taken, or being considered, to relieve the overcrowding." The NCA members told Cummins that while they welcomed mini-schools to alleviate the space crunch, they "regret that these structures occupy space which has been, during school hours, a playground for children, and, during non-school hours, a community recreational resource. The mini-school solution was criticized . . . especially in a community as park and playground poor as Elmhurst."

Cummins replied that school construction "is a central Board of Education role and responsiblity," but she did invite the NCA to suggest potential school sites to SB24. She ended the meeting by commenting on the issue that would soon dominate SB24's agenda, "the sex education curriculum now being developed by a parent-clergy-educator committee in SB24." As reported by the *Newtown Crier,* "she explained why the central board–developed curriculum was regarded by the local board as unacceptable. . . . [She feels] very strongly that a curriculum, to be acceptable, must inculcate values and morality which have strong support in the community."[26]

In 1989 Mary Cummins was reelected to SB24, and Joseph Fernandez became chancellor of the City Board of Education. In 1990 Cummins and Fernandez tangled when he prevented SB24 from making principal and assistant principal appointments without public parental involvement, a decision prompted by parent grievances filed with the BOE. Cummins sued Fernandez in retaliation, using $5,000 in tax-levy SB24 funds, and Fernandez subsequently overturned still more SB24 personnel and budget decisions.[27]

In 1992 they tangled again. A 443-page curriculum guide for first-grade teachers, *Children of the Rainbow,* was unveiled by the BOE in September 1991. Its genesis was a 1985 BOE directive "to bring about elimination of practices which foster attitudes and/or actions leading to discrimination against students, parents, or school personnel on the basis of race, color, religion, national origin, gender, age, sexual orientation and/or handicapped condition." Fernandez's predecessor, Chancellor Richard Green, had begun a five-year program to implement this directive and had planned to introduce the topic of sexual orientation in the sixth grade. Green died in 1989, and during the Green-Fernandez transition three pages on homosexual families were added to the first-grade *Rainbow* curriculum, an action that reviewers of the guide and BOE members and staff later said had escaped their attention.[28]

In February 1992 Mary Cummins received *Children of the Rainbow* and immediately declared it "gay and lesbian propaganda." Again using tax money, she sent a letter to 22,000 SD24 parents announcing, "We will not accept two people of the same sex engaged in deviant sex practices as a 'family.' " Throughout 1992 Cummins refused to provide copies of *Children of the Rainbow* to parents or to discuss it at public SB24 meetings. Teachers and parents in Elmhurst-Corona were divided: some supported Cummins; others wanted a role in reviewing the curriculum guide and deciding how much, if any, was unacceptable. In October 1992 Cummins hired buses for a rally at BOE headquarters where, among signs reading "God Created Adam and Eve, Not Adam and Steven" and "Gays Are Lower Than Animals," Father John Garkowski urged the crowd to "protect the innocence of children as long as possible. . . . It's bad enough you can't pray in school."

Meanwhile, Fernandez consented to allow the thirty-two local school boards to develop alternative curriculum guides. All except SB24 agreed either to use *Children of the Rainbow* as it stood, to delete the pages on gay and lesbian issues and introduce the topic of sexual orientation at higher grade levels, or to present a substitute guide. After SB24 refused to meet his November 1992 deadline to present a plan including tolerance of homosexuality, Fernandez suspended the board. A week later the BOE reversed the suspension and in February 1993 voted 4 to 3 not to renew Fernandez's contract.[29]

During these events the conflict widened. Mayoral challenger Rudolph Giuliani backed the four BOE members who abandoned Fernandez, and incumbent David Dinkins supported the chancellor's modified curriculum plan. John Cardinal O'Connor of the New York Roman Catholic Diocese condemned *Children of the Rainbow,* and praised BOE members who opposed it. Gay activists from ACT-UP and the Lesbian Avengers demonstrated at BOE headquarters and an SB24 meeting in Glendale. Mary Cummins enlisted the conservative Family Defense Council, and it prepared videotapes for the 1993 school board election asserting that Fernandez was "controlled by the homosexual movement" and had been brought to New York by "pro-homosexual" Mayor Dinkins. The national Christian Coalition then teamed with the New York Diocese to endorse school board candidates and campaign for them among Latin American Protestants and Catholics.[30]

As in other districts where "pro-homosexuality" became an issue, turnout in SD24 was up: 17,000 people voted, compared with 6,700 in 1989. Cummins placed first among twenty-two candidates in the May 1993 SB24 election, and Father Garkowski was second. Among other winners, however, Louisa Chan became the first SB24 member of color in a district whose students were only 27 percent white. A Chinese immigrant who had come to the United States in 1968 and worked as a state hospital inspector, Chan was president of the PS13 Parents Association in Elmhurst; she had organized a petition opposing Cummins's suit against Fernandez in 1990, and supported the *Children of the Rainbow* curriculum.[31]

Louisa Chan quickly became a thorn in SB24's side, asking pointed questions about policy and personnel decisions. At a November 1993 meeting Mary Cummins called her "chink eyes" and said, "What would you know, you're only a chink." Cummins later denied having made these racial slurs, but two white board members attested that she had. At a February 1994 meeting Cummins declared Chan "an evil, wicked woman." One white SB24 member who sided with Chan commented, "There is tremendous resentment among the other members about her being on the board." A *Newsday* editorial observed, "Anyone who sits in on the board's public meetings can see that several board members treat Chan like a second-class citizen." As the infighting continued, Asian American activists appeared at meetings demanding an apology from Cummins.[32]

Another source of tension at SB24 was Christian Coalition candidate Frank Borzellieri, a Ridgewood parochial school graduate also elected in 1993. Borzellieri demanded that certain books be banned from school libraries, including a biography of Martin Luther King, and insisted, "We are a white, Christian, British, Protestant nation. . . . Where does it say we have to focus on other cultures?" Perry Buckley, an African American from Sherwood Village and president of the PS14 Parents Association, joined parents, board members, and politicians to denounce Borzellieri, and SB24 president Mary Crowley ruled out of order a Borzellieri resolution stating, "Guidance by the Ten Commandments is superior to paganism; and . . . American history and the American way of life are clearly superior to all others."[33]

As the Cummins-Fernandez war and its aftermath enveloped the board between 1990 and 1996, SD24 registered the largest enrollment increase in the city, much of it concentrated in Elmhurst-Corona. In 1992 it rated sixth worst among the city's thirty-two school districts in physical conditions. By 1994 it was the most crowded, its schools averaging 140 percent of capacity. By 1996 more than half its pupils read below national norms for their grade level. In that year's school board election Mary Cummins and Father John Garkowski were not candidates, and only 6,800 voted. Louisa Chan and Perry Buckley were both elected, and so was Frank Borzellieri, gaining 1,900 votes from white supporters in SD24's southern tier.[34]

Race and Beyond Race

Established white residents in Elmhurst-Corona did not mobilize politically on the basis of ethnicity. No ethnic association of Irish or Italians or Germans or Poles or any other European group was active in CD4's political field.[35] Neither was white racial identity a basis of political organization by the 1980s and 1990s. Race *was* an issue when whites mobilized to keep out public housing in the 1960s. But two decades later, as CD4's political field was becoming increasingly multiracial, the established white population now understood that local quality of life was affected as much by white business owners, police, school board members, mayors, absentee landlords, organized crime groups, and developers as by anyone else.

How did Elmhurst-Corona's established whites see their new neighbors? To start, they used a vocabulary of race, ethnicity, and nationality that was widely shared but also undergoing change.

Latin Americans were "Spanish" or "Hispanics," terms used by Latin Americans themselves when speaking with white residents both informally and in public settings like CB4. ("Latino" had little currency.) Specific nationalities—"Colombian," "Dominican"—were increasingly distinguished when circumstances warranted.

East Asians were "Orientals," although this term was heard less frequently from whites by the 1990s; "Asians" replaced it, and "Chinese" and "Koreans" became more readily distinguished. South Asians were referred to as "Hindus," a term gradually replaced by "Indians." ("Asian" did not ordinarily include "Indians.")

"Blacks," and "African Americans" after this term's endorsement by Jesse Jackson in 1988,[36] referred to the majority of black persons. Persons of African ancestry who were Latin American might be spoken of as "black, but Spanish." Black immigrants were often specified by nationality, such as "Haitians" or "Jamaicans," or for "Africans" by their continent of birth.

White immigrants such as "Greeks" or "Russians" were identified by nationality. Second- and third-generation whites occasionally used European ethnic labels but usually called themselves "Americans." This term was used as well by immigrants when speaking about established whites: officers of the Korean American Association of Mid-Queens spoke of white civic leaders as "American politicians"; a Colombian CB4 member mentioned taking "American" friends to a play.

The boundary around "American," however, could shift as white persons used the term differently in different situations. In informal conversation, "Americans" and "immigrants" were contrasted, with "American" understood as white—although most whites, if asked, would agree that "African Americans" were also "American." For immigrants—of all colors—the use of "American" was more complicated. Mary Cummins considered herself "a first-generation American. . . . My parents were from Ireland." In contrast, many Elmhurst-Corona whites used "first generation" to refer to immigrants, and "second generation" for their U.S.-born offspring. Cummins's usage, reflecting confusion as to which generation is "first," also recalls the nineteenth-century application of "American" to U.S-born whites, and "immigrant" or "foreigner" to the European-born.[37]

During one of her tirades against Louisa Chan, Mary Cummins insisted "I'll say what I like as long as I'm an American." "I'm an American too," Chan retorted, emphasizing a definition that included naturalized citizens.[38] This exchange echoed the one in the McDonald's dispute between lawyer Joseph Morsellino and civic activist Ilsa Vasko: she also responded, "I'm an American too" after Morsellino had used the phrase "here in America." Rose Rothschild's insistence to Korean leaders that they were "Americans of Korean ancestry," just as she was an "American of Italian ancestry," echoed the statements of Chan and Vasko.

Some white CB4 members occasionally spoke about persons of color as "minorities" but spoke less often of themselves or others as "whites." Overall, ethnic and racial terms were rarely used in their meetings.[39] Exceptions occurred when an ethnic organization such as the Korean American Association of Mid-Queens was mentioned. When race was introduced, however, it was often objected to or supressed by whites. At one CB4 meeting, a police officer reporting on drug buyers near Lefrak City began, "We have a large number of white people," and Rose Rothschild immediately cut him off, saying, "We're not talking ethnic." The drug problem was to be defined as affecting Elmhurst-Corona and its residents, not in terms of race. At a CB4 public hearing, Clara Salas, a Cuban, said of school overcrowding, "Maybe [it continues] because the kids are Oriental and Hispanic." Hilda Dietz of the Newtown Civic Association interrupted, "No, that's out of order," and Steve Trimboli responded, "We're not interested in Hispanic or Oriental. We call them all children. . . . The politicians' representatives are here to get the message: 'We need schools.' " Rose Rothschild added, "We fought when the kids were white. We fought when the kids were Hispanic. We still are fighting."

Insistence upon a nonracial discourse among residents of CD4 could thus silence "minority" expression of issues affecting persons because they were not white. To Elmhurst-Corona whites, however, themselves now a numerical minority, nonracial discourse seemed doubly important. It dissolved a racial definition of whites that connected them to whites who supported policies they opposed, especially those that persons of color might label "racist." It also validated the reality of white-white conflicts, which were real to them and in which persons of color could be allies.

This denial of a racial group-versus-group, or "minorities"-versus-"whites," definition of neighborhood issues was also significant to Elmhurst-Corona whites because of their increasing personal interaction with persons of color. By the 1990s veteran CB4 members of different races were embracing as they arrived at meetings. Whites also interacted with persons of color at work. Phil Pirelli's food processing firm employed Latin Americans in jobs formerly held by whites. City employees Ed Gullin and Kenneth Witter worked in multiracial offices where African Americans as well as whites held professional and supervisory positions, and Witter socialized with coworkers across racial lines. Retired nurse Mary Walensa recalled some black colleagues "smarter than I am." College student Steve Aron was hired at Maspeth Bowl by its Puerto Rican owner.

Church and neighborhood were also points of cross-racial contact. Norma Fee, Patsy Baird, and Ed Gullin attended racially diverse Protestant churches, and Joe Frascatti served with Latin Americans on a Roman Catholic parish committee. Phil Pirelli met his diverse neighbors through his block association; Fee and Baird introduced themselves to theirs in personal efforts to maintain their street's appearance. Friendships developed on her apartment floor between Mary Walensa and the Latin American and Korean households whose children she tutored. Younger white residents grew up with friends of color. Kenneth Witter traveled to Ireland with his Chinese friend Art Wong. Steve Aron produced two Korean friends for me to interview, and two of his bowling teammates were Puerto Rican. Interracial marriages among Elmhurst-Corona whites were also evident, among them Ed and Laura Gullin, Wong and his non-Chinese wife, and Norma Fee and Patsy Baird's white minister, married to a Filipina church member.

The shared local culture of Elmhurst-Corona whites was also beginning to include persons of color long resident or born there. At the 110th Precinct demonstration in 1985, Puerto Rican Angela Sonera recalled that everyone knew the cop on the beat when she was a Corona schoolgirl in the 1950s. And at a district cabinet meeting an African American agency representative—backing up Rose Rothschild's recollection that in the 1960s "Roosevelt Avenue used to be nice"—said, "I agree. I grew up in [the] Dorrie Miller [apartments in North Corona]."

Still, white-black ties were few, relative to those between whites and Latin Americans and Asians. By the 1980s whites in Elmhurst-Corona were likely to have Latin American and Asian neighbors, and ties of friendship, church and block association membership, shared memory, and marriage emerged more readily from this base than did similar ties between whites and blacks. Most white-black friendships arose at work rather than from common residence, and bonds resulting from common political activity occurred at the district level of Community Board 4 rather than in block, tenant, or civic associations.

[12]

Continuities in Civic Politics

Since the 1960s New York City mayors have relied more on municipal employee unions than political party clubs to turn out votes, and rising television costs have given increased influence to permanent-government campaign financiers. Party clubs in neighborhood New York shrank from 300 in the early 1970s to half that number in the 1990s (there had been 1,700 clubs during the 1930s). And with civil service hiring and public employees' collective bargaining, clubs retained little power to fill city jobs and influence agency performance. Mayoral patronage under Koch dried up for Queens Democrats after the 1986 Manes scandal, and it remained meager under Dinkins, who received only tepid backing from the Queens Democratic organization.[1]

A sense of estrangement from "the city" and mayoral power existed among white Elmhurst-Corona civic activists by the 1980s. "We are stepchildren, Manhattan is the favored son." "They don't care about the other boroughs." "Mayor Koch and his goddam hoodlums are against Corona." These comments at Community Board 4 meetings reflected the assaults on quality of life which followed the 1975 fiscal crisis. They also indicated a weakened power of numbers in Community District 4. Elmhurst's Democratic Club folded in the 1970s; Corona's Northside Democratic Club survived but with reduced political muscle. And with fewer whites and more immigrants, the total number of votes cast by CD4 residents diminished.[2] "We don't have no political push," one white civic activist lamented. "We're just being plopped on," said another.

In the 1980s most of Corona fell within the 35th Assembly District, where 18,600 persons voted in the 1989 mayoral election. This was the lowest number of votes in all sixteen Queens ADs, nine of which each produced between 30,000 and 40,000 votes. Most of Elmhurst was in the 30th AD, where 22,600 voted, the third lowest Queens AD total. In the 1993 mayoral election Corona and

Elmhurst were divided between the redistricted 35th and 34th ADs, which produced 18,200 and 14,600 votes. No other Queens district produced fewer than 20,500 votes that year, and in seven the turnout was between 30,000 and 41,000.[3]

County, citywide, and statewide officials paid less attention to those ADs where the vote was relatively small. Moreover, most state assembly and city council members representing Elmhurst-Corona, all of them Democrats, owed first allegiance to other parts of their districts. Between 1982 and 1992 the 35th AD was represented in Albany by Helen Marshall, whose club membership and voter base was in the North Corona–East Elmhurst African American community, as were those of her successor, Jeff Aubry. The 30th and 34th ADs were represented by white men whose bases were in Forest Hills, Woodside-Maspeth, and Jackson Heights. For seats on the city council, Elmhurst-Corona was split during the 1980s into three districts, the biggest spanning five community districts and represented by Joseph Lisa Jr., a Corona Northside Democratic Club member. Lisa was rated among the seven least effective council members in a 1987 *Daily News* poll of government officials, policy advocates, and business and labor leaders, and he rated lowest of all in "accessibility" and "concern for local issues." Lacking party support for reelection, he was appointed to a judgeship in 1991. Most of CD4 was then redistricted into two city council seats, one won by Helen Marshall (who moved from the assembly) and the other by John Sabini, a white male from Jackson Heights.[4]

The power of numbers involved more than voting, however, and in response to these electoral circumstances Elmhurst-Corona's "parapolitical" civic activism grew more important. This was not without frustrations: "When we have demonstrations no one comes; we look like idiots," Al Fernicola warned at one CB4 meeting. Still, new civic leaders and associations, and a revival of civic rituals, emerged among CD4's white residents, and this activity began to draw in immigrant and black newcomers.[5]

The Elementary Forms of Civic Political Life

Civic politics began with actions by individuals who, on their own, approached others about "problems that are important to us." Often it was garbage—misplaced, mispackaged, sitting out too long—that provoked this step. Norma Fee and Patsy Baird spoke to new neighbors about garbage and dog litter. Glyn Lloyd, a retired hotel worker, visited each new household in his Elmhurst co-op to explain rules for placing garbage in the incinerator room. Countless others undertook similar activity.

With more serious problems, or where personal requests proved insufficient, the next step was to notify authorities: the Sanitation Department, the 110th Precinct, or the CB4 district office. Police termed persons who did so "block watchers"; district manager John Rowan called them "feelers in the community." They included the Lefrak City residents who surveyed 57th Avenue and recorded drug sellers' descriptions and buyers' license numbers. They also included residents throughout Elmhurst-Corona who reported illegally parked vehicles, prostitution locations, and other quality-of-life problems.[6]

Next came the concerted action of residents whom I refer to as "wardens." Examples abounded. Some collected complaints in their immediate neighborhood and then contacted authorities. Linda Walsh of the New Elmhurst Civic League wrote the city council transportation committee detailing the lack of maintenance along the Long Island Rail Road's South Elmhurst corridor, and the subsequent danger to homes from litter and brush fires and to children who entered the corridor through broken fences. Tony Caminiti, a Democratic Party district leader, relayed a variety of quality-of-life complaints from his Corona Heights constituents to elected officials and CB4, and he informed "his people" of meetings by "putting it in the paper"—placing flyers in copies of the *Daily News* sold at Joyce's candy store.[7]

Other wardens did research. Bill Donnelly mapped dead and dying Elmhurst street trees to pressure the city for pruning and replanting. Steven Castro, a Lefrak City resident, compared prices at the Rego Park and Lefrak City Pathmark stores; he discovered thirteen items with higher prices at Lefrak and publicized his results in a CB4 consumer affairs committee flyer. Some wardens mediated local disputes. Restaurateur Anthony Federici interceded after two Corona Heights Italian greengrocers began a price war and the windows of one were shot out one night; he also sent an employee to request men racing cars on Corona streets to stop, and the problem ended.[8]

Many wardens were members of block, tenant, co-op, and civic associations and operated under their banner. In 1985 CB4 had a list of thirty-five such associations (though some were no doubt inactive). Block associations formed to address problems on their own doorstep. One in Elmhurst was set in motion after "a new family" arrived in 1974. As a resident recounted:

> The sidewalk had become the outdoor storage area for [tires and empty cardboard boxes]. Aggravating the situation was the behavior of the new children [who] raced up and down the sidewalk on their bicycles [and intimidated] some of the children on the block. . . . [One] summer evening, groups of neighbors started discussing the best way of solving this problem. . . . Around nine p.m. the neighbors re-assembled in front of the problem property, about a hundred strong, and selected three representatives to speak with the landlady and the father. . . . After an hour or so, an understanding was reached. The landlady agreed to keep any outside garbage in covered cans and to keep the area in front of her house clean. The father, for his part, agreed to closer supervise his sons and asked to be told of any future problems. . . . Nearly two months after this incident the promises were still being kept.[9]

Block associations persisted if problems did, or through dedicated leadership. Otherwise they waxed and waned.

Tenant associations were similar to block associations in the immediacy of problems addressed but different in that tenants shared a building and a landlord. By 1976 the association at the Carlyle, a seventy-unit Elmhurst building, had enrolled fifty-seven households, elected officers, and retained a lawyer; complaints filed with the city two years earlier of inadequate heat, broken windows, and roof repairs were finally being addressed by the landlord. The association consisted of "white, black, Oriental and Hispanic people," and its newsletter was printed in English, French, and Spanish.[10]

Residents of larger apartment complexes faced more daunting organizational challenges. The Lefrak City Tenants Association had undergone leadership changes by the 1980s, and continuity of floor, building, and section captains required constant attention. In addition to matters of maintenance, security, recreation facilities, parking garage conditions, and garbage collection and storage, the LCTA dealt with quality-of-life issues—such as drug sales on 57th Avenue—that brought it into contact with the 110th Precinct, city agencies, and CB4. In this regard it was a civic association as well as a tenant association.

Cooperative apartments elected boards of directors which also took on civic association functions. The 225-unit Sherwood Village C co-op had an eight-member board elected annually. At the 1987 meeting its president, Helma Goldmark, also a CB4 member, reported on painting and boiler costs, a J-51 tax abatement for new windows, and an increase in garage rent. In addition to these internal matters, she informed the 125-person audience about new housing planned for the nearby Corona high school site, and introduced a 110th Precinct officer who reported on an elevator mugger operating in the area. The majority of co-op members at the meeting were young and elderly whites, and the rest mainly black.

CD4's civic associations proper were territorially defined membership organizations that included homeowners and tenants living within self-designated sections of Elmhurst-Corona. They waxed and waned in size and effectiveness, but most persisted through the 1980s and into the 1990s. Their purview included whatever quality-of-life issues concerned their members, and they used the "city trenches" of CB4, as well as direct appeals to elected officials, to press municipal agencies to respond.[11]

In 1986 only 5 percent of adult Americans were involved in any political activity or organization; a fifth were "totally apolitical," and the remaining three-quarters only marginally interested in politics. Five percent of CD4's adult population amounted to 5,000 persons, and the membership rolls of all local organizations probably approached this number. The total of block watchers and wardens; block, tenant, co-op, and civic association leaders; and community board members was of course smaller. John Mudd, an architect of Lindsay-administration decentralization policies, estimated that in New York's community districts "there were only a small number of civic activists, perhaps fifty to 100, . . . who were willing to give the time and energy to become sufficiently knowledgeable"; these were people frequently "out at meetings every night of the week" and "active in . . . different organizations."[12]

Wardens in Action

Who were Elmhurst-Corona's civic activists? Among white residents they tended to be elderly persons who turned to civic politics after retirement, working-age men who were born or had long resided in the neighborhood, and women who became involved while their children were growing up. Some of these persons were also active in churches or synagogues, or in senior centers, and they all maintained wide networks of acquaintances among neighbors and longtime friends.[13]

Bob Tilitz and the Elmhurst Library

One example is Bob Tilitz, a Veterans Administration social worker who lived in the Elmhurst house to which his family had moved in 1917. After retiring at age sixty-five he became an active member of the Newtown Civic Association in 1976. Among other issues, the NCA was worried about physical deterioration and declining utilization at the Elmhurst Branch Library. When its closure was rumored, NCA leaders urged residents to borrow books to counter this threat, and Tilitz began a campaign to support the library which would continue for the next two decades.

The 1975 cuts had reduced the library's forty-hour weekly schedule to twenty-two hours. In the NCA's *Newtown Crier* Tilitz reminded Elmhurst residents that it had had a sixty-one-hour schedule in the 1950s, and a seventy-two-hour schedule when it opened in 1906. As NCA library committee chair he organized petitions and a letter-writing campaign and lobbied city council members, the Queens Borough Public Library's board of trustees, and Mayor Koch. He won a twenty-five-hour schedule in 1977, thirty-eight hours in 1979, building renovations in 1985, and forty-six hours in 1986. By 1981 annual circulation had recovered to the 1960s level of 100,000 volumes, and in 1989 it topped 300,000. When Dinkins's budget reductions were announced in 1990, Tilitz mobilized library supporters once again and prevented more devastating cuts than the thirty-nine hour schedule imposed in 1991.

In 1978 Bob Tilitz's sister Olga Conway organized a gardening group under the NCA library committee mantle. Older white women and occasional student volunteers turned the bleak half-acre library grounds into a colorful mini-park of tulips, rosebushes, evergreens, an herb garden, birdbaths, and teak benches. Fund-raising drives attracted individual contributors and gifts from telephone company retirees, the Korean Central Presbyterian Church across the street, and McDonald's owner Ira Meyer. In 1983 and 1988 the garden won "Dress Up Your Neighborhood" awards presented at City Hall.

During the 1980s the library expanded services to include lectures, films, art classes, and musical performances. Some were geared to established white Elmhurst residents, but events were also held in Korean, Chinese, and Spanish. Performances by the Chinese Music Ensemble of New York and the Andean musical group Tahuantinsuyo attracted old and new residents. In 1987 the library added several thousand volumes in Spanish and a thousand in Chinese. Soon Korean, Polish, Russian, Gujarati, Hindi, and Urdu materials were available, and non-English books were accounting for a third of circulation by 1989.

Filled with schoolchildren in the afternoons and on Saturdays, and adults attending reading circles, career workshops, and "fitness over 50" classes, the Elmhurst library became a contemporary version of a turn-of-the-century settlement house. In 1979 it offered free English classes and in 1985 added adult literacy instruction. Bob Tilitz reported these developments with news of budget struggles and of the garden committee's progress in his "Library Notes" column for the *Newtown Crier.*

Tilitz served as NCA president during 1980–1981 and for fourteen years chronicled Elmhurst civic politics in the bimonthly *Crier,* of which 10,000 copies circulated to stores, banks, churches, apartments, and 550 NCA member households. He joined the Queens Borough Public Library board in 1980, and CB4 in 1988. Most of his associates in civic activities were white, longtime Elmhurst residents, many of them also senior citizens. As the library was reinvigorated, Tilitz's network expanded to include Linna Yu, the head Elmhurst librarian, and library supporter Louisa Chan, whom he in turn supported in her School Board 24 campaign. His reaching out to new Elmhurst residents, however, began on his own street. In 1984 he organized a summer block party attended by fifty German, Italian, Greek, Chinese, and Latin American neighbors. "As an NCA officer, I try to meet them all. I greet newcomers, especially those on my side of the street. I feel a responsibility to integrate my block. Some are accessible, others less so."

Bob Tilitz died at age eighty-six in 1996, and scores of civic activists and neighbors attended his memorial service at the Elmhurst Branch Library.

Al Fernicola, Richard Italiano, and the St. Leo's Teen Center

Al Fernicola, born in the 1940s, and Richard Italiano, a decade younger, were lifelong Corona Heights residents. Fernicola's warden activities began in 1978 when he started a block association and organized citizen sanitation patrols. He then joined the 110th's auxiliary police corps, a group of volunteers who supplemented diminished patrol strength after the 1975 budget cuts, and continued his membership until 1985. Italiano's family was among the homeowners threatened by the Corona high school plan during 1966–1972; his father was a board member of the Corona Community Development Corporation in the 1980s and his mother a Northside Democrat. Fernicola joined CB4 in 1979 and became chair of its public safety committee; Italiano joined in 1987 and served on the youth committee. Each was later elected to a two-year term as CB4 chair during the 1990s.

With adult concern mounting over nighttime teenage noise and drinking in Corona Heights, in 1986 Father Joseph Calise began a Friday night "teen club" in St. Leo's church basement. He asked Fernicola and Italiano, both parishioners, to help, and each devoted considerable time over the next three years. Members needed written permission from home to attend; numbering more boys than girls, they ranged in age from thirteen to eighteen, and most were high school students. "Spanish" youth—or "Hics" (from "Hispanics") as some white teens derogatorily referred to them—at first outnumbered "Italians."

On the evening I attended in March 1987, about fifty teens were present. They all appeared to know one another and exchanged conversation in passing. But once the loud dance music started (played over a sound system donated by McDonald's owner Ira Meyer), the "Italian" teens gathered at the end of the room near the refeshments and the adults (all of whom were Italian), and the "Spanish" teens congregated at the other end near the music. At the "Spanish" end of the room one girl told me, "I'm half Dominican and half Italian. They [the Italians] like disco, and we like rap music. We like to wear sneakers [pointing to clean white sneakers and socks], and they wear [a term for footwear I did not catch]. They're preppy."

When I visited again in October, about thirty teens were present. There were many new faces (by then, seventy-five were registered members), and the "Spanish" and "Italian" groups were much less separate. When a young Dominican woman arrived late, she circled the room kissing several "Italian" and "Spanish" youth who called out her name.

On both occasions Al Fernicola had arranged speakers. I spoke about Corona's past and present, and two men in their twenties explained how talking to adults about personal problems—violence, underachievement, social isolation—could help young people feel better about themselves. These near-peers awed the youth. When I spoke, they were attentive but restless and full of jokes. In answers to my questions, most said they hoped to leave Corona when they grew up; only a couple of "Italian" girls said they liked Corona "because you know everyone, and always have someone to talk to about your problems." They told me they went to "the city" (Manhattan) to find jobs. For entertainment there were only "pizzerias" in Corona; they went to Forest Hills or Manhattan for movies, and to the Queens Center mall, Flushing, or "the Village" (Greenwich Village) for clothes and jewelry shopping.

In 1988 the teen center moved to a private house near the church and, with city youth services funding from CB4, it continued there for its remaining two years. But by then few Latin American youth were attending—most members were white—and activity was in small groups: board games, pool, video watching, talking. Al Fernicola, Richard Italiano, and other adult volunteers organized the teens to sell Christmas trees (to pay for a ski trip), sing Christmas carols at two Corona nursing homes, and shovel snow for senior citizens. They also sponsored Fourth of July parties, in part to lure boys away from the fireworks at William Moore Park, and they helped some teens find summer jobs.[14]

The Reemergence of Civic Associations

As residents of a defined territory, civic association members claimed to represent a designated *place*. The map of CD4 was divided into civic association domains (see Figure 8), albeit with some areas unrepresented and some overlapping. Such maps overstate realities however. Civic association territories were thinly organized if measured by the numbers that paid dues and attended meetings. They are better understood from their leadership core outward than from an imputed grassroots base.

Like onions, civic associations had layers. At the core was a set of wardens—sometimes only one—who served as officers and chaired committees. Next were active members. Unlike leaders, they rarely talked in public on behalf of the association or spoke out at meetings, but they got things done: taking minutes, conducting correspondence, distributing flyers and newsletters, circulating petitions, joining leaders in lobbying, and attending demonstrations. Beyond these layers were enrolled members who paid dues and received mailings. Some came to the periodic association meetings, held a few times a year, but others rarely if ever attended. When significant events occurred, however—a public hearing about an unpopular zoning change, or a mayoral town meeting—enrolled members often turned out. And so did an outer layer of nonmembers who lived within the civic association territory and read about the event in newspapers or flyers, or heard about it as news traveled along the interpersonal networks of civic association leaders and active members.

Civic associations were notable more for their capacity for action than for their ongoing structure. Leaders appeared, and leaders exited—by moving, by joining other organizations, or because of disputes. Followers rose and fell in number as issues intensified or subsided. A civic association might be dormant, holding few or no meetings, and then reenergize and expand. Sometimes an existing association might arrive to assist and even incorporate a group of residents beginning to agitate and organize around a problem of importance to them. Or a new organization might arise after an older association faded.

During the 1970s and 1980s a new set of civic associations was created by white residents in Elmhurst-Corona, all focusing on quality-of-life issues. But only in small numbers, or in the outer layers, did any Latin American, Asian, or black newcomers appear.

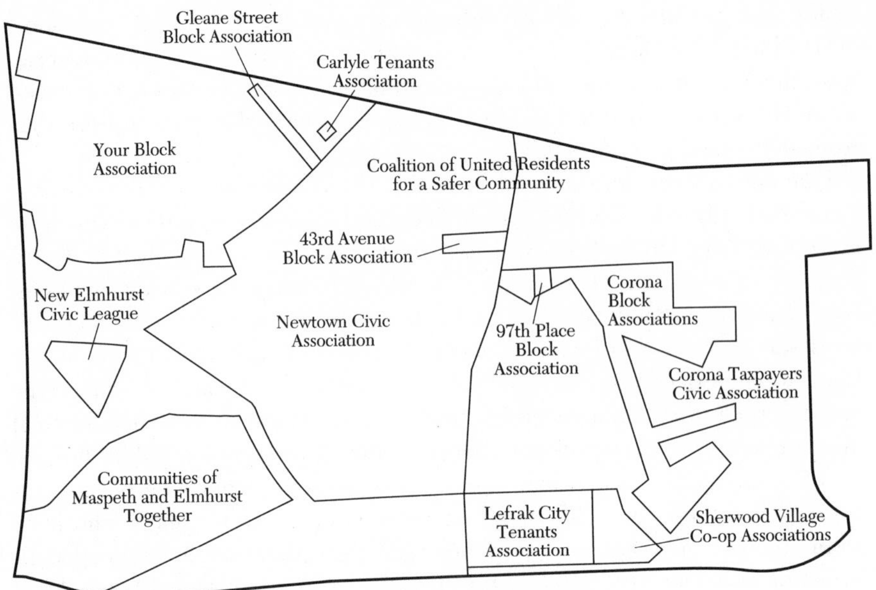

Figure 8. Elmhurst-Corona civic, block, tenant, and co-op associations.

Elmhurst

Four civic associations composed mainly of white residents were active in different parts of Elmhurst during the 1980s and 1990s. The largest, the Newtown Civic Association, was formed in 1970 and met at the American Legion Hall. Its *Newtown Crier* listed the German, Irish, Italian, Eastern European, Jewish, and Greek names of its officers and board members, persons who had grown up in Elmhurst or moved there in the 1940s and 1950s. At first the NCA's territory comprised only the Newtown section and half of Baxter-Roosevelt, but in 1985 it expanded to encompass all of Elmhurst's 11373 zip code.

More than 200 persons came to its early meetings. By the mid-1980s enrolled membership had grown, but only 30 to 100 were attending its five meetings per year. Guest speakers included 110th Precinct commanding officers, school, hospital, and library administrators, city agency representatives, and elected officials; candidate nights were held prior to elections. Depending on the speaker, nonmembers and leaders from other civic associations also attended.

NCA leaders and active members, a group of two dozen, researched city regulations and policies, gathered local intelligence, met with elected officials, wrote letters and organized petitions, demonstrated, and publicized issues in the *Crier.* The efforts of wardens such as Bob Tilitz, around particular issues, occurred under the NCA banner. Women as well as men served as board members and officers and often had ties to other organizations as well; Hilda Dietz, the third female president, for example, was active in the 110th Precinct Community Council, the Elmhurst Memorial League, St. Bart's Parents Association, and her church. She was not a member of CB4, but several NCA activists were, including its first president, Howard Riback; John Costello, who championed the "illegal aliens" issue in the 1970s; Miriam Levenson, Tom McKenzie, Bob Tilitz, and Angie LaChapelle.

The NCA's outer layers included some immigrant newcomers, and a handful of Latin Americans and Asians attended meetings. Others certainly read the *Crier's* news about schools, parks, and houses of worship. In 1981 president Bob Tilitz raised the question of adding Spanish and Chinese pages to the *Crier,* but at the next NCA meeting several members "spoke out strongly against [it], while none spoke in favor." In 1984 president Miriam Levenson noted, "Many of the new arrivals' . . . names appear on NCA membership rolls. Their names do not yet, however, appear [as] NCA officers and board of directors members." In 1988 Victor Kao, a Chinese industrial designer and active NCA member, and Leo Murillo, a Colombian school psychologist, were elected to the board. Kao also joined Tom McKenzie and Angie LaChapelle in voter registration drives. By 1993 the twenty-one officers and board members included Kao and Colombian Luz Leguizamo, also a CB4 member, but all the rest were white.

One matter that particularly incensed the NCA was a twelve-story, 163-unit condominium erected by Chinese developer Thomas Huang on Justice Avenue in Newtown in 1985. Its white architect used every bonus provision of the zoning code to maximize the number of units and minimize the number of required parking spaces. The building was larger than anything around it, and its occupants competed for scarce street parking. Yet it was built "as of right" under R6 zoning provisions and required no variance.[15] Only downzoning could have prevented it.

A second Elmhurst civic association, Your Block Association, was formed in the Broadway-Woodside section in 1977 by Ron Laney, an Elmhurst-raised electronics salesman and member of CB4 during 1976–1982. Laney's first YBA issue was the conversion of an empty factory into condominium housing (see Chapter 5). He also began an annual "Elmhurst Day" festival at the 78th Street playground opposite Elmhurst Hospital, and raised funds for concrete planters and bushes along Broadway and Woodside Avenue. In 1979 Laney and a handful of YBA members confronted the staff of an aluminum siding company at their Ridgewood headquarters to protest advertisements placed illegally on Elmhurst telephone poles and streetlights.

Art Stevens, a retiree, became YBA president in 1982; his vice-president was Dr. Bishwa Bagchee, an immigrant who later returned to India. In 1985 Korean businessmen Sung Jin Chun and Seung Ha Hong joined YBA, and Stevens introduced them to other Elmhurst civic leaders. By then, individual and merchant members numbered 500, but only Stevens and a few active supporters (including Mary Walensa) participated in YBA activities. These included publicizing guest speakers at YBA meetings held at Elmhurst Hospital, assisting residents with petitions for traffic signs, and raising contributions for street trees. Stevens also supervised residents of the Leben Home, a 360-bed facility for mentally disabled adults, in cleanup work in Elmhurst parks, providing small stipends from local merchant contributors (participants also received free lunch at Ira Meyer's McDonald's restaurant). In the 1990s Stevens's health limited his leadership, and YBA became inactive.

Local concern about the Leben Home intensified after 1988. The YBA cleanup program had ended, and unsupervised, often ill-clothed residents were panhandling on Elmhurst streets. In 1989 state inspectors documented inadequate heat, unsatisfactory physical conditions, and poor resident hygiene; seven resident suicides and two murders occurred during 1989–1990. New management took over in 1992, but the following year a decomposed body was discovered by a freezer repairman.[16]

During the late 1980s and 1990s Angie LaChappelle, an Elmhurst warden who had raised four children in her house opposite the Leben Home, monitored conditions there closely. She observed "overmedicated residents . . . allowed to roam the streets at will, often a danger to themselves as they are unable to function safely as can be seen in their crossing the streets and talking out loud to themselves." As a CB4 member since 1987 and NCA officer from 1989, LaChappelle kept both these organizations informed and received cooperation from district manager Rose Rothschild, who had monitored the Leben Home herself during 1981–1983 while chairing CB4's health committee.

After leaving the YBA presidency in the early 1980s, warden Ron Laney continued to be active in civic politics, serving as an NCA officer from 1987 and a CB4 member during 1988–1992. At civic association and CB4 meetings his belligerent questioning of public officials sometimes captured the mood of the audience, and other times pained local leaders seeking a positive response. Under his "Elmhurst Alive, Inc." banner he continued the annual festival in the 78th Street playground. In 1985 it featured carnival games and rides, a multiracial array of vendors, and a young Latin American disc jockey whose booming, triple-turntable sound system attracted more than a hundred teens. In 1989 half the playground was closed for "temporary parking" during Elmhurst Hospital construction. Driving through Elmhurst with a bullhorn on top of his car, Laney organized 150 residents to protest at the hospital and collected 1,000 signatures opposing the playground closure; Elmhurst Alive also filed suits against the Health and Hospitals Corporation and Parks Department. Nevertheless, the scheduled eighteen-month loss of the playground lengthened, and it remained closed through 1995.

A third Elmhurst civic association, the New Elmhurst Civic League (NECL), dated from the 1940s. Its territory comprised five tree-lined blocks of attached homes built in that decade, surrounded by LIRR tracks and commercial real estate. Michael Dowd, CB4's first chair, and Rose Mazzarella, a CB4 member until she moved in 1987, were NECL members. Mazzarella frequently voiced her neighbors' concerns about the L'Amour East rock music club located near them. NECL president Robert Valentino and member Linda Walsh were active in zoning struggles during 1985–1989. Walsh also focused on overoccupancy and street prostitution; she joined CB4 in 1990.

No civic association existed in the rest of South Elmhurst during the 1970s.[17] Many of this neighborhood's white residents, however, were members of its two Roman Catholic parishes, Ascension and St. Adalbert's, and sent their children to parish schools; others belonged to the First Presbyterian congregation. In 1983 a group of South Elmhurst residents asked the NCA to expand its border to include them, but NCA members voted down their request. By then, however, a fourth civic association, Communities of Maspeth and Elmhurst Together, was expanding into South Elmhurst. COMET was active in Community District 5, just over the Elmhurst-Maspeth border, and held meetings at both St. Adalbert's and another Roman Catholic church in Maspeth. (CD5 contains a section that was part of Elmhurst before community district lines were drawn and is referred to there as "South Elmhurst.") COMET was headed by Rosemarie Daraio, a lifelong Maspeth resident, and it operated as an umbrella organization for block associations that sponsored safety patrols and pursued various quality-of-life issues.

A group of forty South Elmhurst residents, including some COMET members, came to the February 1984 CB4 meeting to protest construction of two fifty-foot pollution-control towers at a metal factory in the midst of their neighborhood. The group was mainly white, with Italian, Irish, German, and East European surnames, but included Ed and Laura Gullin, two other Latin Americans, and one Chinese. The federal Environmental Protection Administration had ordered the factory to curtail hydrocarbon emissions, and its management had selected the tower technology in order to meet an EPA deadline. It planned to build the towers on a mapped but nonexistent street within factory property but needed a CB4 vote to "demap" this street. From there the matter would proceed to the City Planning Commission and then to the Board of Estimate, consisting of the mayor, city council president, comptroller, and the five borough presidents. (The Board of Estimate was abolished after passage of a new city charter in 1989.)

CB4 zoning committee chair Charles Stidolph explained that the fifty-three-year-old factory predated the 1961 zoning ordinance and could legally erect the towers, but placing them on the mapped street required a formal city map change. "Explanatory" arguments from the factory spokesperson sought to assure CB4 that the towers would reduce emissions by 90 percent. "Exclamatory" comments from South Elmhurst residents and CB4 members followed. "Move to an industrial area!" "I lost a son to cancer." "Smokestacks in the community impact property values." "People come first. A factory shouldn't be here."

Hoping to prevent construction of the towers, CB4 voted against the demapping. The City Planning Commission reversed the vote, but Queens borough president Donald Manes convinced his colleagues on the Board of Estimate to sustain CB4; a busload of South Elmhurst residents appearing to speak against it at a public hearing had swayed him. Rather than employ a more expensive pollution-control method, the factory moved away from South Elmhurst.

At the February 1984 CB4 meeting, district manager John Rowan had asked the protesters to name a representative. They chose Audrey Hass, whose family had lived in South Elmhurst since the 1880s. Hass organized an Ad Hoc Committee for the Preservation of Our Communities; she continued to attend CB4 meetings and joined the board in 1985. That year the Ad Hoc Commitee affiliated with COMET, which expanded its activity in CD4. In 1986 COMET president Rosemarie Daraio and NECL president Robert Valentino cochaired a meeting on downzoning at St. Adalbert's, and several NCA and CB4 leaders attended. There Daraio announced that COMET safety patrols now operated only in Elmhurst, not Maspeth; signs I saw on telephone poles in South Elmhurst read, "This Block Patrolled by Civilian Patrol COMET."

In 1987 Rosemarie Daraio became a paid community liaison for city council member Walter McCaffrey of Sunnyside. "He doesn't know this end of Queens Boulevard," she explained. She remained COMET president into the 1990s, organizing a "National Night Out" rally in 1988, a forum with mayoral candidate Koch in 1989, and South Elmhurst community meetings on zoning and crime issues. She also led COMET and NECL members, now including several Asians, in protests against massage parlors in 1986 and street prostitution during 1990. As she said in 1994, "We enjoy a certain quality of life, and we're going to fight to keep it."[18]

A fifth arena of Elmhurst civic politics was the interlocking memberships of the Elmhurst Lions Club, the Elmhurst Chamber of Commerce, and the Elmhurst Economic Development Corporation. Formed in 1963, the Lions were a group of white businessmen and professionals with offices on or near Queens Boulevard. Their tire, insurance, real estate, funeral home, optometry, and chiropractic businesses served local customers, but few Lions themselves lived in Elmhurst. They met weekly over lunch at the Pan American Motor Inn, sponsored a mobile hearing-testing unit, and collected old eyeglasses for reuse. During 1986–1987 they made donations to an Elmhurst Boy Scout troop and a senior citizen meals-on-wheels program at St. James Episcopal Church. The same group also formed the Elmhurst Chamber of Commerce in 1970.

Conflict between these business owners and Elmhurst residents arose periodically. At a 1976 CB4 public hearing a dozen South Elmhurst residents protested both the "eyesore" conditions and vehicles parked on the sidewalk at a Queens Boulevard tire company, and its unfulfilled promise to plant street trees. The company's owner, a Lion, was represented by attorney John Blaha, also a Lion and an Elmhurst Chamber of Commerce officer. The owner was requesting a zoning variance to expand his business to a residentially zoned portion of his property, and several South Elmhurst residents returned to oppose it at the next CB4 meeting.

By the 1980s, sentiment among the Lions-Chamber group ran strongly against CB4 and Elmhurst civic associations. During the 1985–1989 zoning wars these business proprietors favored upzoning Queens Boulevard, where several owned commercial property, and opposed downzoning, the position backed by the NCA, NECL, COMET, and CB4 (see Chapter 14). At a Lions meeting in 1985 attorney Blaha told me, "They should do away with community boards," explaining that "people from the area" were "prejudiced" against development.

In 1987 a Korean and an African American became members of the Elmhurst Lions. The core of long-term white members remained, but by the 1990s a third of the two dozen Lions were East and South Asian. In 1995 a Chinese banker was elected president.

Created in 1974, the Elmhurst Economic Development Corporation (EEDC) remained dormant until 1985, when it received New York State funding and retired construction contractor Steve Trimboli became its director. Its board was made up of Elmhurst Lion and Chamber members, and Trimboli was inducted as a Lion. In 1986 the EEDC funded the $6,000 survey of nine hundred businesses along Elmhurst shopping strips conducted by our research team. The EEDC used the data for a mailing list and a shopping guide published in 1987, and I reported on the survey results at a CB4 meeting and in the *Newtown Crier.*

Another EEDC activity was its summer recreation program in Newtown Field, the largest green space in Elmhurst. Beginning in 1985 the EEDC used city youth services funds allocated by CB4 to make the track, baseball field, and basketball courts available to up to sixty young people per day. Visits by Parks Department mobile recreation vehicles were also scheduled, and on one July 1987 day a mobile swimming pool arrived at Newtown Field. Half of the two dozen children who used it, all Latin American and Asian, were from a Parks Department summer program a block away; the rest, all black, were from Lefrak City resident Edna Baskin's summer cleanup team (see Chapter 14). District manager Rose Rothschild, who told Baskin about this opportunity, was on hand for photographs for Trimboli's EEDC newsletter, as were CB4 chair Miriam Levenson and YBA president Art Stevens, who was also a Lion and EEDC board member.

In 1988 the EEDC expanded its activities to afterschool programs in Elmhurst's PS13, PS89, and PS102. In 1991 the Lefrak City Tenants Association began using Newtown Field under EEDC aegis for its summer track-and-field youth activities. That year, however, Parks Department summer programs were eliminated and mobile recreation units cut back. In 1994 severe cuts and delays in city youth services funding curtailed the summer programs of the EEDC and other organizations.

Corona

In 1980 the Corona Heights white population (10,700) was considerably smaller than that of Elmhurst (28,000). The two opposed camps from the 1966–1972 Corona high school struggle continued, and leaders of the pro-Battista faction established the Corona Preservation Senior Center, serving a mainly white elderly population, in 1973.[19] The pro-Cuomo Corona Taxpayers Civic Association remained active and expanded in Corona Heights, where its membership overlapped with that of the Northside Democrats, in whose clubhouse they met. The Corona Taxpayers were represented on CB4 by Tony Caminiti, Lou Simeone, Pat Carpentiere, and Don Mallozzi.

In 1981 city youth services money was made available for local allocation by community boards, and CB4 awarded the Corona Taxpayers funds for afterschool programs at PS14, PS19, and IS61. When questions surfaced in 1983 about the organization's lack of tax-exempt status, a Corona Community Development Corporation (CCDC) was created to administer the programs. A second problem arose in 1984 when the CCDC applied for Community Development Agency (CDA) antipoverty funds for its programs. James Lisa, stepbrother of city council member Joseph Lisa Jr., and Tony Caminiti, serving as assembly member Helen Marshall's representative, sat on the local area policy board that allocated CDA funds. Council member Lisa and Caminiti were both on the CCDC board, which presented a conflict of interest.[20]

In 1985 a new CCDC board was formed, and Steve Trimboli, who had run the Corona Taxpayers' youth programs, moved to the Elmhurst Economic Development Corporation. New CCDC board members included Pat Carpentiere and Leonard Italiano from the Corona Taxpayers, Tony Giordano of the Corona Heights Businessmen's Association, and Rose Rothschild and Carmela George from CB4. With additional city funds for business promotion, the CCDC hired Tom Rodriguez as director in 1986.

A son and grandchild of immigrants from Spain, Rodriguez had grown up in Corona Heights during the 1960s and 1970s and still lived there. He had completed a master's degree in Urban Studies at Queens College and had been a member of our research team. As CCDC director, Rodriguez began a newsletter covering local events and developed flyers and posters for shopping campaigns. He also administered a grant program for upgrading Corona storefronts with funds secured by Helen Marshall. In 1987 he published a shopping directory, drawing in part on a survey of four hundred Corona businesses that our team had conducted after completing the Elmhurst survey. That year Rodriguez also presided at a ceremony in William Moore Park to unveil new Corona and Elmhurst shopping district medallions, which the CCDC placed along CD4's commercial strips; the audience of two dozen included representatives of the governor, mayor, and borough president, plus council member Lisa, CCDC board members, and Elmhurst Lions (among them, three Koreans).

During 1986–1990 Tom Rodriguez expanded Corona youth activities to include afterschool, Saturday, and summer programs at PS14, PS19, IS61, and St. Leo's school. With funding from several sources, up to six hundred children participated in math and reading tutoring, ESL (English as a second language) instruction, dance classes, arts and crafts, and recreational activities. In 1987 I met two Latin American women, both Corona residents, who supervised the CCDC summer program; the majority of children were Latin American, and others were white, black, and Asian. Rodriguez also extended the CCDC umbrella beyond Corona Heights and Corona Plaza. In 1989 it served as fiscal agent for youth activities in Lefrak City, organized by Edna Baskin's Concerned Community Adults. And following "gang" disturbances in 1989 at his alma mater, Newtown High School, Rodriguez met with the principal and helped plan "dialogues" between rival youth groups. He later developed an evening counseling and recreation program at the school, funded by a youth services allocation from CB4.

The CCDC board was all white until Carlos Zamora, proprietor of a Corona Heights electronics firm, joined in 1989. In 1991 Beatrice Abreu, a Dominican, replaced Rodriguez as director. She applied for "crime prevention" monies from Safe Streets, Safe City to replace city funds cut back by Mayor Dinkins, and

CCDC youth programs continued. In 1991 warden Tony Caminiti took 150 Corona youth to a Mets baseball game at nearby Shea Stadium under CCDC auspices.

With the success of the CCDC, the Corona Taxpayers Civic Association waned. Forty persons attended one of its meetings at the Northside Democratic Club in 1985, but the following year president Pat Carpentiere complained, "When the Corona Taxpayers meet, only fifteen people show up." Much of its white membership was aging, and by the late 1980s wardens Simeone and Mallozzi had died, Carpentiere had moved, and the Corona Taxpayers was moribund. In 1990, when residents of a block near William Moore Park objected to an eleven-story condominum, they formed a new "Concerned Citizens of Corona" group to protest its construction.[21]

The Northside Democratic Club, however, persisted and during the late 1980s became a meeting ground between white Corona Heights residents and African Americans from the Lefrak City area. Assembly member Helen Marshall had political ties to both communities, and at the same time that she championed funding for CCDC programs, she also maintained an office and staff liaison at Lefrak. Black wardens from Lefrak City and Sherwood Village came to Northside Club meetings from 1987 on, and by the 1990s black Democratic Party activists Priscilla Carrow, a CB4 member, and Barbara Jackson, now a district leader, were in frequent contact with Northside leader Tony Caminiti. In 1992 a poster for Jeff Aubry, running to succeed Marshall in the state assembly and also an African American, hung in William Moore Park. And in 1996, Northside supported Perry Buckley, another African American, in his successful School Board 24 candidacy.

The Revival of Civic Rituals

During the 1980s white wardens and civic associations revived long-dormant Christmas tree–lighting ceremonies and Memorial and Veterans Day commemorations. For organizers and some white audience members these rituals activated emotion-filled memories of childhood in Elmhurst and Corona, and of World War II and its losses. Symbolically, they recreated the local community's past from a time before racial change and recent immigration. Most children and parents in attendance and even some participants, however, were Latin American, Asian, and black; for them the rituals were meaningful in the present and marked their place within it. The symbolic re-creation of the past was thus only partially accomplished, and current demographic realities intruded upon and transformed these civic rituals. Furthermore, the relationship between World War II–era commemoration organizers and Elmhurst-Corona veterans of the Vietnam War, which was contemporaneous and to some degree identified with racial change and immigration, proved problematic. Indeed, the struggle by white Vietnam veterans for a place in Elmhurst-Corona's civic landscape was enacted in part through these public rituals.

Christmas in Corona Heights

Beginning in 1981 a tree–lighting ceremony was held each year in William Moore Park. It was coordinated by the staff of city council member Joseph Lisa Jr. until 1986, when CCDC director Tom Rodriguez took over. At the 1985 ceremony hundreds of people had filled the park by 7:30 P.M. The adults were mainly white, with many older Italians and a sprinkling of younger, well-dressed men and women. I said hello to Carmela George and her husband and spotted several more CB4 faces in the crowd. At a Parks Department stage in the center of the park, CCDC president Pat Carpentiere greeted the audience, and Corona Taxpayers master of ceremonies Tony Quondamatteo introduced an Italian woman who sang the national anthem in a florid soprano. The head of the Corona VFW post led the pledge of allegiance, and Father Joseph Calise of St. Leo's pronounced the invocation.

The PS14 glee club followed with "Tu Scendi dalle Stelle" in Italian and, with more gusto, "Feliz Navidad" in Spanish; its members were mainly Latin American, with a few Asian and white children. Next, council member Lisa introduced "dignitaries" from the list in the printed program; they included Democratic district leaders Tony Caminiti and Norma Cirino, Northside Democratic Club president Don Mallozzi, the commanding officer of the 110th, principals of PS14 and PS19, and three Corona Lions who presented toys to be distributed to needy children. Then the PS19 glee club sang a Christmas carol and a Hanukkah song.

At this point Tony Giordano of the Corona Heights Businessmen's Association began the tree lighting. First, colored lights on the large Christmas tree flashed on, and then lights on four smaller evergreen bushes. St. Leo's small adult choir sang next, and a booming recorded "Santa Claus Is Coming to Town" followed, with young and old singing and swaying in the cold. Santa Claus, a Corona Lion, arrived in a 110th Precinct van with siren blasting as it circled the park. He walked through the crowd greeting people, and audience members brought donated presents to the stage. Assembly member Helen Marshall gave a rousing thanks to all involved. The ceremony concluded with "Silent Night," and the crowd repaired across the street to the Northside Club, where white women of the old Corona served cookies and hot chocolate to children of the new Corona.

In succeeding years the event followed the same script, with a few variations. Corona wardens were reshuffled in program roles, and while he was CCDC director Tom Rodriguez was emcee. In 1987 a concert band of forty Latin American, Asian, black, and white students from IS61 provided live music, and WABC-TV broadcast the event; in 1988 a representative of St. Leo's Teen Center turned on the tree lights as other members stood by. During the 1990s the number of elderly whites declined, though Northside and VFW women continued to serve refreshments, and the number of Latin American, Asian, and black parents accompanying children increased. At the fifteenth annual tree lighting in 1995, the Corona Lions, Northside Democrats, and city council member Helen Marshall were the event's sponsors.

Christmas in Elmhurst

In 1971 the Newtown Civic Association revived an annual reading of Clement Clarke Moore's 1822 poem "A Visit from St. Nicholas ('Twas the night before Christmas)," combining it with a tree-lighting ceremony in the Elmhurst park located on what was formerly Moore family property. The ritual lapsed in 1977 but was revived again in 1983 by a short-lived Elmhurst Youth Program. Moore's poem was read by Elmhurst Baptist Church minister Kelly Grimsley that year, and a Newtown High School band played, St. Adalbert's Girl Scouts caroled, and NCA and CB4 members attended. In 1984 the event was organized by Your Block Association president Art Stevens, with Elmhurst Lions Club, 110th Precinct, and CB4 assistance. Between 1985 and 1987, Elmhurst Economic Development Corporation director Steve Trimboli conducted the ritual; YBA and other groups, including the Korean American Association of Mid-Queens (KAAMQ), were cosponsors.

In 1985 a white, Asian, and Latin American crowd of 150 gathered at 6:30 P.M. near a Parks Department stage. In the audience were district manager John Rowan, CB4 members Rose Rothschild, Miriam Levenson, and Raoul LaFaye, three 110th Precinct officers, and several Elmhurst Hospital staff members. Joined by Latin American and white Brownie Scouts, the white Elmhurst Branch Library director read the Moore poem. Council member Lisa then explained the historical significance of the site, now officially Clement Clarke Moore Homestead Park. He introduced a choir of twenty from the Ban Suk United Methodist Church who, accompanied by electric piano, sang "O Night Divine" and "Silent Night" in English, then "Jingle Bells" in Korean. In 1987 the choir returned and this time sang "I Wish You a Merry Christmas," "Deck the Halls," and "Go Tell It on the Mountain" in Korean first and then English. That year I stood in the cold with Sung Jin Chun and Seung Ha Hong of the KAAMQ as we watched Santa Claus arrive by fire engine.

Learning there would be no Christmas tree–lighting ceremony in 1988, two 110th C-POP officers asked PS89 teachers to have students make decorations for the tree in Clement Clarke Moore park. In 1991 the ritual was revived once more by the NCA but took place in the Elmhurst Branch Library garden. A score of NCA activists, including Bob Tilitz, Olga Conway, Victor Kao, and Angie LaChapelle, gathered with children around a tree planted in the year the library first opened. After lighting the tree, they joined library director Linna Yu inside for hot chocolate and cookies, and NCA member Bunny Schwartz explained the significance of the Hanukkah menorah lights. The ritual continued in this location during the 1990s.

Elmhurst Memorial Day

During 1985–1988, EEDC director Steve Trimboli also revived Elmhurst's celebration of Memorial Day in Clement Clarke Moore Park.[22] Posters for the May 1986 program listed the Elmhurst Lions and Chamber of Commerce, Your Block Association, the 110th Precinct Community Council, and the KAAMQ as cosponsors. By 2:00 P.M. an audience of two hundred Asians, Latin Americans, a few blacks, and two dozen elderly whites had gathered. The bullhorn atop Ron Laney's car, parked nearby, was connected to the stage microphone. The area around the stage and park flagpole was decorated with ribbons and balloons. A dozen white men from Vietnam Veterans of America (VVA), Chapter 32, organized in Elmhurst in 1981, formed a color guard of flag-bearers with rifle escort. Several of them wore black POW/MIA (Prisoner Of War/Missing In Action) armbands. A Police Department auxiliary band of twenty, including several black and female members, played patriotic music on the stage.

Trimboli, a World War II veteran, introduced Father John Garkowski of St. Bart's, who gave the invocation; remarks followed from city council members Joseph Lisa Jr. and Walter McCaffrey and U.S. Representative Thomas Manton. The 110th's commanding officer, EEDC president John Blaha, and local Boy Scouts and Brownie Scouts were acknowledged. CB4 district manager John Rowan, a Vietnam combat air crew veteran and founding president of VVA Chapter 32, read a list of Elmhurst men killed in Vietnam; it began with "Frenchie" Esnault, and included German, Latvian, Jewish, and four Spanish names. The VVA color guard then lowered the park's American flag to half-mast. More patriotic music from the police band concluded the program.

For Elmhurst-raised Rowan, public recognition of Vietnam veterans in his own community had not come easily. In 1984 Don Fedynak and Ken Troutman of VVA Chapter 32 asked CB4 to request a hold on the upcoming auction of a city-owned property in Corona. They were applying for funds to establish a counseling and twelve-bed treatment program for victims of posttraumatic stress and needed time before they could bid on the site. They also knew that some CB4 members wanted it for a new school.

Don Mallozzi supported the veterans, but other CB4 members raised objections. "We have all kinds of halfway houses in Corona," said Norma Cirino, "mentally retarded, children—more than our fair share. Let the city sell it." "We're all for the Vietnam vets," said Rose Rothschild, "but we need to consider the impact on the community. The Leben House is out of control." Troutman responded, "Sixty thousand have died in the U.S. from suicide. We need to do something for these men. We shunned them. Don't just knock us down. We've had enough of that." The board agreed to schedule a public hearing on the site's use, and the City Planning Commission placed a six-month hold on its disposition.

During the four months preceding the May 1985 public hearing, the city established, unannounced, a shelter for homeless women in Elmhurst, and five new group homes for teenagers opened in Elmhurst apartment buildings. At the hearing Corona residents opposed the VVA treatment center and recommended a school or factory on the site. In June, CB4 supported this position. The site was later rejected by the Board of Education, and a construction firm applied to purchase it.

A second CB4 public hearing in May 1985 had to do with park sites in Elmhurst. Ken Troutman and John Rowan presented a VVA proposal for a memorial honoring Jean-Claude Esnault, the first Elmhurst resident killed in Vietnam. "Esnault was an immigrant from France," Rowan said. "It would be nice to highlight the immigrants in this area. William Moore, who the park is named after in Corona, was the first man killed in World War I in Corona." "Immigrants," added Troutman, "this is what you're dealing with: a guy in my squad gets a notice to renew his green card. There he is, defending his country in Vietnam. A Hispanic guy, and he died a week later."

At the next CB4 meeting Steve Trimboli opposed the Esnault memorial. "It should be for all wars. Everybody is falling over themselves for the Vietnam vets." "I object to that [remark]," responded Judy D'Andrea. (That week marked the tenth anniversary of the U.S. departure from Vietnam, and there was much press and television coverage, and a parade in Manhattan.) "I'm not belittling the Vietnam vets," Trimboli continued, "but we should honor all veterans of all wars." Tom McKenzie countered that there was already a World War I memorial in Elmhurst. CB4 nonetheless supported Trimboli, with only D'Andrea voting no. Sitting through the discussion, district manager Rowan had no voice or vote.

At Trimboli's 1987 Memorial Day ceremony only six Vietnam veterans provided a color guard, and none participated in 1988. The main attraction both these years was Arnie Mig's Serenaders, a fifteen-piece swing band whose $300 fee was contributed by the Elmhurst Lions, Elmhurst Chamber of Commerce, and McDonald's owner Ira Meyer. Composed mostly of white men in their fifties and older, they played World War II–era tunes, such as Glenn Miller's "String of Pearls" and "In the Mood." In 1987 several older white people brought folding chairs, and the music drew a crowd of 150 Asian, Latin American, and black park users, but in 1988 only fifty persons watched and listened. At this last Elmhurst Memorial Day event Trimboli told me that originally he had wanted to hold it at the American Legion Hall, but the commander said, "No, not if the Vietnam vets are in it. They want to take over the post." Trimboli added, "I told him 'You guys took over from the World War I vets.' "

In 1986 VVA Chapter 32 opened a walk-in counseling office for veterans at an

Elmhurst site, one requiring no vote by CB4. In 1989 the chapter moved rent-free into St. James Episcopal's wooden church hall, built in 1734, and members from a range of building trades began renovating this landmark structure. The VVA group also helped establish a residence for homeless veterans in Long Island City. In the early 1990s Ken Troutman became a member of CB4, and with city council member John Sabini's help a memorial to Elmhurst's nine Vietnam War dead was dedicated in 1997 at the site proposed by Rowan and Troutman in 1985.[23]

Elmhurst Veterans Day

Compared with Memorial Day, the Veterans Day ritual begun in 1989 at the American Legion Hall struck a deeper, more responsive chord among older white Elmhurst residents. It was organized by Tom McKenzie, president of the Elmhurst Memorial League, which owned and managed the hall. The November 1990 ceremony began at 10:00 A.M. as an audience of 150 found places at seventeen long folding tables. Most were elderly, white male Legionnaires and female auxiliary members—several of the men wore Post 298 caps, as did a group of ten widows in cream-colored dresses who sat together at one table—but among the men was one Filipino member, a longtime Elmhurst resident. In addition to two Filipina women with him and a handful of Latin Americans—some of whom were part of white family groups—Seung Ha Hong and two other Korean men sat among Elmhurst wardens Steve Trimboli, Bob Tilitz, Angie LaChapelle, and Ron Laney.

Tom McKenzie opened the program. "We are here to honor those who died in World War I and World War II. In front [of the building] you can see the plaque, although we don't keep it polished the way we should, with the names of thirty Elmhurst men who died in World War I. They include names of streets that were named to commemorate these men. Here behind me [on two large tablets] are the names of 600 who died in World War II." During that war, he explained, families of men killed received gold stars to place in their front windows. Today relatives of three Elmhurst men who died in World War II were present; two of the families had been presented gold star pennants by the Elmhurst Memorial League in 1989, and the third was about to receive one. The three names—Tilitz (brother of Bob Tilitz), Rella, and Regan—symbolized the German, Italian, and Irish strands of white Elmhurst. Their family photographs, converted to slides and shown to the audience, transported many in the room back to the 1930s and 1940s and their own youth at PS89 and Newtown High School.

Regan's brother, no longer an Elmhurst resident, told the audience that his family had moved to Elmhurst in 1915. His mother died in 1935, but his stepmother ("She's really my mother too"), now ninety-two and too frail to attend, still lived in the family house. "I remember, during World War II, the silver star families, for those who had a son or husband serving overseas. And then the gold stars for those who lost a loved one."

At 11:00 A.M. an American Legion officer performed the ritual conducted each year since the hall's 1926 opening: he gaveled the podium eleven times and explained, "World War I, the war to end all wars, ended on the eleventh hour, of the eleventh day, of the eleventh month. And that was when the soul of the American Legion was born." Next, a color guard of two men and two women in American Legion caps marched to the dais. A member of the Glenn Miller Memorial Band followed, carrying a large poster photo of the bandleader, which he placed on an easel; Miller, he explained, also died during World War II. The band, courtesy of EEDC director Trimboli and "with two original band members," then played, and a few persons danced to what they called "real music—you never forget it," "not like the junk they play now." A benediction by Father John Garkowski of St. Bart's concluded the ceremony, and people helped themselves to a buffet lunch of cold cuts and sodas.

Corona Memorial Day

In 1989 Council member Lisa organized a sixtieth Memorial Day anniversary of the 1929 dedication of William Moore Park. Of Irish and German parentage, Moore was killed in World War I during a battle in France. The 1989 event brought the French deputy consul general, borough president Claire Shulman, wardens Al Fernicola, Tom Rodriguez, and Art Stevens, and many elderly Italians to the park, which was decorated for the day with red, white, and blue bunting and American and French paper flags.

As the crowd of 250 waited, a marine color guard of four African Americans led a procession of Corona VFW members and the World War II veterans group from St. Leo's, where a special mass had been conducted. Once the marchers had arrived, Lisa was the main speaker; he explained the day's historical background and directed presentations of a French flag to the Corona VFW post and a New York City flag to France's representative. A ninety-four-year-old World War I veteran then told the audience that he remembered playing "hit the cat and baseball" with Moore on Corona streets when they were children.

A flower wreath was placed near the park flagpole at a plaque listing the eight Corona men, with Irish and German names, who died in World War I. "The men above, we do not consider them gone," the VFW post commander said solemnly. "In reality they are very close to us." Corona wardens Tony Caminiti, wearing a VFW cap, and Norma Cirino presented a framed proclamation from the Corona Lions to Moore's only surviving relative. Lisa thanked the Park Side restaurant for its support and Baldi's bakery for the large cake that audience members would enjoy at the Northside Democratic Club after the event.

As at the Christmas tree lighting in this same location, the new Corona was represented by schoolchildren and by scores of Boy Scouts, behind whom stood their Latin American, black, and white mothers. At the culmination of the ceremony three buglers from IS61 played "Taps" while the audience stood at attention. Two of these young Corona boys in white shirt and tie were East Asian, and the third was Latin American.

[13]

Innovations in Civic Politics

By the late 1980s most white-led Elmhurst-Corona civic groups had a small number of Latin American, Asian, or black members, but few had made concerted efforts to expand beyond their established white base. That did occur within block, tenant, and co-op associations—on Gleane Street, in the Carlyle apartment building, in the Sherwood Village C co-op—but multiracial memberships reflecting Elmhurst-Corona's new population mix were not characteristic of Community District 4's large civic associations.

One top-down attempt at cross-racial organizing had taken place in 1973 when the CD3-CD4 district cabinet created a "neighborhood stabilization" committee to "promote understanding and cooperation between different ethnic groups in Elmhurst-Corona." In 1974 the committee sponsored a meeting at which block association leaders from Laurelton, Queens, spoke about their efforts to resist racial blockbusting. This led to a short-lived "Elmhurst-Corona Community Federation" bringing together whites, blacks, and Latin Americans. Its white civic leaders included Howard Riback (representing the Newtown Civic Association), Steve Trimboli (Italian Charities Senior Center), John Rowan (American Legion Post 298), Norma Cirino (Northside Democrats), Lillian Manasseri (Corona Preservation Civic Association), and Tony Quondamatteo (Corona Taxpayers Civic Association), all also CB4 members. The then mainly white Lefrak City Tenants Association and Sherwood Village co-ops were also represented. The federation's African American members were all from North Corona–East Elmhurst in CD3.[1] Leaders of four Latin American organizations joined as well, but only one, Argentinian Peter Nefsky, was active in CD4 civic politics, serving on CB4 during 1972–1975, and heading the 110th Precinct Community Council during the 1980s.

Building Blocks in the New Corona

The federation became moribund as the 1975 fiscal crisis began. But by then, white and black civic activists had begun to meet each other at the newly created district cabinet. Among them was Carmela George, who founded the 97th Place Block Association in 1975. A second-generation Italian born in Corona Heights, she began working at age fifteen alongside German, Italian, Polish, and African American women at a Long Island City factory in 1945. (She completed her GED—General Equivalency Diploma—in 1972.) In 1949 she married at St. Leo's Church. Her husband worked for a utility company, later operated a prepared-food van, and by the 1980s was a taxi driver (his Italian father had changed the family surname to "George" and married a German-French wife). In 1952 their first child was born, and Carmela George left the factory. Over the years, three of her siblings and her mother moved to Long Island, another to California, and her daughter and three grandchildren to Massachusetts. Only her son remained in Corona, living in his parents' home.

Carmela George's family had moved in 1944 to the street where she still lives. Then the block was "all German and Irish. They said we brought the neighborhood down. We were the only Italians on the block. Nobody talked to us." As other Italians moved in, attitudes changed, and in 1960 she and her husband bought their home from a German family who lived across the street from her parents. In 1967 a Puerto Rican family moved to the street, and by the mid-1970s Irish, Italian, Polish, Puerto Rican, Dominican, and Korean families inhabited its thirteen two-family homes. In the mid-1980s there were Chinese and Guyanese Indians as well.

In 1975, at age forty-six, Carmela George was upset by conditions on her street. The Sanitation Department pickup was on Saturday, but people "didn't seem to know there was a regular garbage collection" and put garbage on the curb throughout the week. Illegal dumping had increased along the Long Island Rail Road siding at one end of the block. People did auto repairs on the street, and "it started to look like Gasoline Alley." The last straw arrived when prostitution, drug use, and gambling began in a house owned by an absentee landlord.

Carmela George now went door to door explaining when garbage should be placed outside and collecting $3.00 block association dues. By attending district cabinet meetings she met a 110th Precinct officer, who came to her monthly association meetings, and a Sanitation Department supervisor whom she persuaded to issue summonses more aggressively on her street. One man, after being warned about placing garbage outside, was fined $200 and "came running to me [saying], 'What can *I* do?' I said, 'I told you.' " At the district cabinet she also met Helen Marshall, then an African American Democratic district leader from East Elmhurst, who gave her leads about jobs for teenagers and other practical advice. George began to call city agencies about illegal housing conversions, a broken street light, and removal of abandoned cars.

In 1976 she organized a "Queens Beautification Day" for her own and three adjacent blocks. People cleaned yards and sidewalks, and sanitation trucks carted away bulk refuse. Her son planted six sycamore trees on the street, and she painted murals of landscapes, animals, and antique cars on the LIRR retaining wall to cover graffiti. She had notified the newspapers, and stories about the event appeared in the *Daily News* and *Long Island Press*.[2] In 1977 she received a Citizens Committee for New York City award for her block association work.

Soon block association members were monitoring Corona Plaza stores for sidewalk litter, and George wrote letters to merchants about "eyesore" conditions. In 1977 she organized a community meeting at the Corona Plaza movie theater "to try and involve the Spanish community." Her Police and Sanitation Department contacts spoke, as did the Latin American president of another block association she helped organize. When she repeated her cleanup day, eight block associations participated, and later that year four new associations formed on nearby blocks.

During 1977–1978 the group of block associations continued to meet with sanitation, police, and other officials at St. Leo's, the 110th Precinct house, and the Corona Plaza VFW hall. George's own 97th Place Block Association again received press coverage when thirty neighbors cleared the street of eighteen inches of snow and then shared lamb stew, lasagna, and franks and beans cooked by members.[3] The 1978 cleanup involved all twelve Corona block associations.

That year Carmela George convened meetings of white, black, and Latin American neighborhood wardens, including Helen Marshall and Corona Taxpayers leaders, to plan "a federation" of Corona organizations. The United Corona Association (UCA) was inaugurated in 1979, with George as president. Its letterhead gave her address as headquarters and listed not only the block associations she had organized but CB4, St. Leo's Church, the Corona Preservation and Corona Taxpayers civic associations, the Northside Democrats, the Corona Heights VFW post, three African American organizations from CD3, and the Lefrak City Tenants Association (now under black leadership). Also in 1979 the UCA sponsored a cleanup covering forty streets, including the blocks surrounding Lefrak City and those of several new block associations. The UCA also wrote a letter in support of the 1979 LCTA rent strike. The UCA alliance did not last into the 1980s, however. Carmela George and block association leaders Al Fernicola and Judy D'Andrea joined CB4 in 1979, as did LCTA president Richard Isles. At monthly CB4 meetings George reported on quality-of-life problems such as radio-car double parking and illegal occupancies. She joined CB4's health committee and also headed its cultural affairs committee; from 1983 to 1988 she organized an annual art show in William Moore Park.

During the 1980s and 1990s Carmela George continued to hold the annual cleanup on her own and three adjacent blocks. This took continued effort; she visited the new occupants each time a house was sold or rented, explained about weekly sanitation pickups, and asked them to join the block association. The majority of newcomers were now Latin Americans, and she was helped "a lot" by a Puerto Rican woman neighbor and by Mireya Banks, a Dominican woman on the next block.[4] Before each May cleanup George arranged for Sanitation Department vehicles and "No Parking" signs, and she asked all residents to move their cars before the Saturday event.

When I arrived for the 1986 cleanup, only a few parked cars were left on the four streets. At 11:00 A.M. the blocks' two regular sanitation men, one white and one black, arrived with a heavy-duty vehicle that crushed the refrigerators, furniture, tree branches, rugs, sink tops, tires, paint cans, fenders, and wooden planks that residents loaded into it. The sanitation men also collected refuse along the LIRR siding, still a magnet for illegal dumping (in 1988 men from the same four blocks helped hoist a piano "dropped" at this site into the heavy-duty vehicle).[5] Other people swept dirt from sidewalks and driveways into the street, and soon a mechanical sweeper arrived to clean gutters on the four blocks. Next, the sanitation men connected a hose at each block's fire hydrant and sprayed each street for ten minutes. As they hosed 97th Place, a Guyanese Indian woman, a Chinese man, and a Latin American woman and teenage girl nudged impacted gutter debris with their brooms. Finally the sweeper returned and cleaned both sides of each street once more.

Carmela George was a whirlwind, running from house to house and block to block throughout the morning. She tried to locate owners of the remaining parked cars, distributed plastic trash bags, gave "We Care About New York" T-shirts to children "who help," and collected block association dues from a new Chinese family. At the LIRR wall she met Mireya Banks, who was directing youth in whitewashing over the graffitied murals. That afternoon teenage cousins Ramon Batista and Ralph Nuñez painted emblems of the New York Mets, Yankees, and Jets on the wall, and George added a ten-foot Statue of Liberty.[6]

In 1986 Carmela George was in her mid-fifties and comfortable in her Corona surroundings. She walked to meetings and took a shopping cart to neighborhood stores, driving only to the YMCA to swim. When she traveled to Manhattan she used the subway. Her block and those around her were well kept. Her efforts since 1975 had "really made a difference. But you have to keep at it. A lot of people sell out, and new people come in. It's like in transit."

The pace of transit, moreover, was increasing. During the early 1980s, rising real estate prices rippled outward from Manhattan into Queens. In addition, cuts in the number of building inspectors encouraged illegal units and rooming houses, and CD4's R6 zoning made it profitable to buy and demolish homes and replace them with brick-box infills. All this fed the population implosion and put pressure on city services. In Corona it quadrupled home prices and escalated solicitations from real estate agents.

One-family home prices in Elmhurst-Corona averaged $43,000 in 1977, and two-family homes, $56,000. By 1985 prices in Elmhurst *began* at $180,000. Two years later the median sale price for houses in Corona was $190,000. Developers who bought them could add $30,000 in demolition costs, build a five-unit infill on the lot, and sell it for $425,000 to $475,000; the buyer would then rent each two-bedroom unit for $700 to $900 per month. Some landlords created additional illegal units, and some tenants also rented out rooms; owners of some older homes also added illegal units and rented out rooms. Sale prices and rents continued to escalate. By 1989 median home prices were $240,000 in Corona and $265,000 in Elmhurst; a room in an illegally divided older home rented for $320 a month.[7]

Elmhurst-Corona residents discussed rising home prices at CB4 and civic association meetings, and commented on the amounts that neighbors moving out received. Mary Walensa's sister bought her Elmhurst home for $20,000 in 1955 and sold it for $268,000 in 1987. On Carmela George's block "the sellers are old people, and Spanish who are here ten or fifteen years," she said in 1987. "They say they are retiring and getting their money. A two-family on this block sold for $240,000, another for $280,000."

Those selling were pleased with the rising prices. So was Elmhurst realtor Herbert Ingber, who had started Veterans Reality in 1945 and by the mid-1980s was buying homes in Corona to demolish for infills. And so were lawyer, realtor, and banker members of the Elmhurst Lions.[8] But CD4 residents who wanted to stay, like Carmela George, were not pleased with the barrage of calls, visits, and flyers from beeper-carrying employees of the 130 licensed realties operating in their neighborhood.

Some local wardens remembered attending the 1974 district cabinet meeting on "blockbusting" in Laurelton, where they had learned that New York's secretary of state had banned real estate solicitations in that neighborhood after a formal citizen complaint.[9] In 1985 the Northside Democrats met with Secretary of State Gail Shaffer to discuss the situation in Corona. She outlined procedures for instituting a solicitation ban or, alternatively, a less sweeping "cease-and-desist" order under which the names of residents who did not wish to sell their homes could be placed on a list sent to realties. If a listed homeowner was then contacted, the offending real estate agent faced a loss of license.[10]

To initiate the formal complaint process, Pat Carpentiere of the Corona Taxpayers Civic Association wrote Shaffer about the "real estate companies who deluge our homeowners with almost weekly invitations to sell their homes," enclosing "a sample of the type of material sent to our homeowners on an almost daily basis." This included official-looking certificates for "a Complimentary Evaluation of your property," English and Spanish flyers, and handwritten notes from white, Latin American, and Asian realty agents. These agents offered "quick cash" to sellers and listed nearby properties they had sold. At a Newtown Civic Association meeting Tom McKenzie detailed the same practices in Elmhurst.

In the summer of 1986 Carmela George collected 192 letters from homeowners wishing to be placed on a cease-and-desist list. Early in 1987 the 192 persons were sent registration cards by the secretary of state; George expanded the list to 279 names in CD4 and CD3; and with help in Albany from assembly member Helen Marshall the cease-and-desist list became official in June 1987. For this campaign Carmela George drew on contacts she had made over the years. "I did my own block and friends. I went to meetings and got about forty. Tony Caminiti's sister Francie, at the Northside [Democratic Club], got about forty, and there were a few others [in Corona Heights]. In Elmhurst at the 43rd Avenue [Block] Association, we got thirty-eight there, [and] Lucy [Schilero] helped a lot." Other women also helped—Mireya Banks, George's Dominican friend on the next block; Norma Cirino from CB4 in Corona Heights; a female staff member in council member Lisa's office; Helen Marshall, who collected cards from her East Elmhurst constituents—and Tom McKenzie added a dozen Elmhurst name. The final list included white, Latin American, Chinese, and African American homeowners.

In 1988 Judy D'Andrea complained at CB4 that "cease-and-desist names are getting realtor calls." Violations of the order, with supporting evidence, had to be reported to the secretary of state. But in 1989 the law authorizing cease-and-desist lists was overturned by a court decision, a new law was passed, and registration cards had to be filled out again. In the intervening period Tom McKenzie received forty-five solicitations. The new law held, however, and in 1996 individual requests to be added to cease-and-desist lists continued to be processed by the secretary of state.[11]

While I was visiting Carmela George in 1987, her neighbor José Frias called about a robbery in progress; because she had "better English," he asked her to notify the police. "There's Spanish and Spanish, good Spanish and bad Spanish," she told me. "The Spanish people also worry about their own newcomers. The new Spanish when they come in don't want to listen. They just want to do things their own way. People who have been here for a long time feel differently about the neighborhood." She mentioned a "black Spanish" Colombian man on the next block: "At first when I started talking to him he hated me, but then he became a good friend . . . Spanish people are good, real reliable, if you get them one by one. They like me. The Spanish remind me of Italians a lot—emotional, swearing, carrying on. I pick up a word here and there when they talk."

She also saw good and bad among Chinese. "Chinese are buying, at big prices, and convert a one-family to three units. It's illegal, but they get away with it, sell it like a three-family." Such a case had occurred on her block. "They are careful not to put different buzzers for different names on the door, and they won't let you inside. They say, 'Oh, they are not here.' " On the other hand, she said, "Thank God for the Chinese. They're very clean, they don't make noise. They take care of their garbage. They're very family-oriented people."

Whenever she "fights with someone, the next time I see them I smile and say hello, and sometimes that surprises them. Some people think that I'm a little crazy, but that's what you have to do. You can't really hold it against people." Her husband, she said, "doesn't get involved in my activities, [but] when I began, he said they don't know what they're in for. I found I'm good at this, but I don't get a big head about it. I won't mistreat anybody, or talk down to them, even if they ask the same question over and over, but I feel they have to do it themselves. I got real sharp with this. This was the best education I ever got."

Civic Organizing in the New Elmhurst

The 110th Precinct house is located on 43rd Avenue, an Elmhurst street of one-and two-family homes. With scores of cars belonging to police officers filling up the block, parking was a severe problem for residents. In 1984 Joe Bellacicco, a 43rd Avenue resident, and Carmela George began a petition for a police parking garage. (Bellacicco and George had known each other since childhood, their fathers having emigrated from Italy on the same ship.) Bellacicco called an outdoor meeting of his block's residents to discuss the problem.

Among those attending was Lucy Schilero, a beautician who had grown up on 43rd Avenue in the 1950s and 1960s. She had moved to Jackson Heights when she married in the 1970s and had worked in Queens, in Manhattan (where her customers included Raquel Welch and Jacqueline Onassis), and on Long Island. In 1977 she and her Italian American husband moved back to 43rd Avenue to her grandmother's house. Her Italian immigrant parents lived on the same street.

Thirty-five people came to the 1984 block meeting, but Joe Bellacicco "didn't want an organization," Schilero recalled, "only a meeting for parking. But the people wanted it. We had a second meeting . . . at the 110th Precinct. I sat in the back then. Complaints came out. The old-time Americans felt there was no point, but we the ethnics—my father had an Italian accent—wanted to keep it. The attendance dropped. In the summer of 1985 there were about ten people. Then things started to mushroom in 1986 after we heard the 110th might move."

In 1985 Rose Rothchild, then CB4 chair, proposed converting the existing precinct house into a school and relocating the 110th to Corona. Northside Democratic Club and Corona Taxpayers leaders supported this plan. The Newtown Civic Association favored the school but wanted the precinct moved elsewhere in Elmhurst. In the end, the 110th remained in place, but during 1985–1986 Schilero and her neighbors worried that they might lose the protection the precinct house provided: "We bought homes with . . . a police station there."

After a 110th officer told her, "Talk to Rose [Rothchild]," Schilero began attending CB4 meetings in 1986. There she met Richard Bearak, the City Planning Department liaison for CD4, and began to learn from him about zoning and land-use matters. She reported back to her neighbors, and soon at 43rd Avenue Block Association meetings "we were getting people all the way from [the St. Bart's vicinity in Elmhurst], Jackson Heights, and around PS19 [in Corona], all concerned about the 110th moving." Carmela George and her block association members also began to attend 43rd Avenue association meetings.

Also in 1986 Lucy Schilero circulated a petition to keep the 110th Precinct where it was. She collected 4,000 signatures, mostly in her own Baxter-Roosevelt section of Elmhurst. "I went door to door on the petition. I hit churches, trains [at IRT stations], and stores first, then the houses. St. Bart's helped. Some Newtown Civic Association people were angry about that, but I got 1,500 names in one day in August 1986. I got 150 names from the Elmhurst Baptist Church. All the people on our block helped, fifty people. We had everything in Spanish, Greek, Italian, Chinese, Korean, French. I met Iranians, Turkish [people], to help translate."

She also met tenant association leaders from several Elmhurst apartment buildings. Their groups had formed to fight illegal rent increases and evictions, and to wage rent strikes and court suits against deteriorating services. Some were involved in protracted battles with absentee investors who had purchased blocks of occupied units when buildings were converted to co-ops.[12] "I met the Wallington Tenants Association, the Elmhurst Avenue Tenants Association, the Whitney Tenants Association, and they introduced me to other buildings, including a Cuban tenants association in one building. Now I felt less lonely after [the] Newtown [Civic Association] and Corona [Taxpayers] said no [to keeping the 110th where it was]."

Lucy Schilero's personal network also began to change. She still kept in touch with "Irish, Polish" friends from high school and work, but "my old friends have spread out from Elmhurst. Most moved to Long Island and have homes there, for the schools." But as a result of her organizing,

> now, I have new ethnic friends: Hindu, Spanish (a lot), Chinese. My Ecuadorian neighbor Lucy Galindo is a good friend and in touch with Spanish residents. She translates. Achilles Selearis [a Greek immigrant] went with me door to door. He helped a lot, especially with Muslims, who would not talk to a woman by herself. There are immigrants from France who are my neighbors. . . . [White] friends in Maspeth and Middle Village say to me, "How can you live here? It's like Manhattan." I tell them we have to live with one another or we won't survive. A [white] neighbor said to me, "Lucy, the blacks are moving in." I said, "There's black trash and white trash. Nobody's backyard is clean". . . . I told a Hindu boy who was called "black" that I was called "black guinea" when we moved [here]. [The Irish and Germans] said we would make homemade wine. . . . The Hindus and Shiites are the hardest to relate with. The man at the Geeta Temple, he's been great, but he won't come to meetings. I want to get Haitians, I want to bring one with me on my rounds. Jamaicans are moving in now; I see the Rasta hairdos. . . . I like the diversity of the area. The world is at your doorstep. I haven't tried all the food—I enjoy the ethnic foods. I like the

stores. . . . The newcomers are people we want to keep here. They are hard-working people, like the old immigrants. They [all] have to interrelate; they are now neighbors.

Schilero had volunteered in a literacy program when she lived in Jackson Heights, but her organizing skills were self-taught. "One time I said to a Chinese neighbor, 'The sewer is backing up into my house and into your house.' And he said, 'Oh yeah, bad, bad, bad.' And that's how it started with some of them, that was the beginning of the break. The others saw it and they said, 'How about us?' And we had a whole block."[13]

In 1986 Lucy Schilero formed the Coalition of United Residents for a Safer Community, comprising the 43rd Avenue Block Association and the tenant associations she met through petitioning. She had maintained contact with leaders of all these groups and shared information on quality-of-life issues that mattered to them, particularly drug selling along Roosevelt Avenue, sanitation, police response, and illegal occupancy. Through this coalition network she was able to circulate petitions rapidly, including one to keep open the Elmhurst Hospital pharmacy and walk-in clinics threatened by Dinkins administration cuts in 1991.

In 1987 the 43rd Avenue Block Association meetings officially became coalition meetings. There Schilero reported on what she learned at public hearings and at CB4, which she joined in 1990, and on her contacts with other civic groups and elected officials. And she stressed voter registration. Coalition meetings, held three times year, also featured speakers from the 110th Precinct and various government agencies. At first elected officials were unwilling to come, but soon they were eager to address audiences numbering up to one hundred and more diverse than anywhere else in CD4.

A Puerto Rican CUNY professor living on her street provided Spanish translations of petitions and meeting flyers. Two weeks before each meeting Schilero called leaders of the coalition groups, and several active members expanded this telephone tree along Chinese, Spanish, and Greek branches. During meetings, people at the back of the room translated for non-English speakers. By 1990, Korean, Bengali, Urdu, and Vietnamese were also in use within the coalition's communication network. By this time Lucy Schilero was herself a more effective speaker and meeting organizer: the "ums" and "you knows" of the mid-1980s were gone; printed agendas were more detailed and informative; and audience responses were smoothly integrated into meeting business.[14]

In 1990 the coalition held an awards dinner at the Knights of Columbus Hall in Elmhurst. The audience of 150 was a mix of older whites, many Latin Americans of all ages, Greek and Italian immigrants, and East and South Asians. Joe Bellacicco, the 43rd Avenue Block Association president, introduced Schilero, who in turn introduced CB4 district manager Rose Rothschild, representatives from the Mayor's Community Assistance Unit and the borough president's office (both of whom remarked on the impressive Friday night turnout), the 110th's commanding officer, and the Queens borough police commander, Francis X. Smith, who proclaimed he was "an Elmhurst boy."

Schilero reviewed accomplishments since 1985 and congratulated the audience for supporting the coalition. Then engraved plaques were presented: to two former 110th Precinct commanders and several C-POP and community relations officers; to Rothschild and the borough president's CD4 liaison, Ivonne Garcia; to the head of each coalition organization and to the Vietnamese, Chinese, Bangladeshi, and Latin American members who did translations; and to two Chinese and Greek boys for their help. Throughout the evening Lucy Schilero's mother took photographs.

Many of the same coalition members were present in 1992 when Lucy Schilero organized a nine-block National Night Out march from PS19 to the 110th Precinct house. Before the march began, she explained the precise route to the crowd and used signs to cue groups of children for the television cameras sent by three TV stations to cover the 250 marchers as they set off.

Led by two police vans and four scooters and carrying signs protesting drugs and crime, the throng included older whites, PS19 summer program teachers, and a majority of Latin American and East and South Asian parents and children. One black Latin American man had long dreadlocks, and a few South Asian woman wore Punjabi *salwar-kamiz* pants and blouses. African American CB4 member Priscilla Carrow, who arrived from Sherwood Village to join the marchers, was surprised by the diversity. Twenty 110th officers—white, black, Latin American, and Asian—also marched. Neighborhood residents were added along the route, and Sergeant Pete Petrone counted almost nine hundred as they neared the precinct house. There everyone was invited inside for cookies and soda in the same meeting room where Lucy Schilero had attended her first block association meetings eight years earlier.

Maintaining a responsive police presence was important to Schilero and her coalition. Local drug dealing frequently resulted in intimidation, harassment, and violence. Shootings were well remembered, and at one coalition meeting it was evident that members were still unsettled by a recent killing at a coffee shop one block from 43rd Avenue.

In 1995 CB4's zoning committee recommended against a street marker at the Elmhurst site where journalist Manuel de Dios had been killed by cocaine dealers in 1992; committee chair Lou Walker said they did not want to commemorate a murder, and it was obvious that committee members were unfamiliar with the incident. Then city council member Helen Marshall came to the front of the room. Speaking emotionally, she compared "this Hispanic hero" with Martin Luther King, in whose memory CB4 had stood for a moment of silence at the beginning of the meeting. She urged the board to approve the street marker, as did council member John Sabini. He emphasized that de Dios's death symbolized New York's long-established freedom of the press, and that he and Marshall intended to vote for the marker in the city council.[15]

Lucy Schilero—knowing that there already was a sign with de Dios's name in the public sitting triangle opposite the site of his murder, that a tree-planting ceremony in his memory had occurred in Flushing Meadows–Corona Park, and that marches along Roosevelt Avenue were held each year on the date of his death—objected to one more exercise in symbolic politics. "There are other names," she exclaimed, "Mr. Mendez, and children who died before [de Dios] because of drugs. Who will remember *them?* The drug dealers are still active there, and prostitutes. We need to go further. Can't we use the money to fight drugs?" Helen Marshall responded that the street marker cost only $150, and CB4 then voted to approve it. The two women represented divergent concerns. Marshall, occupying a "Hispanic" city council seat created in 1991, had defeated Latin American primary challengers and was likely to face others in the future. Schilero reflected the views her diverse neighbors expressed in many coalition meetings; they worried more about reducing the danger around them than memorializing it with street markers.

By 1996 Lucy Schilero's coalition included 2,000 members of forty block, tenant, co-op, and business associations in a still-expanding territory in the northern half of Elmhurst-Corona. Her meetings were drawing as many as four hundred people and now included Mexican and Russian immigrants, African Americans from Lefrak City, and whites from Jackson Heights. She maintained a busy schedule of telephone contacts with coalition leaders and conferred face to face with a score of them two weeks before each membership meeting.

The problem of teenagers congregating on corners, which arose in the late 1980s and then subsided, had come back. Without recreation programs or jobs, local teens were drinking beer and playing boomboxes, urinating in public, and vandalizing property with graffiti "tags." Some smoked pot, although it was now heroin that brought outside customers to CD4. Frustrated residents voted at the June 1996 coalition meeting for a nighttime youth curfew to address this problem that mattered to them.

The Entry of Immigrants into Civic Life

Latin Americans and Asians constituted a majority of Elmhurst-Corona's population by 1980, but their involvement in civic politics did not reflect their numbers. Enormous organizational energy did go into a vast world of immigrant associations, houses of worship, and political activity at borough, citywide, and international levels, but this intersected only minimally with neighborhood politics in CD4. There were scores of Colombian, Dominican, Ecuadorian, and other Latin American nationality-based associations in Queens. Leaders and members of these groups focused largely on home country politics, sports, and cultural activities; some—such as the Centro Civico Colombiano, which offered citizenship and English classes and ran the annual Colombian festival in Flushing Meadows-Corona Park—were headquartered in CD4. There was also a handful of pan–Latin American organizations operating primarily at the borough level.[16]

Chinese organizations in Queens drew Elmhurst-Corona members, but most of their activities occurred in Flushing.[17] Associational lines divided South Asian immigrants by country, region, language, and religion, mirroring cultural complexities in their homelands; some of these groups met in CD4, but they drew upon a Queens or New York metropolitan area membership base.[18] Immigrant churches, temples, and mosques were well represented in Elmhurst-Corona, but only the Korean Central Presbyterian Church made an impact on local civic life, by beginning a Sunday afternoon street cleanup in 1991. Echoing the views of many white residents, warden Bob Tilitz said of the new houses of worship, "They are *in* Elmhurst but not of it."

In demographic terms, most Elmhurst-Corona immigrants were young working-age adults and children. Both male and female immigrants worked, frequently at more than one job and often at night or on weekends, when organization meetings were held. Many immigrants, moreover, were relatively recent arrivals, unfamiliar with Elmhurst-Corona civic issues, and the majority were not citizens. They had not lived in New York before the 1975 fiscal crisis and thus lacked the memory and experience against which established residents measured their diminished quality of life. English, which some immigrants did not feel comfortable speaking, was also a barrier to civic participation.

Further, many immigrants regarded Elmhurst-Corona as a temporary point of settlement. Some, intent on sending remittances to relatives in their home country, limited expenses and social involvement here, planning eventually to return to their native lands. Others hoped to move to better housing elsewhere after establishing themselves. Rosalia Almonte, a Dominican garment worker recently arrived in Corona, visited relatives in a New Jersey suburb on social occasions, and her husband dreamed of moving to Long Island.[19] Compared with CD4's whites, the immigrant population was more in flux, with newcomers constantly arriving and others moving up and out. There were far fewer of the kinds of persons who became neighborhood wardens—retirees, housewives, locally reared men—among immigrants than within the white population.

A few Latin Americans and Asians did join civic associations headed by whites, and many immigrant homeowners and long-established tenants were members of the block associations organized by Carmela George and Lucy Schilero's coalition. At the same time, two new organizations arose to address a wider set of issues that mattered to immigrant residents of Elmhurst-Corona, and in the mid-1980s they staked out places in CD4's political field.

Ciudadanos Conscientes de Queens

Born in Puerto Rico, Haydee Zambrana moved to Jamaica, Queens, during her teens. In the 1970s she worked as a paralegal in Manhattan and there encountered many Latin Americans from the growing immigrant population in Elmhurst-Corona and Jackson Heights. She moved to Elmhurst in 1978 and soon met other Latin Americans—Puerto Rican, Colombian, Ecuadorian, Argentinian—who shared her concerns about the lack of social services for Spanish speakers and the need for a Latin American presence in Queens politics. In 1980 Zambrana launched Ciudadanos Conscientes de Queens/Concerned Citizens of Queens (CCQ).

Working nights as a civilian employee at the 110th Precinct, she threw herself into building CCQ and recruiting others to help. From a small Elmhurst office on Roosevelt Avenue she referred people to appropriate government agencies, sometimes providing advocacy and English translation herself. She learned that many immigrants were paying large sums to immigration lawyers and to trade schools, often with nothing to show for it.[20] She canvassed Latin American businesses along Roosevelt Avenue and found they suffered from rising commercial rents and disruptions caused by drug dealing, and lacked a channel of communication with the police. She also took classes in community planning at the Pratt Institute in Brooklyn.

From 1981 on, CCQ offered advice on immigration matters. Latin Americans had been brought in under the visa preference system in 1978, and opportunities to enter the United States through family reunification expanded. CCQ also began processing citizenship applications, and its total during 1984 reached 1,000. That year CCQ received an award from Governor Mario Cuomo for volunteer efforts "in the Hispanic community of Queens." New York State funding followed in 1985, including a contract to provide organizing assistance and court advocacy to Spanish-speaking tenants. By 1986 the number of CCQ's citizenship petitions had tripled, with Colombians and Dominicans accounting for 40 percent each and other Latin Americans for 20 percent.

Haydee Zambrana testified about problems with INS at the Queens hearing of the Mayor's Commission on Hispanic Concerns in 1986. She explained that citizenship applicants were "harassed" in INS interviews by being asked, "Are you a prostitute? Do you deal in drugs?"—questions already answered on their applications. She said she had been unable to obtain a meeting with INS officials, and that Congress members from Queens to whom she sent copies of applicant complaints had not offered to help.

Also in 1986 Zambrana became full-time executive director of CCQ. By then its volunteer and paid staff also provided counseling on entitlement eligibility and vocational training programs, held English classes, conducted seminars for business proprietors, and ran a state–funded hotline informing undocumented immigrants of their rights. For services not covered by government grants, CCQ charged on a sliding scale.

In 1986 the Immigration Reform and Control Act (IRCA) was passed, and legalization became possible for undocumented immigrants who had resided in the U.S. since 1982. In 1987 CCQ received a federal grant to process legalization applications. Over the next two years it handled the cases of 3,000 persons "of all nationalities," 90 percent of whom received temporary green cards. In 1989 CCQ was funded to provide citizenship and English classes for 2,000 newly legalized immigrants who would be eligible for naturalization beginning in 1992.

As CCQ programs multiplied, its staff, mainly women of several Latin American nationalities, also grew. In 1986 Maritza Sarmiento-Radbill, an Ecuadorian, joined Haydee Zambrana and remained as director of immigrant services until 1989. In 1987 CCQ moved to larger offices in Corona Plaza. That year CCQ and CB4 member Clara Salas, a Cuban social worker, conducted a workshop on U.S. licensure for Latin American doctors and other professionals, with support from borough president Claire Shulman. And also in 1987, CCQ joined the Flushing Chinese Business Association and the Queens Borough Chamber of Commerce in presenting forums on the new IRCA law for employers.[21]

Haydee Zambrana enjoyed meeting Asians as a result of the legalization work. "Chinese, Koreans, and Indians all have their own issues and problems. The image is that Asians have money, but there is not really much difference between Asians and Hispanics. Asians are better organized, but the Hispanics in Queens also have money." She noted further the high educational levels of many Latin Americans requesting services at CCQ.

Zambrana was impatient with the nationality-based Latin American organizations in Queens—"We all want our own parade"—believing that little of their energy went to local issues.[22] A few persons in Queens, however, had already begun to organize on a more inclusive basis. Since 1976 a pan–Latin American parade, Desfile Hispano de Queens, was held each year in Jackson Heights, organized by two Puerto Rican women. And in 1977 Nayibe Nuñez-Berger, a Colombian, and Aida Gonzalez, an Ecuadorian, founded the pan–Latin American Ollantay Art Heritage Center in Jackson Heights. These two women also provided one-to-one help to female Spanish-speaking victims of domestic violence at Queens Family Court, where Nuñez-Berger, a psychologist, worked.

In 1986 Haydee Zambrana told the Mayor's Commission on Hispanic Concerns, "My priority is to help the Hispanic community become part of the American political process." She went about this in several ways. When I first met her, she was registering voters at the 1985 Queens Festival in Flushing Meadows–Corona Park. In 1986 she joined Nayibe Nuñez-Berger, Aida Gonzalez (since 1985 Queens County's director of cultural affairs), and others in forming United Latin Americans of Queens (ULAQ), which supported Latin American public office-seekers over the next two years. Although it achieved no victories, borough president Shulman did name Ivonne Garcia, a Nicaraguan, as her advisor on Hispanic affairs.

As the mother of two children, Zambrana also became involved in school board politics. By 1986 Latin American children made up one-quarter of the public school enrollment in Queens, but there was no Latin American on any of the seven Queens school boards. Zambrana persuaded Clara Salas to run for SB24 and Maritza Sarmiento-Radbill for SB30. Both lost, and the Queens school boards remained without Latin American representation. In 1989 Zambrana ran for SB30 herself, but she also lost.[23]

To learn more about local civic politics, Haydee Zambrana began attending CB4 meetings in 1984. She also lobbied borough president Donald Manes to appoint more Latin Americans to Queens community boards, and helped potential members fill out applications. In 1985 she and Clara Salas joined CB4, and that year its Latin American membership doubled to six. Like other members, Zambrana reported on quality-of-life issues, including drug selling on Roosevelt Avenue, conditions in Linden Park, and problems with car services.

After its move to Corona Plaza, CCQ began to take on the trappings of a civic association. Zambrana met with Corona Plaza merchants—Colombian, Dominican, Cuban, Korean, Arab, Greek, Jewish—and conveyed their complaints to the 110th Precinct's commanding officer. In 1989 she began a summer program for forty Corona Plaza children. She also organized an annual Corona Plaza Christmas tree–lighting ceremony, and a score of merchants contributed to that event.

In 1987 the tree stood behind wooden police barriers in the plaza between CCQ's office and the local IRT station. On the night of the ceremony, forty merchants, CCQ staff, and guests gathered at 6:00 P.M. to see the tree lights turned on. In Spanish and English, Haydee Zambrana explained that while Three Kings Day, rather than Christmas, was celebrated in Latin America, "here we do it the North American way." A chorus of CCQ staffers then sang five seasonal Spanish songs, accompanying themselves with drum, tambourine, and *guiro* (scraper). Next, a Filipino CCQ paralegal stepped forward and sang "Silent Night," "Santa Claus Is Coming to Town," and "O Holy Night." His solo performance was followed by a Latin American man singing "The Little Drummer Boy" in Spanish. After this the audience was invited to the CCQ office, where Zambrana announced, "Here we will do it our way. The food is Argentinian, Colombian, Filipino; there is music, so enjoy yourself." A Colombian restaurateur told me, "The girls from Concerned Citizens of Queens did a great job."

In 1990 conflict erupted between Haydee Zambrana and a group of CCQ staff members; she was forced to resign the directorship and left, feeling devastated. CCQ continued as a multiservice center, but its civic activism ended. In 1991 Zambrana formed Latin Women in Action and resumed advocacy and referral activities on a smaller scale. By 1995 her new Corona Plaza office, focusing on immigration, had processed 4,000 citizenship applications.

In 1995 Haydee Zambrana, introduced as "an old board member," spoke to CB4 about voter registration. She stressed the need to reach not only new citizens but also young people approaching voting age and older adults whose registration had lapsed. She asked to use the Northside Democrats' clubhouse for a voter-education workshop by bringing in a voting machine from the Board of Elections, something she had done at CCQ, and Northside leader Tony Caminiti agreed.

The CCQ internal struggle left a vacuum in the Corona Plaza section of CD4. This heavily Latin American area fell within the city council district won in 1991 by Helen Marshall, who, while still in the state assembly, had asked several persons involved in CD3 and CD4 civic politics to form a "Hispanic Task Force." Among them were Tom Rodriguez of the Corona Community Development Corporation, and Ana Lopez, a Dominican who headed the Father Billini Association, a youth program begun in 1979 at Our Lady of Sorrows Church in CD3. With Marshall's help, Lopez received Safe Streets, Safe City funds in 1993 to begin a "Beacon School" youth program at PS19, located in CD4.[24]

By 1995 Latin American membership on CB4 still stood at six. Among them was Luz Leguizamo, a Colombian and a member of the Centro Civico Colombiano in Elmhurst and of the Queens Hispanic Coalition formed in 1991 to replace ULAQ. At CB4 Leguizamo heard a speaker from the Campaign to Save Our Public Hospitals, a citywide advocacy group opposed to the Giuliani privatization plan. Leguizamo knew that large numbers of poor and uninsured Latin American immigrants used Elmhurst Hospital, and she realized that access would be impeded under private management. Consequently, she organized a bilingual forum at the Centro Civico Colombiano where speakers from the Campaign to Save Our Public Hospitals addressed an audience of Centro officers and other Queens Latin Americans. Humberto Suárezmotta of the Asociación de Empresarios Colombo-Americanos, a merchants' organization, also spoke and vehemently opposed the Elmhurst Hospital sale. Later in 1995 city council member Helen Marshall organized another forum with the Campaign to Save Our Public Hospitals, attended by eighty African American, white, and Latin American CD3 and CD4 civic activists. Queens Hispanic Coalition president Nayibe Nuñez-Berger provided English-Spanish translation throughout the day.

The Korean American Association of Mid-Queens

In April 1985 a crowd of 200 Koreans appeared at the 110th Precinct to protest two recent arrests. In October 1984, according to the Ad-Hoc Korean Committee against Police Brutality, which organized the protest, when police intervened in a dispute between a Korean Elmhurst boutique owner and a customer, the storeowner had been addressed in racist terms by 110th officers, beaten at the precinct house, and then charged with disorderly conduct and resisting arrest. In March 1985 a Korean taxi driver, stopped for speeding, had also been addressed in racist terms and then beaten and held for three days at the 110th, the Ad-Hoc Committee contended; he had required six stitches at Elmhurst Hospital. The police contested both assertions; they stated that the taxi driver was intoxicated, and that the officers' behavior in both cases had been appropriate.

Protesters demanded that charges be dropped, the arresting officers reprimanded, and a public apology made to the Korean community. Sensitive to simmering black-Korean tensions elsewhere in the city and eager to make common cause with African Americans, the Ad-Hoc Committee had invited Reverend Herbert Daughtry of the Black United Front to speak. A leader of citywide reputation, he told protesters not to indict the entire police department, but "too many . . . are engaging in this. We pay them not to do violence upon us, but to protect us."[25] The protest was covered by newspapers and television, and white Elmhurst-Corona leaders were aware of the event.

Concern among Elmhurst Koreans over relations with the police and other city agencies was mounting. The boutique owner and taxi driver incidents were reported in the Korean press and widely discussed. But even before this, many Korean storeowners in CD4 felt they were being harassed with unfair Sanitation Department fines for litter on sidewalks in front of their businesses.[26]

In February 1985 the Korean American Association of Mid-Queens (KAAMQ) was founded by Sung Jin Chun and Seung Ha Hong. Chun, a chemist and teacher in Korea, had arrived in Elmhurst in 1970 and established a real estate business; his wife was a nurse at Jamaica Hospital. In 1976 they moved to Bayside, Queens, but he continued to work in Elmhurst as the Korean population there grew.

Hong, immigrating in 1971, had worked for an American baker. In 1984 he bought El Molino Argentinian Bakery in Elmhurst, where he sold both Latin American and U.S.-style pastry; his wife owned an Elmhurst beauty parlor. On the day his bakery opened he received a $50 sanitation fine. He told me that up to two hundred people per minute passed his store, located next to a subway entrance, and it was impossible to keep the sidewalk free of food wrappers and cigarette stubs. Although the law required only that merchants sweep within one hour of opening, which he did, when he complained about the fine to the district Sanitation Department supervisor, the response was, "You want another?" Hong decided he had to create personal relationships with local officials.[27]

Sung Jin Chun and Seung Ha Hong began by visiting Korean businesses throughout Elmhurst and adjoining neighborhoods, listening to their problems, and enrolling them in the KAAMQ. Many were already members of citywide associations of Korean greengrocers, dry cleaners, or other businesses, but they understood the need for a local Korean organization as well. Chun also met with the 110th Precinct commander immediately after the taxi driver incident. Following the protest rally, which was organized by young activist Koreans and not the KAAMQ, Chun was invited to address precinct officers about Korean culture and attitudes toward the police. This opened a continuing 110th-KAAMQ dialogue. When Korean translation was needed or problems involving Koreans arose, 110th commanding officers would call Hong, who both worked and lived in Elmhurst.

Chun and Hong also established personal ties with whites active in Elmhurst civic politics. They met Your Block Association president Art Stevens, who since 1982 had been speaking to local Korean merchants about garbage and litter regulations. Through Stevens, the two Koreans became Elmhurst Lions, attended 110th Precinct Community Council meetings, and participated in the Elmhurst Christmas tree–lighting and Memorial Day rituals.

During their organizing, Sung Jin Chun and Seung Ha Hong met Daok Lee Pak, a Korean Elmhurst resident who had lived ten years in Wyoming before moving to New York. Her long-practiced English was better than that of most Korean immigrants, and she had worked as a court translator since 1982. On her own, she had met with CB4 member Rose Mazzarella to mediate a dispute between a Korean beverage distributor and South Elmhurst residents: CB4 had voted a zoning variance for the business, but neighbors complained that promises about delivery hours and site beautification were not kept.

After becoming a KAAMQ member in 1985, Pak began to attend CB4 meetings, and she joined it in 1986. Chun and Hong also attended CB4 and district cabinet meetings during 1986–1987—Hong often bringing pastry from his bakery—and became friendly with district manager John Rowan and chair Rose Rothschild. In March 1986 Chun, Hong, Pak, Rowan, and Rothschild organized a seminar on sanitation regulations and enforcement for Korean storeowners; the Sanitation Department supervisor for CD4 and Sung Soo Kim, executive director of the Korean American Small Business Service Center, were featured speakers.

Just as the KAAMQ's ties in CD4's political field were solidifying, the Newtown Civic Association discovered the Korean-owned Honeybee massage parlor in Elmhurst. Sung Jin Chun and Seung Ha Hong nonetheless persevered in their civic activities, participating in CB4's 1986 demonstration at the 110th Precinct, sponsoring the first Korean program at the Elmhurst Branch Library, and creating linkages with African American wardens at Lefrak City. The two men also expanded KAAMQ's role within the Korean community. In June 1986 several KAAMQ leaders joined the Young Korean American Service and Education Center of Jackson Heights to organize a Korea pavilion at the Queens Festival in Flushing Meadows–Corona Park. This event, sponsored by the borough president and celebrating cultural diversity, included immigrant groups in its Asian Village and Pueblo Hispano. The intergenerational cooperation between the KAAMQ and the young activists, whose folk music troupe and pavilion posters were critical of South Korea's government, was widely noted by Queens Korean residents.[28]

Chun, Hong, and other KAAMQ leaders also met Korean business colleagues from around the city during the annual *ch'usok* festival in Flushing Meadows–Corona Park. And in 1985 both men joined the board of directors of the citywide Korean American Small Business Service Center. Within CD4 they continued to visit Korean stores and provide their immigrant constituents a link to their home country and culture. In 1987 Seung Ha Hong collected $4,000 from local Korean merchants for victims of a flood in Korea which killed six hundred persons.

The following year the KAAMQ sponsored a Lunar New Year program at Newtown High School, and hundreds of Koreans of all ages attended. A professional band—trumpet, electric guitar, bass, keyboard, and drums—opened the evening with the American and Korean national anthems. Joonku Cho, KAAMQ's new president and an Elmhurst restaurateur, then introduced several Korean guests, including Sung Soo Kim, and five white honorees: Steve Trimboli and John Blaha of the Elmhurst Economic Development Corporation and Lions, the 110th's commanding officer, CB4 chair Miriam Levenson, and me. Next, ten Korean high school girls in red and green gowns performed a traditional fan dance. The main event followed: six "pop tune" singers performed "Kansas City," "What'd I Say," "Unchained Melody," and "Autumn Leaves" in English, and up-tempo and ballad numbers in Korean. Upon request, Elmhurst Lion Blaha sang "I Left My Heart in San Francisco" and "New York, New York," much to the audience's delight. The four-hour evening was broadcast to Korean audiences in six U.S. cities. In the lobby, young activist Koreans registered voters.

In 1988 Daok Lee Pak organized a KAAMQ dinner at a Korean restaurant for the district managers of Community Districts 1, 2, 3, and 4 and other civic leaders. Following speeches by several Koreans, translated into English by Sung Soo Kim, assembly member Helen Marshall spoke. She said this was her first invitation from the Korean community, stressed her own family's Guyanese immigrant roots, and mentioned her Guyanese Chinese cousins. Rose Rothschild reiterated her call for stores to post signs in English so that non-Koreans would feel welcome. Newtown Civic Association warden Bob Tilitz later wrote Pak to congratulate the KAAMQ. "I know of no other [immigrant] group which reaches out as does the [KAAMQ] to the larger community of which it is a part."

In four years Sung Jin Chun and Seung Ha Hong had accomplished much. Sadly, both Chun and Hong suffered heart attacks in 1989 and had to curtail their activities. The two men nonetheless continued to provide leadership to the KAAMQ and serve as channels of communication to the 110th and CD4 civic groups. Still active, the KAAMQ registered 2,000 Korean voters during 1995–1996 and donated a patrol bicycle to the 110th Precinct.

Whites, Immigrants, Blacks

Elmhurst-Corona's numerically declining white population faced post–fiscal crisis assaults on its quality of life and a politically weakened neighborhood by reanimating its parapolitical institutions. Wardens attacked quality-of-life problems, developed new civic associations, and revived old rituals. Most of these associations remained mainly white, but after the mid-1980s a few Latin American and Asian participants could also be counted.

While creating an association for fellow Koreans, Sung Jin Chun and Seung Ha Hong navigated white-led civic arenas to establish relationships with wardens, the 110th Precinct, and CB4. Haydee Zambrana forged similar linkages but also used a familiar local ritual, the Christmas tree lighting, to begin making CCQ not only a Latin American service organization but also a Corona Plaza civic association.

While the KAAMQ and CCQ were finding their places in CD4's political field, and its white civic associations were beginning to reach some Latin American and Asian constituents, Carmela George and Lucy Schilero innovated a different political vision.[29] Beginning on their own blocks, they attempted to include everyone, both established and newcomer. Like those of other block and tenant and co-op associations, George's and Schilero's efforts defined a multiracial constituency from the start. The basis of inclusion was place, not ethnicity or race.

Where did CD4's black newcomers fit? In large part, their wardens, associations, and rituals were found in the Lefrak City vicinity, where their unique housing-market situation concentrated them. They also organized on the basis of place, but their place within CD4 was different from that of everyone else.

Everyone, however, met in the central arena of Elmhurst-Corona's political field, Community Board 4. The story of the African American–CB4 connection, like the stories of Carmela George, Lucy Schilero, and Haydee Zambrana, involved a network of women. And at the same time that female-mediated black-white links were emerging, the leadership of CB4 itself was changing from male to female.

[14]

The Politics of Place

In 1980 Community Board 4 was a mainly white island in a multiracial Elmhurst-Corona sea. Its forty-five members included two newly appointed African Americans. Its three Latin Americans were gone by 1981, replaced by two more who left in 1983. There were no Asians. In contrast, many white members had served through the 1970s; several would continue on CB4 during the 1980s; and ten still remained in 1996.

In the early 1980s, borough president Donald Manes was making little effort to appoint CB4 members who reflected Elmhurst-Corona's new diversity. In the mid-1980s the situation began to change, and African Americans, Latin Americans, and Asians were appointed in growing numbers, both by Manes and his successor Claire Shulman. Some of the newcomers soon chaired CB4 committees, and in the 1990s several were elected to its executive committee. This change resulted from a two-way process: newcomers found their way to CB4, and CB4 became more receptive to them as new leadership appeared.

Limits of the 1970s Leadership

In 1979 Lou Simeone, a Corona Heights accountant, replaced Steve Trimboli as chair of CB4. His first crisis was a Social Security Administration announcement of plans to move 2,600 jobs from Lefrak City to Jamaica, Queens. The impact on local commercial strips would be devastating, and Simeone enlisted Lefrak City Tenants Association president Richard Isles, an African American CB4 member, to lobby with him against the move. They organized a "Save Our Neighborhood" coalition that included Sherwood Village co-op residents and 57th Avenue merchants, and testified at hearings in Washington and Queens.

Manes and other elected officials, however, continued to support the move. A frustrated Simeone concluded, "The politicians have written off Corona and Elmhurst because most of the residents don't vote."[1]

In addition to cooperation with black Lefrak City residents, Simeone cooled the "illegal immigrants" rhetoric that some CB4 members continued to voice. In 1980 Simeone told the *Daily News,* "We had chaos and confusion in a short period. There was an influx of illegal aliens. . . . Many . . . now have been here long enough to marry and have families. All the planning was thrown off [but] this confusion may work itself out. A majority of immigrants are middle-class types and hard workers. They either make money and go back or establish themselves here as citizens. Orientals are . . . buying up houses and stores and maintaining them. That's the best thing that's happening to us."[2]

During his three years as chair Simeone also began negotiations for new construction on the empty Corona high school site. In 1980 Presbyterian Senior Services (PSS) offered to build a federally funded residence for elderly and disabled persons, a use of the site that CB4's Corona Task Force had recommended in 1979. With Simeone's support, CB4 approved the proposal, and the Board of Education released the land for sale to PSS. Now a member of School Board 24, Simeone declined to serve another term as chair of CB4, though he remained a member until his death in 1984. In 1982 Steve Trimboli returned as chair.

CB4 versus LCTA

Between 1982 and 1985 relations between CB4 and Lefrak City African Americans deteriorated. Richard Isles was no longer LCTA's president, and no member of its new leadership was appointed to the board. William Weisberg, chair of CB4's neighborhood stabilization committee and an Elmhurst resident, organized committee "tours" of Lefrak City, inviting fellow Newtown Civic Association members. He criticized the LCTA when it negotiated an agreement with Lefrak management over tenant complaints about security, telling CB4 that the LCTA "went off on its own without informing the [neighborhood stabilization] commitee or anyone else."

At a 1983 CB4 meeting, Trimboli introduced "with great trepidation" a presentation on "the quality of life at Lefrak City." A Lefrak management offical spoke about roof repairs, efforts to secure commercial tenants, and cooperation with the LCTA on security. CB4 member Ken Daniels, a white Lefrak City resident, responded that on the last neighborhood stabilization committee "tour" he had noted missing floodlights in the parking area, graffiti on hall walls, and youth with radios and beer "roaming" lobbies and basements. The Lefrak official responded that security guards could not legally detain youth walking through the complex. He added that the 110th Precinct rated it a "B" sector, with less crime than the surrounding area. Catcalls and signs of disbelief greeted that statement; "They go to our neighborhood and commit crimes there," one member exclaimed. Other white members too responded with hostility. One distinguished "Lefrak City" from "our community." Another said, "We adopted Lefrak City." Several stated that youths should be "questioned." As comments heated up, Rose Rothschild suggested opening the floor to "the people in the audience who live in Lefrak City."

Five black Lefrak City residents were present but until that point had had no place on the agenda. Now one woman told CB4 that the replacement lock supplied by Lefrak management was "so flimsy my nine-year-old son can open it," and that maintenance personnel were unavailable between 9:00 A.M. and 2:30 P.M. But then she said, "I love my apartment. I love the layout, the neighborhood, the school district. We have to work together." Everyone applauded her. Next, the LCTA president, Governor Hendley, explained that ongoing improvements were a result of "signed agreements" with Lefrak management. He called for "working out a solution between the Lefrak organization, the neighborhood stabilization unit, and the tenants association. Yes, there is a youth problem, but we are bickering, and the problems are not solved. The problems cannot be solved by going outside; we must work inside Lefrak City. It was once a beautiful place." He was also applauded.

But then the cooperative spirit dissipated. A white CB4 member said, "I support Lefrak. The tenants do the damage. The tenant association must be able to control the tenants." He went on to assert that "there are several tenant associations." Hendley said this was incorrect. Daniels retorted that voter turnout in the last LCTA election was small. Hendley replied, "The slate ran unopposed."

During 1984, CB4-LCTA relations improved, and the neighborhood stabilization committee now included LCTA members. In 1985 Governor Hendley came again to CB4 when another Lefrak City presentation was on the agenda. Lefrak management officials reported progress on security issues and said that the complex was enjoying a zero vacancy rate. When Daniels again brought up "congregating" youth, an official replied, "There are about 5,000 young people in Lefrak City. They will hang out. This is where they live." Norma Cirino, chair of the CB4 youth services committee, agreed: "The problem is the youth have no place to go." Hendley nodded. But then Cirino added, "We asked for the Outreach program that deals with drug and alcohol problems to get recreation space, but Mr. Lefrak said no." Hendley interjected, "We had one [youth program] and this community board railroaded it out." Cirino replied, "[That] was supposed to be an office for a program, not a hangout. This is Father [Coleman] Costello's program that operates throughout New York City. We need it in Corona."

This exchange reopened an old sore. The "hangout" Cirino referred to was the space occupied by the Youth in Progress Association (YIPA), a program begun by black Lefrak City adults in 1979 to provide job training, tutoring, and recreation for young people of sixteen to twenty-one. It was launched with corporate and foundation grants and in 1980 received city youth services funding. When authority to award these funds was given to community boards in 1981, however, Cirino's committee bypassed YIPA and gave $23,000 to Father Costello's Outreach Project, a substance-abuse program for teens, headquartered in Glendale. The committee also recommended that Outreach replace YIPA in the space provided by Lefrak management, but Lefrak refused.[3] CB4 had thus defunded a program the LCTA backed and had defined the needs of black youth as drug and alcohol prevention rather than career training and recreation. Following Cirino's comments, Hendley was not permitted to speak again. He appeared disgusted, and as the board turned to its next topic, the trust between CB4 and the LCTA established during 1984 seemed to vanish.

"Everybody's Name Is Wang"

Once President Reagan took office in 1981, the PSS senior housing project faced elimination. CB4 members Lou Simeone, Steve Trimboli, and Tony Caminiti lobbied U.S. Representative Gary Ackerman and Senator Alfonse D'Amato to save it, and the project went forward. Federal low-interest housing loans lowered its construction costs, and Section 8 rent subsidies were available for tenants. By September 1984 the PSS housing was ready for its 150 occupants.

Since in moral terms many white Corona Heights residents saw the housing as compensation for the disruption caused by the original high school plan, CB4 had urged a "local preference" block of seventy-four units for Corona applicants, provided they met age or disability and income criteria. As hundreds of applications arrived in spring 1984, however, chair Steve Trimboli told CB4 that some callers were requesting information in Chinese. "Everybody's name is Wang," he said in a joking tone. "I know how to solve their housing problem—call the INS. We want our own people. Chinese have some nerve, saying we don't speak Chinese. We were here first. We want our neighbors in first."[4]

That summer CB4 learned that the Section 8 income eligibility threshold was being lowered from "low income" to "very low income." This cut the maximum allowable income from $17,400 to $11,400 for a couple, and from $15,250 to $10,000 for a single adult. The change was part of the 1981 budget act and took effect in July 1984, just two days after PSS housing applications closed. CB4 leaders who had fought for the project had not known that Corona residents with incomes above "very low" levels would be excluded.[5]

When applicants were selected by lottery during summer 1984, Trimboli was disturbed that fourteen of the first thirty were "green card holders." One "Kim," a Korean, had been in the United States six months and claimed a $4,800 annual income. Trimboli wrote down the address to "check with the INS to see if Kim was legal" and who had sponsored Kim's immigration. PSS "got angry" with Trimboli, and he resigned from the selection committee but began to publicize the Kim case in press interviews and on the Bob Grant radio program.[6]

In September 1984 district manager John Rowan reminded CB4 that Section

8 did not exclude legal immigrants. Lou Simeone, however, sensed that the immigration issue could be used to pressure elected officials to obtain a waiver of the new income threshold. He called for a public hearing "on the issue of preferential treatment of green card holders over our own people," and it was held later that month.

Restoring the old income guideline was the main topic of the hearing, which drew one hundred elderly white Corona Heights residents. Tony Caminiti clarified the legal issues and reported that he, Trimboli, and Simeone had met with Senator D'Amato and received his promise to intercede. PSS announced that it would hold thirty "local preference" units until the matter was resolved. Simeone, a member of the applicant selection committee, told the audience, "As your rep, we're in there pitching for you. If the guidelines are changed back it will be okay for this community." Nonetheless, anti-immigrant sentiment poured out. "Who in Corona is 'very low income?' " one person shouted. "Foreigners!" another responded. "American citizens are being deprived of their rights. In one case a one-year resident Oriental will get an apartment," said a third. Assembly member Helen Marshall tried to calm things down: "Thirty or forty years ago your parents held green cards. That's how America works." She was jeered: "There was room, now it's crowded!"

Of 1,200 applications received by PSS, 275 were from Elmhurst-Corona. Of the first thirty-five residents to arrive during fall 1984, fourteen were legal immigrants. One white Corona resident declined an apartment, saying, "It's a Korean building," but others were pleased to move in. "People are happy and grateful, both Corona people and people from outside," CB4 housing committee chair Judy D'Andrea reported. "It's like one big family." In December 1984 she announced that the income waiver had been granted, and Corona residents denied units earlier would now be recontacted.

The changing relationship of race and place in Elmhurst-Corona was highlighted by the PSS housing controversy. "Local preference" could no longer guarantee that units would go to white residents: "Kim is local now," CB4 member Charles Stidolph said at a 1985 CB4 meeting. "Our own people" as Steve Trimboli defined them, "American citizens [who] gave their blood [and] have a history of paying taxes and Social Security for thirty or forty years," could no longer claim exclusive rights to the fruits of neighborhood victory.

Trimboli's statements about immigrants were made before a community board to which no Asian had ever been appointed and on which few Latin Americans remained for more than a year.[7] Negative comments about blacks had diminished with the presence of African American board members beginning in 1976 and the frequent attendance of Helen Marshall after 1982. I did overhear several white CB4 members laughing at an antiblack joke in 1986, but only in a hallway as the meeting was breaking up. Events about to occur at CB4 would also shift to the sidelines the jokes and negative comments about immigrants. The definition of "our own people" was changing in CD4.

New Leadership Arrives

In 1984 the CB4 nominations committee recommended a slate headed by Steve Trimboli. Then, from the floor, Carmela George nominated Rose Rothschild for chair, and Judy D'Andrea seconded the nomination. Trimboli won by 23 to 7, but the floor revolt continued. George nominated Al Fernicola as vice-chair, Rothschild seconded, and Fernicola lost by the same 23 to 7 vote. Finally, George nominated D'Andrea for secretary, Rothschild again seconded, and D'Andrea lost by 17-13. The revolt had failed.

The 1985 election resulted in victory for the insurgents, but only after a stormy confrontation. This year Carmela George chaired the nominations committee, and Trimboli was ineligible to serve again as chair. George's committee presented a slate of Rothschild for chair, Trimboli for treasurer, and D'Andrea for secretary. Its at-large executive committee nominees were George, Fernicola, Richard Isles (now CB4's only black member), and Raoul LaFaye, an Argentinian architect and one of the three Latin Americans appointed in 1984. No floor nominations were offered.

Then, as balloting was about to begin, Matt McKinley, an aide to city council member Joseph Lisa Jr., requested that the vote be postponed on the grounds that newly appointed council member Walter Crowley had not yet made any appointments to CB4. In fact, he did not know whether Crowley had submitted any appointments, and it became obvious that Lisa objected to Rothschild as chair. (Lisa presumed incorrectly that Rothschild backed a female Democratic challenger whom he defeated later in 1985.) A handful of CB4 members supported McKinley's request and moved to table the election. Amid much clamor, the motion failed by 16 to 4. (The number of votes was low because several Corona CB4 members from Lisa's own Northside Club had absented themselves to avoid this confrontation.) The officer slate was elected, and Rothschild took the aide aside to speak privately.

Rose Renda Rothschild was born and raised in East Harlem, the daughter of an Italian immigrant father and second-generation mother.[8] During the 1950s she moved to Jackson Heights with her German-Italian husband but soon returned to Manhattan. There she became active in her local Roman Catholic parish and Democratic Party club, served as a Brownie leader and Parent Association president after her first daughter began school, and attended Hunter College. In 1961 the Rothschilds moved to the Elmhurst apartment where her second and third children were born and where she has lived since. She continued her neighborhood activism in St. Bart's parish, in local Democratic clubs, and as president of the PS89 Parents Association for five years and the Newtown High School Parent Council for two years.

In 1977 Rose Rothschild became one of thirteen women on CB4. "When I came on the board I joined the youth committee, and then it fell apart. Sister

Thomas Francis [a CB4 member and director of St. John's Hospital] said, 'Take [the] health [and social services committee, which she chaired], I'll teach you.' I only knew about schools. I learned. I got outside [non-CB4] members, people I knew through the schools, and the Elmhurst Guidance Center [a mental health agency]. I had up to thirty people on the committee."

As committee chair during 1981–1985, Rothschild met directors and staff at all health and social service agencies in Elmhurst-Corona, attended forums and public hearings, and learned about funding sources. She invited speakers to address her committee and then "booked" them at senior centers and civic group meetings. She also formed an advisory board for the Leben Home and was appointed to the Community Advisory Board of Elmhurst Hospital.

A major victory for Rothschild was the creation of a residence for mentally retarded adults in Corona Heights. By 1979 CD4 contained thirty-two group homes with a total of 1,300 beds; they ranged from the Leben Home to small foster homes for teenagers in Lefrak City apartments. Feeling pressed by population growth, school overcrowding, and deteriorating city services, CB4 resolved to oppose any more such facilities. The board's claim of "oversaturation" was bolstered by borough statistics showing that the four neighboring community districts combined contained fewer group homes than CD4; only CD12 in southeast Queens had more. In 1980 CD4's group homes amounted to one-quarter of those in all of Queens. Nonetheless, the health committee chair that year, Sister Thomas Francis, persuaded CB4 to suspend its resolution and permit a new residence for retarded adults. Not only had a court decision ordered transfer of one hundred Queens family members into "the community" from the notorious Willowbrook State Hospital, but Sister Thomas Francis knew that additional facilities were needed for mentally retarded adult children of aging parents who could no longer provide care in their homes.[9]

When Rose Rothschild became health committee chair, she took on responsibility for this project. She negotiated among Catholic Charities (the agency that would operate the home), St. Leo's Church (whose empty convent would provide the site), state and city bureaucracies, and CB4. She visited existing residences and held meetings to address local opposition. A major ally was Monsignor Anthony Baretta of St. Leo's, who spoke at these meetings on behalf of the new facility.

Rose Rothschild's policy expertise matured as she defended CB4's annual city budget requests for health and social services. At "borough consultations" she answered questions from municipal agency staff and listened to their exchanges with representatives of other Queens community boards. She soon began attending the consultations for all CB4 budget recommendations, becoming familiar with policy and personnel throughout the gamut of city departments.[10] In 1982 she was elected CB4's treasurer and as an executive committee member saw its inner workings firsthand. "After I was health chair, and [then] saw what was going on, I decided I might as well be chair of the board."[11]

When she was elected chair in 1985, Rothschild had been a CB4 member for eight years. Her health committee included nearly all the women members of CB4 and gave her contact with white, black, Latin American, and Asian staff at health and social service agencies throughout CD4. Her 1984 supporters Carmela George, Al Fernicola, and Judy D'Andrea had joined CB4 in 1979 and were leaders of Corona block associations. Corona-born D'Andrea was the mother of two children, a Queens College graduate, and a teacher at PS19 in Corona Plaza. The youngest member of CB4 and chair of its housing committee, she worked closely with the Neighborhood Preservation Program that the board had fought to establish and with the PSS sponsor of the new senior citizen housing.

Rose and the Board

During 1985, as new chair, Rothschild shared CB4's Elmhurst office with district manager John Rowan. Then in 1986 Rowan accepted a city council staff position. Her youngest child now sixteen, Rothschild applied for the district manager position herself and was hired in a unanimous vote by CB4. Her role at board meetings then changed from outspoken member to staff person, and her job included chairing monthly district cabinet meetings and maintaining contact with city agency personnel. As district manager she served at the pleasure of the board, and her activities involved both consolidation of support among its members and expansion of its role in Elmhurst-Corona civic politics.[12]

Consolidating CB4 Support

Consolidation was facilitated by the promotion of vice-chair Miriam Levenson to CB4 chair upon Rothschild's appointment as district manager. A CB4 member since 1971 and a Newtown Civic Association leader, Levenson had experience in Elmhurst school and Democratic Club activities and was knowledgeable about city budget and zoning technicalities. Some male members were uneasy with two women filling CB4's top positions, but gender-based reservations did not last long. During Rothschild's first year, CB4 member Don Mallozzi declared that a "letter written by our district manager Rose Rothschild is a masterpiece." He added, "It was surprising to see two women carrying on in the tradition they are. Miriam is leaving no stone unturned. We're very lucky to have Rose and Miriam to carry on. Compared to the other community boards in the city we are doing very well." A few months later Tom McKenzie, chair of CB4's environmental affairs committee, complimented Rothschild on her diligence in pursuing water and sewer complaints with city agencies: "It's wonderful."[13]

Mallozzi was a member of the Northside Democrats–Corona Taxpayers CB4 group led by Tony Caminiti. Rose Rothschild worked closely with Caminiti, chair of CB4's parks committee, and suggested naming a new park at the Corona high school site after deceased member Lou Simeone. Council member Lisa wanted the park named for Governor Mario Cuomo's father, but Rothschild's suggestion was supported by Caminiti and CB4. Caminiti and Mallozzi were also members of the public safety committee headed by Al Fernicola, and Rothschild met regularly with all three men. In 1988, when CB4 had to vacate its Elmhurst space, Rothschild moved the office to Corona Heights, and monthly board and district cabinet meetings shifted to the Northside clubhouse, a site arranged by Caminiti.

Rose Rothschild's rapprochement with Corona CB4 members, however, produced an Elmhurst backlash. In 1988, when Miriam Levenson was renominated for a final term as chair, Tom McKenzie objected that there was "only one member from Elmhurst" on the proposed executive committee (although in fact, Clara Salas, an Elmhurst resident, was also nominated). The next year the nominations committee recommended Al Fernicola for chair, and an Elmhurst versus Corona uproar broke out. Charles Stidolph of Elmhurst was nominated from the floor and elected by a 17-to-14 vote that divided Elmhurst and Corona members.

A building engineer in private practice, Stidolph opposed the downzoning proposal about to come before CB4; so did EEDC director Steve Trimboli, who led the Elmhurst revolt. Soon after the election Stidolph reprimanded Rothschild for purchasing a fax machine without executive committee approval, but a CB4 motion to ratify her decision passed easily. Relations between Stidolph and Rothschild later warmed, and in 1991 he backed Rothschild when Elmhurst member Bob Tilitz called for a committee to "monitor" her. In 1992 Fernicola was elected CB4 chair without objection.

Expanding CB4 Membership

Rose Rothschild's accession to board chair and then district manager coincided with the arrival of new Latin American, Asian, and African American CB4 members. In 1985 three Latin Americans joined the three appointed a year earlier, including two women whom Rothschild had met through the Elmhurst Hospital Community Advisory Board and encouraged to submit CB4 applications. One of them was Clara Salas, whom Rothschild also supported for a School Board 24 seat in 1986 and who later became chair of CB4's housing committee, a position she held into the mid-1990s. Another new member was Haydee Zambrana of Ciudadanos Conscientes de Queens; she remained on CB4 until 1990 and was in frequent contact with Rothschild's office, from which callers were referred to CCQ. Before a bilingual CB4 staff member was hired in 1988, Rothschild also occasionally asked Zambrana to translate into Spanish.

In 1986 the first two Asian members joined CB4. Chao-rong Horng, a civil engineer and president of the Chinese American Voters Association, later served as chair of the board's zoning committee.[14] Daok Lee Pak, a member of the Korean American Association of Mid-Queens, helped organize a seminar for Korean merchants immediately after joining CB4. At Horng and Pak's first meeting, Rothschild invited Pak to move from the audience to the tables occupied by the board and then asked the older members to introduce themselves to their two new colleagues. Over the next few years other Chinese and Koreans were appointed to CB4 as well.

At meetings, white members frequently used diminutive nicknames to address one another: Kenneth was "Kenny," Anthony "Tony," Daniel "Danny," and Rose sometimes "Ro." African Americans and long-resident Latin Americans found it easy to use this white working-class code, but recent immigrants, particularly Asians, did not. In order to avoid singling them out with formal "Mr. Horng" or "Mrs. Pak" usage, Rothschild coined nicknames that others also began to use at meetings. Thus Chao-rong Horng became "Chao," Daok Lee Pak "Lee," and B. Ramamoorthy, in 1990 the first Indian member, "Ram."[15]

Rose Rothschild also supported the new Asian members in ways that mattered to them. In 1987 she and Miriam Levenson attended an Organization of Chinese Americans dinner honoring Chao-rong Horng. Rothschild became particularly friendly with leaders of the KAAMQ and at their invitation visited the Korea pavilion at the 1986 Queens Festival and *ch'usok,* both in Flushing Meadows–Corona Park. She also patronized Seung Ha Hong's bakery; concerning a birthday cake bought there, she announced at a district cabinet meeting, "It was so good they almost ate the doily. Usually birthday cake doesn't go, but people ate it all." At a 1993 CB4 meeting "Ram" publicly thanked Rothschild for her letter included in the India Day Parade souvenir book. "It was a gorgeous journal," she said in return.

Beyond personal relationships and courtesies, however, it was Rothschild's action on "problems that are important to us" which solidified support from both old and new CB4 members. Her work to bring three new schools to CD4 and additions to others, her support of local business owners, and her prodding of Police, Sanitation, Environmental Affairs, and Parks Departments and other city agencies spoke for itself.[16]

Tragedy struck Rose Rothschild in 1988 when both her mother and her husband died within one month. Many came to the wakes and services that followed these losses, a mix of white, black, Latin American, and Asian faces. Monsignor Anthony Baretta conducted her husband's funeral mass at St. Leo's Church. As the pallbearers arrived from Guida's funeral home across the street, Rothschild, her children and granddaughter, and a handful of relatives and family friends followed, with Sung Jin Chun and Seung Ha Hong behind them. Other friends in the church included Carmela George, Judy D'Andrea, Al Fernicola, Miriam Levenson, Tony Caminiti, Tom Rodriguez, Haydee Zambrana, Richard Bearak of the City Planning Department, and Ron Baskin from Concerned Community Adults in Lefrak City (his wife, Edna, did not attend open-casket funerals). Guida's funeral home was a thicket of flowers, among them a large wreath from the Lefrak City Tenants Association.

A Bridge to Lefrak City

By 1985, with relations between CB4 and the community's black residents still minimal, the several thousand black voters in the Lefrak area were approaching Elmhurst-Corona's declining white electorate in size. They already formed an important constituency for Helen Marshall, state assembly member. She maintained an office in Lefrak City, where two of her aides lived, and had helped obtain space there for the Lefrak City Senior Center.

Marshall supported Rose Rothschild's 1986 candidacy for district manager and spoke to CB4 members on her behalf. In 1987 she put Rothschild on the agenda of her own Lefrak City town meeting, providing the first large black audience Rothschild addressed as district manager. The two women continued to work closely, and when Rothschild received an award from the Franklin D. Roosevelt Democratic Club in 1995, it was Marshall who detailed her biography to the several hundred Queens party faithful attending the event.

Having visited Lefrak City as chair of CB4's health and social services committee, Rothschild knew and spoke with black audience members who occasionally attended CB4 meetings. As board chair during 1985 and then district manager, she visited the Lefrak area and met with LCTA leaders. She steered the CB4 neighborhood stabilization committee away from LCTA-management issues and toward quality-of-life problems affecting Lefrak tenants as residents of CD4. And in addition to pressing the 110th Precinct about drug selling on 57th Avenue (the LCTA also dealt directly with the 110th on this), she focused on garbage.

The most densely populated portion of CD4, Lefrak's twenty apartment towers generated masses of garbage, which sat awaiting pickup on the street. In 1986 Rothschild pushed the Sanitation Department to add a third weekly collection day at Lefrak City, but Lefrak management still continued to place garbage on the street well before pickup time. In 1987 Helen Marshall informed the district cabinet, "They put out garbage every day. Garbage is flowing and people throw things on top of garbage. People should not have to live with that." Rothschild and Marshall met with Lefrak management to demand that garbage remain in holding areas until the morning it was to be collected, a policy Lefrak did then institute.

Problems at the Lefrak City Branch Library

Edna Baskin, an African American Lefrak City resident since 1979 and an LCTA member, had begun attending CB4 and neighborhood stabilization committee meetings in 1985. In her native Buffalo, New York, she had been active in black community politics and worked in the campaigns of state assembly member Arthur Eve. Frustrated that the LCTA channel to the community board was blocked, she reported what she learned at CB4 to residents of her building, including parents of the children in her home-based day-care business. She wanted to know what to tell "her" parents about youth recreation opportunities as their children grew up and hoped she might find answers at CB4.[17]

In 1986 a crisis was mounting at the Lefrak City branch of the Queens Borough Public Library (QBPL). Many children came there after school, their numbers increasing as the weather grew colder. The librarians were unable to provide supervision, and a QBPL security guard was dispatched to assist them. Then early in 1987 the QBPL announced that the guard would be discontinued. Helma Goldmark, a white Sherwood Village resident and CB4 member, concerned about both young and elderly users of the library, requested that the guard remain.

In February 1987 a QBPL security official came to a meeting of CB4's neighborhood stabilization committee which was attended by Goldmark, Rothschild, Edna Baskin, the branch librarians, and a dozen Lefrak City and Sherwood Village residents, half white and half black. "It's quieted down with a guard," Rothschild began. "Kids today are ten going on forty, but if they see a security guard there will be less playing around." The QBPL official defended the withdrawal of the guard and blamed "the community," "these latchkey kids," and "the parents" for difficulties; moreover, he said, the librarians had a beeper to call central security if necessary.

Rothschild objected. "You are taking a negative approach. So far [you are saying] the kids are from Murder Incorporated. I'm here doing my job, which is to get you to do your job." Edna Baskin followed: "I speak as a parent [of two grown-up sons]. I pass every day. I've seen the librarian physically and verbally assaulted by a 175-pound, six-foot, fourteen-year-old." Rothschild backed her up. "Kids are tired after being closed in all day. My son is six [foot], three [inches tall], seventeen years old. As Edna said, you should try a security guard." Rovenia McGowan, a black Sherwood Village resident and a schoolteacher, and Ken Daniels, the white chair of the neighborhood stabilization committee, added that schools, department stores, and their own buildings had security guards. "If we don't get a guard, we may lose the library," McGowan pleaded.

The QBPL official had attempted to split the white and black residents, blaming black children and parents for the problem. Instead, he encountered local solidarity, with black and white adults requesting help to deal with troublemakers, and to allow black neighborhood children and white senior citizens to use the library in peace. The guard remained.

An African American Warden

In June 1987 Edna Baskin read in the minutes of CB4's youth services committee that no youth group had been found to represent Elmhurst-Corona in a boroughwide summer cleanup contest. First place, including a trip to Disney World for team members and adult leaders, would be determined by Sanitation

Department cleanliness ratings and evidence of community support. Baskin quickly put together a Concerned Community Adults (CCA) team of five- to sixteen-year-olds from families she knew through her child-care business. She filled out the contest application, and youth services committee chair Judy D'Andrea and district manager Rose Rothschild submitted it as CB4's entry. A July 1987 "Kick Off Ceremony" was held at Queens Borough Hall, where borough president Claire Shulman and baseball veteran Cy Block, the contest's sponsor, addressed teams representing eight community districts. Rothschild and CB4 chair Miriam Levenson were there to support the CCA group. "The other teams don't have ten [members]," Rothschild said. "Edna has ten. When we do something we do it right."

Over the next six weeks Baskin's team collected litter three days a week along a twenty-block perimeter of Lefrak City, including its 57th Avenue shopping strip. Appreciative merchants donated haircuts, school supplies, and refreshments, and parents and LCTA volunteers supervised the children at work and during recreational events. The CCA youth matched the first-place team in Sanitation Department scorings but came in second because the winners had made a videotape of their activities.

The CCA team did have community support, however. It was featured in a *Daily News* story with a photo of the children, Rothschild and Levenson, and "Leo the Greek," a lunchwagon proprietor who provided free hot dogs and sodas several times during the summer.[18] And the KAAMQ invited Baskin, the cleanup team members, and a parent supervisor to a dinner at a Korean restaurant. Other guests included Rothschild and Levenson, LCTA secretary Jim Galloway, Bob Tilitz of the Newtown Civic Association, Tom Rodriguez of the Corona Community Development Corporation, a 110th Precinct community affairs officer, Steven Gregory, Kyeyoung Park, and me. KAAMQ members Sung Jin Chun and Seung Ha Hong and CB4 member Daok Lee Pak spoke and presented gifts to the youth. Baskin told me later, "The kids really enjoyed that Korean dinner. They learned to eat seaweed and sushi. They had never eaten raw fish. They said seaweed was like spinach. That's a cultural thing. The kids wanted to go back."[19]

Lefrak management was so impressed with the cleanup that it provided space and food for a celebration dinner. As parents looked on, the children received certificates from state assembly member Helen Marshall, from Ron Baskin on behalf of CCA, and from a Sanitation Department official. Certificates were also presented to adult CCA members who had helped in various ways, the KAAMQ and Daok Lee Pak, and Rose Rothschild and Judy D'Andrea of CB4.

Although there was no contest the following year, Edna Baskin repeated the cleanup. She recruited a new team of fifteen children, including two from a group home in Lefrak City. One hot August day I watched them sweep sidewalks, rake patches of grass, pick up discarded paper and containers, and load collected trash in plastic bags onto a children's wagon, which was also used to carry work tools and cold drinks. The 1988 team included children born in Jamaica, Trinidad, Barbados, Haiti, Ghana, and Puerto Rico; two were Latin American, and the rest were black. Supervision was provided by Baskin and Toyin Chukwuogo, a Nigerian Lefrak City resident. A CCA poster reading "Work with us to keep it clean!" in Spanish, Korean, Chinese, Hindi, Italian, and English (designed at Baskin's request by our research team) was displayed in Lefrak City store windows.

The dinner at summer's end again featured gifts from merchants and certificates from Marshall, but this year representatives of other elected officials also presented proclamations. Ron Baskin gave a bouquet of roses to CCA honoree Rose Rothschild and told the children, "We want you to know that there are adults in the community who will support you. You no longer have to be the best black, the best Hispanic, the best white. You can be the best at what you do." The CCA cleanup continued into the 1990s as both a summer youth activity and a communication channel between Lefrak City residents and merchants.[20]

New Links

After incorporating CCA in 1988, Edna Baskin held fund-raising Black Heritage book sales and began an after-school tutoring program for fifty children at the Lefrak City Branch Library. Here she was joined by scores of black adults, an elderly Jewish widow, an Indian branch librarian (who was also a Sherwood Village resident), a Vietnamese high school student math tutor, and Elena Acosta, a Colombian Queens College student. The tutoring program continued until 1992, when Dinkins's budget cuts reduced afternoon library hours.[21] Baskin also joined CB4 in 1988. That year youth services committee chair Judy D'Andrea recommended that funds returned from the Glendale-based Outreach Project be allocated to CCA's tutoring program. Corona Community Development Corporation director Tom Rodriguez, whom Baskin knew from CB4, administered these funds until CCA obtained tax-exempt status.

Edna Baskin's growing number of activities, contacts, and CCA members was noted by LCTA leaders. In 1987 she organized a youth forum attended by fifty Lefrak City teens and a dozen adults, including Rothschild, Levenson, Pak, and Bob Tilitz. Soon thereafter Governor Hendley asked Baskin to bring CCA under the LCTA umbrella, but she refused.[22] As her independent activity intensified both within the Lefrak City arena and in the district-level political field, the LCTA faced a competing force.

In 1988 LCTA member John Braxton also joined CB4. In 1989 Rovenia McGowan of Sherwood Village became the fourth black CB4 member, followed by LCTA officers James Brown and Lou Walker in 1990. By 1993 there were eight black members, nearly a fifth of CB4's membership. Baskin was elected an at-large member of the executive committee in 1990; Walker joined her in 1992, and Brown in 1994. That year Baskin was elected CB4 treasurer, and in 1996 Walker became vice-chair.

The new receptivity to black voices at CB4 arose because Rose Rothschild made quality-of-life issues at Lefrak City part of CB4's agenda, and she and Judy D'Andrea backed a group of black children as representatives of the Elmhurst-Corona community. The bridge from Lefrak City to CB4 was provided by Edna Baskin and her desire to expand opportunities for black youth. The challenge CCA posed to the LCTA in fact proved beneficial. In 1991 LCTA vice-president Al Blake organized a Lefrak City Summer Classic basketball tournament and a program of track and other sports in which five hundred youths participated. Lefrak management opened basketball and pool facilities to Blake, and his contacts at CB4, which he joined in 1992, led to his sports program's use of Newtown Field.

District Manager and District Cabinet

The first district managers in the early 1970s were mayoral appointees who did not live in the community district where they worked. Their "horizontal" coordination of local city operations was seen as requiring City Hall ties in order to *resist* neighborhood demands. Most district managers were young male college graduates who viewed the job as the first rung on the ladder to a career in public administration.[23] But the 1975 fiscal crisis cuts and continuing Koch-Dinkins-Giuliani budget reductions transformed the district manager's role. Agency coordination remained important, but action on quality-of-life "problems that are important to us," not technocratic administration of austerity, was deemed essential by the community board members who after 1977 hired the district managers. Local knowledge and support became crucial to a district manager's effectiveness.

Rose Rothschild had the necessary knowledge. She had pushed a baby carriage along neighborhood streets and taken her children to play in Elmhurst parks. Her father had endured a ten-hour wait at St. John's Hospital. The Neighborhood Preservation Program inspected her apartment building, found code violations, and negotiated a repair agreement with her landlord. Late-night noise and sidewalk parking occurred at a nightclub on her block; a drug seller was arrested in her building; and her son was approached on the street and asked if he wanted a prostitute.

As district manager, Rothschild's daily routine revolved around complaints called in or made in person by Elmhurst-Corona residents, including CB4 members. These complaints were transmitted to the appropriate city agency, frequently after on-site investigation by Rothschild herself. She and her staff then followed up by keeping in touch with complainants and agency personnel. She also maintained contacts with elected officials and their staffs, school principals, health and social service agency personnel, civic activists, and clergy. She spoke at civic and block association meetings, Lions Club luncheons, senior citizen centers, and public hearings. She talked with scores of 110th Precinct officers and local business proprietors. She met lawyers, developers, builders, and architects in negotiations over zoning variance requests. She attended the Borough Board (consisting of Queens city council members and the chairs of community boards) and Zoning Task Force convened by borough president Claire Shulman. She dealt with the Community Assistance Unit and the Office of Management and Budget staff of Mayors Koch, Dinkins, and Giuliani.[24]

By the 1980s, in keeping with the 1975 city charter, service districts and budgeting for police, sanitation, parks, environmental protection, street maintenance, traffic, housing inspection, and city planning were "coterminous" with community district lines. Each of these agencies was represented at monthly meetings chaired by CB4's district manager. Nonmayoral agencies—including School Board 24, branch libraries, Elmhurst Hospital, the Long Island Rail Road, and the subways—were unaffected by coterminality; occasionally, however, Rothschild invited representatives from these and from private service providers to speak at cabinet meetings.[25]

After she became district manager, Rose Rothschild pruned the 125-name district cabinet mailing list of CB4 members, local wardens, and private agency directors, leaving a dozen or so district-level agency supervisors and a similar number of liaisons of elected officials. The Police, Sanitation, and Parks Departments frequently sent two or more representatives; with occasional guests, attendance averaged between thirty and forty. Reflecting the city work force and elected officials' sensitivity to their diverse constituents, the district cabinet was a multiracial body. At one 1991 meeting, twenty of the thirty-three present were white, eight black, four Latin American, and one Chinese.

Although city agency personnel were required to attend, the district manager had no power to order or discipline them; Rothschild could only "encourage, cajole, and sometimes pressure."[26] She reiterated citizen complaints her office received, asked pointed questions about particular problems, inquired when corrective action would be taken, and sometimes directly criticized agency performance. "Ponce Plaza [a sitting area beneath the elevated IRT] is filthy, get somebody over there," she told a Parks Department supervisor at one district cabinet meeting. "We take out garbage twice a week, and clean the park on Friday," he responded. "There are only two [trash]baskets," she countered. "You need more. Ponce Plaza gets an F."

Rose Rothschild also worked to establish personal relationships with city workers and supervisors. Nicknames were used, in both directions. "I did put [trash]baskets in, Ro," Sanitation Department supervisor Phil Pirozzi interjected during the Ponce Plaza discussion. She met face to face with each set of sanitation inspectors serving six-month rotations on CD4's commercial strips. She requested building code enforcement officers to "come to the office, not just receive the pinks [complaint notices] by mail. We want to develop a rapport with them, and talk about the area." She complimented individuals such as 110th

C-POP officers on work well done. She conferred privately before meetings with agency personnel whose performance she wanted to discuss. And she separated the messenger from the message when service reductions were announced. "I know, Pam, it's not your fault," she told a Human Resources Administration liaison reporting on Giuliani administration cuts, "but you're the bearer of bad news. This is disgraceful."[27]

One of Rothschild's strongest weapons was her sense of humor. One elected official's liaison said there were more laughs than at any of the other district cabinet and community board meetings he attended in three boroughs. She joked informally in small groups and one on one, and openly in meetings. She said aptly of one long-winded warden, "By the time [they have] finished talking the year 2000 has arrived." When a Parks Department official remarked that two female summer recreation workers were helping pick up litter, Rothschild responded, "We're not women's liberation. Get the men in there to clean!" And pressing an LIRR representative about removing trash along the railroad corridor, she said, "I don't see people clean up. It's the same couch [there] for the last twenty years."[28]

Rothschild's district cabinet meetings were noted for her demands for agency accountability. "They know I'm tough all over the city," she said at one cabinet meeting. "That's why I get what I want." After sharp exchanges, however, she would close a meeting with comments such as "Thanks for coming. I know you hate to be badgered, but we get it, and have to give it to you."

One reason for creating district cabinets was to avoid situations where "two district officers whose services either overlapped or were dependent on each other often had not previously met face to face." While this was solved by monthly meetings, district managers still needed "to overcome bureaucratic red tape and secure rapid responses" to problems caused by lack of communication at higher levels of city government.[29] Achieving interdepartment cooperation in such instances gave Rose Rothschild particular satisfaction. "I find in this kind of setting [the district cabinet] everyone seems to coordinate. Our agency people are really good."

In 1989 Rothschild invited an Elmhurst Hospital official to discuss expansion plans. "I am concerned about parking," she began. A Transit Police officer asked if construction would interfere with the emergency subway exit in front of the hospital. The hospital representative had not known that such an exit existed. A Fire Department battalion chief, noting that "we're hearing about most of the construction [for the first time] today," emphasized that his vehicles needed unimpeded access to the emergency exit. The district sanitation supervisor observed that if vehicles displaced from the old parking lot parked on the streets, "with the MD cars, we can't sweep." Rothschild told the hospital representative, "The higher-ups are not filtering down the plans to the local people. This is the first time they're hearing about it. There are going to be problems." The plan to use the 78th Street playground for parking during the construction period resulted from this meeting.

Rose Rothschild's experience with city operations and regulations increased her fund of lubricatory power. As district manager she added to her previous knowledge of schools, health care, and social services. She also drew upon CB4's committee chairs—particularly Judy D'Andrea (housing, youth), Al Fernicola (public safety), and Tony Caminiti (parks)—and on Miriam Levenson's land-use and budget experience.[30] And she attended briefings and seminars, some organized by private organizations such as the Community Service Society and the Vera Institute of Justice. She employed her knowledge of city government in her annual "District Needs" statements, which accompanied CB4's budget recommendations. These documents covered each agency and identified its problem areas.[31]

Rothschild frequently used lubricatory power to make CB4's power of numbers more effective. In 1989, for example, COMET members from South Elmhurst opposed a six-story parking garage behind St. John's Hospital. When CB4 voted on the proposal, a wordy "exclamatory" motion against it passed easily. Several of the motion's reasons for opposing the garage, however, were irrelevant to the technical land-use issue at hand. Rothschild summarized the appropriate arguments in concise "explanatory" terms for the meeting's minutes and later drafted a letter to the City Planning Commission that did not make CB4 "look silly."

Land use and zoning were the most complex matters before CB4. Rose Rothschild found a tutor and ally in Richard Bearak, the young Department of City Planning liaison assigned to CD4 during 1985–1988. (Bearak developed an affection for the neighborhood, and it became the subject of his architectural thesis.)[32] He spoke at nearly every CB4 and district cabinet meeting, and even though glazed looks often followed his precise and detailed reports, Bearak directed his considerable lubricatory power toward aiding Rothschild and other civic activists in the zoning wars of 1985–1989. Soon after he began his CD4 assignment, Rothschild said at a CB4 meeting, "Richy has been very good. We get a lot of information from him." In 1988 she told the district cabinet, "If it wasn't for Richy Bearak, we wouldn't have any [new] school. He went above and beyond the call of duty."

As the 1980s began, the march of infill housing continued, and more "huge, architecturally depressing multiple dwellings," as Bob Tilitz called them, replaced one- and two-family homes. After their downzoning application failed in 1980, CB4 and Newtown Civic Association leaders shifted tactics. Beginning in 1981 they pressed to make Elmhurst-Corona a "special district" requiring eight-foot side yards between buildings in all new construction. Opposition from the Queens County Builders and Contractors Association (QCBCA) led the City Planning Commission to table this request in 1985.

Meanwhile, landlord abandonment and gentrification were leading to a citywide loss of 400 housing units a week, a mounting homeless population, and a vacancy rate of only 2 percent. At the same time, the Koch-era Manhattan boom was adding 30,000 white-collar jobs a year, and ranks of yuppies priced out of Manhattan were looking for housing in the outer boroughs. Facing reelection in 1985, Koch was eager to increase upscale housing alternatives for this growing constituency.[33] Consequently, developer activity in Queens was on the upswing. Builder Thomas Huang, whose 163-unit Elmhurst condominium opened in 1985, was aiming at "middle income . . . Asian and [white] American" buyers with several other new Queens apartments. In CD4 new housing units jumped from 60 a year during 1981–1983 to 280 in 1984, and infills were replacing demolished homes in other neighborhoods as well. Unwilling to compromise on side-yard restrictions, the QCBCA developers were not only producing buildings as large as existing zoning would permit but seeking variances for even bigger projects.[34] The zoning wars were on.

Standoff: Quality Housing and Queens Boulevard Upzoning

In 1983 Koch's Department of City Planning began work on a "Quality Housing" plan to provide a 20 percent floor-area-ratio (FAR) bonus for developers who erected shorter buildings covering more of the building lot; the idea was to mollify civic activists who were increasingly protesting the new "towers" appearing among two- and three-story homes. Then in 1984 the department formulated a second plan: to upzone the one-mile Elmhurst stretch of Queens Boulevard from R6 to R8, a change that would permit new apartments of up to eighteen stories.[35]

The Quality Housing and Queens Boulevard plans were both announced early in 1985. Those CB4 members who understood what they might mean were aghast. Since the early 1970s the board had complained about "honkytonk" fast-food and "garish" auto businesses on Queens Boulevard and urged the Department of City Planning to study *commercial* upzoning for a "better caliber" of businesses and jobs. Now they faced *residential* upzoning that could add thousands of people to a neighborhood where schools were overcrowded, parking scarce, and police, sanitation, parks, subways, and hospitals overburdened.

The Battle Is Joined

In March 1985 zoning committee chair Charles Stidolph alerted CB4 members to the upzoning threat. "We're talking about buildings 40 percent bigger than [Thomas Huang's Justice Avenue condominium. Queens City Planning director] Peter Magnani is hearing from the developers. He's not hearing from you." Steve Trimboli then revealed that "as president of the Elmhurst Economic

Development Corporation" he and several Queens Boulevard property owners had met with Magnani four months earlier for a briefing on the proposal. Though still CB4 chair at the time, Trimboli had not informed Stidolph or other board members.

Peter Magnani and City Planning Commission vice-chair Martin Gallent were invited to the April 1985 CB4 meeting. They explained that a consultant would be hired to study the impact of Queens Boulevard upzoning on traffic, subways, schools, and services. A final proposal would come to CB4 as part of the Uniform Land Use Review Procedure (ULURP) before going to the City Planning Commission and Board of Estimate. "Nothing is set in stone," Magnani said.[36] But the mood of CB4 members and South Elmhurst residents in attendance remained uneasy. As questions poured out, Magnani and Gallent stressed Mayor Koch's emphasis on new housing.[37] "Now the vacancy rate in Queens is 1.25 percent," Gallent explained. "The housing component is essential." "What kind of housing," Ken Daniels asked, "luxury, co-ops, middle income?" "It will be as the market dictates," Gallent responded, but then added that a "sweetening" of property-tax abatements would be offered. "Our best hope is middle-income to upper-middle income."

"Can the people of Elmhurst afford this?" asked Norma Cirino. Rose Rothschild, chairing her first CB4 meeting, answered "No!" and Gallent remained silent. "We have several markets here," John Rowan stated, "one generated by immigrants, one of young middle-class professionals. So I'd like to see a real assessment of what market we're talking about." The mayor's men assured the audience that additional schoolrooms would be part of the final package, and that no homes outside the Queens Boulevard commercial strip would be included in the upzoned area. In fact, Gallent added, "downzoning to reflect existing housing" would be considered "to protect the low-rise areas to the north and south."

After years of unsuccessful campaigns to downzone, CD4's civic activists were wary of City Hall's newfound willingness to "protect" them. The Quality Housing plan would make buying and demolishing existing homes even more profitable, and Queens Boulevard rezoning would transform Elmhurst into an "upscale" area. "Any piece of property will be up for development if this goes through," Charles Stidolph told other zoning committee members in June. "I offer half a million for your property, and you won't sell. Will you sell for $3 million? Every piece becomes salable. All the land that is rezoned will be built to the maximum, and this will mean a great change in Elmhurst."

As more details of the plans emerged, it was learned that the new housing was intended for households earning $61,000 and up, twice CD4's median income. Opposing Koch in the 1985 mayoral primary, city council president Carol Bellamy accused him of "promoting the development of housing for the rich [and] once again the needs of the average New Yorker are ignored."[38] Queens borough president Donald Manes, however, favored upzoning Queens Boulevard. NCA officers and CB4 chair Rothschild met with Manes in July 1985 to demand that schools and other services be brought up to par before any new housing was approved. South Elmhurst wardens also lobbied Manes, and he agreed to add a commercial upzoning option to the $340,000 consultant's study beginning that autumn.

Opposition Gathers

During 1986, concern over Queens Boulevard upzoning mounted in Elmhurst's civic associations. In June new borough president Claire Shulman met with COMET, the NCA, and district manager Rose Rothschild, who conveyed their opposition to upzoning and emphasized that speculation was already occurring on residential streets near the study area.[39] Shulman then formed a Zoning Task Force to which Rothschild and CB4 chair Miriam Levenson were appointed along with other Queens civic activists and developers from the QCBCA.

Meanwhile, the Quality Housing proposal, a long technical document, came to CB4, and an accompanying "environmental impact study" was conducted in Elmhurst-Corona and the other neighborhoods where its 20 percent floor-area bonus would apply. In January 1987 the Quality Housing plan came to CB4 for a vote, the first stage in the ULURP process. The issue was brought up late in the meeting, and Charles Stidolph, the CB4 member who best understood zoning matters, was absent. City Planning liaison Richard Bearak stated that a vote had to be taken that night. He explained that Quality Housing would mean shorter, squatter buildings with enclosed parking but without front or side yards. If it was not approved, he said, more "towers" could be expected like the eight-story "sliver building" that South Elmhurst residents had picketed in 1986. He also reviewed the "20 percent FAR" bonus and added that Quality Housing would be affordable only to the upper 15 percent of New York City households.[40]

Bearak understood that he could not recommend which way to vote; he limited his role to clarification of the plan. His technical explanation, however, passed over many board members' heads. "When I talk to the community board about zoning, it's like a blank wall," he later told me. "They don't understand everything." The board's discussion became fixed on the idea that Quality Housing would "prevent sliver buildings." Quality Housing was then approved by a 9-to-2 vote, with nine members abstaining.[41]

At the March 1987 meeting Bearak announced that Quality Housing was then at the City Planning Commission; if approved there and by the Board of Estimate, it would take effect in Elmhurst-Corona. CB4 members were confused about when and what they had approved. Rose Rothschild told them they still could vote on each new building, but Miriam Levenson said, "No, they build as-of-right if it passes." Rothschild appeared shocked. One member called for a vote to reconsider. Charles Stidolph then asked pointedly, "How many more families?" Bearak replied, "A 20 percent increase in FAR, and six-to-seven units instead of three-to-four." "Quality Housing is really fraud housing," another member exclaimed. CB4 then voted to oppose the plan.

Opposition was gathering elsewhere in Queens as well, particularly in Bayside, an upper-middle-class homeowner neighborhood where housing speculation and demolition for infills were also on the rise. Bayside residents, whose Assembly District vote totals were twice those of Elmhurst-Corona, lobbied borough president Shulman, a Baysider herself. In July 1987 COMET and NCA members attended an anti–Quality Housing rally in Bayside at which hundreds protested. Elmhurst-Corona activists also joined 1,000 demonstrators from Concerned Citizens of Bayside and other Queens civic associations to oppose Quality Housing at a Board of Estimate public hearing in August.

Accepting Shulman's lead, the Board of Estimate reduced the Quality Housing floor-area bonus on residential streets in R6 zones, thus insulating most of Elmhurst-Corona. And following a mass rally of Queens civic activists at City Hall, in October 1987 the Board of Estimate voted restrictions on infill housing in R4 and R5 areas such as Bayside. Mounting their own demonstration in December 1987, protesting QCBCA developers encircled Shulman's Queens Borough Hall office with dozens of bulldozers, cement mixers, and other construction vehicles.[42]

Saved by the Brook

Although the impact of Quality Housing was contained by multineighborhood civic activism, the Queens Boulevard plan still posed a threat to Elmhurst. In February 1987 Richard Bearak informed CB4 of the consultant's estimate that upzoning could result in eighteen new apartment buildings by 1990—"Like Tommy Huang's building!" exclaimed Rose Rothschild—and only one new school was projected. "As long as real estate developers are in it, you won't hear about schools," Norma Cirino responded. "Maybe if this community went up in arms: 'No high rises unless schools!' We should go on record." insisted Howard Riback. Rothschild replied that she and Miriam Levenson repeated this message every month at the Zoning Task Force. "The builders don't care," Levenson added. "They build and move on."

In September 1987 Bearak told CB4 that the Queens Boulevard consultants were still at work. "They are figuring there will be fewer public school children with a middle- to upper-middle-class population." CB4 members knew from experience, however, that higher housing costs were no guarantee that the new residents would be single professionals or couples who would send their children to private schools. "[Several] families will move into an apartment. They won't break it up but will rent rooms to boarders, and share bathrooms," Rose Rothschild stated. CB4's Latin American and Asian members also opposed this potential flood of new housing. "People will buy and rent out to nurses at Elmhurst Hospital," Clara Salas said. "All is double parking [now]," Chao Rong-Horng added. "[Clement Clarke Moore Park] is not so nice—it's really crowded."

In October Bearak told CB4 that additional research on toxic conditions, the result of auto-related uses in half the Queens Boulevard study area, would delay the final report. By June 1988 the consultants had discovered an underground stream and decided that its possible contamination, as well as the cost of building apartment towers over it, needed further study. Horse Brook, the freshwater stream that had made settlement by English farmers possible in 1652, thus saved Elmhurst's contemporary residents from the arrival of 9,000 more inhabitants. When the Queens Boulevard study was completed in 1991, the city's post-1989 job hemorrhage was under way, and demand for upscale outer-borough housing had collapsed.[43] Aside from two new schools, Queens Boulevard in 1996 looked much as it had ten years earlier.

Defeat: The Pool Club Site

While Elmhurst activists were mobilizing against Quality Housing and Queens Boulevard upzoning, a third land-use struggle began in Corona. It concerned the three-acre city-owned site of the Rego-Forest Pool Club, which had survived the Corona high school struggle. Little used by CD4 residents, this private swimming pool was evicted by the city in 1984. By that time the rest of the aborted high school site was filled by Presbyterian Senior Services and Transport Workers Union senior citizen residences, a forty-eight-unit moderate-income condominium set to open in 1986,[44] and a two-acre park to be built by the city's Department of Housing Preservation and Development (HPD).

In 1985 CB4 members and elderly Italian Corona Heights residents met with the HPD architect designing the new park, a Latin American Chinese named José Chung. CB4's parks committee chair Tony Caminiti detailed the history of the high school site and its current status. Neighborhood residents offered suggestions on fencing and entrances and affirmed that the park should be designed for older persons, not toddlers or teenagers.

Construction began in 1986, and "Louis Simeone Park" was dedicated at a 1987 ceremony. The HPD commissioner was master of ceremonies, and among the dignitaries present were CB4 members Caminiti, Steve Trimboli, Norma Cirino, and Tom Rodriguez, district manager Rose Rothschild, Father Joseph Calise of St. Leo's, borough president Claire Shulman, and city council member Joseph Lisa Jr. Seated on folding chairs facing a gazebo in the well-shaded, grassy park were scores of white Corona residents and black, white, and Korean senior citizens from the PSS and TWU residences. Several 110th Precinct officers were also present.

The TWU residents' chorus, equally divided among black, white, and Korean members, sang "The Star-Spangled Banner." The HPD Commissioner thanked park designer José Chung and outlined Mayor Koch's ten-year city housing plan.[45] Shulman emphasized the importance of the Corona high school struggle to the "decentralization movement," and both she and council member Lisa eulogized Lou Simeone. The African American TWU official who had supervised the senior citizen residence project pledged to maintain the park. The TWU chorus then returned and sang "In the Good Old Summertime," "God Bless America," "East Side, West Side," and a song in Korean. Arriving late, a fourth-grade class of Latin American, black, white, East Asian, and South Asian students from PS19 danced a Virginia reel on the park lawn. "Oh, look how cute!" said an elderly Italian woman sitting next to me.

A few minutes earlier Tony Caminiti had told me, "We have another fight, over the pool site." CB4 had long wanted a "multipurpose center" for day care, youth, and senior citizens in the area between Corona Heights and Lefrak City, one on the model of the nearby Forest Hills Community House, which had opened in the early 1970s. Following the pool club's eviction in 1984, CB4 listed a multipurpose center on this location as its first Parks Department budget priority, but it was not included in either the 1985 or the 1986 city budget.

Multipurpose Center versus Housing

In March 1986, CB4 learned that HPD had issued a request for proposals (RFP) to construct residential housing on the pool club site. Rose Rothschild reiterated CB4's support for a multipurpose center: "There is already plenty of housing there. We'll fight any more housing." In July, details of the RFP became public: the pool club site was among twelve city-owned locations on which Municipal Assistance Corporation (MAC) funds would subsidize 1,037 units of privately owned housing. More than a quarter of these units, some 296, would be built in two eight-story apartments at the Corona site. The city's selling price for the three-acre parcel was $296,000 (or $1,000 per apartment), about the same price as a two-family home in CD4.[46]

In September 1986, when CB4 held a public hearing on the plan, an HPD official revealed that the RFP had actually been issued in March 1985, and that Forest City Enterprises of Cleveland, Ohio, had already been chosen to build the housing. (Forest City was also the developer of the Public Development Corporation's MetroTech office complex in downtown Brooklyn.) Tony Caminiti was furious: "We hear of it after the fact. Why does the city hire a developer before coming to the community?" Housing committee chair Judy D'Andrea was also angry. Since 1980 she had represented CB4 in planning 350 units of senior citizen and condominium housing on the high school site. "Why was the community never apprised on the MAC money for housing? The city says forget the community, forget the community board, we'll do what we want."

Some white Corona residents saw the 80 percent moderate-income, 20 percent low-income MAC housing as "a second Lefrak City," and CB4 member Don Mallozzi's opposition echoed the resistance to scattered-site housing of twenty years earlier: "We're afraid if these houses are built, these people will destroy the new park that HPD is building." Others regarded the new housing as gentrification. "The rents are not middle income," Lefrak City resident Ken Daniels pointed out. "The paper says . . . they will run $1,100 a month." But most speakers stressed neighborhood crowding. "We can't handle the amount of children in the schools at the present time," said council member Lisa. "We are the highest [Queens community district] in [population] density that I know of. We're wearing out sidewalks and public transportation." He and assembly member Helen Marshall repeated the call for a multipurpose center.

Rose Rothschild stated that during the past two years CB4 had received neither a response to its multipurpose center budget request nor notification of the housing RFP. "I can't believe the city agencies don't speak to each other," Norma Cirino declared. "Are real estate interests so rich that they can buy whatever they want?" In a fog of bureaucratese, the HPD official replied that his agency, not the Department of Parks, had jurisdiction over the pool club site; hence CB4 had listed its multipurpose center request in the wrong city budget category. "CB4 didn't evaluate the responses properly, and then go to OMB," he said. "We never lied to you." "Cut the bullshit," a man in the audience called out. At the next CB4 meeting Rothschild reported, "[OMB] never answered that it was not Parks [that controlled the pool club site]. They only said [the multipurpose center] can't be funded. I went through the files."

Up Against the Permanent Government

Throughout the fall of 1986 and 1987 CB4 members lobbied against the 296-unit "Queenswood" housing plan. Tony Caminiti, Judy D'Andrea, and new housing committee chair Clara Salas met with the Forest City developers and conveyed the community's concerns about school overcrowding and the lack of youth recreation facilities. Caminiti, Rothschild, Miriam Levenson, and Helen Marshall presented their case at a meeting with borough president Shulman, a Queenswood supporter. She discouraged their suggestion that both a smaller Queenswood and a multipurpose center could be built on the site. "She told us Corona is a 'hot area' [for housing]," Caminiti explained to CB4. "*New York Magazine* also said Corona is hot," Levenson added.

Rothschild then wrote directly to Mayor Koch about the multipurpose center, emphasizing that "the Lefrak City senior center is in a basement" and that increasing numbers of children were coming to the Lefrak City Branch Library after school. CB4 member Helma Goldmark of Sherwood Village wrote to Koch and other elected officials requesting a facility to serve both young and old, adding that "the Forest Hills center works well." Clara Salas and Haydee Zambrana met directly with Koch. "He told us the [Queenswood] rents are reasonable," Salas reported, "and there is a need for housing in Corona. He is 200,000 miles away."

In January 1988 the Queenswood proposal came to CB4 for a vote. At the public hearing an audience of twenty whites, blacks, and Asians applauded CB4 members who opposed it. "If we accept this proposal, it shows we don't care about youth and [crowded] schools. They should have first come with services," declared Ken Daniels.

Judy D'Andrea spoke next. "I'm angry at the whole proposal, the developers, and HPD. They know this community and this site. HPD knew we had as a number-one priority a multipurpose center for four or five years when they did the RFP without consulting the community. Unlike the [condominiums] and senior citizen housing [on the rest of the high school site], these developers are profit-making. [*Audience cheers.*] They will make money, they got the land for $300,000! And Mayor Koch will make money from the real estate taxes. Our community, the children and seniors, will be devastated." She added that the "moderate-income" Queenswood units would be targeted to households well above CD4's median income. "Your mayor wants to help the poor and moderate income. He's building for the rich. He wants to take from this community, from people who live, worked, and sent children to school here. He wants to send us—I don't know where he wants to send us. This is my feeling. The school overcrowding is horrendous."

CB4 voted unanimously against the 296-unit housing development, and Corona wardens, inspired by the success Bayside and Elmhurst activists had enjoyed against the Quality Housing plan in 1987, vowed to continue the fight. The Corona Community Development Corporation's spring 1988 newsletter carried editorials by Pat Carpentiere and Tom Rodriguez warning that Queenswood would generate upward pressure on rents in the surrounding area.[47] D'Andrea, Carpentiere, Rodriguez, Tony Caminiti, and Don Mallozzi spoke against Queenswood at a March 1988 Board of Estimate public hearing. "I wanted [Claire Shulman's] representative to hear," D'Andrea later told CB4. "[But] people were reading the *New York Times* and getting coffee. It was extremely upsetting. When we came up, a Board of Education guy gave [Shulman's representative] his plans, and she said OK. We came prepared to answer questions, and with facts. It was a joke. The people who are paid to be there [and] the HPD guy were unprepared."

Later that month the Board of Estimate approved Queenswood. Claire Shulman, still a supporter, had presented her colleagues there a "compromise" under which the Board of Education would "free" twenty classrooms by transferring administrators to offices in Lefrak City. The classrooms, it turned out, were in Ridgewood in the southern tier of SD24 and did nothing to relieve school crowding in CD4.[48] In May 1988 a sign appeared on the VFW Hall in Corona Heights: "Claire Shulman, Borough President, has knifed Corona in the back."

Unexpectedly, by the time Queenswood opened in 1990 the Manhattan job hemorrhage was occurring, and yuppie spillover into Queens had dried up. Near heavily black Lefrak City and free from private-sector housing discrimination, Queenswood rented mainly to black residents. Children from these families now entered CD4's overcrowded public schools.

The school situation, however, was about to improve somewhat. Opposition to more housing during the first three battles in CD4's zoning wars had prompted Claire Shulman to secure capital funds for a second school and in 1987 a third in Elmhurst-Corona. The outrage of Koch's Commission on Hispanic Concerns over crowded classrooms also helped, and in 1987 Deputy Mayor Robert Esnard was assigned to expedite site selection for schools in CD4. Richard Bearak joined Board of Education staff in identifying locations for schools, and Rose Rothschild rallied support and fended off opposition to each selected site.[49] When these schools finally opened in the mid-1990s, however, they could only take up the existing slack; new overcrowding would soon arise.

Victory: Downzoning at Last

When Richard Bearak was assigned to CD4 by the Queens office of the Department of City Planning in June 1985, his first assignment was to complete the long-delayed study of "special district" side-yard restrictions proposed by the Newtown Civic Association and CB4. He was not told about any downzoning to "protect" residential tracts near Queens Boulevard, as mentioned by Martin Gallent at the April 1985 CB4 meeting. By fall 1985, however, Bearak had requested and received approval from his director Peter Magnani to convert the side-yard research to a rezoning study.

The Bearak Rezoning Plan

Richard Bearak then extended his work to all of CD4 except for the Queens Boulevard commercial strip, a 300-block area containing 12,000 lots. He compared actual lot coverage, floor area, and building uses with what was permissible under the 1961 Zoning Resolution. This required study of building plans and other records, on-site fieldwork on virtually every street in CD4, and computer data-entry and mapping. He discovered that many existing buildings contained less floor area than R6 zoning permitted. This difference, or "development envelope," was what made it profitable for builders to buy and demolish homes and erect infills. Bearak produced a plan to downzone 80 percent of CD4 lots to R4 and R5, which would both reflect existing structures and offer protection against further infill incursion.

Bearak well understood the Queens County Builders and Contractors Association's opposition to any downzoning and the counter-pressure that would be needed from civic activists to enact his plan. In January 1987 he informed

CB4 that his rezoning map was complete, and that it would go first to the Queens Zoning Task Force for comment and then begin the six-month ULURP process with votes by CB4, the City Planning Commission, and the Board of Estimate. Bearak did not anticipate that two years would pass before his plan's ULURP review actually began.

At a March 1987 meeting attended by three hundred mainly white South Elmhurst residents, COMET president Rosemarie Daraio announced that Richard Bearak and the Queens Department of City Planning "are not against us," despite the Queens Boulevard and Quality Housing proposals the mayor was promoting. Bearak told the audience, "You know what present R6 zoning is doing to your neighborhood." Referring to his map, he showed how downzoning could protect most of CD4.

The details of three different zoning proposals confused many in the audience, but their antagonism to Koch's pro-developer stance was palpable. As Elmhurst warden Bob Tilitz summarized it, "We oppose new development until all services are provided for those already here and any new population. The *Daily News* called us 'populist obstructionists.' Welcome, fellow populist obstructionists! Koch claims we oppose all development. This is name-calling, unfair and unjust. They ignore what we have to say about transportation, code enforcement, [and] the need for more schools."

In April 1987 Claire Shulman warned the pro-developer Elmhurst Chamber of Commerce that demands for downzoning were coming from all over Queens, and speculators buying plots to erect infills might find their plans thwarted. That spring the Newtown Civic Association formed a pro-downzoning "Coalition of Community Organizations of Central Queens" together with COMET, the 43rd Avenue Block Association, the New Elmhurst Civic League, and Woodside and Glendale groups. Headed by Bob Tilitz and Lucy Schilero, the coalition joined the Bayside-led fight against Quality Housing which brought victories in the summer and fall of 1987.[50] In August 1987 Borough President Claire Shulman read the political tea leaves and announced her support for neighborhood-by-neighborhood downzoning studies.[51]

That fall the QCBCA placed ads in local newspapers warning that home prices would fall if downzoning was instituted. Tilitz and others disputed this, arguing that any such drop would later reverse because of the strong demand for Elmhurst-Corona homes *as* homes. The very consideration of downzoning, however, stepped up the demolition-infill cycle in Elmhurst-Corona; the number of completed housing units in CD4 jumped from 250 in 1985 to a yearly average of 335 during 1986–1988.[52]

In November 1987 Concerned Citizens of Bayside began a "tie a red ribbon" campaign to demonstrate support for downzoning. Twenty-five civic associations joined, including those in Elmhurst, and 50,000 red ribbons appeared on trees throughout Queens. "This drove the politicians crazy, and attracted attention," a Bayside leader told NCA members. Campaign organizers met with Koch's staff, and in April 1988 the mayor came to Bayside to announce a City Planning study of downzoning in eighteen Queens neighborhoods.

Bearak's Plan Reborn

Meanwhile, pressure from developers on Koch's Department of City Planning had stalled Bearak's downzoning plan. It had not gone to the Queens Zoning Task Force until June 1987, and then the City Planning hierarchy requested more analysis of the combined effects of upzoning and downzoning. Nothing happened for months. But after Koch's Bayside announcement, department higher-ups were suddenly asking Bearak when his study would be ready. In May 1988 his rezoning plan was approved by the department. For Koch, anticipating his 1989 re-election campaign, Queens downzoning had become good politics.

All this added more fuel to the infill fire in CD4. With R4 and R5 neighborhoods now protected, Elmhurst-Corona was one of the few R6 "hot spots" left. "The speculators are buying up homes and lots like crazy," Norma Cirino told the district cabinet in June 1988. "They're paying top dollar because of anticipation of the rezoning." Rose Rothschild added, "We've got demolitions galore. [The] Ramrock [company], he's up to the office every day with demolitions, all over Elmhurst and Corona." Bearak explained that foundations had to be "in the ground" before downzoning took effect in order for construction companies to erect the larger buildings allowable under the old zoning. Beating this deadline, some 400 new Elmhurst-Corona housing units were completed in 1989, and 680 more in 1990.[53]

In May 1989 Bearak's rezoning plan finally came to CB4.[54] "It's an election year, that's why we're getting it," observed Bob Tilitz. Chair Charles Stidolph convened the public hearing at Ascension School in South Elmhurst, where a mainly white audience of 125, including a few Asians, listened as Bearak explained the details. "This area is a real estate phenomenon. They buy the land and pay to knock the building down. Homebuyers are not competing with developers. Now, with downzoning, the value of the house rises as the land value drops. Combined with areas to be upzoned by the proposal, there is still a maximum of about 6,000 potential units [to be built]. The idea is preservation of property, not windfall profits."

CB4 approved Bearak's proposal in June 1989. In July, in the setting of white columns, blue carpet, and long pewlike benches of the City Hall meeting chamber, CB4 members Tilitz, Stidolph, Levenson, and two COMET leaders testified in favor of downzoning before the City Planning Commission, and Richard Bearak joined them. Even though he had opposed downzoning publically,[55] Stidolph stated that it was "supported by the community," and thanked Bearak.

Following the commission's approval, in September 1989 Bearak, Tilitz, Rosemarie Daraio, and Lucy Schilero testified before the Board of Estimate. Tilitiz stated,

> We are proud of the manner in which we adjusted to the transformation of Elmhurst from a community which was home to only a few ethnic groups to one in which scores—literally, scores—of nationalities and cultures are represented. Ours has become a truly rainbow population. . . . But we feel only anger and distress as a result of losses and hardships suffered following the mis-zoning of 1961 which opened the way for enormous overbuilding, . . . extremely overcrowded schools, overburdened public transit, and other services. . . . You have today, in the action you take on the application for the rezoning of Elmhurst-Corona, the means to ease the crisis and to open the way for the comeback of our community.

Bearak's rezoning plan passed, and by 1991 the speculative housing boom in Elmhurst-Corona was over. In 1992 Rose Rothschild announced, "Construction in CB4 has stopped. They put in the foundations to beat the law, and then stopped." By 1993 half of Queens had been downzoned. The QCBCA developers blamed the power of numbers: "members of community boards, civic groups, and neighborhood residents" of Queens.[56]

The Politics of Place

In 1990 the director of the Elmhurst Economic Development Corporation, Steve Trimboli, declared in a letter to *Newsday*, "In this time of budget crunch [the city should] eliminate community boards." Bob Tilitz responded in the *Newtown Crier* that "Community Boards, as they exist today, represent a modest advance toward the goal of neighborhood empowerment. . . . To abolish them . . . would be a disastrous backward step for the movement to humanize municipal government and to reduce the enormous concentration of power in a handful of leaders at the top." At a 1995 CB4 meeting Trimboli repeated his call to abolish community boards. Ignoring him, members resumed discussing their opposition to Mayor Giuliani's plan to sell Elmhurst Hospital.

At the height of the zoning wars in 1988 a commission appointed to revise the city charter had considered elimination of community boards, or abrogration of their public hearing and voting powers on land-use issues. Bob Tilitz attended these hearings and told CB4, "People in high places don't like community boards." Judy D'Andrea added, "The high-power developers in this city are trying to eliminate the ULURP process because we stand in their way. And they make political contributions to high-power officials." Rose Rothschild warned, "If the charter commission has its way, you'll be a little social group that meets once a month for coffee, and that's it."

The 1989 city charter disempowered borough presidents and expanded the city council from thirty-five to fifty-one seats, but it left community boards unaffected. The Giuliani administration, however, sought to limit their power by cutting their budgets and supporting a city council bill to reduce the boards'

ULURP review period to thirty days, making it difficult for them to schedule public hearings and votes during summer recesses. This move was intended to increase mayoral power in land-use matters, and Rose Rothschild publically criticized it.[57]

As I listened to Steve Trimboli's 1995 tirade against community boards, I wondered what Elmhurst-Corona would be like if CB4 had never existed. Would post–fiscal crisis assaults on quality of life have been more severe? Would the three new schools ever have been built? Would rows of Queens Boulevard apartment towers, incursions of Quality Housing, and even more infills have engulfed CD4? Would American-versus-immigrant or white-versus-black tensions have exploded? Had there been no CB4, the emergence of the most diverse multiracial neighborhood in the United States would have occurred with no public forum at which white, black, Latin American, and Asian leaders had a place to interact. Each racial and ethnic group in Elmhurst-Corona would have had to confront mayoral and permanent-government power directly, without the power of numbers and lubricatory expertise that CB4 made possible.

The board had been and still is pivotal to the ongoing creation of a political "community" in this diverse neighborhood. Anthropologist F. G. Bailey explains that members of a political community create "a common culture [and] conceive of themselves as an entity . . . ranged against a non-moral world outside." Those beyond the community "are likely to be judged in an instrumental fashion, not 'in the round.' They are not [interacted with as] human beings to the same extent as those of us who belong within the community."[58]

Elmhurst-Corona in the 1980s and 1990s was not a political community in any complete sense; probably no urban neighborhood ever is. For many of its wardens, however, and for the organizations and networks to which they belonged, lines of race and ethnicity had become crossable. CB4 members knew each other by name and were in a position to see beyond stereotypes of "blacks," "immigrants," and "outer-borough white ethnics." In their common culture of political struggle, they began to see each other "in the round," as persons who resided in the same place and faced the same threats to their quality of life: crowded schools, crowded subways, crowded streets. Individual characteristics other than race were increasingly important. Members joked about the large number of senior citizens on CB4 in the 1980s. "When I came on the board, no one was under eighty," Rose Rothschild said. "I mean, we needed younger people." As the 1990s began, "we got younger ones. We got really nice people, like Al Blake." An LCTA member and organizer of Lefrak City youth activities, Blake was African American.

The zoning wars of 1985–1989 were waged as CB4's new leadership was solidifying and steps toward greater inclusion were beginning. New Latin American and Asian members supported the Quality Housing, Queens Boulevard, and pool club site battles. The opportunity for white-black cooperation that a multipurpose center might have brought was lost, but by 1987 some white CB4 members were beginning to take seriously both issues and leaders from Lefrak City's black population.

The Louis Simeone Park opening brought together white, black, Asian, and Latin American participants, but aside from one song in Korean, racial and ethnic diversity was never mentioned during this quality-of-life ritual. And rarely after 1985 was race or ethnicity broached at CB4 meetings. When "moral outsiders" such as the library security official tried to introduce race divisively, CB4 leaders deflected the effort. Over the next ten years the politics of place grew stronger. At one CB4 meeting, for instance, Clara Salas validated a point she was making not by claiming to represent Latin American residents but by stating, "I've lived in this community for thirty years. I was virtually born here."

Bob Tilitz's 1989 characterization of CD4 at the City Planning Commission as containing "a truly rainbow population" with "scores of nationalities and cultures" was unusual in the discourse of civic politics. But things were changing. Not only was CB4 a meeting point for the racially diverse strands in its political field, but some participants were beginning to value this diversity.

[15]

Bonds of Interracial Cooperation

In May 1996 Edna Baskin and Tony Caminiti organized a dinner to celebrate Rose Rothschild's tenth anniversary as district manager. To begin the formalities, chair Richard Italiano introduced Community Board 4's officers: first vice-chair Lou Walker, second vice-chair Lucy Schilero, executive secretary Clara Salas, treasurer Edna Baskin, and three at-large directors. This group—five white, two black, one Latin American—reflected the racial composition of the forty dinner attendees. After receiving gifts and testimonials, Rose Rothschild told the audience that she was "a girl from East Harlem" who moved to Elmhurst-Corona in 1961 and found that it was "also a multiethnic community, which I enjoy."

Such heralding of Elmhurst-Corona's diversity had rarely been voiced before in the CB4 arena; rather, the watchword had been "We're not talking ethnic." During the preceding dozen years, however, events celebrating multiethnicity had flourished in schools, at Elmhurst Hospital, and in churches. Neighborhood quality-of-life rituals had become increasingly multiracial, as had small-business coalitions. In addition, two high-profile racial incidents in 1991 and race-conscious efforts to redraw electoral and school districts between 1991 and 1994, had heightened awareness of the "multiethnic" nature of CD4.

Rituals of Inclusion

Public schools and hospitals serve all who enter, and in the post-1975 era of budget cuts they needed to rally support from both old and new constituents. Roman Catholic parishes either welcomed newcomers or faced shrinking numbers and collections. During the late 1970s and the 1980s new rituals of inclusion were created in Elmhurst-Corona public schools, Elmhurst Hospital, and

St. Leo's Church in Corona Heights. Symbols of ethnic diversity and exhortations of racial harmony in these rituals acknowledged the changing composition of the community these institutions now served.[1]

Public School Programs

Because of School Board 24's inattention to its northern tier, principals in Elmhurst-Corona primary schools sought support for additional classrooms and programs from local elected officials, wardens, and parents. Some also cultivated reporters, who visited their schools and exposed severe overcrowding.[2] Their most valuable weapon was the children themselves. I never failed to note smiles and "Aren't they cute!" comments from adults observing the rainbow array of pupils at school assemblies or events. Civic leaders and elected officials all seemed as enchanted by the children as were groups of parents.

"Cultural Sharing Day" at Corona's PS19 celebrated Chinese New Year, Dominican Republic Independence Day, and Brotherhood Week. In 1988 the Red Silk Dancers, a professional Chinese troupe, thrilled the assembled children and adults with lion and sword dances. Then the PS19 Dancers—seven Latin American, South Asian, and Chinese girls—demonstrated a Spanish flamenco with castinets, and five girls from the school's Dominican Republic dance group performed a merengue. The PS19 string ensemble of eleven Latin American, East Asian, and black violinists closed the program with a Latin American air.

The roster of guests at Cultural Sharing Day revealed Principal Irene Nash's advocacy on behalf of her school. They included borough president Claire Shulman, whom, Nash noted, "we can thank for the mini-school; it's not easy to get one." Nash also thanked Shulman's office for funds to bring professional arts groups to PS19 and introduced the African American director of that program. Shulman in turn emphasized the day's theme: "Queens County is the most diverse county in the U.S.A. . . . It makes us better, more intelligent, and more understanding to respect all racial and ethnic backgrounds." A framed proclamation from Shulman listed forty countries represented among the PS19 student body.

Nash next introduced city council member Joseph Lisa Jr., who rehearsed the students in saying "Happy New Year" in Chinese, and state assembly member Helen Marshall, whom Nash thanked for hosting an annual PS19 student trip to the state capitol in Albany. Other guests included representatives of Governor Cuomo and Mayor Koch, SB24 member Norma Cirino (who, Nash mentioned, was from "a bilingual home"), Northside Democratic Club leader Tony Caminiti, and district manager Rose Rothschild. Half a dozen Chinese organization leaders and agency officials were also acknowledged, among them Chao-rong Horng of CB4. The event was covered by two Chinese newspapers and featured on television news.

In 1974 Principal Cleonice LoSecco had arrived at Elmhurst's PS89 to find growing numbers of immigrant pupils and a declining cohort of politically active parents. By 1988 her 1,600 students were 54 percent Latin American, the rest mostly Asian, and a few black or "other" (that is, white). The school had several Spanish, Korean, and Chinese bilingual classes from which students "mainstreamed" in two years or less. The ethnic composition of its regular classes mirrored the overall student population.

In 1977 LoSecco held her first "International Festival." The event reoccurred each May, highlighted by a "Parade of Nations" along a twelve-block route around the school. Many children wore home-country dress, but in some classes all pupils donned identical Colombian, Filipino, Greek, or other ethnic costumes for the "folk dances" that followed the parade.

Escorted by 110th Precinct C-POP officers, the 1986 parade began with the *Chariots of Fire* movie theme blaring from an outdoor public address system. Classes bore signs reading "Class 4-141 is a League of Nations"; "We are the World, 4-302"; and "1-106—Bilingual, Bicultural, and Proud of It." Some students carried handmade posters of their home-country flags; their labels identified Argentina, Canada, Chile, China, Colombia, Costa Rica, Cyprus, Cuba, Ecuador, El Salvador, Guatemala, Haiti, Honduras, Hong Kong, India, Japan, Mexico, Pakistan, Peru, the Philippines, Puerto Rico, Spain, and Vietnam. When the first paraders returned, dances began on a street next to the school. Classes filled with Latin American and Asian faces performed a Greek mazurka, Argentine and Colombian dances, a "Philippines Basket Dance," and "Tropical Breezes, from the Caribbean." Third-graders dressed in red, white, and blue, including one Sikh boy in a turban, presented a "Salute to Lady Liberty."

Hundreds of parents—most of them stylishly dressed mothers in their twenties and thirties, including several in South Asian garb—surrounded the dancers. Many held cameras and video recorders. One father called, "José!" and snapped a photo of his white-costumed son performing a "Yugoslavian" dance. Following the performance, parents went inside for "ethnic artifacts displays" and "tasting parties" in each classroom. So did I, and I found the homemade Korean food in a bilingual class and the Indian, Guatemalan, Chinese, and Guayanese dishes in a second-grade room authentically "ethnic" and delicious.

PS89's immigrant parents strongly supported this annual event and raised substantial funds for it. Principal LoSecco struggled, however, to turn this support into parent activism to address problems of doubled-up classrooms, busing of kindergarteners, and the shortage of language specialists. "I feel like a revivalist preacher," she said.

Three Kings Day at Elmhurst Hospital

In 1981 Elmhurst Hospital began celebrating Three Kings Day, or Epiphany, a major holiday among many Christians around the world. This January event involving staff, patients, and the surrounding community was of particular significance to Latin Americans for whom "Los Tres Magos" was the high point of the Christmas season.

The 1986 program in the hospital's auditorium was packed with hospital staff (mainly Latin American and black), children, and a racially mixed group of adults from the community, among them older whites and Rose Rothschild and Miriam Levenson from CB4. Patients, some in wheelchairs, were escorted to the front as the Three Kings (three hospital employees) entered wearing red robes and silver crowns and bearing "gifts of gold, frankincense, and myrrh." Hospital officials welcomed the audience in English and Spanish and recounted the significance of Epiphany, adding that this day also marked "National Migration Week." Ray Bermudez, a Jackson Heights businessman and chair of the hospital's Community Advisory Board, recalled the "boxes of toys" he received on Three Kings Day as a child in Puerto Rico.

Two groups of schoolchildren provided entertainment. A choir of thirty from PS69 in Jackson Heights, half East Asian and nearly half Latin American plus a few South Asian and white faces, delighted the audience with "Frosty the Snowman," "Need a Little Christmas," and a Hanukkah song. Their teacher pointed out that many of these students and their families used Elmhurst Hospital. Next, a dozen costumed dancers from the Father Billini Association folkloric troupe—part of the afterschool program at Our Lady of Sorrows Church in Corona Plaza—came to the stage. Their director, Ana Lopez, explained that the Dominican merengue they performed had African influences, and would be followed by Puerto Rican and Colombian dances. Several Latin American audience members clapped along with the performance.

In 1987 and 1988 hospital patients in wheelchairs sang moving solos of "O Holy Night" and "Noche de Paz (Silent Night)." And each year the program included a message from the hospital chaplain, Sister Catherine Naughton, emphasizing racial harmony. "We gather today as a family," she said in 1987, "young and old, staff, patients, volunteers, neighbors, people of different nationalities, religions, and colors. . . . Our variety and differences make our family richer and more beautiful. . . . God is not Jewish, Catholic, Protestant, Hindu, or Muslim. . . . God is not white, black, brown, or yellow. God is love."

St. Leo's Stations of the Cross

During the 1980s Latin Americans increased from 27 to 41 percent of the 1.5-million-member Roman Catholic Diocese of Brooklyn and Queens, and whites fell from 61 to 43 percent. "We are a diocese of immigrants," Bishop Francis Mugavero proclaimed in 1986, and "we must have the capacity to touch their hearts." Masses were celebrated in seventeen languages, with half the parish churches offering them in Spanish. (Only 2 percent of priests were Latin American, however, and the church was steadily losing members to Spanish-speaking Protestant congregations.)[3] With growing Latin American numbers at St. Leo's in

Corona Heights, Monsignor Anthony Barretta began a "parish renewal program" in 1981 "to coordinate various ethnic groups into a vibrant living community." A statue of Our Lady of Guadalupe, "patroness of the Americas," was placed in the renovated sanctuary, and a Colombian priest and Puerto Rican deacon were added to the pastorate. At the same time, the presence of St. Leo's Italian parishioners remained strong. In 1984 five English, two Italian, and one Spanish mass were celebrated each Sunday, and the weekly bulletin included thirty ads from local white-owned firms and three from Latin American businesses.[4]

In 1986 a pre-Easter "Stations of the Cross" procession through Corona Heights was revived by Italian and Latin American lay leaders at St. Leo's and a new young priest, Father Joseph Calise. This ritual, reenacting Christ's judgment and march to his cruxifiction, had been mounted in earlier years by Italian parishioners but at some point had been dropped. A trilingual English-Italian-Spanish flyer announcing its revival was intended to appeal to all parishioners.

The 1987 procession began in the church parking lot on an April Saturday morning. Monsignor Barretta, who was too ill to march, sprinkled holy water over the crowd of two hundred. Father Calise read the First Station text from a mimeographed packet distributed by organizer Al Fernicola and two female Teen Center members. With a 110th Precinct van in the lead, eight altar boys carrying banners, and marchers singing the First Station verse in English, Father Calise lifted a five-foot wooden cross to his shoulder, and the procession began.

The march stopped at prearranged sites where parishioners had placed tables with crucifixes, candles, and flowers in front of their homes. At each location one of the fourteen Stations texts was recited in English, Italian, or Spanish, and the verse then sung in that language as we marched to the next location. The throng, mostly women, doubled in size along the sixteen-block route. It was more than half Latin American, mainly middle-aged and young adults with a few children in family groups; another quarter was elderly and predominantly Italian, including several widows dressed in black. The Spanish singing was strongest, and the Italian verses loudest among the elderly women, but each group also sang in the other's language. The English choir numbered about ten, and singing in that language was weakest of all. A dozen Filipinos and Chinese also marched in the procession.

Returning to St. Leo's, the crowd filled the church. Before beginning the mass, Monsignor Barretta told the assembly, "There is a lot of talent in this parish. It's my responsibility that it has not been brought forth in the past. . . . The important thing is that all the people of the parish got together today. It didn't make any difference if you were Italian, English-speaking, German, or Spanish. . . . People who never tasted lasagna should taste lasagna. People who never tried *arroz con pollo* should try *arroz con pollo.* If you never have eaten a kosher frank, eat a kosher frank."

Rainbow Protestant Churches

Most Catholics attend their local parish church, and CD4's many Latin American immigrants constituted a stream of new worshipers for its Roman Catholic congregations. Elmhurst-Corona's historically white Protestant churches, however, had no equivalent stream of new members. Protestants might attend churches of their own denomination elsewhere, worship across denominational lines, or form new congregations as many immigrants did. Two of Elmhurst's white Protestant churches lost members and disbanded in the early 1980s. The rest survived by incorporating immigrants.[5]

Many white members of civic assocations and CB4 continued to worship in Elmhurst-Corona's Protestant and Catholic churches as they became arenas of interaction between established residents and newcomers. With smaller congregations than Catholic churches—numbering in the scores or low hundreds rather than thousands—each of the three Protestant churches I attended was a site of such cross-racial interaction.[6]

First Presbyterian Church of Newtown

A monument in front of the stone tower of the First Presbyterian Church on Queens Boulevard commemorated German and Scottish members who died in World War II, and a signboard nearby invited worshipers to attend "An International Church." Each week more than two hundred persons of all races entered and received a church program heralding a membership comprising "Over Thirty-five Nationalities."

When Charles Sorg, of German ancestry, became minister in 1965, the white congregation was aging and shrinking. The first Latin American had joined in 1962, and as new immigrant members arrived, Pastor Sorg welcomed them. He refused to hold services in languages other than English, however, or to rent space to non-English congregations, despite continuing requests. Many newcomers were from English-speaking countries and were often better educated than established white members. Their children revived the Sunday School and the youth choir, and even after moving away, several immigrant families continued to attend First Presbyterian. This "International Church" received attention in the press and from the Presbyterian hierarchy,[7] and its multiracial ethos attracted still more members—some Presbyterian, others not. By the 1980s the core of active members also numbered several interethnic couples: Swedish-Mexican, Italian-Cuban, Puerto Rican–Okinawan, Cuban-WASP.

Pastor Sorg recruited members for his boards of elders and deacons, and during 1987–1988 they included African, Asian, Caribbean, English, and Latin American immigrants as well as white Americans. In addition to their financial and organizational responsibilities, each week one elder read a scripture passage and another greeted members; the deacons collected the offering and prepared the monthly communion service. Other members, also of diverse backgrounds, were recognized in Pastor Sorg's pulpit announcements and in the program as contributors of flowers, choir directors and members, instrumental and vocal soloists, leaders of women's and youth groups, organizers of special events, and church school director and teachers.

At the coffee hour that followed each service the congregation sorted itself as much by age and gender as by ethnicity. Groups of children and teenagers were the most diverse. African mothers of young children, many of whom lived in Lefrak City, sat together, as did Indonesian families. Older white and Latin American members of the church's AARP chapter and the women's association, and a similar group of younger single women, conversed with one another. So did racially mixed groups of church officers.

Despite its diversity, First Presbyterian was not a multicultural church. The service incorporated no liturgy or music that was not traditionally Presbyterian or American. Neither did Pastor Sorg dwell on racial or ethnic harmony in his sermons. His theology was "practical," oriented to Christians existing in a secular culture and a "society that shuns us." He treated all his members as individuals—addressing people by name, asking about work and family, counseling in times of distress. He saw his immigrant congregants as persons who practiced their own cultures in private but otherwise wished to participate in American life.

The one exception was "International Night," an annual ritual of inclusion begun in the late 1970s. Here a buffet of home-cooked ethnic dishes was followed by a "Parade of Nations," with congregants in "traditional" dress introduced in alphabetical order according to country of origin.

The 1987 parade featured African, Asian, Caribbean, European, Latin American, and cowboy-garbed white American church members from twenty-seven countries. At its conclusion, the congregation sang "In Christ There Is No East or West" and "God Bless America." Entertainment followed; in 1988 there was sensuous Indonesian dancing (raising the eyebrows of a few but enthralling others); solo performances of Mexican, Filipino, and German songs; the youth choir—half African and the rest Chinese, Indonesian, Puerto Rican, and white—singing "That's What Friends Are For"; and seven Cameroonian, Ghanaian, Nigerian, and Kenyan women in smashing cloth outfits and headties dancing first in a circle and then one by one. The evening ended with a sing-along of American popular tunes.

Elmhurst Baptist Church

In 1973 Reverend Kelly Grimsley arrived at Elmhurst Baptist Church—part of the American Baptist Churches denomination—to succeed a minister of white southern origin who had been there since 1936. The congregation was then of English and German background, including some members who had come to New York from other states. One Indian family had joined the church in the 1950s, and the new minister soon welcomed the first Filipino and Chinese members.

By 1988 Filipinos made up half of the seventy-member congregation; the others included a score of mainly elderly whites, plus newer Puerto Rican, Nicaraguan, and Jamaican members. Pastor Grimsley had married a Filipina church member in 1983, and there were other interracial couples among the membership. Whites, Asians, Latin Americans, and blacks were deacons, trustees, and choir and women's society members. At the coffee hour following each Sunday service, hugs and conversation crossed racial lines, and ties among longtime members were close. Several whites used the expression "She was raised in this church" when referring to a younger member, denoting a nearly kinlike attachment.

Elmhurst Baptist's old-fashioned American hymns meshed with Grimsley's Social Gospel theology. His messages touched on homelessness, international conflicts, television evangelists, and relations between Elmhurst's old and new residents. He was perhaps more liberal than his members, but his intelligence, humor, and caring attracted their loyalty. He did not introduce multicultural activities, nor did his members demand them. The Filipino contingent did present one program of their homeland's songs and dances in 1980, but the church's recurrent events were annual spaghetti dinners and Easter breakfasts.

Membership numbers, however, were insufficient to maintain the large fieldstone church built in 1900; to augment income, the congregation rented space to AARP, Boy Scout, and Alcoholics Anonymous groups. In 1973 it had begun renting to Christian Testimony Church, a Chinese congregation.[8] A Korean congregation was added in 1978, and a Spanish congregation in 1979. When Christian Testimony bought the nearby Elmhurst Masonic Temple in 1983, a Haitian congregation replaced it as one of Elmhurst Baptist's tenants—of whom only the Spanish congregation was affiliated with the American Baptist Churches. The Korean group was Southern Baptist Convention, the Haitian group Methodist, and the Chinese church an independent body. This multiple use required careful Sunday scheduling. Elmhurst Baptist's congregation worshiped at 11:00 A.M. in the striking octagonal sanctuary, and the Korean group occupied it at 1:00 P.M. The Spanish congregation met in the church hall at 9:00 A.M., and Haitian worshipers in the basement at 10:00 A.M.

The only liturgical tie among these groups was an Advent program: the Spanish, Korean, and Haitian congregations hosted evening musicales on the fourth, third, and second Sundays before Christmas; on the first Sunday at 4:00 P.M. the Elmhurst Baptist choir presented a cantata to which members of all four congregations were invited. At the 1988 Haitian Advent service, half the audience of thirty were white and Filipino Elmhurst Baptist members; the minister teased them about how their French had improved since the previous year. Few members from the tenant congregations were present at the cantata, but the Elmhurst Baptist congregation was out in full force, and four lectors—Filipino, white, Nicaraguan, and Indian—conducted the service.

The Haitian congregation departed for its own building in North Corona in 1993 and was replaced by an Indonesian congregation. In 1995 a fire ruined this church whose "Loving Progressive Multi-ethnic Congregation" was by then being led by Filipino and African American ministers. Meeting at another church, the congregation of two hundred regrouped to plan repairs and renovation.[9]

Bethany Lutheran Church

Still a thriving church of two hundred in the early 1960s, in 1967 Bethany Lutheran abandoned plans to construct a new hall because its mainly German membership was declining. In 1971 a Chinese congregation (subsidized by Bethany's Lutheran–Missouri Synod denomination) and a monthly service in Spanish were added "to serve the new people in the community." Within a year the Chinese group numbered 150. The small Spanish service drew parents of children enrolled in the church's "Bible Story Hour" pre-school, run by a Cuban female Bethany member. Numbers at the English service, however, continued to dwindle. In 1975 the white male pastor became campus minister at Queens College, serving at Bethany only on Sundays until he left in 1983.

For two years Bethany had no pastor; then Reverend Lyn Mehl arrived in 1985. A mother of teenagers and the wife of a Lutheran minister at a church in Woodside, Mehl was newly ordained, and Bethany was her first church. A crisis soon occurred. Bethany had separated from the Missouri Synod to join the Association of Evangelical Lutheran Churches, which was scheduled to merge with two other Lutheran bodies in 1988. The subsidized Chinese congregation remained with the Missouri Synod and now planned to move to another Queens church. Pastor Mehl had a commitment from the new denomination for mission funding, but her vision was of one trilingual church rather than two congregations and a monthly Spanish service.

She nurtured this vision organizationally and liturgically. Using her midwestern high school Spanish, she conducted weekly services with a female Puerto Rican lay minister, encouraged the use of Spanish folk songs *(coritos),* counseled Salvadoran, Ecuadorian, and Mexican women and children, and provided Sunday School and Confirmation instruction. During summers the Spanish and English groups worshiped jointly.[10] After the Chinese congregation left, Mehl worked with Chinese members who elected to stay at Bethany. She organized a Chinese service, attended the group's Sunday meal at the church, and secured a full-time Chinese pastor, who arrived in 1989. The church council's president, a white ESL teacher, also offered free English classes for Bethany's Latin American and Chinese members.

Pastor Mehl continued to minister to the thirty-five who attended the English service. For the elderly Germans she used "old-style Martin Luther hymns" and assisted at the annual bratwurst supper sponsored by the Ladies Guild, its membership now just a handful. She maintained the weekly coffee hour following the service, and her teenage son Philip joined in reviving a Bethany choir. For the younger members she added "contemporary Christian" folk-rock singing, outings to ethnic restaurants, and bowling.

Special occasions brought members of the three Bethany groups together. For the 1988 Pentecost service, Mehl prepared programs in English, Spanish, and Chinese. The seventy-five attending, drawn equally from the three groups, followed in their own language as Venezuelan and Chinese lay leaders translated the minister's opening message and sermon. Hymns, scripture passages, and the Apostle's Creed were sung or read simultaneously in all three languages, and Mehl remarked that this cacophony recalled the Biblical Pentecost. Then she announced, "It has taken seventeen years for this day to come, the first trilingual service. And like beef, beans, and tomatoes, it makes a wonderful stew. People have come from Guyana, Germany, Taiwan, Central America and South America, and the good old U.S. of A." An "International Dinner" followed in the church basement, featuring Chinese, Cuban, and American dishes, and then singing in English, Chinese, German, and Spanish.

The half-dozen Guyanese Indians at the Pentecost service were among two dozen new members, most in their twenties and thirties, who had joined Bethany's English service since 1985. Others included U.S.-born and immigrant Chinese, Latin Americans, and young whites, several of German ancestry. The Spanish service did not survive, and neither would the Chinese congregation. In 1992 the ESL instructor died of AIDS; this disturbed many of the Chinese, and their group later left the church. In 1995, however, Reverend Lyn Mehl's son Philip married a Chinese member of the English-service group. Like First Presbyterian, Elmhurst Baptist, and other historically white Elmhurst-Corona churches, Bethany's congregation persisted by becoming multiracial.

Quality-of-Life Rituals

Rituals celebrating programs and facilities to improve neighborhood quality of life occurred periodically in Elmhurst-Corona; so did marches and rallies to protest assaults on quality of life. They included a playground dedication in Corona (see the Introduction), a CB4 protest at the 110th Precinct (Chapter 7), demonstrations over subway crowding and prostitution (Chapter 9), the National Night Out march organized by Lucy Schilero (Chapter 13), and the Louis Simeone Park opening and dinners honoring Edna Baskin's summer cleanups (Chapter 14).

These events focused on matters of concern to all neighborhood residents.

Ethnicity and race were not highlighted—for the most part they went unmentioned—but participants and audiences were multiethnic and multiracial, and increasingly more so through the 1980s and into the 1990s. Still, not all residents interpreted particular quality-of-life issues in the same way. The dedication ceremony at a Corona residence for mentally retarded adults exemplified the inclusive side of such rituals; two anti-drug marches revealed contrasts in how different leaders and residents defined this quality-of-life problem.

Donald Savio Residence Dedication

In 1987 a ceremony to welcome the new residents of St. Leo's renovated former convent began at 3:00 P.M. Latin American girls in plaid parish school uniforms handed programs to the two hundred guests as they filed into the auditorium. I spotted Father Joseph Calise, CB4 members Tony Caminiti, Miriam Levenson, Carmela George, Al Fernicola, and Richard Italiano, and district manager Rose Rothschild. Diocesan clergy and bureaucrats, government agency officials, and older Italians from Corona Heights were also in the audience. A priest explained that Donald Savio was a retired police officer who had begun a second career at the Catholic Charities Office for Disabled Persons, and died at age fifty-nine. He then introduced a score of dignitaries, among them Monsignor Anthony Barretta of St. Leo's, who told the audience, "It is a blessing to this parish to house these people."

Next the Savio Residence administrator asked his staff to stand, and twenty white, black, and Latin American women and men rose, several of them Corona residents. He then introduced the fourteen mentally retarded residents, ranging in age from twenty-two to sixty-one. As each name was called, the person stood, and several turned to the audience to wave. Two of the men clasped their hands over their heads in a prizefighter's salute; this broke the tension, and the crowd applauded warmly. The residents included two African Americans, two Latin Americans, and five Italians. Half, it was added, were from Corona.

When the ceremony concluded, Bishop Francis Mugavero led the audience to the renovated convent, where he cut a red ribbon, sprinkled holy water, and blessed the new facility. The residents, already inside, stood beaming. People then toured the building, guided by the staff, St. Leo's students, and four Teen Center volunteers.[11]

Marching against Drugs

In 1988 a crowd of two hundred gathered in the PS69 playground in Jackson Heights at 8:00 P.M. for a rally sponsored by the "Anti-Drug Task Force of CB3 and CB4." Handmade signs read "Jackson Heights Says 'No' to Drug Dealers and Users" and "Crack is WACK, Just Say No." The audience of whites, blacks, Latin Americans, and a few East Asians included Lucy Schilero, a white

Elmhurst tenant association leader from her coalition, James Galloway of the Lefrak City Tenants Association, Maritza Sarmiento-Radbill from Ciudadanos Conscientes de Queens, Ana Lopez with ten children from the Father Billini Association afterschool program, and Ray Bermudez of the Jackson Heights Business and Professional Association.

Matt McKinley, the white rally organizer and a candidate for Jackson Heights Democratic district leader, was the first speaker. He defined the area's drug problem as the product of immigrant criminals and called for law-and-order solutions. "You see movable pharmacies [on Roosevelt Avenue]—cocaine, crack, bazooka, marijuana. Also prostitutes, in three forms: female, male, transvestite. We have a livery cab problem; they bring customers to sellers, and you can buy drugs in cabs. Contact [your elected officials] to let them know you want a cabinet-level drug post and more INS officers to assist the police."

Elwanda Young, the African American director of ELMCOR, a social service agency in North Corona–East Elmhurst, also spoke. She explained that ELMCOR operated a drug treatment program serving fifty-four community residents. To her, the drug problem included treating users from the neighborhood as well as apprehending sellers. At countless meetings, 110th Precinct officers had told civic activists that they arrested local buyers from Elmhurst-Corona as well as sellers. Some failed to accept this, blaming everything on "outsiders." Others knew that drug use could entrap neighbors, and even family members, of all races.

Black residents faced an additional drug-related problem that affected few whites. As one young man put it at a community meeting in Lefrak City, "We are stopped by the police, thinking we're selling drugs. They take innocent people and ignore the drug dealers." A woman in her thirties added, "My husband was harassed. We see the same [drug-sellers'] faces. Why is nothing done? I've lived here twelve years."

This broader range of concerns about drugs was evident in several African American–led marches on 57th Avenue during the 1980s and 1990s. In 1992 a "Stop the Violence / Stop the Drugs" Saturday rally was organized by the Officers Coalition Program, a group of eleven black and Puerto Rican Department of Corrections officers, and by the Lefrak City Youth and Adult Activities Association, the sponsor of the Lefrak Classic summer youth program. The 150 marchers gathered at Eternal Light Baptist Church. The majority were African Americans from the Lefrak City vicinity, including CB4 members Priscilla Carrow and Edna Baskin (both members of Eternal Light), James Galloway and Ruby Muhammad of the LCTA, and Democratic district leader Barbara Jackson, also an LCTA member. They were joined by two white senior citizens wearing Lefrak City Senior Center baseball caps, two white elected officials whose districts now included the Lefrak area, and Daok Lee Pak, a Korean former member of CB4.

Sergeant Pete Petrone and a detail of 110th Precinct officers blocked off half of 57th Avenue for the noontime event. The Officers Coalition Program men organized the line of march: first came Boy Scouts with their mothers (including one Filipina woman) and other children, then the Eternal Light youth choir, and, last, local wardens and other adults. Chanting "Stop the Violence, Stop the Drugs, Save the Children, Save the Children," we marched the six-block route to a wooden stage where a large crowd surrounded the booming sound system playing a soul music mix.

Al Blake of the Lefrak City Youth and Adult Activities Association was the emcee. He introduced state assembly member Jeff Aubry, who asked people listening from their Lefrak City apartment balconies to "come down and join us" and implored adults to keep children away from drugs by their own example. LCTA president Governor Hendley spoke next, followed by the two white elected officials and the Eternal Light minister, whose choir then sang several gospel songs. Russell Barnwell, head of the Officers Coalition Program and a Lefrak City resident, then introduced each of the program's members, mentioning that all were parents who volunteered their time and resources for youth activities. Adults need to "watch where they go and walk because children will watch and follow," he told the audience. Barnwell headed a Lefrak City Cadet Corps which over the next three years grew from fifteen to fifty-seven youths. In addition to performing drum-and-bugle drills, they helped feed homeless persons, visited jails to see the consequences of crime, and participated in still more anti-drug rallies.[12]

Small-Business Coalition

In 1985 I attended a meeting of the Coalition for Fair Business Rents at Macedonia AME Church in Flushing. The audience of thirty Asian, white, and Latin American small-business leaders included Sung Jin Chun of the Korean American Association of Mid-Queens, Ray Bermudez of the Jackson Heights Business and Professional Association, and Richard Ong of the Flushing Chinese Business Association.[13] Coalition president Steve Null, the white owner of a health food store, described the escalation of rents which had spread from Manhattan to the rest of the city during the 1980s. Mayor Koch opposed commercial rent regulation, Null explained, but under election-year pressure he had appointed a blue-ribbon commission to study the issue, with recommendations due in 1986. Coalition vice-president Sung Soo Kim reported on the six meetings held since the Koch commission's appointment.

A Korean man said the city's 9,500 Korean small businesses frequently faced double or triple rent increases and demands for "under-the-table money" from landlords. A white upper Manhattan business owner added that his rent rose from $1,800 to $9,000 when his lease was renewed, and something needed to be done. In response, Peter Vallone, the new speaker of the city council, said that "in my opinion" the commercial rent regulation bill favored by other council members "was unconstitutional." Julie Wager, the white owner of a lingerie store in Astoria and a member of Koch's blue-ribbon commission, told the audience that most other members did not believe rent regulation was needed.

When Koch's commission, composed mainly of Manhattan bankers and developers, reported in 1986, it acknowledged that a quarter of small-business owners considered rent increases their most serious problem but nevertheless recommended against rent regulation. Three of the fifteen members dissented, including Wager and John Torres of the Metropolitan Spanish Merchants Association.[14]

Earlier in 1985 Korean leaders had endorsed mayoral candidate Carol Bellamy, who favored commercial rent regulation, over Koch, whom they knew was likely to be reelected. With a 23 percent self-employment rate, most Koreans either owned small businesses or worked in them. By 1987 the city's mainly small Asian-owned businesses numbered 27,000 and Latin American–owned firms numbered 21,000, both totals having doubled since 1982. The 25,000 black-owned businesses had increased 45 percent, with much of the growth coming from black immigrants. Whites still owned a majority of the city's 185,000 small businesses, but issues affecting this sector of New York's real economy now cut across racial and ethnic lines.[15]

In 1986 district manager John Rowan told a reporter there was "zero commercial space available" in CD4. Several mini-malls had expanded the floor space of the Elmhurst-Corona storefronts they replaced during the 1980s, but the tight rental market continued.[16] Stores and offices even sublet portions of their space to other businesses. Steve Trimboli of the Elmhurst Economic Development Corporation told me that some landlords rented to immigrants—who used their savings to buy businesses, paying cash as "key money" or "goodwill"—and then "jacked up the rent at the end of the lease"; the new owners could not afford the increase and forfeited their security deposits. "High rents are destroying the small-business person," warned Salvatore Lombardo, a Corona Heights pharmacist and president of the Corona Community Development Corporation, in 1989.

As rents increased, so did taxes, thanks to a commercial rent tax that existed in no city other than New York. Fines by Department of Sanitation officers were still another cost: in 1984 the Koch administration stepped up sanitation enforcement in what many small-business owners saw as an attempt to boost revenues at their expense; by 1992 such fines added $400 million to city coffers. Small-business proprietors felt oppressed. Overall, the number of small businesses in New York City grew only 4 percent during the 1980s, while nationwide the increase was 24 percent.[17]

A Small-Business "David"

Sung Soo Kim arrived in the United States in 1969 to study political science at the University of Virginia and then Columbia University in New York City. In 1981 he was hired as executive director by the Korean Produce Association. Kim oversaw the interests of nearly 1,000 fruit-and-vegetable-store owners in the Hunts Point wholesale market, organized the annual KPA *ch'usok* festival in Flushing Meadows–Corona Park, negotiated with city agencies over regulations and fines, and helped draft an unsuccessful commercial rent regulation bill. He also represented KPA members in high-profile disputes with black customers and citywide activists in Jamaica, Harlem, and Brooklyn's Flatbush.[18]

After Koch's 1985 mayoral victory, Sung Soo Kim founded the Korean American Small Business Service Center. Formed to give one voice to the city's Korean business owners, Kim's center unified the existing double structure of groups formed by occupation and locality. It comprised fourteen citywide associations of Korean greengrocers, dry cleaners, seafood sellers, garment contractors, restaurateurs, and so on, plus fourteen local associations of Korean businesses of all types which operated in the same neighborhood—including the KAAMQ. Kim mailed 4,000 monthly newsletters, hosted a weekly radio program, sponsored seminars with municipal agency staff and business proprietors, and produced materials in Korean on city laws and regulations. In 1989 he negotiated a 50 percent reduction in outstanding sanitation fines, saving his members $1.5 million.[19]

Many small-business groups, hoping for improved receptivity at City Hall, supported Dinkins against Koch in 1989.[20] That year I attended the fourth anniversary dinner of the Korean American Small Business Service Center at Leonard's catering hall in Great Neck, Long Island. Mayor-elect Dinkins, unable to attend, sent a letter to Sung Soo Kim in which he "look[ed] forward to working together with you to improve the quality of life in our city." The letter was included in the bilingual dinner program, as were photos of the "magnificent seven" city council members who had voted for commercial rent regulation. The program also listed the center's forty-three-member board of directors, among them Seung Ha Hong and Sung Jin Chun.

Korean leaders had found Dinkins helpful in resolving black-Korean conflict in Harlem in 1984–1985 and 1989. In 1990, however, they were disappointed by his months-long inaction with respect to the protracted boycott of a Korean business in Flatbush.[21] They were also upset by his delay in appointing a promised Small Business Advisory Board.

In frustration, Sung Soo Kim founded a five-county, multiethnic Small Business Congress of forty-eight organizations in August 1991. Joining him on the steps of City Hall, Howard Strauss, vice-president of the Joint Council of Kings County Boards of Trade, announced, "No one in city government represents small business, and we want to be heard." Alfred Placeres, president of the New

York State Federation of Hispanic Chambers of Commerce, affirmed that "the Korean greengrocer has so much in common with the Dominican grocer. They live in their business, their life savings are at stake, and often neither one speaks much English." Roy Hastick of the Caribbean American Chamber of Commerce and Industry declared, "Whether you are black, Korean, [or] Hispanic, you have the same problem. . . . The city is putting the small-business owner out of business." Sung Soo Kim summed things up: "We are all Davids, small Davids, but we still believe in the slingshot."[22]

Neighborhood New York versus Megastores

The Mayor's Small Business Advisory Board was at last named at the end of 1991. Its agenda was controlled by Dinkins officials, however, and participants were dissatisfied, wanting action on rents, competition from street vendors, lengthy city permit and loan procedures, the commercial rent tax, and an unincorporated business tax that doubled the city income tax of many owners. Not until 1993, the mayoral election year, did Dinkins allow the board to elect its own chair from its ranks; the members chose Sung Soo Kim. But meanwhile, the city's business failure rate had increased from 1,000 firms a year in 1990 to 3,800 in 1992, with 90 percent of failures occurring among small businesses.[23]

Small-business leaders also worried about proposed zoning changes that would allow megastores of up to 100,000 square feet to locate in the city (typical neighborhood New York stores are 3,000 square feet or less). Announced by Dinkins in 1992, the plan sought to bring giant supermarkets, furniture outlets, and discount warehouses to New York. "We're going to fight it," Sung Soo Kim vowed. As the election neared, many small-business owners decided to support Republican candidate Rudolph Giuliani.[24]

Late in 1993 Dinkins signed a bill reducing the commercial rent tax by $30 million, and Mayor Giuliani gradually eliminated it in the outer boroughs. But Peter Morisi, owner of a Brooklyn pasta factory and head of the Merchants and Entrepreneurs Rights Coalition Inc. (MERCI), stated, "When you measure these tax breaks against the summonses and regulations we pay . . . it's just a drop in the bucket." Steve Null of the Coalition for Fair Business Rents agreed: "It is not at the top of [our] list."

What headed the list for small-business owners was the acceleration of megastore development which Giuliani was advancing on two fronts. Within fifteen months his administration had awarded Industrial and Commercial Incentive Program tax exemptions of $1 million or more to three megastores, including Caldor and Home Depot. Then Giuliani embraced but doubled the megastore zoning proposed by Dinkins: Giuliani's plan would permit megastores of up to 200,000 square feet (equal to five football fields) on manufacturing-zoned land. Existing zoning regulations—limiting stores to 10,000 square feet and requiring community board hearings and votes and city council approval for larger sites—would all be eliminated so that megastores could open "as of right." Fifty-seven megastores on manufacturing-zoned land were projected by 2005.[25]

Peter Morisi of MERCI objected. "I serve on the mayor's Small Business Advisory Council, and he hasn't even come to us to get our feedback on changing the zoning. Big business puts the gun to the city's head every time." Neighborhood groceries, beverage dealers, clothing stores, pharmacies, and hardware stores feared that city-subsidized megastores would force them to close (and after the opening of Home Depot in Queens, fifteen of the city's 130 lumberyards did close). "The big supermarkets abandoned the city in the 1970s, leaving a vacuum that immigrant businesses filled," said Sung Soo Kim. "Now they want to come back, but only on their terms and with a host of unfair subsidies. This is not free competition." Critics also noted that some megastores had opened under existing zoning, and that commercially zoned land was not in shortage in any of the five boroughs. They predicted that under the Dinkins-Giuliani plan, rising rents in manufacturing zones would stifle new factory development and force firms already there to close. Doubts were voiced about a promised net job increase and about one developer's claim that megastores would lure $3 billion in business from the suburbs to the city—a figure the Giuliani administration endorsed but could not document. Many small merchants felt betrayed.[26]

In June 1996, CB4 sided with small business and against the mayor. Some members remembered local stores that had folded after the Queens Center mall opened in 1971. The point many speakers repeated, however, was that megastores utilized "cheap labor," so that any city policy to facilitate them would adversely affect the job market for everyone. Giuliani's proposal received negative votes from twenty-eight of the thirty-eight community boards that contained manufacturing-zoned land and was rejected by all five borough boards. In December 1996 the city council voted down the megastore plan.[27]

In a city marked by high-profile incidents of racial conflict, the low-profile, dozen-year growth of a multiracial small-business coalition went largely unnoticed. But the Korean business proprietors, led by Sung Soo Kim, who played a central role in this development, were ready to oppose even other Koreans on issues that were important to them. In 1994 a Korean-owned 50,000-square-foot wholesale food store opened in Flushing and operated illegally as a retail store. The Korean American Small Business Service Center protested, demanding (unsuccessfully) that it be shut down for evading zoning regulations.[28]

C-Town: Black-Korean Dialogue

In 1989 the Lefrak City Tenant Association's treasurer, James Galloway, chaired a joint meeting with CB4 to discuss incidents of youth violence that had occurred two weeks earlier. The audience included Governor Hendley and other

LCTA leaders, district manager Rose Rothschild, CB4 members Edna Baskin, Ken Daniels, and Daok Lee Pak, several KAAMQ members including Seung Ha Hong and Sung Jin Chun, Captain McNamara and officers of the 110th Precinct, representatives of elected officials, local merchants, and Lefrak City residents. Galloway explained that on Memorial Day a group of youths had attacked a greengrocery owner and his employee, both of whom were hospitalized; later that night windows were smashed at a bank. "This meeting is to find out what protection the police will be providing this summer to the residents and merchants of the Lefrak City area. . . . We have gangs, and we all know it."

The greengrocer, a Korean, told the group that at 9:00 P.M. "a white Hispanic" youth was discovered shoplifting by the employee, a Latin American. Following police advice, they waited until the youth left the store and then told him that if he returned the goods they would do nothing more. The youth refused, went away, and returned with "an iron bar" and "about forty" supporters; he hit the greengrocer, and his friends threw fruit at the store. The greengrocer called 911 and the 110th Precinct several times, but a police officer arrived only an hour later, and an EMS ambulance after that. Captain McNamara said something had gone wrong with the handling of the call and promised to investigate.

The atmosphere at the meeting was tense. Daok Lee Pak felt that the attack was "premeditated. I'm not saying it was racial," she told McNamara, but the youths seemed to know "exactly where to go." The greengrocer stated that police had not been visible on the holiday weekend preceding Memorial Day. McNamara responded that he thought the attack was "spontaneous" and groused about police retirements and a shortage of replacements. Two disgruntled Lefrak City residents complained that bank staff had knocked out the broken window glass at 3:00 A.M., disturbing their sleep. The bank manager said this was "unfortunate" but it "had to be done as soon as possible."

By the end of the meeting the LCTA, Baskin's Concerned Community Adults, local merchants, and the elected officials' liaisons had agreed to write to Mayor Koch and the borough police commander requesting greater police presence. Within two weeks the Tactical Narcotics Team returned and made several drug arrests. Over the next year communication among those who had been at the meeting increased. Galloway and Pak helped revive a 57th Avenue merchants association; the group's Dominican president, a supermarket owner, and several Korean members paid for Christmas street decorations and donated meals and snacks to Baskin's summer cleanup.[29] And two LCTA officers joined CB4.

By the end of the 1980s many 57th Avenue businesses were owned by Koreans. Black customers noted that frequently only family members now worked there, and the employees of former non-Korean owners lost their jobs. In 1988 Francis Ahn, a Korean, opened a C-Town supermarket on the site of the previous Waldbaum's. According to Edna Baskin, black residents who had worked at Waldbaum's "couldn't even get applications" to work at C-Town. "They hired only one black person—from Jamaica [in Queens], not from the area." At a meeting with fifty Lefrak City area merchants in 1989, Rose Rothschild spoke to the new Korean owners. "I explained that Jewish merchants worked there, and hired in the community. If [Koreans] need people, they bring in a 105-year-old grandmother. They can work with Edna Baskin, and get good kids. That would help a lot."

The C-Town Incident

People in Elmhurst-Corona knew that black-Korean conflict occurred elsewhere in the city. Moreover, a merchant targeted by black protesters in Jamaica in 1982 was a member of an Elmhurst Korean church, and another Korean storeowner and Elmhurst resident was killed by a black customer in Manhattan in 1986.[30] During 1990 the boycott of a Korean store in Flatbush received continual press coverage. In January 1991 the owner was acquitted of assaulting a Haitian female shopper, the disputed incident that had spurred the boycott. Four days later Flatbush came to Lefrak City.

On Monday, February 4, an eleven-year-old African American boy named Bobby Yates, claimed that he was chased, beaten, and locked in a freezer by Yong Cha Kim, a fifty-three-year-old Korean produce manager at C-Town. Kim asserted that he saw Yates, an unpaid grocery bag "packer" working for tips, take money from "the fish bucket," a receptacle where shoppers left tips for store employees who cleaned fish. Kim said he scolded the boy, but Yates ran from him and knocked over a bottle of fabric softener, which broke on the supermarket floor. Kim then grabbed Yates and detained him in a "food preparation room" at the rear of the store, telling him he would call his mother and the police.

Bobby's mother, Cynthia Yates, was shopping in the store; she was located and took her son to Elmhurst Hospital, where he was treated for a cut on his ear. Kim, who spoke little English, stated that Yates fell when he slipped on the spilled fabric softener. C-Town owner Francis Ahn insisted that Yates had been disruptive in his store on previous occasions; he had allowed him to be a "packer" in the hope of preventing further problems. The police charged Kim with third-degree assault but found no evidence that Yates had been locked in a freezer.

Cynthia Yates was a member of Reverend Herbert Daughtry's House of the Lord Pentecostal Church in Brooklyn, and she consulted him on what steps to take. Daughtry, a prominent African American citywide activist, introduced her to the lawyer who had represented the Flatbush boycott leaders. He also brought a busful of demonstrators the following Saturday to join Mrs. Yates in a picket line urging a boycott of C-Town. Forty people demonstrated that day, and six the next. On Monday, Ahn announced that he had dismissed Kim, and the boycott ended.[31]

The Community Task Force

After hearing about the C-Town incident, Lefrak City's black wardens affirmed they wanted neither a boycott nor the presence of outside activists. "We don't want this to be a Brooklyn-type situation," said Ruby Muhammad, an LCTA section leader. LCTA acting president and CB4 member James Brown, a retired postal inspector, declared, "We wash our own linen here. We don't need outsiders to come in."

Muhammad called Rose Rothschild and requested that CB4 facilitate negotiations with C-Town owner Ahn. Rothschild in turn asked Edna Baskin, as vice-chair of CB4's neighborhood stabilization committee, to form a fact-finding committee, and it met on the Friday following the incident. Cynthia and Bobby Yates, Daughtry, Ahn and Kim, LCTA leaders, Rothschild, Baskin, Helen Marshall, and representatives from the 110th Precinct and the city and state human rights offices all attended. To continue oversight of the incident and its aftermath, a Community Task Force (CTF) was created.

Five days later Edna Baskin convened a CTF open meeting attended mainly by African American Lefrak City residents. People reviewed their experiences with local merchants and voiced long-simmering frustrations over treatment of customers and the declining number of black employees. Complaint forms were distributed, and the assemblage formulated a list of "demands" to present at a CTF meeting with merchants the following week. They included the "hiring of a Black or Hispanic manager or supervisor to mediate future conflicts," "ceas[ing] unwarranted surveillance of customers," and "hir[ing] employees who speak fluent English, . . . particularly . . . cashiers."

Twenty-five merchants, all but two Korean, attended the next CTF meeting. Francis Ahn of C-Town announced that he had already agreed to the CTF demands. Because only two non-Korean merchants were present, however, other Koreans felt they were being "singled out." The black CTF members, assuring them that the demands applied to all local merchants, formed a committee to monitor stores for compliance with the demands and to head off new problems. The storeowners designated representatives to continue meeting with CTF members and soon revived their (again) moribund merchants association.

At the March 1991 task force meeting, conflict between the LCTA and Baskin surfaced, with Governor Hendley insisting that the CTF deal only with resident-merchant relations, not an expanded agenda of youth programs as Baskin proposed. (In 1992 Baskin ran against Hendley and James Galloway for the LCTA presidency; Hendley won.) Jeff Aubry of the borough president's office, a lifelong East Elmhurst resident and veteran CB3 member, helped smooth the CTF's path by drafting bylaws, approved at the following meeting. Over the next year the task force met monthly, monitored C-Town and other stores, distributed two newsletters reporting on the original incident and the continuing concerns of residents and merchants, and held a seminar on security problems for merchants and a public meeting open to all.[32]

Black-Korean dialogue began at the first CTF fact-finding meeting when C-Town produce manager Yong Cha Kim explained that in Korea any adult may reprimand a child for misbehavior; this was not, he now realized the custom in the United States. Some African American adults remembered that this had been true also in black communities when they were young but admitted that it was not the case today. Al Blake, a paralegal and retired policeman, brought up other problematic "cultural differences" such as objections that Korean merchants placed change on the counter rather than in a customer's hand, and that they did not "smile" enough.

At other meetings CTF members heard complaints from Koreans. Several mentioned shoplifting; they said it occurred with groups of children as well as individual adults and emphasized their need to raise prices for everyone to compensate for losses. CTF members, although they said it existed "in every community, white and nonwhite alike," acknowledged this problem; chair Edna Baskin had seen a group of children leaving an Indian-owned drugstore with stolen merchandise.

Francis Ahn told of customers who returned spoiled perishables, claiming to have bought them that day and asking for refunds. CTF member James Brown backed him up: "I'm in C-Town everyday. I've seen people try to return three-day-old meat." Ahn said he allowed exchanges but not refunds, adding "It is not just a matter of the value of the items. Sometimes when they are respectful, I don't mind if it is a big amount. But if they are cursing and yelling, then I don't want to return even a small amount." Al Blake, who headed the CTF monitoring committee, told Ahn, "That's not fair to you. It's a two-way street. Some customers have an attitude and are looking for trouble."

At the CTF public meeting the Korean president of the merchants' association explained through a translator that the city's economic "depression" (the post-1989 job hemorrhage) prevented more of his members from attending the meeting. Seven of twenty-eight Korean-owned Lefrak-area stores had closed recently, four were near closure, and eight had new owners. "My suggestion to the task force is that rent is our biggest problem. Can you contact the landlords, and ask them also to show they are concerned with the community? We are squeezed. The Korean merchants pay rent and real estate tax for the landlords, yet the landlords are not affected by the depression. They make money in the neighborhood but are not part of the community problem-solving effort."

Race and Quality of Life

Basing their work on resident complaint forms and their own experiences, CTF members pursued problems ranging from individual indignities to quality-of-life issues. The racial or ethnic identity of storeowners, through known to

CTF members, was rarely mentioned, and then only to identify which store was under discussion: the "Asian" check-cashing company, or "that Spanish grocery." Similarly, it was unnecessary to state that most customers were black. In cases of personal affronts and "unwarranted surveillance" it was understood that whites rarely encountered similar treatment. Here direct CTF action was needed.[33] With quality-of-life problems the issues were the same as those addressed by other civic groups, and the CTF enlisted the aid of CB4, elected officials, and the 110th Precinct.

The largest number of complaint forms referred to a check-cashing business which, Ron Baskin observed, had produced dissatisfaction over many years. "They are rude," said Al Blake. "They seem to think there is something wrong if black people have a check over a certain amount." CTF members visited and wrote to the business, but the owner was unresponsive, and complaints continued. When CTF members discovered the firm advertising falsely as an authorized payment location for utility bills, they asked city council member John Sabini to investigate.

"Unwarranted surveillance" occurred at several stores. CTF members objected to a Woolworth security guard's treatment of Ruby Muhammad's eleven-year-old niece: the store's metal detector rang when she entered, and without speaking to the girl the guard searched her pocketbook. Shoppers at a hardware store complained that the Korean owners trailed them; both the minister of Edna Baskin's church and Denise Henderson, a demure corporate employee and CTF member, reported being followed. Al Blake visited the store and learned that a black locksmith watched customers, making the owners' surveillance unnecessary, yet "they do target some people they suspect," Blake reported.

Blake was more successful in changing security procedures at C-Town, where, people complained, guards asked only some people to check the bags they brought into the store. Indeed, when I, a white male, visited C-Town in March 1991, I was not requested to check my shoulder bag, but a Latin American women right behind me *was* asked for her bag, and she objected. After Blake spoke with Francis Ahn, the store instituted a policy of requesting all customers to leave their bags in a holding area; as a result, Ahn told Blake, shoplifting declined.

Other complaints—that "rainchecks" were not given when sale items ran out; that sandwich makers did not wear gloves and hairnets—were brought to the relevant storeowners' attention. A more serious problem of rotten meat at one supermarket resulted in a CTF inspection visit. After Edna Baskin obtained New York State sanitary inspection reports documenting violations under the previous ownership, on our Sunday morning visit we found no scale in the produce section, and uncleaned meat saws flecked with dried meat. "It's a ghetto store; I've felt that way from when I first moved in," said Baskin. "This is a middle-class neighborhood."

Some CTF members objected to a weekend flea market in C-Town's parking lot. "I don't know about you, but I think it diminishes the area," said one. Al Blake replied that Francis Ahn had agreed to let the Lefrak City Boy Scouts sell dresses and jewelry for two weeks, but other vendors had moved in and remained. Members requested that police give summonses. A more dangerous situation existed at a video rental where drug dealers openly conducted sales inside the store. Blake and James Brown, the CTF liaisons to the 110th, informed the commanding officer about both these situations.

A protracted problem arose with a candy store—consistently referred to as "Henry's," although the owner was Chinese—where children were allowed to play video games during school hours, and X-rated videos were displayed near the cash register. CTF members spoke repeatedly to Henry, asked the 110th to send truant officers, and informed district manager Rose Rothschild, who pressed the NYPD public morals division to inspect. No pornography violation was discovered, however, and although CTF members stewed, little changed at Henry's.

C-Town One Year Later

Immediately after the 1991 C-Town incident, Francis Ahn had deployed uniformed security guards and hired a more diverse staff. In March 1991 I noted black, Latin American, and one white in addition to Korean floor staff, and only black and Latin American female cashiers. In June 1991 James Brown told the CTF "everything is moving along smoothly." For this, Helen Marshall credited "the health of the community," referring to earlier contacts between the Korean American Association of Mid-Queens and Edna Baskin's cleanup team, and merchant contributions to the Lefrak City Senior Center. Marshall was also impressed that Francis Ahn fired employees "on the spot" in cases of rudeness and customer harassment.

Complaints about produce and cleanliness at C-Town continued to come to the CTF and were conveyed to Ahn. Then in February 1992 Baskin reported "two incidents at C-Town. Twice, about five kids went in the store, running around. The kids were disruptive of baby carts and the elderly. They ate grapes. The police were called; the manager felt that if *he* stopped them, people would go after him. They were all between nine and thirteen." Al Blake added, "One kid was asked to leave and not come back. His mother objected and called Al Sharpton [an African American citywide activist]. I spoke to the mother. There was no police report, or no complaint filed, so there was little to react to. Then she decided to escalate. She did a handwritten boycott flyer in Section 2 [of Lefrak City]. Then nothing. I told her without a police report there was no case for a lawsuit."

"We've got to educate people," Governor Hendley responded. "They shouldn't let kids in like that. We should write a letter to the parents. We have to protect the merchants. They've lost their bite. The Koreans are scared stiff about another C-Town. The community has the power." As the meeting ended, Blake observed, "People say they now put the change in your hand. I guess the Koreans are more used to dealing with American people."

The Mayi Murder: White–Latin American Conflict

On March 29, 1991, two months after the C-Town incident, a nineteen-year-old Dominican Queens College freshman, Manuel Mayi, was killed by a group of white Corona youth. After Mayi left his girlfriend's house near William Moore Park on a Friday night, he had used a blue marker to inscribe his personal graffiti "tag," MAZE 7, and that of his "clique," RTR (Ready to Rush), on a billboard and on the wall of the Park Side restaurant. A group of young people in the park saw him and chased him along 108th Street—some on foot and others in a van—for sixteen blocks to North Corona, then sprayed a fire extinguisher in his face and hit him with baseball bats. Mayi died of a broken skull and brain contusions.

Detectives from the 115th Precinct located witnesses who had heard the chase and beating, and two who saw the attackers from a distance. Three white youths were arrested, but in a lineup the witnesses identified only Joseph Celso, an eighteen-year-old high school student who lived near the park. In addition, the police were contacted by a young white Corona Heights woman who said she had heard Celso admit to the killing; this witness, however, moved to Italy and refused to return for the trial. In April 1993 a jury of six whites, four blacks, and two Latin Americans acquitted Celso of second-degree murder and manslaughter. The two witnesses who testified had criminal records and were unable to convince the jury of Celso's guilt.[34]

Law Enforcement Interpretations

At the trial and in interviews with reporters, Queens police and prosecutors revealed their theory of the killing: Mayi was a prolific graffiti "writer" in the CB3-CB4 area, and "this was graffiti-motivated as far as we can tell. They took exception to him marking up walls, and set out after him." Investigators found no evidence of racial or ethnic bias and did not consider the white youths part of a gang. Nonetheless, one official told *Newsday* in 1993, "the Park Side . . . is a mob-associated restaurant, which has long been run by Tony Federici, a soldier in the Lucchese organized crime family. . . . [T]he teenagers beat Mayi to impress Federici."[35]

In 1989 *Newsday* columnist Bill Reel quoted a Queens policeman: "The mutts know better than to come into certain neighborhoods. They're afraid of the kind of justice that gets meted out. . . . In the 110th Precinct, around 108th Street and Corona Avenue, the part they call Spaghetti Park. Need I say more? Five blocks in any direction is crime-free. No need to even lock your car."[36] Neighborhood New York has a 150-year history of street-corner toughness from which a few men graduate into criminal activity. As historian Alan Block put it, in this world "the method to secure relationships was to do 'favors' for the already powerful." Several historically Italian neighborhoods such as Corona Heights retain residues of this heritage, much reduced but still occasionally dangerous to outsiders: whites in the past, nonwhites more recently.[37]

But actions that brought investigators into their neighborhoods were not welcomed by criminal entrepreneurs. As sociologist Donald Tricarico notes, these men "had a vested interest in local order" and held younger males "in check." The killing of Manuel Mayi, the killings of black and Ecuadorian men in Howard Beach, Bensonhurst, and Bay Ridge between 1987 and 1994, and the beating of an Italian off-duty policeman in Bay Ridge in 1995—all done by white youths in historically Italian neighborhoods—may represent the loosening of traditional organized-crime control more than its perpetuation.[38]

At any rate, the "Mafia" reputation of Park Side owner Federici was common knowledge in Corona Heights during the 1980s and 1990s. I heard the nickname "Tough Tony" many times, frequently in connection with his Fourth of July fireworks show. Once I even heard a teacher at PS14 jokingly tell another to "ask Tough Tony" for protection from a parent who was annoying her. My research team member Priti Prakash was well aware of Tough Tony's neighborhood reputation from having lived in Corona Heights as a teenager in the early 1980s.

Whether Manuel Mayi was aware of any of this is unknowable. Even if he were, as one police officer put it, "You do have to ask yourself—would he have been killed if he was Italian?"[39]

Latin American Interpretations

Manuel's mother, Altagracia Mayi, was convinced that "they killed my son because he was Spanish. You don't kill someone because he wrote graffiti." At Queens College a Committee for Justice for Manny Mayi, composed of Mayi's counselor and student friends, agreed. They joined his mother in courthouse picket lines and protested what they charged was inadequate investigation of racial bias as a motive for the murder.

Citywide Latin American organizations backed them. The Dominican Women's Caucus and other groups convinced Mayor Dinkins to offer a $10,000 reward for information about the murderers, persuaded the city's Human Rights Commission to declare Mayi's killing "bias-related," and met with the Queens district attorney. The Spanish-language press covered the trial closely, and headlines announcing the acquittal angered many. "Once again, a young man of color is dead and none of his assailants are in jail and the investigation is closed," concluded Richie Pérez, leader of the National Congress for Puerto Rican Rights. "The message to neighborhood segregationists is that institutions of government will not pursue them vigorously."

Two weeks after the 1993 verdict, three hundred protesters marched from the site of Mayi's death to William Moore Park. They included Latin American elected officials, among them Nydia Velasquez, Corona's Congress member since 1992. In the park, well guarded by 110th Precinct officers, Altagracia Mayi demanded justice. With support from Latin American organizations, she had contacted the attorney general's office in Washington and announced that it would investigate the killing as a possible civil rights violation.

Protests continued: in March 1994, 250 mainly Dominican demonstrators marched from NYPD headquarters near City Hall to the lower Manhattan federal office building. They excoriated Mayor Giuliani's refusal to demand a federal Justice Department investigation for Mayi as he had for the 1991 killing of a Jewish man in Crown Heights, Brooklyn. "What is the color of justice?" Altagracia Mayi asked at the rally. "Is it for whites only or for the entire community?" A week later the attorney general's office reported that its investigation had uncovered no grounds for a civil rights case. "Eyewitnesses have alleged that the members of the crowd who chased Mr. Mayi out of the park were yelling at him for defacing the park with graffiti," a federal official wrote the Mayi family. "There is insufficient evidence that this murder was racially motivated."

Altagracia Mayi's outrage and that of others did not end. At his 1994 town meeting in East Elmhurst, Mayor Giuliani was confronted by demonstrators with banners demanding a renewed investigation. "It's the Mafia," Mrs. Mayi told the mayor, holding up a large portrait of her son. Giuliani repeated that police and federal investigators had discovered no evidence of anti–Latin American bias and reiterated that the case was weakened by the refusal of the principal witness to return from Italy and testify. In March 1996 a "Rally for Racial Justice" was held at City Hall on the fifth anniversary of Manuel Mayi's death. The cosponsors included twenty-three citywide Latin American, African American, and Asian organizations, and the rally flyer charged that "one member . . . of the racist gang in Corona [that killed Mayi] has since been appointed to the NYC Police Department."

In Corona the Mayi murder and trial produced prayer vigils and involvement in pickets and marches by Dominican residents. "We have never participated in the political process. Manuel Mayi was the spark that initiated our motivation," said Julio Ferreras, president of Hermanos Unidos de Queens, a Corona-based association of Dominican social clubs founded in 1982 and sponsor of sports activities in Linden Park. In 1996 Ferreras became a member of CB4's youth services committee.[40]

White Corona Interpretations

Graffiti on public surfaces had exploded throughout New York City during the 1970s.[41] It subsided in the early 1980s but returned at the end of the decade; at a 1988 district cabinet meeting Rose Rothschild remarked, "All of a sudden graffiti is all over, a big rash. It's like ten years ago." In Elmhurst-Corona graffiti appeared in parks, on LIRR and highway sidings and overpasses, on houses of worship, and on commercial buildings. Objections were registered by wardens and civic associations in South Elmhurst, the Newtown section of Elmhurst, Corona Heights, and the neighboring areas of Jackson Heights and Forest Hills. Assembly member Helen Marshall purchased two "graffiti-buster" machines to clean building surfaces and made them available to community groups, including Ana Lopez's Father Billini Association youth program. Edna Baskin's 1993 summer cleanup began with a dozen children and adults painting over graffiti on the Long Island Expressway retaining wall opposite Lefrak City.

By the early 1990s graffiti was frequently mentioned as a "quality-of-life" issue, one linked to the lack of youth recreation facilities. The problem was not associated with persons of any particular ethnic or racial identity but was acknowledged to be a citywide concern. Manuel Mayi's graffiti-writing was thus one more instance of a widespread phenomenon. After the 1993 acquittal verdict, one white Corona resident told me, "His tag, MAZE/RTR, was all over Corona Heights, not just at the Park Side. It was even on the street in front of my house. Don't make him a hero. But he didn't deserve to die. They got away with murder."

The proposition that Manuel Mayi was killed because he was a Latin American trespassing in a white neighborhood did not reflect Corona Heights demography. Scores if not hundreds of Latin American residents, many of them Dominican, passed William Moore Park daily. The four Corona Heights census tracts surrounding the park were 56 percent Latin American in 1990, and 30 percent white (in 1980 whites had been 56 percent, and Latin Americans 35 percent). Ironically, at the time of Mayi's murder and of Joseph Celso's trial, citywide Latin American advocacy groups were contending that Corona Heights was a Latin American–majority area and lobbying to include it within "Latino" city council and congressional districts.

Regardless of demographic shifts in Corona Heights, organized-crime gambling operations flourished near William Moore Park, as was evident from police raids in 1987 and 1990. "The men" still frequented a cafe facing the park, and Park Side proprietor Anthony Federici's Fourth of July fireworks continued to attract large crowds into the 1990s. Following *Newsday* reports of Federici's Lucchese-family "soldier" status in 1993, two white Corona Heights residents told me they had known of his "Mafia" reputation but not these specific details—although others, one added, probably did know.

Attitudes among some Corona Heights whites mirrored those that historian Gerald Meyer described for East Harlem Italians in decades past: "As long as they did not hurt the community . . . residents expressed little or no disapproval toward gamblers, even racketeers. Furthermore, they believed the Mafia helped keep the community safe from burglaries and street crime."[42] Other white

Corona residents resisted such attitudes. The St. Leo's Teen Center was formed in part to pull young men away from the lure of organized crime and Fourth of July street bravado. Antagonism to the new majority in Corona Heights certainly existed among some whites as well. In fact, Joseph Celso had been a Teen Center member during 1987–1988; he had heard his Latin American peers there referred to as "Hics" and watched most drift away. Still, as journalist Gasper Signorelli, native of another historically Italian New York neighborhood, wrote after the 1989 murder of black teenager Yusuf Hawkins in Bensonhurst, "The killing of innocent strangers has never been sanctioned by my 'tribe.' People in such neighborhoods do know that living in a city means sticking to certain fundamental values: that killing is wrong, that racism is wrong, that the city belongs to all of us and we should be able to visit any part of it in safety."[43]

After the Celso acquittal and the Latin American march to William Moore Park, elected officials and white Corona wardens lent support to a Community Conciliation Network (CCN) program headed by a Puerto Rican woman and located in quarters facing the park. Offering "conflict resolution" training and afterschool tutoring to a small number of young people, the CCN also sponsored an annual "mini-cultural event" in the park, featuring ethnic foods and music. Tony and Josephine Caminiti, both CB4 members and leaders of the Northside Democratic Club, were the first guests of honor in 1993. Helen Marshall, Rose Rothschild, and other local leaders also attended.

At the district cabinet meeting preceding CCN's 1995 mini-cultural event, Rothschild reported angrily that her CB4 office had received calls repeating a rumor that "they will barricade the park and keep local people out, and that marchers will come to protest the Mayi killing." She told one white caller, "We are a multiethnic community and if another nationality is doing an event in the park, you must live with it. . . . If the mother [Altagracia Mayi] wants to be there, this is America. If it was my son, I'd have a gun ready to shoot."

The event took place with no march and no disturbance. About sixty people—a third of them Italian men gathered as usual at the bocce court—and a dozen police occupied balloon-filled William Moore Park during the Saturday afternoon. Elderly Italians, Latin Americans of all ages, and one Chinese mother and son sat on benches and helped themselves to rice and beans, tamales, and a pasta salad provided by "Mr. Tony from the Park Side." Meat store owner Tony Giordano greeted people on behalf of the Corona Heights Businessmen's Association and the Corona Community Development Corporation. Rose Rothschild, CB4 member Angie LaChappelle, two white Democratic district leaders, and Tony Caminiti spoke briefly, as did African American assembly member Jeff Aubry, who then joined the men playing bocce.

Only one Queens Latin American organization, the Sociedad Puertorriqueña de Queens, endorsed the event, and no local Latin American groups participated. Aside from a stirring performance by a female Mexican singer in *vaquero* (cowboy) garb, Latin American culture was represented only by food and recorded music to which a handful of children lip-synced with a toy microphone while swaying salsa-style. Other selections signaled the event's inclusive mission: Frank Sinatra songs, two African American 1970s disco numbers, and Glenn Miller's 1940s "In the Mood."

Throughout the afternoon a dozen white and Latin American Corona teenagers gathered at a flower shop opposite the park; male and female, they talked quietly, consoling one another. Several times one or two entered the park to place candles and flowers in memory of three friends who two nights earlier had been killed by an LIRR train while standing near the track on the 108th Street overpass and, according to police, dropping eggs on automobiles passing beneath. The three were part of a group known as "the Corona boys," a name used for decades by young men who met in William Moore Park. One was the same age as Manuel Mayi and Joseph Celso, and the other two were several years younger. They had grown up together in Corona Heights; Steven Luparello and Kevin Titus were white, and Jorge Baez was Latin American.[44]

Redistricting and the Containment of Interracial Cooperation

Drawn to reflect historic neighborhoods and manmade boundaries, New York's community district borders have remained fixed for more than three decades. To their residents they define political fields within which wardens and civic groups articulate local viewpoints to elected officials and municipal agencies. The fifty-nine CDs have shifted in population size—by 1990 they ranged from 25,000 to 221,000—but average 124,000. They provide the basic budgeting and service-delivery grid for all city services except fire protection and education. In short, they define local-level government in New York City.

In contrast, electoral districts—city, state, and federal—are drawn without regard to neighborhood borders or service-delivery areas; they slice community districts apart and combine slivers from different CDs. They are reconfigured after each decennial census by politicians seeking to ensure reelection from districts with as many voters of like race, ethnicity, religion, and political party as possible. Local wardens who build ties with one another around district-level concerns are split apart when enlisting support from their respective elected officials. These officials, in turn, take only limited interest in any one CD, only part of which falls within their electoral district.

Before the federal Voting Rights Act of 1965, residential concentrations of black or Puerto Rican New Yorkers were gerrymandered into separate electoral districts to dilute their voting strength. After New York State's 1970 congressional redistricting, the National Association for the Advancement of Colored People (NAACP) and the Puerto Rican Legal Defense and Education Fund

(PRLDEF) challenged the district lines in court. They won a revised set of districts that made more likely the election of black and Puerto Rican congress members. With Voting Rights Act certification of New York's electoral districts thereafter required by the federal Justice Department, a similar sequence of events followed the 1980 census.

City Council Redistricting

In 1991 a commission of lawyers and public policy experts was appointed to map new city council districts, and hearings on proposed district lines were scheduled in each borough.[45] The redrawing was complicated by a 1989 charter provision increasing the number of council seats from thirty-five to fifty-one, a change intended to boost "minority" representation.

After the 1990 census the black and the Latin American redistricting stakes were quite different, however. New York City's black population had increased only from 24 to 25 percent since 1980; an expanded share of "black seats" could not be expected. Many African Americans believed that with a sitting black mayor, six black council members, and black representation on the redistricting commission, their gains would be preserved. The NAACP thus did not enter the redistricting struggles.

In contrast, the city's Latin American population had grown from 20 to 24 percent since 1980. Only three sitting council members were Puerto Rican, and the share of "Latino seats" potentially could grow to one-quarter. In March 1991 the Puerto Rican/Latino Voting Rights Network, a group of seven Puerto Rican organizations including PRLDEF, began meeting to map "predominantly Latino districts."[46] In April it unveiled a plan for thirteen such districts, including two in Queens. One joined Corona Heights, Corona Plaza, and half of Elmhurst and Jackson Heights to produce a 52 percent Latin American district. Latin American registered voters in this and other proposed districts were far less than 50 percent, but the group's strategy was to create districts in which a young and heavily-immigrant population would produce larger numbers of Latin American voters later in the 1990s.

An unintended aspect of the Voting Rights Network's map was to place in separate districts heavily black Lefrak City and North Corona–East Elmhurst, which during the 1980s had fallen within the same city council and state assembly districts. Here black North Corona–East Elmhurst and Lefrak City Democrats had supported white city council member Joseph Lisa Jr., and white Corona Heights Democrats had backed black state assembly member Helen Marshall.

In May 1991 the redistricting commission published its own preliminary map. It included only one "predominantly Latino district" in Queens. This 21st District, 55 percent Latin American, joined Corona Heights and a small portion of Elmhurst with Corona Plaza and North Corona–East Elmhurst. By cutting potential Latin American representation from Queens in half, the plan displeased the Puerto Rican/Latino Voting Rights Network. It also angered African Americans by severing North Corona–East Elmhurst from Lefrak City, which was placed in the Elmhurst–Jackson Heights 25th District. The commission's rationale for these lines was to create "Asian influence" by amassing as many Asian voters as possible in the 25th, where Asians constituted 27 percent of the population.

At the May 1991 commission hearing in Queens, a PRLDEF spokesman argued for the network's "two-district plan." Queens Latin American leaders were present to support this position, including Nayibe Nuñez-Berger of the Queens Hispanic Coalition, Jackson Heights small-business leader Ray Bermudez, and Ana Lopez of the Father Billini Association youth program. When specific questions about district lines were asked, however, it became evident that the PRLDEF spokesperson was familiar with Queens on a computer screen but not on the ground, which hurt the presentation of his case.

A black man from East Elmhurst argued that severing Lefrak City from North Corona–East Elmhurst was at odds with the intent of the 1965 Voting Rights Act. Edna Baskin, Al Blake, Barbara Jackson, and other Lefrak City wardens who were present all supported keeping the two black areas in one council district. At a later City Hall demonstration they joined Helen Marshall, now a candidate in the new 21st District, to protest its configuration. Ron Baskin stated that C-Town and other stores would be in the 21st, and their Lefrak City customers in the 25th. Blake protested, "Our [African American] voice would not be heard in the new [25th] district."

On the redistricting commission's final map Lefrak City was returned to the 21st District, but three commissioners, including two Puerto Ricans, voted against this plan. They called it a move to ensure Helen Marshall's election, and a leader of the Puerto Rican/Latino network condemned what he branded "blatant discriminatory practices against Latino voters." PRLDEF and the network sued under the Voting Rights Act, and in July 1991 the Justice Department rejected the commission's 21st District. The result was that Lefrak City was again moved into the 25th, and the preliminary 21st, with its 55 percent Latin American population, was approved.

Even without Lefrak City votes, Marshall defeated one African American and three Latin American primary challengers to win the 21st District city council seat in 1991 and was reelected in 1993 and 1997. In proportions of registered voters, the 21st District was 38 percent white, 33 percent black, 24 percent Latin American, and 4 percent Asian. Marshall did not consider it either Latin American or black: "I have represented the area [as an assembly member] for nine years, but lived here for thirty-three. You can't win this district by being black, Hispanic, or white. You've got to be able to pick up black votes, Hispanic votes, and white votes to win."[47]

Congressional Redistricting

To avoid court-imposed congressional districts following the 1990 census, the New York State legislature used computers and consultants both to ensure a proportional number of "minority" districts and to protect incumbents, all but one of whom were reelected. Of fourteen newly mapped New York City seats, three were relatively compact black-majority districts in Brooklyn and Queens, made easy to draw by the city's housing segregation patterns. A fourth compact Harlem district contained a 47 percent black voting-age plurality, and its African American representative was reelected. A fifth compact district in the Bronx (and Westchester County) had a more diverse multiracial composition and reelected a white incumbent. Four of these three black and two multiracial compact districts fell within a single county.[48]

White New Yorkers in 1990 were more residentially concentrated than blacks; 53 percent lived in census tracts that were at least 80 percent white, versus 41 percent of blacks in tracts at least 80 percent black.[49] Thus compact white-majority districts would have been easy to map, but instead, only one of the seven newly drawn white-majority districts was relatively compact—a Staten Island–Brooklyn seat. The others were oddly shaped, with three of them spanning three counties. Heavily white southern Brooklyn and northeastern Queens, moreover, were each split among three odd-shaped congressional districts to maximize white representation; two Queens districts were even extended into Westchester, Nassau, and Suffolk Counties to pull in more white voters.

Of the two Latin American–majority districts, one was a compact Bronx seat and the other an odd-shaped district that joined heavily Latin American neighborhoods in Brooklyn and Manhattan's Lower East Side with Elmhurst-Corona. In the 1992 Democratic primary for this seat, five Latin American candidates challenged a white Congress member whose district had been dismantled. Nydia Velasquez won both primary and general elections and was reelected in 1994 and 1996, the first Puerto Rican woman to serve in the U.S. Congress.[50]

Although New York's 24 percent Latin American population proportionally could claim at least three of the city's fourteen congressional seats, drawing even a second Latin American–majority district proved difficult. In 1990 only 22 percent of Latin Americans lived in census tracts where they composed at least 80 percent of the population. As journalist Annette Fuentes put it, "In truth, the dispersion of Latinos and the greater geographic concentration of African Americans made it easier to ensure black representation than Latino."[51]

In Queens, Latin Americans grew more dispersed between 1980 and 1990; as in Elmhurst-Corona their numbers elsewhere in the borough were increasing in historically white neighborhoods. The same pattern of numerical growth with greater dispersion was also true for Asians. In contrast, black population increases in heavily white areas all occurred at the margins of the large southeast

Queens black community. Black Queens residents were more concentrated geographically in 1990 than in 1980.[52]

These trends made solidly Latin American or Asian electoral districts unlikely in the future. Yet in a borough projected to grow from 20 to 26 percent Latin American and 12 to 18 percent Asian by 2000, and with a Latin American now representing part of Queens in Congress, Democratic county chair Thomas Manton sought to channel this demographic surge into his party fold. In 1992 his sixty-four-member county committee consisted of fifty-two white and twelve black locally elected district leaders. In 1993 he added two Chinese and four Colombian, Dominican, and Ecuadorian members-at-large.[53]

School Board Redistricting

In 1994 a New York State commission on redrawing the city's thirty-two school districts held hearings in each borough.[54] Since 1969, when lines were first drawn, some largely white districts had fallen below the statutory 15,000-pupil minimum, and a new law lowered this to 12,000. Others experienced enormous growth and severe crowding, among them School District 24, now projected to reach 40,000 pupils by the year 2000. The commission's public hearing in Queens was packed with hundreds of parents, teachers, and elected officials.

The commission proposed creating a new School District 33 that would join Elmhurst-Corona from SD24 with similarly crowded Jackson Heights and North Corona–East Elmhurst from SD30. The result would be a district in which 96 percent of pupils were "minorities," the majority of them Latin American. The plan was supported by Latin American leaders—including Nayibe Nuñez-Berger of the Queens Hispanic Coalition—but opposed for varying reasons by white, black, and Asian speakers.

White elected officials objected to the increased administrative cost of any new districts and called for building more schools to alleviate overcrowding. Some white teachers protested being moved from SD30, which like SD24 had a white-majority board, to what they anticipated would be a Latin American–majority SD33 board. "You just want a job!" one called out at Nuñez-Berger when she testified. A group of white South Elmhurst parents from PS102 had similar motives and wished to remain in SD24 rather than be included in SD33.

Helen Marshall objected that SD33 would "squeeze all the minority children into one jam-packed overcrowded district." She admitted, "We don't have proper minority representation on School Board 24—no Hispanic and only one Asian—[or] School Board 30, [which] has two blacks and one Hispanic." She proposed "zone reps" to replace at-large elections, which produced "control by just one end of the district." Donald Stewart, the black president of SB30, said the SD33 plan was "discriminatory and racist. This would decrease minority voting strength in School Districts 24 and 30." Harry Stewart, president of the

North Corona–East Elmhurst NAACP, proclaimed, "School District 33 will not add one seat . . . and School District 24 goes to 75 percent white. Segregation has crept in." To cheers, he concluded, "I oppose the many mini-schools as a solution. Build more schools!"

Louisa Chan, the sole Asian member of SB24, agreed. "Don't segregate us in School District 33. Those in the north end [of SD24] may want control and jobs, but this doesn't benefit the children. We tried on the [commission's] computer to divide School District 24, but it is impossible to do so and maintain racial balance and intermediate school feeder patterns. So keep School District 24, even if it is [now] 30,000." She said the Board of Education needed to do more "voter education." An Indian man concurred: "Reform the election system for better minority representation."

Although representing smaller populations than the Latin American speakers, black and Asian spokespersons protested reconfiguring multiracial school districts where, despite white dominance, they had made inroads. Latin American leaders had achieved little electoral success and found no support for reshaping the political arena to make victory more likely. White politicians, teachers, and parents simply defended the status quo. Objections to school redistricting elsewhere in Queens and in other boroughs were also voiced at commission hearings, and no district lines were changed. In 1996, however, the state legislature reduced the powers of the district school boards, transferring authority to the citywide Board of Education and the chancellor.

The Containment of Interracial Cooperation

At the end of the 1991 city council redistricting battles, economist Robert Fitch observed, "Redistricting was meant to boost minorities. It ended up preserving white power."[55] In a city only 43 percent white, thirty of the fifty-one council members elected, or 59 percent, were white. Fitch's dictum also applied to the 1992 congressional redistricting: eight of fourteen Congress members, or 57 percent, were white. Achieving this result entailed creating six odd-shaped white districts, two of which extended into the suburbs to capture additional white voters. Six of the seven white-majority congressional districts, moreover, had populations between 74 and 82 percent white; Alan Gartner, a white staff member of the city council and congressional redistricting bodies, blamed this outcome on "incumbents [who] think they're entitled to landslides, not just a fair shot."[56] In a majority-minority city, such districts could result only from racial gerrymandering to protect white officeholders.

It was Nydia Velasquez's congressional district, however, that was challenged in court on the basis of odd shape and racial gerrymandering—even though, with a registered-voter population 49 percent Latin American, 29 percent white, 16 percent black, and 5 percent Asian, it better reflected the city at large than did any of the white odd-shaped districts. The suit was filed in 1995 by the Campaign for a Color-Blind America, a conservative Texas organization that also challenged black and Latin American districts in other states. In 1997 a federal court declared the district unconstitutional. Velasquez planned an appeal to the Supreme Court, but in view of its previous decisions against black-majority districts, she was doubtful that such an appeal would survive.[57]

In Queens and throughout the city the 1990s redistricting struggles increased racial antagonism and suspicion. "Tensions between blacks and Latinos are worse than ever before because both communities are worse off than twenty years ago, and there are no powerful organizations promoting unity," concluded National Congress for Puerto Rican Rights leader Richie Pérez in 1992. At a 1993 Institute for Puerto Rican Policy forum, Luther Blake, an African American member of the city council redistricting commission, explained, "People are looking around and saying, 'Well how do we keep these people [blacks, Latin Americans, Asians] from getting their fair share of power?' The easiest way. Let them fight among themselves."[58] At the Queens redistricting hearings I attended in 1991 and 1994, this is exactly what happened: before my eyes, civic activists who on other occasions cooperated in quality-of-life struggles now drew apart into their own corners of the room along racial lines.

What if congressional districts had been drawn both to protect historically excluded minorities and to be compact, including intact community districts as much as possible? Would the 1992 results have been seven (rather than twelve) white- or black- or Latin American–majority districts, and seven (rather than two) multiracial districts, pointing toward the city's future? What if the 1969 school districts had been drawn to coincide with the community districts already in existence? Would white, black, Latin American, and Asian Elmhurst-Corona residents by 1994 have had a twenty-five-year history of struggling together to build more schools rather than of battling against a distant white-majority board?

The court decision voiding Nydia Velasquez's seat made unlikely the creation of odd-shaped "minority" districts after the 2000 U.S. census, but odd-shaped white districts remain unchallenged. Only slowly, unevenly, unfairly will New York inch its way toward the future of us all. Yet despite divisions caused by redistricting, voters may be more ready for this future than some politicians and citywide advocates think. Already, black candidates Helen Marshall and Jeff Aubry have won in Elmhurst-Corona's multiracial districts by understanding that "you've got to be able to pick up black votes, Hispanic votes, and white votes to win."

At the 1991 Queens city council redistricting hearing, an older man with a pronounced Spanish accent rose to state that he backed the Puerto Rican/Latino Voting Rights Network's "two-district plan." Then he said, "I live in Jackson Heights where we Hispanics live among many others. Personally, I will support any candidate, Hispanic, white, black, or Asian, who represents the interests of the people in Jackson Heights." He received the longest, most sustained applause of any speaker, and it came from every corner of the room.

Conclusion: The Future of Us All

At no one's request and by no one's design, Elmhurst-Corona was transformed from a solidly white neighborhood in 1960 to "perhaps the most ethnically mixed community in the world" by the 1990s. The United States is still at the early stages of a similar transition. The arrival of a "majority-minority" population on a national scale in the next century will not repeat the story told in this book, nor will the many local transitions from now to then follow any single script. Still, the elements and forces of change that transformed Community District 4 are already at work elsewhere and will recur in varying combinations and patterns in the coming decades. If our goal as citizens and neighbors is indeed, in Lani Guinier's definition, "an integrated body politic in which all perspectives are represented, and in which all people work together to find common ground," we need to ask what lessons may be drawn from the Elmhurst-Corona story.

Government Matters

In contemporary America, government is involved at every step in the movement toward common ground. It is not simply by individual choice that people of so many diverse orgins live together in CD4. Individual whites, blacks, and immigrants indeed chose to move to, stay in, or leave Elmhurst-Corona, but they did so in response to shifting job opportunities, federal highway and housing programs, suburban zoning restrictions, inconsistent fair-housing law enforcement, and changing immigration policies—all the results of government actions.

Neighborhood New Yorkers endured assaults on quality of life resulting from the 1975 fiscal crisis and continuing budget cuts, clearly the product of permanent-government and mayoral decisions. Zoning regulations and diminished housing-code enforcement defined neighborhood realities for all residents of Elmhurst-Corona and set the stage for their struggles to change them. Individuals innovated new alliances and forms of organization but did so within a political field shaped by decentralized community boards, district cabinets, and school boards—structures created by city policies that dated to the very years in which Elmhurst-Corona's majority-minority transition began.

All this occurred within a field of power relationships. The power of resources in New York City faced a major threat as the speculative-electronic economy dispersed nationally and globally, and the office buildings that had housed it began to empty. The power of numbers, divided by race, ethnicity, language, religion, and cultural background, faced new organizational challenges. Lubricatory power, either serving to contain the coalescing power of numbers in neighborhood New York or used on its behalf by wardens, renegade professionals, and citywide advocates, was more important than ever.

Contemporary antigovernment conservatives maintain that declining quality of life in neighborhood New York is inevitable. They expect those who can to practice "choice" and move away, and those who cannot to "trust the market" and "display a healthy respect for the natural economic development of the city."[1] Critics of this view point to the underlying power arrangements that such ideas reinforce. They show how permanent-government projects are promoted as "common sense" and "development" and defended "almost entirely on the basis of how many jobs or how much tax revenue they would produce," whether or not such claims can be substantiated. They also show how any use of public resources for the improvement of neighborhood quality of life is denigrated as "redistribution" to "low-income groups or 'minorities.' "[2]

Elmhurst-Corona civic activists had their own ideas about what was "natural." They did not accept the permanent government's and Queens developers' faith in "market" solutions to inappropriate zoning, unsafe housing, crowded schools, and unresponsive police. They joined other Queens civic activists to defeat the Quality Housing plan and win downzoning. Their local efforts resulted in three new schools and additions to others. And as crime rates rose, they called for "cops on the beat"; with similar pressure from neighborhood New Yorkers elsewhere, the Community Patrol Officer Program was phased in citywide, police numbers were restored to 1975 levels, and crime rates began to fall. Only as power relations and then government policies change do new "truths" about who gets and deserves what begin to seem "natural."

What Brings People Together?

Politics is about more than attitudes. It is also about interpersonal connections and group action. Too much social science research defines only attitude surveys as "real," and brands real-life, real-time ethnographic observation as "anecdotal" or "unrepresentative." The struggles, defeats, and victories that constitute neighborhood politics occur not because attitudes somehow change but because wardens act, leaders innovate, people meet, and numbers coalesce. Those who watch and listen systematically in places where this happens can observe politics unfold. Those who limit themselves to interviews and opinion polls miss all this and are left to design after-the-fact explanations of why political change occurs.

Community District 4's extreme racial and ethnic diversity is unique, but more neighborhoods and cities will "look like Elmhurst-Corona" as America's great transition proceeds. Some whites will resist or move away, but others will increasingly interact with new neighbors across ethnic and racial lines. As this occurs, people first sort one another according to their own sets of racial and ethnic categories; then, over time, they begin to add to their networks actual persons with names, occupations, families, and individual characteristics.[3] Where and how in Elmhurst-Corona does this second step start to happen?

First, self-introductions, exchanges of pleasantries, and sometimes friendships arise between neighbors on blocks and in apartment buildings. New residents frequently next encounter a local warden who offers advice on garbage collection or other immediate street and building matters. Sometimes they are also approached by members of block, tenant, co-op, and civic associations, or they see a newsletter or flyer and find their way to an organization meeting. Only a few will become active members of such groups, but along with neighborly ties these are the residential frontlines in bridging ethnic and racial borders. Categorical and personal relations with others, of course, also emerge in workplaces, and ties there affect the way people view and relate to neighbors.

For many whites, houses of worship are another site of cross-ethnic and cross-racial contact.[4] Immigrants also establish their own houses of worship where languages other than English are spoken and little contact occurs with established white or black Americans—yet even here one often finds diverse congregations sharing space, and second-generation English-speaking youth groups beginning to appear. Just as Dutch, German, Polish, Italian, and other European-language congregations in Elmhurst-Corona's past became English-speaking and multiethnic over time, today's new houses of worship may face similar futures; already non-Chinese worship at Elmhurst's Ch'an Buddhist temple. In both predictable and no doubt unexpected ways, houses of worship will be important locations for solidifying and expanding interethnic and interracial ties.

Neighbor-to-neighbor relationships and houses of worship are "private," but wardens and civic groups involve residents with government policies and with efforts to influence and change them. Wardens ask neighbors to "obey the law" about the placement of garbage for collection and other matters; block watchers and "feelers in the community" form connections to police precincts, district-level city agency personnel, and local government bodies such as community boards and their district managers. Block and civic associations do the same, and tenant and co-op associations, though formed for "private" purposes, make use of public laws and courts and frequently take on civic-association-like activities.[5]

This field of local political action brings participants together across racial and ethnic lines and can be expected to do so even more in coming decades. It is what these wardens and associations actually do, however, not any "joiner" impulse, that motivates them and their supporters. Most important, they struggle against assaults on the quality of life resulting from government shrinkage and budget cuts. In Elmhurst-Corona people of all races want effective policing to control drug trafficking, prostitution, gambling, and illegal dumping; and they want livable neighborhoods where parking, public transportation, schools, recreation facilities, access to hospitals, and a safe, decent housing supply are in balance.

The most universally supported quality-of-life concerns in CD4 focus on children: the two-decades-long struggle, still not over, *against* school overcrowding and *for* more youth programs. White wardens fought for expanded hours at the Elmhurst Branch Library and organized afterschool and summer youth programs and the Teen Center; black wardens ran summer cleanup and sports programs and tutored at the Lefrak City Branch Library; Latin Americans organized afterschool and summer programs; Latin American, Asian, and African American candidates ran for seats on School Board 24, and a Chinese woman from Elmhurst was its first member of color.

Some youth programs drew on CD4's annual two-dollar-per-child city youth services allocation and supplemented this money with volunteer adult effort. The need for sites, programs, and adult involvement, however, is far greater than what exists, and schools and youth programs remain underfunded. In 1989 two-thirds of New York City voters favored tax increases over cuts in programs, and six years later 61 percent of New York City parents were ready to pay higher taxes to improve public education. In 1997 two-thirds of New Yorkers remained dissatisfied with their city's schools.[6] Parents of all races well understand the importance of education to their children's future. Joint efforts to secure more resources for schools and youth programs will promote racial and ethnic comity and accord.

Expect More Rituals

Rituals, ceremonies, commemorations, and demonstrations are "transmitters of culture" in human societies and are "generated in social relations." As culture becomes more variegated and complex and social relations more categorical and unpredictable, new rituals emerge to affirm old beliefs and routines, to integrate new ensembles of cultural elements, and to "bring order into experience" for changing groups of neighborhood co-residents.[7]

Rituals of ethnic celebration are created to mark the presence of new ethnic groups and to affirm the persistence of established ones, and more of these rituals will appear as American communities become more diverse. Their ethnic particularity, however, rubs against the multiethnicity of street neighborhoods and city districts; hence, they migrate to central locations where they draw upon areawide populations; Israeli and St. Patrick's Day parades in Manhattan, the Dominican parade in the Bronx, the West Indian–American Day Carnival in Brooklyn, and ethnic festivals in Flushing Meadows–Corona Park provide examples. Their audiences, however, become more diverse over time; public officials of all races appear as marchers and guests; and their formal properties grow increasingly alike.[8]

Civic rituals such as Christmas tree lightings and Memorial Day observances are organized by established whites and celebrate values of continuity. They are revived when newcomers increase in number and these values are under question, but those that remain inwardly focused are unstable and may not survive. When they do, it is because they begin to incorporate newcomers, not only as audience members but as participants, and the parochial assertion of local priority yields to the communal value of place. When this happens, civic rituals no longer belong exclusively to their creators, and like Corona's tree lighting they continue because they now help "neighborhoods . . . retain their identities and boundaries despite . . . shifts in ethnic composition."[9]

Whereas civic rituals deemphasize ethnicity and race, rituals of inclusion openly celebrate diversity. Cultural Sharing Days, International Nights, and Parades of Nations symbolize multiethnic and multiracial communities and seek to promote tolerance, respect, and harmony. In these quintessentially American rituals the distilled, vestigial form in which European ethnicities survive becomes the model for assimilating new foreign cultures. The living cultures of adult immigrants evident in rituals of ethnic celebration risk trivialization as they are reduced to a song, a sharable food, a dance, a costume, a greeting, and a holiday. Perhaps rituals of inclusion work best when enacted by children, because assemblages of children are in themselves a positive symbol to adults of all races and ethnicities.[10]

If participation matters more than content in rituals of inclusion, content is paramount in quality-of-life rituals. These submerge ethnic and racial diversity to stress common neighborhood identity in celebrating new parks and clean streets, or in protesting drugs, prostitution, subway crowding, and other assaults on quality of life. Neighborhood residents who "share a common fate at the hands of city planners, realtors, [and] politicians" are reminded by these rituals that they "simply cannot ignore each other."[11] The power of numbers is valorized symbolically in quality-of-life rituals, and they bolster the work of wardens and local associations.

Listen to Women (They Listen to Each Other)

Early in my fieldwork, warden Bill Donnelly compared Elmhurst during the 1930s with the contemporary neighborhood:

> In those days. . . . only the rich had telephones. We had no telephone, and yet I couldn't do anything and get home before my mother knew about it, and met me on the way in the door with a smack. So my father called it the mothers' union—all the mothers were plugged into the clothesline, he said. Well, the world hasn't changed. The school bus for the primary school stops in front of my house. So there are eighteen to twenty kids and a good collection of mothers and fathers every morning waiting for the school bus. One morning a year ago, the kids were all lined up, and a mother was coming down the block, a new American from Korea, with a kid late for the bus. . . . And a little [Indian] boy on the end of the line—you could see this little lawyer's mind at work—he peels off and heads for home because he's got a good idea. His mother wasn't there; she didn't come with him; he's going home. So the kids get on the bus, the Korean mother packs her kid on the bus, and then she steps over and says to this little boy who's going up the road, "Where you go?" He says, "Home, I'm sick, I've got a cold." She opens his mouth, looks in, and says, "No sick. On bus." He goes on the bus. And I said to myself the mothers' union is alive and working. . . . The fathers can bitch and belly all they want, but the mothers are going to make sure that it all works out.

In the mid-1970s women began moving into Elmhurst-Corona's district-level political field and unblocking the channels between whites, immigrants, and blacks. As the sociologist Herbert Gans observes, "In communities where similarity of backgrounds . . . is scarce, collective action requires a sizeable amount of interpersonal negotiation and compromise—and leaders who can apply personal skills that persuade people to ignore their differences."[12] It was women more than men who supplied this leadership, and one should be prepared for more female leadership everywhere as America's majority-minority transition unfolds.[13] Male wardens continued to be active in Elmhurst-Corona civic politics, but by the mid-1980s women held key leadership positions, and racial and ethnic relations began to change.

White Women

As district manager Rose Rothschild put it, "Men work, but women are at home, and talk to each other about children and schools." She became a parent leader at PS89 in the early 1970s "as the Spanish were moving into the neighborhood. I was the first to have things translated into Spanish for the parents, using a teacher to do it." After joining CB4 she served as health committee chair in the early 1980s; there she solidified ties with white female CB4 members and met social service and health-care providers of all races. In her 1984 CB4 leadership bid, Rothschild was supported by Carmela George—who had organized block associations with advice from Democratic Party leader Helen Marshall, an African American, and with help from her own white and Latin American female neighbors—and by Judy D'Andrea, another block association leader. As district manager, Rothschild worked closely with black, Latin American, white, and Asian women, including several female CB4 members.

The core of white female leaders in CD4—Rothschild, George, D'Andrea, and Lucy Schilero of the Coalition of United Residents for a Safer Community—were Italian. Two others—Miriam Levenson at CB4 and Helma Goldmark in Sherwood Village—were Jewish. These women belonged to the last two white ethnic groups to arrive in Elmhurst-Corona, both of which had faced hostility and housing discrimination into the 1950s. Jews were long "restricted" from many apartment buildings. And Italians, as Bill Donnelly recalled, endured "the lament of the old established people here [that] we were going to have tomatoes and green peppers grown where the front lawns used to be, grape arbors in the driveways, and a goat grazing in the back yard." Carmela George's family encountered these attitudes from Irish and German neighbors in Corona in the mid-1940s, and Lucy Schilero was called "a black guinea" when her family arrived in Elmhurst in the 1950s. Italians and Jews later constituted most of the "white flight" from Corona Plaza and Lefrak City and were among those antagonistic to black and immigrant arrivals in the mid-1960s and 1970s. Still, when cooperative relations between established whites and newcomers began to form, it was women from these two groups who nurtured them.

Black Women

African American female leadership was also evident by the mid-1980s with Helen Marshall, Edna Baskin, and others active in the Lefrak City Tenants Association, the Democratic Party, and CB4. These women were heirs to the "race woman" tradition of outspokenness and organizational leadership in the black community, and they worked with their "race man" counterparts. Nonetheless, it was women—especially Marshall and Baskin—who formed links between their own networks and Elmhurst-Corona whites, white women in particular.

"Women can relate to each other around shopping, children, and daily neighborhood activities," Baskin explained. "I started organizing my group in the supermarket, putting up signs, and then talking to women on Saturday mornings. . . . [Borough president] Claire Shulman, Rose [Rothschild], and Miriam [Levenson] are the women's leadership that I can relate to. [Women] are the glue that holds things together in this community." When the C-Town incident occurred in 1991, Ruby Mohammad called Rothschild, who then called Baskin;

the Community Task Force was begun, and it included several black female members.

Immigrant Women

Among Latin Americans male leaders dominated the many nationality-based associations, but it was women—Haydee Zambrana, Nayibe Nuñez-Berger, Aida Gonzalez—who formed organizations seeking to unite all Latin Americans. At CB4 it was again women—Clara Salas and Zambrana—who remained members for more than a year or two. Their appointments, moreover, came during the mid-1980s when CB4 was undergoing its own transition to female leadership.

Although Korean leaders were predominantly male, it was a woman—Daok Lee Pak—who became the first Korean CB4 member.[14] Edna Baskin told me that when she first met the male leaders of the Korean American Association of Mid-Queens, "even though Mrs. Pak made the introductions," they asked why women in the United States "took such an active role. I asked my husband [Ron Baskin] to answer them, sensing they would listen better to a man. He told them that women are the glue also."[15]

Why Women?

Why was it women more than men who formed this network of cross-racial ties in Elmhurst-Corona? Sociologist Nancy Chodorow would trace these patterns to maternal socialization, which incorporates daughters into a world of women characterized by "relational" identification and "connection to other people," whereas sons exit this world to adopt male roles emphasizing "positional" identification and individual achievement. Consequently, as linguist Deborah Tannen observes, women's ways of talking are more likely to stress "a community of connection," whereas men's talk operates "to preserve their independence in a hierarchical world." Futhermore, as historian Temma Kaplan posits, "the gender system of their society . . . assigns women the responsibility of . . . guarding their neighbors, children, and mates against danger"; under conditions of change "a sense of community that emerges from shared routines binds women to one another" and "politicizes the networks of daily life." Political scientist Carol Hardy-Fanta concludes that women more than men "focus on . . . connecting people to other people to achieve change" but that such "participatory qualities are [not] the unique realm of women [and] these skills and values are within the abilities of men."[16]

In Elmhurst-Corona women certainly acted to "guard their children." When one district cabinet meeting turned to Parks Department capital projects, Rose Rothschild remarked, "I always suggest preschool buildings [in park reconstruction plans] because I'm a mother. Men never look at that." Nonetheless, men such as Bob Tilitz, Al Fernicola, Richard Italiano, Tom Rodriguez, and Al Blake did champion library, afterschool, and recreation programs for school-age youth. Male wardens, particularly men who grew up or had long resided in the neighborhood, could also possess "a sense of community that emerges from shared routines."[17]

As for race, women moved sooner from categorical to personal ties, relating more readily to women of another race as women than men did to other men. The "positional" and "hierarchial" values that continue to mark race relations in the United States are not only more characteristic of male socialization and gender roles but reinforced by the structural relationships of workplaces and hierarchical organizations. Many of Elmhurst-Corona's women leaders were housewives or worked from their homes; men were more likely to be employed in formal settings. Women who entered civic politics, moreover, had frequently had experience in school, religious, or block association groups where improvisation and abilities to involve others were more important than tables of organization and titled positions.

Strengthen Local Democracy

As the quality of life in neighborhood New York worsened after 1975, local "parapolitical" activity expanded, and the city's 3,500 civic, block, tenant, ethnic, and other associations in 1977 grew to 8,000 by 1995. Community boards, where many of these groups voiced their views on municipal services, land-use issues, and budget recommendations, provided new arenas for local politics at a time when political party clubs were becoming less powerful. Whatever their shortcomings, community boards strengthened local democracy. "Resolution of the grievances experienced at the level of communities," organizer Prudence Posner points out, "requires the exercise of power that can enforce policies, regulations, and restrictions on very powerful economic entities." This power of numbers working through community boards was exemplified in the 1989 downzoning of Elmhurst-Corona and in the 1996 defeat of Mayor Giuliani's megastore plan.[18]

Neighborhood New Yorkers of all races—in 1988, 78 percent of Roman Catholic "white ethnics," 79 percent of Asians, 84 percent of African Americans, and 88 percent of Latin Americans—favored *more* government decentralization.[19] City charters affirming the power of community boards were approved by voters in 1975 and 1989. Eight-year limits for city council members, approved twice by voter referendum, will take effect in 2001, potentially devolving more power to the district-level political field. Still, community boards by the mid-1990s were less inclusive than they could have been. Their members were appointed, not elected, and particularly in racially and ethnically diverse community districts they did not fully "look like New York City."

Making Community Boards More Inclusive

Appointment need not have unrepresentative results if it is directed toward creating "an integrated body politic in which all perspectives are represented." (District school board elections, moreover, *have* produced unrepresentative results and are marked by low turnout.)[20] Community board appointments are made annually by New York City's five borough presidents with advice and consent from the city council members representing each community district. This appointment process certainly broadened CB4's membership after the mid-1980s, but it has not yet produced a board that "looks like Elmhurst-Corona." By the the mid-1990s whites and blacks were overrepresented, and Latin Americans and Asians still underrepresented.

Like other elected officials, city council members have little interest in expanding their electorates and encouraging demands from new groups; doing so could make reelection less likely and empower potential rivals.[21] Council members cannot be expected to produce more diverse results in community board appointments until the power of numbers—registered voters—forces them to do so. Whites and blacks are not so much deliberately overrepresented on CB4 as appointed according to how sitting officials read their electorates. Stronger affirmative pressure toward inclusiveness is needed from the borough presidents, even to the point of turning down all a council member's recommendations if more diverse appointments are not forthcoming.

At the Queens hearings of the Mayor's Commission on Hispanic Concerns in 1986, one commissioner asked an aide representing council member Joseph Lisa Jr., "How many Hispanics are there on Community Board 4?" The aide dissembled, stating, "It is representative of the community." This was not true; Elmhurst-Corona was at least one-third Latin American, but there were only six Latin Americans among thirty-nine CB4 members. Borough president Claire Shulman was more honest. "On community boards, if an Hispanic wants to become a member they can easily be considered," she testified. "They can get [applications] from [my Hispanic liaison]. Five years ago we tried to get Hispanic members. Some did apply, but many work two jobs and can't come to night meetings. I have the power to appoint to commmunity boards, and will appoint if they are interested in community affairs." Shulman's response reflected modest steps to make community boards more representative and identified some of the real barriers to greater immigrant participation.

In 1992 city council member John Sabini told the political scientist Michael Jones-Correa, then studying the many nationality-based Latin American associations in Jackson Heights, that he did not "know of any Latino groups holding regular meetings."[22] Subsequent CB4 appointments reflected not only Sabini's unfamiliarity with the Latin Americans in his district but also his sensitivity to black votes in Lefrak City: African American numbers on CB4 rose; Latin American membership did not.

Reinventing Government from the Bottom Up

"Voting is a relatively inefficient mechanism for communicating voter concerns on particular issues," political scientist Jeffrey Davidson observes. Community board meetings, in contrast, provide both members and audience an arena where "average citizens can be stirred to overcome their apprehension [of government, politics, and politicians] and attempt to make their wishes known."[23] Community boards and district cabinets are also places where "ground truth" can be obtained from persons who are "at the location in question and observe conditions firsthand."[24]

Bottom-up ideas about reinventing city government have received diminishing attention during the last three mayoral administrations. Nonetheless, as David Rogers, a student of New York's decentralization experience, concludes, "Ways must be found to link better the increasingly politicized and agitated neighborhoods with the power elites of the city, [and] to ensure that quality of life considerations are given higher priority in land use and service delivery decisions. As things stand now, the city . . . follows a style of reactive, top down, and crisis management that only triggers off a similarly reactive style from the neighborhoods, lessening the chances for the collaborative planning and service delivery that are so essential to the city's future."[25]

The key to making Rogers's recommendation work is the district manager, the person who receives and filters local ground truth from board members and residents, presides over the district cabinet, and crystallizes policy recommendations in annual District Needs statements. Cuts in the district managers' budgets work against more democratic and effective city government.

The city's fifty-nine district cabinets are also potential sites of municipal unions' involvement in reinventing city government. Here union members work across bureaucratic agency lines to solve local problems. Rather than limiting themselves to salaries and benefits, city workers' unions could enlist their own members' ground truth in proposing service improvements, management strategies, and productivity gains from the bottom up.[26]

Regulating and Inspecting the Quality of Life

Reversing two decades of assaults on the quality of life in neighborhood New York will require improved enforcement of many city regulations. More personnel are needed to supervise and coordinate housing and building code compliance control of illegal dumping, and workplace safety and wage-and-hour inspections.[27] Civic groups, community boards, and district cabinets support this increase. Against them stand "free market" conservatives championing deregulation.[28] Giuliani advisor Peter Salins is correct that "the poor receive much less benefit from the city's regimen of subsidies and price regulations than do the [upper] middle classes and the rich." This, however, is as much an argument for redirecting budget resources and tax expenditures to quality-of-life concerns in neighborhood New York as it is a justification for deregulation and cutting taxes.[29]

In the struggle for reregulation, differences in attitudes toward government between white and black Americans, on one hand, and immigrants, on the other, need to be acknowledged. White and African American civic activists seek to restore an era when government was on their side; most immigrants never experienced such an era. The working- and lower-middle-class white civic activists of Elmhurst-Corona benefited from government policies such as Social Security, workplace regulations, housing and homeowner-loan programs, and the public transportation, higher education, and health care that continued to expand until the 1975 fiscal crisis. Blacks began to enjoy greater access to these benefits as a result of 1960s civil rights laws that also widened their employment and housing opportunities. Indeed, few African Americans at all would live in Elmhurst-Corona if "the market" prevailed rather than the 1968 Fair Housing Act under which discriminatory practices were ended in Lefrak City.

Immigrants arrived mainly after 1975 and have seen only cuts and shrinkage in government services. Many paid substantial sums to navigate the immigration laws, utilize family reunification provisions, and become citizens. Some resent paying taxes, and many bring home-country fears and distancing tactics with respect to government. They ask what their taxes in fact provide as school crowding and other quality-of-life problems worsen. Immigrant small business proprietors object to revenue-producing city fines, which they see as arbitrary and punitive. And some business owners shade or evade the law, and welcome reduced enforcement of housing, zoning, and labor regulations. They find allies in conservatives who lionize immigrant entrepreneurship in order to promote deregulation and tax cuts.[30]

Despite these differences, points of commonality emerge and need to be embraced by established resident and newcomer alike. Korean merchants protest city inaction on a Korean megastore that evades zoning regulations; Chinese Staff and Workers Association organizers target employers who pay subminimum wages; the Centro Civic Colombiano and Queens Hispanic Coalition join other Queens residents to fight privatization of Elmhurst Hospital. Room exists for negotiation and agreement among all neighborhood New Yorkers as to where and how government can improve their quality of life.

Increasing Coterminality

The overlapping boundaries of New York's fifty-nine community districts, fifty-one city council districts, and thirty-two school districts serve to "fragment" and "diffuse" the "loyalities, interests, and demands" of neighborhood New Yorkers seeking to influence city policy.[31] Only community districts have any historic and geographical integrity. School districts have none; city council districts, equally artificial, will again be redrawn after the next census. David Rogers urges that "school districts . . . be integrated into district cabinets to facilitate more needed collaboration with other city agencies," and political scientist Joseph Viteritti argues that "[full] coterminality between community districts, school districts, and council districts is essential in order to achieve effective community government."[32]

In moving toward this goal, the "one-person, one-vote" question arises because community district populations vary in size. The integrity of their existing boundaries would be forfeited if they too were redrawn every ten years, but creative alternatives are imaginable: joining very small adjacent districts; giving very large ones two council seats; grouping several districts into like-sized constituencies with two or more representatives, perhaps elected by proportional representation; new modes of computerized, weighted voting.

After a frustrating 1988 district cabinet discussion of personnel cuts in Elmhurst-Corona parks, Rose Rothschild joked, "I'm going to run for mayor, because I know where the needs are. With my luck, I'd get voted in." As political scientists Susan and Norman Fainstein pointed out, in 1991 New York had not yet "had a mayoral candidate with roots in neighborhood politics."[33] (Unsuccessful 1997 Democratic candidate Ruth Messinger, a former district school board member, was the first.) Steps toward "full coterminality" would make this more likely.

Bid Adieu to a *Longue Durée*

With the dispersal and deconcentration of the speculative-electronic economy that began in the early 1980s, New York City is no longer "the capital of the world," and no single city will replace it. Instead, what Fernand Braudel calls the "coherent and fairly fixed series of relationships between realities and social masses" which shaped New York's permanent government and neighborhoods for three hundred years is now winding down.[34] In its place, neither rhetorical celebrations of "the world city" nor the policies of the last three mayors offer much of a future to the children of Elmhurst-Corona.

In contemporary New York the "giant sucking sound" is that of government subsidies and personal income flowing upward to the fortunate fifth and outward to the suburbs. In addition to the continuing alphabet soup of permanent-government tax breaks and "hardship" property-assessment reductions, the Giuliani administration's twenty-seven corporate "designer packages" through May 1997 totaled $310 million per year in taxes forgone. Subtracting the 61,000 jobs these deals "retained" from the 120,000 private-sector jobs added since 1993, and also subtracting 46,000 government jobs lost since then, New York City had added only 13,000 unsubsidized private-sector jobs.[35]

Against this figure stand the 1989–1992 loss of 330,000 jobs, a labor force participation rate of only 55 percent, and an unemployment rate by July 1997 of 10 percent, or some 320,000 people looking for work. Another 80,000 persons were slated to lose public assistance by 2002 with the expectation that they would move "from welfare to work." For New Yorkers with jobs, the gap between rich and poor continued to widen. Between 1991 and 1996 the wages of persons making $25,000 or less fell by 7 percent, while earnings for those making $75,000 or more rose by as much as 60 percent. And an increasing share of employment was going to commuters. In 1995 they held 21 percent of all New York City jobs; then in the first quarter of 1997 the city gained 20,000 jobs, but resident employment fell by 21,000.[36]

This meager job picture, moreover, occurred in the midst of a speculative-electronic boom. By the end of 1996, 77 million Americans—an all-time peak—had invested in the stock market, and in summer 1997 the Dow-Jones average topped 8,000. Still, employment in the securities industry of New York City rose by only 5,600 during 1996, since nationally and globally dispersed trading was taking place everywhere. And part of even this job growth resulted from the increasing role of the city's investment houses in overseas mergers and acquisitions, activities in which fewer people doing deals in New York City may be anticipated in the future.[37]

New York's *longue durée* was over. The $2 billion a year in subsidies to fill empty Manhattan office buildings and "retain" speculative-electronic firms was not producing enough jobs for neighborhood New Yorkers.[38]

Grow the Real Economy

Beneath events, conjunctures, and even long-lasting social orders, the "sites of cities endure" in relation to "geographical constraint" and the "linkage of the local ecosystem with other [systems] translocally."[39] The natural advantages of its harbor first determined New York City's physical location, and public investment in "the Great Dock" in 1676, the Erie canal in 1825, and three centuries of waterfront development maintained its centrality in overseas trade and the national economy. Countinghouses arose around the port and an expanding hinterland to supply it, and by the twentieth century they had evolved into the downtown-midtown office-building complex and what is still the largest regional economy in the nation. An infrastructure of bridges, tunnels, subways, and highways consolidated employment, land values, wealth, and face-to-face decision-making in the Manhattan core.[40]

All this is now changing, and jobs for neighborhood New Yorkers in the new social order will depend upon renewed attention to the city's geographical constraints and translocal linkages. Moves to cheapen the cost of labor will do little to benefit neighborhood New York, but policies to lower land costs and improve transportation could provide the city's employers with competitive advantages in both the regional and global economies. Instead of subsidizing Manhattan office rents in an effort to retain companies that are leaving anyway, New York could "let the market find its own level" and allow falling rents to spiral outward into the rest of city. An abrupt halt to permanent-government aid, rather than a planned shift of public support to the real economy, would leave a hole in the city's budget: receipts from the property-tax would drop, and so would income tax collections—in 1995, for instance, the heavily subsidized securities sector accounted for only 5 percent of New York's jobs, but 17 percent of all private-sector wages. For neighborhood New Yorkers, however, the budget is already full of holes, and tax money from permanent-government sources will decline in the future. Some speculative-electronic firms will remain in the city because of their executives' life-style preferences, and for them policies could be adopted immediately to award tax benefits only for "job creation" or retention verified by payroll-tax receipts.[41]

Downshifting the city's commercial rents from their artificially high levels could help retain employers and jobs that move to cheaper suburban locations but still require proximity to the region's suppliers, business services, and 18 million consumers.[42] Some jobs do leave New York City for overseas sites, but more move within its regional borders. As the economist Paul Krugman explains, "When you look at the economies of modern cities, what you see is a process of localization: A steadily rising share of the work force produces services that are sold only within that same metropolitan area. [These] activities . . . make up the . . . employment that occupies most people in modern cities."[43]

In addition, U.S. exports increased by 50 percent between 1990 and 1995, and the New York region still houses the largest East Coast port complex, one employing 165,000 workers. Beginning in the mid-1950s, however, overseas shipping shifted from Brooklyn to New Jersey with its direct connections to inland trucking and rail networks. Docks and cranes for containerized exports and imports were erected, and by 1990 more than 90 percent of sea cargo was moving through the Jersey ports.

The rail-freight tunnel that the Port Authority of New York and New Jersey was created to build in the 1920s was never constructed, and both foreign imports and New York City's manufactured goods have to be carried either by rail north to Albany and then south, or more expensively by truck across the George Washington Bridge and over a road system increasingly threatened with deterioration and gridlock. The public administration scholar Annmarie Hauck Walsh notes that "all of the highways, loans, partnerships, industrial parks, and tax abatements that authorities in the city have funded cannot produce a fraction of the economic advantage that low cost and efficient freight access to the container port facilities and to the interstate lines could have provided to manufacturing in the boroughs of New York."

As world trade boomed in the 1990s, the U.S. trucking system approached saturation, and rail-freight traffic revived, increasing to 40 percent of U.S. haulage by 1996. Asian exports arriving on the eastern seaboard for nationwide distribution have grown, and global shipping companies have turned to larger vessels and use fewer ports. By 2000 a new generation of international ships will require fifty-foot deep docks. New Jersey's ports hit bedrock at forty feet, but Brooklyn's underused docks are sixty-five feet deep.

U.S. Representative Jerrold Nadler sees New York City's disadvantaged position in the geography of national distribution and overseas trade as a major cause of its manufacturing job losses, and since the late 1970s he has advocated construction of a Brooklyn–New Jersey rail-freight tunnel. With the larger ships that eventually will service only one East Coast "hub" port linked to trucking, rail, and midsized coastal shipping, existing port jobs in the New York region as well as manufacturing are at risk. The $1 billion costs of either blasting the New Jersey harbor to fifty-foot depths or constructing the trans–Hudson River rail-freight tunnel are similar; other port facilities, moreover, will need to be enlarged at a cost of $3 billion, whether on one or both sides of the harbor. In 1997 Mayor Giuliani endorsed Nadler's plan.[44]

Three years earlier Giuliani had backed another proposed tunnel, one to extend suburban rail lines from Grand Central and Penn Stations to lower Manhattan, and in 1997 Governor George Pataki began planning studies for this "multibillion dollar" project. Whether both tunnels can or should be funded—one to grow the real economy, the other to bail out lower Manhattan's permanent government again and allow commuters to avoid the city's subways—are critical questions for the city's future.[45]

Encourage Small Business

"Where large organizations are relied upon for economic expansion and development, [and] small organizations find little opportunity to multiply, to find financing, and to add new work," Jane Jacobs warned in 1969, "the economy inevitably stagnates." Notwithstanding the flow of economic favors to big landlords and corporations since 1975, during 1993–1995 New York City's small businesses created 80,000 jobs, and large firms lost 38,000.[46] The number of manufacturing jobs held steady at 280,000 after 1992, and experienced a slight increase in 1995 (export-led manufacturing nationwide expanded more robustly). Change within the city's manufacturing sector is intense, however, with an ongoing shift from standardized to "differentiated" production. Mass-market, assembly-line factories continued to leave the city (the Taystee Bread, Farberware, and Swingline Stapler closings, for example, received considerable attention), but smaller, more numerous "batch" manufacturing firms proliferated.

These companies respond to customized local and even international "niche markets" for furniture, metal and glass products, jewelry, commercial printing, microbrewery beer, paper products, construction materials, office furnishings, specialty foods, arts and entertainment supplies, and garment industry innovations.[47] The planner Roberta Brandes Gratz explains that "30 percent of the [city's] former manufacturing buildings vacant in 1985 were reoccupied by 1990. . . . High-productivity manufacturing and the valued jobs it brings are coming back, in new configurations that incorporate new technology. . . . These enterprises employ local residents, train low-skilled workers, provide classic moving-up opportunities, and enjoy the stabilizing effect of being part of or near residential communities. [They] create three to four times as many secondary jobs as the business, financial, or retail sector."[48]

Affordable rents are important to the growth of small firms and differentiated production, and to the nurturing of business districts where suppliers, competitors, and customers are close at hand. Between 1992 and 1996 there was an "explosion of computer, software, and multimedia companies in the city," including some that moved to New York from nearby suburbs and even from California for the "benefits of agglomeration." Despite city subsidies to a "New York Information Technology Center" office building in lower Manhattan, most of these 18,000 new jobs were located neither in downtown nor in midtown but in the lower-rent manufacturing lofts and older office buldings in the "Silicon Alley" area between them.[49]

City initiatives begun in 1995 to reduce organized crime's control of commercial trash haulage and of loading activities at New York's five wholesale food markets are positive governmental moves for small business.[50] So are the transportation policy changes and modest tax breaks to assist manufacturing which were begun by the Giuliani administration in 1995 and 1996.[51] Working against these steps, however, are budget cuts, delays in highway, bridge, and tunnel repairs, and attempts to rezone manufacturing land for megastores.

At the street neighborhood level the city's small retail businesses in neighborhood shopping strips provide points of congregation and personal connection for individuals of all ages, and their owners serve as "street watchers and sidewalk guardians." At the district level, notes Queens storeowner Julie Wager, local merchants "are the people that support the myriad of charities that exist out there, not [like] the trendy franchised stores who just take the bucks and get out." High rents and megastores destroy these strands in the fabric of neighborhood New York.[52]

Plan and Tax a Regional Economy

Economic growth in New York City's future will not arise from maintaining the three hundred-year-old pattern of subsidizing land values in the Manhattan central business district. As Robert Fitch emphasizes, "The city has had a real estate strategy—expand the CBD / shrink manufacturing—which it has presented as a jobs strategy. . . . 'Growth' is not the aim. . . . What's really at stake is making certain parcels of land worth more, which is something very different."[53] As economic activity increasingly deconcentrates, locally, nationally, and globally, the vitality of New York's regional economy will depend upon reducing internal barriers to the movement of labor, materials, and products. Lower, unsubsidized land costs, improved transportation linkages, restored and expanded local quality of life, and a healthy, well-educated work force will be needed throughout the region.

What stands in the way of regional economic expansion is what the economist Carol O'Cléireacáin calls "the growing discontinuity between city boundaries and the functioning of the real economy." A divided political structure of city, suburban, and state jurisdictions reinforces inequalities in wealth, public amenities, and education.[54] It also disadvantages New York in the global arena. Most large cities around the world already benefit from regional planning and governance, as do many U.S. cities, particularly those with growing economies.[55] New York City last expanded its political boundaries in 1898, and it is improbable that this will happen again. Decisive political power over the city, therefore, will continue to reside in the state capital in Albany.[56]

"In New York," O'Cléireacáin explains, "the state controls all city taxes, even charging a fee to administer the income and sales taxes, and setting rules for the property tax." In 1983 New York State passed a 10 percent capital gains tax on the sale of buildings worth $1 million or more, virtually all of which were located in New York City; it thus captured billions in tax benefits from the city's 1980s real estate boom. Other tax revenues that could tap economic activity located within the city have been blocked by the state: the city's income tax has been cut and made less progressive; the stock transfer tax, which by the mid-1990s would have been worth $2 billion per year, was repealed by the state in 1980; business and legal services are excluded from the sales tax; elite nonprofit organizations pay no property or sales taxes.[57]

Commuter income, amounting to more than a third of the city's $220 billion in annual personal earnings, continues to be taxed at a small fraction of the resident rate; even economists Charles Brecher and Raymond Horton of the Citizens Budget Commission agree that "present commuter rates are unreasonably low."[58] In the absense of a unified regional tax base to support infrastructure and human capital investment, equalization of New York's commuter and resident tax rates would add $1 billion to the city's annual budget—but this is unlikely to happen. As O'Cléireacáin emphasizes, "State legislators from suburban New York feel the anti-tax mood so strongly they do not want to vote for any tax increase on their constituents." They are willing, however, to raise transit fares and City University tuition for New York City residents.[59]

Conservative economists rail against any tax increases on the city's expanding economic sectors or its fortunate fifth. They argue that "the combined load of New York City and State income, sales, and property taxes is the highest in the country," and cite studies finding that "the tax burden in New York [State] is . . .

34 percent above the national average [in 1996]."[60] What they do not emphasize is that output per worker in New York City is 46 percent higher than nationwide, and average wages are 57 percent higher. With much of this substantially higher city income concentrated at the top of the economic ladder, New York's taxes are much less out of line than antitax advocates suggest.[61]

"Taxes are not just dead weights," holds the economist Robert Heilbroner. "They are the means by which a society gathers its resources for public purposes. They are the ways we pay for our defense, education, roads, . . . clean streets, policemen, water supplies, . . . and old-age . . . support."[62] As taxes shrink, so does the quality of life in neighborhood New York. "Personal responsibility" cannot build schools, fund sufficient youth programs, put cops on the beat, reduce subway crowding, inspect unsafe homes and workplaces, or eradicate illegal dumping, gambling, and drug dealing. Over the past two decades, Elliot Sclar and Walter Hook explain, America's "tax-cutting approach [and] drop in public revenues [have] led to a loss of critical public investments in both the infrastructure and work force, making our economic activities more costly and less efficient. In addition, the upward redistribution of income implied by such policies has not led to a new burst of productive private investment. Instead, it has caused domestic consumer demand to stall, which has further postponed economic revitalization. . . . More progressive tax policy would help stimulate economic growth."[63]

Color-full before Color-blind

Suppose the worst. In 2080 the all-white fortunate fifth is ensconced in gated suburbs and edge cities. Its schools, police, health-care and recreation facilities, and transportation and communication links are all private. Taxes everywhere are a pittance. For the rest of the population—now 37 percent white, 29 percent Latin American, 19 percent black, and 15 percent Asian—public schools, hospitals, parks, sanitation services, and mass transit barely function. Most wages permit only minimal subsistence. Crime and the underground economy sustain enormous numbers, and the few police officers and government inspectors do not interfere. Government statistics on income, poverty, and race are neither published nor collected. The era of big government is over. "Individual choice" and "the market" reign. People live in a "color-blind" society.[64]

Things in 2080 will not be this clear-cut. The power of numbers can be contained but not eliminated by the power of resources and its lubricatory allies. The fortunate fifth, no matter how wealthy and politically powerful, will not be solely white. And as intermarriage and cross-racial kinship blur the lines, the population may not fit so easily into current racial categories. Within the working- and lower-middle-class majority, several alternative scenarios may all find advocates and occur simultaneously: racial and ethnic group competition (encouraged by the fortunate fifth), unity among "people of color," dark-light rather than black-white polarization, rising "mixed" and "multiracial" self-identification, Latin American–styled views of "race" as appearance rather than ancestry, and the confrontation of "people of all colors" with the power of resources.[65]

The more divided the power of numbers, the more likely it is that the worst will prevail. No racial or ethnic group will be able to counter this on its own. As the political philosopher Cornel West puts it, "There will be no fundamental change in America unless we come together. It's a fact—we just have to face it." Only the fortunate fifth can afford to be "color-blind." To the extent that others find themselves only in settings filled with people who look like themselves, they will be doomed to political ineffectiveness. People will need to ensure that block and civic associations, local government bodies, ritual audiences, workplaces, and leadership slates are color-*full.*

"Ultimately, reform of our cities must arise from broad-based citizen movements for change," writes the urban politician-scholar David Rusk. "People who share a common goal find they have common enemies," asserts Robert Fitch. "A sense of what New York means could be created by community movements from below."[66] In Elmhurst-Corona people have been moving in this direction, some more consciously than others, and learning from both successes and failures. An exchange at Community Board 4 following the pool club site defeat in 1988 highlighted the need to strengthen the power of numbers.

> *Judy D'Andrea:* The high-power developers in this city are trying to eliminate the ULURP process because we stand in their way and they make political contributions to high-power politicians.
>
> *Ron Laney:* We have no power. The Board of Estimate and the Mayor opposed us.
>
> *Judy D'Andrea:* It goes back to the community. They [Bayside] get buses and go. We are not like that. We had seven people at the Board of Estimate. If we had 7,000 it would be different.

Welcome a Multiethnic, Multilingual City

Coalescing the power of numbers among whites, immigrants, and blacks, whether in Elmhurst-Corona, in New York City, or nationwide, will require reciprocal recognition of one another's concerns as well as common goals. Angelo Falcón, founder of the Institute for Puerto Rican Policy, raised this matter at a 1990 forum:

> [We] need to . . . understand that our strength is in our community and in our identification as Latinos in terms of our numbers. . . . The fact that we're 25 percent of the city's population is something we've got to find ways of leveraging [to] create some sort of counterforce. . . . The question of language policy—for

> years our people can't get services. . . . You'd think by this time that New York would already have a mechanism for incorporating new populations who don't speak the language. . . . If we're successful in getting New York to adopt a language policy . . . we're leaving a legacy . . . for future generations, . . . for the Asian community, [and] for other communities. . . . We need to frame our own issues in that broader context.[67]

Many white Americans today believe that immigrants resist learning English and that bilingual education perpetuates "linguistic separatism." In fact, of the 41 percent of New Yorkers who spoke another language at home in 1990, three-quarters *also* spoke English. The quarter who did not turned to adult English classes and the public schools to learn, but by 1993 only 30,000 English-class seats were available for 600,000 non-English-speaking adults; government support for these classes amounted to only $20 million per year, and waiting lists ranged from four months to three years. Federal bilingual education funds for the 150,000 "limited English proficiency" students in New York City's public schools had been cut by half during the 1980s, even while the number of children availing themselves of such programs continued to rise.

Children of primary school age acquire English rapidly: in New York City most of them "mainstream" from bilingual to regular classes in three years or less; many do so more quickly in Elmhurst-Corona, where the large number of different languages facilitates English learning among children themselves in both school and neighborhood play groups. Older youth have a harder time, and many immigrant high school students take longer to graduate (although their drop-out rate is lower) than U.S.-born students. Long Island Congress member and "English Only" advocate Peter King distorts the issue by emphasizing that sixth- to ninth-grade immigrant teenagers take longer than three years to "mainstream" in the crowded, underfunded city schools of the 1990s. The alternative—English-language "immersion"—works well when trained instructors, full-day programs, and small teacher-pupil ratios are provided. Even immersion proponent Diane Ravitch admits, "It is not a new [English-only] law that is needed, but better education in the English language for children and adults."[68]

Notwithstanding the meager assistance government provides, in fact today's "immigrants and their children may be acquiring English faster than in the past," Philip Martin and Elizabeth Midgley point out. Although the immigrant parents or grandparents of Elmhurst-Corona whites "rarely learned English well during their lifetimes," their children were fully or partly bilingual, and the third generation was monolingual in English. Most third-generation Latin Americans also speak English exclusively. Today, however, "the handicaps of not knowing English" are increasing, and much evidence suggests that "the three-generation shift to English may shrink to two generations by 2000."[69] Still, as the linguist Ana Celia Zentella advocates, steps to preserve the linguistic resources of America's 40 million bilingual residents could prove advantageous in the global economy of the twenty-first century. By the 1980s less than one-fifth of U.S. students studied a second language as compared with four-fifths earlier in this century.[70]

Large numbers of white Americans also believe that the country is "saturated" with foreign-born newcomers, even though today's 8 percent immigrant population is less than the 14 percent of 1910 and is not likely to reach that level before the 2040s. (New York City's higher 33 percent foreign-born population in 1995 is also below its 41 percent foreign-born peak in 1910.) Further, many mistakenly believe that the majority of newcomers are "illegal aliens." In 1995 the Census Bureau estimated that 4 million of the nation's 23 million immigrants were undocumented, or only 1 in 6. In New York City the ratio was also 1 in 6, but here 90 percent of undocumented immigrants were "overstayers" who had entered the country legally with nonresident visas, versus just 40 percent nationally. Two of New York's three largest undocumented groups, moreover, were white—Italians and Poles—and together they accounted for 1 in 9 of the city's "illegal alien" population.[71]

In Elmhurst-Corona three-quarters of the population by 1990 consisted of immigrants and their children.[72] The cries against "illegal aliens" that stirred numbers of whites in the mid-1970s continued to be raised occasionally at public meetings, by both whites and Latin Americans, but with little effect. At a 1988 school-site hearing one man asked, "How many who will go here are children of illegal aliens? . . . If they did a survey, how many would be deported along with their parents, and free up space for other children?" Only one audience member applauded, and the meeting's business resumed. CB4 did pass a resolution in 1994 calling on Mayor Giuliani to end Mayor Koch's 1985 executive order that prevented city agencies from reporting undocumented immigrants to federal authorities in cases not involving criminal activity. But later that year, when an audience member introduced "illegal aliens" as a quality-of-life problem, CB4 members Luz Leguizamo and Clara Salas objected, and the discussion ended.

Support for decreasing immigrant admissions rose from 42 to 61 percent nationally between 1977 and 1993 but has fallen since.[73] Leadership makes a difference in fanning or dampening anti-immigrant sentiments, and they run lower in New York City, where Mayor Dinkins continued the Koch executive order; so did Mayor Giuliani, who objected publicly both to its nullification by a federal court in 1997 and to the anti-immigrant positions of several national Republican leaders.[74] In Elmhurst-Corona, Carmela George and Lucy Schilero both depended on bilingual members of their block associations, and Schilero invited immigration-rights speakers to her coalition meetings. White civic associations using only English saw their numbers contract.

The 1990 and 1996 federal immigration laws raised yearly admission ceilings but restricted opportunities for family reunification. The 1990 act increased the annual number of occupational visas from 54,000 to 140,000, and by the mid-1990s U.S. technical and professional workers found their employers sponsoring lower-paid immigrants to replace them. An attempt in the 1996 bill to reduce this number and increase funds for scientific and technical U.S. education was killed by business lobbyists and supply-side conservatives who wanted even more such "quality" immigrants. The impact of this policy, curtailing "market" demands to invest in education, is enormous and affects both the U.S.-born and immigrants already here. "The question is, should immigration be encouraged or should national policy encourage training to allow those here, including blacks, to take those jobs?" asked the African American economist Arthur Brimmer. "My own view is that we should do both." Whether both are done will depend upon coalescing the power of numbers against the power of resources.[75]

In 1994, 69 percent of whites and 61 percent of blacks nationwide were registered to vote, as were only 53 percent of Latin Americans and Asians. California's Proposition 187 limiting immigrant rights, which passed in 1994, and similar national legislation proposed by Republicans and passed in 1996 have frightened legal immigrants and increased naturalization rates. The number of immigrants becoming citizens jumped nationally from 270,000 in 1990 to 1.1 million in 1996; in the New York metropolitan area the numbers rose from 30,000 in 1991 to 141,000 in 1995, and a million more immigrants were eligible for citizenship.[76]

The power of numbers in the coming century will need to cross language borders and welcome ethnic alliance. As the journalist Ellis Cose advises, "If we are wise . . . we will realize that the problems of blacks, or Latinos, or whites, or Asian-Americans, inevitably, in an inextricably interrelated society, affect us all."[77]

Overcome the Impasse of Race and Place

There are two versions of the American story. The first is one of inclusion: according to David Ward, "American nationality [is] founded on the idea of political participation rather than on common origins."[78] INS Commissioner Doris Meissner phrased it succinctly in 1996: "We have to be absolutely certain that new people learn that we live in a democratic society where there are certain things we do—vote, send kids to school, pick up the trash, join the PTA."[79] Civic politics in Elmhurst-Corona embodies this view. As district manager John Rowan put it, "The sooner those newcomers can start sharing some civic responsibilities with their older neighbors, the stronger our entire neighborhood will be." And in the words of COMET's president, Rosemarie Daraio, "We don't care who moves in as long as they obey the rules."[80]

The second version of the American story is one of exclusion, the denial of political participation on the basis of race. For Native Americans, African Americans, and Puerto Ricans dispossessed of land, personhood, and sovereignty, and for Asians who could not become citizens until 1952, opportunities for "political participation" arrived only recently—mainly after the civil rights revolution of the 1950s and 1960s—and are still being contested.

The two versions of the American story unfolded simultaneously, and both are true. In the future of us all, believers in the first version must be willing to admit the continuing existence of the second if the power of numbers is to coalesce. They must be prepared to broaden the quality-of-life agenda, which everyone can support, to include concerns of immigrants and blacks. If they do not, then civic politics itself becomes one more destructive episode within the American story of exclusion.[81]

Immigrant concerns will continue to include language issues and family reunification. For African Americans the most glaring point of exclusion in Elmhurst-Corona, as elsewhere, is residential segregation. Most black residents live in one tiny portion of Community District 4—in and around Lefrak City. The situation mirrors that of Queens generally: there is little or no income differential between blacks and whites, yet there are still concentrated black neighborhoods.[82] The situation is perpetuated by the real estate industry. People are "steered" to different neighborhoods; different financial data are utilized for whites and blacks; different information on housing availability and loans is given to persons of different races. All of this is illegal, but it continues unless lawsuits are mounted, tester evidence is collected, and real estate agents' and landlords' records are inspected by government agencies.

The national situation is well documented. Major books detailing what their titles suggest are the sociologists Douglas Massey and Nancy Denton's *American Apartheid* (1993) and economist John Yinger's *Closed Doors, Opportunities Lost* (1995). The first emphasizes that "residential segregation is the most important item remaining on the nation's civil rights agenda" and that policies to end it "do not require major changes in legislation. What they require is political will." The second concludes that "discrimination in housing and mortgage markets . . . imposes costs on us all. A balanced, comprehensive attack on this . . . would make a vital contribution to the goals of fair treatment and equal opportunity which remain central to our potential as a free, democratic—and diverse—nation."[83]

Enforcement of fair housing laws means preventing whites who discriminate from doing so. We cannot expect progress toward "an integrated body politic . . . in which all people work together to find common ground" when black people are excluded from that common ground, as even conservative urban policy scholar Roger Starr insists: "The city should make clear that all housing will be open to all who can afford to pay . . . without discrimination by race, ethnicity, or religion."[84]

How much testing and inspection are necessary? As much as for parking meters. If there were no inspections, no one would put coins in meters, but not every meter has to be checked every day to ensure compliance. Only enough inspection is needed to convince potential lawbreakers that they risk being caught. (The same is true for housing code, workplace, and other quality-of-life violations.) And when landlord and realty operations are inspected, the procedures used by bank examiners need to be followed: "The examination . . . is always begun without prior notice and in a manner that will preserve the element of surprise. . . . The examination staff should assemble near the bank as briefly and inconspicuously as possible. . . . At the beginning . . . it is important to obtain immediate control of . . . all records."[85]

People Can Change

"I think what happened in the course of the 1970s and 1980s was that the United States really redefined itself as a multiracial society," the economist Michael Piore observed in 1990. "I don't want to say there's no resentment. There is a lot. [And] the problems of working out a multiracial and multiethnic society are immense."[86] Whites confront the biggest change: after 2080 they will no longer be the majority but one of several numerical minorities. Elmhurst-Corona whites made this transition in the 1970s, and white New Yorkers in the 1980s.

After the 1986 killing of a black immigrant by white youths in Howard Beach, Jesse Jackson noted, "There is, in fact, more integration in Queens County than in the board rooms of . . . any Wall Street firm. Those good, comfortable people . . . work in more segregated offices, send their children to more segregated schools, [and] go home to more segregated communities" than do many white residents of Queens.[87] Elmhurst-Corona whites live among Latin American and Asian neighbors, and they encounter racial diversity at work and in their churches. Many work with black colleagues, and white civic leaders interact with their African American counterparts on Community Board 4 and in the Democratic Party. Their encounters with immigrants and blacks have different sources, but many whites have moved from categorical to personal relations with individual African Americans and immigrants.

Many of these whites insist they treat their acquaintances of color as individuals—as they do other whites—and not as members of groups. "You can't generalize. I don't have any bias; I judge people individually," explained Mary Walensa. Elmhurst warden Bill Donnelly told me, "It's the old problem of the gray eyes. I don't walk around thinking of myself having gray eyes, largely because I can't see them. I figure the rest of the world is the same way. I don't figure Koreans walk around thinking of themselves as Koreans. I think it's probably like the Australian Aborigines who consider themselves 'people.' "

But whites who do treat individual immigrants and African Americans in personal rather than categorical terms must be prepared to admit that others do not. Certainly the white real estate industry, many white employers, and those whites who routinely use ethnic and racial slurs do not. At one public hearing, for instance, a white CB4 member referred to a Colombian radio-car company as "a bunch of sleaze-bag Third World lowlifes." Among themselves, some white

Elmhurst-Corona leaders joked negatively about blacks. And on one occasion a white Corona grandmother I had met at a school assembly program stopped me on the street to ask about rumors that Lefrak City would be sold as cooperative apartments: "Does this mean the blacks are moving out? They cause trouble, and things are getting worse with them. We pay all our tax money for police to watch them. It's a shame."

People moving from categorical to personal relationships are sometimes caught in mid-transition. Some white Elmhurst-Corona leaders who joked privately about blacks also kissed African American Helen Marshall when greeting her. Elmhurst resident Mary Walensa told me, "The Orientals are of a higher class; the Spanish are lower, but not all, not Rosie," her Puerto Rican neighbor. And at a CB4 meeting one Latin American member announced, "We met with the Lefrak City Tenants Association. They were very nice people. I was pleasantly surprised." Black LCTA officers responded angrily, "What did you expect?" and Edna Baskin said, "I take that as an insult."

When people are spoken of and treated in negative categorical terms, they may respond in kind. As Cornel West explains, "Oftentimes, when we run up against this deep white supremacist sensibility and behavior, we then tar the whole white community with white supremacy, as if there hadn't been [any exceptions]. How easy it is to somehow generate our own homogeneous blob and call it whiteness—in the same way that white supremacy creates its homogeneous blob of blackness. That mentality says all black folk come out of that blob—one stereotype holds for all and our humanity is then rendered invisible. Our individuality is held at arm's length."[88]

The point is not to be color-blind; race, after all, is something one learns to see from childhood, and racial categories are in constant use. The goal, rather, should be to see racial identity as one among the many characteristics of every person and to appreciate the full range of human physical diversity in what always has been and is increasingly now an interconnected, color-full world.

People usually move from categorical to personal relationships not because of mysterious inner changes but because of the changing circumstances around them. Despite Mary Walensa's belief that "the ones that stay in Elmhurst don't have the prejudice," I have no reason to believe that white Elmhurst-Corona residents are fundamentally different from white residents of Flushing, Jackson Heights, Howard Beach, or Ridgewood; both tolerance and prejudice are alive in all neighborhoods, if my exposure since 1972 to white college students from all over Queens is any guide. Still, the intolerant tendencies of the 1970s *were* reversed in Elmhurst-Corona as CB4 and its civic politics acquired new leaders and more diverse participants, developing what Cornel West calls "a public sphere in which critical exchange and engagement take place. . . . Principled alliances—tension ridden, yes, but principled alliances and coalitions. That's the new kind of public sphere that we are talking about. There will be no fundamental social change in America unless we come together [within it]."[89]

The public sphere of decentralized government and civic politics moved one warden from railing against "people pollution" and "Kim" and "Wang" to welcoming black and immigrant children to a summer program and attending a four-hour program in Korean. It is also this public sphere in which black state assembly member Jeff Aubry could place on CB4's quality-of-life agenda the issue of racial discrimination should Mount Sinai Hospital buy and privatize Elmhurst Hospital: "I am concerned, with privatization, about the equality of care. If the privates don't provide it, then we don't want them taking over."

Race divides, but people can change. This book, beginning as an ethnography of one neighborhood's majority-minority transition, became a study of the roots, and weeds, of local democracy. "The political strength of citizens can only be aggregated by assembling the collective aspirations of the many into a coherent, reliable whole," writes the journalist William Greider. "This is the daunting challenge of democracy and it is difficult to do in any era. But it is not impossible."[90]

Early in my fieldwork Bill Donnelly told me, "All of life, everyplace, is the same thing—trying to get people to see that we're all in the same damn thing together. I've been standing on the street corners and hollering for fifty years, and it doesn't amount to nothing. [But] let one [other] person [say], 'Yeah, we're in the same boat together,' then everyone says, 'Hot damn, we're in this same boat together. Let's get together and paddle this boat.' "

Nothing is impossible if we believe that people can change.

Notes

Each note covers all sources between it and the preceding note.

CHE	*Chronicle of Higher Education*	*NYO*	*New York Observer*
CL	*City Limits*	*NYP*	*New York Post*
CNYB	*Crain's New York Business*	*NYT*	*New York Times*
DCP	Department of City Planning	*NYTM*	*New York Times Magazine*
DN	*New York Daily News*	*VV*	*Village Voice*
ND	*New York Newsday*	*WSJ*	*Wall Streeet Journal*
NTC	*Newtown Crier*		

Acknowledgments

1. See Goode 1990; Goode and Schneider 1994; Hagan 1994; Lamphere 1992; Lamphere, Stepick, and Grenier 1994; Stull 1990; Stull et al. 1990.
2. See Daun, Ehn, and Klein 1992; Sanjek 1992.
3. See Sanjek 1989b, 1989a.
4. Lloyd-Jones 1981:90.

Introduction: A Window on America's Great Transition

1. Bouvier and Gardner 1986:27; O'Hare 1992:18; see also Frey 1995:283. A 1996 Census Bureau study projects that whites will constitute just 53 percent of the population in 2050 (*NYT*, 3/14/96).
2. See Falcón 1985b; Tobier 1984:103–5.
3. Salvo, Ortiz, and Vardy 1992:4. For population data here and throughout the book I use City Planning Commission 1969, 1979; DCP 1984, 1992a, 1993b; Rosenwaike 1972; Salvo, Ortiz, and Vardy 1992.
4. During 1983–1989 the Elmhurst and Corona zip codes (11373, 11368) received 5.2 percent of the immigrants who arrived in New York City; a different set of figures shows that CD4's 1990 population of Latin Americans (excluding Puerto Ricans), Asians, West Indians, and

Africans—all predominantly post-1965 immigrants—amounted to 5.2 percent of their New York City total. Community District 4 (slightly smaller than the two zip code areas) contained only 1.7 percent of the city's 1980 population, however, and 1.9 percent of its 1990 total.

5. In the late twentieth century four large immigrant concentrations stand out: Chinatown; central Brooklyn, magnet to Haitians, Jamaicans, and other West Indians; Washington Heights and adjacent areas, where Dominicans predominate; and northwest Queens, where Latin Americans, Asians, other immigrants, and white and black Americans produce a mix found nowhere else in the city. See Salvo, Ortiz, and Vardy 1992: esp. Map 5-1.

6. Kornblum and Beshers 1988; Rieder 1985.

7. Foner 1987:28–29; Guinier 1994:6.

8. It was, however, the method I had chosen for researching interethnic relations in Accra, Ghana; there I studied one street of eleven apartment buildings, a population of 423 persons. See also Susser 1982.

9. Jacobs 1961:117–21. Anthropologists envision any political "field" they study as a set of linked "arenas" in which ongoing political events may be observed; the field also extends beyond these immediate "enclaves of action" to include "encapsulating" structures of power at larger-scale levels; see Swartz 1968. As Turner phrases it, "The arena is a scene for the making of a decision. . . . The field [is] the totality of coexisting entities, . . . channels of communication, [and] ideological views about the desirability or undesirability of the extant stratification [of power. Anthropologists] are interested in . . . concatenations of . . . events, relationships, [and] groups . . . which bring actors into field relationships with one another and form nodes of intersection between [arenas and] fields" (1974:102, 126–41). See also Bailey 1968:293–94, and 1969:9–16, on "political structure" and "environment."

10. Jacobs 1961:122–34.

11. Rieder acknowledges that his study concerns "the most activist and defensive cadres in Canarsie" and not "the more generous and progressive strains in the community," and that it "does not truly reflect the range of Canarsie opinion." He states, moreover, "Resistance to integration declined in the late 1970s," and by 1980 "an Italian PTA leader puts it like this. 'The race issue is way down in Canarsie. People just aren't panicking like before' " (1985:8, 201, 254–55). Hacker 1975:75–77. Mollenkopf (1988b:243) provides a portrait similar to Hacker's but distinguishes "Catholics of Italian, Irish and other ethnic backgrounds" from Jews. Sleeper (1990:143) also distinguishes "white ethnics" from Jews. Elmhurst-Corona's Jewish population was small, and in civic politics Jewish participants were indistinguishable from their white Catholic or Protestant counterparts.

12. Mikulski qtd. in Seifer 1973:viii.

13. Rita Manning, "Average Income by Race/90 Census," computer-produced chart, Department of Urban Studies, Queens College. For readability, I have rounded off income and population figures throughout.

14. Jacobs 1961:150–221. Still, the 36 dwelling units per net residential acre in CD4 yield a density considerably below the 124 to 254 units in Greenwich Village, or the 275 in Boston's North End.

15. See Chen 1989, 1992; Danta 1989a, 1989b; Gregory 1992, 1993, 1994a, 1994b, 1998; Khandelwal 1989, 1991, 1994; Park 1989, 1997; Ricourt 1989, 1994.

16. See Acosta 1989; Yuan 1986.

17. Richards notes that meetings "are often the most striking manifestations of the political structure, values, and activities of the society in question" (1971:4). Like Schwartzman (1990:161), I spent half my fieldwork time at meetings.

18. Gluckman 1940. See Kertzer 1988; Moore and Myerhoff 1977. I follow Kertzer's view of rituals "as important means of channeling emotion, guiding cognition, and organizing social groups. [This approach takes] a middle path between an overly restrictive definition, which would limit ritual to the religious sphere and identify it with the supernatural, and an overly broad definition, labeling as ritual any standardized human activity" (1988:8–9).

19. See Bloch 1974; Irvine 1979:778–79; Moore and Myerhoff 1977:7–8; Simon Ottenberg, "Secular Ritual" course materials, Department of Anthropology, University of Washington, 1986.

20. For classic examples of this approach, see Fortes 1936; Tambiah 1970. Sanjek 1992 presents fuller discussion.

21. See Asad 1979; Bloch 1977; Irvine 1979:784–85; Moore and Myerhoff 1977:1–9, 14–17.

22. Schieffelin thus sees the participatory dimension of ritual as primary: "The work of a performance, what it does and how it does it, can never be discovered only by examining the text, or the script, or the symbolic meanings embodied in the ritual. . . . The participants may not all experience the same significance or efficacy from it. . . . The performance receives its validation socially . . . when they acknowledge that they have shared in its action and intensity" (1993:293).

23. See Sanjek 1990, 1996. As Bailey observes, "It is one of the difficulties of anthropological fieldwork that, even if you happen to know the language well, you can still listen in to a conversation and not know what is being said. The conversation consists of allusions, hints, fragments, all of which serve perfectly well as a means of communication for those on the inside: but effectively they rule the stranger out of comprehension" (1971:13).

24. Whyte 1955:303.

25. Fenton 1962 uses "upstreaming" to refer to interpretations of earlier written records made by persons with direct ethnographic knowledge of a particular community or people.

26. Cf. Richards 1971:7–8.

27. Questions about the choices and responsibilities that fieldworkers confront have been no better posed, or answered, than in de Laguna 1957. See also Bailey 1991:112–15; Sanjek 1990, 1991, 1995, 1996.

28. Leeds 1980, 1994; Sanjek 1994b.

29. See Braudel [1967] 1980:3–4, 10–12, 16–17, 26–34, 48, 50–51, 74–77, 93–94, 209–10, in which "social time" and "cycle" are synonyms for conjuncture, and "structure" for *longue durée.* Anthropologists have made little use of this set of concepts. Comaroff (1985:17–18) cites Braudel when contrasting event and structure but does not employ other elements of his approach; Ohnuki-Tierney (1990) mentions the three temporal levels but focuses on the *longue durée;* Sahlins (1985:xiv, 125) differentiates his use of "structure" and "conjuncture" from that of Braudel.

30. On African Americans since the 1940s, see Jaynes and Williams 1989; on New York population projections, Bouvier and Boggs 1988:35.

31. Katznelson 1981; Pecorella 1994:3.

32. Elias and Scotson [1965] 1994:xviii, xxx–xxxi, xxxv, xxxviii, xlvii, 158.

33. Leeds 1994:218–19. Cf. Bierstedt 1967; Fried 1967:13; Parsons 1951:121; Wolf 1990:586–87. See Leeds 1994: chaps. 3–7 for discussions of power, acknowledging Bierstedt's tripartite formulation, and of classes and social order; see also Sanjek 1994b.

34. Several scholars have called attention to what Leeds terms lubricatory power; see Bailey 1983:210–14; Davidson 1979:20, 114; Gordon 1973:11–12, 300–305; Greider 1992:54–56, 212–13; Irvine 1989:257–58; Pecorella 1994:17. For general views of power compatible with that of Leeds, see Bailey 1991:101–2; Bridges 1984:14; David and Bellush 1971:7–10; Fardon 1985:8–9.

1. Elmhurst-Corona, 1652–1960

1. This historical sketch draws on Albion 1939; Armbruster 1923; Cohen 1981; Goodfriend 1992; Grumet 1981; Innes 1898; Karatzas 1990; Kroessler 1993; Kross 1983; Munsell 1882; Riker 1852; Sanjek 1993; Seyfried 1984, 1987, 1995; Sherman 1929; Shiel 1983; Stankowski 1977; Thompson 1918; White 1991; Willis 1920; Zim, Lerner, and Rolfes 1988; the *Newtown Crier;* and materials from the Long Island Collection of the Queens Borough Public Library.

2. The Social Order of New York City

1. On the historical development of New York's classes and social order, see Sanjek (forthcoming).

2. The title page of McCabe's *Lights and Shadows of New York Life* ([1872], 1970) touts its

coverage of the city's "Splendors and Wretchedness; Its High and Low Life; Its Marble Palaces and Dark Dens; Its Attractions and Dangers." On the contemporary "dual city," see Mollenkopf and Castells 1991a, 1991b, 1991c.

3. This is exemplified in influential formulations of Robert Merton, Herbert Gans, and Andrew Hacker. Merton defined the cosmopolitan-local dichotomy in 1949: "The localite largely *confines* his interests to the community. . . . Devoting little thought or energy to *the Great Society,* he is *preoccupied* with local problems, to the virtual *exclusion* of the national and international scene. He is, strictly speaking, *parochial.*" In contrast, the cosmopolitan "maintain[s] a *minimum* of relations within the community [and] is oriented *significantly* to the world outside. . . . He resides [locally] but lives *in the Great Society.* If the local type is parochial, the cosmopolitan is *ecumenical*" ([1949] 1968:447; emphasis added). Drawing on ethnographic research, Gans contrasted upper- and lower-middle-class "subcultures" of a New York City suburb in similar terms. The upper middle class consisted of college-educated managers and professionals who "as cosmopolitans . . . want to shape the community by national values which may not respect local traditions. . . . [T]hose of the [lower middle class] participate [in civic ventures] only when there is a political threat to their homes and families." This lower middle class, nonetheless, was "active in church and in voluntary associations," the PTA, organized youth groups, and "community service" organizations, activities shunned by cosmopolitans (1967:24); see also Gans 1988:xii, 153–54, 196. Hacker celebrated New York's cosmopolitans, even arguing, "Civilization depends on subsidizing entertainment for [this] class . . . just as it needs an exploited class to hold down the costs." His overview of neighborhood New York concluded "that the city has become too democratic, with too many participants and too much participation" (1975:14–15, 72–82, 89–91, 133–39, 146–48).

4. Suttles 1976:4–5.

5. Chen 1992; LaRuffa 1988; Padilla 1958; Valentine 1978.

6. Jacobs 1961:29–88, 119–21; Suttles 1972:55–58.

7. Jacobs 1961:132; Suttles 1972:50–54, 58–64.

8. On conceptualizing this occupational continuum, see Brint 1991:156, 162–67; Gans 1979:7–8; Halle 1984:10, 16–19; Levison 1974; Parker 1972.

9. Clearly disliking the "lower" qualifier, member Tom McKenzie objected at a 1984 CB4 meeting that "the *New York Times* called this 'a *lower*-middle-class neighborhood.' Yet that same paper is advertising $200,000 homes in Elmhurst." Playing on the ambiguity of the term "middle class" for their own purposes, politicians and lubricatory specialists often make use of the desire of neighborhood New Yorkers to be identified simply as "middle class." At a 1985 CB4 meeting a mayoral spokesperson said of proposed new housing that only upper-middle-class newcomers, not local residents, could afford, "It's mainly for middle-class people."

10. On "the hidden elderly poor," see Mudd 1984:126, 186; Settlement Housing Fund 1985. In 1990, 1 in 9 white New Yorkers lived in poverty, and they amounted to one-fifth of the city's poor (Falcón 1992).

11. The largest localized population of Asians in New York City, the 45,000 Chinese in Manhattan's CD3—concentrated in Chinatown—still formed only 30 percent of this community district's population.

12. In 1990 New York City was 43 percent white, 25 percent black, 24 percent Latin American, and 7 percent Asian. CD3 in Queens was 28 percent white, 16 percent black, 44 percent Latin American, and 12 percent Asian.

13. See Domhoff 1967, 1974; Mills 1956; Ostrander 1984; Joselit 1983; Rischin 1962.

14. Newfield and DuBrul 1977:75–77. The formulation of these two liberal journalists is echoed by mainstream political scientists: Danielson and Doig 1982:273; Pecorella 1994:9; Walsh 1990:211, 215.

15. Newfield and DuBrul 1977:82.

16. Fitch 1976, 1987, 1993:49–51; see also Sanjek (forthcoming). The model of U.S. urban political economy in Logan and Molotch 1987 is compatible with ideas presented in this chapter and throughout; I read their study after completing this book and give priority to Fitch 1976 and Newfield and DuBrul 1977 (whom they do not cite) for influencing my thinking over many years.

17. Newfield and DuBrul 1977:83.
18. Fitch 1976:250.
19. Newfield and Barrett 1988.
20. Fitch 1989:709.
21. These processes are well described for Manhattan's Lower East Side in Abu-Lughod 1994, esp. the articles by Smith, Duncan and Reid, Mele, and Sites. They focus on smaller-fry developers and landlords who feed economically off policies promoted by permanent-government big fish.
22. See Brint 1991:160–62.
23. On these suburban reentrants, see Fava and DeSena 1984.
24. See Brecher and Horton 1993:31–32; Brint 1991:172–73 on "liberal" and "egalitarian" professional "cultures"; Danielson and Doig 1982:336–37; Fitch 1993:62; Shefter 1985:49–56.
25. Mollenkopf 1988a:277; cf. Gans 1988:68; Piven and Cloward 1988:176–77, 215.
26. Cox 1948:311; see also Sinnreich 1980:72–74.
27. See Gregory 1992 on the relationship between empowerment and quality-of-life politics in the North Corona–East Elmhurst African American community.

3. Racial Change and Decentralization

1. Caro 1974:961–83, 1005–25; Homefront 1977; Mudd 1984:136–37; Schaffer 1973; Sullivan 1991:233–35.
2. Abrams 1966; Bellush 1971:108–9; Connolly 1977; Gordon 1973:267; Homefront 1977; Mudd 1984:137–38; Reider 1985:20–26; Schoener 1979:216.
3. Cuomo 1974:37–38, 55; Gregory 1992; Schoener 1979:212–13.
4. Tobier 1984.
5. Rogers 1968.
6. Clark 1966; Fleming 1965; Reed 1986.
7. Community Council of Greater New York 1958; City Planning Commission 1963; Gregory 1992.
8. Fischer 1966:31; Rogers 1968:67–95; Shefter 1985:67–68; *NYT*, 5/10/64.
9. Rieder 1986 covers similar white groups in Canarsie.
10. City Planning Commission 1963, 1968; Corona–East Elmhurst Development Committee 1969; Gregory 1992.
11. Bellush 1971:110–11; Cuomo 1974 ignores this 1965 episode.
12. Green and Wilson 1989:21–23; Hacker 1975; Rogowsky, Gold, and Abbott 1971; Shefter 1985:68.
13. David 1971; Ehrenreich and Ehrenreich 1970:191–213, 268–79; Gittell 1971; Gordon 1973:107–66; Hacker 1975:84–89; Katznelson 1981:135–89; Mudd 1984; Rogers and Chung 1983.
14. Bellush 1971; Cuomo 1974.
15. Abrams 1966; Cuomo 1974:196.
16. This account draws on Bellush 1971; Cuomo 1974; and newspaper clipping files at the Long Island History Collection, Queens Borough Public Library, Jamaica.
17. Green and Wilson 1989:19–20; Morris 1980:72; Schoener 1979:233–35.
18. Fleming 1965.
19. Gordon 1973:132–36; Katznelson 1981:137–41; Morris 1980:28, 74–78; Mudd 1984:16, 57–64.
20. Fuentes 1980; Gitell 1971; Katznelson 1981:153–78; Mudd 1984:48–51; Pecorella 1994:99–104; Rogers and Chung 1983.
21. Katznelson 1981:141–44; Mudd 1984:44–48; Percorella 1994:123–26; Rogers 1990:169.
22. This section is based on Newfield and Barrett 1988; *DN Special Report*, 12/14/86; *VV*, 2/4/86, 9/22/87; and the author's files of newspaper clippings.
23. On Groh, see Auletta 1979:168; Morris 1980:217.
24. On Lazar, see Auletta 1979:168. PVB proceeds in 1995 were $281 million (*NYT*, 11/3/95).

25. Mudd 1984:65–189; Pecorella 1994:104–10; Rogers 1990:163–64.

26. Morris 1980:211–12; Mudd 1984:73–74, 85, 155–56, 181–83, 192, 203–7; Pecorella 1994:126–36.

27. Mudd 1984:152–55, 184: Rogers 1990:164–65.

28. Mudd 1984:192, 197–203; Rogers 1990:169–70.

29. These same bases for community board membership continued into the 1980s; see Pecorella 1994:170–71.

30. Mudd 1984:194.

31. Another 3,400 lived in North Corona on the CD3 side of seven census tracts extending across Roosevelt Avenue from CD4; by 1980 this black population had fallen to 2,700. Information on Lefrak City in the 1960s–1970s is from newspaper clipping files at the Long Island History Collection, and CB4 and district cabinet minutes. See also Gregory 1993.

32. *Long Island Daily Press,* 11/17/61.

33. *NYT,* 9/30/70.

34. Nixon documents declassified in 1996 reveal his hatred of Lindsay (*DN,* 10/18/96).

35. Quoted in *NYT,* 10/24/71.

36. *NYT,* 2/1/76.

37. *New York Magazine,* 3/12/73; *NYT,* 10/24/71; *Long Island Press,* 10/27/75.

38. In 1976 some 633 units remained unoccupied (City Planning Commission 1979).

39. Gordon 1973:262; Hacker 1975:96–97, 102–4; Mudd 1984:126, 186; Williams 1994.

40. Cuomo 1974:59–60, 148; Gordon 1973:255–93; Morris 1980:119, 143.

41. By 1979 there were eleven group homes in Lefrak City, occupying a score of apartment units and serving ninety-five teenagers or mentally retarded adults (City Planning Commission 1979).

42. Cuomo 1974:149.

43. Gregory 1992.

44. Bailey and Waldinger 1991:56–62; Connolly 1977:186–93; Hacker 1975:41, 121–22; Morris 1980:66; Sassen 1988:86; Wilson 1980:126–34, 167–79. Bailey and Waldinger, Connolly, and Wilson each stress an economic "deepening schism" in the 1970s between poor, and working- and lower-middle-class African Americans. See Gregory 1992.

4. The Impact of the New Immigration

1. Chen 1992:37–38; Wong 1982.

2. Georges 1990:37–41; Grasmuck and Pessar 1991:31–33; Gregory 1992:259; Hendricks 1974:81; Ricourt 1989; Seyfried 1987:96.

3. On immigration legislation, see Abrams 1980; Bouvier and Gardner 1986; Cruz 1980; Davis, Haub, and Willette 1983; Glazer 1988:56–57; Hendricks 1974:53–70; Keely 1980; Kraly 1987; Portes and Rumbaut 1990:116–23; Reimers 1985:63–154, 161; Salvo, Ortiz, and Vardy 1992:127–55; Sung 1980; Warren 1980; Winnick 1990:xiii–xvii; Wong 1980.

4. In the years immediately after the 1965 U.S. invasion of the Dominican Republic the American embassy began a liberal visa policy as a safety valve to permit political opponents of the regimes in power to emigrate; see Georges 1990:38–39; Grasmuck and Pessar 1991:2–3, 31–33.

5. Chaney 1976:96, 98, 110, 119; Cruz 1980; Fisher 1980:11–12, 18–20; Glaser 1980; Goodman 1979; Hernandez 1980:480; Kim 1980:143–78; Park 1997; Pido 1983; Portes 1978:17–23; Reimers 1985:35–36, 97, 100–102, 110, 114; Salas 1991:63–64; Saran 1980; Wong 1980; Youssef 1992:142.

6. Crewsdon 1983:30–42, 115–16, 136–39, 281; Georges 1990:40–41, 81–97; Hendricks 1974:53–70; Laguerre 1984:33–48, 72–73; Preston 1979:11–12, 29; Reimers 1985:36, 138. See also Fix and Passel 1994:25.

7. *Long Island Press,* 7/9/68; *DN,* 7/12/70; *NYP,* 2/24/75, 2/28/75; *NYT,* 4/4/79.

8. New York Times et al. 1973. See Waldinger 1986:14, 19–21, 27–32; and 1987b.

9. The eleven Latin American travel agencies in CD4 provided an array of services including airline tickets, translation, notary public, income tax preparation, driving instruction, real estate

and rental information, foreign periodicals, money orders, preparation of immigration forms, loans, arrangement of job offers for would-be immigrants, and sale of foreign lottery tickets; cf. Hendricks 1974:123–26; Chaney 1976:108.

10. On South American restaurants and groceries in Elmhurst, see Stern 1980:242–51.

11. The Elmhurst-Corona picture is consistent with comparative insights of Aldrich and Waldinger 1990. See Chen 1992; Hendricks 1974:76, 81, 113–14; Khandelwal 1991; Park 1997; Ricourt 1995. See also Kim 1980:101–21, 1987; Waldinger 1986:135–37; Young 1983.

12. On similar prejudice toward Haitian newcomers in predominantly white neighborhoods, see Stafford 1987:146–47.

13. *NYT*, 4/4/79; cf. Waldinger 1987a:4.

14. Chaney 1976:112–13; Hendricks 1974:81.

15. For Queens, Latin American census responses were 5 percent black, 60 percent white, and 32 percent other; for New York City, 6 percent black, 45 percent white, and 49 percent other. The proportion of Elmhurst-Corona Latin Americans who identified themselves as "white" ranged from 86 percent in South Elmhurst to 39 percent in Lefrak City. "Black" Latin American census responses were 4 percent or lower throughout CD4 except in Lefrak City, where they amounted to 18 percent. On Latin American census choices of "other" versus "black" or "white," see Rodríguez 1989:49–84.

16. Lâguerre 1984:21–23, 56, 143–50; Reimers 1985:36, 147–49; Stafford 1987; Trouillot 1990:109–36.

17. I thank May Guerrier for this information. See also Colen 1990; Reimers 1985:149.

18. Chaney 1976:116–18; Hendricks 1974:118–19. See also Acosta 1989.

19. Chen 1992:163–81.

20. For a portrait of a Spanish Pentecostal congregation in Corona, see Danta 1989a. On Korean Protestant churches, see Kim 1980:187–207; Park 1989, 1997.

21. See Gregory 1992.

22. Fisher 1980:144–45; see also Shankar 1989.

23. *DN*, 3/23/61; *ND*, 11/23/79, 11/25/79.

24. Auletta 1979:194; City Planning Commission 1969, 1979.

25. Community school boards oversee primary and intermediate schools, but high schools are run directly by the citywide Board of Education.

26. *ND*, 4/13/86, 4/21/89; Rogers and Chung 1983:204–5, 216–18.

27. *DN*, 8/25/74; see Preston 1979:28–29.

28. Crewsdon 1983:125; Papademetriou 1983:3–4.

29. Crewsdon 1983:98–111; Hauser 1981:55; Passel 1986; Waldinger 1986–87:399, 1989b:53–55; Youssef 1992:39–42.

30. Crewsdon 1983:99, 107–8; Preston 1979:2, 6; Reimers 1985:215; *NYT*, 12/29/74. This hyperbole had an effect on public opinion: see Crewsdon 1983:15; Harwood 1986.

31. *DN*, 11/17/74.

32. On the lack of a federal immigrant policy or targeted impact aid, see Crewsdon 1983:328; Fix and Passel 1994:16, 57, 71.

33. Abrams 1980; Bouvier and Gardner 1986:28–32; Brinkley-Carter 1980; Crewsdon 1983:19, 239–77; Marshall 1983; Petras 1980; Piore 1980; Preston 1979:2–4, 16–17, 34; Sassen 1980, 1988:31, 37–43, 47, 191; Sternlieb and Hughes 1976:162; Waldinger 1986–87.

34. Sassen 1991b:81; *NYT*, 3/15/81, 7/4/82, 9/10/86.

35. "On the national level, population growth has been declining since the 1950s and since 1972 fertility levels have been below replacement level. . . . The forecast is that the United States will have a negative rate of increase by the year 2030" (Youssef 1992:157). See also Abrams 1980:28, 33; Bouvier and Gardner 1986:17; Keely 1980:24, 488; North 1979; Reimers 1985:72–74; Simon 1986; Stolnitz 1980:51–52. On more restrictive immigrant worker policies of European and Arab Gulf nations, see Sassen 1988:50–52.

36. Crewsdon 1983; Wells 1996.

37. Colen 1990; Connolly 1977; Crewsdon 1983:235–38, 251; Hendricks 1974:62; Marshall 1983:23–24; Reimers 1985:139, 143.

38. Buck 1979; Carey 1976:15–16; Marshall 1983; Sassen 1991b:88–89; Waldinger 1986, and personal communication, 6/17/86.

39. Buck 1979; Chaney 1976:126–27; Chen 1992; Grasmuck and Pessar 1991:184–85; Park 1997; Preston 1979:34–43; Ricourt 1995.

40. Bienstock 1977; Bernstein and Bondarin 1975; Ginzberg 1976, 1977, 1979; Gordon 1979.

41. Chaney 1976:113, 120–21, 1980:289; Chen 1992; Fitch 1993:279; Hendricks 1974:76; Marshall 1983; Preston 1979; Ricourt 1995; Sassen 1988:85–93.

42. Bonacich, Light, and Wong 1980; Chaney 1976, 1980; Chen 1992; Grasmuck and Pessar 1991; Hendricks 1974; Kim 1980; Park 1997; Pessar 1987a, 1987b; Reimers 1985:138–39, 141–43; Sung 1980:48; Waldinger 1986:4, 31–32, 39–40, 108, 171, and 1986–87:390.

43. Bonacich, Light, and Wong 1980:179; Bouvier and Gardner 1986:28–32; Crewsdon 1983:239–77; Grasmuck and Pessar 1991:186; Hacker 1975:101–2, 147–48; Keely 1982; Marshall 1983; Petras 1980; Piore 1980; Preston 1979; Sassen 1980, 1988:31, 37–43, 47, 191. See also Fix and Passel 1994:47–54.

44. Bailey and Waldinger 1991:56–62; Balmori 1983; Chaney 1976:120; Crewsdon 1983:264; Fix and Passel 1994:50–51; Frey 1995:299; Grasmuck and Pessar 1991:168; Hacker 1975:23; Hendricks 1974:78; Institute for Puerto Rican Policy 1991; Waldinger 1986:112–16, 156, 1986–87:386, 1987b, 1989b:64–69; Waldinger, "The Jobs Immigrants Take," *NYT,* 3/11/96.

45. Bailey and Waldinger 1991:56–62; Crewsdon 1983:267; Ginzberg 1980; Waldinger 1986–87. See also Bernstein and Bondarin 1975:4–5. Preston (1979:38) and Waldinger (1986:111) point out that welfare payments exceeded minimum wage earnings during the 1970s. Although in some cases this may have affected the willingness of New York-raised African Americans and Puerto Ricans to take minimum-wage "bad jobs" (assuming no employer preferences for immigrants), it was among *males* in these two groups that employment dropped, not females, who constituted most of those eligible for AFDC. The proportion of employed African American women actually rose in New York City during the 1970s, from 50 to 58 percent; it also rose for Puerto Rican women, from 30 to 38 percent. Where "good" jobs were available to African Americans, they took them; while total white-collar jobs declined by 68,000 in New York over the 1970s, African American white-collar employment rose from 206,000 to 242,000. Much of this job growth was in the public sector, where racial discrimination was less intense than in private-sector employment; see Waldinger 1986–87. See also Waldinger, "How Immigration Hurts African-Americans," *ND,* 6/26/95.

46. Sassen 1988:22, 40, 126–70, 1991b. For a well-reasoned, quantitatively supported alternative view to Sassen, see Bailey and Waldinger 1991.

47. Balmori 1983; Fitch 1993:280; Sassen 1991b:88, 100; Waldinger 1986:23–24, 1986–87:395–96.

48. Bouvier and Gardner 1986:32; Crewsdon 1983:106, 270–75; Fix and Passel 1994:57–67; Keely 1982; Preston 1979:31; Simon 1986:19.

49. Crewsdon 1983:35, 245, 252–55, 338; Waldinger 1986–87.

50. Ginzberg 1977, 1980; Hacker 1975:147–48; Keely 1980:488; Kim 1980, 1987; Waldinger 1986–87; Young 1983. Opportunities for black retail employment were also scarce in predominantly black neighborhoods; see Sullivan 1989. In 1980, 1 in 30 African American males in New York City were self-employed as compared with 1 in 8 foreign-born males. In Waldinger's view, ethnic borders in all job niches tightened during the 1970s, and hiring following ethnic lines more closely than before.

51. Bienstock 1977; Ginzberg 1979; Sassen 1988:126–70; Waldinger 1986:2, 1986–87.

52. Bouvier and Gardner 1986:22–26; Crewsdon 1983:44–45; Glaser 1980; Goodman 1979; Kim 1980:147–70; Pido 1983; Portes 1978:17–23; Reimers 1985:100–102; Simon 1986:26–27; Youssef 1992:138.

53. Abrams 1980; Brinkley-Carter 1980; Kim 1980:154–55; Petras 1980; Winnick 1990:42. "The United States saved an estimated $850 million in investment costs in both 1971 and 1972 by admitting technical and professional immigrants from low-wage countries" (Sassen 1988:190). See also Fix and Passel 1994:36, 52; *ND,* 8/22/94.

54. Bouvier and Gardner 1986:26; Reimers 1985:249; Yousef 1992:158; *CHE,* 5/24/91, 9/29/93, 7/14/95, 6/7/96.

55. Castleman 1982; Chen 1992; Ginzberg 1980:47–48; Leacock 1969; Sieber 1978; Sullivan 1989; *NYT,* 8/4/92.

5. Fiscal Crisis and Land-Use Struggles

1. Auletta 1979:31, 40, 72; Chinitz 1965:107–9; Danielson and Doig 1982:35, 45, 61, 138, 262; Drennan 1991; Edel 1976:233–34; Harris 1991; Netzer 1990:32, 39; Schultze et al. [1972] 1976:201–4.

2. Alcaly and Bodian 1976:42; Auletta 1979:39; Beinstock 1977:3–9; Danielson and Doig 1982:51; Fitch 1993:243, 279; Harris 1991; Waldinger 1986; Willis 1988:36–37.

3. Housing segregation still persists; see *NYT,* 2/15/94, 3/17/94.

4. Danielson and Doig 1982:14, 28–29, 52, 61, 78, 87, 90–91, 95–96, 98, 105–6, 165, 262.

5. Morris 1980:34–35, 56.

6. Auletta 1979:29; Beinstock 1977:16–17; Danielson and Doig 1982:260; Fainstein and Fainstein 1988:172–74; McNickle 1993:116–17; Morris 1980:18, 44–46, 145; Netzer 1990:28; Piven 1973; Shefter 1985:86, 112–13.

7. Alcaly and Bodian 1976:30; Auletta 1979:14, 29, 36, 52–53, 55–56, 58, 95; Morris 1980:22, 36–37, 127–39, 170, 199–201, 215, 222–23; Newfield and DuBrul 1977:18–28; Netzer 1990:41–45; Shefter 1985:61; Sinnreich 1980:85–86, 98, 100; Zevin 1976:18.

8. Auletta 1979:193; Danielson and Doig 1980:275–77; Morris 1980:68–71, 118–19, 169, 185–86, 190; Netzer 1990:34–37; Sinnreich 1980:111; Tabb 1982:22.

9. Alcaly and Bodian 1976:40; Auletta 1979:45–50, 66–68, 75, 119, 185–86, 217, 233–34, 325; Beinstock 1977:13–15; Brecher and Horton 1993:245, 250–51; Congressional Budget Office [1975] 1976:295; Curvin and Porter 1979:69; Fuchs 1992; Lichten 1980:157; Maier 1984:357; McNickle 1993:157; Morris 1980:83–107, 120–21, 125, 136, 172–85; Netzer 1990:44–45; Piven 1973:327, 345–46; Schultze et al. [1972] 1976:196–200; Shefter 1985:88, 95–96, 116–19; Sinnreich 1980:85, 98–99; Tabb 1982:61–65; Zevin 1976:18. Comparative research showed that the ratio of city workers to residents was higher in New York than in many though not all other cities, but these studies did not figure in the services to the many suburban commuters to Manhattan.

10. Auletta 1979:65; Beinstock 1977:4–6, 9–10, 18; Danielson and Doig 1982:46; Drennan 1991:31–33; Fitch 1993:279; Mollenkopf 1976:128; Morris 1980:139–40; Netzer 1990:27; Sinnreich 1980:103; Whyte 1976; Willis 1988:37–38.

11. Auletta 1979:200; Beinstock 1977:6; Edel 1976:232, 236–37; Netzer 1990:32; Sinnreich 1980:48–50, 53, 106, 116–18, 122.

12. Brecher and Horton 1993:191, 204–5; Chinitz 1965:111; Danielson and Doig 1982:49; Drennan 1991:25; Fitch 1993:xvi, 20, 41, 53; Morris 1980:29–31, 151–52; Schultze et al. [1972] 1976:191; Sinnreich 1980:60, 102, 105; Tabb 1982:77.

13. See Sanjek (forthcoming).

14. Danielson and Doig 1982:260, 279; Fitch 1993:252–54; Zevin 1976:19.

15. Danielson and Doig 1982:37, 46–47, 196–99, 273–74; Epstein 1976:67–68; Fitch 1993:xiv–xv, 28–29, 42, 74, 120–21, 130–44, 206; Newfield and DuBrul 1977:87–97; Shefter 1985:58–60.

16. Auletta 1979:85; Danielson and Doig 1982:316–22; Epstein 1976; Fitch 1993:xiv, 30, 44; Grossman 1980:223–24; Newfield and DuBrul 1977:91; Tabb 1982:60, 1984:328.

17. Chinitz 1965:109; Danielson and Doig 1982:37–38; Epstein 1976:61, 69; Fitch 1993:101–2, 280; Lichten 1980:147; Tabb 1982:60, 1984:343; Willis 1988:32.

18. Danielson and Doig 1982:37; Whyte 1976:98–99. See also Beinstock 1977:18; Brecher and Horton 1993:30; Carey 1976:16–18; Fitch 1993:79, 89 n 49, 106, 108–11, 122–24. On the Lindsay administration's faith in this viewpoint, see Fainstein and Fainstein 1988:178–79.

19. Edel 1976:235; Fitch 1993:58–59; Morris 1980:139–41, 143. See also Harrison and Bluestone 1988:10.

20. Auletta 1979:131; Brecher and Horton 1993:91–94; Danielson and Doig 1982:251; Morris 1980:219–20.

21. Auletta 1979:103–5, 118; Brecher and Horton 1993:31; Edel 1976:239; Morris 1980:199–201; Newfield and DuBrul 1977:28; Shefter 1985:62–65, 131; Tabb 1982:22–23, 1984:326–27; Zevin 1976:24.

22. Alcaly and Bodian 1976:53, 57; Auletta 1979:85–86, 88–89, 105–7, 113–14; Lichten 1980:145, 153–54, 170; Morris 1980:222–24; Newfield and DuBrul 1977:45–46 Tabb 1982:24–25.

23. Lichten 1980:156–60, 1984:198–205; Morris 1980:219, 222, 223, 228; Newfield and DuBrul 1977:173; Shefter 1985:131.

24. Auletta 1979:87–90; Lichten 1980:158–61; Morris 1980:226–30; Netzer 1990:46; Newfield and DuBrul 1977:18–28.

25. Alcaly and Bodian 1976:31, 47; Auletta 1979:90–91; Bellush 1990:312–14; Lichten 1980:163–67; Maier 1984:347; Morris 1980:232–34; Netzer 1990:47–50; Newfield 1976:300–302; Newfield and DuBrul 1977:78, 178–91; Shefter 1985:132–34, 247; Tabb 1982:25–26, 28.

26. Auletta 1979:277; Bellush 1990:312, 314–15; Friedman 1976; Lichten 1984:206–10; Shefter 1985:129.

27. Auletta 1979:90–91, 136–37, 186, 286; Bellush 1990:314–15; Lichten 1980:167–68, 1984:205–12; Morris 1980:234; Newfield and DuBrul 1977:68–69; Shefter 1985:134–36; Tabb 1982:27–28.

28. Auletta 1979:138, 277–78, 284, 320; Bellush 1990:315–16; Brecher and Horton 1993:40–41, 143–49; Morris 1980:235–36; Netzer 1990:50; Shefter 1985:139, 163–66; *VV*, 11/26/91.

29. Bellush 1990:313; Brecher and Horton 1993:26; Lichten 1980:166; Morris 1980:233; Newfield and DuBrul 1977:184–86.

30. Auletta 1979:15, 217, 278; Brecher and Horton 1993:166, 230, 304–5, 311, 333; Danielson and Doig 1975:283; Grossman 1980:179–82, 209; Netzer 1990:50; Newfield 1976:297; Newfield and DuBrul 1977:191–97; Shefter 1985:142, 146; Tabb 1982:30, 42–53, 93.

31. Curvin and Porter 1979:13; Newfield and DuBrul 1977:4; Shefter 1985:146; Tabb 1982:30.

32. Auletta 1979:5–7; Bellush 1990:318; Fainstein and Fainstein 1988:184; Harris 1991:140; Sieber 1987; Sinnreich 1990:37–38; Twentieth Century Fund 1980:4–5; Waldinger 1986–87:372–73.

33. Fainstein and Fainstein 1988:185; Shefter 1985:142, 151, 163, 197, 199; Sinnreich 1980:145; Tabb 1982:83, 1984:337–38; *NYT*, 12/2/80.

34. Baxter and Hopper 1981; Domurad et al. 1981; Domurad and Russianoff 1982; Fainstein and Fainstein 1988:183–85; Sinnreich 1980:78; Twentieth Century Fund 1980:18.

35. Lichten 1980:169–70.

36. City Planning Commission 1969.

37. Tauber and Kaplan 1966.

38. See Sanjek (forthcoming); DCP 1976; Fitch 1993:134–36; Huxtable 1987; Marcus 1993; Strickland 1993.

39. *DN*, 1/28/80.

40. In 1987 the Queens Department of City Planning estimated that CD4 contained 150,000 inhabitants.

6. New York's Three Economies

1. Phillips 1994:79–84; Vilain 1991:62; cf. Harrison and Bluestone 1988:13, 53–59, 111; *ND*, 1/12/97.

2. Bluestone and Harrison 1982:207–8; Bowles, Gordon, and Weisskopf 1990:123–24, 162–64, 200–204; Harrison and Bluestone 1988:14, 86–87, 153–54; Lekachman 1982; Levy 1995:10–11; Phillips 1990:49, 120–25, 139–45; Sassen 1988:153 and 1991a:35, 37–39, 155–57; Vogel 1993:57–58; Willis 1988:43; *ND*, 1/27/92; *NYT*, 7/10/78, 7/8/79, 4/28/93.

3. Barlett and Steele 1992:118; Garreau 1991:78; Greider 1992:60–78, 91; Harrison and

Bluestone 1988:56, 66–67; Phillips 1990:95–98; Sassen 1991a:64, 82; *ND,* 8/12/92; *NYT,* 6/3/82, 8/9/82, 10/14/82, 1/1/84.

4. Barlett and Steele 1992:41–61, 195–200, 218; Bluestone and Harrison 1982:199, 209–10; Bowles, Gordon and Weisskopf 1990:129–30, 200, 203, 213, 219; Greider 1992:91, 97; Harrison and Bluestone 1988:90, 93–94, 131, 152; Lekachman 1982:57–78; Phillips 1990:46, 57, 78–79, 90–91; *NYT,* 12/16/81, 2/7/82, 8/8/82.

5. Barlett and Steele 1992:12, 14, 18–19, 27–30, 41–42, 46, 55, 99–101, 134–61, 163, 171–83, 190–91, 217–18; Bluestone and Harrison 1982:6, 11, 40–41, 125–26, 149–59; Bowles, Gordon, and Weisskopf 1990:90–91; Fitch 1994:25–26; Greider 1992:39–42; Harrison and Bluestone 1988:19, 24–25, 57–66; Obey 1996; Phillips 1990:68–70, 1994:85–88; Sassen 1991a:120–21; *DN,* 1/2/97; *Entrepreneurial Economy,* 10/82; *ND,* 5/12/96; *NYT,* 1/10/82, 9/29/82, 10/6/82, 12/28/82, 5/2/95, 10/31/95; *WSJ,* 1/2/96.

6. Drennan 1991:33–38; Lekachman 1982:143; Sassen 1991a:11, 131–39, 203; Vilain 1991:54; Vogel 1993:67; Willis 1988:31, 35–36, 40–44; *NYT,* 7/14/82, 3/22/83.

7. Brint 1991:159–61; Fitch 1994:23–24; Garreau 1991:22; Harris 1991:140–42; McNickle 1993:282; Sassen 1991a:9, 185–86; 260–64, 279; Tabb 1982:77–78; Tobier 1984:108; Twentieth Century Fund 1980; Tyler 1987:467; Winnick 1988:8–10, 20–21, 29; *ND,* 11/27/94; *NYT,* 11/28/83, 7/8/84, 7/26/84, 12/23/92; *NYTM,* 11/4/82.

8. Bluestone and Harrison 1982:294 n 12; Epstein and Duncombe 1991:178–79, 181, 195; Garreau 1991:112; Harrison and Bluestone 1988:144; Phillips 1994: 82, 84, 217; Shefter 1985:59; Sinnreich1980:128–29; *Fortune,* 6/27/94; *ND,* 6/29/86, 12/16/96; *NYT,* 1/23/76, 8/5/79, 9/6/82, 4/18/93, 9/19/93, 5/15/95, 2/2/97, 3/18/97; *NYTM,* 5/21/95.

9. Drennan 1990:38–39.

10. Barlett and Steele 1992:106; Brecher and Horton 1993:7; Fitch 1993:4, 9–10, 22, 1994:17, 34, 44–46; Greider 1992:68–78; Harrison and Bluestone 1988:58–59, 142; Phillips 1994:87; Sassen 1991a:82–83, 121–23; Willis 1988:33; *City Project Bulletin,* 2/24/97; *DN,* 1/13/95, 1/2/96; *ND,* 7/1/91, 2/22/92, 1/25/93, 1/24/94, 3/26/95, 5/4/95, 12/29/95; *NYO,* 6/3/96, 12/2/96; *NYT,* 6/26/88, 12/21/90, 6/12/94, 5/4/95, 5/7/95, 5/9/95, 5/25/95, 5/31/95, 1/23/97; *VV,* 2/4/97.

11. Fitch 1993:7, 1994:18, 21, 22–23; Phillips 1994:85; *CNYB,* 7/22/96, 10/21/96; *ND,* 1/27/92, 7/20/92, 4/16/93, 4/19/93, 7/26/93, 4/25/94, 10/24/94, 1/7/95, 5/17/95, 6/20/95; *NYO,* 9/23/91; *NYP,* 4/19/95, 4/28/95, 5/6/95; *NYT,* 4/16/92, 4/18/93, 4/28/93, 6/12/94, 7/27/94, 10/29/94, 2/23/95, 3/17/95, 3/22/95, 3/28/95, 4/18/95, 5/9/95, 6/15/95, 7/12/95, 2/19/96, 10/21/96, 1/23/97, 3/7/97; *WSJ,* 9/25/95, 1/2/96, 12/12/96.

12. Fitch 1994:35; Frey 1995:290, 303, 334; Garreau 1991:5, 17–68, 111–31, 237, 509; Greider 1992:394; Harris 1991:133–34; Kahler 1993:39–40; Kasarda 1995:216, 230–32, 235–37, 246; Phillips 1990:132; Sassen 1991a:138, 148–49, 152–54, 159, 164; Shefter 1985:205; Vogel 1993; Willis 1988:41, 53, 50; *CNYB,* 11/28/94; *Fortune,* 6/27/94; *ND,* 8/3/92, 8/12/92, 4/19/93; *NYO,* 9/23/91; *NYT,* 3/22/83, 12/12/83, 1/20/85, 4/25/94, 11/11/96, 3/7/97; *NYTM,* 5/21/95, 12/1/96; *WSJ,* 2/12/97.

13. Barlett and Steele 1992:190–95, 206–11; Bluestone and Harrison 1982:180; Greider 1992:35–59, 258–64, 341–45; Obey 1996; Phillips 1990:46–48, 1994:xv–xvi, 38–45, 60–65, 87, 91–110; Piven and Cloward 1988:10–11, 158–59, 214; *ND,* 5/14/95.

14. Bluestone and Harrison 1982:244; Bowles, Gordon, and Weisskopf 1990:27; Harrison and Bluestone 1988:131; Phillips 1994:83, 85–86, 88; *NYT,* 11/20/83, 7/26/84, 6/26/88, 8/25/91.

15. Bluestone and Harrison 1982:159, 188–89, 198; Bowles, Gordon, and Weisskopf 1990:148–51, 156–60, 205, 220; Harrison and Bluestone 1988:16–17, 88–93, 143–44, 147–51, 153–54; Levy 1995:11, 38; Phillips 1990:120–25, 167; Vogel 1993:49–50; *Financial World,* 6/20/95; *NYT,* 4/18/81, 3/16/86, 4/2/95.

16. Barlett and Steel 1992:xi, 18; Bluestone and Harrison 1982:95; Bluestone, Harrison, and Gorham 1984:13, 16, 31, 33; Epstein and Duncombe 1991:200 n 4; Harrison and Bluestone 1988:55–56, 69–72; Kasarda 1995:215; Phillips 1990:18–20, 167; Sassen 1991a:9; *NYT,* 9/18/83, 8/28/85, 10/27/85, 3/24/94.

17. Brecher and Horton 1993:7, 194; Fitch 1993:273; Kasarda 1995:241; *NYT,* 7/14/82, 10/17/82, 12/15/87; *VV,* 4/15/81.

18. Fitch 1994:20–21; see also Fitch 1993:11–12, 22–25, 153.

19. Barlett and Steel 1992:31–39; Bluestone and Harrison 1982; Bluestone, Harrison, and Gorham 1984:11, 18; Bowles, Gordon, and Weisskopf 1990:9–10, 63–66, 90–91, 205, 260 n 11; Fitch 1994:38; Gordon 1996:187–97; Greider 1992:377–93, 399–400; Harrison and Bluestone 1988:7–11, 29–33, 205 n 5; Garreau 1992:30; Krugman 1996; Levy 1995:9; Moss 1994:11–12; Phillips 1990:117–18, 127, 129–30, 167, 1994:204–5; *ND*, 4/30/95; *NYT*, 6/24/83, 6/27/83, 8/8/84, 11/15/93, 1/26/96.

20. Bluestone and Harrison 1982:25–27; Bluestone, Harrison, and Gorham 1984:8; Bowles, Gordon, and Weisskopf 1990:87, 90, 206; Drennan 1991:31; Garreau 1991:5–7; Kasarda 1995:215–19, 220, 231, 234–39; Leinberger 1992; New York Times 1996; Sassen 1991a:201; Willis 1988:36–37; *NYT*, 3/3/91, 3/27/92, 12/21/92, 12/23/92, 9/26/94, 4/5/95, 8/23/96; *NYTM*, 6/6/82.

21. Brecher and Horton 1993:30–31, 41, 185–87, 195, 196; Fainstein and Fainstein 1988:190; Garreau 1992; Greider 1992:88; Kasarda 1995:224–31; Kieschnick 1981:12, 24, 26, 29, 37–39, 50–57, 62–63, 69–73, 83–84, 87; Phillips 1994:207; Sinnreich 1980:102–4; Willis 1988:48–50; *ND*, 10/24/94; *NYT*, 4/4/76, 5/18/87, 2/8/95, 4/17/95.

22. Fitch 1993:xii, 13, 39–49, 116–19, 134–35, 153–55, 255–56, 259–61, 1994:38–39; Kahler 1993:32–35; Macchiarola 1988:162; Netzer 1990:53–54; Wagner 1988:33–34, 44–46; Walsh 1990:213; *NYT*, 2/28/80, 8/25/91, 8/4/94, 8/24/94, 9/13/94, 10/4/94, 2/19/95.

23. Bluestone and Harrison 1982:18, 116–18; Bowles, Gordon, and Weisskopf 1990:57; Garreau 1992:30, 133–34; Harrison and Bluestone 1988:26 n, 71–72; Kasarda 1995:231; Levy 1995:7, 11, 13, 43–45; Phillips 1994:87; *CNYB*, 11/28/94; *DN*, 1/25/94, 10/28/94; *Fortune*, 6/27/94; *ND* 6/29/86, 11/17/94; *NYP*, 8/12/95; *NYT*, 4/18/81, 5/16/83, 8/17/83, 10/7/85, 1/31/93, 9/5/93, 9/19/93, 7/18/94, 10/8/94, 10/17/94, 10/6/95, 3/20/96.

24. Barlett and Steele 1992; Greider 1992:70, 82–83, 92–93; Harrison and Bluestone 1988; Levy 1995:25; Phillips 1990, 1994; Wolff 1995; *NYT*, 4/21/92, 10/7/94, 8/21/95, 3/13/96, 3/28/96, 6/22/96; *WSJ*, 11/22/96, 12/23/96.

25. Barlett and Steele 1992:4; Phillips 1990:157, 163–64; Wolff 1995; *NYT*, 2/28/82, 4/4/84, 1/11/91, 5/11/92; *NYTM*, 11/19/95.

26. Gordon 1996:100; Tobier 1984; *Honolulu Advertiser*, 2/3/92; *NYT*, 8/25/82, 12/11/83, 8/3/84, 9/27/90, 9/27/91, 7/26/92, 10/5/93, 1/4/95, 4/17/95, 7/2/95; *WSJ*, 9/27/96.

27. Barlett and Steele 1992:7, 19–20; Bluestone and Harrison 1982:4–5, 17, 147; Bowles, Gordon, and Weisskopf 1990:38, 137–43, 156, 157–59; Gordon 1996; Greider 1992:86, 92–94, 396–97; Harrison and Bluestone 1988:5–11, 79, 94–97, 110, 112, 117, 149–51; Kasarda 1995:240, 250, 256; Levy 1995:1, 15–16, 21, 37–38, 41–43, 48; Obey 1996; Phillips 1990:14–20, 80–87, 168, 179–80, 1994:86–87; Williams 1994; Wolff 1995:2, 17; *ND*, 4/29/87, 11/18/93, 8/6/95; *NYT*, 4/25/82, 11/17/91, 5/12/92, 7/20/93, 3/31/94, 10/17/94, 1/8/95, 4/17/95, 6/16/95, 6/23/95, 6/25/95; *NYTM*, 11/19/95; *WSJ*, 2/22/96, 6/2/97.

28. Barlett and Steele 1992:xiv, 7; Bluestone and Harrison 1982:19, 180–90; Bowles, Gordon, and Weisskopf 1990:38–40, 124–29; Gordon 1996; Greider 1992:193; Harrison and Bluestone 1988:39–52; Levy 1995:5; Obey 1996; Phillips 1990:20, 21; *CNYB*, 11/28/94; *Fortune*, 6/27/94; *ND*, 10/5/90; *NYT*, 5/7/78, 3/13/80, 8/14/83, 12/12/83, 4/5/84, 10/24/85, 2/1/87, 10/3/89, 9/5/90, 12/1/94, 7/3/95; *WSJ*, 12/12/95.

29. Frey 1995; Levy 1995:3; *NYT*, 6/28/92; *NYTM*, 1/20/91.

30. Barlett and Steele 1992:2, 33; Bluestone and Harrison 1982:203; Phillips 1990:23–25; *Landlines*, 9/95; *NYT*, 9/3/95; *NYTM*, 11/19/95.

31. Fitch 1993:5, 7, 19–20; Phillips 1990:170; Weitzman 1989:30–31; *DN*, 3/31/94, 1/31/95, 12/3/95; *ND*, 7/14/95; *NYP*, 7/13/95; *NYT*, 6/26/88, 12/25/94, 3/1/95, 5/9/95, 5/29/95, 12/5/95; *Westsider*, 4/13/95.

32. Fitch 1994:17–19; Rosenberg 1987, 1989, 1992; Tobier 1984; Weitzman 1989; *DN*, 11/11/91; *ND*, 3/5/95, 3/26/95, 3/17/97; *NYT*, 5/23/82, 7/26/84, 4/12/94, 7/14/95, 10/21/96.

33. DCP 1993b; Rothschild 1996.

34. Committee on Banking, Finance, and Urban Affairs 1984:8; Kasarda 1995:263; Tyler 1987:468–70; *CNYB*, 11/28/94; *ND*, 6/29/86; *NYO*, 2/5/96; *NYT*, 7/8/84, 2/28/94. On underground

economic activities supplementing welfare and low-paid jobs in poor New York City neighborhoods, see Sharff 1981, 1987; Sullivan 1989; Valentine 1978. On the economic impact of organized crime, see Shaffer 1973.

35. Ferman, Henry, and Hoyman 1987; Greider 1992:85–86; *ND,* 8/7/94; *NYT,* 3/15/81, 5/9/81, 7/4/82, 9/10/86.

36. Ferman, Henry, and Hoyman 1987; Tyler 1987:468–70; *DN,* 3/15/87, 7/16/95; *ND,* 8/7/94. For a narrow view of New York City's "informal economy" focusing primarily on immigrants, see Sassen 1991a:279–83, 288–94, and 1991b. See also Winnick 1988:13–14, 19–20, 21–23.

37. *DN,* 6/9/94, 2/8/96; *ND,* 4/26/95; *NYT,* 6/16/93, 8/3/94.

38. *DN,* 4/27/94, 5/26/96, 7/18/96; *ND,* 3/4/93, 4/26/95; *NYT,* 4/8/84.

39. *DN,* 4/12/91, 6/27/91; *NYP,* 8/24/94; *NYT,* 12/15/82, 5/12/87, 11/23/93, 10/19/95.

40. Chen 1992:86–87; Hoyman 1987:68; *ND,* 8/7/94; *NYT,* 3/15/81, 6/16/93. On tax evasion by Italian immigrants in Queens and Brooklyn, see Fortuna 1991:84–88; Hutchens 1977:124.

41. Chinese Staff and Workers Association 1990:4.

42. Buck 1979; Chen 1992:123; Chinese Staff and Workers Association 1990; Colen 1990; Park 1997; Smith 1992; *DN,* 9/23/90, 9/24/90; *ND,* 5/4/88, 6/28/90, 10/18/91, 6/10/93, 7/24/96; *NYT,* 5/30/90, 5/19/91, 5/26/92, 6/9/93, 6/13/93, 6/15/93, 7/16/95; *VV,* 4/26/94. On Italian illegal immigrants working below minimum wage in Italian-owned businesses, see Fortuna 1991:84–86, 88, 92; Hutchens 1977:155–56.

43. Ricourt 1995; *Community [Assistance Unit] News,* 4/85; *DN,* 7/4/94; *ND,* 12/17/90; *NYT,* 11/24/80, 12/9/84, 5/13/86.

44. *ND,* 4/13/93; *NYT,* 8/4/76, 7/14/80, 8/27/82.

45. *DN,* 4/12/91, 8/2/91, 6/3/92; *ND,* 5/5/92; *NYT,* 5/30/81, 6/14/83, 8/2/83, 7/20/87, 9/24/90, 6/14/93, 4/16/95, 9/28/95.

46. Collier and Buitron 1971; Salomon 1973; *ND,* 2/15/87, 2/4/91, 5/23/94; *NYT,* 12/15/81.

47. On similar merchant-peddler conflict in the 1820s and 1890s–1910s, see Blackmar 1989:171–72; Bluestone 1992:295–97.

48. Giuliani and Bratton 1994; *ND,* 2/15/87; *NYT,* 12/1/80, 2/12/83, 4/14/83, 7/31/86, 12/1/86, 12/19/86, 12/25/86, 2/7/93, 5/9/94.

49. Tanenbaum 1995; *DN,* 6/30/91; *ND,* 1/11/90; *NYT,* 8/28/91.

50. *DN,* 4/12/94, 8/17/94; *NYT,* 8/28/7, 7/29/85, 11/11/92.

51. *ND,* 3/12/95; *NYT,* 9/24/84, 9/13/90, 6/13/93, 9/5/94, 8/8/95.

52. *DN,* 9/12/95; *ND,* 10/13/87, 8/7/88; *NYT,* 12/6/92, 11/12/95.

53. *DN,* 4/7/91, 6/13/93; *ND,* 7/20/92; *NYT,* 9/23/92, 2/26/95, 9/2/95, 9/3/95, 9/24/95, 4/29/96.

54. *DN,* 7/12/93; *NYT,* 3/11/79, 5/1/93.

7. *Mayoral Ideologies*

1. Brower 1989; Marcuse, Medoff, and Pereira 1981; Newfield and DuBrul 1977:324; Tabb 1982:37–39; Weitzman 1989. This redirection of city antipoverty funds, however, resulted in a firestorm of protest, and by 1982 NSA designations were awarded to thirty-two neighborhoods (*CL,* 4/79).

2. Twentieth Century Fund 1980:23.

3. Twentieth Century Fund 1980; cf. Sassen 1988:153–58, 173–74, 177. See also Fitch 1993:159–63.

4. Twentieth Century Fund 1980; Sinnreich 1980:157–60.

5. Walsh 1990:209–11; *NYT,* 7/14/82, 3/22/83. See also Suttles 1984:296–97.

6. Wagner 1988:8, 22–47, 149; cf. Winnick 1990:49–52. See also Arian et al. 1990:29–36; Fitch 1993:165–69.

7. Salins 1988; Willis 1988; Winnick 1988.

8. Drennan 1991; Mollenkopf 1988b; Mollenkopf and Castells 1991b.

9. Haig 1926:427; Harrison and Bluestone 1988:67–68, 214; Hymer 1979; Sassen 1991a.

10. Sassen 1991a; Willis 1988:44. See Frey 1995:276–77; Kasarda 1995:226, 235–38; *CNYB,* 5/1/95; *DN,* 5/25/95.

11. Vogel 1993:53, 65; he nonetheless contended, "For the foreseeable future, [New York] is likely to remain both America's and the world's *most* important financial center"(69). Kahler (1993:39–44) made similar points but concluded, "The advent of national banking will mean that not only will New York banks be able to operate in other regions, but also the headquarters of a larger number of major banks will be located elsewhere."

12. Fitch 1993, 1994.

13. Vilaine 1991:vi, 62–79; see *WSJ*, 3/6/96.

14. *DN*, 4/2/95, 1/26/97; *ND*, 4/5/93; *NYO*, 10/16/95; *NYT*, 8/5/94, 12/14/94, 10/13/95.

15. Fuentes 1980; Gittell 1971; Glazer 1993; Green and Wilson 1989:23–27; Kasinitz 1992:xii–xv; *NYT*, 1/27/92.

16. Green and Wilson 1989:73, 103, 109, 133; *Crítica*, 1/95, 2/95, 3/95; *DN*, 7/17/95; *ND*, 10/19/87, 12/26/87; *NYT*, 1/27/85, 6/7/94.

17. Glazer 1993:177; *DN*, 8/4/92; *ND*, 1/25/87, 4/3/90; *NYT*, 3/29/87.

18. Green and Wilson 1989:109–10, 133–34; Mills 1987; *DN*, 9/21/94; *ND*, 7/7/87, 12/22/87, 11/11/94; *NYT*, 12/21/86.

19. *DN*, 7/2/89, 5/6/90, 8/2/91; *DN Magazine*, 3/17/85; *ND*, 11/4/87, 2/9/90, 1/25/91, 7/28/91, 7/14/92, 7/15/92; *NYT*, 1/9/85, 12/21/88, 7/28/91, 7/29/91, 8/4/91; *VV*, 8/27/91.

20. Arian et al. 1990:20–68; City of New York 1986:89–128; Falcón 1985a, 1985b; Green and Wilson 1989:89–95, 133; Harrington 1987; Mills 1987:480; Stafford 1989:11–18, 63–64; *NYTM*, 4/8/90.

21. Chen 1992:152, 216; Park 1997; *NYT*, 8/19/84.

22. Falcón 1985a:14; Institute for Puerto Rican Policy 1987a:2; Office of the Mayor press release 425–85, 10/4/85; *NYT*, 12/12/82.

23. City of New York 1986, 1987; Institute for Puerto Rican Policy 1987; Stafford 1989:11; *DN*, 12/18/86, 3/10/87; *NYT*, 8/3/86, 3/10/87.

24. *ND*, 1/25/87, 8/9/91; *NYT*, 5/14/85, 3/29/87, 4/1/87, 6/28/90.

25. *CL*, 4/80; *ND*, 1/26/87, 7/5/92; *NYT*, 11/3/91.

26. *CL*, 11/85, 8/87, 4/91; *DN*, 7/2/92, 7/14/95; *ND*, 10/12/86, 1/26/87, 6/24/88, 12/30/90, 1/27/91, 3/17/91, 7/15/91; *NYT*, 10/25/84, 3/13/89, 2/25/90, 7/1/92, 7/5/92, 6/6/94.

27. Bailey and Waldinger 1991; Stafford 1985; *ND*, 5/11/92.

28. Stafford 1989; Waldinger 1986–87; *DN*, 1/27/94; *ND*, 6/17/95; *NYT*, 8/4/92, 7/17/94.

29. *DN*, 5/9/95; *ND*, 1/25/87, 1/27/87, 10/11/92; *NYT*, 5/14/85, 3/29/87, 2/25/90.

30. *ND*, 12/15/87, 7/20/92; *NYT*, 7/29/91.

31. Arian et al. 1990:44–45, 69–114, 201–5; Falcón 1989a:4, 1989b; *ND*, 5/16/90.

32. Falcón 1989b; *ND*, 6/17/95.

33. Sung Soo Kim to David Dinkins, 4/19/89; *Crítica*, 3/95; *DN*, 5/6/90; *ND*, 10/10/90, 10/11/92; *NYT*, 1/28/92.

34. Arian et al. 1990:94; Falcón 1989b:3; *ND*, 6/14/93; *DN*, 11/4/93, 11/8/93.

35. *Crítica*, 7/94, 8/94, 12/94, 4/95, 8/94; *DN*, 8/16/94, 1/2/96; *ND*, 6/9/95, 6/17/95, 4/29/96, 5/1/96; *NYO*, 3/25/96; *NYP*, 6/24/95; *NYT*, 8/23/94, 4/4/95, 3/12/97.

36. Morris 1980:167–68; Newfield and DuBrul 1977:157–62; *NYT*, 6/7/94.

37. *DN*, 2/5/85, 2/7/85, 3/8/90, 9/2/92, 10/15/92, 7/20/93, 7/23/93; *ND*, 3/8/90; *NYT* 1/27/85.

38. A 110th Precinct Community Council dating from 1964 consisted of local residents who during the 1980s gave awards to individual officers and supported precinct-sponsored youth activities; it did not serve as a channel for citizen complaints.

39. *ND*, 8/11/87.

40. *ND*, 4/10/86.

41. *ND*, 4/3/90; *NYT*, 8/31/89.

42. Brecher and Horton 1991:107, 111; 1993:26–27, 166–67, 241–62, 279–80, 283–86; Netzer 1990:50; Shefter 1985:140–41; Stafford 1989:22–23; Willis 1988:34; *DN*, 9/3/89; *ND*, 6/20/91.

43. Vilain 1991:45, 48; *ND*, 10/4/90, 4/26/91; *NYT*, 8/3/92.

44. *ND* 6/21/91, 3/25/92, 10/2/92, 5/8/93, 5/11/93.

45. Tanenbaum 1995:172–84; *DN*, 1/24/94, 12/11/94, 12/30/94, 7/16/95; *ND*, 7/16/95, 1/14/96, 1/16/96; *NYP*, 7/8/95; *NYT* 1/25/94, 4/8/95.

46. *ND,* 12/7/94, 7/14/95; *NYT,* 8/7/94, 1/1/95, 3/15/95, 7/8/95, 7/23/95.

47. Giuliani and Bratton 1994; *DN,* 8/19/94, 9/21/94, 9/28/94, 3/30/95; *ND,* 10/24/94; *NYT,* 1/1/95, 5/18/97; *VV,* 9/6/94.

48. *ND,* 8/17/94, 9/19/94; *NYT,* 6/6/95.

49. *ND,* 3/19/96, 9/17/96, 9/18/96, 9/23/96, 10/2/96, 10/13/96, 2/14/97.

8. Mayoral Practice

1. Bellush 1990:316–19, 321; Fitch 1993:280; Sleeper 1987; Walsh 1990:215; *NYT,* 11/17/80, 8/8/82, 11/20/83.

2. Bellush 1990:321, 332; Brecher and Horton 1993:202; Fainstein and Fainstein 1988:185; Leichter 1995; Sleeper 1987; Tabb 1982:85; Twentieth Century Fund 1980:16; Willis 1988:34; *CL,* 10/84; *NYT,* 4/6/82, 1/25/83, 11/28/83.

3. Bellush 1990:322–23, 332–33; Brecher and Horton 1993:201, 209–17; Brower 1989:14–16, 21; Curvin and Porter 1979:121, 125; Fainstein and Fainstein 1988:183–84; Harrison and Bluestone 1988:105; Leichter 1995; Newfield and DuBrul 1977:132–35; Sanjek 1984; Sleeper 1987; *CL,* 8/83, 10/83, 11/83, 8/85; *ND,* 4/17/91; *NYO,* 8/21/95, 9/11/95; *NYT,* 8/30/92. "Between 1982 and 1985, Edward Koch's campaign committee received . . . close to $1 million in large contributions from real estate interests" (Eichenthal 1990a:81).

4. Bellush 1990:327; Brecher and Horton 1993:11; Fitch 1993:46; Leichter 1995; Shefter 1985:177; Sleeper 1987; Walsh 1990:210; *CL,* 4/86, 4/88, 4/90; *NYT,* 4/9/95.

5. Harrison and Bluestone 1988:184; Kieschnick 1981; *CL,* 4/88.

6. *DN,* 1/25/87, 4/29/90; *ND,* 3/22/87; *NYT,* 8/27/83; *VV,* 4/15/81.

7. Salvo, Ortiz, and Vardy 1992:162.

8. *ND,* 12/21/86, 10/5/87.

9. Brecher and Horton 1993:266, 270, 292, 317; *ND,* 12/21/86, 2/26/89; *NYT,* 8/31/89.

10. Arian et al. 1990; Falcón 1989a, 1989b; Institute for Puerto Rican Policy 1990:23–24; *VV,* 11/26/91.

11. Fitch 1993:6, 145–46; Garreau 1992:446; *ND,* 7/1/91, 1/27/92, 7/20/92, 1/25/93, 5/9/93, 7/26/93, 1/24/94, 1/28/94, 3/27/95; *NYT,* 12/21/90, 11/7/91, 12/20/91.

12. Bach and West 1993; Brecher and Horton 1993:192; Kasarda 1995:232–33; *ND,* 5/26/92; *NYT,* 5/3/92.

13. Leichter 1995; *DN,* 6/19/92, 12/9/93; *ND,* 3/5/91, 12/17/91, 6/19/92; *NYT,* 3/1/92, 12/22/93.

14. Leichter 1995; *DN,* 7/12/92, 12/29/92, 7/21/94; *ND,* 4/17/91, 3/27/95.

15. *ND,* 5/26/92, 8/21/92, 12/1/92; *NYO,* 9/23/9; *NYT,* 9/12/91, 10/13/91, 8/2/92, 5/9/93.

16. Vilain 1991:10–11, 15, 52, 108–9; *ND,* 9/24/91; *NYT,* 2/1/92, n.d./92.

17. Fitch 1993:95, 135, 186–205; New York Times 1996:37–96; *DN,* 7/12/94, 7/21/94; *ND,* 4/5/93, 7/16/94, 12/12/94; *NYO,* 12/2/96; *NYP,* 8/29/95; *NYT,* 8/6/92.

18. Leichter 1995; *DN,* 9/6/91, 7/18/93, 7/21/94, 12/21/94; *ND,* 8/3/92, 4/5/93, 6/11/93, 7/26/93; *NYT,* 4/28/93, 5/3/93, 8/5/94.

19. Brecher and Horton 1993:307–24; Vilain 1991:48; *DN,* 7/19/94, 9/25/94; *NYT,* 7/7/9, 7/21/91, 3/21/93.

20. *DN,* 6/6/85, 5/11/92, 8/23/93, 9/7/93; *ND,* 8/9/88, 3/15/91, 9/14/90, 5/9/91, 5/10/91, 5/16/91, 8/21/91, 4/23/92, 9/8/93, 3/15/91, 6/9/92, 6/11/92, 5/12/93, 6/23/93, 9/2/93, 12/23/93; *NYT,* 8/24/86, 2/22/91, 10/22/92, 2/20/91, 9/4/91, 8/29/93; *Queens Environmental Campaign Green Letter,* August–September 1991; *Queens Tribune,* 2/21/91; *Woodside Herald,* 6/28/91.

21. Leichter 1995; *DN,* 4/2/95; *ND,* 3/27/95; *NYT,* 7/5/95.

22. Brecher and Horton 1993:30.

23. *CNYB,* 11/26/94; *DN,* 8/1/94, 12/16/94; *ND,* 7/25/94, 10/24/94, 12/5/94, 6/8/95, 6/9/95, 6/30/95; *NYT,* 5/15/94, 12/16/94, 12/29/94, 10/15/95.

24. Leichter 1995; *ND,* 12/12/94, 12/16/94; *NYT,* 5/15/94.

25. Leichter 1995; *DN,* 5/11/95; *ND,* 6/9/95, 6/30/95; *NYO,* 11/27/95; *NYT,* 12/31/94, 7/5/95.

26. *CNYB,* 12/23/96, 1/13/97; *DN,* 2/3/97; *ND,* 1/7/96, 1/20/96, 2/5/96; *NYT,* 1/5/96, 11/10/96, 3/23/97.

27. Leichter 1995; *CL,* 3/97; *DN,* 12/21/94, 6/8/95, 9/8/95, 4/5/96; *ND,* 3/27/95, 5/10/95, 6/18/95, 5/11/97; *NYP,* 4/10/95, 8/9/95, 11/11/96; *NYT,* 6/6/94, 4/7/97, 4/25/97, 6/6/97; *VV,* 6/11/96. Six more Giuliani designer packages went unannounced in the press.

28. Rothschild 1996; *City Project Bulletin,* 2/5/97, 2/24/97; *DN,* 2/11/95, 2/15/95, 6/14/95, 7/12/95; *ND,* 10/26/93, 2/10/95, 3/12/95, 7/4/95, 12/4/94; *NYO,* 4/22/96; *NYP,* 10/6/94, 9/15/95; *NYT,* 9/5/94, 8/9/95, 9/1/95, 2/9/97; *VV,* 12/14/93.

29. *DN,* 5/3/95, 6/20/95, 9/13/95, 10/29/95; *ND,* 2/18/93, 1/20/94, 8/12/94, 8/28/94, 9/4/94, 4/5/95, 6/4/96, 9/4/96, 9/21/96, 4/28/97; *NYP,* 6/22/95, 9/4/95; *NYT,* 3/28/91, 3/20/94, 5/15/94, 5/16/95, 6/19/95, 6/22/95, 7/18/95, 11/3/95, 6/12/96, 1/14/97, 4/13/97, 4/14/97.

30. Brecher and Spiezio 1995; *CL,* 11/94; *DN,* 2/20/94, 11/30/94, 1/20/95, 2/23/95; *ND,* 7/7/91, 4/20/94, 2/25/95; *NYT,* 10/6/82, 3/30/94, 2/24/95, 2/28/95, 9/9/95, 10/31/95, 10/7/96.

31. *ND,* 3/7/96, 4/28/96, 1/12/97, 1/16/97.

32. Brower 1989:23–32, 42–47; *DN,* 3/22/95; *ND,* 4/2/95, 6/16/95; *NYP,* 3/4/95; *NYT,* 3/28/95.

33. *DN,* 7/30/95, 8/13/95; *NYT,* 8/8/95, 9/21/95, 4/14/97.

34. *NYP,* 4/29/95; *VV,* 3/14/95, 5/9/95; *ND,* 3/27/95.

35. *Inside City Hall,* NY-1 television, 4/28/95; *ND,* 4/29/95.

9. *Assaults on the Quality of Life*

1. Quality-of-life surveys in other city neighborhoods turned up similar concerns; *DN,* 5/28/95; *NYT,* 8/4/94, 8/7/94, 10/30/94, 10/8/96.

2. DCP 1993b; *ND,* 6/20/93; *NYT,* 1/1/95, 2/16/97.

3. *NYT,* 12/14/91; on crowded conditions at these two stations in the 1950s, see Caro 1974:931.

4. *ND,* 9/23/94, 3/9/97.

5. DCP 1976, 1993b; Rothschild 1996. There were more than 23,625 cars in 1980, and more than 28,475 in 1990; between these years the number of persons driving to work alone increased from 8,090 to 13,200.

6. *DN,* 8/8/85, 9/15/86, 9/26/95, 10/19/95; *ND,* 11/20/91, 5/11/93, 2/17/95; *NYT,* 4/18/82, 12/13/83, 12/17/83, 8/8/85, 8/12/94, 3/19/95, 7/10/95, 12/17/95.

7. Chen 1992:96–99, 122–26; Park 1997; Ricourt 1995; see Weitzman 1989:13, 16. Such arrangements are ancient history in New York City; see Blackmar 1989:62–68.

8. *ND,* 4/3/91; *NYT,* 10/15/92, 4/27/97.

9. Bach and West 1993:102; Rothschild 1993; *ND,* 1/11/94, 4/2/95, 4/24/97; *NYT,* 10/7/96, 4/23/97; see also Brecher and Horton 1993:293. During the 1990s the press rediscovered every two years that up to 60,000 persons, mainly immigrants, lived in illegal cubicles and basement units: *ND,* 6/26/90; *NYT,* 3/23/92, 3/12/94, 10/6/96. On Chinatown, see Chen 1992:92–93.

10. *Newsday* reporters traced the Almonte family during 1986–1987 in monthly articles; see esp. *ND,* 10/26/86, 2/1/87, 3/29/87.

11. Brecher and Horton 1991:119–21; Fitch 1993:46–47, 119, 150, 206–31, 1994:38, 41; Goldberger 1988:135–36; Newfield and DuBrul 1977:121–22, 238; Waldinger 1986:107, 116; Willis 1988:52; *CL,* 11/85; *DN,* 10/4/87, 4/29/90; *ND,* 5/29/91; *NYT,* 10/12/83, 6/28/84, 12/25/86, 9/16/87, 11/12/91.

12. Harrison and Bluestone 1988:160; *DN,* 3/20/88, 6/27/89, 8/19/92; *ND,* 5/31/96; *NYT,* 2/26/81, 2/5/90; *VV,* 2/10/82, 2/3/87.

13. Newfield and DuBrul 1977:260–61; Rothschild 1996; *DN,* 12/17/95; *ND,* 8/21/94; *NYP,* 7/22/96; *NYT,* 4/13/93, 4/20/93.

14. Chen 1992: 29–30; *DN,* 2/22/85; *NYT,* 6/19/92.

15. Allen 1993:169–70; Halle 1984:41–42, 141; La Ruffa 1988:105–10; Tricarico 1984:41, 53, 64–65; Valentine 1978:23–24; *DN,* 9/17/93; *NYT,* 4/29/80, 11/20/87, 10/12/94.

16. *DN,* 3/1/87; *ND,* 3/1/87, 2/28/90.

17. *ND,* 9/20/89.

18. Newfield and DuBrul 1977:251–66; *DN,* 12/12/93, 7/25/94, 1/29/96, 10/2/96, 12/10/96; *ND,* 4/29–5/1/86, 9/8–11/86, 4/16/87, 1/21/92, 2/2/92, 5/6/92, 5/31/92, 7/28/93, 11/4/94, 1/29/96; *NYT,* 3/9/80, 10/27/80, 2/14/82, 4/25–27/82, 9/30/84, 12/19/86, 11/25/92, 8/3/94, 11/2/94, 11/17/94; *NYTM,* 7/26/92.

19. *DN,* 6/7/93; *ND,* 9/8/86; *VV,* 9/21/93.

20. *DN,* 10/25/84, 6/16/92, 4/13/93, 12/14/93; *ND,* 3/16/87; *NYP,* 12/25/96; *NYT,* 10/4/84, 6/10/87, 11/20/88, 12/21/88, 10/22/90, 10/21/91, 11/1/92, 1/24/93, 5/29/94, 9/3/95.

21. Chen 1992:111.

22. *DN,* 10/4/84, 10/24/93, 3/22/97; *ND,* 11/22/89; *NYT,* 9/2/90, 1/1/94; *VV,* 9/21/93.

23. *DN,* 8/3/94; *ND,* 8/13/92, 1/[n.d.]/95; *NYT,* 8/12–14/92, 8/2/94.

24. *ND,* 3/5/97.

25. Sullivan 1991:226, 232–33, 239–40; *NYT,* 9/14/79, 11/24/82; "The Big Business of Illicit Drugs," *NYTM,* [n.d.]/83.

26. *DN,* 12/14/89; *NYT,* 11/17/88, 8/3/92.

27. *DN,* 8/12/88; *ND,* 8/15/88.

28. *DN,* 12/18/86, 3/25/92; *ND,* 5/28/90, 4/12/92; *NYT,* 9/11/84, 7/25/86, 1/11/90; *VV,* 8/4/87; *Woodside Herald,* 3/3/78.

29. Chaney 1976:88, 136; Thomas Tilitz, c. 1982, "Paper on Elmhurst" (typescript in author's files); *ND,* 2/23/86, 5/17/86, 7/2/88, 4/18/91, 5/12/92, 11/28/94, 9/5/96; *NYT,* 11/20/86, 2/13/87, 5/21/88, 8/24/88, 9/27/94, 9/15/95.

30. *DN,* 12/8/86, 3/12/92, 12/5/93, 3/12/96; *ND,* 6/19/86, 2/8/87, 4/10/87, 5/26/91, 7/16/91, 3/13/92, 3/26/92, 5/11/93, 1/27/94, 3/6/94, 9/27/94; *NYT,* 3/24/87, 8/23/88, 9/27/91, 4/16/93, 5/12/93, 11/25/95, 2/25/96, 12/29/96.

31. *DN,* 7/29/88, 11/20/91, 9/29/92, 4/2/93, 1/25/94, 6/26/94, 3/11/97; *ND,* 6/19/86, 8/12/86, 4/8/87, 5/4/88, 1/6/89, 7/14/90, 2/16/91, 7/23/91, 3/15/92, 1/13/96; *NYT,* 6/14/81, 8/18/82, 11/24/85, 11/21/86, 12/9/86, 8/22/88, 12/5/88, 11/6/89, 1/31/90, 9/27/90, 11/28/94, 7/30/95, 4/20/97.

32. *DN,* 4/29/92, 1/10/94, 4/12/94, 4/28/94, 5/28/95; *ND,* 6/21/93, 8/5/94; *NYT,* 4/10/87, 6/17/93, 12/1/94, 3/11/97.

33. *DN,* 11/20/87, 5/19/88; *ND,* 10/24/88, 5/21/94, 3/6/95; *NYT,* 7/19/87.

34. *DN,* 1/5/85, 7/11/87, 2/22/89, 5/16/92, 8/13/95; *ND,* 7/11/87, 11/18/87, 9/16/88, 2/22/89, 11/17/89, 5/26/92, 8/14/92, 1/23/94, 9/5/96, 9/16/96; *NYT,* 11/5/82, 11/11/82, 6/6/85, 8/9/87, 2/28/89, 3/15/95, 3/18/95, 8/14/95, 11/2/95, 12/3/95, 2/11/96; *WSJ,* 8/26/96.

35. *DN,* 4/26/92; *ND,* 1/13/86, 1/31/86, 2/20/86, 4/26/86, 7/12/86, 2/4/89, 3/19/89; *NYT,* 12/28/86, 5/28/95.

36. *DN,* 11/26/92, 5/15/94, 6/14/94, 8/24/96; *ND,* 4/26/86, 9/2/96, 11/24/96; *NYT,* 1/30/92, 6/17/93.

37. *DN,* 6/8/90; *ND,* 9/19/88, 6/8/90, 7/28/92.

38. Baxter and Hopper 1981; Hopper 1988; Hopper, Susser, and Conover 1985; Sanjek 1984; Susser 1991:213–15; *CNYB,* 11/11/96; *NYT,* 11/16/93, 3/13/94.

39. *CL,* 3/87.

40. *City Project Bulletin,* 11/6/96; *DN,* 6/14/95, 8/9/95, 8/30/95; *ND,* 11/3/91, 2/16/92; *NYT,* 9/5/94, 9/7/95, 3/10/97.

41. *DN,* 9/21/94, 9/8/95, 9/6/96; *ND,* 9/26/96; *NYT,* 3/30/91, 5/15/94, 6/8/94.

42. *DN,* 5/23/86, 11/21/86, 7/19/89; *ND,* 11/26/89.

43. *DN,* 1/25/89, 1/5/90, 9/8/90; *ND,* 9/7/90, 10/10/90, 10/24/90, 1/24/95; *NYT,* 9/6/90.

44. *DN,* 6/28/87, 7/24/89; *ND,* 3/31/87, 5/18/91; *NYT,* 1/4/88, 1/6/91, 4/1/92; *New Yorker,* 11/16/92.

45. *ND,* 8/29/93, 10/17/93, 10/18/93, 2/22/94.

46. DCP 1992a; *ND,* 9/30/93.

47. I watched this meeting on NY-1 television.

48. *NYT,* 8/20/95.

49. *DN,* 3/15/95, 5/28/95, 9/15/95, 10/27/95; *ND,* 3/15/95; *NYP,* 1/10/96; *NYT,* 3/12/97, 4/13/97.

10. The New Multicultural Geography of Elmhurst-Corona

1. Winnick 1990:69.

2. DCP 1992a, 1992c, 1992d, 1993a, 1993b; Salvo, Ortiz, and Vardy 1992:4, 203.

3. See Sanjek 1992.

4. Kim 1981:112–21, 237–57; Park 1997.

5. Park 1997; Korean Harvest and Folklore Festival programs for 1985, 1986, 1991, and 1993. The 1993 program was twice the size and four times the length of the 1985 program, and contained far more paid ads from both Korean and non-Korean businesses.

6. I am not sure when the first of these celebrations occurred in William Moore Park, but hanging in the Corona Pizzeria was a photograph dated "July 4, 1984," showing men (including Anthony Federici) carrying a fifty-foot sandwich with Italian and American flags stuck in it.

7. *ND,* 8/9/89. In 1993 *Newsday* reported that Anthony Federici "was identified in 1988 as a Lucchese soldier by the U.S. Senate Permanent Subcommittee on Investigations. A law-enforcement source in the Queens district attorney's office told *New York Newsday* this week that Federici is now a capo with strong ties to the Genovese crime family. Asked if Federici is connected to any mob family, Federici's attorney, Harold Borg, said, 'Of course he's not' " (*ND,* 4/11/93). In 1992 Federici joined the Flushing Hospital board of directors. When its chair, Joseph Tanenbaum, was "questioned by a reporter about Federici's reputed mob links, [he] said he confronted the restaurateur. 'He didn't say yes or no. He let it go by,' Tanenbaum said" (*ND,* 5/14/93).

8. This event bears similarity to the more famous Fourth of July celebration sponsored since 1971 by Gambino crime boss John Gotti in Howard Beach, Queens. In 1996 Mayor Giuliani declared "zero tolerance" and halted all Fourth of July fireworks throughout the city (*ND,* 7/3/96, 7/4/96, 7/5/96).

9. Still, as Paine points out, "There are ways in which one 'says' through doing rather than by saying" (1981:18). Bloch (1974, 1977) stresses the separation of "ritual communication" from daily "practical activities" where social arrangements different from those enacted in ritual may obtain. The "formalized" strutting and interaction of the fireworks men, and the lack of verbal communication with their stationary, non-Italian audience, were in Bloch's terms ritual representations of the neighborhood's "traditional authority" and "a form of social control"; in short, "what is being said [or done] is the right thing because . . . it has become the only thing," and silence places traditional authority "beyond logic," with no room for response or contradiction. Asad (1979:616) points out there need be no "integrated system of 'shared meaningful ideas' " in any particular cultural setting, and "historic forces and relations" may undermine traditional authority as "radically opposed" views not expressed in one ritual emerge at other times or places; the 1993 march of Latin American activists to William Moore Park following the Mayi murder acquittal (see Chapter 15) used the location of the Fourth of July event to challenge what these protestors saw as "traditional authority" in Corona Heights. In the multiracial transition the United States is undergoing, rituals of ethnic assertion in multiethnic neighborhoods may well be "unstable, unable to reach the clinching together of people and ideas that characterizes established rituals" (Bloch 1985:36). Other forms of ritual that do this more effectively are discussed in later chapters.

10. Hannerz 1992. For other critiques of the "mosaic" metaphor, see Gans 1979; Goode 1990.

11. *DN,* 5/12/97; *NYT,* 11/24/96.

12. *ND,* 1/23/93; *NYT,* 6/1/93.

13. *DN,* 7/3/90, 7/4/90, 7/6/93, 9/6/93; *DN Magazine,* 7/23/89; *ND,* 6/1/89, 7/9/90, 5/15/94, 5/16/94, 5/26/94, 6/17/94, 6/22/94, 6/27/94, 6/30/94, 11/10/96.

14. DCP 1984. Comparable 1990 figures are not readily available.

15. DCP 1992d; Thomas Tilitz, c. 1982, "Paper on Elmhurst"; *ND,* 9/23/90; *NYT,* 12/24/82, 4/1/87, 3/13/89, 7/15/92, 6/6/94.

11. Solidarity and Conflict among White Americans

1. Thomas Tilitz, c. 1982, "Paper on Elmhurst." Cf. Jacobs 1961:138–39; Winnick 1990:137–38.

2. On relations between Italian immigrants and Italian-Americans, see Alba 1983; Fortuna 1991; Hutchens 1977; LaRuffa 1988; Tricarico 1984. "Yuppies" included "gentrifiers," who renovate older homes (few did so in Elmhurst-Corona); condominium and co-op apartment purchasers (like some in Sherwood Village and other CD4 buildings); and apartment renters, including persons who expected to move out of the city when they had children or who lacked sufficient income to purchase upscale real estate (some of whom lived in Elmhurst). See Allen 1993:219; Fava and DeSena 1984; Hacker 1975:137–39; Sieber 1978, 1987; Zukin 1987.

3. DCP 1984; 1980 census tract data, CUNY Data Service; Rothschild 1993.

4. Myers 1982. On senior citizens in neighborhood New York, see Cantor 1975; Tricarico 1984:85–86, 96–97, 117, 142, 159–60. A 1993 poll found that 42 to 45 percent of New Yorkers aged eighteen to sixty, if given the chance to live elsewhere, would remain in their neighborhood; among those sixty-one and over, however, 58 percent would remain (*ND*, 12/21/93).

5. Names in these portraits are pseudonyms. Subjects were selected to reflect variety in age, gender, ethnicity, religion, housing tenure, geographic location, and local attachment. Interviews were conducted at the subjects' homes or a location chosen by them; notes were taken by hand.

6. At least a third of the 3,200 persons listing English and the 2,100 listing French ancestry resided in census tracts whose racial composition suggests that they were black Caribbeans. In 1990 census data for CD4 (covering an area slightly different from the thirty-five 1980 census tracts), European nationality totals lumped unmixed and partial ancestry, but the same relative order as in 1980 persisted: 7,600 Italians, 4,250 Irish, 3,250 Germans, 2,000 Poles, 1,450 Greeks, 1,600 Russians and Ukrainians listed together, 560 Hungarians, 385 Romanians, 385 Yugoslavians [*sic*], 325 Austrians, 300 Czechs, 285 Slovaks, 270 Scots, 220 Scotch-Irish, 190 Dutch, 160 Swedes, 100 Lithuanians, and 100 Norwegians. Portuguese did not appear, and 740 English and 1,000 French again probably included some black residents. Census data are from 1980 census tract tables prepared by the CUNY Data Service and DCP 1993b; on the wider Queens County picture for 1980, see Kornblum and Beshers 1988:206–13.

7. White ethnic intermarriage is well studied; see Alba 1981, 1985, 1990; Lieberson 1985; Lieberson and Waters 1986, 1988; Sanjek 1994c; Waters 1990; Yancey, Ericksen, and Leon 1985. The incidence of Jewish marriage to non-Jews has grown from 10 percent in 1945 to 50 percent in 1995 (*NYT*, 7/17/95).

8. Maria Matteo, manuscript (in author's files), 1989.

9. Halle 1984:270–71; cf. Alba 1985:160. This view is consistent with Yancey, Ericksen, and Juliani 1976, and Yancey, Ericksen, and Leon 1985, on the changing structural underpinnings of white American identities. For other critiques of the opposing view of white ethnic persistence, see Gans 1979; Patterson 1979; Sanjek 1994a:8–9; references in note 7.

10. See Halle 1984:272–74; Kornblum and Beshers 1988:214–15.

11. Gans 1979:1–3.

12. Tricarico 1984:161; see also Alba 1985:viii, 75–76, 92.

13. Maria Matteo, manuscript, 1989.

14. *DN*, 7/3/85, 4/7/93, 6/15/96, 12/29/96; *ND*, 8/9/89, 6/3/92. See also Harlow 1995.

15. See Tricarico 1984 on the commercialization of Italianness in South Greenwich Village, and LaRuffa 1988 on Belmont in the Bronx.

16. Gans 1979:9; cf. Alba 1985:172–73; Tricarico 1984:165–66.

17. Hutchens (1977:77) quotes a second-generation Italian who assumed Irish ethnicity in the late 1940s: "When I was about sixteen, I loved to go to Irish dances and pretend to be Irish. I usually got away with it, too." Hebard (1990) describes Irish "traditional" dance groups that recruit among Irish and part-Irish Americans, but it is unclear whether the "Germans, Jews, Italians, [and] Polish" who join have any Irish ancestry. See also Gans 1979:6–13.

18. Prins 1965:4.

19. "Territory, then, is not neutral to its inhabitants and cumulative effects of changes and crit-

ical historical events are obvious in people's awareness of their localism" (Ekman 1991:22–23; see also 12–13, 92–93, 100–101). Cf. Suttles 1972:36–37.

20. I learned about the First United Methodist center from the fieldwork of Ruby Danta; see also Ricourt 1995.

21. On Davidoff's connections and lobbying, see *DN,* 12/16/91; *VV,* 4/7/92.

22. DCP 1989.

23. Davidson 1979:100–107. See also Bailey 1981, 1983:103–22; Suttles 1990:48–49.

24. Morris 1980:86, 94–95.

25. *ND,* 8/4/94; *NYT,* 7/17/94, 10/10/94.

26. *NTC,* May–June 1987.

27. *DN,* 6/4/90; *ND,* 6/7/90; *VV,* 4/23/93.

28. *ND,* 12/17/92.

29. *DN,* 11/24/92; *ND,* 9/1/92, 10/7/92, 11/10/92, 11/14/92, 11/26/92, 11/30/92, 12/1/92, 12/2/92, 12/4/92, 12/8/92; *NYT,* 10/6/92, 11/17/92, 12/3/92, 12/11/92, 12/27/92, 2/12/93; *VV,* 12/22/92, 4/20/93.

30. *DN,* 11/30/92, 12/2/92, 1/3/93; *ND,* 11/30/92, 12/1/92, 12/8/92, 12/18/92, 5/19/93; *NYT,* 12/5/92, 4/29/96; *VV,* 4/20/93.

31. *ND,* 4/11/93, 5/18/93; *NYT,* 4/18/93.

32. *DN,* 12/1/93; *ND,* 12/2/93, 3/2/94, 3/8/94, 3/27/94, 6/9/94; *NYT,* 2/19/94, 3/6/94.

33. *DN,* 2/14/94, 6/22/94; *ND,* 5/17/94, 5/20/94, 6/24/94.

34. *ND,* 2/5/92, 2/18/93, 4/25/96, 5/29/96; *NYT,* 3/28/91, 5/15/94.

35. Some whites did join ethnic societies at work (e.g., Kenneth Witter belonged to an Irish group) or ethnically based county, city, or national fraternal-sororal and charitable organizations. As members of an ethnic group paralleling those of other whites, Jews joined similar societies and organizations; as adherents of a religion, they were members of Jewish congregations as well. On ethnic solidarity and mobilization, see Olzak 1983.

36. *NYT,* 12/21/88, 1/31/89, 1/29/91.

37. Allen 1993:236; *DN,* 2/25/94. For views of "American" among other whites, see Halle 1984:203, 233–37; Lieberson 1985; Lieberson and Waters 1986, 1988; Tricarico 1984:19, 102, 139.

38. *NYT,* 2/19/94.

39. Cf. Goode 1990:135.

12. Continuities in Civic Politics

1. Auletta 1979:45–49; Gans 1988:17; Katznelson 1981:125–28; McNickle 1993:325; Mollenkopf 1988a:275–77, 1991:350–51; Mudd 1984:18–21; Pecorella 1994:27–28, 87–88; Wade 1990; *ND,* 6/17/92, 6/21/92.

2. In 1990 only 30 percent of Elmhurst-Corona's immigrant residents were citizens; this compared to 42 percent of immigrants in the city at large (DCP 1993b).

3. Institute for Puerto Rican Policy 1989b: 11; *DN,* 11/4/93. ADs are the standard unit by which election results are reported; for similar turnout differences among Queens ADs in other elections, see *DN,* 9/11/85; Institute for Puerto Rican Policy, "1990 Election Analysis," 11/8/90.

4. *DN,* 1/18/87; *ND,* 6/8/91, 6/12/91, 11/6/91. CD4 also falls within state senate district lines, but this body had a Republican majority, and CD4's Democratic state senator had little clout.

5. Bailey (1968:281) locates "parapolitical" activity in the "lesser arenas, . . . those which are partly regulated by, and partly independent of, large encapsulating political structures; and which . . . fight battles with these larger structures in a way which . . . seldom ends in victory, rarely in dramatic defeat, but usually in a long drawn stalemate and defeat by attrition"; cf. Suttles 1972:67. Scholars who limit politics to elections include Arian et al. (1991); Brecher and Horton (1993:79–80); McNickle (1993). For wider definitions of politics, see Bailey 1968, 1969; Davidson 1979:9–19; Hardy-Fanta 1993; Morgen and Bookman 1988; Piven and Cloward 1988:xii; Swartz, Turner, and Tuden 1966; Whyte 1943, 1946. On civic activism "outside regular politics," see Greider 1992:161–62, 169, 201, 206–7, 214–15; on parapolitical pressuring of elected leaders in New York City, see Fainstein and Fainstein 1991:323–24.

6. Cf. DeSena 1990:80–82; Mudd 1984:117.

7. There are four elected district leaders in each AD, two of whom must be male and two female. On the social significance of the *Daily News* among working-class whites in the New York area, see Halle 1984:48, 141; Tricarico 1984:34, 41, 95, 109.

8. Cf. Gregory 1992:272 n 12; Tricarico 1984:68–69, 126–37.

9. *NTC,* September–October 1974; Suttles 1972:36, 37, 55–57.

10. *NTC,* July–August 1975, May–June 1976; Suttles 1972:57–58;.

11. Katznelson 1981; Suttles 1972:58–59. The balance of power varies within each of New York City's community districts between its community board and local wardens, civic and block associations, political party clubs, elected officials, merchant associations, community school boards, police precinct councils, and public hospital advisory boards. Nonetheless, as political scientists Susan and Norman Fainstein emphasize, "community board meetings offer a forum, attended by administrative and elected officials, in which other neighborhood organizations raise issues of concern on topics ranging from police to housing to sanitation" (1991:320–21). Political scientist Ira Katznelson studied the newly established Lindsay-era decentralization structures in Washington Heights during 1971–1974, before the assaults on neighborhood quality of life which followed the 1975 fiscal crisis, and the linking of community boards and district cabinets in 1977. On later political developments in Washington Heights, see Georges (1984, 1988), who, unlike other anthropologists studying immigrants in New York City, devotes attention to community board and parapolitical civic arenas.

Five fieldwork-based studies of "white ethnic neighborhoods" in New York also cover wardens and civic politics but, except for Tricarico 1984, do not address their relationship to local community boards or place their activities within the district-level political field these boards define. See Susser 1982 on "Greenpoint-Williamsburg" (Brooklyn CD1) but concerning principally one Greenpoint block (fieldwork during 1975–1978); Tricarico 1984 on South Greenwich Village (fieldwork 1970–1978); Rieder 1985 on Canarsie, Brooklyn (fieldwork 1975–1977); LaRuffa 1988 on Belmont, the Bronx (fieldwork 1981–1982); and DeSena 1990, also on Greenpoint (fieldwork 1983). Of these studies only Susser's deals with the 1975 fiscal crisis, and none cites Katznelson's book on the political role of the new "city trenches."

12. Greider 1992:170; Mudd 1984:51–52. See also Pecorella (1994:14–17), who refers to civic activists as "attentive nonelites." Mudd's numerical estimate accords with Jacobs 1961. Gans also cites a 5 percent figure for political activism and organizational membership but describes "middle American" civic politics as more ad hoc and more dependent on outside organizers than was true in CD4. Elmhurst-Corona's working- and lower-middle-class white, black, Latin American, and Asian civic activists were certainly not "liberals," and "microsocial" family and neighborhood ties did matter a great deal to them, but they did not conform to Gans's view of "middle Americans" as people who are "unwilling and unable to organize" and who find "political action . . . morally and psychologically unsatisfying" (1988:ix–xi, 2–8, 43, 56, 72–78, 153–54). Still, thousands more CD4 residents had no involvement in civic politics, and many no doubt were unaware of CB4 and Elmhurst-Corona civic organizations.

13. Cf. Suttles 1972:37–41. Halle (1984) studied New York–area male, blue-collar workers who evince interest in political issues during workplace discussions but are uninvolved in neighborhood civic politics.

14. Also see Acosta 1989. Columnist Juan Gonzales described another Corona warden, Dominican immigrant Maria Evora, who from the mid-1980s to her death in 1995 offered music lessons and a Friday night gathering spot to Latin American teens in her home on the Corona Heights–Corona Plaza border. She also counseled youth with drug or other problems, referring some to a Catholic retreat center, and coached a choral group that performed at masses in St. Leo's (*DN,* 12/15/95).

15. *NYT,* 2/15/85.

16. *CL,* 3/90; *DN,* 6/22/90, 8/10/93.

17. A South Elmhurst United Civic Association dating from the 1930s became moribund sometime after 1969: *Brooklyn Eagle,* 7/22/32; *Long Island Press,* 9/7/69.

18. *NYT,* 11/9/94.

19. The Corona Homeowners Civic Association, which pressured against proposed low-income housing in 1965, became inactive after the early 1970s; its president served on CB4 during 1970–1971.

20. *CL,* 11/84; *NYT,* 3/2/79.

21. *DN,* 1/11/90; *ND,* 4/16/90.

22. Nationwide, most white Americans no longer participate in Memorial Day public events; see Halle 1984:251, 286.

23. *DN,* 4/28/85; *ND,* 4/10/89.

13. Innovations in Civic Politics

1. On civic politics in this community, see Gregory 1992, 1994a, 1994b, 1997.

2. *DN,* 10/5/76; *Long Island Press,* 10/24/76.

3. *NYP,* 2/9/78.

4. On Mireya Banks's network among Latin Americans in Corona, see Ricourt 1995.

5. For a fieldnote description of the 1988 cleanup, see Sanjek 1990:135. That year only one other block in CD4 held a similar annual cleanup day.

6. *DN,* 5/18/86.

7. City Planning Commission 1979; Edel 1987; *DN,* 1/28/90; *ND,* 11/6/90; *NYT,* 8/4/85, 10/27/87.

8. *DN,* 3/25/86; *NYT,* 1/2/87.

9. John P. Lomenzo, Secretary of State, "PUBLIC HEARING To Declare East Flatbush-Crown Heights-Brooklyn and Cambria Heights-Laurelton, L.I. NON-SOLICITATION AREAS," Department of State, New York State, 7/8/71 (typescript). The orders were authorized under a New York State anti-blockbusting law passed in 1969.

10. *ND,* 4/24/85. Objecting to both procedures, the New York State Association of Realtors challenged the state laws authorizing them, claiming First Amendment "free speech" protection, and the nonsolicitation ban was declared unconstitutional by the U.S. Supreme Court in 1994. This action was supported by advocates of fair housing, who argued that the ban was used in white neighborhoods to keep out nonwhite newcomers (*DN,* 2/12/90, 6/24/94; *ND,* 2/14/90, 6/24/94, 11/15/94). In CD4 and CD3, the cease-and-desist list was used by white, black, Latin American, and Asian homeowners who wished to stay.

11. *DN,* 2/13/95.

12. *NYT,* 10/13/85; *CL,* 12/85, 1/90.

13. *ND,* 7/1/90.

14. In Bailey's terms, Schilero had moved from wielding the "influence" of an "informal leader," which began with petition organizing, to exercising the "authority" of office as coalition president. "The informal leader has to lead without being seen to do so. . . . [But] beyond a certain point the leader has no alternative but to dispense with influence and take on the mask of authority" (1971: 299–300; see also 283, 285).

15. On such tactical displays of passion in political events, see Bailey 1983:11–12, 23–24, 37–38, 40.

16. See Chaney 1976:118–19; Hendricks 1974:107–12; Jones-Correa 1998; Ricourt 1995.

17. Chen 1992. When Louisa Chan was elected to SB24 in 1993, her victory was the result of her activism as a public school parent, not as a candidate of Chinese organizations.

18. Fisher 1980; Khandelwal 1991, 1994; Sridhar 1988.

19. Chaney 1976:119–25; Hendricks 1974: 24, 40–49, 84–91, 104; Jones-Correa 1998; *ND,* 4/27/86. See Park 1997 on the Korean ideology of *anjong,* or upward mobility, in the United States.

20. See *ND,* 6/22/86.

21. *CCQ In Action,* 5/86; *DN,* 10/22/89; *ND,* 9/13/86, 5/28/87.

22. *NYT,* 8/15/86.

23. *ND,* 1/31/86, 3/14/89.

24. *DN,* 6/26/94; *NYT,* 8/20/94.

25. *New York Nichibei,* 4/25/85; Park 1997. On Daughtry, see Green and Wilson 1989:73–74.

26. On sanitation regulations affecting stores, see *ND,* 6/18/95.

27. Cf. Pecorella 1994:185–86.

28. On the Queens Festival, see Chen 1992; on the New York City Korean community, see Park 1997.

29. "Innovation is a special kind of . . . planned and consciously intended [change which] carries connotations of discontinuity. . . . Innovations occur when [people] come to realize that they are no longer or may soon not be getting what will satisfy them out of [their] environment: they are then ready to experiment with new rules for their mutual interaction. . . . [An innovation] may be judged not . . . on its own merits but by the reputation and credit of those sponsoring it" (Bailey 1973:9, 313).

14. The Politics of Place

1. *DN,* 1/31/80; *ND,* 2/2/80. The move to Jamaica took place in 1988, but political considerations led Governor Mario Cuomo and Mayor Edward Koch to shift state and city offices to Lefrak City to replace those lost (*NYT,* 3/11/84, 1/21/90; *VV,* 9/18/90).

2. *DN,* 5/4/80.

3. *DN,* 9/12/79, 10/9/79; *DN Magazine,* 3/29/87. The Costello program never established an office in CD4, but the youth services committee continued to fund it until 1987, when Judy D'Andrea replaced Cirino as chair. Unable to monitor the Outreach Project's Elmhurst-Corona activities, D'Andrea recommended reduced support that year, and funding ended in 1988.

4. As Bailey notes, "Assertive rhetoric . . . is a rhetoric of belonging, of including in the congregation those who choose to believe and excluding the rest either by ignoring them, ridiculing them, or making them the objects of anger and contempt. . . . [I]t is inappropriate to ask whether an argument advanced in this form of rhetoric is valid. . . . The proper question to ask . . . concerns effectiveness" (1983:135–36).

5. In October 1984 when a federal offical asked CB4, "Didn't anyone tell you about the congressional guidelines change?" there was no response.

6. Cf. Bailey 1988:20–23.

7. One of the Latin American CB4 members appointed in 1982 later told the borough president's Latin American advisor that he left in 1983, feeling he received no respect and was not taken seriously.

8. On the East Harlem Italian community, see Meyer 1989; Orsi 1985.

9. See Vega 1987.

10. On the budget consultation process, see Mudd 1984:197–203; Pecorella 1994:151–53.

11. Compare Siefer 1973:21–22, quoting Kathleen McCourt.

12. "The leader's aim is both to keep his [*sic*] group strong and his own position secure" (Bailey 1969:66).

13. Thus, "Values and beliefs may yield to circumstances and new styles of leadership may become customary" (Bailey 1988:42).

14. See Chen 1992.

15. For comparative insights on how such usages convey "solidarity or intimacy," demarcate "a particular culture or sub-culture," and accomplish "redefinition" of previously distant relationships, see Parkin 1980. Also see Bailey 1988:84–85; Irvine 1979:785.

16. "Successful leadership is a matter of . . . creating confidence . . . that the leader can deliver the goods. This faith is reinforced when the leader does in fact deliver" (Bailey 1969:76).

17. Edna Baskin personified the African American female community activist defined by Gilkes (1980:223, 1988:57). Such women "act on whatever level they happen to find themselves," and typically become politically involved through concerns about youth. They "organize blacks in the community to work for specific changes while making demands against the white community in order to effect change. . . . The respect they acquire through working for the community confers upon them the privilege of publically criticizing the black community and raising the community's consciousness." Baskin was also what Sacks calls a "centerwoman. . . . The role in-

volves keeping people together, ensuring that obligations are fulfilled, and acting to express the group consensus" (1988:121–22, 132–33).

18. *DN,* 7/24/87.

19. This event resulted from some applied anthropology. I suggested to Pak that the KAAMQ might help the CCA team in some way; I then conferred with Gregory, who thought Pak should contact Baskin directly, since the two women already knew each other through CB4. Before I called Pak back, Gregory talked to Baskin, and she called Pak. The dinner occurred two weeks later and was repeated in 1988.

20. *DN,* 6/2/91, 7/6/94; *ND,* 9/9/88, 8/16/89, 6/18/90; *DN,* 7/23/90.

21. *ND,* 1/26/92.

22. Gregory 1993.

23. Mudd 1984; Pecorella 1994:165.

24. See *CL,* 6/82; Pecorella 1994:151–53; cf. Gans 1988:124. On Koch's increasing antagonism to community boards and Shulman's support, see Rogers 1990:173–75.

25. In some agencies supervisors were responsible for more than one community district. Fire Department districts were exempt from coterminality but not from attendance at district cabinet meetings. See Mudd 1984:203–7; Pecorella 1994:162–66.

26. Mudd 1984:106. Even though it made no formal collective decisions, the district cabinet conformed to Bailey's "arena council" model, each representative being "steered by the heavy rudder of those [agency cohorts] whose interests he represents." CB4 exhibited both district-level "elite council" and particularistic arena council characteristics; it was marked by consensus on some occasions and by strict majority voting on others. See Bailey 1965:9–14 and 1983:83–84, 93–94, 207–8; Kuper 1971:13–23; Schwartzman 1989:25–26, 61–64.

27. In bureaucratic settings such as the district cabinet, Bailey argues, "leadership begins where the formal rules stop"; in order to establish her own "goals and values," a leader employs " 'intuition,' 'flair,' 'gift,' and 'knack' . . . to make up for the insufficiencies of bureaucracy" and develops "informal—that is, personal—linkages" (1988:66, 71).

28. On forms and uses of humor in political events, see Bailey 1983:78, 87–94; Miller 1967.

29. Mudd 1984:103–5; Pecorella 1994:166.

30. On the importance of "a close circle of advisors," see Bailey 1988:121–22, 124.

31. See Rothschild 1993, 1996. As Mudd put it, "Occupying a unique position between the city administration and the community, [district managers] would know more about agency operations and neighborhood concerns than anyone else" (1984:91).

32. The thesis included historical maps of the area's landscape from colonial times to the present. Bearak deposited a set of the maps at the CB4 office and also gave a set to me.

33. Winnick 1990:57–58, 111; *CL,* 5/85, 8/85; *NYT,* 11/18/84.

34. DCP 1992b:15; *NYT,* 4/14/85, 2/2/86.

35. *CL,* 6/87; *DN,* 11/3/85; *NYT,* 10/21/84, 3/3/85.

36. On ULURP and the powers of community boards, see Mudd 1984:193–97; Pecorella 1994:140, 146–49.

37. On the 1985 Koch housing plans, see *NYT,* 4/14/85.

38. Brower 1989:143.

39. See *NYT,* 12/1/85

40. *DN,* 3/12/86; *ND,* 1/19/87.

41. Bailey observes that "experts have a set of common understandings, which enable them to communicate with one another with brevity. . . . [W]hile the sophisticated code . . . tends to grow in bulk . . . its mode of communication . . . moves in the other direction" (1983:184). And Paine notes, "Audiences, on the whole, do not like to be asked to examine arguments *in extenso* [and] prefer persuasive capsules" (1981:16).

42. *DN,* 8/9/87, 12/18/87; *ND,* 4/12/87, 10/31/87; *NYT,* 7/12/87, 8/2/87, 8/12/87, 10/4/87, 10/30/87.

43. See Winnick 1990:125.

44. *NYT,* 10/11/85.

45. For a critique of this as "subsidized housing for the privileged, displacing the poor," see Brower 1989.

46. *ND,* 7/30/86. Richard Bearak estimated that the city could have sold this property for "better than ten times" this amount on the private market.

47. Cf. Brower 1989:95, 97.

48. *ND,* 3/17/88, 3/30/88. In response to Bearak's prodding, HPD did free its remaining quarter-acre of the Corona high school land as a community recreational site to be maintained by Queenswood's developer.

49. *DN,* 2/8/88, 8/21/89, 2/9/90.

50. *DN,* 4/7/87, 7/9/87.

51. *ND,* 8/12/87.

52. DCP 1992b.

53. DCP 1992b.

54. DCP 1989.

55. *NYP,* 5/4/89.

56. *DN,* 12/12/93.

57. See Fitch 1989; Pecorella 1994:146–49; Viteritti 1990; *Queens Gazette,* 3/28/96; *NYO,* 3/25/96; *NYT,* 1/3/93. Giuliani advisor Peter Salins advocated elimination of ULURP altogether (1993:170).

58. Bailey 1981:7, 13–15, 24.

15. Bonds of Interracial Cooperation

1. These and other recurring events formed a cultural "civic calendar" that I followed faithfully. Unlike similar events studied by Goode and her Philadelphia team, however, Elmhurst-Corona's rituals of inclusion arose within the community; they were not "imposed by . . . outside human relations agencies" (Goode 1990:126).

2. PS19: *DN,* 11/16/88, 4/27/89; *ND,* 2/5/90; *NYT,* 1/17/85, 6/17/88, 5/25/92, 3/20/94. PS89: *DN,* 5/28/87, 10/24/93, 11/28/93, 12/12/93, 1/2/94, 2/20/94, 5/29/94; *NYT,* 10/28/82, 9/9/86.

3. *ND,* 2/22/91, 10/14/91; *NYT,* 8/25/86. More than language was involved in Latin American conversion to Protestantism; a 1991 *Newsday* poll found that 44 percent of Latin American New Yorkers attended English-language religious services. See Danta 1989a, 1989b.

4. St. Leo's church bulletin, 4/29/84; *Tablet,* 1/26/85. On youth activities at St. Leo's, see Acosta 1989.

5. In 1990 the adult population of Queens was 52 percent Roman Catholic and 23 percent Protestant. Its 409 Protestant churches, however, outnumbered the borough's 122 Roman Catholic parishes (*DN,* 1/28/90).

6. According to Gans (1988:10), 30 to 40 percent of "middle Americans" attend church weekly; a 1996 poll of adult New Yorkers found that 38 percent attend religious services at least once a week (*DN,* 1/19/97). DeSena (1990:110) points out that studies of white ethnic neighborhoods, such as Susser 1982 (one may add Halle 1984 and Rieder 1985), "barely mention the existence of religious facilities" and do not discuss their role in local social or political life. She exempts Whyte 1955 but fails to cite LaRuffa 1988, Orsi 1985, and Tricarico 1984, who discuss Roman Catholic churches in historically Italian New York City neighborhoods.

7. *DN,* 12/27/81; *NYT,* 11/15/82; *A.D.* August 1976. On the Latin American membership of this church, see Danta 1989a, 1989b.

8. See Chen 1992:160–63.

9. *NYT,* 11/19/95, 4/14/96. Grimsley left in 1988. See Acosta 1989 on the youth group at this church.

10. See Danta 1989a, 1989b. On the original Chinese group, see Chen 1992:159–60.

11. An attempt by New York State to open a group home for twenty-four mentally retarded adults, without prior community involvement and CB4 approval, met with opposition in 1990.

Led by state assembly member Joseph Crowley, 250 Elmhurst residents rallied in protest, and the state agency backed off (*ND*, 9/28/90, 11/24/90). On siting issues, see Vega 1987.

12. *NYT*, 8/20/95.

13. See Chen 1992:185–215.

14. *CL*, 5/84, 6/85; *NYT*, 6/5/86.

15. Park 1997; Salvo, Ortiz, and Vardy 1992:160–61; Wong 1986:162.

16. *DN*, 2/12/86; *NYT*, 5/3/91.

17. Brecher and Horton 1993:206–8; *DN*, 10/10/84; *ND*, 6/18/95; *NYT*, 5/3/93.

18. Park 1997; *DN Magazine*, 3/17/85; *ND*, 4/14/86; *NYT*, 1/19/85, 9/21/85.

19. *ND*, 10/17/89; *NYT*, 8/15/90; *Queens Tribune*, 11/19/87.

20. *ND*, 7/17/89.

21. *DN*, 5/6/90; *NYT*, 1/19/85, 9/25/90.

22. *DN*, 9/27/91, 10/4/91; *ND*, 9/5/91. On Haystick, see Kasinitz 1992:181–88.

23. *DN*, 7/18/93; *ND*, 6/11/93, 6/14/93, 7/26/93.

24. *ND*, 7/20/92; *NYT*, 3/22/93.

25. Leichter 1995; *CNYB*, 5/12/97; *DN*, 3/24/94; *ND*, 2/17/95, 4/29/95; *NYP*, 4/10/95; *NYT*, 2/19/95. The Caldor ICIP deal soured when the discount chain announced it was closing two of eight New York City sites (*DN*, 2/12/97).

26. Morisi 1994a, 1994b (which reprints testimony from a 1994 congressional hearing on the impact of discount superstores on small business and local communities); *DN*, 6/3/94, 10/5/94, 11/2/94, 2/1/95, 2/26/95, 3/8/95, 5/7/95, 10/9/95, 2/11/96, 5/19/96; *ND*, 7/2/94, 7/27/94, 8/8/94, 2/22/95, 9/5/96; *NYP*, 9/26/96, 11/28/96; *NYT*, 9/13/94, 10/4/94, 2/19/95, 4/18/95, 11/24/96.

27. *DN*, 12/5/96; *ND*, 5/1/96, 6/19/96, 12/8/96; *NYO*, 12/9/96; *NYT*, 9/26/96, 11/19/96.

28. *DN*, 4/15/96; *ND*, 3/6/95, 3/19/95; *NYT*, 12/11/94. The store's owner was the sole Korean member of Mayor Giuliani's Small Business Advisory Council.

29. *ND*, 7/1/90.

30. *ND*, 4/14/86, 12/1/86.

31. *ND*, 2/10/91, 2/11/91, 2/12/91, 2/14/91, 3/13/91, 4/2/91; *NYT*, 2/10/91, 2/12/91.

32. At Edna Baskin's request I spoke at the March 1991 meeting, joined the CTF, and attended subsequent meetings. In addition to the core of a dozen black Lefrak City residents and Aubry, and occasional attenders Rose Rothschild and Helen Marshall, Ruby Danta and Madhulika Khandelwal also came to CTF meetings after March 1991.

33. The unique circumstances of black people in the United States could arouse ironic, ingroup gallows humor. At one CTF meeting the abrupt closure after twenty-seven years of Lefrak City's Jack LaLanne health club was aired: "They were selling new memberships right up to the announcement, after they knew it would be closing," reported Al Blake. A petition drive for membership refunds had already gained 500 signatures, and a suit was under discussion with the state attorney general's office. Noting the company response that memberships could be transferred to other branches, Helen Marshall joked, "Take a busload of us to the Bayside [a mainly white neighborhood] branch, and see how quickly they reopen at Lefrak City."

34. *DN*, 2/14/93, 3/23/93; *Latino News*, 12/10/91; *ND*, 5/1/91, 9/26/91, 3/23/93, 4/9/93, 4/11/93, 4/12/93.

35. *Latino News*, 12/10/91; *ND*, 5/1/91, 9/26/91, 4/12/93.

36. *ND*, 2/29/89.

37. See Sanjek (forthcoming); Block 1980:222; LaRuffa 1988:5–6, 57–61; Rieder 1985: 178–83; Sleeper 1990:130–31; Tricarico 1984:42–44.

38. See Chapter 7; *ND*, 6/30/95. In a 1994 survey of quality-of-life issues in Brooklyn, "disorderly youth" was mentioned as a major problem in largely white Bay Ridge, Bensonhurst, Dyker Heights, and Midwood (*NYT*, 10/30/94).

39. *ND*, 9/26/91.

40. *DN*, 2/14/93, 3/23/93, 3/29/94; *Latino News*, 12/10/91; *ND*, 9/26/91, 4/29/92, 3/23/93, 4/9/93, 4/11/93, 4/12/93, 4/5/94.

41. See Castleman 1982 on the origins of subway graffiti in the 1970s.

42. Meyer 1989:129.

43. *ND*, 8/13/89, qtd. in Sleeper 1990:131.

44. *DN*, 9/30/95; *ND*, 9/30/95, 3/29/96.

45. Fitch 1989; Santiago 1993.

46. On city council redistricting, see Fitch 1991; NYC Latino Districting Committee 1991; Santiago 1993; *News from the New York City Districting Commission*, May–July 1991; *DN*, 7/24/91; *NYT*, 7/18/91, 7/19/91, 9/4/91.

47. *NYT*, 7/19/91.

48. On congressional redistricting, see Hanson and Falcón 1992; Santiago 1993; *NYT*, 2/29/97.

49. *ND*, 3/17/91.

50. *ND*, 8/11/92.

51. Fuentes 1992:31.

52. In 1980, 53 percent of the borough's Latin Americans lived in its multiracial northwest quadrant (CDs 1–4), 31 percent in the heavily white southwest (CDs 5, 6, 9, 10) and northeast (CDs 7, 8, 11) sectors, and 17 percent in largely black southeast Queens (CDs 12–14); in 1990 the Latin American figures shifted to 50 percent, 36 percent, and 16 percent respectively. Of black Queens residents, 16 percent lived in the multiracial northwest quadrant in 1980, 12 percent in the heavily white southwest and northeast sectors, and 72 percent in largely black southeast Queens; in 1990 these figures dropped to 14 percent (northwest), increased to 15 percent (southwest/northeast), and remained at 72 percent (southeast).

53. *DN*, 8/5/93; *ND*, 9/19/91, 6/17/92, 10/29/92, 4/5/93, 5/8/96. See Chen 1992:220–23.

54. *Queens Tribune*, 10/6/94.

55. Fitch 1991.

56. Santiago 1993:31.

57. *ND*, 2/27/97, 2/28/97, 3/3/97; *NYT*, 7/2/96, 9/8/96, 2/29/97.

58. Fuentes 1992:32; Santiago 1993:26. See also Falcón 1985a, 1985b; Institute for Puerto Rican Policy 1990:43–44.

Conclusion: The Future of Us All

1. For statements of this viewpoint, see Hacker 1975:140–48, and Salins, who also sees "the tidy working-class neighborhoods of Queens" as "natural products of the market only modestly shaped by zoning" (1993:168, 171). Elmhurst-Corona wardens clearly did not believe such nostrums.

2. See Fardon 1985:14–15; Suttles 1990: esp. 13. Gans (1988:34) points out that Americans "are exposed to far more anti-government than anti-business propaganda."

3. On categorical and personal relations, see Mitchell 1966:51–56; in workplaces and other organizational settings, people also locate themselves and others according to what Mitchell terms structural relationships. On racial and ethnic categories used by Queens Koreans, see Park 1997.

4. In 1997 one-third of Americans reported that they worshiped with immigrants (*DN*, 6/16/97).

5. I refrain from referring to these forms of organization collectively as "civil society" or, in this book, engaging political debate concerning civil society, "mediating institutions," or "the private sector." Much of that debate is framed in abstract terms contrasting "the state" and "civil society" and focusing on national-level organizations and "movements," whereas I deal with local political action and the specific levels and policies of government which affect Elmhurst-Corona. As many argue concerning "civil society," however, this sphere of activity certainly "exists . . . against the state, in partial independence from it [and] includes those dimensions of social life which cannot be confounded with, or swallowed up in the state"; the purpose of these activities, moreover, is to "determine or inflect the course of state policy" (Taylor 1990: 95, 100).

6. Arian et al. 1990:104–5; *DN*, 9/15/95; *NYT*, 4/13/97.

7. Douglas 1973:42, 73; see also 179–80.

8. See Estades 1980; Kasinitz 1992:140–59; Kasinitz and Freidenberg-Herbstein 1987. As Barth notes, "When political groups articulate their opposition in terms of ethnic criteria, the di-

rection of cultural change is also affected. . . . [Ethnic groups] tend to become structurally similar, and differentiated only by a few clear diacritica" (1969:35).

9. Suttles 1972:27.

10. Douglas's approach to ritual suggests that rituals of inclusion will become less common as "informality . . . familiarity, [and] intimacy" develop among newcomers and established residents, and categorical relationships give way to personal ones; see Douglas 1973:99–100, 103.

11. Suttles 1972:35, 50.

12. Gans 1988:111; Gans also notes the price such leaders may pay: "At times the viability of collective action may ride on the ability or charisma of the leadership [and the] heavy burdens placed on leaders can also breed suspicions of their motives and thus impair attempts to work together." Several efforts to limit or "monitor" district manager Rose Rothschild were waged by male CB4 members; Haydee Zambrana was ousted from her leadership position at CCQ. They and other female leaders were subjects of controversy and rumor. On the difference leadership makes in diverse neighborhoods, see Reider 1985:263.

13. The 1970s witnessed a large-scale movement of working- and lower-middle-class women into grassroots politics. It included what Perlman terms both bottom-up "neighborhood organizing," like that in Elmhurst-Corona, and top-down "community organizing" by staff and local chapters of such groups as ACORN, National People's Action, and the Gray Panthers, many of which drew on 1960s civil rights movement and Office of Economic Opportunity experiences and participation. See Perlman 1976, 1979; Seifer 1974. Kling and Posner's *Dilemmas of Activism* (1990), a volume of essays on "class, community, and the politics of local mobilization," focuses on community organizing from the top-down perspective, and not the elementary forms of civic political action that I studied. Conceptualizing and actualizing connections between these two political worlds—between local wardens and associations and their "inherent ideologies" on one hand, and organizers and advocates and their "derived ideologies" on the other—remain an overarching "dilemma of activism": how do working- and lower-middle-class formations of the power of numbers become linked to each other, and harnessed to effective lubricatory power?

14. Several Chinese women, including Elmhurst residents, were leaders in Chinese organizations, Democratic politics, and civic politics in Queens, but their activities centered in Flushing (see Chen 1992) with the exception of Elmhurst's SB24 member Louisa Chan.

15. Ron Baskin was the only husband of any of the women leaders I knew who was at all active in civic politics; husbands of others were supportive but not involved. Similarly, few wives of male wardens or CB4 members were active in the district-level civic political field.

16. Chodorow 1974; Hardy-Fanta 1993:13, 191; Kaplan 1982:545–47; Tannen 1990:277.

17. Cf. Suttles 1972:37–41.

18. Posner 1990:15; *NYT*, 2/25/96.

19. Waldinger 1989b:70–71.

20. Rogers 1990:158.

21. As Gans (1988:68) points out, "Many political organizations discourage direct face-to-face participation . . . because citizens can behave unpredictably. . . . Although they cannot admit it, elected officials can sometimes do without active citizen participation of any kind." See also Piven and Cloward 1988:76–77, 215.

22. Jones-Correa 1998.

23. Davidson 1979:23, 185.

24. Johnson 1995:15–16. In July 1997 massive press coverage and mayoral posturing followed discovery of two homes in Jackson Heights and North Corona where nearly sixty deaf Mexican immigrants lived "in servitude and terror" under crowded conditions, and were forced by the ring of persons who had smuggled them across the border to beg and to sell items in subway cars. Neighbors had noticed comings and goings at the two sites, and a Colombian community board member who was also president of a local civic association had notified CB3's district manager about the houses six months earlier (*NYT* 7/21/97).

25. Rogers 1990:184.

26. The labor-versus-capital model fits public employee unions poorly. Capital's resources, via

taxation, are already on the side of the working class, to be used for the common good. Municipal workers enjoy the right to bargain for higher wages and benefits, but when they "win" these by diminishing neighborhood quality of life, including their own (unless they are suburban residents, and there's the rub), capital concedes nothing.

27. During 1994–1995 business license inspections fell by 23 percent; during 1995–1996 the fire department's building inspections dropped by 26 percent. In 1996 the Giuliani administration cut restaurant inspections and lowered fines for violations. That year it also unveiled a housing deregulation plan that included builder "self-certification" to reduce city inspections; Claire Shulman denounced it as legalizing "dangerous, substandard housing." In 1997 a Buildings Department official told the Queens Borough Board that "self-certification" also applied to homeowners cited for illegal conversions; if they notified Buildings that they had corrected the problem, no reinspection would be made. See *City Project Bulletin,* 11/6/96; *CNYB,* 2/26/96, 11/11/96; *ND,* 7/16/97; *NYP,* 9/15/95; *NYT,* 12/24/96, 12/27/96.

28. See Hochman 1988; Salins 1988, 1993.

29. Salins 1988:3; see also Brecher and Horton 1991:126.

30. E.g., Winnick 1988, 1990. On immigrant entrepreneurs more generally, see Waldinger 1986; on differing attitudes toward private power groups among whites, blacks, and immigrants, Waldinger 1989b:73.

31. Suttles 1972:60, 67; cf. Mudd 1984:51.

32. Rogers 1990:259; Viteritti 1991:38; cf. Rogers and Chung 1983:219; Viteritti 1990:426.

33. Fainstein and Fainstein 1991:326.

34. Braudel [1967] 1980:31; on this 300-year history, see Sanjek (forthcoming).

35. *ND,* 5/11/97. Of one Giuliani corporate retention package, Peter Salins noted, "They mention jobs as the rationale for the deal. But the real fear is not the loss of thousands of jobs, it's the loss of the whole concept of the integrated financial sector" (*NYO,* 10/23/95).

36. *Crain's Market Facts,* July 1995; *DN,* 1/2/97; *ND,* 3/27/97, 5/30/97; *NYT,* 7/23/97.

37. *NYP,* 12/13/96; *NYT,* 12/27/96; *VV,* 2/4/97; *WSJ,* 1/5/96. Outstanding stock to company assets, or "book value," ratios stood at 4.8 to 1 by the end of 1996, exceeding the 4.2-to-1 ratio that preceded the 1929 crash; investor gurus Henry Kaufman and George Soros warned of "an unsustainable financial bubble" and "a panic" (*NYP,* 7/8/97; *WSJ,* 11/25/96, 12/16/96).

38. *VV,* 6/11/96.

39. Braudel [1967] 1980:12, 31, 51–52; Leeds 1980:135.

40. See Albion 1939:16–37; Garreau 1991:283–84; Pratt 1911:12–14; Sanjek (forthcoming).

41. These changes were proposed in 1995 by city council members Steve DeBrienza and Ronnie Eldridge, and similar limitations for corporate "retention packages"— including payback provisions if jobs were eliminated or transferred elsewhere—were advocated by State Senator Franz Leichter (Leichter 1995: pt. 2, 15–18; *ND,* 3/27/95; *NYP,* 1/9/96). In 1996 corporate "designer packages" under Clay Lifflander's successor Charles Millard began to include some modest "conditionality" provisions (*DN,* 5/15/96; *NYP,* 11/11/96; *NYT,* 4/11/97, 4/25/97).

42. On rent and on market size and accessibility as factors in business location decisions, see Bowles, Gordon, and Weisskopf 1990:225; Haig 1926; Hoover and Vernon 1959; Jacobs 1969:56, 205; Kieschnick 1981:53–55, 57, 87; Pratt 1911; Vernon 1957; Vilain 1991:19–21. On metropolitan area employment in the 1990s, see Leinberger 1992; *NYT,* 12/21/92, 2/18/94.

43. Krugman 1996:211–13. For parallel arguments that also emphasize the power of resources versus the power of numbers, see Gordon 1996: esp. 188–202. On NAFTA and its impact on the U.S. labor market, see Krugman 1996:113–15, 150–65; *NYT,* 10/9/95; *WSJ,* 10/26/95, 6/17/97.

44. Vilain 1991:22–25; Walsh 1990:213; *CL,* 1/91; *Empire State Report,* 9/91; *DN,* 7/24/95, 4/30/96, 1/14/97; *NYO,* 1/27/97; *NYT,* 7/30/95, 11/1/96, 1/15/97; *WSJ,* 9/19/96, 10/2/96, 10/18/96, 1/3/97, 3/7/97.

45. *NYP,* 7/14/97. Giuliani's feuding with the Port Authority and with New Jersey complicate the Brooklyn port and tunnel plan; see *CNYB,* 3/17/97, 4/7/97; *DN,* 6/7/96, 10/14/96; *ND,* 2/2/97; *NYP,* 8/24/95, 10/30/96.

46. Jacobs 1969:78–79; *VV,* 2/4/97. Cf. Leichter 1996:3–4; *NYT,* 8/17/94.

47. Fitch 1993:25–26, 245–46, 269; Jacobs 1969:242, 245; Moss 1994; Sinnreich 1980:120; Winnick 1990:158–60; *CNYB*, 11/28/94; *DN*, 2/17/95; *ND*, 2/21/93, 4/5/95, 6/30/95, 7/17/97; *NYT*, 8/19/83, 4/17/94, 9/4/95, 6/7/96, 4/8/97. On similar developments in Tokyo, see Sassen 1991a:212.

48. *ND*, 3/21/95. See also Isabel Hill's 1993 film *Made in Brooklyn*.

49. Fitch 1993:103–8; Jacobs 1969:49–51, 125–27, 137–40; Vernon 1960:22–23; *CNYB*, 5/1/95; *DN*, 7/9/95; *NYT*, 7/23/95, 4/15/96.

50. Similiar Dinkins-era plans were not approved by the city council or were dropped when the Giuliani administration took office. See *DN*, 7/22/94, 7/24/94, 12/1/95, 12/17/95, 3/1/96, 3/19/96, 7/10/96; *NYT*, 1/23/94, 11/30/95, 6/25/95, 7/1/96, 10/27/96, 4/16/97.

51. Commenting on this policy shift, Deputy Mayor Fran Reiter observed, "The financial sector was where we really concentrated our resources. The city made a conscious decision that that's the kind of economy we wanted. It was foolish" (*DN*, 11/20/95, 5/6/96; *NYT*, 5/1/96).

52. Jacobs 1961:36–41, 55–73; *ND*, 3/22/88.

53. Fitch 1993:49.

54. O'Cléireacáin 1993:168; see also Fuchs 1992:289–90; Leinberger 1992; Sclar and Hook 1993; Vernon 1957:20–21, 29. Phillips points out that U.S. state-level government—unique in relation to other industrial democracies—encourages self-defeating tax-concession wars and preserves what "are now some of the oldest borders in the world" (1994:128–33, 148–50, 199–201).

55. Danielson and Doig 1982:138–39; Rusk 1993; Schultze et al. [1972] 1976:207–9; *NYT*, 5/14/72, 1/23/76, 4/4/76.

56. On the legal and political dominance of New York State over New York City, see Benjamin 1990; Eichenthal 1990b:90–92, 100; O'Cléireacáin 1993; Walsh 1990.

57. Communications Workers of America 1994; Fitch 1995; O'Cléireacáin 1993:170–71, 175; *CL*, 6/97. The 10 percent building sales tax produced $792 million in 1987; it was repealed in 1996 (*CNYB*, 10/21/96).

58. Brecher and Horton 1993:205. At least one municipal workers union, economist Robert Fitch, former Koch and Dinkins official Harvey Robins, and 1997 mayoral candidate Sal Albanese agreed. See Communications Workers of America 1994; Fitch 1995; *CL*, 6/97; *DN*, 2/16/97.

59. O'Cléireacáin 1993:178.

60. *NYP*, 11/20/96; *NYT*, 10/24/87. In fact, average city and state taxes for New Yorkers with incomes of $25,000 or less are *lower* than in Atlanta, Chicago, Philadelphia, or Milwaukee; it is New Yorkers with incomes of $100,000 or more who pay higher taxes than in those cities (*Crain's Market Facts*, July 1995).

61. Average New York City worker output was $68,800 versus $47,100 nationwide in 1994, and average wages were $49,000 versus $31,000 in 1996 (*Crain's Market Facts*, July 1995; *DN*, 1/2/97). Brecher and Horton find that since 1960 "the general trend is towards a more progressive tax system" in New York City (1991:118). Anti-tax activists and supporters of increased tuition and transit fares seek to reverse this.

62. *NYT*, 10/19/81.

63. Sclar and Hook 1993:66, 68. The importance of expanding demand at the bottom rather than cutting taxes at the top is also stressed by Bluestone and Harrison (1982:198), and Greider (1992:102–3). In this regard, U.S. economic policy contrasts with that of western Europe. With 45 percent of the overall economy going to taxes, Europeans have higher wages, less income inequality, nearly free health care and higher education, better public transportation, higher levels of welfare and unemployment benefits, higher union membership, cooperative labor-management relations, shorter work hours, modest or miniscule militaries, and less than 1 percent of the labor force in prison or on parole. With 31.6 percent of the U.S. economy going to taxes, its citizens have stagnant wages, rising income inequality, increasingly unaffordable health insurance and higher education, worse public transportation, a shrinking safety net, lower union membership, antagonistic labor-managment relations, longer work hours, an enormous military, and 4 percent of the labor force in prison or on parole. See Bluestone and Harrison 1982:14; Gordon 1996; Greider 1992:153–54, 193; Harrison and Bluestone 1988; Krugman 1996:192;

Phillips 1990:127; *DN*, 7/9/91; *ND*, 11/18/93; *NYT*, 5/13/73, 6/13/76, 6/27/82, 12/1/94, 2/16/95, 5/14/95, 8/10/95, 6/22/97; *WSJ*, 6/19/97.

64. This or some other future will arrive primarily because of internal power alignments in the United States. "None of the important constraints on American economic and social policy come from abroad," writes Paul Krugman. "We have the resources to take far better care of our poor and unlucky than we do; if our policies have become increasingly mean-spirited, that is a political choice, not something imposed on us by anonymous forces. We cannot evade responsibility for our actions by claiming that global markets made us do it" (*NYT* 2/13/97).

65. See Sanjek 1994c.

66. Rusk 1993:3; *VV*, 4/12/94.

67. Institute for Puerto Rican Policy 1990:25–28; see also *NYT*, 5/8/97.

68. DeCamp 1991; Fix and Zimmerman 1993; DCP 1993a, 1993b; *Business Week*, 7/13/92, *DN*, 4/28/93, 2/23/95; *ND*, 3/12/95; *NYT*, 3/1/81, 5/6/83, 8/29/93, 12/5/95.

69. Martin and Midgley 1994:37–38.

70. Crewsdon 1983:289; *CHE*, 11/23/88.

71. Passel and Edmonston 1992; Salvo, Ortiz, and Vardy 1992:175; *ND*, 7/21/97; *NYT*, 7/1/86, 6/27/93, 8/2/93, 8/30/95, 2/8/97; *NYTM*, 10/27/96. Evidence relating to the widely subscribed-to beliefs that immigrants take jobs from Americans and are a net tax "burden" is less clear-cut. A 1997 National Academy of Sciences study found that "immigration added perhaps $10 billion a year to the nation's output. . . . Job prospects of low-skilled native-born workers were sometimes hurt by competition with immigrants and . . . the incomes of native-born workers tended to fall as a result. . . . The vast majority of Americans are enjoying a healthier economy as a result of the increased supply of labor and lower prices that result from immigration [but] some black workers have lost their jobs to immigrants, especially in . . . New York City . . . where they compete for the same jobs" (*NYT* 5/18/97). The immigration scholar Wayne Cornelius concludes, "The proportion of immigrants using some form of public assistance has been estimated . . . at 5.1 percent by . . . Michael Fix and Jeffrey Passel and at 26.1 percent by George Borjas. . . . These and others disagree about the proper unit of analysis (should it be individuals or households?), which kinds of immigrants to include . . . (should political refugees, who have disproportionately high rates of welfare use, be excluded?), and even about which government programs should be classified as 'welfare' " (*CHE*, 11/15/96). Undocumented immigrants are ineligible for welfare benefits other than Medicaid for emergency treatment. Legal immigrants do not qualify for most welfare benefits during their first three years, and they lose opportunities to sponsor relatives when they do; the majority never do qualify. See Fix and Zimmerman 1993; Martin and Midgley 1994:28–34; *Business Week*, 7/13/92; *NYT*, 9/22/80, 8/2/84.

72. DCP 1992a, 1993b.

73. *DN*, 6/16/97; *ND*, 5/20/92; *NYT*, 7/1/86, 6/27/93.

74. *ND*, 2/27/94; *NYT*, 3/10/96, 7/5/97, 7/19/97.

75. Salvo, Ortiz, and Vardy 1992:17–20, 67; Youssef 1992:1–2, 161–62; *DN*, 8/28/95; *ND*, 8/22/94; *NYT*, 12/21/86, 3/16/88, 10/14/90, 8/28/95, 9/13/95, 2/26/96, 3/29/96, 3/16/97; *WSJ*, 10/9/95, 12/18/95, 1/3/96.

76. Leadership Education for Asian Pacifics, "Reframing the Immigration Debate," 1996; *DN*, 12/29/95; *ND*, 11/27/93, 2/21/96; *NYT*, 9/25/95, 3/10/96, 9/13/96, 10/26/96; *NYTM*, 10/27/96; *Washington Post*, 2/24/94.

77. *DN*, 3/1/92.

78. Ward 1989:15.

79. *NYTM*, 10/27/96.

80. *NYT*, 10/9/94.

81. See Goode 1990:126, 134; Jones-Correa 1998.

82. *NYT*, 6/6/94.

83. Massey and Denton 1993:234–35; Yinger 1995:252. See also Hacker 1992:35–38; Halle 1984:26–30, 226, 299; Jaynes and Williams 1989:115–56; Rusk 1993:29–31, 33–38, 78–79, 125; Yancey, Ericksen, and Leon 1986.

84. Starr 1988:184.
85. Mayer 1974:379.
86. *NYT,* 10/14/90.
87. *NYT,* 1/28/87.
88. West 1993:5–6.
89. West 1993:6.
90. Greider 1992:220–21.

References

Abrams, Charles. 1966. The Housing Problem and the Negro. *Daedalus* 95:64–76.

Abrams, Franklin. 1980. Immigration Law and Its Enforcement: Reflections of American Immigration Policy. In Bryce-Laporte, ed., 27–35.

Abu-Lughod, Janet, et al. 1994. *From Urban Village to East Village: The Battle for New York's Lower East Side.* Cambridge, Mass.: Basil Blackwell.

Acosta, Elena. 1989. The Socialization of Youth in Two Queens Churches. In Sanjek, ed., 80–91.

Alba, Richard. 1981. The Twilight of Ethnicity among American Catholics of European Ancestry. *Annals of the American Academy of Political and Social Sciences* 454:86–97.

——. 1985. *Italian Americans: Into the Twilight of Ethnicity.* Englewood Cliffs, N.J.: Prentice-Hall.

——. 1990. *Ethnic Identity: The Transformation of White America.* New Haven: Yale University Press.

Albion, Robert Greenhalgh. 1939. *The Rise of New York Port [1815–1860].* Boston: Northeastern University Press.

Alcaly, Roger, and Helen Bodian. 1976. New York's Fiscal Crisis and the Economy. In Alcaly and Mermelstein, eds., 30–58.

Alcaly, Roger, and David Mermelstein, eds. 1976. *The Fiscal Crisis of American Cities: Essays on the Political Economy of Urban America with Special Reference to New York.* New York: Vintage.

Aldrich, Howard, and Roger Waldinger. 1990. Ethnicity and Entrepreneurship. *Annual Review of Sociology* 16:111–35.

Allen, Irving Lewis. 1993. *The City in Slang: New York Life and Popular Speech.* New York: Oxford University Press.

Arian, Asher, Arthur Goldberg, John Mollenkopf, and Edward Rogowsky. 1991. *Changing New York City Politics.* New York: Routledge.

Armbruster, Eugene. 1923. *Long Island Landmarks, Part 1. The Town of Newtown.* N.p.

Asad, Talal. 1979. Anthropology and the Analysis of Ideology. *Man* 14:607–27.

Auletta, Ken. 1979. *The Streets Were Paved with Gold.* New York: Vintage.
Bach, Victor, and Sherece West. 1993. *Housing on the Block: Disinvestment and Abandonment Risks in New York City Neighborhoods.* New York: Community Service Society.
Bailey, F. G. 1965. Decisions by Consensus in Councils and Committees. In *Political Systems and the Distribution of Power,* ed. Michael Banton, 1–20. London: Tavistock.
——. 1968. Parapolitical Systems. In Swartz, ed., 281–94.
——. 1969. *Stratagems and Spoils: A Social Anthropology of Politics.* Oxford: Basil Blackwell.
——. 1971. Gifts and Poisons; The Management of Reputations and the Process of Change. In *Gifts and Poison: The Politics of Reputation,* ed. F. G. Bailey, 1–25, 281–301. Oxford: Basil Blackwell.
——. 1973. Promethean Fire: Right and Wrong; Debate, Compromise, and Change. In *Debate and Compromise: The Politics of Innovation,* ed. F. G. Bailey, 1–15, 309–28. Oxford: Basil Blackwell.
——. 1981. Dimensions of Rhetoric in Conditions of Uncertainty. In Paine, ed., 25–38.
——. 1983. *The Tactical Uses of Passion: An Essay on Power, Reason, and Reality.* Ithaca: Cornell University Press.
——. 1988. *Humbuggery and Manipulation: The Art of Leadership.* Ithaca: Cornell University Press.
——. 1991. *The Prevalence of Deceit.* Ithaca: Cornell University Press.
Bailey, Thomas, and Roger Waldinger. 1991. The Changing Ethnic/Racial Division of Labor. In Mollenkopf and Castells, eds., 43–78.
Balmori, Diana. 1983. *Hispanic Immigrants in the Construction Industry: New York City, 1960–1982.* New York: Center for Latin American and Caribbean Studies, New York University.
Barlett, Donald, and James Steele. 1992. *America: What Went Wrong?* Kansas City: Andrews & McMeel.
Barth, Fredrik. 1969. Introduction. In *Ethnic Groups and Boundaries,* ed. Fredrik Barth, 1–38. Boston: Little, Brown.
Baxter, Ellen, and Kim Hopper. 1981. *Private Lives / Public Spaces: Mentally Disabled Adults on the Streets of New York City.* New York: Community Service Society.
Bellush, Jewell. 1971. Housing: The Scattered-Site Controversy. In Bellush and David, eds., 98–133.
——. 1990. Clusters of Power: Interest Groups. In Bellush and Netzer, eds., 296–338.
Bellush, Jewell, and Stephen David, eds. 1971. *Race and Politics in New York City: Five Studies in Policy-Making.* New York: Praeger.
Bellush, Jewell, and Dick Netzer, eds. 1990. *Urban Politics New York Style.* Armonk, N.Y.: M. E. Sharpe.
Benjamin, Gerald. 1990. The State/City Relationship. In Bellush and Netzer, eds., 223–44.
Bernstein, Blanche, and Arley Bondarin. 1975. Income Distribution in New York City. *City Almanac* 9 (6): 1–13.
Bienstock, Herbert. 1977. New York City's Labor Market: Past Trends, Current Conditions, Future Propects. *City Almanac* 12 (4): 1–18.
Bierstedt, Robert. 1967. Power and Social Class. In *Social Structure, Stratification, and Mobility,* ed. Anthony Leeds, 77–93. Washington, D.C.: Pan American Union.

Blackmar, Elizabeth. 1989. *Manhattan for Rent, 1785–1850.* Ithaca: Cornell University Press.

Bloch, Maurice. 1974. Symbols, Song, Dance, and Features of Articulation: Is Religion an Extreme Form of Traditional Authority? *European Journal of Sociology* 15:55–81.

——. 1977. The Past and the Present in the Present. *Man* 12:278–92.

——. 1985. From Cognition to Ideology. In Fardon, ed., 21–48.

Block, Alan. 1983. *East Side–West Side: Organizing Crime in New York City, 1930–1950.* New Brunswick, N.J.: Transaction Books.

Bluestone, Barry, and Bennett Harrison. 1982. *The Deindustrialization of America: Plant Closings, Community Abandonment, and the Dismantling of Basic Industry.* New York: Basic Books.

Bluestone, Barry, Bennett Harrison, and Lucy Gorham. 1984. *Storm Clouds on the Horizon: Labor Market Crisis and Industrial Policy.* Brookline, Mass.: Economic Education Project.

Bluestone, Daniel. 1992. The Pushcart Evil. In *The Landscape of Modernity: Essays on New York City, 1900–1940,* ed. David Ward and Olivier Zunz, 287–312. New York: Russell Sage.

Boggs, Vernon, Gerald Handel, and Sylvia Fava, eds. 1984. *The Apple Sliced: Sociological Studies of New York City.* New York: Praeger.

Bonacich, Edna, Ivan Light, and Charles Choy Wong. 1980. Korean Immigrant Small Business in Los Angeles. In Bryce-Laporte, ed., 167–84.

Bookman, Ann, and Sandra Morgen, eds. 1988. *Women and the Politics of Empowerment.* Philadelphia: Temple University Press.

Bouvier, Leon, and Vernon Briggs Jr. 1988. *The Population and Labor Force of New York: 1990–2050.* Washington, D.C.: Population Reference Bureau.

Bouvier, Leon, and Robert Gardner. 1986. *Immigration to the U.S.: The Unfinished Story.* Washington, D.C.: Population Reference Bureau.

Bowles, Samuel, David Gordon, and Thomas Weisskopf. 1990. *After the Waste Land: A Democratic Economics for the Year 2000.* Armonk, N.Y.: M. E. Sharpe.

Braudel, Fernand. 1977. *Afterthoughts on Material Civilization and Capitalism.* Baltimore: Johns Hopkins University Press.

——. [1967] 1980. *On History.* Chicago: University of Chicago Press.

Brecher, Charles, and Raymond Horton. 1991. The Public Sector. In Mollenkopf and Castells, eds., 103–27.

Brecher, Charles, and Raymond Horton, with Robert Cropf and Dean Mead. 1993. *Power Failure: New York City Politics and Policy since 1960.* New York: Oxford University Press.

Brecher, Charles, and Sheila Spiezio. 1995. *Privatization and Public Hospitals: Choosing Wisely for New York City.* New York: Twentieth Century Fund.

Bressi, Todd, ed. 1993. *Planning and Zoning New York City: Yesterday, Today, and Tomorrow.* New Brunswick, N.J.: Center for Urban Policy Research.

Bridges, Amy. 1984. *A City in the Republic: Antebellum New York and the Origins of Machine Politics.* Ithaca: Cornell University Press.

Brinkley-Carter, Christina. 1980. The Economic Impact of the New Immigration on "Native" Minorities. In Bryce-Laporte, ed., 211–21.

Brint, Steven. 1991. Upper Professionals: A High Command of Commerce, Culture, and Civic Regulation. In Mollenkopf and Castells, eds., 155–76.

Brower, Bonnie. 1989. *Missing the Mark: Subsidizing Housing for the Privileged, Displacing the Poor: An Analysis of the City's 10-Year Plan.* New York: Association for Neighborhood and Housing Development.

Bryce-Laporte, Roy Simon, ed. 1979. *Sourcebook on the New Immigration: Book II.* Washington, D.C.: Smithsonian Institution.

——. 1980. *Sourcebook on the New Immigration.* New Brunswick, N.J.: Transaction Books.

Cantor, Marjorie. 1975. *The Formal and Informal Social Support System of Older New Yorkers.* New York: New York City Office for the Aging.

Carey, George. 1976. *A Vignette of the New York–New Jersey Metropolitan Region.* Cambridge, Mass.: Ballinger.

Caro, Robert. 1974. *The Power Broker: Robert Moses and the Fall of New York.* New York: Vintage.

Castells, Manuel, and John Mollenkopf. 1991. Conclusion: Is New York a Dual City? In Mollenkopf and Castells, eds., 399–418.

Castleman, Craig. 1982. *Getting Up: Subway Graffiti in New York.* Cambridge: M.I.T. Press.

Chaney, Elsa. 1976. Colombian Migration to the United States (pt. 2). In *The Dynamics of Migration,* 87–141. Washington, D.C.: Smithsonian Institution.

——. 1980. Colombians in New York City: Theoretical and Policy Issues. In Bryce-Laporte, ed., 285–94.

——. 1983. Colombian Outpost in New York City. In Howard, ed., 67–76.

Chen, Hsiang-shui. 1989. A Changing Congregation: Taiwanese, Tamils, and Americans in a Queens Church. In Sanjek, ed., 19–29.

——. 1992. *Chinatown No More: Taiwan Immigrants in Contemporary New York.* Ithaca: Cornell University Press.

Chinese Staff and Workers Association. 1990. *New York City in the 1990's: Problems of Chinese Workers and Minorities Seeking Equal Opportunity and a Living Wage.* New York: Chinese Staff and Workers Association.

Chinitz, Benjamin. 1965. New York: A Metropolitan Region. In *Cities,* 105–21. New York: Knopf.

Chodorow, Nancy. 1974. Family Structure and Feminine Personality. In *Woman, Culture, and Society,* ed. Michelle Rosaldo and Louise Lamphere, 43–66. Stanford: Stanford University Press.

Cisneros, Henry, ed. 1993. *Interwoven Destinies: Cities and the Nation.* New York: Norton.

City of New York. 1986. *Report of the Mayor's Commission on Hispanic Concerns.* New York: City of New York.

——. 1987. *City Response to the Report of the Mayor's Commission on Hispanic Concerns.* New York: City of New York.

City Planning Commission. 1963. *Corona–East Elmhurst Area Extension Urban Renewal Designation.* New York: City of New York.

——. 1968. Corona and East Elmhurst: "Chance for Change." Consultant's report, typescript.

——. 1969. *Plan for New York City: Queens Community Planning District 4.* New York: City of New York.

——. 1979. *Portfolio, An Information System for Community Districts: Queens Community District 4.* New York: City of New York.

Clark, Kenneth. 1966. The Civil Rights Movement: Momentum and Organization. *Daedalus* 95:239–67.

Cohen, David Steven. 1981. How Dutch Were the Dutch of New Netherland? *New York History* 62:43–60.

Colen, Shellee. 1990. "Housekeeping" for the Green Card: West Indian Household Workers, the State, and Stratified Reproduction in New York City. In *At Work in Homes: Household Workers in World Perspective,* ed. Roger Sanjek and Shellee Colen, 89–119. Washington, D.C.: American Anthropological Association.

Collier, John, and Anibal Buitron. [1946] 1971. *The Awakening Valley.* Quito, Ecuador: Instituto Otavaleño de Antropologia.

Comaroff, Jean. 1985. *Body of Power, Spirit of Resistance: The Culture and History of a South African People.* Chicago: University of Chicago Press.

Committee on Banking, Finance, and Urban Affairs, House of Representatives. 1984. *The New York City Housing Crisis.* Washington, D.C.: Government Printing Office.

Communications Workers of America. 1994. *Reclaiming What Is Ours.* New York: Local 1180.

Community Council of Greater New York. 1958. *Queens Communities.* New York: Community Council of Greater New York.

Congressional Budget Office. [1975] 1976. New York City's Fiscal Problem. In Alcaly and Mermelstein, eds., 285–95.

Connolly, Harold. 1977. *A Ghetto Grows in Brooklyn.* New York: New York University Press.

Corona–East Elmhurst Development Committee. 1969. A Community Conservation Program. Typescript.

Cox, Oliver. 1948. *Caste, Class, and Race: A Study in Social Dynamics.* New York: Monthly Review Press.

Crewsdon, John. 1983. *The Tarnished Door: The New Immigrants and the Transformation of America.* New York: Times Books.

Cruz, Carmenines. 1980. The Migration Process in Colombia: Some Considerations about Its Causes and Consequences. In Bryce-Laporte, ed., 85–97.

Cuomo, Mario. 1974. *Forest Hills Diary: The Crisis of Low-Income Housing.* New York: Vintage.

Curvin, Robert, and Bruce Porter. 1979. *Blackout Looting, New York City, July 13, 1977.* New York: Gardner.

Danielson, Michael, and Jameson Doig. 1982. *New York: The Politics of Urban Regional Development.* Berkeley: University of California Press.

Danta, Rosalia. 1989a. Conversion and Denominational Mobility: A Study of Latin American Protestants in Queens, New York. M.A. thesis, Queens College, City University of New York.

——. 1989b. Latin Americans in Protestant Churches: Reaffirmation of Culture, or Acculturation? In Sanjek, ed., 30–42.

Daun, Åke, Billy Ehn, and Barbro Klein, eds. 1992. *To Make the World Safe for Diversity: Towards an Understanding of Multi-Cultural Societies.* Stockholm: Ethnology Institute, Stockholm University.

David, Stephen. 1971. Welfare: The Community-Action Program Controversy. In Bellush and David, eds., 25–58.

David, Stephen, and Jewell Bellush. 1971. Introduction: Pluralism, Race, and the Urban Political System. In Bellush and David, eds., 3–24.

Davidson, Jeffrey. 1979. *Political Partnerships: Neighborhood Residents and Their Council Members.* Beverly Hills, Calif.: Sage.

Davis, Cary, Carl Haub, and JoAnne Willette. *U.S. Hispanics: Changing the Face of America.* Washington, D.C.: Population Reference Bureau.

DeCamp, Suzanne. 1991. *The Linguistic Minorities of New York City.* New York: Community Service Society.

de Laguna, Frederica. 1957. Some Problems of Objectivity in Ethnology. *Man* 57:179–82.

Department of City Planning. 1976. *Zoning Handbook.* New York: City of New York.

——. 1984. *Community District Statistics: A Portrait of New York City from the 1980 Census.* New York: City of New York.

——. 1989. *Elmhurst/Corona, Queens.* New York: City of New York.

——. 1992a. *Demographic Profiles: A Portrait of New York City's Community Districts from the 1980 and 1990 Censuses of Population and Housing.* New York: City of New York.

——. 1992b. *New Housing in New York City, 1990–1991.* New York: City of New York.

——. 1992c. *Total Asians by Specified Asian Group.* New York: City of New York.

——. 1992d. *Total Population by Single, First, and Second Ancestry.* New York: City of New York.

——. 1993a. *Language Spoken at Home for Persons 5 Years of Age and Over.* New York: City of New York.

——. 1993b. *Socioeconomic Profiles: A Portrait of New York City's Community Districts from the 1980 and 1990 Censuses of Population and Housing.* New York: City of New York.

DeSena, Judith. 1990. *Protecting One's Turf: Social Strategies for Maintaining Urban Neighborhoods.* Lanham, Md.: University Press of America.

Domhoff, William. 1967. *Who Rules America?* Englewood Cliffs, N.J.: Prentice-Hall.

——. 1974. *The Bohemian Grove and Other Retreats: A Study in Ruling-Class Cohesiveness.* New York: Harper Colophon.

Domurad, Frank, David Fleischer, Gene Russianoff, and Loretta Simon. 1981. *City of Unequal Neighbors: A Study of Residential Property Tax Assessments in New York City.* New York: New York Public Interest Research Group.

Domurad, Frank, and Gene Russianoff. 1982. *City of Unequal Neighbors, One Year Later: A Study of Residential Property Tax Assessments in New York City.* New York: New York Public Interest Research Group.

Douglas, Mary. 1973. *Natural Symbols.* New York: Vintage.

Drennan, Matthew. 1991. The Decline and Rise of the New York Economy. In Mollenkopf and Castells, eds., 25–41.

Edel, Matthew. 1976. The New York Crisis as Economic History. In Alcaly and Mermelstein, eds., 228–45.

——. 1987. *An Economic and Demographic Profile of Queens.* Flushing: Department of Urban Studies, Queens College, City University of New York.

Ehrenreich, Barbara, and John Ehrenreich. 1970. *The American Health Empire: Power, Profits, and Politics.* New York: Vintage.

Eichenthal, David. 1990a. Changing Styles and Strategies of the Mayor. In Bellush and Netzer, eds., 63–85.

——. 1990b. The Other Elected Officials. In Bellush and Netzer, eds., 86–106.

Ekman, Ann-Kristin. 1991. *Community, Carnival, and Campaign: Expressions of Belonging in a Swedish Region.* Stockholm: Stockholm University Studies in Social Anthropology.

Elias, Norbert, and John Scotson. [1965] 1994. *The Established and the Outsiders: A Sociological Enquiry into Community Problems.* London: Sage.

Epstein, Cynthia Fuchs, and Stephen Duncombe. 1991. Women Clerical Workers. In Mollenkopf and Castells, eds., 177–203.

Epstein, Jason. 1976. The Last Days of New York. In Alcaly and Mermelstein, eds., 59–76.

Estades, Rosa. 1980. Symbolic Unity: The Puerto Rican Day Parade. In Rodríguez, Sánchez Korrol, and Alers, eds., 82–89.

Fainstein, Norman, and Susan Fainstein. 1988. Governing Regimes and the Political Economy of Development in New York City, 1946–1984. In Mollenkopf ed., 161–99.

——. 1991. The Changing Character of Community Politics in New York City: 1968–1988. In Mollenkopf and Castells, eds., 315–32.

Falcón, Angelo. 1985a. *Black and Latino Politics in New York City: Race and Ethnicity in a Changing Urban Context.* New York: Institute for Puerto Rican Policy.

——. 1985b. Puerto Rican and Black Electoral Politics in NYC in the "Decade of the Hispanic." *Hunter College Centro de Estudos Puertorriqueños Newsletter,* June, 7–10, 23.

——. 1989a. *Puerto Ricans and the 1989 Mayoral Election in New York City.* New York: Institute for Puerto Rican Policy.

——. 1989b. *The 1989 Mayoral Election and Charter Revision Vote in New York City.* New York: Institute for Puerto Rican Policy.

——. 1992. *Puerto Ricans and Other Latinos in New York City Today.* New York: Institute for Puerto Rican Policy.

——. 1993. The Puerto Rican Community: A Status Report. *Diálogo* 7:1, 5, 10–13.

Fardon, Richard. 1985a. Introduction: A Sense of Relevance. In Fardon, ed., 1–20.

——, ed. 1985b. *Power and Knowledge: Anthropological and Sociological Approaches.* Edinburgh: Scottish Academic Press.

Farley, Reynolds, ed. 1995. *State of the Union: America in the 1990s,* vol. 2. New York: Russell Sage.

Fava, Sylvia, and Judith DeSena. 1984. The Chosen Apple: Young Suburban Migrants. In Boggs, Handel, and Fava, eds., 305–22.

Fenton, William. 1962. Ethnohistory and Its Problems. *Ethnohistory* 9:1–23.

Ferman, Louis, Stuart Henry, and Michele Hoyman, eds. 1987. The Informal Economy. *Annals of the American Academy of Political and Social Science* 483:1–172.

Fischer, John. 1966. Race and Reconciliation: The Role of the School. *Daedalus* 95:24–44.

Fisher, Maxine. 1980. *The Indians of New York City: A Study of Immigrants from India.* Columbia, Mo.: South Asia Books.

Fitch, Robert. 1976. Planning New York. In Alcaly and Mermelstein, eds., 246–84.

——. 1987. New York 2000: The Secret Life of Urban Real Estate. *Village Voice,* 17 November, 26–34.

——. 1989. Foundations and the Charter: Making New York City Safe for Plutocracy. *Nation,* 11 December, 709–14.
——. 1991. Mauling the Mosaic. *Village Voice,* 18 June, 11–15.
——. 1993. *The Assassination of New York.* New York: Verso.
——. 1994. Explaining New York City's Aberrant Economy. *New Left Review* 207:17–48.
——. 1995. "Spread the Pain"? Tax the Gain! *Nation,* 8 May, 628–32.
Fix, Michael, and Jeffrey Passel. 1994. *Immigration and Immigrants: Setting the Record Straight.* Washington, D.C.: Urban Institute.
Fix, Michael, and Wendy Zimmerman. 1993. *After Arrival: An Overview of Federal Immigration Policy in the United States.* Washington, D.C.: Urban Institute.
Fleming, Harold. 1965. The Federal Executive and Civil Rights: 1961–1965. *Daedalus* 94:921–48.
Foner, Nancy. 1987a. Introduction: New Immigrants and Changing Patterns in New York City. In Foner, ed., 1–33.
——, ed. 1987b. *New Immigrants in New York.* New York: Columbia University Press.
Fortes, Meyer. 1936. Ritual Festivals and Social Cohesion in the Hinterland of the Gold Coast. *American Anthropologist* 38:590–604.
Fortuna, Giuseppe. 1991. *The Italian Dream: The Italians of Queens, New York City.* San Francisco: Mellen Research University Press.
Frey, William. 1995. The New Geography of Population Shifts. In Farley, ed., 271–336.
Fried, Morton H. 1967. *The Evolution of Political Society.* New York: Random House.
Friedman, Robert. 1976. Pirates and Politicians: Sinking on the Same Ship. In Alcaly and Mermelstein, eds., 327–38.
Fuchs, Ester. 1992. *Mayors and Money: Fiscal Policy in New York and Chicago.* Chicago: University of Chicago Press.
Fuentes, Annette. 1992. New York: Elusive Unity in La Gran Manzana. *Report on the Americas* 26 (2): 27–33.
Fuentes, Luis. 1980. The Struggle for Local Political Control. In Rodríguez, Sánchez Korrol, and Alers, eds., 111–20.
Gans, Herbert. 1962. Urbanism and Suburbanism as Ways of Life: A Re-Evaluation of Some Definitions. In *Human Behavior and Social Processes,* ed. Arnold Rose, 625–48. Boston: Houghton Mifflin.
——. 1967. *The Levittowners: Ways of Life and Politics in a New Suburban Community.* New York: Vintage.
——. 1979. Symbolic Ethnicity: The Future of Ethnic Groups and Culture in America. *Ethnic and Racial Studies* 2:1–20.
——. 1988. *Middle American Individualism: Political Participation and Liberal Democracy.* New York: Oxford University Press.
Garreau, Joel. 1991. *Edge City: Life on the New Frontier.* New York: Anchor.
Georges, Eugenia. 1984. *New Immigrants and the Political Process: Dominicans in New York.* New York: Center for Latin American and Caribbean Studies, New York University.
——. 1988. *Dominican Self-Help Association in Washington Heights: Integration of a New Immigrant Population in a Multiethnic Neighborhood.* Austin: University of Texas Center for Mexican American Studies.
——. 1990. *The Making of a Transnational Community: Migration, Development, and Cultural Change in the Dominican Republic.* New York: Columbia University Press.

Gilkes, Cheryl Townsend. 1980. "Holding Back the Ocean with a Broom": Black Women and Community Work. In *The Black Woman,* ed. La Frances Rodgers-Rose, 217–31. Beverly Hills, Calif.: Sage.

——. 1988. Building in Many Places: Multiple Commitments and Ideologies in Black Women's Community Work. In Bookman and Morgen, eds., 53–76.

Ginzberg, Eli. 1976. The Pluralistic Economy of the U.S. *Scientific American* 235 (6) :25–29.

——. 1977. The Job Problem. *Scientific American* 237 (5): 43–51.

——. 1979. The Professionalization of the U.S. Labor Force. *Scientific American* 240 (3): 48–53.

——. 1980. Youth Unemployment. *Scientific American* 242 (5): 43–49.

Gittell, Marilyn. 1971. Education: The Decentralization-Community Control Controversy. In Bellush and David, eds., 134–63.

Giuliani, Rudolph, and William Bratton. 1994. *Police Strategy No. 5: Reclaiming the Public Spaces of New York.* New York: City of New York.

Glaser, William. 1980. International Flows of Talent. In Bryce-Laporte, ed., 59–67.

Glazer, Nathan. 1988. The New New Yorkers. In Salins, ed., 54–72.

——. 1993. The National Influence of Jewish New York. In Shefter, ed., 167–92.

Gluckman, Max. 1940. Analysis of a Social Situation in Modern Zululand. *Bantu Studies* 14:1–30.

Goldberger, Paul. 1988. Shaping the Face of New York. In Salins, ed., 127–40.

Goode, Judith. 1990. A Wary Welcome to the Neighborhood: Community Responses to Immigrants. *Urban Anthropology* 19:125–53.

Goode, Judith, and Jo Anne Schneider. 1994. *Reshaping Ethnic and Racial Relations in Philadelphia: Immigrants in a Divided City.* Philadelphia: Temple University Press.

Goodfriend, Joyce. 1992. *Before the Melting Pot: Society and Culture in Colonial New York City, 1664–1730.* Princeton: Princeton University Press.

Goodman, Louis. 1979. The Impact of Immigration Doctors on the U.S. Medical Profession. In Bryce-Laporte, ed., 10–21.

Gordon, David. 1979. *The Working Poor: Toward a State Agenda.* Washington, D.C.: Council of State Planning Agencies.

——. 1996. *Fat and Mean: The Corporate Squeeze of Working Americans and the Myth of Managerial "Downsizing."* New York: Free Press.

Gordon, Diana. 1973. *City Limits: Barriers to Change in Urban Government.* New York: Charterhouse.

Grasmuck, Sherri, and Patricia Pessar. 1991. *Between Two Islands: Dominican International Migration.* Berkeley: University of California Press.

Green, Charles, and Basil Wilson. 1989. *The Struggle for Black Empowerment in New York City: Beyond the Politics of Pigmentation.* New York: Praeger.

Gregory, Steven. 1992. The Changing Significance of Race and Class in an African American Community. *American Ethnologist* 19:255–74.

——. 1993. Race, Rubbish and Resistance: Empowering Difference in Community Politics. *Cultural Anthropology* 8:24–48.

——. 1994a. Race, Identity and Political Activism: The Shifting Contours of the African American Public Sphere. *Public Culture* 7:147–64.

——. 1994b. "We've Been Down This Road Already." In Gregory and Sanjek, eds., 18–38.

——. 1998. *Black Corona: Race and the Politics of Place in an Urban Community.* Princeton: Princeton University Press.

Gregory, Steven, and Roger Sanjek, eds. 1994. *Race.* New Brunswick, N.J.: Rutgers University Press.

Greider, William. 1992. *Who Will Tell the People? The Betrayal of American Democracy.* New York: Simon & Schuster.

Grossman, David. 1980. Capital Construction Needs of New York City in the 1977–86 Period. In Twentieth Century Fund Task Force on the Future of New York City, 175–230.

Grumet, Robert Steven. 1981. *Native American Place Names in New York City.* New York: Museum of the City of New York.

Guinier, Lani. 1994. *The Tyranny of the Majority: Fundamental Fairness in American Democracy.* New York: Free Press.

Hacker, Andrew. 1975. *The New Yorkers: A Profile of an American Metropolis.* New York: Mason/Charter.

——. 1988. Looking Backward—and Forward. In Salins, ed., 203–18.

——. 1992. *Two Nations: Black and White, Separate, Hostile, Unequal.* New York: Scribner.

Hagan, Jacqueline Maria. 1994. *Deciding to Be Legal: A Maya Community in Houston.* Philadelphia: Temple University Press.

Haig, Robert. 1926. Toward an Understanding of the Metropolis. *Quarterly Journal of Economics* 40:179–208, 402–34.

Halle, David. 1984. *America's Working Man: Work, Home, and Politics among Blue-Collar Property Owners.* Chicago: University of Chicago Press.

Hannerz, Ulf. 1992. *Culture, Cities, and the World.* Amsterdam: Centrum voor Grootstedelijk Onderzoek.

Hanson, Christopher, and Angelo Falcón. 1992. *Latinos and the Redistricting Process in New York City.* New York: Institute for Puerto Rican Policy.

Hardy-Fanta, Carol. 1993. *Latina Politics, Latino Politics: Gender, Culture, and Political Participation in Boston.* Philadelphia: Temple University Press.

Harlow, Ilana. 1995. *The International Express: A Guide to Ethnic Communities along the 7 Train.* Woodhaven, N.Y.: Queens Council on the Arts.

Harrington, Michael. 1987. When Ed Koch Was Still a Liberal. *Dissent* 34:595–602.

Harris, Richard. 1991. The Geography of Employment and Residence in New York Since 1950. In Mollenkopf and Castells, eds., 129–52.

Harrison, Bennett, and Barry Bluestone. 1988. *The Great U-Turn: Corporate Restructuring and the Polarization of America.* New York: Basic Books.

Harwood, Edwin. 1986. American Public Opinion and U.S. Immigration Policy. *Annals of the American Academy of Political and Social Sciences* 487:201–12.

Hauser, Philip. 1981. The Census of 1980. *Scientific American* 245 (5):53–61.

Hebard, Erin McGauley. 1990. Irish-Americans and Irish Dance: Self-Chosen Ethnicity. In *Encounters with American Ethnic Cultures,* ed. Philip Kilbride, Jane Goodale, and Elizabeth Ameisen, 116–32. Tuscaloosa: University of Alabama Press.

Hendricks, Glenn. 1974. *The Dominican Diaspora: From the Dominican Republic to New York City—Villagers in Transition.* New York: Teachers College Press.

Hernandez, Frank. 1980. International Commentary. In Bryce-Laporte, ed., 478–80.

Hochman, Harold. 1988. Clearing the Regulatory Clutter. In Salins, ed., 93–108.

Homefront. 1977. *Housing Abandonment in New York City.* New York: Homefront.

Hoover, Edgar, and Raymond Vernon. 1959. *Anatomy of a Metropolis.* New York: Anchor.

Hopper, Kim. 1988. More Than Passing Strange: Homelessness and Mental Illness in New York City. *American Ethnologist* 15:155–67.

Hopper, Kim, Ezra Susser, and Sarah Conover. 1985. Economies of Makeshift: Deindustrialization and Homelessness in New York City. *Urban Anthropology* 14:183–236.

Howard, John, ed. 1983. *Awakening Minorities: Continuity and Change.* New Brunswick, N.J.: Transaction Books.

Hoyman, Michele. 1987. Female Participation in the Informal Economy: A Neglected Issue. *Annals of the American Academy of Political and Social Science* 483:64–82.

Hutchens, Nancy. 1977. Recent Italian Immigrants in Brooklyn. Ph.D. diss., Rice University.

Huxtable, Ada Louise. 1987. Stumbling toward Tomorrow: The Decline and Fall of the New York Vision. *Dissent* 34:453–61.

Hymer, Stephen. 1979. *The Multinational Corporation.* Cambridge: Cambridge University Press.

Innes, J. H. 1898. Ancient Newtown. *Newtown Register,* 20 January–31 March.

Institute for Puerto Rican Policy. 1987. *A Community Guide to the Report of the NYC Mayor's Commission on Hispanic Concerns,* pts. 1–3. New York: Institute for Puerto Rican Policy.

——. 1990. *The Dinkins Administration and the Puerto Rican Community: Lessons from the Puerto Rican Experiences with African-American Mayors in Chicago and Philadelphia.* New York: Institute for Puerto Rican Policy.

——. 1991. *New York as a "Majority Minority" City: 1990 Census Tract Databook.* New York: Institute for Puerto Rican Policy.

Irvine, Judith. 1979. Formality and Informality in Communicative Events. *American Anthropologist* 81:773–90.

——. 1989. When Talk Isn't Cheap: Language and Political Economy. *American Ethnologist* 16:248–67.

Jacobs, Jane. 1961. *The Death and Life of Great American Cities.* New York: Vintage.

——. 1969. *The Economy of Cities.* New York: Vintage.

Jaynes, Gerald, and Robin Williams, eds. 1989. *A Common Destiny: Blacks and American Society* Washington, D.C.: National Academy Press.

Johnson, Allen. 1995. Explanation and Ground Truth: The Place of Cultural Materialism in Scientific Anthropology. In Murphy and Margolis, eds., 7–20.

Jones-Correa, Michael. 1998. *Between Two Nations: The Political Predicament of Latino Immigrants in New York City.* Ithaca: Cornell University Press.

Joselit, Jenna Weissman. 1983. *Our Gang: Jewish Crime and the New York Jewish Community, 1900–1940.* Bloomington: Indiana University Press.

Kahler, Miles. 1993. New York City and the International System: International Strategy and Urban Fortunes. In Shefter, ed., 27–47.

Kaplan, Temma. 1982. Female Consciousness and Collective Action: The Case of Barcelona, 1910–1918. *Signs* 7:545–66.

Karatzas, Daniel. 1990. *Jackson Heights: A Garden in the City.* New York: n.p.

Kasarda, John. 1995. Industrial Restructuring and the Changing Location of Jobs. In Farley, ed., 215–67.

Kasinitz, Philip. 1992. *Caribbean New York: Black Immigrants and the Politics of Race.* Ithaca: Cornell University Press.

Kasinitz, Philip, and Judith Freidenberg-Herbstein. 1987. The Puerto Rican Parade and West Indian Carnival: Public Celebrations in New York City. In Sutton and Chaney, eds., 327–49.

Katznelson, Ira. 1981. *City Trenches: Urban Politics and the Patterning of Class in the United States.* Chicago: University of Chicago Press.

Keely, Charles. 1980. Immigration Policy and the New Immigrants, 1965–75; Comment. In Bryce-Laporte, ed., 15–25, 487–88.

——. 1982. Illegal Migration. *Scientific American* 246 (3): 41–47.

Kertzer, David. 1988. *Ritual, Politics, and Power.* New Haven: Yale University Press.

Khandelwal, Madhulika [Shankar]. 1989. Hindu Religious Activities of Indians in Queens. In Sanjek, ed., 43–55.

——. 1991. Indian Immigrants in New York City: Patterns of Growth and Diversification, 1965–1990. Doctor of Arts diss., Carnegie-Mellon University.

——. 1994. Indian Immigrants in Queens, New York City: Patterns of Spatial Concentration and Distribution, 1965–1990. In *Nation and Migration: The Politics of Space in the South Asian Diaspora,* ed. Peter van der Veer, 178–96. Philadelphia: University of Pennsylvania Press.

Kieschnick, Michael. 1981. *Taxes and Growth: Business Incentives and Economic Development.* Washington, D.C.: Council of State Planning Agencies.

Kim, Illsoo. 1980. *New Urban Immigrants: The Korean Community in New York.* Princeton: Princeton University Press.

——. 1987. The Koreans: Small Business in an Urban Frontier. In Foner, ed., 219–42.

Kling, Joseph, and Prudence Posner, eds. 1990. *Dilemmas of Activism: Class, Community and the Politics of Local Mobilization.* Philadelphia: Temple University Press.

Kornblum, William, and James Beshers. 1988. White Ethnicity: Ecological Dimensions. In Mollenkopf, ed., 201–21.

Kraly, Ellen. 1987. U.S. Immigration Policy and the Immigrant Populations of New York. In Foner, ed., 35–78.

Kroessler, Jeffrey. 1993. Baseball and the Blue Laws. *Long Island History Journal* 5:168–77.

Kross, Jessica. 1983. *The Evolution of an American Town: Newtown, New York, 1642–1775.* Philadelphia: Temple University Press.

Krugman, Paul. 1996. *Pop Internationalism.* Cambridge: MIT Press.

Kuper, Adam. 1971. Introduction: Council Structure and Decision-Making. In Richards and Kuper, eds., 13–28.

Laguerre, Michel. 1984. *American Odyssey: Haitians in New York City.* Ithaca: Cornell University Press.

Lamphere, Louise, ed. 1992. *Structuring Diversity: Ethnographic Perspectives on the New Immigration.* Chicago: University of Chicago Press.

Lamphere, Louise, Alex Stepick, and Guillermo Grenier, eds. 1994 *Newcomers in the Workplace: Immigrants and the Restructuring of the U.S. Economy.* Philadelphia: Temple University Press.

LaRuffa, Anthony. 1988. *Monte Carmelo: An Italian-American Community in the Bronx.* New York: Gordon & Breach.

Leacock, Eleanor. 1969. *Teaching and Learning in City Schools: A Comparative Study.* New York: Basic Books.

Leeds, Anthony. 1980. Systems Levels Interaction in the Texas Hill Country Ecosystem: Structure, History, and Evolution. In *Beyond the Myths of Culture: Essays in Cultural Materialism,* ed. Eric Ross, 103–38. New York: Academic Press.

——. 1994. *Cities, Classes, and the Social Order.* Ed. Roger Sanjek. Ithaca: Cornell University Press

Leichter, Franz. 1995. *Corporate Welfare: The Other AFDC (Aid to Financially Dependent Companies).* Albany, N.Y.: Office of State Senator Franz Leichter.

——. 1996. *Business Blues: A Report on the Effects of the New York State Economic Policies on Small Business.* Albany, N.Y.: Office of State Senator Franz Leichter.

Leinberger, Christopher. 1992. Business Flees to the Urban Fringe. *Nation,* 6 July, 10–14.

Lekachman, Robert. 1982. *Greed Is Not Enough: Reaganomics,* New York: Pantheon.

Levison, Andrew. 1974. *The Working Class Majority.* New York: Penguin.

Levy, Frank. 1995. Incomes and Income Inequality. In Farley, ed., 15–57.

Lichten, Eric. 1980. The Development of Austerity: Fiscal Crisis in New York City. In *Power Structure Research,* ed. G. William Domhoff, 139–71. Beverly Hills, Calif.: Sage.

——. 1984. Fiscal Crisis, Power, and Municipal Labor. In Boggs, Handel, and Fava, eds., 196–213.

Lieberson, Stanley. 1985. Unhyphenated Whites in the United States. *Ethnic and Racial Studies* 8:159–80.

Lieberson, Stanley, and Mary Waters. 1986. Ethnic Groups in Flux: The Changing Ethnic Responses of American Whites. *Annals of the American Academy of Political and Social Sciences* 487:79–91.

——. 1988. *From Many Strands: Ethnic and Racial Groups in Contemporary America.* New York: Russell Sage.

Lloyd-Jones, David. 1981. The Art of Enoch Powell: The Rhetorical Structure of a Speech on Immigration. In Paine, ed., 87–111.

Logan, John, and Harvey Molotch. 1987. *Urban Fortunes: The Political Economy of Place.* Berkeley: University of California Press.

Macchiarola, Frank. 1988. Making the Schools Work. In Salins, ed., 153–69.

McCabe, James D., Jr. [1872] 1970. *Lights and Shadows of New York Life.* New York: Farrar, Straus & Giroux.

McNickle, Chris. 1993. *To Be Mayor of New York: Ethnic Politics in the City.* New York: Columbia University Press.

Maier, Mark. 1984. Management Strategies in Public Sector Labor Law. In *Marxism and the Metropolis,* ed. William Tabb and Larry Sawers, 346–63. New York: Oxford University Press.

Marcus, Norman. 1993. Zoning from 1961 to 1991: Turning Back the Clock—but with an Up-to-the-Minute Social Agenda. In Bressi, ed., 61–102.

Marcuse, Peter, Peter Medoff, and Andrea Pereira. 1981. *Triage: Programming the Death of Communities.* Washington, D.C.: National Citizens' Monitoring Project.

Marshall, Adriana. 1983. *Immigrants in a Surplus-Worker Labor Market: The Case of New York.* New York: Center for Latin American and Caribbean Studies, New York University.

Martin, Philip, and Elizabeth Midgley. 1994. *Immigration to the United States: Journey to An Uncertain Destination.* Washington, D.C.: Population Reference Bureau.

Massey, Douglas, and Nancy Denton. 1993. *American Apartheid: Segregation and the Making of the Underclass.* Cambridge: Harvard University Press.

Mayer, Martin. 1974. *The Bankers.* New York: Ballantine.

Merton, Robert. [1949] 1968. Patterns of Influence: Local and Cosmopolitan Influentials. In Robert Merton, *Social Theory and Social Structure,* 441–74. New York: Free Press.

Meyer, Gerald. 1989. *Vito Marcantonio: Radical Politician, 1902–1954.* Albany: State University of New York Press.

Miller, Frank. 1967. Humor in a Chippewa Tribal Council. *Ethnology* 6:263–71.

Mills, C. Wright. 1956. *The Power Elite.* New York: Oxford University Press.

Mills, Nicolaus. 1987. Howard Beach–Anatomy of a Lynching. *Dissent* 34:479–85.

Mitchell, J. Clyde. 1966. Theoretical Orientations in African Urban Studies. In *The Social Anthropology of Complex Societies,* ed. Michael Banton, 37–68. New York: Praeger.

Mollenkopf, John. 1976. The Crisis of the Public Sector in America's Cities. In Alcaly and Mermelstein, eds., 113–31.

——. 1988a. The Place of Politics and Politics of Place. In Mollenkopf, ed., 273–83.

——. 1988b. The Postindustrial Transformation of the Political Order in New York City. In Mollenkopf ed., 223–58.

——, ed. 1988c. *Power, Culture, and Place: Essays on New York City.* New York: Russell Sage.

Mollenkopf, John, and Manuel Castells, eds. 1991a. *Dual City: Restructuring New York.* New York: Russell Sage.

——. 1991b. Introduction. In Mollenkopf and Castells, eds., 3–22.

——. 1991c. Political Inequality. In Mollenkopf and Castells, eds., 333–58.

Moore, Sally, and Barbara Myerhoff. 1977. Secular Ritual: Forms and Meanings. In *Secular Ritual,* ed. Sally Moore and Barbara Myerhoff, 3–24. Assen, Netherlands: Van Gorcum.

Morgen, Sandra, and Ann Bookman. 1988. Rethinking Women and Politics: An Introductory Essay. In Bookman and Morgen, eds., 3–29.

Morisi, Peter. 1994a. *Rezoning.* Brooklyn: M.E.R.C.I. [Merchants and Entrepreneurs Rights Coalition Incorporated].

——. 1994b. *Rezoning Part 2.* Brooklyn: M.E.R.C.I.

Morris, Charles. 1980. *The Cost of Good Intentions: New York City and the Liberal Experiment, 1960–1975.* New York: McGraw-Hill.

Moss, Mitchell. 1994. *Made in New York: The Future of Manufacturing in the City of New York.* New York: Taub Urban Research Center, New York University.

Mudd, John. 1984. *Neighborhood Services: Making Big Cities Work.* New Haven: Yale University Press.

Munsell, William. 1882. *History of Queens County, New York.* New York: Munsell.

Murphy, Martin, and Maxine Margolis, eds. 1995. *Science, Materialism, and the Study of Culture.* Gainesville: University Press of Florida.

Myers, Phyllis. 1982. *Aging in Place: Strategies to Help the Elderly Stay in Revitalizing Neighborhoods.* Washington, D.C.: Conservation Foundation.

Netzer, Dick. 1990. The Economy and the Governing of the City. In Bellush and Netzer, eds., 27–59.

Newfield, Jack. 1976. How the Power Brokers Profit. In Alcaly and Mermelstein, eds., 296–315.

Newfield, Jack, and Wayne Barrett. 1988. *City for Sale: Ed Koch and the Betrayal of New York.* New York: Harper & Row.

Newfield, Jack, and Paul DuBrul. 1977. *The Abuse of Power: The Permanent Government and the Fall of New York.* New York: Viking.

New York Times. 1996. *The Downsizing of America.* New York: Times Books.

New York Times, New York City Planning Department, and New York City Economic Development Administration. 1973. *New York Market Analysis.* New York: New York Times Company.

North, David. 1979. Comment in Bicentennial Planning Conference (transcript). In Bryce-Laporte, ed., 207–73.

NYC Latino Districting Committee. 1991. *Citywide Latino NYC Council District Plan.* New York: Puerto Rican/Latino Voting Rights Network.

Obey, David. 1996. *Who Is Downsizing the American Dream?* Washington, D.C.: Center for National Policy.

O'Cléireacáin, Carol. 1993. Cities' Role in the Metropolitan Economy and the Federal Structure. In Cisneros, ed., 167–86.

O'Hare, William. 1992. *America's Minorities—The Demographics of Diversity.* Washington, D.C.: Population Reference Bureau.

O'Hare, William, Kelvin Pollard, Taynia Mann, and Mary Kent. 1991. *African Americans in the 1990s.* Washington, D.C.: Population Reference Bureau.

Ohnuki-Tierney, Emiko. 1990. Introduction: The Historicization of Anthropology. In *Culture through Time,* ed. Emiko Ohnuki-Tierney, 1–25. Stanford: Stanford University Press.

Olzak, Susan. 1983. Contemporary Ethnic Mobilization. *Annual Review of Sociology* 9:355–74.

Orsi, Robert. 1985. *The Madonna of 115th Street: Faith and Community in Italian Harlem, 1880–1950.* New Haven: Yale University Press.

Ostrander, Susan. 1984. *Women of the Upper Class.* Philadelphia: Temple University Press.

Padilla, Elena. 1958. *Up from Puerto Rico.* New York: Columbia University Press.

Paine, Robert. 1981. When Saying Is Doing. In Paine, ed., 9–23.

——, ed. 1981. *Politically Speaking: Cross-Cultural Studies of Rhetoric.* Philadelphia: Institute for the Study of Human Issues.

Papademetriou, Demetriou. 1983. *New Immigrants to Brooklyn and Queens.* Staten Island, N.Y.: Center for Migration Studies.

Park, Kyeyoung. 1989. "Born Again": What Does It Mean to Korean Americans in New York City? *Journal of Ritual Studies* 3:289–303.

——. 1997. *The Korean American Dream: Immigrants and Small Business in New York City.* Ithaca: Cornell University Press.

Parkin, David. 1980. The Creativity of Abuse. *Man* 15:45–64.

Parsons, Talcott. 1951. *The Social System.* New York: Free Press.

Passel, Jeffrey. 1986. Undocumented Immigration. *Annals of the American Academy of Political and Social Sciences* 454:181–200.

Passel, Jeffrey, and Barry Edmonston. 1992. *Immigration and Race in the United States.* Washington, D.C.: Urban Institute.

Patterson, James. 1979. A Critique of "The New Ethnicity." *American Anthropologist* 81:103–5.

Pecorella, Robert. 1994. *Community Power in a Post Reform City: Politics in New York City.* Armonk, N.Y.: M. E. Sharpe.

Perlman, Janice. 1976. Grassrooting the System. *Social Policy,* September–October, 4–20.

——. 1979. Grassroots Empowerment and Government Response. *Social Policy,* September–October, 16–21.

Pessar, Patricia. 1987a. The Dominicans: Women in the Household and the Garment Industry. In Foner, ed., 103–29.

——. 1987b. The Linkage between the Household and the Workplace of Dominican Women in the U.S. In Sutton and Chaney, eds., 255–77.

Petras, Elizabeth. 1980. Toward a Theory of International Migration: The New Division of Labor. In Bryce-Laporte, ed., 439–49.

Phillips, Kevin. 1990. *The Politics of Rich and Poor: Wealth and the American Electorate in the Reagan Aftermath.* New York: HarperCollins.

——. 1994. *Arrogant Capital: Washington, Wall Street, and the Frustration of American Politics.* Boston: Little, Brown.

Pido, Antonio. 1983. Brain Drain Philippinos. In Howard, ed., 119–27.

Piore, Michael. 1980. The Economic Role of Migrants in the U.S. Labor Market. In Bryce-Laporte, ed., 427–38.

Piven, Frances Fox. [1973] 1974. The Urban Crisis: Who Got What, and Why. In Richard Cloward and Frances Fox Piven, *The Politics of Turmoil,* 314–51. New York: Vintage.

Piven, Francis Fox, and Richard Cloward. 1988. *Why Americans Don't Vote.* New York: Pantheon.

Portes, Alejandro. 1978. Migration and Underdevelopment. *Politics and Society* 8:1–48.

Portes, Alejandro, and Ruben Rumbaut. 1990. *Immigrant America: A Portrait.* Berkeley: University of California Press.

Posner, Prudence, 1990. Introduction. In Kling and Posner, eds., 3–20.

Pratt, Edward. 1911. *Industrial Causes of Congestion of Population in New York City.* New York: AMS Press.

Preston, Julia. Undocumented Immigrant Workers in New York City. *Report on the Americas* 12 (6): 2–46.

Prins, A. H. J. 1965. *Sailing from Lamu: A Study of Maritime Culture in Islamic East Africa.* Assen, Netherlands: Van Gorcum.

Reed, Adolph, Jr. 1986. The "Black Revolution" and the Reconstitution of Domination. In *Race, Politics, and Culture: Critical Essays in the Radicalism of the 1960s,* ed. Adolph Reed Jr., 61–95. Westport, Conn.: Greenwood.

Reimers, David. 1985. *Still the Golden Door: The Third World Comes to America.* New York: Columbia University Press.

Report of the National Advisory Commission on Civil Disorders [Otto Kerner, Chairman]. 1968. New York: Bantam.

Richards, Audrey. 1971. Introduction: The Nature of the Problem. In Richards and Kuper, eds., 1–12.

Richards, Audrey, and Adam Kuper, eds. 1971. *Councils in Action.* Cambridge: Cambridge University Press.

Ricourt, Milagros. 1989. Latin American Protestant Women and Community Needs in Corona. In Sanjek, ed., 92–103.

——. 1994. The Creation of a Pan-Latino Ethnicity: Gender, Class, and Politics in Corona, Queens. Ph.D. diss., City University of New York.

Rieder, Jonathan. 1986. *Canarsie: The Jews and Italians of Brooklyn against Liberalism.* Cambridge: Harvard University Press.

Riker, James, Jr. 1852. *The Annals of Newtown in Queens County, New York.* New York: Fanshaw.

Rodríguez, Clara. 1989. *Puerto Ricans: Born in the U.S.A.* Boston: Unwin Hyman.

Rodríguez, Clara, Virginia Sánchez Korrol, and José Oscar Alers, eds. 1980. *The Puerto Rican Struggle: Essays on Survival in the U.S.* Maplewood, N.J.: Waterfront Press.

Rogers, David. 1968. *110 Livingston Street: Politics and Bureaucracy in the New York City School System.* New York: Vintage.

——. 1990. Community Control and Decentralization. In Bellush and Netzer, eds., 143–87.

Rogers, David, and Norman Chung. 1983. *110 Livingston Street Revisited: Decentralization in Action.* New York: New York University Press.

Rogowsky, Edward, Louis Gold, and David Abbott. 1971. Police: The Civilian Review Board Controversy. In Bellush and David, eds., 59–97.

Rosenberg, Terry. 1987. *Poverty in New York City: 1980–1985.* New York: Community Service Society.

——. 1989. *Poverty in New York City, 1985–1988.* New York: Community Service Society.

——. 1992. *Poverty in New York City, 1991.* New York: Community Service Society.

Rosenwaike, Ira. 1972. *Population History of New York City.* Syracuse, N.Y.: Syracuse University Press.

Rothschild, Rose. 1993. District Needs Statement. In *Community District Needs,* 61–80. New York: Department of City Planning.

——. 1996. District Needs Statement. In *Community District Needs,* 67–86. New York: Department of City Planning.

Rusk, David. 1993. *Cities without Suburbs.* Washington, D.C.: Woodrow Wilson Center Press.

Sacks, Karen Brodkin. 1988. *Caring by the Hour: Women, Work, and Organizing at Duke Medical Center.* Urbana: University of Illinois Press.

Sahlins, Marshall. 1985. *Islands of History.* Chicago: University of Chicago Press.

Salas, Miguel Tinker. 1991. El immigrante latino: Latin American Immigration and Pan-Ethnicity. *Latino Studies Journal* 2 (3): 58–71.

Salins, Peter. 1988a. Introduction. In Salins, ed., 1–6.

——. 1993. Zoning for Growth and Change. In Bressi, ed., 164–84.

——, ed. 1988b. *New York Unbound: The City and the Politics of the Future.* New York: Basil Blackwell.

Salomon, Frank. 1973. Weavers of Otavalo. In *Peoples and Cultures of Native South America,* ed. Daniel Gross, 463–92. New York: Natural History Press.

Salvo, Joseph, Ronald Ortiz, and Francis Vardy. 1992. *The Newest New Yorkers: An*

Analysis of Immigration into New York City during the 1980s. New York: Department of City Planning.

Sanjek, Roger. 1984. *Crowded Out: Homelessness and the Elderly Poor in New York City.* New York: Coalition for the Homeless.

——. 1989a. Christians from Four Continents: Americans and Immigrants in Protestant Churches of Elmhurst, Queens. In Sanjek, ed., 4–18.

——. 1990. The Secret Life of Fieldnotes; On Ethnographic Validity. In *Fieldnotes: The Makings of Anthropology,* ed. Roger Sanjek, 187–270, 385–417. Ithaca: Cornell University Press.

——. 1991. The Ethnographic Present. *Man* 26:609–28.

——. 1992. The Organization of Festivals and Ceremonies among Americans and Immigrants in Queens, New York. In Daun, Ehn, and Klein, eds., 123–43.

——. 1993. After Freedom in Newtown, Queens: African Americans and the Color Line, 1828–1899. *Long Island History Journal* 5:157–67.

——. 1994a. The Enduring Inequalities of Race. In Gregory and Sanjek, eds., 1–17.

——. 1994b. The Holistic Anthropology of Anthony Leeds. In Leeds 1994, 27–45.

——. 1994c. Intermarriage and the Future of Races in the United States. In Gregory and Sanjek, eds., 103–30.

——. 1995. Politics, Theory, and the Nature of Cultural Things. In Murphy and Margolis, eds., 39–61.

——. 1996. Ethnography. In *Encyclopedia of Social and Cultural Anthropology,* ed. Alan Barnard and Jonathan Spencer, 193–98. London: Routledge.

——. Forthcoming. *The Shape of New York City History.* Ithaca: Cornell University Press.

——, ed. 1989b. *Worship and Community: Christianity and Hinduism in Contemporary Queens.* Flushing, N.Y.: Asian/American Center, Queens College.

Santiago, John, ed. 1993. *Redistricting, Race, and Ethnicity in New York City.* New York: Institute for Puerto Rican Policy.

Saran, Parmatma. 1980. New Ethnics: The Case of the East Indians in New York City. In Bryce-Laporte, ed., 303–12.

Sassen[-Koob], Saskia. 1980. Immigrant and Minority Workers in the Organization of the Labor Process. *Journal of Ethnic Studies* 8:1–34.

——. 1988. *The Mobility of Labor and Capital: A Study in International Investment and Labor Flow.* Cambridge: Cambridge University Press.

——. 1991a. *The Global City: New York, London, Tokyo.* Princeton: Princeton University Press.

——. 1991b. The Informal Economy. In Mollenkopf and Castells, eds., 79–101.

Schaffer, Richard. 1973. *Income Flows in Urban Poverty Areas: A Comparison of the Community Income Accounts of Bedford–Stuyvesant and Borough Park.* Lexington, Mass.: Lexington.

Schieffelin, Edward. 1993. Performance and the Cultural Construction of Reality: A New Guinea Example. In *Creativity/Anthropology,* ed. Smadar Lavie, Kirin Narayan, and Renato Rosaldo, 270–95. Ithaca: Cornell University Press.

Schultze, Charles, Edward Fried, Alice Rivlin, Nancy Teeters, and Robert Reischauer. [1972] 1976. Fiscal Problems of Cities. In Alcaly and Mermelstein, eds., 189–212.

Schwartzman, Helen. 1989. *The Meeting: Gatherings in Organizations and Communities.* New York: Plenum.

Sclar, Elliott, and Walter Hook. 1993. Toward an Urban Policy. In Cisneros, ed., 48–80.

Seifer, Nancy. 1973. *Absent from the Majority: Working Class Women in America.* New York: American Jewish Committee.

Settlement Housing Fund. 1985. *Elderly Homeowners in New York: Profile, Problems, Policy.* New York: Settlement Housing Fund.

Seyfried, Vincent. 1984. *300 Years of Long Island City, 1630–1930.* New York: Edgian Press.

——. 1987. *Corona: From Farmland to City Suburb, 1650–1935.* New York: Edgian Press.

——. 1995. *Elmhurst: From Town Seat to Mega-Suburb.* Merrick, N.Y.: Traction Yearbook.

Sharff, Jagna. 1981. Free Enterprise and the Ghetto Family. *Psychology Today* 15 (3): 40–47.

——. 1987. The Underground Economy of a Poor Neighborhood. In *Cities of the United States: Studies in Urban Anthropology,* ed. Leith Mullings, 19–50. New York: Columbia University Press.

Shefter, Martin. 1985. *Political Crisis, Fiscal Crisis: The Collapse and Revival of New York City.* New York: Basic Books.

——, ed. 1993. *Capital of the American Century: The National and International Influence of New York City.* New York: Russell Sage.

Sherman, Franklin. 1919. *Building Up Greater Queens Borough.* New York: Brooklyn Biographical Society.

Shiel, John. 1983. Horse Creek and Horse Brook. *Long Island Forum,* August.

Sieber, R. Timothy. 1978. Schooling, Socialization, and Group Boundaries: A Study of Informal Social Relations in the Public Domain. *Urban Anthropology* 7:67–98.

——. 1987. Urban Gentrification: Ideology and Practice in Middle-Class Civic Activity. *City and Society* 1:52–63.

Simon, Julian. 1986. Basic Data concerning Immigration into the United States. *Annals of the American Academy of Political and Social Sciences* 454:12–56.

Sinnreich, Masha. 1980. Background Paper. In Twentieth Century Fund Task Force on the Future of New York City, 35–173.

Sleeper, Jim. 1987. Boom and Bust with Ed Koch. *Dissent* 34:437–52.

——. 1990. *The Closest of Strangers: Liberalism and the Politics of Race in New York.* New York: Norton.

Smith, Robert. 1992. New York in Mixteca; Mixteca in New York. *Report on the Americas* 26 (1): 39–41, 48–49.

Sridhar, Kamal. 1988. Language Maintenance and Language Shift among Asian-Indians: Kannadigas in the New York Area. *International Journal of the Sociology of Language* 69:73–87.

Stafford, Susan Buchanan. 1987. The Haitians: The Cultural Meaning of Race and Ethnicity. In Foner, ed., 131–58.

Stafford, Walter. 1985. *Closed Labor Markets: Underrepresentation of Blacks, Hispanics and Women in New York City's Core Industries and Jobs.* New York: Community Service Society.

Stafford, Walter, with Edwin Dei. 1989. *Employment Segmentation in New York City Municipal Agencies.* New York: Community Service Society.

Stankowski, Barbara. 1977. *Maspeth . . . Our Town.* New York: Maspeth Federal Savings and Loan Association.

Starr, Roger. 1988. Easing the Housing Crisis. In Salins, ed., 170–86.

Stern, Zelda. 1980. *The Complete Guide to Ethnic New York.* New York: St. Martin's.

Sternleib, George, and James Hughes. 1976. Metropolitan Decline and Inter-Regional Job Shifts. In Alcaly and Mermelstein, eds., 145–64.

Stolnitz, George. 1980. International Migration Policies: Some Demographic and Economic Consequences. In Bryce-Laporte, ed., 51–55.

Strickland, Roy. 1993. The 1961 Zoning Revision and the Template of the Ideal City. In Bressi, ed., 48–60.

Stull, Donald, ed. 1990. When the Packers Came to Town: Changing Ethnic Relations in Garden City, Kansas. *Urban Anthropology* 19:303–427.

Stull, Donald, Janet Benson, Michael Broadway, Arthur Campa, Ken Erickson, and Mark Grey. 1990. *Changing Relations: Newcomers and Established Residents in Garden City, Kansas.* Lawrence: Institute for Public Policy and Business Research, University of Kansas.

Sullivan, Mercer. 1989. *"Getting Paid": Youth Crime and Work in the Inner City.* Ithaca: Cornell University Press.

——. 1991. Crime and the Social Fabric. In Mollenkopf and Castells, eds., 225–44.

Sung, Betty Lee. 1980. Polarity in the Makeup of Chinese Immigrants. In Bryce-Laporte, ed., 37–49.

Susser, Ida. 1982. *Norman Street: Poverty and Politics in an Urban Neighborhood.* New York: Oxford University Press.

——. 1991. The Separation of Mothers and Children. In Mollenkopf and Castells, eds., 207–24.

Suttles, Gerald. 1972. *The Social Construction of Communities.* Chicago: University of Chicago Press.

——. 1976. Urban Ethnography: Situational and Normative Accounts. *Annual Review of Sociology* 2:1–18.

——. 1984. The Cumulative Texture of Local Urban Culture. *American Journal of Sociology* 90:283–304.

——. 1990. *The Man-Made City: The Land-Use Confidence Game in Chicago.* Chicago: University of Chicago Press.

Sutton, Constance, and Elsa Chaney, eds. 1987. *Caribbean Life in New York City.* New York: Center for Migration Studies.

Swartz, Marc. 1968a. Introduction. In Swartz, ed., 1–46.

——, ed. 1968b. *Local-Level Politics.* Chicago: Aldine.

Swartz, Marc, Victor Turner, and Arthur Tuden. 1966. Introduction. In *Political Anthropology,* ed. Marc Swartz, Victor Turner, and Arthur Tuden, 1–41. Chicago: Aldine.

Tabb, William. 1982. *The Long Default: New York City and the Urban Fiscal Crisis.* New York: Monthly Review Press.

——. 1984. The New York City Fiscal Crisis. In *Marxism and the Metropolis,* ed. William Tabb and Larry Sawers, 323–45. New York: Oxford University Press.

Tambiah, S. J. 1970. *Buddhism and the Spirit Cults in North-east Thailand.* Cambridge: Cambridge University Press.

Tanenbaum, Susie. 1995. *Underground Harmonies: Music and Politics in the Subways of of New York.* Ithaca: Cornell University Press.

Tannen, Deborah. 1990. *You Just Don't Understand: Women and Men in Conversation.* New York: Ballantine.

Tauber, Gilbert, and Samuel Kaplan. 1966. *The New York City Handbook.* New York: Doubleday.

Taylor, Charles. 1990. Modes of Civil Society. *Public Culture* 3:95–118.

Thompson, Benjamin. 1918. *History of Long Island.* New York: Robert Dodd.

Tobier, Emanuel. 1984. *The Changing Face of Poverty: Trends in New York City's Population in Poverty, 1960–1990.* New York: Community Service Society.

Tricarico, Donald. 1984. *The Italians of Greenwich Village: The Social Structure and Transformation of an Ethnic Group* Staten Island, N.Y.: Center for Migration Studies.

Trouillot, Michel-Rolph. 1990. *Haiti: State against Nation.* New York: Monthly Review Press.

Turner, Victor. 1974. *Dramas, Fields, and Metaphors: Symbolic Action in Human Society.* Ithaca: Cornell University Press.

Twentieth Century Fund Task Force on the Future of New York City. 1980. *New York—World City.* Cambridge, Mass.: Oelgeschlager, Gunn & Hain.

Tyler, Gus. 1987. A Tale of Three Cities: Upper Economy, Lower—and Under. *Dissent* 34:463–70.

Valentine, Bettylou. 1978. *Hustling and Other Hard Work: Life Styles in the Ghetto.* New York: Free Press.

Vega, Gina. 1987. *The Big Stick: Placing Persons with Mental Retardation in Communities.* Flushing: Department of Urban Studies, Queens College, City University of New York.

Vernon, Raymond. 1957. Production and Distribution in the Large Metropolis. *Annals of the American Academy of Political and Social Science* 314:15–29.

Vilain, Pierre. 1991. *New York City 1991: The World's Capital in Transition.* New York: New York City Economic Policy and Marketing Group.

Viteritti, Joseph. 1990. The New Charter: Will It Make a Difference? In Bellush and Netzer, eds., 413–28.

——. 1991. *Community Government, the City Council, and the Reform Agenda.* New York: Robert Wagner School of Public Service, New York University.

Vogel, David. 1993. New York City as a National and Global Financial Center. In Shefter, ed., 49–70.

Wade, Richard. 1990. The Withering Away of the Party System. In Bellush and Netzer, eds., 271–95.

Wagner, Robert, Jr., et al. 1988. *New York Ascendant: The Commission on the Year 2000.* New York: Harper & Row.

Waldinger, Roger. 1986. *Through the Eye of the Needle: Immigrants and Enterprise in New York's Garment Trades.* New York: New York University Press.

——. 1986–87. Changing Ladders and Musical Chairs: Ethnicity and Opportunity in Post-industrial New York. *Politics and Society* 15:369–401.

——. 1987a. Beyond Nostalgia: The Old Neighborhood Revisited. *New York Affairs* 10:1–12.

——. 1987b. Minorities and Immigrants—Struggle in the Job Markets. *Dissent* 34:519–22.

——. 1989a. Immigration and Urban Change. *Annual Review of Sociology* 15:211–32.

——. 1989b. Race and Ethnicity. In *Setting Municipal Priorities, 1990,* ed. Charles Brecher and Raymond Horton, 50–78. New York: New York University Press.

Walsh, Annmarie Hauck. 1990. Public Authorities and the Shape of Decision Making. In Bellush and Netzer, eds., 188–219.

Ward, David. 1989. *Poverty, Ethnicity, and the American City, 1840–1925: Changing Conceptions, of the Slum and the Ghetto.* Cambridge: Cambridge University Press.

Warren, Robert. 1980. Volume and Composition of U.S. Immigration and Emigration. In Bryce-Laporte, ed., 1–14.

Waters, Mary. 1990. *Ethnic Options: Choosing Identities in America.* Berkeley: University of California Press.

Weitzman, Phillip. 1989. *Worlds Apart: Housing, Race/Ethnicity, and Income in New York City, 1978–1987.* New York: Community Service Society.

Wells, Miriam. 1996. *Strawberry Fields: Politics, Class, and Work in California Agriculture.* Ithaca: Cornell University Press.

West, Cornel. 1993. Audacious Hope and a Sense of History. *Crossroads* 35:2–6.

White, Shane. 1991. *Somewhat More Independent: The End of Slavery in New York City, 1770–1810.* Athens: University of Georgia Press.

Whyte, William Foote. 1943. A Challenge to Political Scientists. *American Political Science Review* 37:692–97.

——. 1946. Politics and Ethics. *American Political Science Review* 40:301–7.

——. 1955. *Street Corner Society: The Social Structure of an Italian Slum.* Chicago: University of Chicago Press.

Whyte, William H. 1976. End of the Exodus: The Logic of Headquarters City. *New York Magazine,* 20 September, 88–99.

Williams, Brett. 1994. Babies and Banks: The "Reproductive Underclass" and the Raced, Gendered Masking of Debt. In Gregory and Sanjek, eds., 348–65.

Willis, Mark. 1988. New York's Economic Renaissance. In Salins, ed., 30–53.

Willis, Walter. 1920. *Queens Borough, New York City, 1910–1920.* New York: Chamber of Commerce of the Borough of Queens.

Wilson, William Julius. 1980. *The Declining Significance of Race.* Chicago: University of Chicago Press.

Winnick, Louis. 1988. New York Unbound. In Salins, ed., 7–29.

——. 1990. *New People in Old Neighborhoods: The Role of New Immigrants in Rejuvenating New York's Communities.* New York: Russell Sage.

Wolf, Eric. 1990. Facing Power—Old Insights, New Questions. *American Anthropologist* 92:586–96.

Wolff, Edward. 1995. *Top Heavy: A Study of the Increasing Inequality of Wealth in America.* New York: Twentieth Century Fund Press.

Yancey, William, Eugene Ericksen, and Richard Juliani. 1976. Emergent Ethnicity: A Review and Reformulation. *American Sociological Review* 41:391–403.

Yancey, William, Eugene Ericksen, and George Leon. 1985. The Structure of Pluralism: "We're All Italian Around Here, Aren't We, Mrs. O'Brien." *Ethnic and Racial Studies* 8:94–116.

Yinger, John. 1995. *Closed Doors, Opportunities Lost: The Continuing Costs of Housing Discrimination.* New York: Russell Sage.

Young, Philip K. Y. 1983. Family Labor, Sacrifice and Competition: Korean Greengrocers in New York City. *Amerasia* 10:53–71.

Youssef, Nadia. 1992. *The Demographics of Immigration: A Socio-Demographic Profile of the Foreign-Born Population in New York State.* Staten Island, N.Y.: Center for Migration Studies.

Yuan, Xiaoxia. 1986. A Profile of Businesses in Elmhurst and Corona, Queens. M.A. thesis, Queens College, City University of New York.

Zevin, Robert. 1976. New York City Crisis: First Act in a New Age of Reaction. In Alcaly and Mermelstein, eds., 11–29.

Zim, Larry, Mel Lerner, and Herbert Rolfes. 1988. *The World of Tomorrow: The 1939 New York World's Fair.* New York: Harper & Row.

Zukin, Sharon. 1987. Gentrification: Culture and Capital in the Urban Core. *Annual Review of Sociology* 13:129–47.

Index

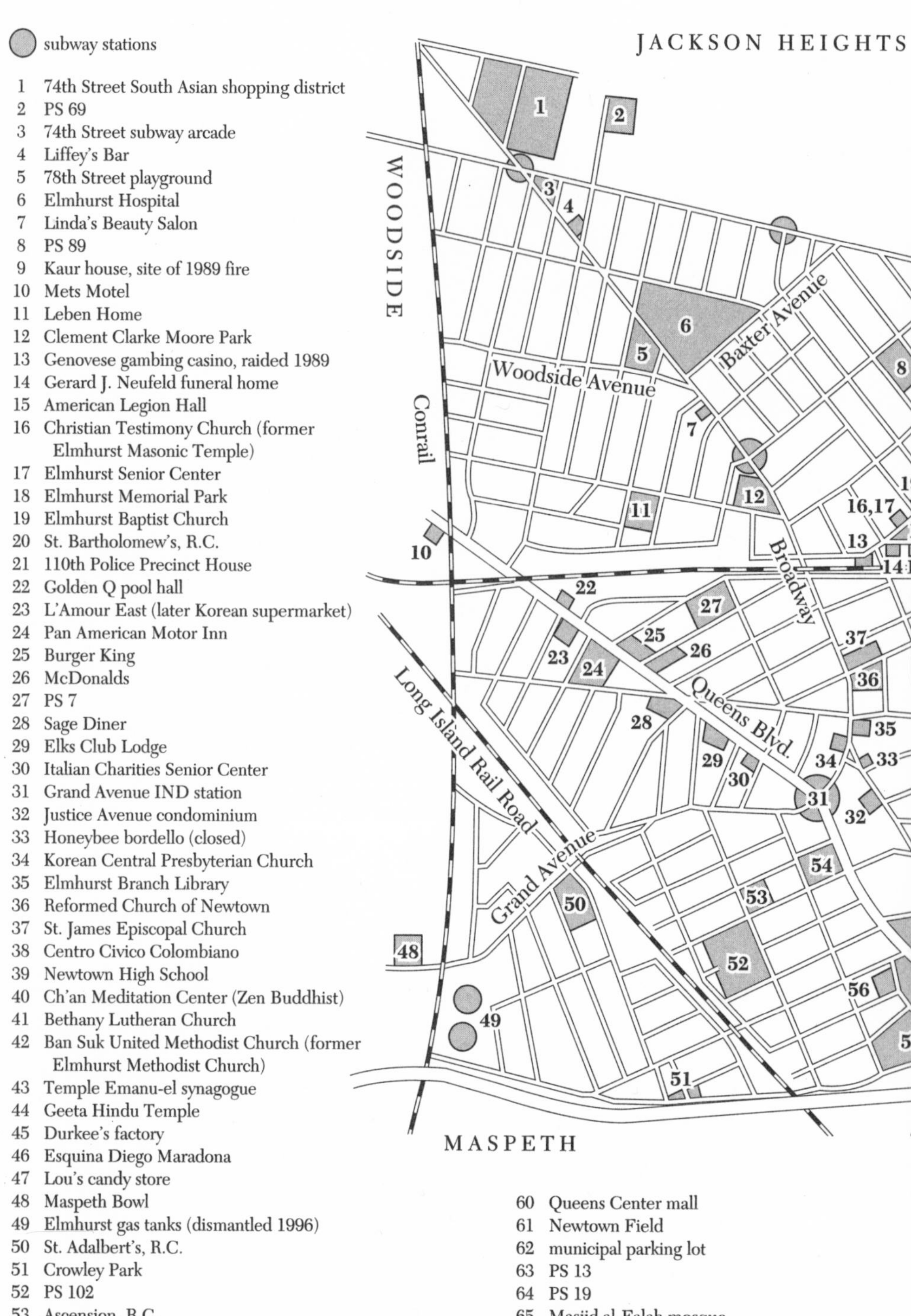
subway stations
1 74th Street South Asian shopping district
2 PS 69
3 74th Street subway arcade
4 Liffey's Bar
5 78th Street playground
6 Elmhurst Hospital
7 Linda's Beauty Salon
8 PS 89
9 Kaur house, site of 1989 fire
10 Mets Motel
11 Leben Home
12 Clement Clarke Moore Park
13 Genovese gambing casino, raided 1989
14 Gerard J. Neufeld funeral home
15 American Legion Hall
16 Christian Testimony Church (former Elmhurst Masonic Temple)
17 Elmhurst Senior Center
18 Elmhurst Memorial Park
19 Elmhurst Baptist Church
20 St. Bartholomew's, R.C.
21 110th Police Precinct House
22 Golden Q pool hall
23 L'Amour East (later Korean supermarket)
24 Pan American Motor Inn
25 Burger King
26 McDonalds
27 PS 7
28 Sage Diner
29 Elks Club Lodge
30 Italian Charities Senior Center
31 Grand Avenue IND station
32 Justice Avenue condominium
33 Honeybee bordello (closed)
34 Korean Central Presbyterian Church
35 Elmhurst Branch Library
36 Reformed Church of Newtown
37 St. James Episcopal Church
38 Centro Civico Colombiano
39 Newtown High School
40 Ch'an Meditation Center (Zen Buddhist)
41 Bethany Lutheran Church
42 Ban Suk United Methodist Church (former Elmhurst Methodist Church)
43 Temple Emanu-el synagogue
44 Geeta Hindu Temple
45 Durkee's factory
46 Esquina Diego Maradona
47 Lou's candy store
48 Maspeth Bowl
49 Elmhurst gas tanks (dismantled 1996)
50 St. Adalbert's, R.C.
51 Crowley Park
52 PS 102
53 Ascension, R.C.
54 First Presbyterian Church of Newtown
55 Macy's (later Stern's)
56 Elmwood movie theater
57 St. John's Hospital
58 Hoffman Park
59 Woodhaven Boulevard IND station
60 Queens Center mall
61 Newtown Field
62 municipal parking lot
63 PS 13
64 PS 19
65 Masjid al-Falah mosque
66 Ciudadanos Conscientes de Queens
67 Corona Plaza movie theater
68 Linden Park
69 First United Methodist Church of Corona
70 Our Lady of Sorrows, R.C.
71 Corona Preservation Senior Center
JACKSON HEIGHTS
WOODSIDE
MASPETH
Conrail
Woodside Avenue
Baxter Avenue
Broadway
Queens Blvd.
Long Island Rail Road
Grand Avenue